DRUGS AND
SOCIETY

TWELFTH EDITION

PART 2

GLEN R. HANSON, PhD, DDS

Professor, Department of
Pharmacology and Toxicology
Associate Dean, School of Dentistry
Director, Utah Addiction Center
University of Utah
Salt Lake City, Utah
Senior Advisor, National Institute
on Drug Abuse
National Institutes of Health
Bethesda, Maryland

PETER J. VENTURELLI

Associate Professor, Department of
Sociology and Criminology
Valparaiso University
Valparaiso, Indiana
Board Member
Baldwin Research Institute

ANNETTE E. FLECKENSTEIN, PhD

Professor, Department of Pharmacology
and Toxicology
University of Utah
Salt Lake City, Utah

World Headquarters
Jones & Bartlett Learning
5 Wall Street
Burlington, MA 01803
978-443-5000
info@jblearning.com
www.jblearning.com

Jones & Bartlett Learning books and products are available through most bookstores and online booksellers. To contact Jones & Bartlett Learning directly, call 800-832-0034, fax 978-443-8000, or visit our website, www.jblearning.com.

Production Credits

Chief Executive Officer: Ty Field
President: James Homer
Chief Product Officer: Eduardo Moura
Executive Publisher: William Brottmiller
Publisher: Cathy L. Esperti
Editorial Assistant: Jillian Porazzo
Production Editor: Jill Morton
Senior Marketing Manager: Andrea DeFronzo
VP, Manufacturing and Inventory Control: Therese Connell
Composition: Laserwords Private Limited, Chennai, India
Cover Design: Kristin E. Parker
Photo Research and Permissions Coordinator: Amy Rathburn
Cover and Title Page Images: Background, © Eky Studio/
ShutterStock, Inc.; A rocks glass, © Yeko Photo Studio/
ShutterStock, Inc.; Three pills, © Maksud/
ShutterStock, Inc.; An iced coffee, © Yeko Photo Studio/
ShutterStock, Inc.; Rolling a joint, © Nikita Starichenko/
ShutterStock, Inc.; Steroids used by an athlete,
© Jupiterimages/liquidlibrary/Thinkstock;
An aisle of pills, © Jupiterimages/Photos.com/
Thinkstock; A spray can, © Mikael Damkier/
ShutterStock, Inc.; A cigarette, © Mariusz
Szachowski/ShutterStock, Inc.; A drug user,
© iStockphoto/Thinkstock
Printing and Binding: Manufactured in the United States by LSC Communicat
Cover Printing: Manufactured in the United States by LSC Communications

To order this product, use ISBN: 978-1-284-10183-6

6048

Printed in the United States of America
22 21 20 19 18   10 9 8 7 6 5 4 3

BRIEF CONTENTS

CONTENTS

CHAPTER 12
Hallucinogens (Psychedelics) 371

CHAPTER 13
Marijuana 403

CHAPTER 14
Inhalants 447

CHAPTER 18
Treating Drug Dependence   612

CHAPTER 9

Narcotics (Opioids)

© ermingut/iStockphoto.com

Did You Know?

▶ The release of natural substances called endorphins activate opioid receptors and can mimic the effects of narcotics such as heroin or morphine.

▶ By the end of the 19th century, almost 300,000 Americans were addicted to opiates, primarily due to the use of patent medicines that contained opium products.

▶ Narcotics are among the most potent analgesics available today.

▶ In the past decade, treatment for nonmedical use of prescription pain relievers has increased more than four-fold and currently accounts for two-thirds of prescription abuse in the United States.

▶ Because of concern about abusing prescription narcotic analgesics, many clinicians are hesitant to prescribe sufficient quantities of these drugs to adequately manage severe, long-term pain.

▶ Addiction to prescription narcotic analgesics rarely happens when these medications are used properly to treat pain.

▶ There is evidence that acupuncture reduces pain by activating a natural opioid system.

▶ Many heroin addicts have been exposed to the AIDS virus.

▶ Heroin supplies today are more potent, cheaper, and more readily available than a decade ago.

▶ One designer drug, made from the narcotic fentanyl, is 6000 times more potent than heroin.

▶ Some heroin addicts have to be treated with the narcotics methadone or buprenorphine for the rest of their lives to keep them from abusing heroin.

▶ Dextromethorphan (a common over-the-counter cough medicine chemically related to codeine), when taken in high doses, can cause phencyclidine (PCP)-like hallucinations.

 Drugs and Society Online is a great source for additional drugs and society information for both students and instructors. Visit **go.jblearning.com /hanson12** to find a variety of useful tools for learning, thinking, and teaching.

Learning Objectives

On completing this chapter you will be able to:

❯ Describe the principal pharmacological effects of narcotics, their biological targets, and their main therapeutic uses.

❯ Identify the major side effects of narcotics, in particular their abuse potential.

❯ Distinguish between narcotic physical dependence and addiction.

❯ Identify the abuse patterns for heroin.

❯ Outline the stages of heroin dependence.

❯ List the withdrawal symptoms that result from narcotic dependence, list potential treatments, and discuss the significance of tolerance.

❯ Describe and compare the use of methadone and buprenorphine in treating narcotic addiction.

❯ Identify the unique features of fentanyl that make it appealing to illicit drug dealers but dangerous to narcotic addicts.

❯ Describe how "designer" drugs have been associated with narcotics and Parkinson's disease.

❯ Describe why dextromethorphan in cough medicines is abused.

❯ Identify the opioid features of tramadol and its potential for abuse.

Introduction

The proportion of persons admitted for substance abuse treatment whose principal problem was nonmedical use of prescription pain medication (i.e., narcotic analgesics) has gone from 2.2% to almost 10% in the past decade (Ostrow 2012). Consequently, abuse of prescription painkillers has been described as an epidemic by the Centers for Disease Control and Prevention (CDC) and is viewed as a gateway for abuse of potent narcotics such as heroin (Naggiar 2012). What are these drugs, where do they come from, and how do they work?

The term *narcotic* in general means a central nervous system (CNS) depressant that produces insensibility or stupor. The term has also come to designate those drugs and substances with pharmacological properties related to opium ingredients and their drug derivatives. All opioid narcotics activate opioid receptors and have abuse potential. Narcotics are frequently prescribed for pain relief (**analgesics**), to reduce coughing (**antitussive**), and to reduce diarrhea.

In this chapter, we introduce the opioid narcotics with a brief historical account. The pharmacological properties and therapeutic uses of these drugs are discussed, followed by a description of, and distinction between, their side effects and problems with tolerance, withdrawal, dependence, and addiction. Narcotic abuse, its risks and outcomes, is presented in detail, with special emphasis on heroin. In addition, treatment approaches for narcotic addiction, dependence, and withdrawal are included. This chapter concludes with descriptions of other commonly used opioid narcotics and related drugs.

What Are Narcotics?

The word *narcotic* has been used to label many substances, from opium to marijuana to cocaine. The translation of the Greek word *narkoticos* is "benumbing or deadening." The term *narcotic* is sometimes used to refer to a CNS depressant, producing insensibility or stupor, and at other times to refer to an addicting drug. Most people would not consider marijuana among the narcotics today, although for many years it was included in this category. Although pharmacologically cocaine is not a narcotic either, it is still legally classified as such. Perhaps part of this confusion is due to the fact that cocaine, as a local anesthetic, can cause a numbing effect.

For purposes of the present discussion, the term *narcotic* is used to refer to those naturally occurring substances derived from the opium poppy and their synthetic substitutes. These drugs are referred to as the **opioid** (or opiate) narcotics because of their association with opium. They have similar pharmacological features, including abuse potential, pain-relieving effects (referred to as analgesics), cough suppression, and reduction of intestinal movement, often causing constipation, but useful in reducing severe diarrhea. Some of the most commonly used opioid narcotics are listed in **Table 9.1**.

The History of Narcotics

The opium poppy, *Papaver somniferum*, from which opium and its naturally occurring narcotic derivatives are obtained, has been cultivated for millennia. A 6000-year-old Sumerian tablet has an ideograph for the poppy shown as "joy" plus "plant," suggesting that the addicting properties of this substance have been appreciated for millennia. The Egyptians listed opium along with approximately 700 other medicinal compounds in the famous Ebers Papyrus (circa 1500 BC).

The Greek god of sleep, Hypnos, and the Roman god of sleep, Somnus, were portrayed as carrying containers of opium pods, and the Minoan goddess of sleep wore a crown of opium pods. During the so-called Dark Ages that followed the collapse of the Roman Empire, Arab traders actively engaged in traveling the overland caravan routes to China and to India, where they introduced opium. Eventually, both China and India grew their own poppies.

KEY TERMS

analgesics
drugs that relieve pain without affecting consciousness

antitussives
drugs that block the coughing reflex

opioid
relating to the drugs that are derived from opium

TABLE 9.1 Commonly Used Opioid Narcotic Drugs and Products

Narcotic Drugs	Common Names	Most Common Uses
Heroin	Horse, smack, junk (street names)	Abuse
Morphine	Several	Analgesia
Methadone	Dolophine	Treat narcotic dependence
Meperidine	Demerol	Analgesia
Oxycodone	Percodan, OxyContin	Analgesia
Propoxyphene	Darvon	Analgesia
Codeine	Several	Analgesia, antitussive
Loperamide	Imodium A-D	Antidiarrheal
Diphenoxylate	Lomotil	Antidiarrheal
Opium tincture	Paregoric	Antidiarrheal
Buprenorphine	Suboxone	Treat narcotic dependence
Tramadol	Ultram	Analgesia (Note: considered to have weak, but significant, opioid properties)

■ Opium in China

The opium poppy had a dramatic impact in China, causing widespread addiction (Karch 1996). Initially, the seeds were used medically, as was opium later. However, by the late 1690s, opium was being smoked and used for diversion. The Chinese government, fearful of the weakening of national vitality by the potent opiate narcotic, outlawed the sale of opium in 1729. The penalty for disobedience was death by strangulation or decapitation. Despite these laws and threats, the habit of opium smoking became so widespread that the Chinese government went a step further and forbade its importation from India, where most of the opium poppy was grown. In contrast, the British East India Company (and later the British government in India) encouraged cultivation of opium. British companies were the principal shippers to the Chinese port of Canton, which was the only port open to Western merchants. During the next 120 years, a complex network of opium smuggling routes developed in China with the help of local merchants, who received substantial profits, and local officials, who pocketed bribes to ignore the smugglers.

Everyone involved in the opium trade, but particularly the British, continued to profit until the Chinese government ordered the strict enforcement of the edict against importation. Such actions by the Chinese caused conflict with

the British government and helped trigger the Opium War of 1839 to 1842. Great Britain sent in an army, and by 1842, 10,000 British soldiers had won a victory over 350 million Chinese. Because of the war, the island of Hong Kong was ceded to the British, and an indemnity of $6 million was imposed on China to cover the value of the

© forbis/Shutterstock, Inc.

Opium poppies such as these are used as a source for natural opioid narcotic drugs such as heroin, morphine, and codeine.

A famous cartoon, showing a British sailor shoving opium down the throat of a Chinese man, which dates back to the Opium War of 1839–1842.

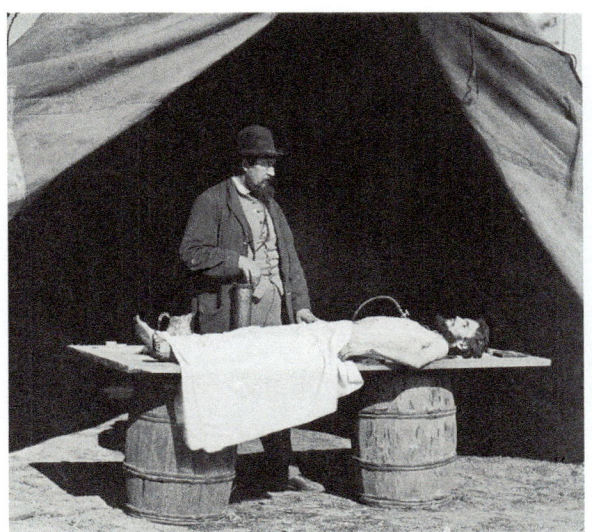

With the development of the hypodermic needle and its use during the Civil War, heroin addiction became more likely and more severe.

destroyed opium and the cost of the war. In 1856, a second Opium War broke out. Peking was occupied by British and French troops, and China was compelled to make further concessions to Britain. The importation of opium continued to increase until 1908, when Britain and China made an agreement to limit the importation of opium from India (Austin 1978).

American Opium Use

Meanwhile, in 1803, a young German named Frederick Serturner extracted and partially purified the active ingredients in opium. The result was 10 times more potent than opium itself and was named *morphine*, after Morpheus, the Greek god of dreams. This discovery increased worldwide interest in opium. By 1832, a second compound had been purified and named *codeine*, after the Greek word for "poppy capsule" (Maurer and Vogel 1967).

The opium problem was aggravated further in 1853, when Alexander Wood perfected the hypodermic syringe and introduced it first in Europe and then in America. Christopher Wren and others had worked with the idea of injecting drugs directly into the body by means of hollow quills and straws, but the approach was never successful or well received. Wood perfected the syringe technique with the intent of preventing morphine addiction by injecting the drug directly into the veins rather than using oral administration (Golding 1993). Unfortunately, just the opposite happened; injection of morphine increased the potency and the likelihood of dependence (Maurer and Vogel 1967).

The hypodermic syringe was used extensively during the Civil War to administer morphine to treat pain, dysentery, and fatigue (Kosten and Hollister 1998). A large percentage of the soldiers who returned home from the war were addicted to morphine (National Institute on Drug Abuse [NIDA] 2013). Opiate addiction became known as the "soldier's disease" or "army disease."

By 1900, an estimated 300,000 Americans were dependent on opiates (NIDA 2013). This drug problem was made worse because of (1) Chinese laborers, who brought opium with them to the United States to smoke (it was legal to smoke opium in the United States at that time); (2) the availability of purified morphine and the hypodermic syringe; and (3) the lack of controls on the large number of patent medicines that contained opium derivatives (Karch 1996). Until 1914, when the Harrison Narcotic Act was passed (regulating opium, coca leaves, and their products), the average opiate addict was a middle-aged, Southern, white woman who functioned well and was adjusted to her role as a wife and mother. She bought opium or morphine legally by mail order from Sears and Roebuck or at the local store, used it orally, and caused very few problems. A number of physicians were addicted as well. One of the best-known morphine addicts was William Holsted, a founder of Johns Hopkins Medical School. Holsted was a very productive surgeon and innovator, although secretly an addict for most of his career. He became dependent on morphine as a substitute for his cocaine dependence (Brecher 1972).

Chinese laborers often smoked heroin at the turn of the 20th century.

Heroin use by soldiers fighting in Afghanistan is a great concern.

Looking for better medicines, chemists found that modification of the morphine molecule resulted in a more potent compound. In 1898, diacetylmorphine was placed on the market as a cough suppressant by Bayer. It was to be a "heroic" drug, without the addictive potential of morphine—it thus received the name *heroin.*

Heroin was first used in the United States as a cough suppressant and to combat addiction to other substances (Hubbard 1998). However, its inherent abuse potential was quickly discovered. When injected, heroin is more addictive than most of the other narcotics because of its ability to enter the brain rapidly and cause a euphoric surge (DiChiara and North 1992). Heroin was banned from U.S. medical practice in 1924, although it is still prescribed legally as an analgesic or for treatment of narcotic dependence (like methadone) in other countries (Drug War Facts 2012).

The Vietnam War was an important landmark for heroin use in the United States (Hubbard 1998). It has been estimated that as many as 40% of the U.S. soldiers serving in Southeast Asia at this time used heroin to combat the frustrations and stress associated with this unpopular military action. Although only 7% of the soldiers continued to use heroin after returning home, those who were addicted to this potent narcotic became a major component of the heroin-abusing population in this country (Golding 1993).

Heroin smoking became popular in the mid-1980s in response to the acquired immune deficiency syndrome (AIDS) epidemic. This was due to a fear of HIV infection when using infected needles to administer the drug intravenously (Hubbard 1998). The effect resulting from inhalation is as intense as that caused by injection, although a very pure drug is required for smoking. Smoking continues to be a favorite form of heroin administration today.

As experience has shown, problems with the opiate drugs such as heroin are closely linked with war and its associated miseries and pains. As our country again finds itself in the middle of an extended and increasingly less popular military engagement in the Middle East, particularly Afghanistan, problems with heroin are becoming more and more apparent (RT 2013). As during previous wars, soldiers turn to drugs like heroin to cope and even to survive emotionally in a war zone. This is reflected in comments such as: "Life is unbearable. You don't know whether you're going to be alive in 10 minutes' time or not." "Life has few pleasures; you're uncomfortable . . . the food is pretty awful, the ever-present smell of death and you see some of your closest buddies die before your very eyes." "So life is really unbearable and heroin is cheap" (Edwards 2010).

Pharmacological Effects

Even though opioid narcotics have a history of being abused, they continue to be important therapeutic agents.

■ Narcotic Analgesics

The most common clinical use of the opioid narcotics is as analgesics to relieve pain. These drugs are effective against most varieties of pain, including *visceral* (associated with internal organs of the body) and *somatic* (associated with skeletal muscles, bones, skin, and teeth) types. Used in sufficiently high doses, narcotics can even relieve the intense pain associated with some types of cancer (Gutstein and Akil 2006).

The opioid narcotics relieve pain by activating the same group of receptors that are controlled by the endogenous substances called *endorphins* (Trigo et al. 2010). The endorphins are a family of peptides (small proteins) that are released in the brain, in the spinal cord, and from the adrenal glands in response to stress and painful experiences. When released, the endorphins serve as transmitters and stimulate receptors designated as opioid types. Activation of opioid receptors by either the naturally released endorphins or administration of the narcotic analgesic drugs blocks the transmission of pain through the spinal cord or brain stem and alters the perception of pain in the "pain center" of the brain. Because the narcotics work at multiple levels of pain transmission, they are potent analgesics against almost all types of pain.

Interestingly, the endorphin system appears to be influenced by psychological factors as well. Thus, natural activation of opioid receptors also contributes to the regulation of emotional behaviors such as stress, learning, and memory as well as the regulation of the brain's reward circuits (Trigo et al. 2010). It is possible that pain relief caused by administration of placebos or nonmedicinal manipulation such as acupuncture is due in part to the natural release of endorphins (Eshkevari and Heath 2005). This relationship suggests that physiological, psychological, and pharmacological factors are intertwined in pain management through the opioid system, which makes it impossible to deal with one without considering the others.

Although the narcotics are very effective analgesics, they do cause some side effects that are particularly alarming; thus, their clinical use usually is limited to the treatment of moderate to severe pain (Schumacher, Basbaum, and Way 2012). Other, safer drugs, such as the aspirin-type analgesics, are preferred for pain management when possible. Often, the amount of narcotic required for pain relief can be reduced by combining a narcotic, such as codeine, with aspirin or acetaminophen (the active ingredient in Tylenol). Such combinations reduce the chance of significant narcotic side effects while providing adequate pain relief (Schumacher et al. 2012).

Morphine is a particularly potent pain reliever and often is used as the analgesic standard to which other narcotics are compared (Gutstein and Akil 2006). With continual use, tolerance develops to the analgesic effects of morphine and other narcotics, sometimes requiring a dramatic escalation of doses to maintain adequate pain control (Schumacher et al. 2012).

Because pain is expressed in different forms with many different diseases, narcotic treatment can vary considerably. Usually, the convenience of oral narcotic therapy is preferred but often is inadequate for severe pain. For short-term relief from intense pain, narcotics are effective when injected subcutaneously or intramuscularly. Narcotics can also be given intravenously for persistent and potent analgesia or administered by transdermal patches for sustained chronic pain (*Drug Facts and Comparisons* 2010). Despite the fact that most pain can be relieved if enough narcotic analgesic is properly administered, physicians frequently underprescribe narcotics or are not well trained in proper pain management or how to use the opioid narcotics responsibly (Meier 2010; Young 2007). Because of fear of causing narcotic addiction or creating legal problems with federal agencies such as the Drug Enforcement Administration (DEA) (see "Here and Now: Are Restrictions on Pain Pills Too Painful?"), many patients in the United States are often inadequately treated for their pain (Jointogether.org 2010). An important rule of narcotic use is that adequate pain relief should not be denied because of concern about the abuse potential of these drugs (Schumacher et al. 2012). Indeed, addiction to narcotics is rare in patients receiving these drugs for therapy unless they have a history of drug abuse or have an underlying psychiatric disorder (Gutstein and Akil 2006).

Occasionally, there are outbreaks of abuse of commonly prescribed narcotic products such as OxyContin (Brady 2010; "'Oxy' Kids Crisis" 2007). This product includes the opiate oxycodone, which has the approximate narcotic potency of morphine and can be obtained with relative ease. Authorities claim that the illegal pills come from doctors' offices, from dealers who fake illness to get legal prescriptions or who are writing phony orders, and from others who steal the supplies from pharmacies. OxyContin has been called *oxys*, *O.C.*, and *killers* on the street and is popular with narcotic abusers because of its rapid and potent effect. However, many, if not most, of those who use prescriptions drugs for nonmedical purposes obtain their painkillers from the medicine cabinets of a family member or a friend (*Alcoholism and Drug Abuse Weekly* 2010). On the street, the drug can cost 10 times its prescription price. Because of its potent ability to suppress respiration, OxyContin appears to have

HERE AND NOW

Are Restrictions on Pain Pills Too Painful?

Because of a spiraling increase in the abuse of prescription painkillers, the DEA has warned doctors who specialize in pain management that they risk special investigation if they do not comply with DEA guidelines. For example, the DEA recommends avoiding the use of opioid analgesics for the treatment of pain in patients who have a history of abusing these drugs. In addition, the DEA frowns upon the practice of doctors writing prescriptions for these pain drugs that can be filled on a future date. These and other restrictive DEA policies are viewed by some pain doctors as overregulation. Some are concerned that physicians will hesitate to prescribe even needed pain medication for fear of being investigated and charged with breaking the law. They worry that the DEA's actions are sending a chilling message that could result in withholding opioid narcotics from millions of patients who cannot be adequately treated by other drugs.

Data from Kaufman, M. "New DEA Statement Has Pain Doctors More Fearful." *Washington Post* (30 November 2004): A-17; and Borigini, M. "Prescribing Narcotics: A Doctor's Point of View." Health Central, Chronic Pain Connection. 27 October 2008. Available http://www.healthcentral.com/chronic-pain/c/91/46424/prescribing-view. Accessed March 14, 2011.

been involved in overdose deaths throughout the country, although there is some evidence that other drugs were also involved in many of these cases. Critics claim that part of the abuse problem with OxyContin stems from overuse in situations that should be managed by a less potent and less addicting opioid analgesic.

■ Other Therapeutic Uses

Opioid narcotics are also used to treat conditions not related to pain. For example, these drugs suppress the coughing center of the brain, so they are effective antitussives. Codeine, a natural opioid narcotic, is commonly included in cough medicine. In addition, opioid narcotics slow the movement of materials through the intestines, a property that can be used to relieve diarrhea or can cause the side effect of constipation (Schumacher et al. 2012). Paregoric contains an opioid narcotic substance and is commonly used to treat severe diarrhea.

When used carefully by the clinician, opioid narcotics are very effective therapeutic tools. Guidelines for avoiding unnecessary problems with these drugs include the following (Rolfs 2008):

- Opioid pain relievers should only be used for pain when severity warrants and after consideration of other nonopioid pain medications such as aspirin, ibuprofen, or acetaminophen (e.g., Tylenol).
- Doses and duration of use should be limited as much as possible while permitting adequate therapeutic care.

- The patient should be counseled to store the medications securely, not share with others, and dispose of drugs properly when the pain has subsided and the medication is no longer needed.
- Long-duration opioid drugs should not be used to treat acute pain, except in situations where adequate monitoring can be conducted.
- The use of opioids should be reevaluated if pain persists beyond the anticipated time period for acute pain management.
- A comprehensive evaluation should be conducted before initiating opioid treatment.
- The provider should consider conducting a screen for risk of abuse or addiction before initiating opioid treatment.
- A treatment plan should be established between the doctor and patient that includes measurable goals for reduction of pain and improvement of function.
- The patient, and if appropriate, family members, should be informed of the risks and benefits of the opioid treatment. Sometimes a written contract identifying these elements should be prepared and signed.
- Opioid treatment should be discontinued if the terms of the contract are not being met by the patient.
- If significant abuse is suspected, the clinician should discuss the concerns with the patient and help the patient find appropriate treatment.

■ Abuse of Prescription Opioid Painkillers

As already mentioned, the abuse of prescription opioid painkillers has become a major problem in the United States and has been described by the U.S. Drug Czar (i.e., director of the Office of National Drug Control Policy [ONDCP]), R. Gil Kerlikowske, as the "nation's fastest-growing drug problem" (*USA Today* 2010). An example of what has become all too common is the tragic narcotic overdose death of Leslie Cooper near Portsmouth, Ohio. She was never known to wander the streets or dark alleys to get her opioid narcotics. She received her drugs "legally" from multiple doctors and "pain-management clinics." Her problem with these prescription analgesics started when doctors prescribed potent painkillers to deal with the severe discomfort after a difficult surgery. More surgeries were necessary, which meant continual demand for, and access to, the opioid pain relievers. Something went terribly wrong and Leslie paid the price with her life. In her system was found a deadly combination of depressant drugs prescribed for muscle relaxation and depression, and two very potent narcotic analgesics. Leslie fell asleep and did not wake up. This is an example of why the misuse of these painkillers has led to a doubling of emergency room visits since 2004 (*USA Today* 2010), and also has caused some critics to question whether many doctors who prescribe such drugs are sufficiently trained in either proper pain or substance abuse management (Meier 2010).

Abuse problems with these drugs are partially due to the facts that these narcotic analgesics are very popular and account for about 7% of all prescribed drugs and that the number of patients who are taking the long-lasting versions of the agents (e.g., OxyContin) has increased 30% during the past decade (Meier 2010). This means that these drugs are more readily available and their use more widely accepted than ever before. However, it is important to appreciate that when used properly (i.e., as prescribed), the likelihood of becoming addicted to these narcotics for most people is very small (likely less than 1%). But there are risk factors that make some patients more likely to have problems with these drugs; for those with these risk factors the rate of addiction jumps to 25% (see "Prescription for Abuse: What Makes People Vulnerable?") (Sify News 2010).

PRESCRIPTION FOR ABUSE

What Makes People Vulnerable?

For most patients, the responsible use of prescription opioid analgesics is very helpful in the management of moderate to severe pain; however, a relatively small population has factors that can increase the danger of becoming addicted to these drugs as much as 25-fold. The risks that lead to this vulnerability include:

- Family history of substance abuse problems, which suggests the likelihood of genetic vulnerability (Levran et al. 2009)
- Dependence on nicotine, alcohol, or sleeping pills
- Depression
- Use of psychiatric medications
- Younger than 65 years of age

The value of identifying these risks is they may help warn clinicians about which patients require special consideration and caution when prescribing narcotics to treat their pain.

....

Data from Sify News. "Risk Factors for Painkiller Addiction Identified." 28 August 2010. Available http://sify.com/news/risk-factors-for-painkiller-addiction-identified-news-scitech-ki3pEjahbic.html. Accessed March 14, 2011; Reuters. "Do Smokers Use More Prescription Painkillers?" 17 June 2010. Available http://www.reuters.com/article/idUSTRE65G5RQ20100617. Accessed March 14, 2011; Medical News Today. "Study Identifies Risk Factors for Painkiller Addiction and Links the Addiction to Genetics." 28 August 2010. Available http://www.medicalnewstoday.com/articles/199263.php. Accessed March 14, 2011; and American Academy of Pain Medicine. "Psychiatric Factors Linked to Increased Risk for Misuse of Opioid Medications." 23rd Annual Meeting. Abstract 151. 7 February 2007.

Abuse of prescription opioid narcotics such as OxyContin and illicit narcotics such as heroin might seem to some people very different because one comes from a doctor and the other from drug dealers in the street. But in reality, because both types of drugs are opiates, they both can cause similar addiction, overdoses, and even death. In fact, a surprising rise in heroin abuse is occurring across the United States, which is likely in part the result of people who become addicted to the prescription opioid painkillers and switch to heroin because it is more accessible and easier to obtain.

SIGNS & SYMPTOMS

Narcotics

Possible Signs of Use	Possible Signs of Overdose
Euphoria	Low and shallow breathing
Drowsiness	Clammy skin
Respiratory depression	Convulsions
Constricted pupils	Coma
Nausea	Death

Heroin also can cost as little as one-fifth the price of prescription medications. All too often cases of heroin overdose deaths appear to have their origins from the victim first being exposed to the opioid narcotics during a chronic treatment for pain often associated with sports-related injuries (Valenzuela 2010; Willis 2008).

■ Mechanisms of Action

As mentioned earlier, the opioid receptors are the site of action of the naturally occurring endorphin peptide transmitters and are found throughout the nervous system, intestines, and other internal organs. Because narcotic drugs such as morphine and heroin enhance the endorphin system by directly stimulating opioid receptors, these drugs have widespread influences throughout the body.

For example, the opioid receptors are present in high concentration within the limbic structures of the brain. Stimulation of these receptors by narcotics causes release of the transmitter dopamine in limbic brain regions. This effect contributes to the rewarding actions of these drugs and leads to dependence and abuse (see "Signs & Symptoms: Narcotics") (Trigo et al. 2010; Zocchi et al. 2003).

■ Side Effects

One of the most common side effects of the opioid narcotics is constipation. Other side effects include drowsiness, mental clouding, respiratory depression (suppressed breathing is usually the cause of death from overdose), nausea and vomiting, itching, inability to urinate, a drop in blood pressure, and constricted pupils (Kral and Ghafoor 2013;

Schumacher et al. 2012). This array of seemingly unrelated side effects is due to widespread distribution of the opioid receptors throughout the body and their involvement in many physiological functions (Gourlay 2004; Trigo et al. 2010). With continual use, tolerance usually develops to some of these undesirable narcotic responses.

Drugs that selectively antagonize the opioid receptors can block the effects of natural opioid systems in the body and reverse the effects of narcotic opiate drugs (*Drug Facts and Comparisons* 2010). When an opioid antagonist such as the drug naloxone is administered alone, it has little noticeable effect. The antiopioid actions of naloxone become more apparent when the antagonist is injected into someone who has taken a narcotic opioid drug. For example, naloxone will cause (1) a recurrence of pain in the patient using a narcotic for pain relief, (2) the restoration of consciousness and normal breathing in the addict who has overdosed on heroin, and (3) severe withdrawal effects in the opioid abuser who has become dependent on narcotics (Kral and Ghafoor 2013). Because of the ability of these antagonists to block the effects of opioid drugs, they are also used as treatment for some opioid-dependent patients (Kral and Ghafoor 2013).

An interesting recent use of opioid antagonists is to treat alcohol dependence. The Food and Drug Administration (FDA) has approved the use of naltrexone (a narcotic antagonist) in a regular and extended-release formulation to relieve the craving of alcoholics for excessive alcohol consumption (Schumacher et al. 2012).

Abuse, Tolerance, Dependence, and Withdrawal

All the opioid narcotic agents that activate opioid receptors have abuse potential and are classified as scheduled drugs (see **Table 9.2**). Their patterns of abuse are determined by the ability of these drugs to cause tolerance, dependence, withdrawal effects, and eventually addiction. However, it is important to recognize that even though a patient treated by these drugs for pain develops physical dependence and experiences significant withdrawal when the drug is abruptly removed, they are not necessarily addicted (Hitti 2010). In fact, relatively few patients properly receiving the opioid narcotics for pain relief will go on to become truly

TABLE 9.2 Schedule Classification of Some Common Narcotics

Narcotic	Schedule
Heroin	I
Morphine	II, III
Methadone	II
Fentanyl	II
Hydromorphone	II
Meperidine	II
Codeine	II, III, V
Buprenorphine	III
Pentazocine	IV
Tramadol	Unscheduled
Narcotics combined with nonsteroidal anti-inflammatory drugs	III

Drug Enforcement Administration (DEA). Controlled Substances Act. 1 February 2010. Information and Legal Resources (May 2013). Available http://www.deadiversion.usdoj.gov /schedules/#list

addicted, even though they may develop physical dependence and are temporarily uncomfortable when the narcotic treatment is discontinued. This distinction between physical dependence and the compulsive need to use the opioid narcotics despite very negative consequences (i.e., addiction) is very important and needs to be appreciated in order to provide proper pain management, especially for severe long-term pain conditions (Drug War Facts 2010b).

The process of tolerance literally begins with the first dose of a narcotic, but tolerance does not become clinically evident until after 2 to 3 weeks of frequent use (either therapeutic- or abuse-related). Tolerance occurs most rapidly with high doses given in short intervals and is a common result of the extended clinical use of prescription opioid painkillers. It also is caused by abuse of these narcotics in addicted persons. The result of tolerance is that doses of these drugs must be increased (sometimes several-fold) to retain or regain the therapeutic or nonmedicinal narcotic effects. Physical dependence invariably accompanies severe tolerance (Schumacher et al. 2012). Psychological dependence can also develop with continual narcotic use because these drugs can cause euphoria and relieve stress. Such psychological dependence

leads to compulsive use (Luscher 2012). Because all narcotics affect the same opioid systems in the body, developing tolerance to one narcotic drug means the person has cross-tolerance to all drugs in this group.

The development of psychological and physical dependence makes stopping the drug uncomfortable due to resulting unpleasant withdrawals. Someone who has used potent narcotics for a long time, like a major long-term addict, will experience severe withdrawal effects such as exaggerated pain responses, agitation, anxiety, stomach cramps and vomiting, joint and muscle aches, runny nose, and an overall flu-like feeling. Although these withdrawal symptoms are not fatal, they are extremely aversive and encourage continuation of the narcotic habit (Luscher 2012).

Overall, the narcotics have similar actions; there are differences, however, in their potencies, severity of side effects, likelihood of being abused, and clinical usefulness.

■ Heroin Abuse

My parents had no idea. My mom thought I was smoking a lot of weed and taking diet pills, because who would've thought that such a bad drug (heroin) could be so easily accessible to me. Growing up, everything is pushed on you. You're trying to be the smartest, trying to compete with everyone. Heroin was an escape.

It hits you hard, but it's so smooth and enticing at the same time. It hits you like a train of false love.

Believe it or not, as a high school teenager, it is easier for us to get than alcohol. (*Quotes from three young people in rehabilitation in New York; Buckley 2009*)

These quotes from three young people illustrate the powerful attraction of heroin and help explain why it is so frequently abused. They also illustrate that the use of heroin, especially by teenagers and young adults, appears to be increasing. The likely explanations for this recent rise in popularity include the facts that high-grade heroin has become very cheap and readily available (Suhr and Salter 2012). In addition, it appears that elevated heroin use is an indirect consequence of the increase in the abuse of prescription opioid painkillers. Thus, as more people abuse the prescribed narcotics they increase their consumption because they develop tolerance. This makes their habit more expensive and makes it more difficult to obtain enough of the prescription drugs to satisfy their nonmedical (addiction) needs. Consequently, these people frequently switch to street heroin, which is a fraction of the cost while being reasonably pure and potent (Daly 2013). Of course, this switch to heroin increases the risk of getting a bad batch of drug that is much more potent than expected or contains other drugs that are more dangerous. The unintended outcomes can be, at the least, very dangerous and result in a trip to the emergency room, or in the extreme, can cause an accidental overdose fatality (Bernstein 2010; Caldwell and Salter 2010).

Heroin is currently classified as a Schedule I drug by the DEA (see Table 9.2). It is not approved for any clinical use in the United States, is one of the most widely abused illegal drugs in the world, and is reported to account for more than $120 billion in global sales each year (Chossudovsky 2006; GlobalSecurity.org 2010). It is also thought to be associated with some of the highest mortality rates and most emergency room visits of any of the illegal drugs of abuse in the United States (NIDA 2005). Heroin was illicitly used more than any other drug of abuse in the United States (except for marijuana) until 20 years ago, when it was unseated by cocaine (DiChiara and North 1992). In 2012, 0.6% of high school seniors reported having used heroin during the previous year, and 1.1% indicated that they had used this drug sometime during their life (Johnston 2013).

From 1970 through 1976, most of the heroin reaching the United States originated from the Golden Triangle region of Southeast Asia, which includes parts of Burma, Thailand, and Laos. During that period, the United States and other nations purchased much of the legal opium crop from Turkey in an effort to stop opium from being converted into heroin. From 1975 until 1980, the major heroin supply came from opium poppies grown in Mexico. The U.S. government furnished the Mexican government with helicopters, herbicide sprays, and financial assistance to destroy the poppy crop. Changes in political climates have shifted the source of supply back to the Golden Triangle and Latin American countries (e.g., Colombia; Seper 2003) and more recently to Afghanistan, where 92% of the world's heroin is currently produced (Christensen 2010), accounting for approximately $3 billion in revenue for local farmers (Agence France-Presse [AFP] 2010).

Heroin produced in Afghanistan has taken a heavy toll on the Afghan people (Christenson 2010) (see "Here and Now: Afghans' Drug War"). It has been speculated that heroin trafficked from Afghanistan has killed more than a million people worldwide in the past decade (AFP 2010), and as previously discussed, is a substantial problem for U.S. and NATO soldiers fighting in the Afghan War (Edwards 2010). Despite these disturbing effects, the United States has stopped its previous policy of crop eradication because it alienated the poorest Afghan populations, who rely on this crop to survive and support their families. Eradication tended to turn them against the efforts of the U.S./European-supported government to eliminate insurgent groups such as the Taliban. More recently, the U.S. government and military have been trying to convince farmers to replace their opium poppies with other profitable crops (AFP 2010; Starikov 2010). Despite these efforts to be more "compassionate and understanding," many experts question the effectiveness of these strategies (Starikov 2010).

HEROIN COMBINATIONS

Heroin is typically smuggled into the United States from one of four foreign sources: Mexico, South America, Southeast Asia (e.g., Burma), or Southwest Asia (e.g., Afghanistan). It is carried into the United States hidden in commercial and private vehicles driven from Mexico or Canada or carried by couriers traveling on commercial flights. Pure heroin is a white powder. Other colors, such as brown Mexican heroin, result from unsatisfactory processing of morphine or from adulterants. Heroin is usually "cut" (diluted) with lactose (milk sugar) to give it bulk and thus increase profits. When heroin first enters the United States, it can be up to 95% pure; by the time it is sold to users, its purity can be as low as 3% or (recently) as high as 70% (Good Drugs Guide 2013; Schneider 2009). If users are unaware of the variance in purity and do not adjust doses accordingly, the results can be extremely dangerous and occasionally fatal (Bernstein 2010; NIDA 2005).

Heroin has a bitter taste, so sometimes it is cut with quinine, a bitter substance, to disguise the fact that the heroin content has been reduced. Quinine can be a deadly adulterant. Part of the "flash," or immediate rush, from direct injection of heroin may be caused by this contaminant. Quinine is an irritant, and it causes vascular damage, acute and potentially lethal disturbances in

HERE AND NOW

Afghans' Drug War

How goes the "war" in Afghanistan? The answer may be quite different depending on whether you are referring to the military war being fought against the Taliban with guns, explosives, and military maneuvers or the drug war being fought against poor opium farmers trying to survive on meager earnings that come from the few acres they are able to cultivate. Opium crops are particularly well suited to this land and historically brought good prices. Consequently, it is difficult to convince the poor farmers that crops that allow them to feed their families are evil and should be stopped. Despite the fact that efforts by both the Afghan and U.S. governments to educate opium farmers and help them develop profitable alternative crops reduced poppy cultivation by 22% in 2009, production of Afghan opium has risen dramatically during the Afghan War and currently is thought to provide 92% of the world's heroin. Just because they produce the opium, the Afghan people are not immune to its problems. It is speculated

Courtesy of Lance Cpl. Kowshon Ye/U.S. Department of Defense

that 1 in 25 Afghans is an addict, and there are very few resources to provide adequate treatment or initiate effective prevention programs. Statistics such as these are powerful evidence that the Afghans' drug war goes very badly indeed.

Data from Constable, P. "A Poor Yield for Afghans' 'War on Drugs.'" *Washington Post* (19 September 2006): 14A; and Christenson, S. "Heroin Addiction Takes Brutal Toll on Afghanistan." *San Antonio Express-News.* 24 May 2010. Available http://www.mysanantonio.com/news/local_news/in_kabul_regrets_rehab_and_redemption_94714589.html?showFullArticle=y. Accessed March 14, 2011.

heartbeat, depressed respiration, coma, and death from respiratory arrest. Opiate poisoning causes acute pulmonary edema as well as respiratory depression. To counteract the constipation caused by heroin, sometimes mannitol is added for its laxative effect.

Another potentially lethal combination emerges when heroin is laced with the much more potent artificial narcotic fentanyl. This adulterated heroin can be extremely dangerous due to its unexpected potency (NIDA 2004).

Frequently, heroin is deliberately combined with other drugs when self-administered by addicts (Hickman et al. 2007). According to the National Institute on Drug Abuse (NIDA)–sponsored Drug Abuse Warning Network (DAWN) survey of emergency rooms in the United States, 41% of the reported heroin abuse cases involved other drugs of abuse in combination with this narcotic. Heroin is most frequently used with alcohol, but it is often combined with CNS stimulants, such as cocaine (Good Drugs Guide 2012). Some crack cocaine smokers turn to heroin to ease the jitters caused

Courtesy of DEA

Crude heroin is dark, whereas purified heroin is a white powder.

by the CNS stimulant. It also has been reported that heroin addicts use cocaine to withdraw or detoxify themselves from heroin by gradually decreasing amounts of heroin while increasing amounts of cocaine. This drug combination is called **speedballing**, and addicts claim the cocaine provides relief from the unpleasant withdrawal effects that accompany heroin abstinence in a dependent user (Rowlett et al. 2010).

PROFILE OF HEROIN ADDICTS

An estimated 600,000 to 1 million active heroin addicts live in the United States, a figure that has remained relatively stable despite changes in the number of infrequent and moderate users. Heroin addicts often search for a better and purer drug; however, if they do find an unusually potent batch of heroin, there is a good chance they will get more than they bargained for. Addicts are sometimes found dead with the needle still in the vein after injecting a particularly potent batch of heroin (Caldwell and Salter 2010). More than 3000 deaths occur annually in the United States from heroin overdoses (Caldwell 2010). Death associated with heroin injection is usually due to concurrent use of alcohol or barbiturates—not the heroin alone—and frequently occurs after an addict has gone weeks or months without the drug and injects the same amount of heroin he or she used before, not realizing that tolerance has worn off (Rombey 2003b).

Hard-core addicts often share a common place where they can stash supplies and equipment for their heroin encounters. These locations, called *shooting galleries,* serve as gathering places for addicts (Cowan and Carvel 2006). Shooting galleries can be set up in homes, but are usually located in less established locations such as abandoned cars, cardboard lean-tos, and weed-infested vacant lots. An entrance charge often is required of the patrons. Conditions in shooting galleries are notoriously filthy, and these places are frequented by intravenous heroin users with bloodborne infections that can cause AIDS or hepatitis. Because of needle sharing and other unsanitary practices, shooting galleries have become a place where serious communicative diseases are spread to a wide range of people of different ages, races, genders, and socioeconomic statuses (Nakamura 2008). In some countries such as the United Kingdom, there are controversial efforts to develop government-regulated shooting galleries in order to assure sanitary conditions and clean needles for the heroin addicts to prevent their exposure to the dangers

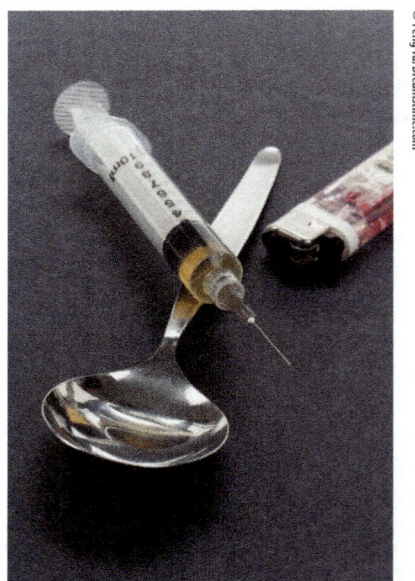

Heroin paraphernalia is usually simple and crude but effective: a spoon on which to dissolve the narcotic and a makeshift syringe with which to inject it.

of contracting devastating and potentially deadly diseases (Leach 2009).

The heroin in shooting galleries is typically prepared by adding several drops of water to the white powder in an improvised container (such as a metal bottle cap), and lightly shaking the container while heating it over a small flame to dissolve the powder. The fluid is then drawn through a tiny wad of cotton to filter out the gross contaminants into an all-too-often used syringe where it is ready for injection.

Some addicts become fixated on the drug's paraphernalia, especially the needle. They can get a psychological high from playing with the needle and syringe. The injection process and syringe plunger action appear to have sexual overtones for them. As one reformed user explained, "I think what I miss more than heroin sometimes is just the ritual of shooting up." A current user concurred, explaining, "You get addicted to the needle . . . Just the process of sticking something into your vein, having such a direct involvement with your body . . ." ("Mary" 1996, p. 42; Winkler et al. 2011).

HEROIN AND CRIME

In 1971, the Select Committee on Crime in the United States released a report on methods used to combat the heroin crisis that arose in the 1950s and 1960s. This report was a turning point in setting up treatment programs for narcotic addicts. The report stated that drug arrests for heroin use had increased 700% since 1961, and that the cost

KEY TERM

speedballing
combining heroin and cocaine

TABLE 9.3 Prevalence of Heroin and Other Opioid Abuse Among High School Seniors

Year	Annual Use		Lifetime Use	
	Heroin	Other Opioids	Heroin	Other Opioids
1989	0.6%	4.4%	1.3%	8.3%
1995	1.1%	4.7%	1.6%	7.2%
1999	1.1%	6.7%	2.0%	10.2%
2002	1.0%	9.4%*	1.7%	13.5%*
2007	0.9%	9.2%	1.5%	13.1%
2009	0.7%	9.2%	1.2%	13.2%
2012	0.6%	7.9%	1.1%	12.2%

* In 2002, the question text was changed in half of the questionnaire forms. The list of examples of narcotics other than heroin was updated: Talwin, laudanum, and paregoric—all of which had negligible rates of use by 2001—were replaced with Vicodin, OxyContin, and Percocet. The 2002 data presented here are based on the changed forms only; N is one-half of N indicated. In 2003, the remaining forms were changed to the new wording. Data based on all forms beginning in 2003.

Data from Johnston, L. D., P. M. O'Malley, J. G. Bachman, and J. E. Schulenberg. Monitoring the Future. "Trends in Lifetime Prevalence of Use of Various Drugs in Grades 8, 10, and 12 (Table 1)." Ann Arbor, MI: University of Michigan, 2010. Available http://monitoringthefuture.org /data/10data/pr10t1.pdf. Accessed April 22, 2011.

of heroin-related crimes to U.S. society was estimated to exceed $3 billion per year. Other studies since that time have linked heroin addiction with crime (McMurran 2007).

Although many young heroin addicts come from affluent or middle-class families (Weiss 1995), research shows heavy users (usually addicts who inject their heroin) are frequently poorly educated with minimal social integration and live in neighborhoods surrounded by poverty (Nandi et al. 2010). Because of these disadvantages, these heroin addicts often have a low level of employment, exist in unstable living conditions, and socialize with other illicit drug users. Clearly, such undesirable living conditions encourage criminal activity. However, three other factors also likely contribute to the association between heroin use and crime:

1. The use of heroin and its pharmacological effects encourage antisocial behavior that is crime related. Depressants such as heroin diminish inhibition and cause people to engage in activities they normally would not. The effects of heroin and its withdrawal make addicts self-centered, demanding, impulsive, and governed by their "need" for the drug.
2. Because heroin addiction is expensive, the user is forced to resort to crime to support the drug habit (McMurran 2007).
3. A similar personality is driven to engage in both criminal behavior and heroin use.

Often, heroin addicts start heroin use about the same time they begin to become actively involved in criminal activity. In most cases, the heroin user has been taking other illicit drugs, especially marijuana, years before trying heroin (Reid, Elifson, and Sterk 2007).

These findings suggest that for many heroin addicts, the antisocial behavior causes the criminal behavior rather than the criminal behavior resulting from the heroin use. Thus, the more a drug such as heroin is perceived as being illegal, desirable, and addictive, the more likely it will be used by deviant criminal populations. However, typically heroin users are not violent, although they may participate in criminal activity to fund their drug habit. Violence is more likely associated with heroin trafficking and distribution because of the criminal groups involved in this activity.

■ Patterns of Heroin Abuse

It has become apparent that problems with narcotics are no longer confined to the inner cities, but have infiltrated suburban areas and small towns and afflict both rich and poor (see "Here and Now: Heroin Use in a Small Town"). The following are recent heroin trends (see **Table 9.3**):

• Heroin use among adolescents and young adults, after holding steady through much of the first decade in 2000, is thought to be rising due to a decrease in cost, and increases in purity and availability (Cole 2010; Schneider 2009).

- Heroin has become purer (60–70% purity) and cheaper ($10/bag [~100 mg]) (Schneider 2009).
- Thanks to the greater purity, new users are able to administer heroin in less efficient ways, such as smoking and snorting, and avoid the dangers of intravenous use (Cole 2010). Many youths believe that heroin can be used safely if it is not injected.
- Because of its association with popular fashions and entertainment, heroin has been viewed as glamorous and chic, especially by many young people, despite its highly publicized lethal consequences. The look of being "wasted" and unkempt has been referred to as "heroin chic" (Urban Dictionary 2005). However, this "druggy look" and malnourished appearance has fallen out of fashion within the glamour business because of its very negative implications and health consequences (Quinion 2005).
- Approximately 190,000 emergency room visits each year are due to heroin overdoses (MyAddiction.com 2010).

STAGES OF DEPENDENCE

Initially, the early effects of heroin are often unpleasant, especially after the first injection (Gutstein and Akil 2006). It is not uncommon to experience nausea and vomiting after administration; gradually, however, the euphoria overwhelms the aversive effects (Quinion 2005). There are two major stages in the development of a psychological dependence on heroin or other opioid narcotics:

1. In the rewarding stage, euphoria and positive effects occur in at least 50% of users. These positive feelings and sensations increase with continued administration and encourage use.
2. Eventually, the heroin or narcotic user must take the drug to avoid withdrawal symptoms that start about 6 to 12 hours after the last dose. At this stage, it is said that "the monkey is on his back." This stage is psychological dependence. If 1 grain of heroin (about 65 milligrams) is taken over a 2-week period on a daily basis, the user becomes physically dependent on the drug.

METHODS OF ADMINISTRATION

Many heroin users start by sniffing the powder or injecting it into a muscle (intramuscular) or under the skin ("skin popping"). Because of the increased purity and decreased cost, many of today's heroin users are administering their drug by smoking and snorting (Caldwell and Salter 2010; Schneider 2009).

HERE AND NOW

Heroin Use in a Small Town

Heroin is supposed to be a "big town" drug, but is gaining popularity in smaller towns. This is very disturbing to those who have chosen to live the rural life with the belief that such an environment will somehow protect them from the ugliness, fear, and pain of typical metropolitan drug problems. They are finding out that drugs such as heroin can be anywhere and used by anybody. Stories like that of Sandi Daost are tragic: her 19-year-old son Robby died from a heroin overdose after months of going in and out of rehab centers trying to stay clean. He grew up in the typical small town—Springville, Utah. The family believed that Robby finally had kicked the habit. He had been clean for 7 months and laughed and joked with the family again. He had a job and a cute girlfriend and was attending church with his family. One Sunday, he told his mother he was going to play golf with a friend. Robby didn't go golfing, but made his last trip to meet his heroin connection. He was found in his bed the next morning, dead from a heroin overdose. The citizens of Springville were bewildered and shocked because within a relatively short time, five other heroin overdose deaths occurred to young men also in their late teens or early 20s. We expect this type of thing in Los Angeles or New York, but no one seems to have an answer to "why in Springville?"

Data from Rombey, D. "Heroin Is Silent Scourge of Sheltered Springville." *Deseret News* (9 June 2003): A-1; Rombey, D. "Heroin Takes Toll on Families." *Deseret News* (10 June 2003): A-1; and Van Hollen, J. "Heroin Abuse Now a Rural Threat Too." *The Cap Times*. 3 October 2010. Available http://host.madison.com/ct/news/opinion/mailbag/article_c47ae879-6bf7-5bf3-a2e5-87c2bebf92a0.html. Accessed March 14, 2011.

Most established heroin addicts still prefer to **mainline** the drug (intravenous injection) (Community Epidemiology Work Group [CEWG] 2002). The injection device can be made from an eyedropper bulb, part of a syringe, and a hypodermic needle. Mainlining drugs causes the thin-walled veins to become scarred and, if done frequently, the veins will collapse. Once a vein is collapsed, it can no longer be used to introduce the drug into the blood. Addicts become expert in locating new veins to use: in the feet, the legs, the neck, even the temples. When addicts do not want "needle tracks" (scars) to show, they inject under the tongue or in the groin ("Opioids" 1996).

HEROIN ADDICTS AND AIDS

As noted previously, because needle sharing is common among heavy heroin users, the transmission of deadly communicable diseases such as AIDS is a major problem. The CDC reports that more than 250,000 AIDS patients in the United States contracted the HIV virus through drug injection; most were heroin users (Drug War Facts 2010a). Fear of contracting this deadly disease has contributed to the increase in administering this drug by smoking and snorting (Tree 2010); however, many heroin users who start by smoking and snorting eventually progress to intravenous administration due to its more intense effects (Leland 1996).

HEROIN AND PREGNANCY

Devin acts like any normal two-year-old. He particularly enjoys the fast-food Chick-fil-A restaurant and playing with the barbecue sauce containers. Looking at Devin gives no clue that his mother had become addicted to prescription painkillers when she discovered her pregnancy. She was urged by her sister to seek professional help immediately. Devin was born on time and was undersized at 5 pounds and 5 ounces. Devin was able to avoid the worst withdrawal symptoms after birth because he was immediately placed on methadone and gradually weaned to allow his small body to adjust to not having the painkillers that his mother had been using throughout her pregnancy. Devin was lucky: other babies under similar circumstances who do not receive proper medical care suffer through serious feeding problems, vomiting, diarrhea, muscle stiffness, and severe tremors. These babies cry constantly as they

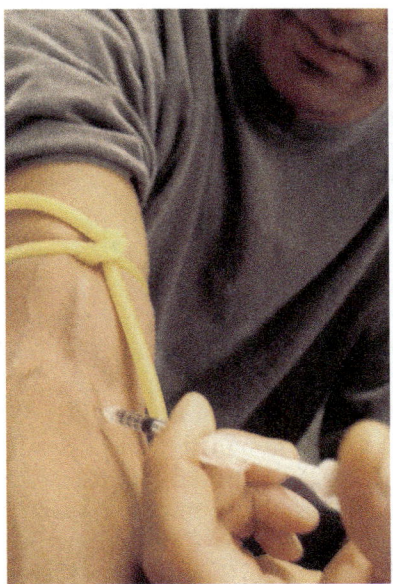

A heroin addict "mainlining" his drug.

experience dangerous narcotic withdrawal, and in extreme cases they may even suffer seizures. (Colon 2011)

Many women use heroin during their pregnancy. In the United States, as many as 7000 infants are born each year to women who chronically used either heroin or other opioid drugs during their pregnancies (Bhuvaneswar et al. 2008). There is no evidence that prenatal exposure to opioid drugs causes overt structural damage, although incidents of lower birthweights or even reduced head size have been reported in infants born to mothers using opioid drugs (Wang 2010). The most devastating consequence of heroin or opioid use during pregnancy appears to be physical dependence in the newborn, resulting in withdrawal symptoms usually immediately after birth. These symptoms are characterized by high-pitched crying, inconsolability, tightened muscle tone, tremors, vomiting, and even seizures. Elements of this withdrawal persist for weeks (Wang 2010). Treatment for such withdrawal problems generally includes low doses of a long-lasting opioid narcotic to reduce the intensity of the symptoms and then a gradual tapering of the dose to eventually wean the infant from the drug. For heroin, this typically takes up to 2 weeks (Pain and Central Nervous

KEY TERM

mainline
to inject a drug of abuse intravenously

#8

System 2005; Wang 2010). In addition, there is some evidence that the use of heroin during pregnancy increases the likelihood of sudden infant death syndrome (SIDS) in offspring (American SIDS Institute 2005).

WITHDRAWAL SYMPTOMS

After the effects of heroin wear off, the addict usually has only a few hours in which to find the next dose before severe withdrawal symptoms begin. A single "shot" of heroin lasts only 4 to 6 hours. It is enough to help addicts "get straight" or relieve the severe withdrawal symptoms called dope sickness but is not enough to give a desired high (Bearak 1992). Withdrawal symptoms start with a runny nose, tears, and minor stomach cramps. The addict may feel as if he or she is coming down with a bad cold (Galanter and Kleber 2008). Between 12 and 48 hours after the last dose, the addict loses all of his or her appetite, vomits, has diarrhea and abdominal cramps, feels alternating chills and fever, and develops goose pimples all over (going "cold turkey"). Between 2 and 4 days later, the addict continues to experience some of the symptoms just described, as well as aching bones and muscles and powerful muscle spasms that cause violent kicking motions ("kicking the habit"). After 4 to 5 days, symptoms start to subside, and the person may get his or her appetite back. However, attempts to move on in life will be challenging because compulsion to keep using the drug remains strong.

The severity of the withdrawal varies according to the purity and strength of the drug used and the personality of the user. The symptoms of withdrawal from heroin, morphine, and methadone are summarized in **Table 9.4**. Withdrawal symptoms from opioids such as morphine, codeine, meperidine, and others are similar, although the time frame and intensity vary (Galanter and Kleber 2008; Gutstein and Akil 2006).

■ Treatment of Heroin and Other Narcotic Dependence

The ideal result of treatment for dependency on heroin or other narcotics is to help the addict live a normal, productive, and satisfying life without drugs (Galanter and Kleber 2008). Unfortunately, the minority of heroin addicts receive adequate treatment for their addiction. Of those who are treated, relatively few heroin users become absolutely "clean" from drug use; thus, therapeutic compromise often is necessary (see **Figure 9.1**). In the real world, treatment of heroin dependency is considered successful if the addict does the following:

- Stops using heroin
- No longer associates with dealers or users of heroin
- Avoids dangerous activities often associated with heroin use (such as needle sharing, injecting unknown drugs, and frequenting shooting galleries) (Tur 2010)
- Improves employment status
- Refrains from criminal activity
- Is able to enjoy normal family and social relationships

For more than 30 years, many heroin addicts have achieved these goals by substituting a long-lasting synthetic narcotic, such as methadone, for

TABLE 9.4 Symptoms of Withdrawal from Heroin, Morphine, and Methadone

Symptoms	Time in Hours		
	Heroin	**Morphine**	**Methadone**
Craving for drugs, anxiety	4	6	24–48
Yawning, perspiration, runny nose, tears	8	14	34–48
Pupil dilation, goose bumps, muscle twitches, aching bones and muscles, hot and cold flashes, loss of appetite	12	16	48–72
Increased intensity of preceding symptoms, insomnia, raised blood pressure, fever, faster pulse, nausea	18–24	24–36	≥ 72
Increased intensity of preceding symptoms, curled-up position, vomiting, diarrhea, increased blood sugar, foot-kicking ("kicking the habit")	26–36	36–48	–

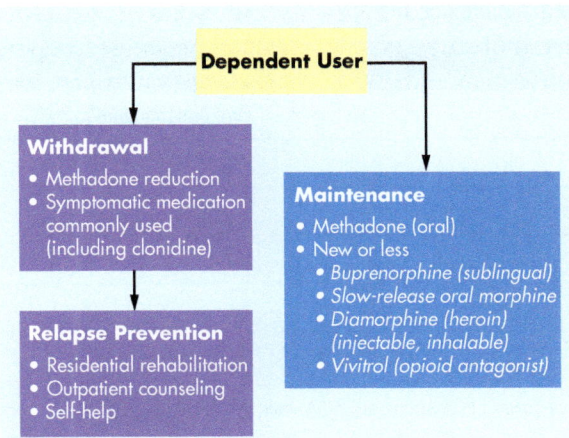

FIGURE 9.1 Treatment of heroin addiction. The principal aspects of treating heroin addiction include minimizing the very aversive withdrawal effect (usually with drug adjuncts); preventing relapse (usually with behavioral modification); and if necessary, providing maintenance support with other opioid-like drugs that have longer action than heroin.

the short-acting heroin (Galanter and Kleber 2008; Zickler 1999). The maintenance ("substitute") narcotic is made available to heroin-dependent people through drug treatment centers under the direction of trained medical personnel. The dispensing of the substitute narcotic is tightly regulated by governmental agencies. The rationale for the substitution is that a long-acting drug such as methadone can conveniently be taken once a day (Galanter and Kleber 2008) to prevent the unpleasant withdrawal symptoms that occur within 4 hours after each heroin use (see Table 9.4). Although the substitute narcotic may also have abuse potential and be scheduled by the DEA (see Table 9.2), it is given to the addict in its oral form; thus, its onset of action is too slow to cause a rush like that associated with heroin use, which means that its abuse potential is substantially less (Galanter and Kleber 2008). In addition, the cost to society is dramatically reduced. According to one study, an untreated heroin addict costs the community $21,000 for 6 months, but the cost of methadone maintenance for a person dependent on heroin is only about $1000 for the same period (Hubbard 1998; Substance Abuse and Mental Health Services Administration [SAMHSA] 2008).

Currently, methadone is approved by the FDA for "opiate maintenance therapy" in the treatment of heroin (or other narcotic) dependency (Galanter and Kleber 2008). It has been used in heroin treatment for more than 30 years. Although it is not the best treatment for every person dependent on

an opiate drug, it is an effective tool for managing many heroin addicts (Benfield 2010). Proper use of methadone has been shown to effectively decrease illicit use of narcotics and other undesirable behavior related to drug dependence (Galanter and Kleber 2008). Although methadone does not tend to make users high, it helps heroin addicts by reducing their drug craving (Benfield 2010). Often methadone-assisted therapy will be long-term and even for the rest of the addict's life. The methadone is typically well tolerated, although if misused it can be problematic and has been associated with a startling number of overdose deaths across the country (Colberg 2009).

A second narcotic, buprenorphine, which is used as an analgesic, also has been approved for treatment of narcotic dependence (Hanson 2003). Because buprenorphine is both an opioid agonist and antagonist, it has minimal potential for dependence and is easy to manage, which makes this drug a desirable substitute for heroin (*Drug Facts and Comparisons* 2010). Efforts are being made to provide education and training to primary care physicians so they will be able to use buprenorphine to treat patients addicted to narcotics in their own offices (SAMHSA 2010). This novel strategy opens the door to physicians heretofore not involved in the treatment of drug addiction to become familiar with substance abuse management and hopefully increase the opportunities to diagnose and treat these patients. There is considerable discussion as to how buprenorphine products compare to methadone in treatment of dependence on, and addiction to, opioids in general and heroin in particular. Although the issues clearly require further study, there is some evidence that buprenorphine is usually the better and safer strategy for detoxification (i.e., treatment of withdrawal) and treatment for infants of opiate-addicted mothers (Boughton 2010; Meader 2010). However, such claims are disputed by some experts in the field (Bates 2010b; More 2008).

A third, and very different drug approved in 2010 by the FDA to treat heroin and other opioid addictions is Vivitrol, an extended-release form of naltrexone, an opioid antagonist (National Center for Biotechnology Information [NCBI] 2013; Rubin 2010). In 2006, Vivitrol was originally approved as a treatment for alcoholism because of its ability to reduce alcohol craving and its consumption (Drugs.com 2010a; Rubin 2010). Vivitrol has been found to also reduce craving for narcotic drugs such as heroin. Its administration consists of a monthly deep muscle injection. Some of the

TABLE 9.5 Comparison of Narcotic Substitutes Used in Opiate Maintenance Therapy

Properties	Methadone	Buprenorphine
Administration	Oral	Oral or sublingual
Frequency of doses	Daily	Daily
Other uses	Analgesic	Analgesic
Physical dependence	Yes	Little
Causes positive subjective effects	Yes	Yes
Abuse potential	Yes	Limited

Data from Swan, N. "Two NIDA-Tested Heroin Treatment Medications Move Toward FDA Approval." *NIDA Notes* (March/April 1993): 45.

potential side effects of using Vivitrol include: (1) interference with thinking or reactions, (2) wheezing, (3) enhanced pain, and (4) mood changes (Drugs.com 2010a).

Table 9.5 compares the opioids that have been used for maintenance therapy. Other drugs used less frequently for similar maintenance therapy of heroin addicts include slow-release oral morphine and even heroin itself for addicts who do not respond to the other maintenance opioid drugs (Bammer et al. 1999).

Some people, including some professionals involved in drug abuse therapy, view heroin or narcotic addiction as a "failure of the will" and see methadone treatment as substituting one addiction for another. However, evidence has demonstrated that this approach is very effective in preventing the spread of infectious diseases such as AIDS and hepatitis and helps the heroin addict to return to a normal productive life (McClure 2009). Unrealistic treatment expectations are sometimes imposed on heroin addicts, leading to high failure rates. For example, some methadone treatment programs distribute inadequate methadone doses to maintain heroin or narcotic abstinence (Recovery Helpdesk 2010); alternatively, narcotic-dependent patients may be told their methadone will be terminated within 6 months regardless of their progress in the program. Such ill-advised policies often drive clients back to their heroin habits and demonstrate that many professionals who treat heroin and narcotic dependency do not understand that methadone is not a cure for heroin addiction but is a means to achieve a healthier, more normal lifestyle (McClure 2009).

It also is essential to understand that even proper treatment does not guarantee resolution of heroin or narcotic addiction (see "Case in Point: Heroin Addiction: Not a Funny Matter"). To maximize the possibility of successful treatment, clients must also participate in regular counseling sessions to help modify the drug-seeking behavior and receive on-site care from professionals, including job training, career development, education, general medical care, and family counseling. These supplemental services dramatically improve the success rate of narcotic dependence treatment (Grinspoon 1995; Partnership 2003; McLellan et al. 1993).

Other Narcotics

A large number of nonheroin narcotics are used for medical purposes. However, many are also distributed in the streets, such as morphine, methadone, codeine, hydromorphone (Dilaudid), meperidine (Demerol), and other synthetics (hydrocodone [Vicodin] and oxycodone [Oxy-Contin]). A few of the most commonly abused opioids are discussed briefly in the following sections. Except where noted, they are all Schedule II or III drugs.

▌ Morphine

As noted earlier, morphine is the standard by which other narcotic analgesic agents are measured (Way, Fields, and Way 1998). It has been used to relieve pain since it was first isolated in 1803. Morphine has about half the analgesic potency of heroin but 12 times the potency of codeine. It is commonly used to relieve moderate to intense pain that cannot be controlled by less potent and less dangerous narcotics. Because of its potential for serious side effects, morphine is generally used in a hospital setting where emergency care can be rendered, if

► CASE IN POINT

Heroin Addiction: Not a Funny Matter

Artie Lange, who used to be a "funnyman" on "The Howard Stern Show," was discovered by his mother bleeding on his Hoboken apartment floor. According to paramedics, Lange had been stabbed nine times with a kitchen knife. Police investigators concluded the wounds were self-inflicted and called it a suicide attempt. Lange had experienced multiple bouts of serious depression associated with a heroin addiction. Despite treatment, Lange manifested self-destructive tendencies that apparently led to this attempt to take his own life. His behavior had been compared to other self-destructive comics such as Chris Farley and John Belushi, who both experienced untimely deaths apparently by accidental causes linked to their drug/heroin use.

Data from Relative, S. "Artie Lange Stabbed Himself Nine Times, Attempted Suicide Confirmed." Associated Content, Arts and Entertainment. 8 January 2010. Available http://www.associatedcontent.com/article/2568063/artie_lange_stabbed_himself_nine_times.html. Accessed February 16, 2011.

necessary. Most pain can be relieved by morphine if high enough doses are used (Reisine and Pasternak 1995; Way et al. 1998); however, morphine is most effective against continuous dull pain.

The side effects that occur when using therapeutic doses of morphine include drowsiness, changes in mood, and inability to think straight. In addition, therapeutic doses depress respiratory activity; thus, morphine decreases the rate and depth of breathing and produces irregular breathing patterns. Like the other narcotics, it can create an array of seemingly unrelated effects throughout the body, including nausea and vomiting, constipation, blurred vision, constricted pupils, and flushed skin (*Drug Facts and Comparisons* 2010; Way et al. 1998).

The initial response to morphine is varied. In normal people who are not suffering pain, the first exposure can be unpleasant, with nausea and vomiting being the prominent reactions. However, continual use often leads to a euphoric response and encourages dependence. When injected subcutaneously, the effects of heroin and morphine are almost identical; this situation occurs because heroin is rapidly metabolized in the body into morphine. After intravenous administration, the onset of heroin's effects is more rapid and more intense than that of morphine because heroin

is more lipid-soluble and enters the brain faster. Because heroin is easier to manufacture and is more potent, it is more popular in illicit trade than morphine. Even so, morphine also has substantial abuse potential and is classified as a Schedule II substance (McEvoy 2003).

Tolerance to the effects of morphine can develop very quickly if the drug is used continuously. For example, an addict who is repeatedly administering the morphine to get a "kick" or maintain a high must constantly increase the dose. Such users can build up to incredible doses. One addict reported using 5 grams of morphine daily; the normal analgesic dose of morphine is 50 to 80 milligrams per day (Jaffe and Martin 1990). Such high doses are lethal in a person without tolerance to narcotics.

■ Methadone

Methadone was first synthesized in Germany in 1943, when natural opiate analgesics were not available because opium could not be obtained from the Far East during World War II. Methadone was first called *Dolophine*, after Adolf Hitler; one company still uses that trade name. (On the street, methadone pills have been called dollies.) As previously described, methadone is often substituted for heroin in the treatment of narcotic-dependent people (*Drug Facts and Comparisons* 2010). It is an effective analgesic, equal to morphine if injected and more potent if taken orally (*Drug Facts and Comparisons* 2010; Way et al. 1998).

The physiological effects of methadone are the same as those of morphine and heroin. As a narcotic, methadone produces psychological dependence, tolerance, and then physical dependence and addiction if repeated doses are taken (Belluck 2003; *Drug Facts and Comparisons* 2010). It is effective for about 24 to 36 hours; therefore, the addict must take methadone daily to avoid narcotic withdrawal. It is often considered as addictive as heroin if injected; consequently, because methadone is soluble in water, it is formulated with insoluble, inert ingredients to prevent it from being injected by narcotic addicts.

Among methadone's most useful properties are cross-tolerance with other narcotic drugs and a less intense withdrawal response (Recovery Helpdesk 2010). If it reaches a sufficiently high level in the blood, methadone blocks heroin euphoria. In addition, withdrawal symptoms of patients physically dependent on heroin or morphine and the postaddiction craving can be suppressed by oral administration of methadone (Meader 2010). The effective dose for methadone maintenance is 50 to 100 milligrams per day to treat severe withdrawal symptoms (*Drug Facts and Comparisons* 2010; Way et al. 1998; Zickler 1999).

The value of substituting methadone for heroin lies in its longer action. Because addicts no longer need heroin to prevent withdrawal, they often can be persuaded to leave their undesirable associates, drug sources, and dangerous lifestyles. The potential side effects from methadone are the same as those from morphine and heroin, including constipation and sedation; yet if properly used, methadone is usually a safe drug (*Drug Facts and Comparisons* 2010).

When injecting methadone, some people feel the same kind of euphoria that can be obtained from heroin. Methadone addicts receiving maintenance treatment sometimes become euphoric if the dose is increased too rapidly. There are cases of people who injected crushed methadone pills and developed serious lung conditions from particles that lodged in the tissue, creating a condition somewhat like emphysema. The number of deaths from methadone overdose have increased substantially in recent years. Data from the CDC demonstrate methadone-related deaths in the

United States increased more than five-fold in the past decade. The reasons for this startling increase include the following (Zielinski 2010):

- Large quantities of methadone are being stolen from legitimate businesses such as hospitals and pharmacies for personal use or to sell.
- Excessive amounts of methadone are being accumulated and abused by doctor-shopping, prescription fraud, or illegal Internet pharmacy web sites.
- It is being misused by patients who received their methadone by legitimate prescriptions for pain.
- Because of increases in pain management clinics, it has become easier to obtain methadone.

Like heroin, methadone overdoses can be reversed by the antagonist naloxone if the person is treated in time.

▪ Fentanyls

The fentanyls belong to a family of very potent narcotic analgesics (more than 200 times the potency of morphine) that are often administered intravenously for general anesthesia. These synthetic opioid narcotics include drugs such as sufentanil and alfentanil (Gutstein and Akil 2006). Fentanyls are also used in transdermal systems (patches on the skin) and as lollipops in the treatment of chronic pain (Adams 2010). Occasionally, reports surface of individuals abusing a fentanyl patch by licking, swallowing, or even smoking it (Hull et al. 2007).

It is estimated that some 100 different active forms of fentanyl could be synthesized; up to now, about 10 derivatives have appeared on the street. They are considered to be "designer" drugs. Because of their great potency, ease of production, and low costs, the fentanyls have sometimes been used to replace heroin (Fodale 2006). Fentanyl-type drugs can appear in the same forms and colors as heroin, so there is nothing to alert users that they have been sold a heroin substitute (NIDA 2007). Due to their powerful effects, these drugs are especially dangerous, and incredibly small doses can cause fatal respiratory depression in an unsuspecting heroin user (Adams 2010; Fodale 2006). It is likely that hundreds have died from overdosing with heroin laced with fentanyl. Because of an enhanced high, addicts are tempted to use these lethal combinations (Boddigger 2006). Because these drugs are sometimes very difficult to detect in the blood owing to the small quantities used, there is no reliable information regarding the extent of fentanyl abuse. Fentanyl is so potent that abusing the patch has caused overdoses and even death (AboutLawsuits 2010; Douglas 2006).

■ Hydromorphone

Hydromorphone (Dilaudid) is prepared from morphine and used as an analgesic and cough suppressant. It is a stronger analgesic than morphine and is used to treat moderate to severe pain. Nausea, vomiting, constipation, and euphoria may be less marked with hydromorphone than with morphine (Karch 1996; Way et al. 1998). It is becoming more popular with opiate addicts due to its potency; however, combination with other CNS depressants can be fatal. On the street, it is taken in tablet form or injected.

■ Oxycodone

Oxycodone (OxyContin) is a moderate narcotic analgesic that in the past decade has been increasingly abused as the proprietary product OxyContin and has created considerable controversy (see "Here and Now: OxyContin Controversy Rages"). OxyContin is a long-lasting version of oxycodone and is considered to be an important and effective therapy for the treatment of severe pain from cancer or other lingering diseases (DrugLib 2010; *Drug Facts and Comparisons* 2010). Abuse of OxyContin has been a considerable cause for alarm by officials. Street names for OxyContin include *OC, kicker, Oxy-Cotton,* and *hillbilly heroin* (CBS News 2007). This drug can be easily abused by simply crushing the tablet, and then ingesting, injecting, inhaling, or placing it rectally. However, recent modifications have made the drug in OxyContin less available by this process and thereby have reduced its appeal to those who intend to abuse it (Diep 2013).

The problems with OxyContin are underscored by the report that in 2012, 2.9% of high school students abused this drug (Johnston 2013). Interestingly, the abuse rate by this population for the less potent Vicodin (hydrocodone plus acetaminophen) was almost double that for OxyContin, likely due to easier access (Johnston 2013). Concern has been further heightened with reports of drug rings, including physicians, illegally distributing OxyContin (McCartney and Risling 2010). Deaths and trips to the emergency room caused by Oxy-Contin have been common and are concerning to both medical and law enforcement organizations (DEA 2012). However, these reports of adverse events associated with OxyContin use must be put into perspective by the knowledge that the vast majority of these emergency events are associated with drug abuse or physical causes (e.g., cancer) in addition to the effects of OxyContin (*Biotech Week* 2003). As a result, the FDA and DEA control Oxy-Contin at the same level as morphine.

■ Meperidine

Meperidine (Demerol) is a synthetic drug that frequently is used as an analgesic for treatment of moderate pain; it can be taken in tablet form or injected. Meperidine is about one-tenth as powerful as morphine, and its use can lead to dependence (Schumacher et al. 2012). This drug is sometimes given too freely by some physicians because tolerance develops, requiring larger doses to maintain its therapeutic action. With continual use, it causes physical dependence. Meperidine addicts may use large daily doses (3–4 grams per day). Repeated use of high doses of meperidine can cause seizures (*Drug Facts and Comparisons* 2010; Gutstein and Akil 2006).

■ Buprenorphine

Buprenorphine, a mild-to-moderate narcotic analgesic, was available as a Schedule V pain reliever for years. As discussed earlier, after extensive research, this drug was approved in 2002 as an effective medication for the treatment of narcotic abuse and dependence (Schumacher et al. 2012). Buprenorphine has been shown to be effective in relieving the cravings for narcotic pain relievers with minimal tendency to cause addiction itself (Bates 2010a). Although buprenorphine has been reported to have a minimal high (Leinweind 2006) when used properly, there have been isolated reports of occasional deaths, especially when combined with other CNS depressant drugs (Williams 2009). Despite buprenorphine's significant safety record and its minimal propensity for abuse, its new FDA-approved indication would cause it to be dispensed to patients with drug abuse histories, so the DEA revised its classification to a Schedule III drug.

Of particular importance is the fact that buprenorphine (in the form of Subutex and Suboxone, a combination of buprenorphine and the opioid antagonist, naloxone) has been approved for the treatment of opiate dependence in an office setting. Trained physicians are allowed to treat up to 100 narcotic-dependent patients with buprenorphine in their medical offices. This means opioid addictions and dependence can now be treated with a prescribed medication by trained primary care physicians, in the offices of private doctors. This is an important step in what may become a revolution in addiction treatment, allowing patients to discreetly receive help from a family doctor for their substance abuse problem (Bates 2010a). Because buprenorphine was approved in 2002 as the first office-based treatment for opiate addiction, only about 300,000 patients have received prescriptions for this drug (Bates 2010a). Currently, almost 20,000 physicians are certified to prescribe it for treatment of opioid drug dependence (Kuehn 2010). With time, it is hoped that use of buprenorphine by primary care physicians will become rather routine (Anderson 2007).

MPTP: A "Designer" Tragedy

Attempts to synthesize illicit designer versions of meperidine by street chemists have proved tragic for some unsuspecting drug addicts. In 1976, a young drug addict with elementary laboratory skills attempted to make a meperidine-like drug by using shortcuts in the chemical synthesis. Three days after self-administering his untested drug product, the drug user developed a severe case of tremors and motor problems identical to Parkinson's disease, a neurological disorder generally occurring in the elderly. Even more surprising to attending neurologists was that this young drug addict improved dramatically after treatment with levodopa, a drug that is very effective in treating the symptoms of traditional Parkinson's disease. After 18 months of treatment, the despondent addict committed suicide. An autopsy revealed he had severe brain damage that was almost identical to that occurring in classical Parkinson's patients. It was concluded that a by-product resulting from the sloppy synthesis of the meperidine-like designer narcotic was responsible for the irreversible brain damage.

This hypothesis was confirmed by a separate and independent event on the West Coast in 1981, when a cluster of relatively young heroin addicts (ages 22–42) in the San Francisco area also developed symptoms of Parkinson's disease. All of these patients had consumed a new "synthetic heroin" obtained on the streets, which was produced by attempting to synthesize meperidine-like drugs (Aminoff 1998; Langston et al. 1983). Common to

both incidents was the presence of the compound MPTP, which was a contaminant resulting from the careless synthesis. MPTP is metabolized to a very reactive molecule in the brain that selectively destroys neurons containing the transmitter dopamine in the motor regions of the basal ganglia. Similar neuronal damage occurs in classical Parkinson's disease over the course of 50 to 70 years, whereas ingestion of MPTP dramatically accelerates the degeneration to a matter of days (Goldstein 1994). As tragic as the MPTP incident was, it was heralded as an important scientific breakthrough—MPTP is now used by researchers as a tool to study why Parkinson's disease occurs and how to treat it effectively (Lane and Dunnett 2008).

Codeine

Codeine is a naturally occurring constituent of opium and the most frequently prescribed of the narcotic analgesics. It is used principally as a treatment for minor to moderate pain and as a cough suppressant. Maximum pain relief from codeine occurs with 30 to 50 milligrams. Usually, when prescribed for pain, codeine is combined with either a salicylate (such as aspirin) or acetaminophen (Tylenol). Aspirin-like drugs and opioid narcotics interact in a synergistic fashion to give an analgesic equivalence greater than what can be achieved by aspirin or codeine alone.

Although not especially powerful, codeine may still be abused. Codeine-containing cough syrup is currently classified as a Schedule V drug. Because the abuse potential is considered minor, the FDA has ruled that codeine cough products can be sold without a prescription; however, the pharmacist is required to keep them behind the counter and must be asked in order to provide codeine-containing cough medications. Despite the FDA ruling, many states have more restrictive regulations and require that codeine-containing cough products be available only by prescription.

Although codeine dependence is possible, it is not very common; most people who abuse codeine developed narcotic dependence previously with one of the more potent opioids. In general, large quantities of codeine are needed to satisfy a narcotic addiction; therefore, it is not commonly marketed on the street.

Pentazocine

Pentazocine (Talwin) was first developed in the 1960s in an effort to create an effective analgesic with low abuse potential. When taken orally, its analgesic effect is slightly greater than that of codeine. Its effects on respiration and sedation are similar to those of the other opioids, but it does not prevent withdrawal symptoms in a narcotic addict. In fact, pentazocine will precipitate withdrawal symptoms if given to a person on methadone maintenance (Gutstein and Akil 2006). Pentazocine is not commonly abused because its effects can be unpleasant, resulting in dysphoria. It is classified as a Schedule IV drug.

■ Propoxyphene

Propoxyphene (Darvon, Dolene) is structurally related to methadone, but it is a much weaker analgesic, about half as potent as codeine (Gutstein and Akil 2006). Like codeine, propoxyphene is frequently given in combination with aspirin or acetaminophen. Although it was once an extremely popular analgesic, the use of propoxyphene declined as its potency was questioned. Research suggested that this narcotic was no more effective in relieving pain than aspirin (Gutstein and Akil 2006). To a large extent, new, more effective nonnarcotic analgesics replaced propoxyphene. In very high doses, it caused delusions, hallucinations, and convulsions and even fatal heart problems. Alone, propoxyphene caused little respiratory depression; however, when combined with alcohol or other CNS depressants, this drug could depress respiration. Due to these negative properties, the FDA requested the removal of this controversial painkiller, and it was removed from the market in 2010 (Stein 2010).

■ Tramadol

Tramadol (Ultram) was first introduced into the U.S. market in 1994 as a synthetic, moderately effective analgesic sometimes used as a substitute for opioid painkillers (Smith 2010). Although tramadol itself causes some activation of opioid receptors in the brain, it appears that its analgesic properties are related to more than just its opioid actions. For example, tramadol alters GABA, noradrenaline, and serotonin transmitter systems as well, in a manner that might contribute to its atypical analgesic properties. For this reason, tramadol may have some antidepressant effects that augment its analgesic abilities (DEA 2013).

Tramadol is frequently prescribed for patients who either do not respond well or have difficulty with the opioid painkillers. Despite the fact that opioid action likely is not the sole basis of its analgesia, it is significant enough to cause some dependence issues. For example, there is an illegal street market for this substance, where it is known by names such as *chill pills* or *ultra*. There are clinicians who claim that for some patients tramadol can cause a serious opioid-like dependence (DEA 2013). Such conclusions are based on findings such as: (1) from 1998 to 2006 there was a six-fold increase in admissions for treatment of tramadol-related dependence; (2) for teens, tramadol is easier to get than alcohol and easy to sell on the streets; (3) emergency room visits nationwide that included tramadol as a significant component went from about 5000 in 2004 to about 16,250 in 2010; and (4) there is evidence that regular daily use of tramadol can cause physical dependence and withdrawals when discontinued abruptly (DEA 2013). These increases in tramadol-related problems correspond to an explosion in its popularity, resulting in about 26 million prescriptions being dispensed by retailers in 2008 (Smith 2010). Tramadol is available as both regular and extended-release tablets (Drugs.com 2010b).

Even though tramadol is marketed as an opioid drug with low risk of dependence and some health authorities consider it to have a relatively low dependence liability, it is clear that many patients can become addicted to this analgesic (DEA 2013). Thus, several states have designated tramadol as either Schedule IV or V (DEA 2013). Currently, tramadol is available only by prescription, but is not scheduled by the DEA even though the prescribing information typically warns that tramadol "may induce psychological and physical dependence of the morphine-type." In some countries, tramadol is actually available over the counter (Breakthrough Addiction Recovery 2010). Because of many clinical complaints across the country, the DEA is reviewing the status of tramadol products in order to determine if scheduling of these drugs would be appropriate.

Narcotic-Related Drugs

Although not classified as narcotics, the following drugs are either structurally similar to narcotics (dextromethorphan) or are used to treat narcotic withdrawal (clonidine) or overdose (naloxone).

▮ Dextromethorphan

Dextromethorphan is a synthetic used in cough remedies since the 1960s and can be purchased without prescription. Although its molecular structure resembles that of codeine, this drug does not have analgesic action nor does it cause typical narcotic dependence (Encyclopedia Britannica 2010).

Although dextromethorphan is not traditionally considered a major drug abuse problem, recent studies are cause for concern. They reveal that many young people have used OTC products containing dextromethorphan to get high (Phillips 2013). Overdose of dextromethorphan-containing cough medicines has been reported in the United States and other countries, sometimes resulting in deadly consequences (see "Here and Now: Dextromethorphan: Nothing to Cough At"). From 1998–2008, 72 cases of dextromethorphan-related deaths were identified. The majority of these cases were suicides, often involving multiple substances (Traynor 2010). Abuse of dextromethorphan typically occurs among adolescents and young adults (Traynor 2010). The relatively few cases of addiction reveal a pattern of high-dose use for months to even years. The principal symptoms of abuse include altered perceptions, sense of floating, hallucinations, visual distortions, and even paranoia and psychotic reactions. Its effects have been described to be similar to those of phencyclidine (PCP) and the general anesthetic ketamine (Morgan, Porritt, and Poling 2006). There is some suggestion that both physical and psychological dependence can occur with dextromethorphan, resulting in withdrawal when its use is discontinued (Mutschler et al. 2010). Dextromethorphan is sometimes mixed with drugs such as alcohol, amphetamines, and cocaine to give unusual psychoactive interactions.

As of 2013, the DEA had taken no steps to restrict the use of dextromethorphan in OTC products; in fact, advisers to the FDA voted against placing this drug in a schedule of controlled substances, which likely will preclude the DEA from making a change in its category (DEA 2013; Traynor 2010).

Young people are becoming aware of dextromethorphan's abuse potential from web sites on the Internet. A growing number of these sites have promoted dextromethorphan as a powerful OTC mind-altering drug. Included on these sites are personal experiences of users as well as directions on how to use the drug, predictions about what to expect, warning signs of adverse

HERE AND NOW

Dextromethorphan: Nothing to Cough At

Dextromethorphan, a key active ingredient in cough suppressants, is the reason why many young people are using OTC cough medicines to get high. The substance—also known as robo, skittles, dxm, dex, and tussin—is found in at least 80 OTC products. Dextromethorphan usually produces a disassociative feeling (roboing, robo rolling, robo tripping) or a feeling of intoxication, but its abuse can also lead to psychotic behavior. When large amounts of dextromethorphan are taken, the drug attaches to receptors in the central nervous system—the same receptors to which PCP attaches. In the long term, this effect can cause depression, memory problems, and suicidal tendencies. Dextromethorphan abuse also can result in death: in 2005, five teenage boys from three different states died after ingesting dextromethorphan powder from an

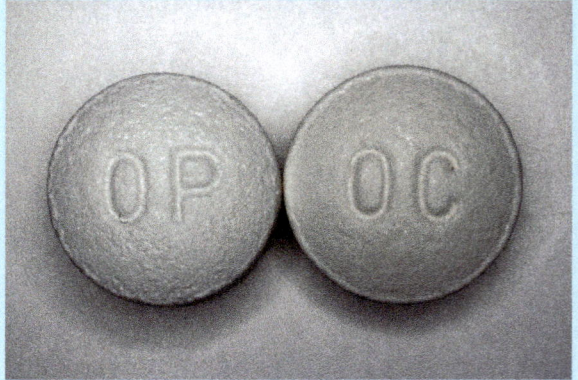

online source that illegally sold the drug in bulk. The company was closed down the next year.

Data from Magnus, E. "Addicted to Cough Medicine?" MSNBC News. 27 March 2004. Available http://www.msnbc.msn.com/id/4608341. Accessed March 14, 2011; and Traynor, K. "Advisers Vote Against Declaring Dextromethorphan a Controlled Substance." American Society of Health Pharmacists. 2010. Available http://www.ashp.org/import/news/HealthSystemPharmacyNews/newsarticle. aspx?id=3418. Accessed March 14, 2011.

reactions, and instructions on how to extract dextromethorphan from OTC cough medicines (Vaults of Erowid 2007).

■ Clonidine

Clonidine (Catapres) was created in the late 1970s. It is not a narcotic analgesic and has no direct effect on the opioid receptors; instead, it stimulates receptors for noradrenaline. Its principal use is as an oral antihypertensive (Benowitz 2012). Clonidine is mentioned here because it is a nonaddictive, noneuphorigenic prescription medication with demonstrated efficacy in relieving some of the physical effects of opiate withdrawal (such as vomiting and diarrhea). However, clonidine does not alter narcotic craving or the generalized aches associated with withdrawal (O'Shea, Law, and Melichar 2010). The dosing regimen is typically a 7- to 14-day inpatient treatment for opiate withdrawal. Length of treatment can be reduced to 7 days for withdrawal from heroin and short-acting opiates; the 14-day treatment is needed for the longer-acting methadone-type opiates. Because tolerance to clonidine may develop, opiates are discontinued abruptly at the start of treatment. In this way, the peak intensity of withdrawal will occur while clonidine is still maximally effective (McEvoy 2003).

One of the most important advantages of clonidine over other treatments for opiate withdrawal detoxification is that it shortens the time for withdrawal to 14 days compared with several weeks or months using standard procedures, such as methadone treatment (O'Shea et al. 2010). The potential disadvantage of taking clonidine is that it can cause serious side effects of its own, the most serious being significantly lowered blood pressure, which can cause fainting and blacking out (*Drug Facts and Comparisons* 2010). Overall, its lack of abuse potential makes clonidine particularly useful in rapid treatment of narcotic dependence; however, the long-term benefit is controversial (Gowing et al. 2003).

■ Naloxone/Naltrexone

Naloxone and the related drug naltrexone are relatively pure narcotic antagonists. These drugs attach to opiate receptors in the brain and throughout the body. They do not activate the receptors, but rather prevent narcotic drugs, such as heroin and morphine, from having an effect. By themselves, these antagonists do not cause much change, but potently block or reverse the effects of all narcotics. Because of its antagonistic properties, naloxone is a useful antidote in the treatment of narcotic overdoses; its administration rapidly reverses life-threatening, narcotic-induced effects on breathing and the cardiovascular system (Schumacher et al. 2012). However, if not used carefully, this antagonist will also block the analgesic action of the narcotics and initiate severe withdrawals in narcotic-dependent people (Way et al. 1998). Its use has been proposed to prevent addicts from experiencing the effects of heroin and other potent opioid narcotics (Schumacher et al. 2012); in fact, as discussed earlier in this chapter, an extended form of naloxone (its effect persists for 1 month) called Vivitrol was approved by the FDA for the treatment of heroin addiction (Rubin 2010). However, many individuals dependent on heroin are not interested in using this drug because it can precipitate withdrawal symptoms. But a recent study found that of those heroin addicts who received six monthly injections, 70% did not go back to heroin use (this was twice the success rate of heroin addicts given placebo), and they claimed that the Vivitrol reduced their cravings for the opiate drug (Rubin 2010).

An interesting use of naloxone has been to combine it with buprenorphine in small quantities (Suboxone). As long as this product is taken as prescribed, the quantity of naloxone is too small to have an antagonistic effect; however, if Suboxone is consumed in high doses, such as would occur if it were being abused, there would be sufficient naloxone to block the opioid effect (Center for Substance Abuse Research [CESAR] 2003). The FDA also has approved Suboxone to reduce the craving for alcohol in the treatment of chronic alcoholism (*Drug Facts and Comparisons* 2010). There are additional reports suggesting that opioid receptors may contribute to other drug addictions such as those caused by nicotine and psychostimulants. At this time it is not clear if an opioid antagonist like naloxone would be effective in treating these other addictions.

Natural Narcotic Substances

Although many herbal preparations can cause drowsiness or have some analgesic properties, few of these actually contain opioid narcotic drugs.

The naturally occurring opioid drugs include morphine, codeine, heroin, papaverine, and thebaine and are found only in the opium poppy, *Papaver somniferum.* Although several varieties of opium-yielding poppies exist, they are typically winter crops in the Southern Hemisphere and do best in climates that have warm days and cool nights. All of the plants thrive in sandy soil. Most of the active drugs are found in the seepage from the seed heads located beneath the flower petals of the poppy flowers, although small amounts of these active ingredients are found in other parts of the plant such as the stem and leaves. Although this species of plant can survive in the United States if the environment is rigidly controlled, the vast majority of the supplies of the naturally occurring narcotic drugs are brought into the country, either legally and sold as legitimate pharmaceuticals or smuggled across borders and sold as illicit narcotics.

The sap oozing from this opium poppy pod contains the natural narcotic drugs.

LEARNING PORTFOLIO

Discussion Questions

1. Why do narcotics have high abuse potential?
2. What are the principal clinical uses of the opioid narcotics?
3. What is the relationship between endorphin systems and the opioid narcotics?
4. Why do the opioid pain relievers account for two-thirds of prescription drug abuse?
5. What effect has the rising abuse of prescription narcotic analgesics had on legitimately prescribing these drug for pain management?
6. What is the difference between opioid addiction and opioid physical dependence?
7. Why was there a substantial increase in heroin abuse in the United States throughout the 1990s?
8. Why does heroin addiction contribute to criminal activity?
9. What are the principal withdrawal effects when heroin use is stopped in addicts?
10. How does methadone maintenance work for the treatment of narcotic dependence? Explain a possible drawback to this approach.
11. How does buprenorphine compare to methadone as treatment for narcotic addictions?
12. How does naloxone (e.g., Vivitrol) compare to methadone maintenance treatment for heroin/opioid addiction?
13. What is considered to be successful treatment for heroin addiction?
14. How does morphine compare with heroin?
15. How does tramadol compare to other opioid analgesics? What should determine whether it should be scheduled by the federal government?
16. Why is dextromethorphan potentially addicting, and what should the federal government do to stop its abuse?
17. What does the fact that naloxone is effective in the treatment of alcoholism suggest about the role of endogenous opioid systems in alcohol dependence?

Key Terms

analgesics	273
antitussives	273
mainline	287
opioid	273
speedballing	284

Summary

1. The term *narcotic* refers to naturally occurring substances derived from the opium poppy and their synthetic substitutes. These drugs are referred to as the opioid (or opiate) narcotics because of their association with opium. For the most part, the opioid narcotics possess abuse potential, but they also have important clinical value and are used to relieve all kinds of

pain (they are analgesic), suppress coughing (they are antitussive), and stop diarrhea.

2. The principal side effects of the opioid narcotics, besides their abuse potential, include drowsiness, respiratory depression, nausea and vomiting, constipation, inability to urinate, and sometimes a drop in blood pressure. These side effects can be annoying or even life-threatening, so caution is required when using these drugs.

3. Heroin is the most likely of the opioid narcotics to be severely abused; it is easily prepared from opium and has a rapid, intense effect. It is a Schedule I drug.

4. When narcotics such as heroin are first used by people not experiencing pain, the drugs can cause unpleasant, dysphoric sensations. However, euphoria gradually overcomes the aversive effects. The positive feelings increase with narcotic use, leading to psychological dependence. After psychological dependence, physical dependence occurs with frequent daily use, which reinforces the narcotic abuse. If the user stops taking the drug after physical dependence has occurred, severe withdrawal symptoms result.

5. Tolerance to narcotics can occur rapidly with intense use of these drugs. This tolerance can result in the use of incredibly large doses of narcotics that would be fatal to a nontolerant person.

6. Methadone and buprenorphine are frequently used to help narcotic addicts stop using heroin or one of the other highly addicting drugs. Oral methadone relieves the withdrawal symptoms that would result from discontinuing narcotics. Methadone can also cause psychological and physical dependence, but it is less addicting than heroin and easier to control. Buprenorphine is distinct from methadone in that it has been approved for use in primary care settings and may be safer for treating women who use opioid narcotics during pregnancy.

7. Fentanyls are very potent synthetic opioid narcotics. They can be easily synthesized and converted into drugs that are as much as 3000 to 6000 times more potent than heroin itself. Detection and regulation of these fentanyl derivatives by law enforcement agencies are very difficult. The fentanyl-type drugs are used as heroin substitutes and have killed narcotic addicts because of their unexpected potency.

8. Attempts to create designer narcotics have led to the synthesis of very potent fentanyl-like drugs that are responsible for a number of overdose deaths. In addition, attempts to synthesize a meperidine (Demerol) designer drug resulted in the inadvertent creation of MPTP, a very reactive compound that causes a dramatic onset of Parkinson's disease in its users.

9. Tramadol is an atypical opioid-like analgesic that has some antidepressant actions that might contribute to its effectiveness as a moderately potent pain killer. It likely has less addicting properties than most of the other opioid narcotics, but its dramatic rise in popularity has revealed a potential for causing dependence and withdrawal in some patients. Although not currently scheduled by the Federal Government, the DEA is considering its addition to the list of controlled substances.

10. Dextromethorphan is a codeine-related drug used as an antitussive in OTC cough medicines. In very high doses, dextromethorphan can cause PCP-like hallucinations and sensory distortions. The abuse of this drug has not been substantial enough to result in its removal or special control by federal agencies.

References

AboutLawsuits. "Fentanyl Pain Patch Wrongful Death Lawsuit Results in $13.3 Million Verdict." 28 October 2010. Available http://www.aboutlawsuits.com/fentanyl-pain-patch-wrongful-death-lawsuit-results-in-133-million-verdict-1560

Adams, K. "Search for Answers in Fentanyl Death Raises More Questions." *Virginian-Pilot.* 18 May 2010. Available http://hamptonroads.com/2010/05/search-answers-fentanyl-death-raises-more-questions

Agence France-Presse (AFP). "Afghan Heroin Took Million Lives Last Decade: Russia." 8 June 2010. Available http://www.google.com/hostednews/afp/article/ALeqM5jJR7-F4pCliXVIW-uLrVyWQAM6GA

Alcoholism and Drug Abuse Weekly. "Marijuana, Prescription Painkiller Abuse Rises in 2009." 20 September 2010. Available http://onlinelibrary.wiley.com/doi/10.1002/adaw.20250/abstract

American Academy of Pain Medicine. "Psychiatric Factors Linked to Increased Risk for Misuse of Opioid Medications." 23rd Annual Meeting, Abstract 151. 7 February 2007.

American SIDS Institute. "Reducing the Risk of SIDS." 2005. Available http://www.sids.org/prevent.htm

Aminoff, M. "Pharmacologic Management of Parkinsonism and Other Movement Disorders." In *Basic and Clinical Pharmacology,* 7th ed., edited by B. Katzung, 450–463. Stamford, CT: Appleton and Lange, 1998.

Anderson, L. "A Drug-War Setback: Red Tape, Doctors Say, Cuts Buprenorphine Prescription." *Baltimore Sun.* 20 June 2007. Available http://articles.baltimoresun.com/2007-06-20/news/0706200045_1_buprenorphine-drug-addiction-medicaid

Austin, G. A. *Perspective on the History of Psychoactive Substance Use.* NIDA Research Issues No. 24. Washington, DC: U.S. Department of Health, Education, and Welfare, 1978.

Bammer, G., A. Dobler-Mikola, M. Fleming, J. Strang, and A. Uchtenhagen. "The Heroin Prescribing Debate: Integrating Science and Politics." *Science* 284 (1999): 1277–1278.

Bates, B. "NIDA Seeks Family Physicians to Treat Opioid-Dependent Youth." *Family Practice News* 40 (2010a): 1–51.

Bates, B. "Psychiatrists Still 'Out of Sync' on Buprenorphine." Elsevier Global Medical News. 22 April 2010b. Available http://www.thefreelibrary.com/Attitudes+'out+of+sync'+on+buprenorphine-a0228519234

Bearak, B. "Junkies Playing Roulette with Needles." *Salt Lake Tribune* (29 November 1992): A-4.

Belluck, P. "Methadone, Once the Way Out, Suddenly Grows as a Killer Drug." *New York Times* (9 February 2003): 8.

Benfield, P. "Methadone: Is It Really a Proper Treatment for Heroin Addicts." Helium.com. 25 June 2010. Available http://www.helium.com/items/1871881-methadone-for-heroin-withdrawal

Benowitz, N. "Antitensive Agents." In *Basic and Clinical Pharmacology,* 12th ed., edited by B. Katzung, 169–192. New York: McGraw-Hill, 2012.

Bernstein, M. "Heroin Kills More Oregonians in 2009 Than Cocaine and Meth Combined." *The Oregonian.* 5 April 2010. Available http://www.oregonlive.com/portland/index.ssf/2010/04/heroin_kills_more_oregonians_i.html

Bhuvaneswar, C., G. Chang, L. Epstein, and T. Stern. "Cocaine and Opioid Use During Pregnancy: Prevalence and Management." *Primary Care Companion to the Journal of Clinical Psychiatry* 10 (2008): 59–65.

Biotech Week. "Purdue Pharma: OxyContin Rarely the Sole Cause of Drug Abuse Deaths." (19 March 2003): 1.

Boddigger, D. "Fentanyl-Laced Street Drugs Kill Hundreds." *Lancet* 368 (2006): 1237–1238.

Borigini, M. "Prescribing Narcotics: A Doctor's Point of View." Health Central, Chronic Pain Connection. 27 October 2008. Available http://www.healthcentral.com/chronic-pain/c/91/46424/prescribing-view

Boughton, B. "Buprenorphine Treatment Safer Than Methadone for Infants of Opiate-Addicted Mothers." Medscape. 21 May 2010. Available http://www.medscape.com/viewarticle/722213

Brady, S. "New Formulation for OxyContin." 8 June 2010. Available http://www.highbeam.com/doc/1P3-2066505411.html

Breakthrough Addiction Recovery. "Tramadol." 1 November 2010. Available http://www.breakthroughaddictionrecovery.com/content-page-188-Tramadol.html

Brecher, E. M. *Licit and Illicit Drugs.* Boston: Little, Brown, 1972.

Buckley, C. "Young and Suburban, and Falling for Heroin." *New York Times.* 27 September 2009. Available http://www.nytimes.com/2009/09/27/nyregion/27heroin.html

Caldwell, A. "Deadly, Ultra-Pure Heroin Arrives in US." Huffington Post. 24 May 2010. Available http://www.huffingtonpost.com/2010/05/24/deadly-ultrapure-heroin-a_n_587648.html

Caldwell, A., and J. Salter. "Cheap, Ultra-Pure Heroin Kills Instantly." Associated Press, Today People. 24 May 2010. Available http://today.msnbc.msn.com/id/37319358/ns/us_news-crime_and_courts

CBS News. "OxyContin: Pain Relief vs. Abuse." 11 June 2007. Available http://www.cbsnews.com/stories/2007/06/19/health/webmed/main2953950.shtml

Center for Substance Abuse and Research (CESAR). "Buprenorphine Now Available for Treating Heroin Dependence in U.S." *CESAR FAX* 12 (31 March 2003): 1.

Chossudovsky, M. "Who Benefits from the Afghan Opium Trade?" Global Research. 21 September 2006. Available http://www.globalresearch.ca/index.php?context=va&aid=3294

Christenson, S. "Heroin Addiction Takes Brutal Toll on Afghanistan." *San Antonio Express-News.* 24 May 2010. Available http://www.mysanantonio.com/news/local_news

/in_kabul_regrets_rehab_and_redemption_94714589
.html?showFullArticle=y

Colberg, S. "Methadone Deaths Climb, Oklahoma Officials Say People Get Drugs from Many Sources." *The Oklahoman.* 27 September 2009. Available http://newsok .com/methadone-deaths-climb-oklahoma-officials-say /article/3404370

Cole, C. "Heroin Back on Streets." *Arizona Daily Sun.* 30 May 2010. Available http://azdailysun.com/news/local /article_729609c8-078e-5b95-b1ca-3c5753b9ce4d.html

Colon, D. "Number of Newborns Addicted to Painkillers Rising." NPR. 16 February 2011. Available http://www .npr.org/2011/02/16/133805289/number-of -newborns-addicted-to-painkillers-rising

Community Epidemiology Work Group (CEWG). *Highlights and Executive Summary.* Vol. 1. NIDA, NIH Publications No. 03-5109A. Bethesda, MD: National Institutes of Health, December 2002.

Constable, P. "A Poor Yield for Afghans' War on Drugs." *Washington Post* (19 September 2006): 14A.

Cowan, R., and J. Carvel. "Heroin Addicts Could Inject Themselves at Supervised Centres in Police-Backed Plans." Guardian Unlimited. 23 May 2006. Available http://www.guardian.co.uk/society/2006/may/23 /drugsandalcohol.drugs

Daly, E. "Heroin Deaths Surge in Florida Following Pill Crackdown." Oxy Watch Dog. 13 May 2013. Available http://oxywatchdog.com

DiChiara, G., and A. North. "Neurobiology of Opiate Abuse." *Trends in Pharmacological Sciences* 13 (May 1992): 185–193.

Diep, F. "How Do You Make a Painkiller Addiction-Proof?" *Popular Science.* 13 May 2013. Available http://www.popsci .com/science/article/2013-05/science-un-crushable -oxycontin

Douglas, J. "Painkiller Patch Abuse Blamed for Deaths." *Los Angeles Times* (15 June 2006).

Drug Enforcement Administration (DEA). "OxyContin." 2012. Available http://www.justice.gov/dea/divisions /sd/2012/sd_oxycontin_brochure.pdf

Drug Enforcement Administration (DEA). "Tramadol." Office of Diversion Control. March 2013. Available http://www.deadiversion.usdoj.gov/drug_chem_info /tramadol.pdf

Drug Facts and Comparisons. St. Louis, MO: Wolters Kluwer, 2010 (Pocket Version): 244–247, 520–590.

DrugLib. "OxyContin (Oxycodone Hydrochloride)— Summary." 2010. Available http://www.druglib.com /druginfo/oxycontin

Drugs.com. "Vivitrol." 22 October 2010a. Available http:// www.drugs.com/vivitrol.html

Drugs.com. "What's Tramadol?" 1 November 2010b. Available http://www.drugs.com/tramadol.html

Drug War Facts. "HIV/AIDS and Injection Drug Use." 2010a. Available http://www.drugwarfacts.org/cms /node/48

Drug War Facts. "Pain Management." 2010b. Available http://www.drugwarfacts.org/cms/node/59

Drug War Facts. "Heroin Assisted Treatment/Heroin Management." 2012. Available http://www.drugwarfacts .org/cms/heroin_maintenance#sthash.LJWKNnvQ .dphs

Edwards, M. "Soldiers At Risk of Getting Hooked on Heroin." 7 June 2010. Available http://www.abc.net.au /news/2010-06-03/soldiers-at-risk-of-getting-hooked-on -heroin/853234

Encyclopedia Britannica. "Dextromethorphan." 2010. Available http://www.britannica.com/EBchecked/topic /160532/dextromethorphan

Eshkevari, L., and J. Heath. "Use of Acupuncture for Chronic Pain: Optimizing Clinical Practice." *Holistic Nursing Practice* 19 (2005): 217–221.

Fodale, V. "Killer Fentanyl: A Lesson from Anesthesiology." *Lancet* 368 (2006): 1237–1238.

Galanter, M., and H. Kleber. *The American Psychiatric Publishing Textbook of Substance Abuse Treatment.* Arlington VA: American Psychiatric Publishing, 2008.

GlobalSecurity.org. "Afghanistan Drug Market." 2010. Available http://www.globalsecurity.org/military/world /afghanistan/drugs-market.htm

Golding, A. "Two Hundred Years of Drug Abuse." *Journal of the Royal Society of Medicine* 86 (May 1993): 282–286.

Goldstein, A. *Addiction from Biology to Drug Policy.* New York: Freeman, 1994: 137–154.

Good Drug Guide. "Basic Heroin Information." Available http://www.thegooddrugguide.com/heroin/basics .htm

Gourlay, G. "Advances in Opioid Pharmacology." *Supportive Care for Cancer* (21 December 2004): 153–159.

Gowing, L., M. Farrell, R. Ali, and J. White. "Alpha 2 Adrenergic Agonists for the Management of Opioid Withdrawal." *Cochrane Database Systems Review* 2 (2003).

Grinspoon, L. "Psychotherapy for Methadone Patients— Part II." *Harvard Mental Health Letter* 12 (October 1995): 7.

Gutstein, H., and H. Akil. "Opioid Analgesics." In *The Pharmacological Basis of Therapeutics,* 11th ed., edited by L. Brunton, J. Lazo, and K. Parker, 547–590. New York: McGraw-Hill, 2006.

Hanson, G. R. "Opening the Door to Mainstream Medical Treatment of Drug Addiction." *NIDA Notes* 17 (January 2003): 3, 4.

Hickman, M., S. Carrivick, S. Paterson, N. Hunt, D. Zador, L. Cusick, and J. Henry. "London Audit of Drug-Related Overdose Deaths: Characteristics and Typology, and Implications for Prevention and Monitoring." *Addiction* 102 (2007): 317–323.

Hitti, M. "Prescription Painkiller Addiction: 7 Myths." 2 August 2010. Available http://www.care2.com/c2c/groups/disc.html?gpp=15009&pst=879478

Hubbard, R. "Focus on Heroin: Increase in Users and Changing Treatment System Present New Challenges for Services Researchers." *Connection* (a semiannual newsletter published by the Association for Health Services Research) (June 1998): 1–2.

Hull, M., M. Juhascik, F. Mazur, M. Flomenbaum, and G. Behonick. "Fatalities Associated with Fentanyl and Coadministered Cocaine on Opiates." *Journal of Forensic Science* 52 (2007): 1383–1388.

Jaffe, J., and M. Martin. "Opioid Analgesics and Antagonists." In *The Pharmacological Basis of Therapeutics,* 8th ed., edited by A. Gilman, T. Rall, A. Nies, and P. Taylor, 522–573. New York: Pergamon, 1990.

Johnston, L. "Monitoring the Future 2012." 2013. Available http://www.monitoringthefuture.org/data.html

Jointogether.org. "Moral Judgment Still Plays a Role in Prescribing Pain Meds." 1 March 2010. Available https://www.drugfree.org/join-together/addiction/moral-judgment-still-plays-a

Karch, S. "Narcotics." In *The Pathology of Drug Abuse,* 281–408. New York: CRC, 1996.

Kosten, T., and L. Hollister. "Drugs of Abuse." In *Basic and Clinical Pharmacology,* 7th ed., edited by B. Katzun, 516–531. Stamford, CT: Appleton & Lange, 1998.

Kral, L. and Ghafoor, V. "Pain and Its Management." In *Applied Therapeutics, The Clinical Use of Drugs,* 10th ed., edited by B. Alldredge et al., 112–146. Philadelphia, PA: Wolters Kluwer, 2013.

Kuehn, B. "Buprenorphine May Boost HIV Treatment." *Journal of the American Medical Association* 304 (2010): 261–263.

Lane, E., and S. Dunnett. "Animal Models of Parkinson's Disease and L-dopa Induced Dyskinesia. How Close Are We to the Clinic?" *Psychopharmacology* 199 (2008): 303–312.

Langston, J., P. Ballard, J. Tetrud, and I. Irwin. "Chronic Parkinsonism in Humans Due to a Product of Meperidine-Analogue Synthesis." *Science* 219 (1983): 979–980.

Leach, B. "Heroin 'Shooting Galleries' Should Be Introduced." *Telegraph.* 14 September 2009. Available http://www.telegraph.co.uk/news/uknews/crime/6185533/Heroin-shooting-galleries-should-be-introduced.html

Leinweind, D. "Baltimore Has New Way to Treat Addict." *USA Today.* 5 October 2006: 5a.

Leland, J. "The Fear of Heroin Is Shooting Up." *Newsweek* (26 August 1996): 55–56.

Levran, O., D. Londono, K. O'Hara, M. Randesi, J. Rotrosen, P. Casasonte, et al. "Heroin Addiction in African Americans: A Hypothesis-Driven Association Study." *Genes Brain and Behavior* 8 (2009): 531–540.

Luscher, C. "Drugs of Abuse." In *Basic and Clinical Pharmacology,* edited by B. Katzung, 565–580. New York: McGraw-Hill, 2012.

"Mary." *Rolling Stone* 30 (1996): 42–43.

Maurer, D., and V. Vogel. *Narcotics and Narcotic Addiction,* 3rd ed. Springfield, IL: Thomas, 1967.

McCartney, A., and G. Risling. "Corey Haim's OxyContin Obtained Through Major Drug Ring." Huffington Post. 28 October 2010. Available http://www.huffingtonpost.com/2010/03/13/corey-haims-oxycontin-obt_n_497813.html

McClure, C. "Global Drug Policy and the HIV/IDU Epidemic in Eastern Europe and Central Asia." International AIDS Society. 2009. Available http://www.iasociety.org/Web/WebContent/File/CraigMcClure_SODAK%202009.pdf

McEvoy, G., ed. "Opiate Agonists and Antagonists." In *American Hospital Formulary Service Drug Information,* 2022–2097. Bethesda, MD: American Society of Hospital Pharmacists, 2003.

McLellen, T., O. Arndt, D. Metzger, G. Woody, and C. O'Brien. "The Effects of Psychosocial Services in Substance Abuse Treatment." *Journal of the American Medical Association* 269 (21 April 1993): 1953–1959.

McMurran, M. "What Works in Substance Misuse Treatments for Offenders." *Criminal Behavior and Mental Health* 17 (2007): 225–233.

Meader, N. "A Comparison of Methadone, Buprenorphine and Alpha2 Adrenergic Agonists for Opioid Detoxification: A Mixed Comparison Meta-analysis." *Drug and Alcohol Dependence* 108 (2010): 110–114.

Medical News Today. "Study Identifies Risk Factors for Painkiller Addiction and Links the Addiction to Genetics." 28 August 2010. Available http://www.medicalnewstoday.com/articles/199263.php

Meier, B. "Move to Restrict Pain Killers Puts Onus on Doctors." *New York Times.* 28 July 2010. Available http://www.nytimes.com/2010/07/29/business/29pain.html

More, J. "The Debate Over Drug Abuse Treatment: Methadone vs. Buprenorphine." Treatment Solutions Network. 28 July 2008. Available http://www.treatmentsolutionsnetwork.com/blog/index.php/2008/07/23/the-debate-over-drug-abuse-treatment-methadone-vs-buprenorphine

Morgan, T., M. Porritt, and A. Poling. "Effects of Dextromethorphan on Rats' Acquisition of Responding with Delayed Reinforcement." *Pharmacology and Biochemical Behavior* 85 (2006): 637–642.

Mutschler, J., A. Koopmann, M. Grosshans, D. Hermann, K. Mann, and F. Kiefer. "Dextromethorphan Withdrawal and Dependence Syndrome." *Deutsches Ärzteblatt International* 107 (2010): 537–540.

MyAddiction.com. "Heroin Addiction Stats and Facts." 2010. Available http://www.myaddiction.com/education/articles/heroin_statistics.html

Naggiar, S. "Opiate Addiction: How Prescription Painkillers Pave the Way to Heroin." NBCNews. 7 June 2012. Available http://www.nbcnews.com/health/opiate-addiction-how-prescription-painkillers-pave-way-heroin-817543

Nakamura, D. "City to Spend $650,000 on Needle Exchange Programs." *Washington Post*. 3 January 2008. Available http://www.washingtonpost.com/wp-dyn/content/article/2008/01/02/AR2008010201905.html

Nandi, A., T. Glass, S. Cole, H. Chu, S. Galea, D. Celentano, et al. "Neighborhood Poverty and Injection Cessation in a Sample of Injection Drug Users." *American Journal of Epidemiology* 171 (2010): 391–398.

National Center for Biotechnology Information (NCBI). "Naltrexone (Injection)." PubMed Health. Available http://www.ncbi.nlm.nih.gov/pubmedhealth/PMHT0011328/

National Institute on Drug Abuse (NIDA). "Research Report Series—Heroin Abuse and Addiction." December 2004. Available http://www.drugabuse.gov/ResearchReports/heroin/heroin5.html

National Institute on Drug Abuse (NIDA). "NIDA InfoFacts: Heroin." January 2005. Available http://www.drugabuse.gov/Infofax/heroin.html

National Institute on Drug Abuse (NIDA). "Fentanyl." 2007. Available http://www.drugabuse.gov/drugpages/fentanyl.html

National Institute on Drug Abuse (NIDA). "What Is the History of Opioid Addiction in the United States." January 2013. NIDA International Program. Available http://www.drugabuse.gov/international/question-2-what-history-opioid-addiction-in-united-states

"Opioids." *Medical Letter* 38 (10 May 1996). Accessed May 17, 2013.

O'Shea, J., F. Law, and J. Melichar. "Lofexidine/Clonidine for Withdrawal." ClinicalEvidence, Mental Health. 2010. Available http://clinicalevidence.bmj.com/ceweb/conditions/meh/1015/1015_I5.jsp

Ostrow, N. "Prescription Painkiller Abuse Surged in U.S., Study Finds." Bloomberg. 25 June 2012. Available http://www.bloomberg.com/news/2012-06-25/prescription-painkiller-abuse-surged-in-u-s-study-finds.html

"'Oxy' Kids Crisis." *New York Post*. 18 June 2007. Available http://www.nypost.com/p/news/regional/item_2RyopB29Z8esHu8oe50qkK

Pain and Central Nervous System. "Helping Opiate-Addicted Babies." *Pain and Central Nervous System Week* (5 September 2005). Available http://www.newsrx.com/newsletters/Pain-and-Central-Nervous-System-Week/2005-09-05/09052005333968W.html

Partnership. "Medication with Counseling May Improve Heroin Treatment." 2003. Available http://www.drugfree.org/join-together/drugs/medication-with-counseling

Phillips, K. "Abuse of DXM Cold Medicines." Focus Treatment Centers. 29 April 2013. Available http://focustreatmentcenters.com/abuse-of-dxm-cold-medicines/

Quinion, M. "Heroin Chic." World Wide Words. January 2005. Available http://www.worldwidewords.org/turnsofphrase/tp-her1.htm

Recovery Helpdesk. "10 Things You Should Know About Methadone: A Low Methadone Dose Is Not Necessarily the Best Methadone Dose." 2010. Available http://www.recoveryhelpdesk.com/2010/05/14/series-10-things-you-should-know-about-methadone-number-10

Reid, L., K. Elifson, and C. Sterk. "Ecstasy and Gateway Drugs: Initiating the Use of Ecstasy and Other Drugs." *Annals of Epidemiology* 17 (2007): 74–80.

Reisine, T., and G. Pasternak. "Opioid Analgesics and Antagonists." In *The Pharmacological Basis of Therapeutics*, 9th ed., edited by J. Hardman and L. Limbird, 521–555. New York: McGraw-Hill, 1995.

Relative, S. "Artie Lange Stabbed Himself Nine Times, Attempted Suicide Confirmed." Yahoo! Voices. 8 January 2010. Available http://www.associatedcontent.com/article/2568063/artie_lange_stabbed_himself_nine_times.html

Reuters. "Do Smokers Use More Prescription Painkillers?" 17 June 2010. Available http://www.reuters.com/article/idUSTRE65G5RQ20100617

Rolfs, R. "Utah Clinical Guidelines on Prescribing Opioids." 2008. Available http://health.utah.gov/prescription/pdf/Utah_guidelines_pdfs.pdf

Rombey, D. "Heroin Is Silent Scourge of Sheltered Springville." *Deseret News* (9 June 2003a): A-1.

Rombey, D. "Heroin Takes Toll on Families." *Deseret News* (10 June 2003b): A-1.

Rowlett, J., S. Negus, T. Shippenberg, N. Mello, S. Walsh, and R. Spealman. "Combined Cocaine and Opioid Abuse: From Neurobiology to the Clinic." 2010. Available http://www.opioids.com/speedballs/index.html

RT. "1mn Died from Afghan Heroin, Drug Production '40 Times Higher' Since NATO Operation." 3 April 2013. Available http://rt.com/news/afghanistan-heroin-production-increased-266

Rubin, R. "FDA OKs Vivitrol to Treat Heroin, Narcotic Addictions." *USA Today*. 13 October 2010. Available http://www.usatoday.com/yourlife/health/2010-10-14-opioid14_ST_N.htm

Schneider, E. "OPINION: Heroin Has Never Been So Cheap, Pure and Easy to Find." *Newsday*. 27 September 2009. Available http://www.newsday.com/opinion/opinion-heroin-has-never-been-so-cheap-pure-and-easy-to-find-1.1476468

Schumacher, M., Basbaum, A. and Way, W. " Opioid Analgesics and Antagonists." In *Basic and Clinical Pharmacology*, 12th ed., edited by B. Katzung, 543–564. New York: McGraw-Hill, 2012.

Seper, J. "Colombia Policy Cited for Rise in Heroin Use; Investigators Hit Focus on Cocaine." *Washington Times* (26 May 2003): A-1.

Sify News. "Risk Factors for Painkiller Addiction Identified." 28 August 2010. Available http://sify.com/news/risk-factors-for-painkiller-addiction-identified-news-scitech-ki3pEjahbic.html

Smith, C. "Experts Push for Painkiller Tramadol to Be on Controlled List." *Pittsburgh Tribune-Review*. 28 March 2010. Available http://www.questia.com/library/1P2-21460255/experts-push-for-painkiller-tramadol-to-be-on-controlled

Starikov, N. "The United States and Afghan Heroin." OrientalReview.org. 23 March 2010. Available http://orientalreview.org/2010/03/23/the-united-states-and-afghan-heroin-2

Stein, R. "Painkiller Is Pulled Off Market at FDA's Request." *Washington Post*. 20 November 2010. Available http://www.washingtonpost.com/wp-dyn/content/article/2010/11/19/AR2010111906786.html

Substance Abuse and Mental Health Services Administration (SAMHSA). "The Costs of Alcohol and Drug Treatment." About.com: Alcoholism. 31 December 2008. Available http://alcoholism.about.com/od/pro/a/blsam040527.htm

Substance Abuse and Mental Health Services Administration (SAMHSA). "Physician Waiver Qualifications." 2010. Available http://buprenorphine.samhsa.gov/waiver_qualifications.html

Suhr, J., and J. Salter. "Heroin Use: Police, Prosecutors Shift to More Aggressive Tactics to Tackle Dangerous Drug." Huffington Post. 14 April 2012. Available http://www.huffingtonpost.com/2012/04/14/heroinuse-police-prosecutors_n_1425678.html

Traynor, K. "Advisers Vote Against Declaring Dextromethorphan a Controlled Substance." *American Journal of Health-System Pharmacy* 67 (2010): 1788.

Tree. "Heroin: One of the Most Dangerous Addictive Drugs." 9 August 2010. Available http://www.tree.com/health/substance-abuse-heroin.aspx

Trigo, J. M., E. Martin-Garcia, F. Berrendero, P. Robledo, and R. Maldonado. "The Endogenous Opioid System: A Common Substrate in Drug Addiction." *Drug and Alcohol Dependence* 108 (2010): 183–194.

Tur, K. "Saving Lives with Heroin Needles." NBC New York. 19 August 2010. Available http://www.nbcnewyork.com/news/local-beat/The-Syringe-Exchange-Saved-My-Life-101112079.html

Urban Dictionary. "Heroin Chic." 5 October 2005. Available http://www.urbandictionary.com/define.php?term=heroinchic

USA Today. "Our View on Drug Addiction: Doctors Abet Growing Abuse of Pain Medication." 20 June 2010. Available http://www.usatoday.com/news/opinion/editorials/2010-06-21-editoril21_ST_N.htm?loc=interstitialskip

Valenzuela, B. E. "Heroin Use on the Rise." *Daily Press* (Victorville, CA). 28 August 2010. Available http://www.vvdailypress.com/news/use-21415-rise-heroin.html

Van Hollen, J. "Heroin Abuse Now a Rural Threat Too." *Cap Times*. 3 October 2010. Available http://host.madison.com/ct/news/opinion/mailbag/article_c47ae879-6bf7-5bf3-a2e5-87c2bebf92a0.html

Vaults of Erowid. "Dextromethorphan." 6 January 2007. Available http://www.erowid.org/chemicals/dxm/dxm.shtml

Wang, M. "Perinatal Drug Abuse and Neonatal Drug Withdrawal." eMedicine from WebMD. 12 April 2010. Available http://emedicine.medscape.com/article/978492-overview

Way, W., H. Fields, and E. L. Way. "Opioid Analgesics and Antagonists." In *Basic and Clinical Pharmacology,* 7th ed., edited by B. Katzung, 496–515. Stamford, CT: Appleton & Lange, 1998.

Weiss, E. "Seattle Scene Represents Nation's Rising Heroin Use." All Things Considered, National Public Radio. 2 January 1995.

Williams, S. "Suboxone Abuse Grows After Outpatient Use Authorized." JSOnline, *Milwaukee-Wisconsin Journal Sentinel.* 2 April 2009. Available http://www.jsonline.com /news/milwaukee/42366057.html

Willis, M. "OxyContin Users Turning to Heroin." Drug-Rehabs. 2008. Available http://www.drug-rehabs.com /HeroinReplacesOxycontin.htm

Winkler, M., P. Weyers, R. Mucha, B. Stippekohl, and P. Pauli. "Conditioned Cues for Smoking Elicit Preparatory Responses in Healthy Smokers." *Psychopharmacology* (Berl.) 213 (February 2011): 781–789.

Young, D. "Scientists Examine Pain Relief and Addiction." *American Society of Health-System Pharmacists* 64 (2007): 796–798.

Zickler, P. "High-Dose Methadone Improves Treatment Outcomes." *NIDA Notes* 14 (1999): 81–82.

Zielinski, N. "Methadone Deaths Increase in the US." Examiner.com. 1 August 2010. Available http://www .examiner.com/public-health-in-grand-rapids/methadone -deaths-increase-the-us

Zocchi, A., E. Girlanda G. Varnier, I. Sartori, L. Zanetti, G. Wildish, et al. "Dopamine Responsiveness to Drugs of Abuse: A Shell-Core Investigation in the Nucleus Accumbens of the Mouse." *Synapse* 50 (2003): 293–302.

© GRAZVYDAS/iStockphoto.com

Did You Know?

▶ The first therapeutic use of amphetamines was in inhalers to treat nasal congestion.

▶ Illegal methamphetamine can be easily made from drugs found in common over-the-counter (OTC) decongestants and some herbal products.

▶ Methylphenidate (Ritalin), a drug prescribed to treat hyperactive children (those with ADHD), is sometimes used illegally by college students to suppress fatigue while studying long hours for exams.

▶ Ecstasy has both psychedelic and stimulant properties.

▶ Products with names such as *bath salt* or *ivory wave* contain designer amphetamine- and cocaine-like drugs that have not been well studied and are potentially very dangerous.

▶ Smoking "freebased" or "crack" cocaine is more dangerous and more addicting than other forms of administration.

▶ Using high doses of amphetamines or cocaine can cause behavior that resembles schizophrenia.

▶ Caffeine is the most frequently used stimulant in the world.

▶ Caffeine is the principal active ingredient in most "energy drinks."

▶ Herbal stimulants promoted as "natural highs" contain CNS stimulants such as caffeine or guaraná.

▶ Ephedrine found in natural herbal products has caused fatal cardiovascular problems in unsuspecting athletes and was removed from the list of FDA-approved OTC products.

Learning Objectives

On completing this chapter you will be able to:

❯ Explain how amphetamines work.

❯ Identify the FDA-approved uses for amphetamines.

❯ Recognize the major side effects of amphetamines on brain and cardiovascular functions.

❯ Identify the terms *speed*, *ice*, *run*, *high*, and *tweaking* as they relate to amphetamine use.

❯ Explain what "designer" amphetamines are and how Ecstasy compares to methamphetamine.

❯ Discuss the unique dangers of products like "bath salts."

❯ Explain what "club drugs" are.

❯ Describe why stimulants are used as "performance enhancers" and why they should be considered dangerous.

❯ Explain how methylphenidate (e.g., Ritalin) compares to methamphetamine.

❯ Trace the changes in attitude toward cocaine abuse that occurred in the 1980s and explain why they occurred.

❯ Compare the effects of cocaine with those of amphetamines.

❯ Identify the different stages of cocaine withdrawal.

❯ Discuss the different approaches to treating cocaine dependence.

❯ Identify and compare the major sources of the caffeine-like xanthine drugs.

❯ List the principal physiological effects of caffeine.

❯ Compare caffeine dependence and withdrawal to that associated with the major stimulants.

❯ Describe the beverages known as "energy drinks" and relate their potential risks.

❯ Understand the potential dangers of using herbal stimulants such as ephedra.

❯ Identify the role of the Food and Drug Administration (FDA) in regulating herbal stimulants.

 Drugs and Society Online is a great source for additional drugs and society information for both students and instructors. Visit **go.jblearning.com /hanson12** to find a variety of useful tools for learning, thinking, and teaching.

Introduction

Stimulants are substances that cause the user to feel energized and experience a sense of increased energy and a state of euphoria, or "high." This effect is likely due to the ability of these drugs to release dopamine (Deslandes, Pache, and Sewell 2002). When used excessively, the user may also feel restless and talkative and have trouble sleeping. High doses administered over the long term can produce personality changes or even induce violent, dangerous, psychotic behavior. Persons addicted to potent stimulants make notoriously bad decisions that hurt them and their loved ones. The following is a quote from a former stimulant (i.e., methamphetamine) user:

> For 5 months I hung out with a crew who cooked meth. My job was to write bad checks to get ingredients to make it. This was my life. My house was a mess and I couldn't take care of anyone including myself. I weighed 100 pounds and stayed up for weeks at a time because I never ran out of gas. . . . I also picked my eye for no reason, until it would get so swollen and red it would stay shut for days. I had my first son when I was 26 and later gave up my second son for adoption because I was such a mess. . . . My mother called social services and made sure that I was not allowed to take care of my children. (Snider 2007)

Many users self-medicate psychological conditions (for example, depression or attention deficit hyperactivity disorder [ADHD]) with stimulants. Because the initial effects of stimulants are so pleasant, these drugs are repeatedly abused, leading to dependence.

In this chapter, you will learn about two principal classifications of stimulant drugs. Major stimulants, including amphetamines and cocaine, are addressed first, given their prominent role in current illicit and prescription drug abuse problems in the United States. The chapter concludes with a review of minor stimulants—in particular, caffeine. The stimulant properties of over-the-counter (OTC) sympathomimetics and "herbal highs" also are discussed.

KEY TERM

uppers
CNS stimulants

Major Stimulants

All major stimulants increase alertness, excitation, and euphoria; thus, these drugs are referred to as **uppers**. The major stimulants are classified as either Schedule I ("designer" amphetamines or major ingredients in bath salts–like products) or Schedule II (amphetamine, cocaine, and methylphenidate [Ritalin]) controlled substances because of their abuse potential. Although these drugs have properties in common, they also have unique features that distinguish them from one another. The similarities and differences of the major stimulants are discussed in the following sections.

▮ Amphetamines

More than 12 million Americans have abused methamphetamine, and 1.5 million of these users are addicted to this potent stimulant. Since 2009, use of amphetamine has declined due to increased concern regarding its potential toxicity (Johnston 2013). Amphetamines are potent synthetic central nervous system (CNS) stimulants capable of causing dependence due to their euphorigenic properties and ability to eliminate fatigue. Despite their addicting effects, amphetamines can be legally prescribed by physicians for appetite control in weight-loss programs, narcolepsy, and hyperactivity disorders. Consequently, amphetamine abuse occurs in people who acquire their drugs by both legitimate and illicit means.

THE HISTORY OF AMPHETAMINES

The first amphetamine was synthesized by the German pharmacologist L. Edeleano in 1887, but it was not until 1910 that this and several related compounds were tested in laboratory animals. Another 17 years passed before Gordon Alles, a researcher looking for a more potent substitute for ephedrine (used as a decongestant at the time), self-administered amphetamine and gave a firsthand account of its effects. Alles found that when inhaled or taken orally, amphetamine dramatically reduced fatigue, increased alertness, and caused a sense of confident euphoria (Grinspoon and Bakalar 1978).

Because of Alles's impressive findings, the Benzedrine (amphetamine) inhaler became available in 1932 as a nonprescription medication in drugstores across the United States. The Benzedrine inhaler, marketed for nasal congestion, was widely abused for its stimulant action but continued to be available OTC until 1949. Because of a loophole in a law that was passed later, not until 1971 were all potent amphetamine-like compounds in nasal inhalers withdrawn from the market (Grinspoon and Bakalar 1978; McCaffrey 1999).

Owing to the lack of restrictions during this early period, amphetamines were sold to treat a variety of ailments, including obesity, alcoholism, bed-wetting, depression, schizophrenia, morphine and codeine addiction, heart block, head injuries, seasickness, persistent hiccups, and caffeine mania. Today, most of these uses are no longer approved as legitimate therapeutics but would be considered forms of drug abuse.

World War II provided a setting in which both the legal and "black market" use of amphetamines flourished (Grinspoon and Bakalar 1978). Because of their stimulating effects, amphetamines were widely used by the Germans, Japanese, and British in World War II to counteract fatigue. By the end of World War II, large quantities of amphetamines were readily available without prescription in seven types of nasal inhalers (Rich and Jordan 2010).

In spite of warnings about these drugs' addicting properties and serious side effects, the U.S. armed forces issued amphetamines on a regular basis during the Korean War and, in fact, may still make it available to pilots in the Air Force to relieve fatigue (Rich and Jordan 2010). Amphetamine use became widespread among truck drivers making long hauls; it is believed that among the earliest distribution systems for illicit amphetamines were truck stops along major U.S. highways. High achievers under continuous pressure in the fields of entertainment, business, and industry often relied on amphetamines to counteract fatigue. Homemakers used them to control weight and to combat boredom from unfulfilled lives. At the height of one U.S. epidemic in 1967, some 31 million prescriptions were written for **anorexians** (diet pills) alone.

Today, a variety of related drugs and mixtures exist, including amphetamine substances such as dextroamphetamine (Dexedrine), methamphetamine (Desoxyn), and amphetamine itself. Generally, if doses are adjusted, the psychological effects of these various drugs are similar, so they will be discussed as a group. Other drugs with some of the same pharmacological properties are phenmetrazine (Preludin) and methylphenidate (Ritalin). Not only are illicit stimulants a significant drug abuse problem, but legal stimulants are the second most frequently abused drug on college campuses, with 15–20% of students using these drugs.

Common slang terms for amphetamines include *speed, crystal, meth, bennies, dexies, uppers, pep pills, diet pills, jolly beans, copilots, hearts, footballs, white crosses, crank,* and *ice.*

HOW AMPHETAMINES WORK

Amphetamines are synthetic chemicals that are similar to natural neurotransmitters such as norepinephrine (noradrenaline), dopamine, and the stress hormone epinephrine (adrenaline). The amphetamines exert their pharmacological effect by increasing the release and blocking the metabolism of these catecholamine substances as well as serotonin, both in the brain and in nerves associated with the sympathetic nervous system. Because amphetamines cause release of norepinephrine from sympathetic nerves, they are classified as sympathomimetic drugs. The amphetamines generally cause an arousal or activating response (also called the *fight-or-flight response*) that is similar to the normal reaction to emergency situations, stress, or crises. Amphetamines also cause alertness so that the individual becomes aroused and hypersensitive to stimuli, and feels "turned on." These effects occur even without external sensory input. This activation may be a very pleasant experience in itself, but a continual high level of activation may convert to anxiety, severe apprehension, or panic.

Amphetamines have potent effects on dopamine in the reward (pleasure) center of the brain. This action probably causes the "flash" or sudden feeling of intense pleasure that occurs when amphetamine is taken intravenously. Some users describe the sensation as a "whole-body orgasm," and many associate intravenous methamphetamine use with sexual feelings. The actual effect of these drugs on sexual behavior is quite variable and dependent on dose (McCaffrey 1999).

WHAT AMPHETAMINES CAN DO

A curious condition commonly reported with heavy amphetamine use is **behavioral stereotypy**, or getting hung up. This term refers to a simple activity that is done repeatedly. An individual

KEY TERMS

anorexians
drugs that suppress the activity of the brain's appetite center, causing reduced food intake

behavioral stereotypy
meaningless repetition of a single activity

who is "hung up" will get caught in a repetitious thought or act for hours. For example, he or she may take objects apart, like radios or clocks, and carefully categorize all the parts, or sit in a tub and bathe all day, persistently sing a note, repeat a phrase of music, or repeatedly clean the same object. This phenomenon seems to be peculiar to potent stimulants such as the amphetamines and cocaine. Similar patterns of repetitive behavior also occur in psychotic conditions, which suggests that the intense use of stimulants such as amphetamines or cocaine alters the brain in a manner like that causing psychotic mental disorders (American Psychiatric Association [APA] 2013) and can lead to violent behavior.

Chronic use of high doses of amphetamines decreases the brain content of the neurotransmitters dopamine and serotonin, which persists for months even after drug use is stopped (Krasnova and Cadet, 2009). These decreases have been shown to reflect damage to the CNS neurons that release these transmitters. It is not clear why this neuronal destruction occurs, although there is evidence that the amphetamines can stimulate production of very reactive molecules, called *free radicals*, which in turn damage brain cells (National Institute on Drug Abuse [NIDA] 2010b).

APPROVED USES

Until 1970, amphetamines were prescribed for a large number of conditions, including depression, fatigue, and long-term weight reduction. In 1970, the Food and Drug Administration (FDA), acting on the recommendation of the National Academy of Sciences, restricted the legal use of amphetamines to three medical conditions: (1) narcolepsy, (2) attention deficit hyperactivity disorder (ADHD), and (3) short-term weight reduction programs (Ballod 2013).

NARCOLEPSY

Amphetamine treatment of narcolepsy is not widespread because this condition is a relatively rare disorder. The term **narcolepsy** comes from the Greek words for numbness and seizure. A person who has narcolepsy falls asleep as frequently as 50 times a day if he or she stays in one position

KEY TERM

narcolepsy
a condition causing spontaneous and uncontrolled sleeping episodes

for very long. Taking low doses of amphetamines helps keep narcoleptic people alert.

ATTENTION DEFICIT HYPERACTIVITY DISORDER

This common behavioral problem in children and adolescents involves an abnormally high level of physical activity, an inability to focus attention, and frequent disruptive behavior. Four to six percent of children and adults have ADHD (Polanczyk and Rohde 2007). The drug commonly used to treat children with ADHD is the amphetamine-related methylphenidate or Ritalin (discussed later in this chapter).

WEIGHT REDUCTION

The most common use of amphetamines is for the treatment of obesity. Amphetamines and chemically similar compounds are used as anorexiants to help obese or severely overweight people control appetite. Amphetamines are thought to act by affecting the appetite center in the hypothalamus of the brain, which causes the user to decrease food intake. The FDA has approved short-term use of amphetamines for weight loss programs but has warned of their potential for abuse. Many experts believe that the euphoric effect of amphetamines is the primary motivation for their continued use in weight reduction programs. It is possible that many obese people have a need for gratification that can be satisfied by the euphoric feeling this drug produces (Wang et al. 2004). If the drug is taken away, these individuals return to food to satisfy their need and sometimes experience "rebound," causing them to gain back more weight than they lost. Some persons who become addicted to amphetamine-like substances begin illicit use of these drugs by trying to prevent weight gain or to lose weight on their own without the guidance of a physician (APA 2013).

SIDE EFFECTS OF THERAPEUTIC DOSES

The two principal side effects of therapeutic doses of amphetamines are (1) abuse, which has already been discussed at length, and (2) cardiovascular toxicities. Many of these effects derive from the amphetamine-induced release of epinephrine from the adrenal glands and norepinephrine from the nerves associated with the sympathetic nervous system. The effects include increased heart rate, elevated blood pressure, and damage to vessels, especially small veins and arteries (Drug War Facts 2004; Drugs.com 2010). In users with a history of heart attack, coronary arrhythmia, or hypertension, amphetamine toxicity can be severe or even fatal.

Meth and Crime

Uncontrolled abuse of methamphetamine damages the brain in such a manner that the user becomes impulsive and often reacts to situations in a violent unpredictable way. Such reactions result in tragic consequences, such as a 62-year-old man who was charged with second-degree assault in connection with a stabbing after a fight broke out. Or another man who stabbed an acquaintance with a kitchen knife during an argument. Or two young men who attacked and severely wounded a 17-year-old high school student because of a drug deal that went bad. Police are frustrated because of the frequency of such crimes and the fact that their jails are filled with methamphetamine users. The ultimate solution is clearly not to hire more police and build more jails, but rather to try to provide proper drug treatment to get meth addicts off of this destructive drug, or better still, to develop better proactive strategies that prevent people from abusing methamphetamine in the first place.

Data from Klouda, N., and S. Pearson. "Crimes Rise with Meth Addiction." *Homer Tribune*. 28 July 2010. Available http://homertribune.com/2010/07/crimes-rise-with-meth-addiction. Accessed March 16, 2011.

CURRENT MISUSE

Because amphetamine drugs can be readily and inexpensively synthesized in makeshift laboratories for illicit sale, can be administered by several routes, and cause a more sustained effect than cocaine, they are more popular than cocaine in many parts of the United States (Johnston 2010). Surveys suggest that there was a decline in the abuse of amphetamines in the late 1980s and early 1990s in parallel with a similar trend in cocaine abuse (Johnston 2013). By 1993, the declines were replaced by a rise in the number of persons abusing amphetamines. However, abuse again declined by 2012, as indicated by the finding that approximately 2.5% of high school seniors were using amphetamines monthly compared to 5.6% in 2001 (Johnston 2013). Of those who abuse methamphetamine and become addicted, many end up in the criminal justice system (Klouda and Pearson 2010; see "Here and Now: Meth and Crime").

Because of the potential for serious side effects, U.S. medical associations have asked all physicians to be more careful about prescribing amphetamines. Presently, use is recommended only for narcolepsy and some cases of hyperactivity in children (Hoffman and Lefkowitz 1995). In spite of FDA approval, most medical associations do not recommend the use of amphetamines for weight loss. Probably less than 1% of all prescriptions now written are for amphetamines, compared with 8% in 1970.

Amphetamine abusers commonly administer a dose of 10 to 30 milligrams. Besides the positive effects of this dose—the "high"—it can cause hyperactive, nervous, or jittery feelings that encourage the use of a depressant such as a benzodiazepine, barbiturate, or alcohol to relieve the discomfort of being "wired" (Hoffman and Lefkowitz 1995; Office of National Drug Control Policy [ONDCP] 2010).

A potent and commonly abused form of amphetamine is **speed**, an illegal methamphetamine available as a white, odorless, bitter-tasting crystalline powder for injection. Methamphetamine is a highly addictive stimulant that is often cheaper and much longer lasting than cocaine. The profit for the speed manufacturer is substantial enough to make illicit production financially attractive (Ordonez 2008). Because the cost ranges from $10 to $20 a dose, it is sometimes known as the "poor man's cocaine" (Leinwand 2007). Despite this image of being a particular problem of the working class, there are many examples of rich and famous people who also abuse this potent stimulant (see "Here and Now: Agassi Admits Using Meth").

Methamphetamine is relatively easy and inexpensive to make. The illicit manufacturers are usually individuals without expertise in chemistry. Such people, referred to as "cookers," can produce methamphetamine batches by using cookbook-style recipes (often obtained in jail or over the

KEY TERM

speed
an injectable methamphetamine used by drug addicts

HERE AND NOW

Agassi Admits Using Meth

In his autobiography, Andre Agassi, the tennis star, admitted to using crystal methamphetamine and lying about it to tennis authorities after failing a drug test. Agassi said that for a moment he was worried about how fans would respond to the revelation that he used drugs, but the concern did not last long. This very popular athlete described his methamphetamine experience as follows: "I snort some. I ease back on the couch and consider the Rubicon I've just crossed. There is a moment of regret, followed by vast sadness. Then comes a tidal wave of euphoria that sweeps away every negative thought in my head. I've never felt so alive, so hopeful—and I've never felt such energy. I'm seized by a desperate desire to clean. I go tearing around my house, cleaning it from top to bottom. I dust the furniture. I scour the tub. I make the beds."

© Brandon_Parry/ShutterStock, Inc.

Data from Wyatt, B. "Agassi Admits Using Crystal Meth." CNN.com. (October 28, 2009). Available http://www.cnn.com/2009/SPORT/10/28/tennis.agassi .crystal.meth/index.html. Accessed February 17, 2011.

Internet). The most popular recipe uses common OTC ingredients—ephedrine, pseudoephedrine, and phenylpropanolamine—as **precursor chemicals** for the methamphetamine. To discourage the illicit manufacture of this potent stimulant, the Comprehensive Methamphetamine Control Act was passed in the United States in October 1996. This law increases penalties for trafficking in methamphetamine and in the precursor chemicals used to create this drug and gives the government authority to regulate and seize these substances (Designer-drug.com). Despite the success in shutting down larger neighborhood operations with this and similar local laws, there are still drug users who make their own meth in small batches using simpler and cruder methods that consist of what has become known as "shake and bake" approaches. These scaled down recipes require relatively small numbers of decongestant pills that are crushed and mixed with common household chemicals; the procedure can be done in inconspicuous places such as a bathroom or in a car. Although no flame is required to "cook" the mixture, the

procedure sometimes can produce powerful explosions, fires, and toxic waste (Juozapavicius 2009). For example, a man in southeast Missouri was seen jumping from his car with his crotch on fire holding a flaming bottle, which he quickly dumped before immediately returning to his car and driving away. Upon closer inspection, the bottle was a "shake and bake" effort to make methamphetamine (Keybol 2013).

Due to the ease of production and the ready availability of chemicals used to prepare methamphetamine, this drug at times has been particularly problematic in the United States and was declared the number 1 drug problem in the majority of counties across the country in 2006 (Rutledge 2006). Traditional methamphetamine users in the United States have been white, male, blue-collar workers over 26 years of age; some adolescents (Johnston 2013); and young adult women. The most recent methamphetamine epidemic appeared to begin in the western states and move east (NIDA Community Epidemiology Workgroup [CEWG] 2007). Despite pockets of severe problems, in general, methamphetamine abuse is still less common on the East Coast (Leinwand 2007; NIDA CEWG 2007).

When discovered, the so-called meth or speed labs are raided by law enforcement agencies across the country. In 2003, the DEA funded the

KEY TERM

precursor chemicals
chemicals used to produce a drug

HERE AND NOW

Chemical Toxins Associated with Meth Labs

Methamphetamine labs can be set up almost anywhere and pose a serious threat to occupants as well as to law officers and emergency personnel. The following are some of the chemicals often present and their toxic potentials.

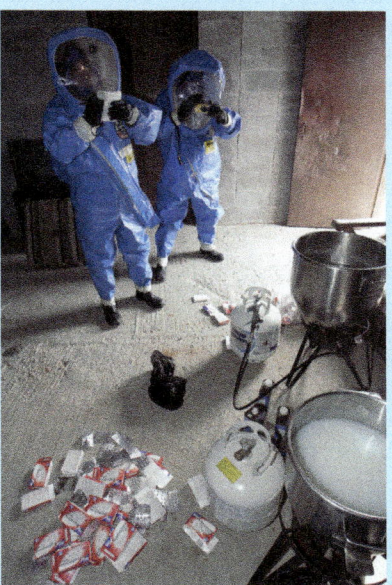

© Kyle Carter/The Meridian Star/AP Photos

Chemicals	Toxic Reactions
Sodium hydroxide	Irritant to skin and eyes
Ammonia	Induces vomiting and nausea
Ether, acetone, and alcohol	Flammable
Chloroform	Carcinogen and volatile
Mercuric chloride	Poisonous (used as insecticide)
Cyanide gas	Extremely poisonous if breathed
Acids	Potent irritants
Iodine	Irritant; causes nausea, headaches, and dizziness
Phosphene gas	Poisonous, flammable (used as nerve gas)

Data from Office of National Drug Control Policy (ONDCP). Synthetic Drug Control Strategy. June 2006. Available http://www.justice.gov/olp/pdf/synthetic_strat2006.pdf. Accessed October 20, 2013.

cleanup of approximately 12,000 illegal methamphetamine labs, most of which were in the western United States. This number decreased to 3866 in 2008 (Doyle 2010) but has since increased again (U.S. Department of Justice 2010). The laboratory operators are usually well armed, and the facilities are frequently booby-trapped with explosives. Not surprisingly, these operations pose a serious threat to their neighbors (U.S. Department of Justice 2003a) and to residents, especially children, in the structure that contains the lab (U.S. Department of Justice 2002). Law enforcement personnel and firefighters are also at risk when dealing with methamphetamine labs owing to ignitable, corrosive, reactive, and toxic chemicals that might explode, start a fire, emit toxic fumes, or cause serious injury at the site. The toxic chemicals can create fumes that contaminate neighboring buildings, the water supply, or soil. These labs are especially dangerous when they are set up in poorly ventilated rooms (see "Here and Now: Chemical Toxins Associated with Meth Labs").

Although still a problem, as already mentioned, the incidence of "mom and pop" neighborhood methamphetamine labs has dramatically decreased across the nation since 2003. This is mainly due to federal and state laws that limit access to large quantities of precursor drugs found in OTC decongestants. The statutes require these decongestant products be kept behind the pharmacy counter, and the quantity sold to a customer must be minimal in order to limit access (Leinwand 2007) (see "Holding the Line: Cold Restrictions"). Although successful in decreasing the number of small neighborhood meth labs in the United States, this strategy unfortunately appears to have had minimal effect on actual supplies of this drug for illegal sales. Methamphetamine is being smuggled across the U.S. border from Mexico (Berkes 2007) and is being manufactured by criminal organizations from chemicals diverted by the ton from Asian pharmaceutical companies (Huus 2007; Randolph 2007; Savage and Gordon 2010). It is estimated that currently the vast majority of meth is imported, keeping supplies abundant, purity high, and costs low (Leinwand 2007; U.S. Department of Justice 2010). In addition, small neighborhood labs are making a significant comeback, particularly in the Midwest, due to a strategy referred to as "smurfing." Smurfs are often well organized and enlist the help of many friends and associates to purchase the methamphetamine precursor chemicals such as pseudoephedrine (e.g., in decongestants) in quantities below the legal limits. In this way large amounts of these chemicals can be accumulated and then sold to methamphetamine producers (U.S. Department of Justice 2010). Due to strategies such as shake-and-baking and smurfing, the number of methamphetamine lab seizures and busts skyrocketed to over 2000 in Tennessee alone in 2010 (Salter 2011).

PATTERNS OF HIGH-DOSE USE

Amphetamines can be taken orally, intravenously, or by smoking. The intensity and duration of effects vary according to the mode of administration. The methamphetamine addict frequently uses chronic, high doses of amphetamines intravenously and can be infected with human immunodeficiency virus (HIV) (The Body 2010). Another approach to administering amphetamines is smoking **ice**, which can cause effects as potent, but perhaps more prolonged and erratic, than intravenous doses. The initial effect (after 5 to 30 minutes) of these potent stimulants is called the **rush** and includes a racing heartbeat and elevated blood pressure, metabolism, and pulse. During this phase, the user has powerful impressions of pleasure and enthusiasm. The next stage is the **high** (4 to 16 hours after drug use) when the person feels aggressively smarter, energetic, talkative, and powerful and may initiate

and complete highly ambitious tasks. The amphetamine addict tries to maintain the high for as long as possible, with continual drug use leading to extended mental and physical hyperactivity; this is referred to as a **run** or **binge** and can persist from 3 to 15 days. Persistent use of these drugs, such as methamphetamine, to maintain the high for long periods of time is called **tweaking.** The tweaker often has neither slept nor eaten much for 3 to 15 days and can be extremely irritable and paranoid and have an elevated body temperature, a condition known as **hyperpyrexia.** This is a potentially dangerous stage for medical personnel or law enforcement officers because if the tweaker becomes agitated, he or she can respond violently to the efforts of others to help. To relieve some of the side effects of the extensive use of methamphetamine, tweakers often use a depressant such as alcohol, barbiturates, benzodiazepines, or opioid narcotics (O'Brien and Anthony 2009). The consequences of such a drug combination are to intensify negative feelings and worsen the dangers of the drug. Tweakers are frequently involved in domestic violence and frequently injure their children and partners (Transitions 2007). Withdrawal follows for 30 to 90 days, including feelings of depression and lethargy. During this phase, craving can be intense and the abuser may even become suicidal. Because a dose of methamphetamine often relieves these symptoms, many addicts in treatment return to abusing this stimulant.

After the first day or so of a run, unpleasant symptoms become prominent as the dosage is increased. Symptoms commonly reported at this stage are teeth grinding, disorganized patterns of thought and behavior, stereotypy, irritability, self-consciousness, suspiciousness, and fear. Hallucinations and delusions that are similar to a paranoid psychosis and indistinguishable from schizophrenia can occur (APA 2013; NIDA 2010b). The person is likely to show aggressive and antisocial behavior for no apparent reason, although recent brain imaging studies have revealed that addictions to the amphetamines can cause long-term damage to the brain's inhibitory control centers (Kuehn 2007; NIDA 2010b). Severe chest pains, abdominal discomfort that mimics appendicitis, and fainting from overdosage are sometimes reported. "Cocaine bugs" represent one bizarre effect of high doses of potent stimulants such as amphetamines: The user experiences strange feelings, like insects crawling under the skin. The range of physical and mental symptoms experienced from low to high doses is summarized in "Signs and Symptoms:

KEY TERMS

ice
a smokable form of methamphetamine

rush
initial pleasure after amphetamine use that includes racing heartbeat and elevated blood pressure

high
lasts for 4 to 16 hours after drug use; includes feelings of energy and power

run
intense use of a stimulant, consisting of multiple administrations over a period of days

binge
similar to a run, but usually of shorter duration

tweaking
repeated administration of methamphetamine to maintain the high

hyperpyrexia
elevated body temperature

HOLDING THE LINE
Cold Restrictions

Starting on September 30, 2006, it became somewhat more difficult for a person with a cold, and a lot more difficult for persons desiring to make methamphetamine from decongestant ingredients, to readily obtain adequate OTC cold medicine for their needs. This is due to a federal law to stop the manufacture of methamphetamine in illegal meth labs found in homes, garages, or basements. To achieve this objective, the restrictions require customers to show a picture ID to purchase cold medicine such as NyQuil Cold & Flu, Actifed Cold & Allergy, and Claritin-D. These and similar decongestant products that contain drugs that can be converted into methamphetamine must be kept behind the store counters in most states. Customers must sign a logbook identifying what they purchased and where they live. The logbook remains on file for 2 years. This law restricts purchase to 3–6 grams of product/day and 9 grams/month. In Oregon and Mississippi these medicines are only available by prescription.

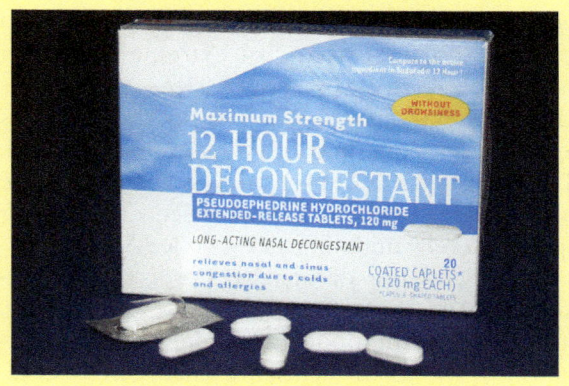

Data from Health & Wellness. "Why Cold Medicines Have Moved Behind the Counter." *Women's Health*. (2013). Available www.sheknows.com/health-and-wellness/articles/7629/why-some-cold-medicines-have-moved-behind-the-counter

SIGNS & SYMPTOMS

Summary of the Effects of Amphetamines on the Body and Mind

	Body	Mind
Low dose	Increased heartbeat	Decreased fatigue
	Increased blood pressure	Increased confidence
	Decreased appetite	Increased feeling of alertness
	Increased breathing rate	Restlessness, talkativeness
	Inability to sleep	Increased irritability
	Sweating	Fearfulness, apprehension
	Dry mouth	Distrust of people
	Muscle twitching	Behavioral stereotypy
	Convulsions	Hallucinations
	Fever	Psychosis
	Chest pain	
	Irregular heartbeat	
High dose	Death due to overdose	

Summary of the Effects of Amphetamines on the Body and Mind."

Toward the end of the run, the adverse symptoms dominate. When the drug is discontinued because the supply is exhausted or the symptoms become too unpleasant, an extreme crash can occur, followed by prolonged sleep, sometimes lasting several days. On awakening, the person is lethargic, hungry, and often severely depressed. The amphetamine user may overcome these unpleasant effects by smoking ice or injecting speed, thereby initiating a new cycle (APA 2013).

Continued use of massive doses of amphetamine often leads to considerable weight loss, sores on the skin, poor oral hygiene and deterioration of the teeth (Rauscher 2006; Shetty et al. 2010), nonhealing ulcers, liver disease, hypertensive disorders, cerebral hemorrhage (stroke), heart attack, kidney damage, and seizures (Fox 2010; Hall and Hando 1993; Kinkead and Romboy 2004). For some of these effects, it is impossible to tell if they are caused by the drug, poor eating habits, or other factors associated with the lifestyle of people who inject methamphetamine.

Speed freaks are generally unpopular with the rest of the drug-taking community, especially "acid-heads" (addicts who use lysergic acid diethylamide [LSD]), because of the aggressive, unpredictable behavior associated with use of potent stimulants (Elias 2010). In general, drug abusers who take high doses of these agents, such as amphetamines or cocaine, are more likely to be involved in violent crimes than those who abuse other drugs (Substance Abuse and Mental Health Services Administration [SAMHSA] 2010). Heavy users are generally unable to hold steady jobs because of their drug habits and often have a parasitic relationship with the rest of the illicit drug-using community.

Although claims have been made that amphetamines do not cause physical dependence, it is almost certain that depression (sometimes suicidal), lethargy, muscle pains, abnormal sleep patterns, and, in severe cases, suicide attempts occur after high chronic doses as part of withdrawal (NIDA 2000). During withdrawal from amphetamine use, the dependent user often turns to other drugs for relief (Cantwell and McBride 1998). Rebound from the amphetamines is opposite to that experienced with withdrawal from CNS depressants.

Although the effects of amphetamines on the unborn fetus are difficult to evaluate and not fully understood (Science Daily 2010a), some human studies suggest that there is a possibility of serious problems in the offspring. This research shows that babies born to methamphetamine-using mothers are much more likely to be preterm and less likely to survive. In addition, almost 40% of the meth-exposed babies are at least temporarily removed from their mothers to be adopted or placed in Child Protective Services or foster care (Harding 2010). Studies on the long-term effects on the offspring of methamphetamine moms have been more difficult to conduct, but suggest that brain structures are altered, particularly if these women are also consuming alcohol. These congenital problems could lead to long-term cognitive or behavioral problems (Science Daily 2010a). The methamphetamine-abusing expectant mothers are also vulnerable to serious pregnancy problems of their own such as uncontrolled high blood pressure and delivery complications (Harding 2010).

There is evidence that repeated high-dose use of amphetamines, such as methamphetamine, by adolescents or adults causes long-term and perhaps permanent damage to both the dopamine and serotonin neurotransmitter systems of the brain (Cohen 2006; Hanson, Rau, and Fleckenstein 2004). This brain damage may result in persistent episodes of psychosis (NIDA 2010b; Yui et al. 1997) as well as long-lasting memory, motor impairment, and cognitive deficits (Hanson et al. 2004; Volkow et al. 2001). Abuse of amphetamines often seriously damages personal relationships with friends, associates, and even family members. Particularly disturbing is the increasing methamphetamine use by young mothers. Moms on meth have claimed that use of this stimulant makes them feel invincible, and like they can run around the world—and then do it again. They claim to lose weight, but they also can lose their instinct to mother their children as they become obsessed

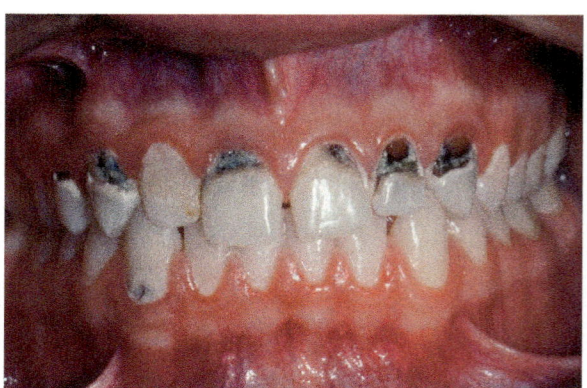

Devastation of oral structures called "meth mouth" sometimes is associated with methamphetamine addiction.

HERE AND NOW

Small Town, Big Problems: The Female Methamphetamine Epidemic

Methamphetamine has caused a drug-related epidemic never before experienced in this country. Its abuse and devastating social effects have taxed public social services in unanticipated ways. One of the most striking aspects of this drug's abuse is its appeal to young adult women, many of whom have children. Typically, the number of women seeking treatment for drug addiction is considerably lower than the number of men in the same situation; however, in many regions roughly equal numbers of men and women seek help for methamphetamine as their primary addiction. Clearly, the destructive influence of methamphetamine abuse is taking an enormous toll on homes and families. Consequently, criminal justice systems for women offenders have been overwhelmed.

Women who are addicted to methamphetamine often do not do well in conventional drug treatment. Because of the potent addicting properties of this drug, they typically struggle with the requirements of probation or parole and often end up back in prison and their children end up in family services and foster care. Although it is not clear why this stimulant is so seductive to young women, women who use methamphetamine typically have:

- A history of chronic unemployment
- A live-in partner who also uses drugs
- A history of physical and sexual abuse
- A history of suicide attempts
- Motivation to use methamphetamine for weight control
- Psychiatric drug-related problems

For female methamphetamine addicts, "this drug is a massive black hole. It's swallowing these people alive and takes a miracle to put these families back together again."

Data from "Escalation in Methamphetamine Use Also Leads to Escalation in Social Service." Health & Medicine Week (14 February 2005); and Rowan-Szal, G., G. Joe, W. Simpson, J. Greener, and J. Vance. "During-Treatment Outcomes Among Female Methamphetamine-Using Offenders in Prison-Based Treatments." Journal of Offender Rehabilitation 48 (2009): 388–401.

with the drug (Holt 2005). Consequently, children are being exposed to dangerous levels of this drug in many forms (see "Here and Now: Small Town, Big Problems") at a tremendous emotional cost (see "Signs and Symptoms: A Daughter's Plea to a Meth Mother").

TREATMENT

Admissions for treatment of methamphetamine addiction more than doubled from 2000 to 2005 (Join Together 2006). However, after this time, there was evidence that efforts in both the United States and neighboring Mexico to restrict access to the decongestant drugs used to synthesize methamphetamine significantly reduced the number of methamphetamine addicts who have voluntarily

entered treatment (Cunningham et al. 2010). But more recent findings suggest that both domestic and Mexican methamphetamine labs are finding ways to get around the laws and avoid detection, resulting in a significant resurgence in methamphetamine supplies and purity in the United States.

The dependence disorder caused by the amphetamines is very hard, but not impossible, to treat successfully. Many methamphetamine addicts have significant impairment of their decision-making ability and do not self-refer, but are forced into treatment by drug courts and other components of the criminal justice system (Newswise 2007; Science Daily 2009). Presently, the most effective treatments for amphetamine addiction are

SIGNS & SYMPTOMS
A Daughter's Plea to a Meth Mother

One can only imagine the frustration, anger, and pain that are suffered by the children of mothers who are addicted to methamphetamine. The children's lives are filled with uncertainty such as the lies of parents who swear that they are clean or will stop their drug habit because they "love their children so much and they don't want to hurt them anymore"; but their addiction always seems to crowd out the "love for the child." Often the children try to 'tough' it out and smile on the outside even though on the inside they being torn apart. How long should a child have to tolerate this emotional and even physical abuse? When does it become too much and how can a child escape? Recently a poem was posted on the Internet that beautifully expressed these terrible struggles of a child with a mother who is a drug addict. This poem is entitled "My Mother vs. Meth" and can be accessed at www.familyfriendpoems.com/poem/my-mother-vs-meth.

behavioral interventions to help modify thinking patterns, improve cognitive skills, change expectations, and increase coping with life's stressors. Amphetamine support groups also appear to be successful as adjuncts to behavioral therapies. There currently are no well-established pharmacological treatments for amphetamine dependency (Elkashef et al. 2008). Approaches used for cocaine have been tried with some success. Antidepressant medication may help relieve the depression that occurs during early stages of withdrawal (NIDA 2006; Raskin 2005).

The persistence of the methamphetamine effects makes this addiction especially difficult to address effectively. The word on the street has been that many of the effects of this stimulant are permanent and its cognitive damage might not be reversible. Although there is ample evidence that hard-core use of methamphetamine for extended periods does have devastating effects on decision making, impulsivity, memory, and other functions, evidence is accumulating that suggests that recovery from these effects is possible. However, effective treatment is not simple or cheap, and typically requires more than a year of intense intervention consisting of drug abstinence; cognitive, emotional, and motivational rehabilitation; and often career and skills development (McManis 2009).

AMPHETAMINE COMBINATIONS

As previously mentioned, amphetamines are frequently used in conjunction with a variety of other drugs such as barbiturates, benzodiazepines, alcohol, and heroin (Nuckols and Kane 2003; Science Daily 2010a). Amphetamines intensify, prolong, or otherwise alter the effects of LSD, and the two types of drugs are sometimes combined. The majority of speed users have also had experience with a variety of psychedelics or other drugs. In addition, people dependent on opiate narcotics frequently use amphetamines or cocaine. These combinations are sometimes called **speedballs**.

"DESIGNER" AMPHETAMINES

Underground chemists can synthesize drugs that mimic the psychoactive effects of amphetamines. Although the production of such drugs diminished in the early 1990s, their use by American teens surged in the late 1990s and early 2000s, as reflected in the fact that more than 9% of high school seniors used the designer amphetamine known as MDMA (Ecstasy) in 2001. This rate dramatically decreased to 3% in 2005, reflecting a concern about its potential harmful effects. However, the rate of annual use rose to 5.3% in 2011 but dropped back again to 3.8% in 2012 (Johnston 2013), suggesting that the concerns about the risk of recreational use of the designer amphetamines have been vacillating (Johnston 2013).

Designer amphetamines sometimes differ from the parent compound by only a single element. These "synthetic spinoffs" pose a significant abuse problem because often several different designer amphetamines can be made from the parent compound and still retain the abuse potential and physical risks of the original substance.

For many years, the production and distribution of designer amphetamines were not illegal, even though they were synthesized from controlled substances. In the mid-1980s, however, the DEA actively pursued policies to curb their production

KEY TERM

speedballs
combinations of amphetamine or cocaine with an opioid narcotic, often heroin

and sale. Consequently, many designer amphetamines were outlawed under the Substance Analogue Enforcement Act of 1986, which makes illegal any substance that is similar in structure or psychological effect to any substance already scheduled, if it is manufactured, possessed, or sold with the intention that it be consumed by human beings (Beck 1990).

The principal types of designer amphetamines are:

- Derivatives from amphetamine and methamphetamine that retain the CNS stimulatory effects, such as methcathinone ("cat") or mephedrone (methyl-methcathinone)
- Derivatives from amphetamine and methamphetamine that have prominent psychedelic effects in addition to their CNS stimulatory action, such as MDMA (Ecstasy)

Because the basic amphetamine molecule can be easily synthesized and readily modified, new amphetamine-like drugs frequently appear on the streets. Although these designer amphetamines are thought of as new drugs when they first appear, in fact most were originally synthesized from the 1940s to the 1960s by pharmaceutical companies trying to find new decongestant and anorexiant drugs to compete with the other amphetamines. Some of these compounds were found to be too toxic to be marketed but have been rediscovered by "street chemists" and are sold to unsuspecting victims trying to experience a new sensation. **Table 10.1** lists some of these designer amphetamines.

Some designer drugs of abuse that are chemically related to amphetamine include DOM (STP), methcathinone (called cat or bathtub speed), mephedrone (methylmethcathinone, called "Meow Meow" or drone and found in products such as ivory wave or bath salts), MDA, and MDMA (or methylenedioxymethamphetamine, called Ecstasy, X, E, XTC, or Adam). As of 2013 most of these drugs had been classified as Schedule I agents.

MDMA (ECSTASY)

Among the designer amphetamines, MDMA continues to be the most popular. It gained widespread popularity in the United States throughout the 1980s, and its use peaked in 1987 despite its classification as a Schedule I drug in 1985 by the DEA. At the height of its use, 39% of the undergraduates at Stanford University reported having used MDMA at least once (Randall 1992a). In the late 1980s and early 1990s, use of MDMA declined in this country, but about this time it was "reformulated." This reformulation was not in a pharmacological sense but in a cultural context.

The "rave" scene in England provided a new showcase for MDMA or Ecstasy (Randall 1992a). Partygoers attired in "Cat in the Hat" hats and psychedelic jumpsuits paid $20 to dance all night to heavy, electronically generated sound mixed with computer-generated video and laser light shows. An Ecstasy tablet could be purchased for the sensory enhancement caused by the drug (Randall 1992b). At one time, it was estimated that as many as 31% of English youth from 16 to 25 years old had used

TABLE 10.1 Designer Amphetamines

Amphetamine Derivative	Properties
Methcathinone ("cat")	Properties like those of methamphetamine and cocaine
Methylenedioxymethamphetamine (MDMA, "Ecstasy")	Stimulant and hallucinogen
Methylenedioxyamphetamine (MDA)	More powerful stimulant and less powerful hallucinogen than MDMA
4-methylaminorex	CNS stimulant like amphetamine
N,N-dimethylamphetamine	One-fifth the potency of amphetamine
4-thiomethyl-2, 5-dimethoxyamphetamine	Hallucinogen
Para-methoxymethamphetamine	Weak stimulant
Mephedrone	Potent stimulant and hallucinogen (found in products such as bath salts)

Ecstasy (Grob et al. 1996). The British rave counterculture and its generous use of Ecstasy were exported to the United States in the early 1990s. High-tech music and video trappings were encouraged by low-tech laboratories that illegally manufactured the drug and shipped it into this country. Because of these sensory-enriched environments, Ecstasy became the drug of choice for many young people in the United States (Cloud 2000) and globally (United Nations Office on Drugs and Crime 2009) looking for a novel "chemical" experience. To this day the rave phenomenon continues to be a major attraction to youthful participants and an excuse for heavy MDMA use (*Journal of the American Medical Association* [JAMA] 2010).

The international seizures of MDMA in 2007 almost doubled those reported for 1998, suggesting that the global abuse of Ecstasy continues to escalate (United Nations Office on Drugs and Crime 2009). Currently, more than 90% of these illegal drugs originate in European countries such as the Netherlands and Belgium, which are the principal source for Ecstasy smuggled into the United States (United Nations Office on Drugs and Crime 2009). However, recently there has been an increase in U.S. homegrown labs, which produce MDMA and methamphetamine despite the fact that the process of making MDMA is very hazardous and the chemicals used for synthesis are difficult to obtain (Friends of Narconon 2010). Besides sensory enhancement, the association of Ecstasy with raves—where there is intense dancing, crowded conditions, and plenty of drugs—all too often results in Ecstasy-related medical emergencies and on rare occasions even death (JAMA 2010).

Because of its frequent association with raves, clubs, and bars, MDMA is known as a club drug. At its peak in 2001, Ecstasy was used by 9.2% of all U.S. high school seniors; since this time its abuse has been reduced by more than half (Johnston 2013).

Some have compared the rave culture and its use of MDMA to the acid-test parties of the 1960s and the partygoers' use of LSD and amphetamines (JAMA 2010). Some say this drug is not likely to cause significant dependence for most casual users, but intense use appears to be able to lead to addiction. Part of the explanation for the dramatic reduction in MDMA use by young populations is likely a reaction to some highly publicized overdoses of Ecstasy and a perceived increase in the risk of this drug (Johnston 2013).

MDMA was first inadvertently discovered in 1912 by chemists at E. Merck in Darmstadt, Germany (Grob et al. 1996). No pharmaceutical company has ever manufactured MDMA for public marketing, and the FDA has never approved it for therapy. MDMA was first found by the DEA on the streets in 1972 in a drug sample bought in Chicago (Beck 1990). The DEA earnestly began gathering data on MDMA abuse a decade later, which led to its classification as a Schedule I substance in 1985, despite the very vocal opposition of a number of psychiatrists who had been giving MDMA to patients since the late 1970s to facilitate communication, acceptance, and fear reduction (Beck 1990). Some health professionals believe that MDMA should be made available to clinicians for the treatment of some psychiatric disorders such as fear and anxiety (Carey 2012). In fact, with FDA approval, small trial studies have been conducted to test the safety of this drug and its potential value in treating conditions such as posttraumatic stress disorder (Carey 2012), although the outcome of these clinical trials has yet to be determined.

MDMA and related designer amphetamines are somewhat unique from other amphetamines in that, besides causing excitation, they have prominent psychedelic effects (Tancer and Johanson 2007). These drugs have been characterized as combining the properties of amphetamine and LSD (Schifano et al. 1998). The psychedelic effects of MDMA are likely caused by release of the neurotransmitter serotonin (Tancer and Johanson 2007). After using hallucinogenic amphetamines, the mind is often flooded with irrelevant and incoherent thoughts and exaggerated sensory experiences and is more receptive to suggestion.

MDMA often is viewed as a "smooth amphetamine" and does not appear to cause the severe depression, "crash," or violent behavior (U.S. Department of Justice 2003b) often associated with frequent high doses of the more traditional amphetamines. As mentioned earlier, MDMA was originally

Because of its frequent association with raves, clubs, and bars, MDMA is known as a club drug.

© anthonymooney/Shutterstock, Inc.

Dancers at a "rave" often consume Ecstacy for sensory enhancement.

thought to be nonaddictive; however, some reports suggest that addiction does occur when high doses of this drug are used (Everything Addiction 2010; Jansen 1999). Many users tend to be predominantly positive when describing their initial MDMA experiences (Cloud 2000). They claim the drug causes them to dramatically drop their defense mechanisms or fear responses while they feel an increased empathy for others (Benedetti 2002). Combined with its stimulant effects, this action often increases intimate communication and association with others (Cloud 2000; Science Daily 2010a). However, heavy users often experience adverse effects, such as loss of appetite, grinding of teeth, muscle aches and stiffness, sweating, rapid heartbeat, hostility, anxiety, and altered sleep patterns (NIDA 2013a). In addition, fatigue can be experienced for hours or even days after use. In high doses, MDMA can cause panic attacks and severe anxiety (NIDA 2010b, 2013a). There is evidence that these high doses can significantly damage serotonin neurons or other systems in the brain and cause long-term memory deficits and psychological disturbances in some people (Lyles and Cadet 2003; Montgomery et al. 2010; Turillazzi et al. 2010). The duration of these high-dose CNS effects has not been determined and may vary based on the intensity of the bingeing (Kish et al. 2010).

Recreational use of Ecstasy has been linked to physical emergencies and even occasional fatalities that are similar to those caused by amphetamines and cocaine (King and Corkery 2010; Schifano et al. 2010). The leading causes of deaths associated with MDMA use appear to be complications from hyperthermia (related to heatstroke), metabolic problems, or underlying heart problems (DEA 2003; Kaye, Darke, and Duflou 2009; King and Corkery 2010).

Because of its popularity, occasional "spinoff" Ecstasy drugs show up in dance clubs frequented by young people. For example, a substance called "Frenzy" or "Nemesis" has been used in the Detroit area and is thought to be smuggled across the Canadian border. The official name of the drug is n-benzylpiperazine or BZP. It is sold in the shape of cartoon characters and has a chemistry that resembles MDMA. BZP is not available in pharmacies, but can be purchased over the Internet and has been used in the club scene since the 1990s. However, the pharmacology of this drug looks more like that of the amphetamines than MDMA in that it has stimulant effects that cause feelings of euphoria, alertness, and increased energy. With high doses, BZP induces a state of paranoia and anxiety accompanied by increased heart rate, blood pressure, and body temperature.

METHYLPHENIDATE: A SPECIAL AMPHETAMINE

Methylphenidate (Ritalin) is related to the amphetamines but is a relatively mild CNS stimulant, especially when used orally, that has been used to alleviate depression. Research now casts doubt on its effectiveness for treating depression, but it is effective in treating narcolepsy (a sleep disorder). As explained previously, Ritalin has also been found to help calm children and adults suffering from attention deficit hyperactivity disorder (ADHD). ADHD is characterized by an inability to focus attention and increased impulsivity. These features make it difficult to stay on-task, impair learning abilities, and can lead to social and personal frustrations (Tye et al. 2009). Like Adderall (amphetamine) and Provigil (modafinil), Ritalin is routinely used to treat this condition in both children and adults. Use of these drugs can improve scholastic performance in 70% of those with ADHD. Ritalin is frequently the drug of choice for this indication (NIDA 2009). The stimulant potency of Ritalin lies between that of caffeine and amphetamine. Although it is not used much on the street by hardcore drug addicts, there are increasingly more frequent reports of use by high school and college students because of claims that it helps them to "study better," "party harder," and enhance their "performance" in general (Oremus 2013). However, there is no evidence that when used properly and taken orally this drug will cause serious dependence or addiction (Volkow and Swanson 2008). Recent statistics from the Monitoring the Future Survey suggest that 2.6% of high school seniors used this drug for nonmedical purposes in 2012 (Johnston 2013). Because of its potential for abuse, some critics claim its medical use in the treatment of childhood ADHD may increase the likelihood that patients will later abuse drugs; however, this has not been found to be the case (Volkow and Swanson 2008). High doses of Ritalin can cause tremors, seizures, and strokes. Ritalin has been classified as a Schedule II drug, like the other prescribed amphetamines. Its principal mechanism of action is to block the reuptake of dopamine and noradrenaline into their respective neurons; thus, its pharmacological action is more like cocaine than methamphetamine.

PERFORMANCE ENHANCERS

Performance enhancers is a term frequently used to describe stimulants, or other drugs, taken to increase physical or mental endurance to embellish one's performance and achieve a more positive outcome. As illustrated in the following real-life example, some college students have come to rely on these drugs to get through the stressful challenges of school.

> Janell (real name withheld), a college sophomore, is only one of all too many students who pray for a miracle every finals week to help them cram in the studying time to survive this very demanding ritual. The miracle that Janell, and others like her, are hoping for comes from the stimulant effects of drugs such as Ritalin and Adderall. Recognizing the use of these substances comes with significant risk, Janell says, "I am afraid that if I keep taking Adderall during stressful times, I will become addicted." Although these "performance enhancing" drugs can be legally prescribed, the way Janell is using them is not medically sanctioned and can do her great harm. But, despite the potential for very serious consequences for this form of drug abuse, Janell responds, "If you expect me to pass five major tests in one week, you better believe that I am going to take Adderall. I need to get in the zone. Nothing else seems to work for me." (Keenan 2010)

KEY TERM

performance enhancers
drugs taken to increase physical or mental endurance to embellish one's performance

Unfortunately, many students and adults do not appreciate the full adverse potential of this practice, or they choose to ignore the possibility that they might become addicted, experience psychosis, or have a severe cardiovascular reaction if they routinely use the prescription stimulants for illegal nonmedical purposes (Oremus 2013). If these drugs are not being obtained legally by prescription, how do those who use them as performance enhancers obtain them? Often the supply comes from other students who have ADHD and a legitimate prescription, and are willing to sell, or sometimes give away, their extra pills.

There is no argument that the popularity of these "performance-enhancing" substances has been increasing with many college, and even high school students (Ricker and Nicolino 2010); however, the value and safety of this practice are being debated (see "Prescription for Abuse: Colleges Are Laboratories for Drug Neuroenhancing").

BATH SALTS: A POTPOURRI OF POTENT STIMULANTS

Bath salts is a term often used to describe a group of stimulant-containing products that frequently include drugs related to synthetic cathinones (e.g., khat), such as mephedrone, MDPV (methylenedioxypyrovalerone), and other not-yet-identified analogs (NIDA 2013b). Because these designer drugs of the amphetamine class typically have not been well studied in either humans or laboratory animals, their pharmacological effects are not precisely known. However, recent reports suggest that abuse of bath salts–related products can have both the stimulant and addicting properties of methamphetamine, with the hallucinogenic actions of MDMA or LSD (Hadlock et al. 2011). The following account in the general press illustrates this point. In 2012 a naked, "zombie-like" man in Miami, Florida, attacked another man by biting off portions of his face. The attacker ignored commands from police officers to stop the violence and was stopped only when shot dead by the officers. The police reported that the attacker was likely under the influence of bath salts that he had in his possession (Curley 2012).

The bath salts products are packaged in colorful small plastic or foil containers, frequently marketed as "not for human consumption" and labeled as "plant food" or "jewelry cleaner," but in reality, buyers typically self-administer the contents of these products by oral, inhalation, or

PRESCRIPTION FOR ABUSE

Colleges Are Laboratories for Drug Neuroenhancing

Although everyone agrees that unsupervised use of stimulants to help with studying or to improve one's performance in other intellectual or physical ways is potentially dangerous, does it actually help improve the likelihood of success in the classroom, on the playing field, or in the workplace? The answer to this question is being debated, but there is good evidence that those who have some degree of ADHD do benefit from stimulant medications like Adderall or Ritalin and will perform better in academic endeavors (Oremus 2013). What about everyone else? It is said that college campuses have become laboratories for researching pharmacological neuroenhancement. Although evidence is equivocal, a commentary in 2008 in a prestigious journal called the use of cognitive enhancement drugs inevitable and stated that ". . . Society must respond to the growing demand . . . by rejecting the idea that 'enhancement' is a dirty word." The authors of this article went on to clarify that their statement was intended to encourage a rational and realistic approach to what they perceived as an inevitability, that is, that in the future our society will realize that these cognitive enhancing drugs are ". . . increasingly useful for improved quality of life and extended work productivity" (Sederer 2009). Others counter with the argument that "advocates fail to recognize the severe personal and societal consequences that such availability would generate, looking instead to a pharmaceutical solution that would, in the end, cause more problems than it would solve" (Hessert 2009).

© Photos.com

even injection means, even though some of the stimulant ingredients in these products have been classified as Schedule I substances by the federal government; other ingredients have not even been identified yet. Some of the common product names are Ivory Wave, Bloom, Cloud, Cloud Nine, Lunar Wave, and White Lightning, just to mention a few. The use of these bath salts products has resulted in thousands of alarming visits to emergency rooms across the United States by persons with a syndrome known as excited delirium and symptoms including paranoia, hallucinations, psychotic behavior, dehydration, muscle damage, kidney failure, and even death (NIDA 2013b). Government and law enforcement agencies are scrambling to develop strategies to address what appears to be a growing and rapidly changing emergency.

■ Cocaine

In the past, cocaine eradication has been considered to be a top priority. This cocaine policy reflected the fact that from 1978 to 1987 the United States experienced the largest cocaine epidemic in history. Antisocial and criminal activities related to the effects of this potent stimulant were highly visible and widely publicized.

As recently as the early 1980s, cocaine use was not believed to cause dependency because it does not cause gross withdrawal effects, as do alcohol and narcotics (Goldstein 1994). In fact, a 1982 article in *Scientific American* stated that cocaine was "no more habit forming than potato chips" (Van Dyck and Byck 1982). This perception has clearly been proven false; cocaine is so highly addictive that it is readily self-administered not only by human beings, but also by laboratory animals (Cumming, Caprioli, and Dalley 2010). Surveys suggested that during 2000, 2.7 million chronic and 3.0 million casual cocaine users lived in the United States (ONDCP 2003). There is no better substance than cocaine to illustrate the "love–hate" relationship that people can have with drugs. Many lessons can be learned by understanding the impact of cocaine and the social struggles that have ensued as people and societies have tried to determine their proper relationship with this substance.

THE HISTORY OF COCAINE USE

Cocaine has been used as a stimulant for thousands of years. Its history can be classified into three eras, based on geographic, social, and therapeutic considerations. Learning about these eras can help us understand current attitudes about cocaine (Emedicinehealth 2010; Gilbert 2011).

THE FIRST COCAINE ERA

The first cocaine era was characterized by an almost harmonious use of this stimulant by South American Indians living in the regions of the Andean Mountains, and dates back to about 2500 BC in Peru. It is believed that the stimulant properties of cocaine played a major role in the advancement of this isolated civilization, providing its people with the energy and motivation to realize dramatic social and architectural achievements while being able to endure tremendous hardships in barren, inhospitable environments. The *Erythroxylum coca* shrub (cocaine is found in its leaves) was held in religious reverence by these people until the time of the Spanish conquistadors (Golding 1993).

The first written description of coca chewing in the New World was by the explorer Amerigo Vespucci in 1499:

> They were very brutish in appearance and behavior, and their cheeks bulged with the leaves of a certain green herb, which they chewed like cattle, so that they could hardly speak. Each had around his neck two dried gourds, one full of that herb in their mouth, the other filled with a white flour-like powdered chalk. . . . [This was lime, which was mixed with the coca to enhance its effects.] When I asked . . . why they carried these leaves in their mouth, which they did not eat, . . . they replied it prevents them from feeling hungry, and gives them great vigor and strength. (Aldrich and Barker 1976, p. 3)

It is ironic that there are no indications that these early South American civilizations had significant social problems with cocaine, considering the difficulty it has caused contemporary civilizations. There are three possible explanations for their lack of significant negative experiences with coca:

1. The Andean Indians maintained control of the use of cocaine. For the Incas, coca could only be used by the conquering aristocracy, chiefs, royalty, and other designated honorables (Aldrich and Barker 1976).

An Andean chews coca leaves.

2. These Indians used the unpurified, and less potent, form of cocaine in the coca plant.
3. Chewing the coca leaf was a slow, sustained form of oral drug administration; therefore, the effect was much less potent, and less likely to cause serious dependence, than the snorting, intravenous injection, or smoking techniques most often used today.

THE SECOND COCAINE ERA

A second major cocaine era began in the 19th century. During this period, scientific techniques were used to determine the pharmacology of cocaine and identify its dangerous effects. It was also during this era that the threat of cocaine to society—both its members and institutions—was first recognized (DiChiara 1993; Musto 1998). At about this time, scientists in North America and Europe began experimenting with a purified, white, powdered extract made from the coca plant.

In the last half of the 19th century, Corsican chemist Angelo Mariani removed the active ingredients from the coca leaf and identified cocaine. This purified cocaine was added into cough drops and into a special Bordeaux wine called Vin Mariani (Musto 1998). The Pope gave Mariani a medal in appreciation for the fine work he had done developing this concoction. The cocaine extract was publicized as a magical drug that would free the body from fatigue, lift the spirits, and cause a sense of well-being, and the cocaine-laced wine became widely endorsed throughout the civilized world (Fischman and Johanson 1996). Included in a long list of luminaries who advocated this product for an array of ailments were the Czar and Czarina of Russia; the Prince and Princess of Wales; the Kings of Sweden, Norway, and Cambodia; commanders of the French and English armies;

The "refreshing" element in Vin Mariani was coca extract.

Sigmund Freud was an early advocate of cocaine, which he referred to as "cure-all."

President McKinley of the United States; H. G. Wells; August Bartholdi (sculptor of the Statue of Liberty); and some 8000 physicians.

The astounding success of this wine attracted imitators, all making outlandish claims. One of these cocaine tonics was a nonalcoholic beverage named Coca-Cola, which was made from African kola nuts and advertised as the "intellectual beverage and temperance drink"; it contained 4 to 12 milligrams per bottle of the stimulant (DiChiara 1993). By 1906, Coca-Cola no longer contained detectable amounts of cocaine, but caffeine had been substituted in its place. In 1884, the esteemed Sigmund Freud published his findings on cocaine in a report called "Uber Coca." Freud enjoyed the way cocaine made him feel and recommended this "magical drug" for an assortment of medical problems, including depression, hysteria, nervous exhaustion, digestive disorders, hypochondria, "all diseases which involve degeneration of tissue," and drug addiction (PBS Newshour 2011).

In response to a request by Freud, a young Viennese physician, Karl Köller, studied the ability of cocaine to cause numbing effects. He discovered that it was an effective local anesthetic that could be applied to the surface of the eye and permitted painless minor surgery to be conducted. This discovery of the first local anesthetic had tremendous worldwide impact. Orders for the new local anesthetic, cocaine, overwhelmed pharmaceutical companies.

Soon after the initial jubilation over the virtues of cocaine came the sober realization that with its benefits came severe disadvantages. As more people used cocaine, particularly in tonics and patent medicines, the CNS side effects and abuse liability became painfully evident. By the turn of the 20th century, cocaine was being processed from the coca plant and purified routinely by drug companies. People began to snort or inject the purified form of this popular powder, which increased both its effects and its dangers. The controversy over cocaine exploded before the American public in newspapers and magazines.

As medical and police reports of cocaine abuse and toxicities escalated, public opinion demanded that cocaine be banned. In 1914, the Harrison Act misleadingly classified both cocaine and coca as narcotic substances (cocaine is a stimulant) and outlawed their uncontrolled use.

Although prohibited in patent and nonprescription medicines, prescribed medicinal use of cocaine continued into the 1920s. Medicinal texts included descriptions of therapeutic uses for cocaine to treat fatigue, vomiting, seasickness, melancholia, and gastritis. However, they also included lengthy warnings about excessive cocaine use, "the most insidious of all drug habits" (Aldrich and Barker 1976).

Little of medical or social significance occurred for the next few decades (Fischman and Johanson 1996). The medicinal use of cocaine was replaced mostly by the amphetamines during World War II because cocaine could not be supplied from South America. (Cocaine is not easily synthesized, so even today the supply of cocaine, both legal and illegal, continues to come from the Andean countries of South America.) During this period, cocaine continued to be employed for its local anesthetic action, was available on the "black market," and was used recreationally by musicians, entertainers, and the wealthy. Because of the limited supply, the cost of cocaine was prohibitive for most would-be consumers. Cocaine abuse problems continued as a minor concern until the 1980s.

THE THIRD COCAINE ERA

With the 1980s, came the third major era of cocaine use. This era started much like the second in that the public and even the medical community were naive and misinformed about the drug. Cocaine was viewed as a glamorous substance and portrayed by the media as the drug of celebrities. Its use by prominent actors, athletes, musicians, and other members of a fast-paced, elite society was common knowledge. By 1982, more than 20 million Americans had tried cocaine in one form or another, compared with only 5 million in 1974 (Green 1985).

The following is an example of a report from a Los Angeles television station in the early 1980s, which was typical of the misleading information being released to the public:

> Cocaine may actually be no more harmful to your health than smoking cigarettes or drinking alcohol; at least that's according to a 6-year study of cocaine use [described in *Scientific American*]. It concludes that the drug is relatively safe and, if not taken in large amounts, it is not addictive. (Byck 1987)

With such visibility, an association with prestige and glamour, and what amounted to an indirect endorsement by medical experts, the stage was set for another epidemic of cocaine use. Initially, the high cost of this imported substance limited its use. With increased demand, however, came increased supply, and prices tumbled from an unaffordable $100 per "fix" to an affordable $10. The epidemic began.

By the mid-1980s, cocaine permeated all elements of society. No group of people or part of the country was immune from its effects. Many tragic stories were told of athletes, entertainers, corporate executives, politicians, fathers and mothers, high school students, and even children using and abusing cocaine. It was no longer the drug of the laborer or even the rich and famous. It was everybody's drug and everybody's problem (Golding 1993). As one user recounted:

> I think I was an addict. I immediately fell in love with cocaine. I noticed right away it was a drug that you had power with, and I wanted more and more. (*From Venturelli's research files, male, age 22*)

Cocaine availability decreased sharply in the United States in 2009, resulting in an increase in price for a pure gram of cocaine from about $95 in 2006 to $175 toward the end of 2009. The purity of cocaine also diminished during this time, from 68% to 46%. The reasons for the shortages of cocaine at this time were thought to relate to several factors including decreased production in Colombia and increased seizures of cocaine destined for Mexico and trafficking into the United States (Beckusen 2013). However, it is important to appreciate that these trends can reverse very quickly and that the United States by far is the largest consumer of cocaine in the world (see **Table 10.2**; Bradley 2012).

COCAINE PRODUCTION

Because cocaine is derived from the coca plant, which is imported from the Andean countries, the United States' problems with this drug have had a profound effect on several South American countries. With the dramatic rise in U.S. cocaine demand in the early 1980s, coca production in South America increased in tandem. The coca crop is by far the most profitable agricultural venture in some of these countries. In addition, it is easily cultivated and maintained (the coca plant is a perennial and remains productive for decades) and can be harvested several times a year (on average, two to four). The coca harvest has brought many jobs and some prosperity to these struggling economies.

It has been claimed that the U.S. coca eradication program has seriously influenced the fragile economies of poor Latin American countries, such as Bolivia and Peru, causing anti-American sentiment, especially in poor rural communities that depend on money from their coca crops (Ceasar 2002). In addition, the spraying of herbicides from U.S.-piloted aircraft to destroy coca harvests is suspected of posing health hazards to the native populations (DeYoung 2003). Because of these problems, there is evidence that the attempts by the U.S. government to control cocaine abuse by eliminating coca crops have not been as successful

TABLE 10.2 National Rankings of Cocaine Consumption: 2012

Country	Share of World's Cocaine Demand (%)	Percentage of Population That Uses	Average Annual Consumption (in grams)
United States	36.8	1.5	42
Brazil	17.7	1.4	35
United Kingdom	5.3	1.5	30
Italy	5.1	1.4	30
Spain	4.9	1.8	30
Mexico	3.1	0.4	39
Germany	2.5	0.5	30
France	2.1	0.6	30
Colombia	1.6	0.5	35
Argentina	1.6	0.6	35
Algeria	1.4		
Canada	1.2		
Rest of the world	16.6		

Reproduced from Bradley, T. "Brazil Now Consumes 18% of the World's Cocaine." Quartz. (Sept. 23, 2012). Available http://qz.com/5058/brazil-now-consumes-18-of-worlds-cocaine/

as hoped and have been extremely costly (Smith 2010). Thus, although there are claims that after 10 years of effort, by 2008 cocaine cultivation in Colombia had decreased by about 30%, there were corresponding increases in cocaine production in the neighboring countries of Bolivia and Peru (Just the Facts 2010). In addition, in this region a literal war has been ongoing between government military and law enforcement groups and drug traffickers as well as illegal paramilitary groups. Thousands of people on both sides have been killed during fighting, as have almost 20,000 innocent civilians (Smith 2010). Although there has been some progress, government officials are clearly frustrated, as is apparent in the following quote from a highly regarded Latin American analyst:

We've tried everything. Aggressive aerial spraying of fields, manual eradication, as well as softer measures to entice producers to adopt other crops, and it's all failed. As long as the price of cocaine remains inflated by prohibition, there is big profit and big incentive for producers and traffickers to grow the plant and export the product to the US and elsewhere. . . . I don't see this is a battle that can be won. (Smith 2010)

Trafficking of illegal cocaine is very profitable and often very dangerous (see "Here and Now: Bloody 'Drug War' Fought in Streets of Mexico"). Because of the highly addictive nature of cocaine and the profits associated with the illegal purchasing and selling of this drug, criminal groups frequently engage in violent struggles for control of the cocaine market (Smith 2010; Weiner 2003). In some ways it is like "playing whack-a-mole." As efforts to shut down drug cartels in Mexico intensify, they tend to pop up elsewhere. For example, with increased cocaine seizures in Mexico, the Dominican Republic has developed into a main transit point for shipping this drug into both the United States and Europe. As a result, drug-related crime has been increasing in Caribbean countries. Of particular concern is the recent rapid rise of cocaine trafficking through the Dominican Republic (Voxxi 2013). From 2001 to 2009, the Dominican Republic's homicide rate nearly doubled and the country has become overwhelmed with an increase in drug-trafficking violence and organized crime, while the police are making the biggest

HERE AND NOW

Bloody "Drug War" Fought in Streets of Mexico

Drug cartels ship hundreds of tons of cocaine to the United States. Because of the billions of dollars that can be made from this illegal market, gangs fight each other for control of the production and merchandising of this substance. This competition frequently turns violent. In Mexico during a particularly bloody week in 2010, 15 people were killed in a car wash, 14 were massacred at a teenager's birthday party, 13 were shot dead at a drug rehabilitation center, 7 were mowed down in the street, 4 factory workers were slaughtered on a bus, and 9 police officers died in an ambush. Such blatant violence has become almost a way of life in some parts of Mexico, but perhaps the most shocking aspect of these acts of wanton homicide is that most of the victims had nothing whatsoever to do with the drug cartels or the government forces fighting each other over drug-related issues. These people just happened

to be in the wrong place at the wrong time and were innocently killed. Such violence has everyone wondering how this can be stopped. Is victory even possible in the war against the drug cartels?

Data from Tuckman, J. "Mexico's Drug Wars: The End of an Exceptionally Bloody Week." Guardian.co.uk. 29 October 2010. Available http://www.guardian.co.uk /world/2010/oct/29/mexico-drug-wars-bloody-week. Accessed March 16, 2011.

---

drug busts in the country's history. A similar increase in drug-related problems is also occurring in Puerto Rico, another affected Caribbean country (Fieser 2010). Solutions are elusive, and it is clear that without a significant reduction in demand the profit from producing, trafficking, and selling cocaine will remain high and attractive to illegal and dangerous groups (see Table 10.2).

COCAINE PROCESSING

Cocaine is one of several active ingredients from the leaves of *Erythroxylum coca* (its primary source). The leaves are harvested two or four times per year and used to produce coca paste, which contains as much as 80% cocaine. The paste is processed in clandestine laboratories to form a pure, white hydrochloride salt powder (Hatsukami and Fischman 1996). Often, purified cocaine is **adulterated** (or "cut") with substances such as powdered sugar, talc, arsenic, lidocaine, strychnine, and

methamphetamine before it is sold on the streets. Adverse responses to street cocaine are sometimes caused by the additives, not the cocaine itself. The resultant purity of the cut material ranges from 10% to 85%.

Cocaine is often sold in the form of little pellets, called *rocks*, or as flakes or powder. If it is in pellet form, it must be crushed before use. Street names used for these cocaine products have included *blow, snow, flake, C, coke, toot, white lady, nuggets, tornado, rock(s)*, and *fat bags*.

Cocaine is often sold in a form that appears like small rocks.

KEY TERM

adulterated
contaminating substances are mixed in to dilute the drugs

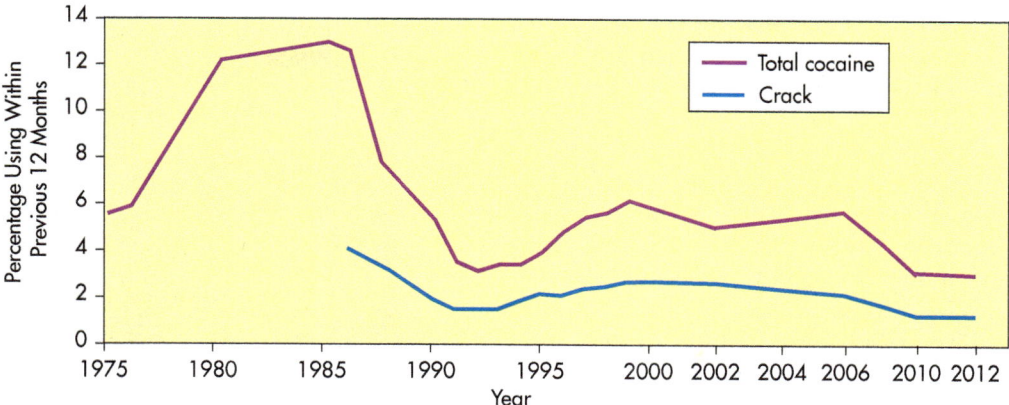

FIGURE 10.1 Trends in cocaine and crack use by high school seniors, 1975–2010. These data represent the percentages of high school seniors surveyed who reported using cocaine during the year.

Data from Johnston, L. D., P. M. O'Malley, J. G. Bachman, and J. E. Schulenberg. Monitoring the Future: National Survey Results on Drug Use, 1975–2012: Volume I: Secondary School Students. Ann Arbor, MI: Institute for Social Research, The University of Michigan, 2013.

CURRENT ATTITUDES AND PATTERNS OF ABUSE

Given contemporary medical advances, we now have a greater understanding of the effects of cocaine and its toxicities and the dependence it produces. The reasons for abusing cocaine are better understood as well. For example, it has been suggested that some chronic cocaine users are self-medicating their psychiatric disorders, such as depression, attention deficit disorders, or anxiety (AddictionInfo 2010). Such knowledge helps in identifying and administering effective treatment. The hope is that society will never again be fooled into thinking that cocaine abuse is glamorous or an acceptable form of entertainment. Attempts are being made to use this understanding (either recently acquired or merely relearned) to educate people about the true nature of cocaine. Such education was likely responsible for trends of declining cocaine use observed from 1987 to 1991 (see **Figure 10.1**). Decreases occurred in virtually every age group evaluated during this period. Surveys during this time revealed that, in general, cocaine use became less acceptable; these changes in attitude almost certainly contributed to the dramatic reduction in use. From 1992 to 1999 cocaine use rose, but leveled off during much of the first decade of the 2000s and had dropped again by 2012 to 2.4% in high school seniors (Johnston 2013). This was likely due to increased cocaine seizures, a reduction in availability, and an increase in cost (Just the Facts 2010). Despite decreased cocaine use, the United States still leads the world in cocaine consumption and spends $37 billion annually, although the European market of $34 billion is not too far behind (Fieser 2010).

COCAINE ADMINISTRATION

Cocaine can be administered orally, inhaled into the nasal passages, injected intravenously, or smoked. The form of administration is important in determining the intensity of cocaine's effects, its abuse liability, and the likelihood of toxicity (NIDA 2010c).

Oral administration of cocaine produces the least potent effects; most of the drug is destroyed in the gut or liver before it reaches the brain. The result is a slower onset of action with a milder, more sustained stimulation. This form is least likely to cause health problems and dependence. South American Indians still take cocaine orally to increase their strength and for relief from fatigue. Administration usually involves prolonged chewing of the coca leaf, resulting in the consumption of about 20 to 400 milligrams of the drug (Encyclopedia Britannica 2010). Oral use of cocaine is not common in the United States.

"Snorting" involves inhaling cocaine hydrochloride powder into the nostrils, where deposits form on the lining of the nasal chambers and approximately 100 milligrams of the drug passes through the mucosal tissues into the bloodstream (NIDA 2010c, 2013c). Substantial CNS stimulation occurs in several minutes, persists for 30 to 40 minutes, and then subsides. The effects occur more rapidly and are shorter-lasting and more intense than those achieved with oral administration because more of the drug enters the brain more quickly. Because concentrations of cocaine in the body are higher after snorting than after oral ingestion, the side effects are more severe.

One of the most common consequences of snorting cocaine is rebound depression, or "crash," which is of little consequence after oral consumption. As a general rule, the intensity of the depression correlates with the intensity of the euphoria (A.D.A.M. 2010).

According to studies performed by the National Institute on Drug Abuse, 10% to 15% of those who try intranasal (snorting) cocaine go on to heavier forms of dosing, such as intravenous administration. Intravenous administration of cocaine is a relatively recent phenomenon because the hypodermic needle was not widely available until the late 1800s. This form of administration contributed to many of the cocaine problems that appeared at the turn of the 20th century. Intravenous administration allows large amounts of cocaine to be introduced very rapidly into the body and causes severe side effects and dependence. Within seconds after injection, cocaine users experience an incredible state of euphoria. The "high" is intense but short-lived; within 15 to 20 minutes, the user experiences dysphoria and is heading for a "crash." To prevent these unpleasant rebound effects, cocaine is readministered every 10 to 30 minutes. Readministration continues as long as there is drug available (NIDA 2010c).

This binge activity resembles that seen in the methamphetamine "run," except it is usually shorter in duration. When the cocaine supply is exhausted, the binge is over (Zickler 2001). Several days of abstinence may separate these episodes; the average cocaine addict binges once to several times a week, with each binge lasting 4 to 24 hours. Cocaine addicts claim that all thoughts turn toward cocaine during binges; everything else loses significance. This pattern of intense use is how some people blow all of their money on cocaine. **Freebasing** is a method of reducing impurities in cocaine and preparing the drug for smoking. It produces a type of cocaine that is more powerful than normal cocaine hydrochloride. One way to "freebase" is to treat the cocaine hydrochloride with a liquid base such as sodium carbonate or ammonium hydroxide. The cocaine dissolves, along with many of the impurities commonly found in it (such as amphetamines, lidocaine, sugars, and others). A solvent,

Freebasing paraphernalia. A water pipe is often used to smoke freebased cocaine, or "crack." Cocaine administered by smoking is very potent and fast-acting; the effect lasts for 10 to 15 minutes, after which depression occurs. This is the most addicting form of cocaine.

such as petroleum or ethyl ether, is added to the liquid to extract the cocaine. The solvent containing the cocaine floats to the top and is drawn off with an eyedropper; it is placed in an evaporation dish to dry, and crystalized cocaine residue is then crushed into a fine powder, which can be smoked in a special glass pipe (Enotes 2010).

The effects of smoked cocaine are as intense or more intense than those achieved through intravenous administration (Fischman and Johanson 1996). The onset is very rapid, the euphoria is dramatic, the depression is severe, the side effects are dangerous, and the chances of dependence are high (NIDA 2007b). The reason for these intense reactions to inhaling cocaine into the lungs is that the drug passes rapidly through the lining of the lungs and into the many blood vessels present; it is then carried almost directly to the brain.

Freebasing became popular in the United States in the 1980s due to the fear of diseases such as AIDS and hepatitis, which are transmitted by sharing contaminated hypodermic needles. But freebasing involves other dangers. Because the volatile solvents required for freebasing are very explosive, careless people have been seriously burned or killed during processing. Street synonyms used for freebased cocaine include *coke, crystal, happy dust, snow, stuff, sugar, white horse,* and *wings* (Thesaurus.com 2010).

KEY TERM

freebasing
conversion of cocaine into its alkaline form for smoking

CRACK COCAINE

Between 1985 and 1986, a special type of free-based cocaine known as crack appeared on the streets (Hatsukami and Fischman 1996). By 1999, approximately 2.7% of high school seniors had tried crack. As of 2012 this number was down to 1.2% (Johnston 2013). Crack can be smoked without the dangerous explosive solvents mentioned earlier in the discussion of freebasing. It is made by taking powdered cocaine hydrochloride and adding sodium bicarbonate (baking soda) and water. The paste that forms removes impurities as well as the hydrochloride from the cocaine. The substance is then dried into hard pieces called rocks, which may contain as much as 90% pure cocaine. Other slang terms for crack include *big C, blow, nose candy, snow, Lady,* and *rock.* Like freebased cocaine, crack is usually smoked in a glass water pipe. When the fumes are absorbed into the lungs, they act rapidly, reaching the brain within 8 to 10 seconds. An intense "rush" or "high" results, and later a powerful state of depression, or "crash," occurs. The high may last only 3 to 5 minutes, and the depression may persist from 10 to 40 minutes or longer in some cases. As soon as crack is smoked, the nervous system is greatly stimulated by the release of dopamine, which seems to be involved in the rush. Cocaine prevents resupply of this neurotransmitter, which may trigger the crash.

Because of the abrupt and intense release of dopamine, smoked crack is viewed as a drug with tremendous potential for addiction and antisocial behavior (NIDA 2010c); some users consider it to be more enjoyable than cocaine administered intravenously. Crack and cocaine marketing and use are often associated with criminal activity (APA 2013) such as robberies and homicides (Swan 1995).

In general, crack use has been more common among African American and Hispanic populations than among white Americans. Of special concern is the use of crack among women during pregnancy. Children born under these circumstances have been referred to as crack babies. Even though the effects of crack on fetal development are not fully understood, many clinicians and researchers have predicted that these crack babies will impose an enormous social burden as they grow up. However, other experts have expressed concern that the impact of cocaine on the fetus is grossly overstated and have suggested that behavioral problems seen in these children are more a consequence of social environment than direct pharmacological effects (Vidaeff and Mastrobattista 2003). This issue is discussed in greater detail later in this section.

It is not coincidental that the popularity of crack use paralleled the AIDS epidemic in the mid-1980s. Because crack administration does not require injection, theoretically the risk of contracting HIV from contaminated needles is avoided. Even so, HIV infection still occurs in crack users because many crack smokers also use cocaine intravenously, thereby increasing their chances of becoming infected with HIV. Another reason for HIV infection (as well as other sexually transmitted diseases, such as syphilis and gonorrhea) among crack users is the dangerous sexual behavior in which these people engage (Science Daily 2010b). Not only is crack commonly used as payment for sex, but its users are also much less inclined to be cautious about their sexual activities while under the influence of this drug (Ladd and Petry 2003).

MAJOR PHARMACOLOGICAL EFFECTS OF COCAINE

Cocaine can have profound effects on several vital systems in the body (Emedicinehealth 2010). With the assistance of modern technology, the mechanisms whereby cocaine alters body functions have become better understood. Such knowledge may eventually lead to better treatment of cocaine dependence.

Most of the pharmacological effects of cocaine use stem from enhanced activity of catecholamine (dopamine, noradrenaline, adrenaline) and serotonin transmitters. It is believed that the principal action of the drug is to block the reuptake and inactivation of these substances following their release from neurons. Such action prolongs the activity of these transmitter substances at their receptors and substantially increases their effects. The summation of cocaine's effects on these four transmitters causes CNS stimulation (Woolverton and Johnston 1992). The increase of noradrenaline activity following cocaine administration increases the effects of the sympathetic nervous system and alters cardiovascular activity.

KEY TERMS

crack
already processed and inexpensive "freebased" cocaine, ready for smoking

crack babies
infants born to women who used crack cocaine during pregnancy

CNS EFFECTS

Because cocaine has stimulant properties, it has antidepressant effects as well. Some users self-administer cocaine to relieve severe depression or the negative symptoms of schizophrenia (Markou and Kenny 2002), but in general its short-term action and abuse liability make cocaine unsatisfactory for the treatment of depression disorders. The effects of stimulation appear to increase both physical and mental performance while masking fatigue. High doses of cocaine cause euphoria (based on the form of administration) and enhance the sense of strength, energy, and performance. Because of these positive effects, cocaine has intense reinforcing properties, which encourage continual use and dependence (Nathan, Bresnick, and Battei 1998).

Cocaine addicts can often distinguish between the two phenomena of the rush and the high associated with cocaine administration. Both the rush and the high peak about 3 minutes after use. The rush seems to be associated with elevated heart rate, sweating, and feelings of "speeding" or "being out of control"; the high includes feelings of euphoria, self-confidence, well-being, and sociability. Drug craving also occurs rapidly and is evident as soon as 12 minutes after administration. Interestingly, brain scans of cocaine users have demonstrated that specific brain regions are associated with these drug effects; thus, the rush and craving are linked with different regions of the limbic system in the brain (Stocker 1999).

The feeling of exhilaration and confidence caused by cocaine can easily become transformed into irritable restlessness and confused hyperactivity (APA 2013). In addition, high chronic doses alter personality, frequently causing psychotic behavior that resembles paranoid schizophrenia (Leard-Hansson 2006). For example, in an interview with Peter Venturelli, a 17-year-old female explained that a cocaine-abusing friend ". . . was so coked up that he carved the word 'pain' in his arm and poured coke on it. He thought it symbolized something." In addition, cocaine use heightens the risk of suicide, major trauma, and violent crimes (APA 2013; MedlinePlus 2010). In many ways, the CNS effects of cocaine resemble those of amphetamines, although perhaps with a more rapid onset, a more intense high (due partially to the manner in which the drugs are administered), and a shorter duration of action (APA 2013). Besides dependence, other notable CNS toxicities that can be caused by cocaine use include headaches, temporary loss of consciousness, seizures, and death.

CARDIOVASCULAR SYSTEM EFFECTS

Cocaine can initiate pronounced changes in the cardiovascular system by enhancing the sympathetic nervous system, increasing the levels of adrenaline, and causing vasoconstriction (Luscher 2012). The initial effects of cocaine are to increase heart rate and elevate blood pressure. While the heart is being stimulated and working harder, the vasoconstriction effects deprive the cardiac muscle of needed blood (Fischman and Johanson 1996). Such a combination can cause severe heart arrhythmia (an irregular contraction pattern) or heart attack. Other degenerative processes have also been described in the hearts and blood vessels of chronic cocaine users (Kloner and Rezkalla 2003). In addition, the vasoconstrictive action of this sympathomimetic can damage other tissues, leading to stroke, lung damage in those who smoke cocaine, destruction of nasal cartilage in those who snort the drug, and injury to the gastrointestinal tract (Goodger, Wang, and Pogrel 2005).

LOCAL ANESTHETIC EFFECTS

Cocaine was the first local anesthetic used routinely in modern-day medicine (Drasner 2012). There is speculation that in ancient times, Andes Indians of South America used cocaine-filled saliva from chewing coca leaves as a local anesthetic for surgical procedures (Aldrich and Barker 1976); however, this assumption is contested by others (Byck 1987). Even so, cocaine is still used as a local anesthetic for minor pharyngeal (back part of the mouth and upper throat area) surgery due to its good vasoconstriction (reduces bleeding) and topical, local numbing effects. Although relatively safe when applied topically, significant amounts of cocaine can enter the bloodstream and, in sensitive people, cause CNS stimulation, toxic psychosis, or, on rare occasions, death (Mayo Clinic 2010a).

COCAINE WITHDRAWAL

Considerable debate has arisen as to whether cocaine withdrawal actually happens and, if so, what it involves. With the most recent cocaine epidemic and the high incidence of intense, chronic use, it has become apparent that nervous systems do become tolerant to cocaine and that, during abstinence, withdrawal symptoms occur (Narconon 2013a). In fact, because of CNS dependence, the use of cocaine is less likely to be stopped voluntarily than is the use of many other

TABLE 10.3 Cocaine Abstinence Phases

Phase 1: "Crash"	Phase 2: Withdrawal	Phase 3: Extinction
24–48 hours since last binge	1–10 weeks since last binge	Indefinite since last binge
Initial	*Initial*	Normal pleasure, mood swings, occasional craving, cues trigger craving
Agitation, depression, anorexia, suicidal thoughts	Mood swings, sleep returns, some craving, little anxiety	
Middle	*Middle and late*	
Fatigue, no craving, insomnia	Anhedonia, anxiety, intense craving, obsessed with drug seeking	
Late		
Extreme fatigue, no craving, exhaustion		

Data from Garwin, F. "Cocaine addiction: Psychology and Neurophysiology." *Science* 251 (1991): 1580–1586.

illicit drugs (Sofuoglu et al. 2003). Certainly, if the withdrawal experience is adverse enough, a user will be encouraged to resume the cocaine habit.

The extent of cocaine withdrawal is proportional to the duration and intensity of use. The physical withdrawal symptoms are relatively minor compared with those caused by long-term use of CNS depressants and by themselves are not considered to be life-threatening (MedlinePlus 2007). Short-term withdrawal symptoms include depression (chronic cocaine users are 60 times more likely to commit suicide than are nonusers), sleep abnormalities, craving for the drug, agitation, and anhedonia (inability to experience pleasure). Long-term withdrawal effects include a return to normal pleasures, accompanied by mood swings and occasional craving triggered by cues in the surroundings (APA 2013; Mendelson and Mello 1996; Narconon 2013a).

Of particular importance to the treatment of chronic cocaine users is that abstinence after bingeing appears to follow three unique stages, each of which must be dealt with in a different manner if relapse is to be prevented. These phases are classified as phase 1, or "crash" (occurs 24 hours to 2 days after drug use is stopped); phase 2, or withdrawal (1 to 10 weeks); and phase 3, or extinction (indefinite). The basic features of these phases are outlined in **Table 10.3** (APA 2013).

TREATMENT OF COCAINE DEPENDENCE

Cocaine dependence is classified as a psychiatric disorder by the American Psychiatric Association (APA 2013) and results in many persons seeking treatment for drug addiction (Platt, Rowlett,

and Spealman 2002). Treatment of this condition has improved as experience working with these patients has increased. Even so, success rates vary for different programs. The problem with program assessments is that they often do not take into account patients who drop out. Also, no clear-cut criteria for qualifying success have been established. For example, is success considered to be abstaining from cocaine for 1 year, 2 years, 5 years, or forever?

No one treatment technique has been found to be significantly superior to others or universally effective (MedlinePlus 2010; NIDA 2010a), nor is there a particularly effective medication to treat cocaine addiction (Platt et al. 2002). Consequently, substantial disagreement exists as to what is the best strategy for treating cocaine dependency. There is a major ongoing effort by federal agencies and scientists to find effective therapy for cocaine addiction. Most treatments are directed at relieving craving. Major differences in treatment approaches include (1) whether outpatient or inpatient status is deemed appropriate, (2) which drugs and what dosages are used to treat patients during the various stages of abstinence, and (3) what length of time the patient is isolated from cocaine-accessible environments.

It is important to treat each individual patient according to his or her unique needs. Some questions that need to be considered when formulating a therapeutic approach include the following:

- Why did the patient begin using cocaine, and why has dependency occurred?
- What is the severity of abuse?
- How has the cocaine been administered?

- What is the psychiatric status of the patient? Are there underlying or coexisting mental disorders, such as depression or attention deficit disorder?
- What other drugs are being abused along with the cocaine?
- What is the patient's motivation for eliminating cocaine dependence?
- What sort of support system (family, friends, coworkers, and so on) will sustain the patient in the abstinence effort?

OUTPATIENT VERSUS INPATIENT APPROACHES

The decision as to whether to treat a patient who is dependent on cocaine as an outpatient or an inpatient is based on a number of factors. For example, inpatient techniques allow greater control than outpatient treatment; thus, the environment can be better regulated, the training of the patient can be more closely supervised, and the patient's responses to treatment can be more closely monitored. In contrast, the advantages of the outpatient approach are that supportive family and friends are better able to encourage the patient, the surroundings are more comfortable and natural, and potential problems that might occur when the patient returns to a normal lifestyle are more likely to be identified. In addition, outpatient treatment is less expensive.

Cocaine-dependent patients should be matched to the most appropriate strategy based on their personalities, psychiatric status, and the conditions of their addiction. For instance, a cocaine addict who lives in the inner city, comes from a home with other drug-dependent family members, and has little support probably would do better in the tightly controlled inpatient environment. However, a highly motivated cocaine addict who comes from a supportive home and a neighborhood that is relatively free of drug problems would probably do better on an outpatient basis.

■ Therapeutic Drug Treatment

Several drugs have been used to treat cocaine abstinence, some of which are themselves active on dopamine systems, but none has been found to be universally effective (NIDA 2013c). Besides relieving acute problems of anxiety, agitation, and psychosis, drugs can diminish cocaine craving; this effect is achieved by giving drugs such as bromocriptine or levodopa, which stimulate the dopamine transmitter system, or the narcotic buprenorphine. As mentioned, the pleasant aspects of cocaine likely relate to its ability to increase the activity of dopamine in the limbic system. When cocaine is no longer available, the dopamine system becomes less active, causing depression and anhedonia, which result in a tremendous craving for cocaine. The intent of these cocaine substitutes is to stimulate dopamine activity and relieve the cravings. Although this approach sometimes works initially, it is temporary. In the third phase of cocaine abstinence, antidepressants such as desipramine are effective for many cocaine-dependent patients in relieving underlying mood problems and occasional cravings.

The beneficial effects of these drugs are variable and not well studied (NIDA 2013c). There is some debate over their use. Drugs are, at best, only adjuncts in the treatment of cocaine dependence. Successful treatment of cocaine abuse requires intensive counseling; strong support from family, friends, and coworkers; and a highly motivated patient (NIDA 2013c). It is important to realize that a complete "cure" from cocaine dependence is not likely; ex-addicts cannot return to cocaine and control its use.

RECOVERY FROM COCAINE DEPENDENCE

Although numerous therapeutic approaches exist for treating cocaine addiction, successful recovery is not likely unless the individual will substantially benefit by giving up the drug. Research has shown that treatment is most likely to succeed in patients who are middle-class, employed, and married; for example, 85% of addicted medical professionals recover from cocaine addiction. These people can usually be convinced that they have too much to lose in their personal and professional lives by continuing their cocaine habit. In contrast, a severely dependent crack addict who has no job, family, home, or hope for the future is not likely to be persuaded that abstinence from cocaine would be advantageous, so therapy is rarely successful. As mentioned earlier, there currently is no uniformly effective pharmacological treatment available to deal with long-term cocaine addiction, although intensive research to identify such therapeutic agents is under way (NIDA 2013c).

POLYDRUG USE BY COCAINE ABUSERS

Treatment of most cocaine abusers is complicated by the fact that they are *polydrug* (multiple drug) users. It is unusual to find a person who abuses only cocaine. For example, many cocaine abusers also use alcohol (Pennings, Leccese, and Wolff 2002). In general, the more severe the alcoholism, the greater the severity of the cocaine dependence. Alcohol is used to relieve some of the unpleasant cocaine effects, such as anxiety, insomnia, and mood disturbances (Pennings et al. 2002). This drug combination can be dangerous for several reasons (Pennings et al. 2002):

- The presence of both cocaine and alcohol (ethanol) in the liver results in the formation of a unique chemical product called cocaethylene, which is created in the reaction of ethanol with a cocaine metabolite. Cocaethylene often is found in high levels in the blood of victims of fatal drug overdoses and appears to enhance the euphoria as well as the cardiovascular toxicity of cocaine.
- Both cocaine and alcohol can damage the liver; thus, their toxic effects on the liver are likely to add together when the drugs are used in combination.
- The likelihood of damaging a fetus is enhanced when both drugs are used together during pregnancy.
- Cardiovascular stress is increased in the presence of both drugs.

Like users of amphetamines, cocaine abusers frequently coadminister narcotics, such as heroin; this combination is called a speedball and has been associated with a high risk for HIV infection (NIDA 2007a). Cocaine users sometimes combine their drug with other depressants, such as benzodiazepines, or marijuana to help reduce the severity of the crash after their cocaine binges. Codependence on cocaine and a CNS depressant can complicate treatment but must be considered.

COCAINE AND PREGNANCY

One of the consequences of widespread cocaine abuse is that since the mid-1980s many babies in the United States have been born to mothers who used cocaine during pregnancy (Winkel 2010). Cocaine use during pregnancy is highest in poor, inner-city regions. Many of these cocaine babies have been abandoned by their mothers and left to the welfare system for care. It is still not clear exactly what types of direct effects cocaine has on the developing fetus (Winkel 2010). Some early studies have been criticized because (1) the pregnant populations examined were not well defined and properly matched, (2) use of other drugs (such as alcohol) with cocaine during pregnancy was often ignored, and (3) the effects of poor nutrition, poor living conditions, and a traumatic lifestyle were not considered when analyzing the results. Due to these problems, much of the earlier work examining

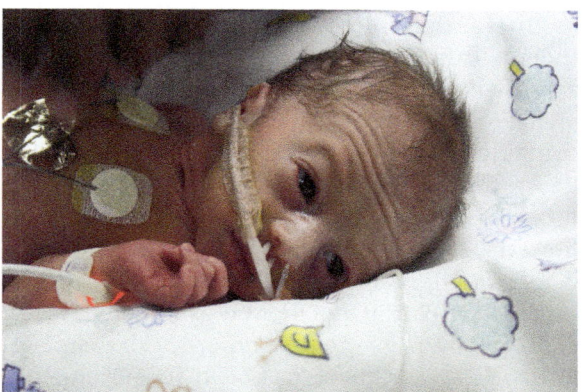

Infants born to crack-using mothers are often premature.

prenatal effects of cocaine is flawed, and the conclusions are questionable (University of Florida 2006; Vidaeff and Mastrobattista 2003).

It is known that cocaine use during pregnancy can cause vasoconstriction of placental vessels, thereby interfering with oxygen and nutrient exchange between mother and child, or contraction of the uterine muscles, resulting in trauma or premature birth. Current data also suggest that infants exposed to cocaine during pregnancy are more likely to suffer a small head (microencephaly), reduced birthweight, increased irritability, and subtle learning and cognitive deficits (March of Dimes 2003; Singer et al. 2004). Other findings also suggest that children who experienced prenatal cocaine exposure have problems with some motor skills, subtle deficits in IQ, and some minor problems with language development, attention span, and ability to gather and use information (March of Dimes 2003). Clearly, many individuals exposed to cocaine during fetal development can function normally in society, but they sometimes require special help, especially if they are allowed to be raised by their cocaine-addicted mother (Kronstadt 2013; Winkel 2010).

Minor Stimulants

Minor stimulants enjoy widespread use in the United States because of the mild lift in mood provided by their consumption. The most popular of these routinely consumed agents are

KEY TERM

cocaine babies
infants born to women who used cocaine during their pregnancy

methylxanthines (commonly called *xanthines*), such as caffeine, which are consumed in beverages made from plants and herbs (*U.S. News and World Report* 2012). Other minor stimulants are contained in OTC medications, such as cold and hay fever products. Because of their frequent use, some dependence on these drugs can occur; however, serious dysfunction due to dependence is infrequent. Consequently, abuse of xanthines such as caffeine is not viewed as a major health problem by most health experts (Medicinenet 2010). However, there has been recent concern that many people, especially adolescents and young adults, do not appreciate that caffeine is a drug and consume it more like food, resulting in side effects and even trips to the emergency room (Hitti 2006).

Caffeine-Like Drugs (Xanthines)

Caffeine is the world's most frequently used stimulant and perhaps its most popular drug (Medicinenet 2010). Beverages and foods containing caffeine are consumed by almost all adults and children living in the United States today (see Table 10.4). In this country, the average daily intake of caffeine is approximately 289 mg (the equivalent of approximately two or three cups of coffee), with as many as 30% of Americans consuming 600 mg or more per day (Medicinenet 2010). Almost 80% of the world's population consumes caffeine daily (Medicinenet 2010). The most common sources of caffeine include coffee beans, tea plants, kola nuts, maté leaves, guaraná paste, yoco bark, and an array of herbal and so-called "natural products."

Although the consumption of caffeine-containing drinks can be found throughout history, the active stimulant caffeine was identified by German and French scientists in the early 1820s. Caffeine was described as a substance with alkaloid (basic) properties that was extracted from green coffee beans and referred to as *kaffebase* by Ferdinand Runge in 1820 (Gilbert 1984). In the course of the next 40 to 60 years, caffeine was identified in several other genera of plants that were used as sources for common beverages. These included

KEY TERM

xanthines
the family of drugs that includes caffeine

TABLE 10.4 Caffeine Content of Beverages and Chocolate

Beverage (Mg/Cup)	Caffeine Content	Amount
Brewed coffee	90–135	5 oz
Instant coffee	35–164	5 oz
Decaffeinated coffee	1–6	5 oz
Tea	25–70	5 oz
Cocoa	5–25	5 oz
Coca-Cola	45	12 oz
Pepsi-Cola	38	12 oz
Mountain Dew	70	12 oz
Energy drinks	80–160	8–16 oz
Excedrin (OTC medication)	65	
NoDoz (OTC medication)	34	
Vivarin (OTC medication)	200	
Chocolate bar	1–35	1 oz

Reproduced from MedicineNet. "Caffeine." 2010. Available http://www.medicinenet.com/caffeine/article.htm. Accessed March 16, 2011.

tea leaves (originally the caffeine-like drug was called *thein*); guaraná paste (originally the drug was called *guaranin*); Paraguay tea, or maté; and kola nuts. Certainly, the popularity of these beverages over the centuries attests to the fact that most consumers find the stimulant effects of this drug desirable.

THE CHEMICAL NATURE OF CAFFEINE

Caffeine belongs to a group of drugs that have similar chemical structures and are known as the **xanthines**. Besides caffeine, other xanthines are *theobromine* (which means "divine leaf"), discovered in cacao beans (used to make chocolate) in 1842, and *theophylline* (which means "divine food"), isolated from tea leaves in 1888. These three agents have unique pharmacological properties (which are discussed later), with caffeine being the most potent CNS stimulant.

BEVERAGES CONTAINING CAFFEINE

To understand the unique role that caffeine plays in U.S. society, it is useful to gain perspective on its most common sources: unfermented beverages.

COFFEE

Coffee is derived from the beans of several species of coffea plants. The *Coffea arabica* plant grows as a shrub or small tree and reaches 4 to 6 meters in height when growing wild. Coffee beans are primarily cultivated in South America and East Africa and constitute the major cash crop for exportation in several developing countries.

The name *coffee* was likely derived from the Arabian word *kahwa* or named after the Ethiopian prince Kaffa. From Ethiopia, the coffee tree was carried to Arabia and cultivated (Kihlman 1977); it became an important element in Arabian civilization and is mentioned in writings dating back to 900 AD.

Coffee probably reached Europe through Turkey and was likely used initially as a medicine. By the middle of the 17th century, coffeehouses had sprung up in England and France—places to relax, talk, and learn the news. These coffeehouses turned into the famous "penny universities" of the early 18th century where, for a penny a cup, you could listen to some of the great literary and political figures of the day.

Coffee was originally consumed in the Americas by English colonists, although tea was initially preferred. Tea was replaced by coffee following the Revolutionary War. Because tea had become a symbol of English repression, the switch to coffee was more a political statement than a change in taste. The popularity of coffee grew as U.S. boundaries moved west. In fact, daily coffee intake continued to increase until it peaked in 1986, when annual coffee consumption averaged 10 pounds per person. Although concerns about the side effects associated with caffeine use have since caused some decline in coffee consumption, this beverage still plays a major role in the lifestyles of most Americans (Medicinenet 2010), with approximately 56% of adults in the United States being coffee drinkers in 2006 (Painter 2006).

TEA

Tea is made from the *Camellia sinensis* plant, which is native to China and parts of India, Burma, Thailand, Laos, and Vietnam. Tea contains two xanthines: caffeine and theophylline. As with coffee, the earliest use of tea is not known.

Although apocryphal versions of the origin of tea credit Emperor Shen Nung for its discovery in 2737 BC, the first reliable account of the use of tea as a medicinal plant appears in an early Chinese manuscript written around 350 AD. The popular use of tea slowly grew. The Dutch brought the first tea to Europe in 1610, where it was accepted rather slowly; with time, it was adopted by the British as a favorite beverage and became an integral part of their daily activities. In fact, the tea trade constituted one of the major elements of the English economy. Tea revenues made it possible for England to colonize India and helped to bring on the Opium Wars in the 1800s, which benefited British colonialism.

The British were constantly at odds with the Dutch as they attempted to monopolize the tea trade. Even so, the Dutch introduced the first tea into America at New Amsterdam around 1650. Later, the British gained exclusive rights to sell tea to the American colonies. Because of the high taxes levied by the British government on tea being shipped to America, tea became a symbol of British rule.

SOFT DRINKS

The second most common source of caffeine is soft drinks. In general, the caffeine content per 12-ounce serving ranges from 30 to 60 milligrams (see Table 10.4). Soft drinks account for most of the caffeine consumed by U.S. children and teenagers; for many people, a can of cola has replaced the usual cup of coffee. Recently, because of its general acceptance, caffeine has been added to juices, water, and even combined with alcoholic drinks.

Super-caffeinated energy drinks have dramatically increased in popularity, with names like Red Bull, Monster, Full Throttle, Rockstar, and Amp. Approximately one-third of 12- to 24-year-olds regularly consume these beverages, accounting for $3 billion in sales annually in the United States (Parker-Pope 2008a). Although manufacturers of these high-dose caffeine drinks claim they do not specifically target teenagers in their marketing strategies, the reality is that adolescents are heavy consumers of "energy" drinks (Griffith 2008) and do not appreciate how high the caffeine doses are in these caffeine-rich products (Today Health 2012). This is evident from the reports by poison control systems and emergency rooms of dramatic increases in calls and visits by young people complaining of caffeine-related overdose symptoms such as shakiness, tremors, dizziness, nausea, vomiting, agitation, increased heart rate, and elevated blood pressure (Goodman 2011).

Another concern relates to observations that consumption of these drinks is associated with what has become known as *toxic jock* behavior: a combination of behaviors that reflect an inclination to engage in dangerous risk taking such as unprotected sex, substance abuse, and violence (Parker-Pope 2008b). These observations do not mean that the caffeine causes this poor decision making, but it does appear that kids who are heavily involved in consuming these beverages are more likely to ignore basic rules of common sense related to their health and safety (Parker-Pope 2008b).

As mentioned previously, caffeine also has been added to alcoholic beverages with names such as Four Loco and Joose. Despite claims by the manufacturers that a combination of caffeine and alcohol was "generally recognized as safe," evidence has been accumulating that, especially in underage consumers, these products pose a significant health risk. After a year-long review of evidence, complaints, and claims, the FDA concluded that this drug combination may mask feelings of drunkenness, prompting consumers to engage in dangerous activities such as driving while under the influence of alcohol. As a result of this FDA conclusion, the caffeine–alcohol combination products have been removed from the market (Kesmodel 2010).

SOCIAL CONSEQUENCES OF CONSUMING CAFFEINE-BASED BEVERAGES

It is impossible to accurately assess the social impact of consuming beverages containing caffeine, but certainly the subtle (and sometimes not so subtle) stimulant effects of the caffeine present in these drinks have some social influence. These beverages have become integrated into social customs and ceremonies and are recognized as traditional drinks.

Today, drinks containing caffeine are consumed by many people with ritualistic devotion first thing in the morning, following every meal, and at frequent interludes throughout the day known as "coffee breaks" or "tea times." The immense popularity of these products is certainly a consequence of the stimulant actions of caffeine. Both the dependence on the "jump-start" effect of caffeine and the avoidance of unpleasant withdrawal consequences in the frequent user ensure the continual popularity of these products.

OTHER NATURAL CAFFEINE SOURCES

Although coffee and tea are two of the most common sources of natural caffeine in the United States, other caffeine-containing beverages and food are popular in different parts of the world.

Some of the most common include guaraná from Brazil; maté from Argentina, Southern Brazil, and Paraguay; and kola nuts from West Africa, West Indies, and South America (Kihlman 1977).

CHOCOLATE

Although chocolate contains small amounts of caffeine (see Table 10.3), the principal stimulant in chocolate is the alkaloid theobromine, named after the cocoa tree, *Theobroma cacao*. (*Theobroma* is an Aztec word meaning "fruit of the gods.") The Aztecs thought very highly of the fruit and seed pods from the cacao tree, and they used the beans as a medium of exchange in bartering. The Mayan Indians adopted the food and made a warm drink from the beans that they called *chocolatl* (meaning "warm drink"). The original chocolate drink was a very thick concoction that had to be eaten with a spoon. It was unsweetened because the Mayans apparently did not know about sugar cane.

Hernando Cortés, the conqueror of Mexico, took some chocolate cakes back to Spain with him in 1528, but the method of preparing them remained a secret for nearly 100 years. It was not until 1828 that the Dutch worked out a process to remove much of the fat from the kernels to make a chocolate powder that was the forerunner of the cocoa we know today. The cocoa fat, or cocoa butter as it is called, was later mixed with sugar and pressed into bars. In 1847, the first chocolate bars appeared on the market. By 1876, the Swiss had developed milk chocolate, which is highly popular in today's confectioneries.

OTC DRUGS CONTAINING CAFFEINE

Although the consumption of beverages is by far the most common source of xanthines, a number of popular OTC products contain significant quantities of caffeine. For example, many OTC analgesic products (e.g., Anacin and Excedrin) contain approximately 30–60 milligrams of caffeine per tablet. Higher doses of 100–200 milligrams per tablet are included in stay-awake (NoDoz) and "picker-upper" (Vivarin) products (Kirkwood and Melton 2012; Wilkinson 2012). The use of caffeine in these OTC drugs is highly controversial and has been criticized by clinicians who are unconvinced of caffeine's benefits. Some critics believe that the presence of caffeine in these OTC drugs is nothing more than a psychological gimmick to entice customers through mild euphoric effects provided by this stimulant.

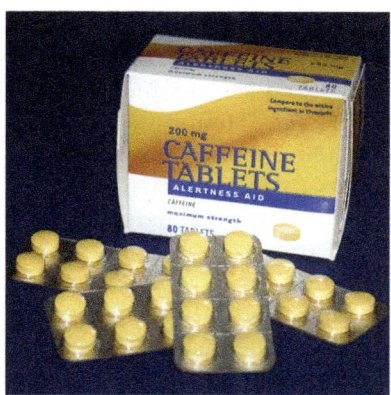

OTC caffeine products frequently contain the equivalent of 2–3 cups of coffee and are used to stay awake.

Despite this criticism, it is likely that caffeine has some analgesic (pain-relieving) properties of its own (Dunwiddie and Masino 2001). Studies suggest that 130 milligrams, but not 65 milligrams, of caffeine is superior to a placebo in relieving non-migraine headaches. In addition, the presence of caffeine has been shown to enhance aspirin-medicated relief from surgical pain (such as tooth extraction). Based on such findings, some clinicians recommend the use of caffeine in the management of some types of headaches and minor to moderate pains (Zhang 2001).

PHYSIOLOGICAL EFFECTS OF THE XANTHINES

The xanthines significantly influence several important body functions. Although the effects of these drugs are generally viewed as minor and short-term (Goldstein 1994), when used in high doses or by people who have severe medical problems, these drugs can be dangerous. The following sections summarize the responses of the major systems to xanthines.

CNS EFFECTS

Among the common xanthines, caffeine has the most potent effect on the CNS, followed by theophylline; for most people, theobromine has relatively little influence. Although the CNS responses of users can vary considerably, in general 100 to 200 milligrams of caffeine enhances alertness, causes arousal, and diminishes fatigue (Medicinenet 2010). Caffeine is often used to block drowsiness and facilitate mental activity, such as when cramming for examinations into the early hours of the morning. In addition, caffeine stimulates the formation of thoughts but does not improve learning ability in the wide-awake student. The effects of caffeine are most pronounced in unstimulated, drowsy consumers (Medicinenet 2010). The CNS effects of caffeine also diminish the sense of boredom (Medicinenet 2010). Thus, people engaged in dull, repetitive tasks, such as assembly-line work, or nonstimulating and laborious exercises, such as listening to a boring professor, often consume caffeinated beverages to help compensate for the tedium. Most certainly, xanthine drinks are popular because they cause these effects on brain activity.

Adverse CNS effects usually occur with doses greater than 300 milligrams per day. Some of these include insomnia, increased tension, anxiety, and initiation of muscle twitches. Doses over 500 milligrams can be dysphoric (unpleasant) and can cause panic sensations, chills, nausea, and clumsiness. Extremely high doses of caffeine, from 5 to 10 grams, frequently result in seizures, respiratory failure, and death (APA 2013).

CARDIOVASCULAR AND RESPIRATORY EFFECTS

Drugs that stimulate the brain usually stimulate the cardiovascular system as well. The response of the heart and blood vessels to xanthines is dependent on dose and previous experience with these mild stimulants. Tolerance to the cardiovascular effects occurs with frequent use (Medicinenet 2010). With low doses (100–200 milligrams), heart activity can either increase, decrease, or do nothing; at higher doses (more than 500 milligrams), the rate of contraction of the heart increases. Xanthines usually cause minor vasodilation in most of the body. In contrast, the cerebral blood vessels are vasoconstricted by the action of caffeine. In fact, cerebral vasoconstriction likely accounts for this drug's effectiveness in relieving some minor vascular headaches caused by vasodilation of the cerebral vessels. For most consumers the effects of caffeine on the cardiovascular system are minor, but for some with underlying heart disease, caffeine can be dangerous (Today Health 2012).

Among the xanthines, theophylline has the greatest effect on the respiratory system, causing air passages to open and facilitate breathing. Because of this effect, tea has often been recommended to relieve breathing difficulties, and theophylline is frequently used to treat asthma-related respiratory problems.

OTHER EFFECTS

The methylxanthines have noteworthy—albeit mild—effects on other systems in the body. They cause a minor increase in the secretion of digestive juices in the stomach, which can be significant to individuals suffering from stomach ailments such as ulcers. These drugs also increase urine formation (as any heavy tea drinker undoubtedly knows).

CAFFEINE INTOXICATION

Consuming occasional low doses of the xanthines (the equivalent of two to three cups of coffee per day) is relatively safe for most users (Kluger 2004). However, frequent use of high doses causes psychological as well as physical problems called **caffeinism**. This condition is found in about 10% of the adults who consume coffee (APA 2013).

The CNS components of caffeine intoxication are recognized as "caffeine use disorder" in the *DSM-5* criteria established by the American Psychiatric Association (2013). The essential features of this disorder are restlessness, nervousness, excitement, insomnia, flushed face, diuresis, muscle twitching, rambling thoughts and speech, and stomach complaints. These symptoms can occur in some sensitive people following a dose as low as 250 milligrams per day. Caffeine doses in excess of 1 gram per day may cause muscle twitching, rambling thoughts and speech, heart arrhythmias, and motor agitation. With higher doses, hearing ringing in the ears and seeing flashes of light can occur. Some researchers suggest consuming large quantities of caffeine is associated with cancers of the bladder, ovaries, colon, and kidneys. These claims have not been reliably substantiated (Medicinenet 2010; Nawrot et al. 2003; Painter 2006).

One problem with many such studies is that they assess the effect of coffee consumption on cancers rather than the effect of caffeine itself. Because coffee contains so many different chemicals, it is impossible to determine specifically the effect of caffeine in such research (Medicinenet 2010). Other reports claim that caffeine promotes cyst formation in women's breasts. Although these conclusions have been challenged, many clinicians advise patients with breast cysts to avoid caffeine (Pruthi 2010). Finally, some reports indicate that very high doses of caffeine given to pregnant laboratory animals can cause stillbirths or offspring with low birthweights or limb deformities. However, studies found that moderate consumption of caffeine (less than 300 milligrams per day) did not significantly

affect human fetal development (Medicinenet 2010). Generally, expectant mothers are advised to avoid or at least reduce caffeine use during pregnancy just to be safe (Medicinenet 2010).

Based on the information available, no strong evidence exists to suggest that moderate use of caffeine leads to disease (Medicinenet 2010). In fact, some research has suggested that moderate caffeine consumption may even reduce the risk of degenerative diseases of the brain such as Parkinson's disease and Alzheimer's disease (Fackelmann 2006; Painter 2006). There are, however, implications that people with existing severe medical problems—psychiatric disorders (such as severe anxiety, panic attacks, and schizophrenia), cardiovascular disease, and possibly breast cysts—may be at greater risk when consuming caffeine. Realistically, other elements, such as alcohol and fat consumption and smoking, are much more likely to cause serious health problems (Gurin 1994; Today Health 2012).

CAFFEINE DEPENDENCE

Caffeine causes limited dependence, which, for most people, is relatively minor compared with that of the potent stimulants; thus, the abuse potential of caffeine is much lower and dependence is less likely to interfere with normal daily routines (Kluger 2004; Medicinenet 2010). Despite this, caffeine use is thought to be able to produce a significant addiction in some people (*U.S. News and World Report* 2012). Consequently, 50% of those consuming one to three cups of coffee each day develop headaches when withdrawing and 10% become significantly depressed, anxious, or fatigued without their coffee (Narconon 2013b). Some people experience elements of withdrawal every morning before their first cup and claim caffeine gives them an edge at work or in school (Hartney 2013; Shute 2007). However, caffeine is so readily available and socially accepted (almost expected) that the high quantity of consumption has produced many modestly dependent users. In fact, we are seeing younger and younger persons consuming more and more caffeine; from 2004 to 2007 the percentage of 18- to 24-year-olds who consumed caffeine daily went from 16% to 31% (Shute 2007; see "Here and Now: Caffeine Emergencies").

The degree of physical dependence on caffeine is highly variable but related to dose. With typical caffeine withdrawal, adverse effects can persist for several days (see **Table 10.5**). Although these symptoms are unpleasant, they usually are not

KEY TERM

caffeinism
symptoms caused by taking high chronic doses of caffeine

HERE AND NOW

Caffeine Emergencies

Because of the increased popularity of caffeine-containing products, especially with teenagers, poison control centers across the country are reporting increased numbers of people presenting at emergency rooms with rapid heart rates and nausea from caffeine overdose. Such was the case when a 14-year-old boy recently showed up at a Minneapolis emergency room having difficulty with breathing after washing down several caffeine pills with so-called "energy drinks" in order to continue playing video games all night. But instead of having a night of video recreation with friends, he spent the evening in an intensive care unit intubated until the caffeine cleared from his system and normal breathing was restored.

Data from Shute, N. "Americans Young and Old Crave High-Octane Fuel, and Doctors Are Jittery." *U.S. News and World Report* (29 April 2007): 58-68.

severe enough to prevent most people from giving up their coffee or cola drinks if motivated. It is noteworthy, however, that many of those patients who are treated for caffeinism relapse into their caffeine-consuming habits (Wheeler 2010).

VARIABILITY IN RESPONSES

Caffeine is eventually absorbed entirely from the gastrointestinal tract after oral consumption. In most users, 90% of the drug reaches the bloodstream within 20 minutes and is distributed into the brain and throughout the body very quickly (Sawynok and Yaksh 1993). The rate of absorption of caffeine from the stomach and intestines differs from person to person by as much as sixfold. Because of the wide variations in the rate at which caffeine enters the blood from the stomach, this likely accounts for much of the variability in response to this drug.

∎ OTC Sympathomimetics

Although often overlooked, the sympathomimetic decongestant drugs included in OTC products such as cold, allergy, and diet aid medications have stimulant properties like those of caffeine. For most people, the CNS impact of these drugs is minor, but for those people who are very sensitive to these drugs, they can cause jitters and interfere with sleep. For such individuals, OTC products containing the sympathomimetics should be avoided before bedtime (Answers.com 2010).

The common OTC sympathomimetics are shown in **Table 10.6** and include ephedrine, pseudoephedrine, and phenylephrine. In the past, these drugs have been referred to as "look-alikes," suggesting they have effects similar to the more potent stimulants such as amphetamine. Although

TABLE 10.5 Caffeine Withdrawal Syndrome

Symptom	Duration
Headache	Several days to 1 week
Decreased alertness	2 days
Decreased vigor	2 days
Fatigue and lethargy	2 days
Nervousness	2 days

Data from Holtzman, S. "Caffeine as a model drug of abuse." *Trends in Pharmacological Sciences* 11 (1990): 355–356.

TABLE 10.6 Common OTC Sympathomimetics

Drug	OTC Product (Form)
Ephedrine	Before being removed from market, was used as a decongestant (oral, nasal spray, or nasal drops)
Naphazoline	Decongestant (nasal spray or nasal drops)
Oxymetazoline	Decongestant (nasal spray or nasal drops)
Phenylephrine	Decongestant (oral, nasal spray, nasal drops, or eye drops)
Pseudoephedrine	Decongestant (oral)
Tetrahydrozoline	Decongestant (eye drops)

Data from Scolaro, K. "Disorders Related to Colds and Allergy." In *Handbook of Nonprescription Drugs,* 17th ed., 179–204. Washington, DC: American Pharmaceutical Association, 2012.

HERE AND NOW

Diet Pills Are Russian Roulette for Athletes

Steve Bechler, a 23-year-old pitcher for the Baltimore Orioles of the American League, died in 2003 after collapsing on the field during running drills due to "multiple organ failure resulting from heat stroke," says the autopsy report. Ephedrine was found in Bechler's body and likely contributed to his death. He was reported to be using an ephedrine supplement called Xenadrine RFA-1. Although advised not to use it by his trainer, Bechler was taking this ephedrine-containing product to get his weight down after being criticized by coaches for being too heavy and not performing well in preseason drills. A teammate explained that heavy athletes like Bechler are under a lot of pressure to control their weight to make big-league teams. Although at the time of Bechler's death use of ephedrine was not prohibited by Major League Baseball, it was prohibited by the National Football League in 2002. The NFL's ban came after Korey Stringer, a lineman for the Minnesota Vikings who was taking an ephedrine product, died after collapsing during a training camp workout

© Jerry Wachter/Sports Imagery/Landov

in 2001. Ephedrine in OTC dietary supplements has since been made illegal by the FDA due to serious side effects and death.

Data from Shipley, A. "Bechler's Diet Pills Draw Scrutiny." *Washington Post* (19 February 2003): D-1; and Mayo Clinic Health. "Ephedra (Ephedra sinica)/ma Huang." Health Information (2010b). Available http://www.mayoclinic.com/health/ephedra/NS_patient-ephedra. Accessed May 3, 2011.

much less potent than amphetamines (even though they can be used as precursor chemicals to make methamphetamine), these minor stimulants can be abused and have caused deaths (Cucchiara and Levine 2011). Attempts to keep these drugs from being promoted as potent stimulants resulted in passage of the federal and state Imitation Controlled Substances Acts. These statutes prohibit the packaging of OTC sympathomimetics to look like amphetamines.

Despite these laws, occasionally other products containing the OTC sympathomimetics are promoted on the street as "harmless speed" and "OTC uppers." It is likely that use of such products can lead to the abuse of more potent stimulants.

As previously mentioned, some of the sympathomimetics that are included in cold medicines can be readily converted into methamphetamine. For this reason, since 2006 federal statutes have required these products be secured in a locked case behind the counter and sold in limited quantities (Baldauf 2006).

▌ Herbal Stimulants

Some OTC sympathomimetics occur naturally and are also found in herbal stimulants or dietary supplements sold by mail and in novelty stores, beauty salons, health food stores, online, and sometimes by health professionals, including physicians. (To appreciate this point, complete an Internet search for "herbal stimulant.") These pills have been sold under many names such as "Rave Herbal Stimulant," "Legal Herbal Weed," and "Herbal Ecstasy," and often contain stimulants such as ephedrine, ephedra, or ma huang. These products are promoted as natural highs to be used as diet aids, energy boosters, or performance enhancers for athletes (Legal Herbal Drugs 2013). Excessive use of these products can cause seizures, heart attacks, and strokes (Banar 2011). In fact, several deaths and many cases of severe reactions have been reported in the United States from excessive use of these products (*Washington Times* 2003). The death of a major league baseball player (see "Here and Now: Diet Pills Are Russian Roulette for Athletes") resulted in particularly strong pressure to ban OTC products, including dietary supplements, containing either the herb ephedra or the active ingredient ephedrine (Shipley 2003). In response to these pressures, the FDA banned the use of ephedrine or ephedra in OTC products; however, it is difficult to actually remove herbal stimulants from the marketplace because of a 1994 federal law that prohibits such action until the FDA conclusively proves the dangers of these substances (Miller and Longtin 2010). Numerous lawsuits have been filed against herbal companies that manufactured products containing ma huang and the drug ephedrine. These legal actions claim that such products have caused serious illness and even death. Several of these lawsuits have been settled out of court, reportedly for millions of dollars. Even before the FDA ban, because ephedrine can be converted into methamphetamine, the Comprehensive Methamphetamine Act passed in 1996 regulated the amount of ephedrine that could be purchased or sold at one time (Sprague, Harrod, and Teconchuk 1998).

Organizations of the United Nations, such as its Office on Drugs and Crime, work with countries around the world to identify critical drug problems and to develop global solutions that cross international borders.

Global Stimulant Abuse

Like the United States, other countries have been seriously impacted by the abuse of stimulant drugs, causing governments and law enforcement agencies around the world and international organizations such as the United Nations Office on Drugs and Crime to search for solutions (United Nations Office on Drugs and Crime 2009). For the most part these drugs are referred to as amphetamine-type stimulants (ATS) or cocaine and their various forms. The ATS drugs include amphetamines such as methamphetamine, methcathinone, and MDMA and related substances.

■ Stimulant Production

Because most ATS drugs are synthetics, they can be produced anywhere and are relatively inexpensive. As mentioned before, for this reason these drugs are often perceived as a "poor-man's cocaine." It is estimated that about 650 metric tons of the ATS drugs were manufactured globally in 2007, of which about 130 metric tons were MDMA (United Nations Office on Drugs and Crime 2009). A pattern exists of shifting manufacturing from developed to developing countries to take advantage of these poorer countries' vulnerabilities and less sophisticated law enforcement

strategies to fight organized crime organizations and their inability to stop manufacturing and sale of these substances. This is illustrated by the shift from the small neighborhood methamphetamine labs in the United States of 2000–2005 to the more recent large sophisticated meth labs run by organized drug cartels and crime syndicates in Mexico (United Nations Office on Drugs and Crime 2009).

In contrast, because cocaine is a natural substance derived from a plant, its production is limited to those regions that have climate and geographic conditions conducive to coca cultivation. The countries that produce the vast majority of the world's cocaine supply are Bolivia, Peru, and Colombia. The global cocaine supply decreased to 845 metric tons in 2008. These recent declines were largely due to a 28% reduction in cocaine production in Colombia as a result of pressure from the United States (United Nations Office on Drugs and Crime 2009).

■ Stimulant Trafficking

Global seizures of ATS have been increasing since 2000, with amphetamine and methamphetamine leading the way (United Nations Office on Drugs and Crime 2009), accounting for 84% of all seizures. However, 2007 saw a dramatic jump in international seizures of MDMA (16% of all ATS confiscated). Typically, trafficking of ATS drugs is intraregional because they can readily be manufactured locally and usually do not need to be smuggled across international borders. In contrast, the precursor chemicals from which ATS drugs are synthesized are typically diverted from legitimate markets for decongestant and cold medicines in Asia (United Nations Office on Drugs and Crime 2009).

Cocaine trafficking patterns are somewhat opposite of those for the ATS drugs. Following several years of expansion, the quantity of cocaine seized in 2006 decreased and remained reduced in 2007 and 2008. This reflects the reduction in cocaine production mentioned earlier and the resultant increases in cocaine prices and purity (United Nations Office on Drugs and Crime 2009).

▌ Global Stimulant Consumption

It is roughly estimated that globally between 72 and 250 million persons annually consume illicit drugs. This figure includes the entire gamut of users from casual abusers to heavy consumers who have become problematic drug addicts (United Nations Office on Drugs and Crime 2009). The intense users are likely very dependent on their drug of choice, cause a serious drain on public health and law enforcement resources, and would benefit from proper treatment. It is estimated that globally there are 13 to 38 million of these problem drug users, ages 15–64 years (United Nations Office on Drugs and Crime 2009).

Different drugs tend to cause problems for different global regions. Marijuana is particularly troubling for Africa and Australia; heroin is especially problematic for Asia and Europe; the ATS drugs are a major problem for Asia, North America, and Australia; and cocaine causes the greatest problem in North and South America, with the United States being the largest consumer in absolute numbers (United Nations Office on Drugs and Crime 2009). By comparison, the ATS drugs are consumed by almost twice as many people around the world (about 40 million annually) as cocaine (about 20 million). For comparison, the global use of MDMA is similar to that for cocaine (United Nations Office on Drugs and Crime 2009).

▌ Global Drug Policy

Like the United States, most countries around the world are looking for solutions to the personal and social consequences of drug abuse in general and the stimulant problems in particular. Lively discussions about demand, production, and trafficking occur between countries to try to stem the tide of drug abuse/addiction and its devastating consequences. The causes are many and the solutions are complex and evasive. There are heated discussions between nations on topics such as (1) who is principally at fault for the problems (i.e., the nations that produce or consume), (2) should these drugs be legalized or at least be decriminalized, and (3) can taxing of such drug products be used to raise needed public revenues. The international discussions resemble those occurring throughout the United States. What has become evident to everyone is that although specific solutions are difficult, all nations are in this together. Drug problems and drug policies to address these problems cross national borders, impacting global efforts to find solutions; thus, to be successful in our attempts to mitigate these drug problems we must have global cooperation and work together.

LEARNING PORTFOLIO

Discussion Questions

1. Should the FDA continue to approve amphetamines for the treatment of obesity? Why?
2. How are methamphetamine and Ecstasy similar, and how do they differ?
3. Should children be taken from mothers who are addicted to methamphetamine or cocaine?
4. What have past experiences taught us about cocaine? Do you think we have finally learned our lesson concerning this drug?
5. If clinical trials demonstrate that MDMA is effective in the treatment of stress and anxiety, should the FDA approve its use by prescription? What would be the effect on recreational MDMA use by young people if the FDA approved MDMA for treating PTSD?
6. Why does the method of cocaine administration make a difference in how a user is affected by this drug? Use examples to substantiate your conclusions.
7. Why do people use crack cocaine, and what are the major toxicities caused by the use of high doses of this stimulant?
8. How is cocaine dependence treated? What are the rationales for the treatments?
9. How does caffeine compare with cocaine and amphetamine as a CNS stimulant?
10. Because of caffeine's potential for abuse, do you think the FDA should control it more tightly? Defend your answer.
11. Do you feel that herbal stimulants, such as ephedra and ma huang, should have been removed from OTC products?
12. How do global efforts to address stimulant abuse problems affect the people and policies in the United States?

Key Terms

Summary

1. Amphetamines, originally developed as decongestants, are potent stimulants. Some amphetamines have been approved by the FDA as (a) diet aids to treat obesity, (b) treatment for narcolepsy, and (c) treatment for attention deficit hyperactivity disorder in children.
2. In therapeutic doses, amphetamines can cause agitation, anxiety, and panic owing to their effects on the brain; in addition, they can cause an irregular heartbeat, increased blood pressure, heart attack, or stroke. Intense, high-dose abuse of these drugs can cause severe psychotic behavior, stereotypy, and seizures as well as the severe cardiovascular side effects just mentioned.

3. Speed refers to the use of intravenous methamphetamine. Ice is smoked methamphetamine. A run is a pattern of intense, multiple dosing over a period of days that can cause serious neurological, psychiatric, and cardiovascular consequences.

4. Tweakers are individuals who repeatedly self-administer methamphetamine to maintain the high. They often have not slept or eaten for days, are very irritable, and sometimes are paranoid or even violent.

5. "Designer" amphetamines are chemical modifications of original amphetamines. Some designer amphetamines, such as Ecstasy, have some abuse potential and are marketed on the street under exotic and alluring names.

6. Ecstasy has both psychedelic and stimulant properties due to its ability to release serotonin and dopamine in the brain. This combination of pharmacological effects makes this drug particularly attractive to younger populations engaging in sensory-rich activities, such as dances called raves.

7. In the early 1980s, cocaine was commonly viewed by the U.S. public as a relatively safe drug with glamorous connotations. By the mid-1980s, it became apparent that cocaine was a very addicting drug with dangerous side effects.

8. The CNS and cardiovascular effects of both amphetamines and cocaine are similar. However, the effects of cocaine tend to occur more rapidly, be more intense, and wear off more quickly than those of amphetamines.

9. The intensity of the cocaine effect and the likelihood of dependence occurring are directly related to the means of administration. Going from least to most intense effect, the modes of cocaine administration include chewing, snorting, injecting, and smoking (or freebasing).

10. Crack is cocaine that has been converted into its "freebase" form and is intended for smoking.

11. Cocaine withdrawal goes through three main stages: (a) the "crash," the initial abstinence phase consisting of depression, agitation, suicidal thoughts, and fatigue; (b) withdrawal, including mood swings, craving, anhedonia, and obsession with drug seeking; and (c) extinction, when normal pleasure returns and cues trigger craving and mood swings.

12. Treatment of cocaine dependence is highly individualistic and has variable success. The principal strategies include both inpatient and outpatient programs. Drug therapy often is used to relieve short-term cocaine craving and to alleviate mood problems and long-term craving. Psychological counseling and support therapy are essential components of treatment.

13. Caffeine is the most frequently consumed stimulant in the world. It is classified as a xanthine (methylxanthine) and is added to a number of beverages, including water, and has even been added to alcoholic drinks. It is also included in some OTC medicines such as analgesics and "stay-awake" products. Caffeine causes minor stimulation of cardiovascular activity, kidney function (it is a diuretic), and gastric secretion.

14. Dependence on caffeine can occur in people who regularly consume large doses. Withdrawal can cause headaches, agitation, and tremors. Although unpleasant, withdrawal from caffeine dependence is much less severe than that from amphetamine and cocaine dependence.

15. OTC sympathomimetics such as ephedrine have been consumed in high doses and used as "legal" highs. Although not as potent as the major stimulants, the recreational use of these drugs can be dangerous. Because of those potential dangers, the FDA has prohibited the use of ephedrine in OTC products.

16. Stimulant abuse and addiction are problems that are global in nature. Because these drugs are manufactured around the world and trafficked across international borders, it is impossible to find lasting solutions to these problems without working with other

countries to help stem the production and smuggling of these illegal substances.

References

A.D.A.M. "Cocaine Withdrawal." *New York Times*, Health Guide. 13 December 2010. Available http://health.nytimes.com/health/guides/disease/cocaine-withdrawal/overview.html

AddictionInfo. "Self Medication Hypothesis, ADHD and Cocaine." AddictionInfo.org. 2010. Available http://www.addictioninfo.org/search/node/self%20medication%20ADHD

Aldrich, M., and R. Barker. In *Cocaine: Chemical, Biological, Social and Treatment Aspects,* edited by S. J. Mule, 3–10. Cleveland, OH: CRC, 1976.

American Psychiatric Association. "Conditions for Further Study." In *Diagnostic and Statistical Manual of Mental Disorders*, 5th ed., text revision, 792–795. Washington, DC: American Psychiatric Association, 2013.

Answers.com. "Decongestant." 2010. Available http://www.answers.com/topic/decongestant

Baldauf, S. "Vanished Behind the Counter." *US News and World Report.* 2 October 2006. Available http://health.usnews.com/usnews/health/articles/060924/2cold.htm

Ballod, M. "Obesity." In *Applied Therapeutics*, 10th ed, edited by B. Alldredge, 872–883. Philadelphia, PA: Lippincott Williams & Wilkins, 2013.

Banar, M. "What Are the Potential Dangers of Herbal Stimulants." Livestrong.com. 7 August 2011. Available http://www.livestrong.com/article/510464-what-are-the-potential-dangers-of-herbal-stimulants

Beck, J. "The Public Health Implications of MDMA Use." In *Ecstasy*, edited by S. Peroutka, 77–103. Norwell, MA: Kluwer, 1990.

Beckhusen, R. "As Colombian Drug Gangs Collapse, Mexican Cartels Get Tons of Cheap Coke. WIRED. (April 2013). Available http://www.wired.com/dangerroom/2013/04/colombian-bacrim-gangs/

Benedetti, W. "Ecstasy Supporters Hope FDA-Approved Study Will Vindicate Drug." *Seattle Post-Intelligencer.* 9 May 2002. Available http://seattlepi.nwsource.com/lifestyle/69629_ecstasystudy.shtml

Berkes, H. "Mexican 'Ice' Replaces Home-Cooked Meth in U.S." National Public Radio (3 April 2007).

Bradley, T. "Brazil Now Consumes 18% of the World's Cocaine." Quartz. 23 September 2012. Available http://qz.com/5058/brazil-now-consumes-18-of-worlds-cocaine/

Byck, R. "Cocaine Use and Research: Three Histories." In *Cocaine: Chemical and Behavioral Aspects*, edited by S. Fisher, 3–17. London: Oxford University Press, 1987.

Cantwell, B., and A. McBride. "Self Detoxification by Amphetamine-Dependent Patients: A Pilot Study." *Drug and Alcohol Dependence* 49 (1998): 157–163.

Carey, B. "A Party Drug May Help the Brain Cope with Trauma." *New York Times.* 19 November 2012. Available http://www.nytimes.com/2012/11/20/health/ecstasy-treatment-for-post-traumatic-stress-shows-promise.html?pagewanted=all&_r=0

Ceasar, M. "US Finds Anger in South America." *Toronto Globe and Mail* (31 August 2002). Available http://www.commondreams.org/headlines.shtml?/headlines02/0831-06.htm

Cloud, J. "The Lure of Ecstasy." *Time* 155 (5 June 2000): 60.

Cohen, G. "A Front-Line Physician's Perspective on the Crystal Meth Epidemic." *Counselor* 7 (October 2006): 51, 52.

Cucchiara, B., and S. Levine. "Stroke Associated with Drug Abuse." MedMerits. 2011. Available http://www.medmerits.com/index.php/article/stroke_associated_with_drug_abuse/

Cumming, P., D. Caprioli, and J. W. Dalley. "What Have PET and 'Zippy' Told Us About the Neuropharmacology of Drug Addiction?" *British Journal of Pharmacology* 10 (2010): 1476–5381.

Cunningham, J., L. Bojorquez, O. Campollo, L. Liu, and C. Maxwell. "Mexico's Methamphetamine Precursor Chemical Interventions: Impacts on Drug Treatment Admissions." *Addiction* 105 (2010): 1973–1983.

Curley, A. "Why 'Bath Salts' Are Dangerous." CNN. 2012 May 29. Available http://thechart.blogs.cnn.com/2012/05/29/why-bath-salts-are-dangerous/

Designer-drug.com. Comprehensive Methamphetamine Control Act (MCA). Available http://designer-drug.com/pte/12.162.180.114/dcd/chemistry/dojmeth1.txt

Deslandes, P., D. Pache, and R. Sewell. "Drug Dependence: Neuropharmacology and Management." *Journal of Pharmacy and Pharmacology* 54 (2002): 885–895.

DeYoung, K. "U.S.: Coca Cultivation Drops in Colombia." *Washington Post* (28 February 2003): A-19.

DiChiara, G. "Cocaine: Scientific and Social Dimensions." *Trends in Neurological Sciences* 16 (1993): 39.

Doyle, M. "Report: 2006 Anti-meth Law Reduced Number of U.S. Labs." McClatchy. 6 July 2010. Available http://www.mcclatchydc.com/2010/07/06/97092/report-2006-anti-meth-law-reduced.html

Drasner, K. "Local Anesthetics." In *Basic and Clinical Pharmacology*, 12th ed., edited by B. Katzung, S. Masters, and

A. Trevor, 449–464. New York: McGraw-Hill Medical, 2012.

Drug Enforcement Agency (DEA). "Ecstasy Statistics." 19 July 2003. Available http://theDEA.org/statistics.html

Drug War Facts. "Methamphetamine." 2004. Available http://www.drugwarfacts.org/methamph.htm

Drugs.com. "Amphetamine Side Effects." 15 November 2010. Available http://www.drugs.com/sfx/amphetamine-side-effects.html

Dunwiddie, T., and S. Masino. "The Role and Regulation of Adenosine in the Central Nervous System." *Annual Review of Neuroscience* 24 (2001): 31–55.

Elias, P. "One of the 'Speed Freak Killers' to Be Freed." SFGate.com. 12 September 2010. Available http://www.sfgate.com/news/article/One-of-the-Speed-Freak-Killers-to-be-freed-3253092.php

Elkashef, A., F. Vocci, G. Hanson, J. White, W. Wickes, and J. Tiihonen. "Pharmacotherapy of Methamphetamine Addiction: An Update." *Substance Abuse* 29 (2008): 31–49.

Emedicinehealth. "Cocaine Abuse." 2010. Available http://www.emedicinehealth.com/cocaine_abuse/article_em.htm

Encyclopedia Britannica. "Science and Technology: Cocaine." Encyclopedia Britannica Academic Edition. 2010. Available http://www.britannica.com/EBchecked/topic/123441/cocaine

Enotes. "Freebasing (Encyclopedia of Drugs, Alcohol, and Addictive Behavior)." 2010. Available http://www.enotes.com/drugs-alcohol-encyclopedia/freebasing

Everything Addiction. "MDMA: A Stimulant Drug You Should Avoid." 19 July 2010. Available http://www.everythingaddiction.com/drugs-addiction/club-drugs/mdma-a-stimulant-drug-you-should-avoid

Fackelmann, K. "Can Caffeine Protect Against Alzheimer's?" *USA Today* (6 November 2006): 4D.

Fieser, E. "Drug Wars in Mexico, Colombia Push Drug Trade to Dominican Republic." *Christian Science Monitor.* 5 November 2010. Available http://www.csmonitor.com/World/Americas/2010/1105/Drug-wars-in-Mexico-Colombia-push-drug-trade-to-Dominican-Republic

Fischman, M., and C. Johanson. "Cocaine." In *Pharmacological Aspects of Drug Dependence: Towards an Integrated Neurobehavior Approach Handbook of Experimental Pharmacology,* edited by C. Schuster and M. Kuhar, 159–195. New York: Springer-Verlag, 1996.

Fox, M. "Amphetamines Could Damage Heart Artery: U.S. Study." *Promises.* 18 August 2010. Available http://promises.com/promisesnews/articles/amphetamines/amphetamine-abuse-can-cause-serious-damage-to-aorta-in-young-people

Friends of Narconon. "Ecstasy/MDMA Manufacturing and Statistics." Friends of Narconon. 2010. Available http://www.friendsofnarconon.org/drug_education/news/latest_news/ecstasy%10mdma_manufacturing_and_statistics

Gilbert, J. "Cocaine: A Brief History of Blow." WLTX. 24 October 2011. Available http://www.wltx.com/news/health/article/156304/291/Cocaine-A-Brief-History-of-Blow

Gilbert, R. "Caffeine Consumption." In *The Methylxanthine Beverages and Foods: Chemistry, Consumption, and Health Effects,* edited by G. Spiller, 185–213. New York: Liss, 1984.

Golding, A. "Two Hundred Years of Drug Abuse." *Journal of the Royal Society of Medicine* 86 (May 1993): 282–286.

Goldstein, A. *Addiction from Biology to Drug Abuse.* New York: Freeman, 1994.

Goodger, N., J. Wang, and M. Pogrel. "Palatal and Nasal Necrosis Resulting from Cocaine Misuse." *British Dental Journal* 198 (2005): 333–334.

Goodman, B. "Energy Drinks Send Thousands to the ER Each Year." WebMD. 22 November 2011. Available http://www.Webmd.com/mental-health/alcohol-abuse/news/20111121/energy-drinks-send-thousands-to-the-er-each-year

Green, E. "Cocaine, Glamorous Status Symbol of the 'Jet Set,' Is Fast Becoming Many Students' Drug of Choice." *Chronicle of Higher Education* 13 (November 1985): 1, 34.

Griffith, D. "Energy Drinks Implications." *Sacramento Bee.* 11 May 2008. Available http://thesportdigest.com/article/energy-drinks-implications-student-athletes-and-athletic-departments

Grinspoon, L., and J. Bakalar. "The Amphetamines: Medical Use and Health Hazards." In *Amphetamines: Use, Misuse and Abuse,* edited by D. Smith, 18–33. Boston: Hall, 1978.

Grob, C., R. Poland, L. Chang, and T. Ernst. "Psychobiological Effects of 3,4-Methylenedioxymethamphetamine in Humans: Methodological Considerations and Preliminary Observations." *Behavioral Brain Research* 73 (1996): 103–107.

Gurin, J. "Coffee and Health." *Consumer Reports* (October 1994): 650–651.

Hadlock G., K. Webb, L. McFadden, P. Chu, J. Ellis, S. Allen, D. Andrenyak, et al. "4-Methylmethcathinone (mephedrone): neuropharmacological effects of a designer stimulant of abuse." *Journal of Pharmacology and Experimental Therapeutics* 339 (2011): 530–536.

Hall, W., and J. Hando. "Illicit Amphetamine Use Is a Public Health Problem in Australia." *Medical Journal of Australia* 159 (1993): 643–644.

Hanson, G. R., K. Rau, and A. Fleckenstein. "The Methamphetamine Experience: A NIDA Partnership." *Neuropharmacology* 47 (2004): 92–100.

Harding, A. "Meth Use in Pregnancy Endangers Mom and Baby." Reuters Health. 29 July 2010. Available http://www.reuters.com/article/2010/07/29/us-meth-pregnancy-idUSTRE66S5M720100729

Hartney, E. "What to Expect from Caffeine Withdrawal." About.com Addictions. 20 January 2013. Available http://addictions.about.com/od/Caffeine/a/What-To-Expect-From-Caffeine-Withdrawal.htm

Hatsukami, D., and M. Fischman. "Crack Cocaine and Cocaine Hydrochloride." *Journal of the American Medical Association* 276 (1996): 1580–1588.

Hessert, A. "The New Performance Enhancing Drugs." *Neuroanthropology*. 4 June 2009. Available http://neuroanthropology.net/2009/06/04/the-new-performance-enhancing-drugs

Hitti, M. "Caffeine Abuse: Buzz Gone Wrong." WebMD. 16 October 2006. Available http://www.webmd.com/content/article/128/117124

Hoffman, B., and R. Lefkowitz. "Catecholamines, Sympathomimetic Drugs, and Adrenergic Receptor Antagonists." In *The Pharmacological Basis of Therapeutics*, 9th ed., edited by J. Hardman and L. Limbird, 199–248. New York: McGraw-Hill, 1995.

Holt, L. "Former Meth Addicts Jenny Madonecky and Faye Benner Speak About Crystal Meth Addiction." *Saturday Today Show*, NBC (8 October 2005).

Huus, K. "Crystal Cartels Alter Face of U.S. Meth Epidemic." MSN.com. 2007. Available http://www.msnbc.msn.com/id/14817871

Jansen, K. "Ecstasy (MDMA)." *Drug and Alcohol Dependence* 53 (1999): 121–124.

Johnston, L. "Monitoring the Future 2009." 2010. Available http://monitoringthefuture.org/data/09data/pr09t3.pdf

Johnston, L. "Monitoring the Future 2012." 2013. Available http://monitoringthefuture.org/pubs/monographs/mtf-overview2012.pdf

Join Together. "Study Says More Seeking Meth Treatment." 6 March 2006. Available http://www.drugfree.org/join-together/addiction/study-says-more-seeking-meth

Journal of the American Medical Association. "Ecstasy Overdoses at a New Year's Eve Rave—Los Angeles, California, 2010." 304 (2010): 629–632.

Juozapavicius, J. "New Meth Formula Avoids Anti-Drug Laws." ABC News (U.S.). 24 August 2009. Available http://www.standard.net/authors/justin-juozapavicius

Just the Facts. "Coca Cultivation and Counter-Drug Efforts in the Andean Region." 2 March 2010. Available http://justf.org/blog/2010/03/02/coca-cultivation-and-counter-drug-efforts-andean-region

Kaye, S., S. Darke, and J. Duflou. "Methylenedioxymethamphetamine (MDMA)-Related Fatalities in Australia: Demographics, Circumstances, Toxicology and Major Organ Pathology." *Drug and Alcohol Dependence* 104 (2009): 254–261.

Keenan, B. "Adderall Is 'Secret Miracle' for Illegal Use." The Breeze. 22 April 2010. Available http://www.breezejmu.org/article_8d88baa4-757c-554f-9d36-9e48c47fb35a.html

Keybol. "How to Make Shake and Bake Meth." Keybol.org. Accessed October 3, 2013. Available http://www.keybol.org/2009/08/how-to-make-shake-and-bake-meth.html

Kesmodel, D. "FDA Bans Mixing Caffeine, Alcohol." *Wall Street Journal.* 18 November 2010. Available http://online.wsj.com/article/SB10001424052748704648604575620673854960904.html

Kihlman, B. *Caffeine and Chromosomes.* Amsterdam: Elsevier, 1977.

King, L. A., and J. M. Corkery. "An Index of Fatal Toxicity for Drugs of Misuse." *Human Psychopharmacology* 25 (2010): 162–166.

Kinkead, L., and D. Romboy. "Meth Emergency." *Deseret Morning News* 153 (14 November 2004): A1, A15–A17.

Kirkwood, C., and S. Melton. "Insomnia, Drowsiness and Fatigue." In *Handbook of Nonprescription Drugs*, edited by D. Krinsky, 867–883. Washington, DC: American Pharmacists Association, 2012.

Kish, S., J. Lerch, Y. Furukawa, J. Tong, T. McCluskey, and D. Wilkins. "Decreased Cerebral Cortical Serotonin Transporter Binding in Ecstasy Users: A Positron Emission Tomography/[11-C]DASB and Structural Brain Imaging Study." *Brain* 133 (2010): 1779–1797.

Kloner, R., and S. Rezkalla. "Cocaine and the Heart." *New England Journal of Medicine* 348 (2003): 487–488.

Klouda, N., and S. Pearson. "Crimes Rise with Meth Addiction." *Homer Tribune.* 28 July 2010. Available http://homertribune.com/2010/07/crimes-rise-with-meth-addiction

Kluger, J. "The Buzz on Caffeine." *Time* (20 December 2004): 62.

Krasnova, N., and J. Cadet. "Methamphetamine Toxicity and Messengers of Death." *Brain Research Reviews* 60 (2009): 379–407.

Kronstadt, D. "Complex Developmental Issues of Prenatal Drug Exposure." Future of Children. Updated November 2013. Available http://futureofchildren.org/publications/journals/article/index.xml?journalid=69&articleid=499jouralid

Kuehn, B. "Brain Scans, Genes Provide Addiction Clues." *Journal of the American Medical Association* 297 (2007): 1419–1421.

Ladd, G., and N. Petry. "Antisocial Personality in Treatment-Seeking Cocaine Abusers: Psychosocial Functioning and HIV Risk." *Journal of Substance Abuse Treatment* 24 (2003): 323–330.

Leard-Hansson, J. "Cocaine-Induced Psychosis and Schizophrenia." *Clinical Psychiatry News.* February 2006. Available http://www.questia.com/library/1G1-149202577/cocaine-induced-psychosis-and-schizophrenia

Legal Herbal Drugs. Available http://legalherbaldrugs.net/

Leinwand, D. "Feds Score Against Homegrown Meth." *USA Today* (2 July 2007): A3.

Luscher, C. "Drugs of Abuse." In *Basic & Clinical Pharmacology*, 12th ed. edited by B. Katzung, S. Masters and A. Trevor, 565–580. New York: McGraw Hill Medical, 2012.

Lyles, J., and J. Cadet. "MDMA Neurotoxicity: Cellular and Molecular Mechanisms." *Brain Research Review* 42 (2003): 155–168.

March of Dimes. "Illicit Drug Use During Pregnancy." July 2003. Available http://www.marchofdimes.com/professionals/14332_1169.asp

Markou, A., and P. Kenny. "Neuroadaptations to Chronic Exposure to Drugs of Abuse: Relevance to Depression Symptomology Even Across Psychiatric Diagnostic Categories." *Neurotoxicology Research* 4 (2002): 297–313.

Mayo Clinic. "Cocaine (Topical Route)." 15 December 2010a. Available http://www.mayoclinic.com/health/drug-information/DR600467

Mayo Clinic. "Ephedra (Ephedra Sinica)/Ma Huang." 2010b. Available http://www.mayoclinic.com/health/ephedra/NS_patient-ephedra

McCaffrey, B. "Methamphetamine." ONDCP, Drug Policy Information Clearinghouse. NCJ-1756677 (May 1999): 1–3.

McManis, S. "For Former Meth Users, 'Give It a Year.'" *Sacramento Bee.* 23 August 2009. Available http://www.facesandvoicesofrecovery.org/resources/in_the_news/2009/2009-08-23_former_meth.php

MedicineNet. "Caffeine." 2010. Available http://www.medicinenet.com/caffeine/article.htm

MedlinePlus. "Cocaine Withdrawal." U.S. National Library of Medicine. 2007. Available http://vsearch.nlm.nih.gov/vivisimo/cgi-bin/query-meta?v%3Aproject=medlineplus&query=cocaine+withdrawal+

MedlinePlus. "Cocaine Withdrawal." 15 November 2010. Available http://www.nlm.nih.gov/medlineplus/ency/article/000947.htm

Mendelson, J., and N. Mello. "Management of Cocaine Abuse and Dependence." *New England Journal of Medicine* 334 (1996): 965–972.

Miller, H., and D. Longtin. "Death By Dietary Supplement." Forbes.com. 2010. Available http://www.forbes.com/2010/03/23/dietary-supplemetns-herbal-fda-opinions-contributors-henry-i-miller-david-longtin.html

Montgomery, C., N. P. Hatton, J. E. Fisk, R. S. Ogden, and A. Jansari. "Assessing the Functional Significance of Ecstasy-Related Memory Deficits Using a Virtual Paradigm." *Human Psychopharmacology* 25 (2010): 318–325.

Musto, D. "International Traffic in Coca Through the Early 20th Century." *Drug and Alcohol Dependence* 49 (1998): 145–156.

Narconon. "Does Cocaine Have Withdrawal Symptoms?" Narconon (2013a). Available http://www.narconon.org/drug-rehab/does-cocaine-have-withdrawal-symptoms.html

Narconon. "Does Caffeine Have Withdrawal Symptoms?" Narconon (2013b). Available http://www.narconon.org/drug-rehab/does-caffeine-have-withdrawal-symptom.html

Nathan, K., W. Bresnick, and S. Battei. "Cocaine Abuse and Dependence." *CNS Drugs* 10 (1998): 43–59.

National Institute on Drug Abuse (NIDA). "Diagnosis and Treatment of Drug Abuse in Family Practice." May 2000. Available http://www.nida.nih.gov/Diagnosis-Treatment/Diagnosis.html

National Institute on Drug Abuse (NIDA). "Methamphetamine Abuse and Addiction." 2006. Available http://www.nida.nih.gov/researchreports/methamph/Methamph.html

National Institute on Drug Abuse (NIDA). "DrugFacts: Cocaine." 2007a. Available http://www.nida.nih.gov/infofacts/cocaine.html

National Institute on Drug Abuse (NIDA). "NIDA Info-Facts: MDMA (Ecstasy)." 2007b. Available http://www.nida.nih.gov/infofacts/ecstasy.html

National Institute on Drug Abuse (NIDA). "DrugFacts: Stimulant ADHD Medications—Methylphenidate and Amphetamines." 2009. Available http://www.drugabuse.gov/Infofacts/ADHD.html

National Institute on Drug Abuse (NIDA). "Cocaine: Abuse and Addiction." September 2010a. Available http://www.drugabuse.gov/publications/research-reports/cocaine-abuse-addiction/what-treatments

National Institute on Drug Abuse (NIDA). "Methamphetamine: Abuse and Addiction." NIDA Research Report Series. 13 November 2010b. Available http://drugabuse.gov/researchreports/methamph/methamph3.html

National Institute on Drug Abuse (NIDA). "DrugFacts: Cocaine." March 2010c. Available http://drugabuse.gov/infofacts/cocaine.html

National Institute on Drug Abuse. "Topics in Brief: Methamphetamine Addiction: Progress, But Need to Remain Vigilant." November 2011. Available http://www.drugabuse.gov/publications/topics-in-brief/methamphetamine-addiction-progress-need-to-remain-vigilant

National Institute on Drug Abuse (NIDA). "DrugFacts: MDMA (Ecstasy or Molly)." March 2013a. Available http://drugabuse.gov/infofacts/ecstasy.html

National Institute on Drug Abuse (NIDA). "Synthetic Cathinones ('Bath Salts')." 20 February 2013b. Available http://www.drugabuse.gov/publications/drugfacts/synthetic-cathinones-bath-salts

National Institute on Drug Abuse (NIDA). "Cocaine: Abuse and Addicting." April 8, 2013c. Available http://www.drugabuse.gov/publications/research-reports/cocaine-abuse-addiction

National Institute on Drug Abuse (NIDA), Community Epidemiology Work Group (NIDA CEWG). "Proceedings of the Epidemiology Work Group on Drug Abuse." January 2007. Available http://www.drugabuse.gov/about/organization/cewg/Reports.html

Nawrot, P., S. Jordan, J. Eastwood, J. Rotstein, A. Hugenholtz, and M. Feeley. "Effects of Caffeine on Human Health." *Food Additives and Contaminants* 20 (2003): 1–30.

Newswise. "Researchers See Trends in Synthetic Stimulant Misuse." 27 March 2007. Available http://www.newswise.com/articles/view/528426/?sc=mwtn

Nuckols, C., and J. Kane. "Methamphetamine Addiction: 'Speed' Still Kills." *Counselor* 4 (2003): 14–18.

O'Brien, M., and J. Anthony. "Extra-medical Stimulant Dependence Among Recent Initiates." *Drug and Alcohol Dependence* 104 (2009): 147–155.

Office of National Drug Control Policy (ONDCP). "Cocaine." ONDCP Drug Policy Information Clearinghouse. 2003. Available http://www.whitehousedrugpolicy.gov/drugfact/cocaine/index.html

Office of National Drug Control Policy (ONDCP). Synthetic Drug Control Strategy. June 2006. Available http://dhs.alabama.gov/pdf/info/synthetic_strategy.pdf

Office of National Drug Control Policy (ONDCP). "Street Terms: Drugs and the Drug Trade." November 2010. Available http://www.whitehousedrugpolicy.gov/streetterms/ByType.asp?intTypeID=24

Ordonez, F. "Mexican Gangs Provide Most U.S. 'Meth.'" McClatchy Newspapers. 29 April 2008. Available http://www.mcclatchydc.com/2008/04/29/35281/mexican-gangs-provide-most-us.html

Oremus, W. "The New Stimulus Package." Slate. 27 March 2013. Available http://www.slate.com/articles/technology/superman/2013/03/adderall_ritalin_vyvanse_do_smart_pills_work_if_you_don_t_have_adhd.html

Painter, K. "Good News, Coffee Lovers." *USA Today* (6 November 2006): 4D.

Parker-Pope, T. "Energy Drinks Linked to Risky Behavior Among Teenagers." *New York Times* (27 May 2008a). Available http://www.nytimes.com/2008/05/27/health/27iht-27well.13247828.html

Parker-Pope, T. "New Teen Health Worry: Energy in a Can." *New York Times* (26 May 2008b). Available http://well.blogs.nytimes.com/2008/05/27/new-teen-health-worry-energy-in-a-can

PBS Newshour. "Cocaine: How 'Miracle Drug' Nearly Destroyed Sigmund Freund, William Halsted." 17 October 2011. Available http://www.pbs.org/newshour/bb/health/july-dec11/addiction_10-17.html

Pennings, E., A. Leccese, and F. Wolff. "Effects of Concurrent Use of Alcohol and Cocaine." *Addiction* 97 (2002): 773–783.

Platt, D., J. Rowlett, and R. Spealman. "Behavioral Effects of Cocaine and Dopaminergic Strategies for Preclinical Medication Development." *Psychopharmacology* 163 (2002): 265–282.

Polanczyk, G., and L. Rohde. "Epidemiology of Attention-Deficit/Hyperactivity Disorder Across the Lifespan." *Current Opinions of Psychiatry* 20 (2007): 386–392.

Pruthi, S. "Does Caffeine Cause Breast Cysts?" Mayo Clinic. 2010. Available http://www.mayoclinic.com/health/breast-cysts/AN00889

Randall, T. "Ecstasy-Fueled 'Rave' Parties Become Dances of Death for English Youths." *Journal of the American Medical Association* 268 (1992a): 1505–1506.

Randall, T. "'Rave' Scene, Ecstasy Use, Leap Atlantic." *Journal of the American Medical Association* 268 (1992b): 1506.

Randolph, T. "Hazelden Study Suggests Drop in Meth Use." Minnesota Public Radio. 19 June 2007. Available http://minnesota.publicradio.org/display/web/2007/06/19/methdecline/?dssource=1

Raskin, A. "Study Suggests Antidepressant May Help Treat Meth Addiction." *Los Angeles Times.* 23 November 2005. Available http://articles.latimes.com/2005/nov/23/science/sci-meth23

Rauscher, M. "Methamphetamine Hard on the Teeth." Reuters Health. 5 October 2006. Available http://www.medicineonline.com/news/12/6307/methamphetamine-hard-on-the-teeth.html

Rich, T., and M. Jordan. "Mother's Little Helper—The History of Amphetamine and Antidepressant Use in America." Wellcorps. 13 November 2010. Available http://www.wellcorps.com/Mothers-Little-Helper-The-History-of-Amphetamine-and-Anti-Depressant-Use-in-America.html

Ricker, R., and V. Nicolino. "Adderall: The Most Abused Prescription Drug in America." Huffington Post. 21 June 2010. Available http://www.huffingtonpost.com/dr-ronald-ricker-and-dr-venus-nicolino/adderall-the-most-abused_b_619549.html

Rowan-Szal, G., G. Joe, W. Simpson, J. Greener, and J. Vance. "During-Treatment Outcomes Among Female Methamphetamine-Using Offenders in Prison-Based Treatments." *Journal of Offender Rehabilitation* 48 (2009) 388–401.

Rutledge, J. "Counties Call Meth Top Drug Problem." *Washington Times.* 19 July 2006. Available http://www.highbeam.com/doc/1G1-148374058.html

Salter, J. "Tennessee Overtakes Missouri in Meth Lab Seizures Numbers." *Southeast Missourian.* 2 March 2011. Available http://www.semissourian.com/story/1707095.html

Savage, C., and M. Gordon. "U.S. Delays Release of Report Tying Meth to Mexico." *New York Times.* 8 June 2010. Available http://www.nytimes.com/2010/06/09/world/americas/09mexico.html

Sawynok, J., and T. Yaksh. "Caffeine as an Analgesic Adjuvant: A Review of Pharmacology and Mechanisms of Action." *Pharmacological Reviews* 45 (1993): 43–85.

Schifano, F., J. Corkery, V. Naidoo, A. Oyefeso, and H. Ghodse. "Overview of Amphetamine-Type Stimulant Mortality Data—UK, 1997–2007." *Neuropsychobiology* 61 (2010): 122–130.

Schifano, F., L. Furia, G. Forza, N. Minicuci, and R. Bricolo. "MDMA ('Ecstasy') Consumption in the Context of Polydrug Abuse: A Report on 50 Patients." *Drug and Alcohol Dependence* 52 (1998): 85–90.

Science Daily. "Brain Functions That Can Prevent Relapse Improve After a Year of Methamphetamine Abstinence." 29 June 2009. Available http://www.sciencedaily.com/releases/2009/06/090629165114.htm

Science Daily. "Brain Abnormalities Identified That Result from Prenatal Methamphetamine Exposure." 17 March 2010a. Available http://www.sciencedaily.com/releases/2010/03/100316174208.htm

Science Daily. "Crack and Cocaine Use a Significant HIV Risk Factor for Teens." 1 April 2010b. Available http://www.sciencedaily.com/releases/2010/03/100331141006.htm

Sederer, L. "Paying the Piper: Brain 'Neuroenhancers.'" Huffington Post. 1 June 2010. Available http://www.huffingtonpost.com/lloyd-i-sederer-md/paying-the-piper-brain-ne_b_209702.html

Shetty, V., L. Moohey, C. Zigler, T. Belin, D. Murphy, and R. Rawson. "The Relationship Between Methamphetamine Use and Increased Dental Disease." *Journal of the American Dental Association* 141 (2010): 307–309.

Shipley, A. "Bechler's Diet Pills Draw Scrutiny." *Washington Post* (19 February 2003): D-1.

Shute, N. "Americans Young and Old Crave High-Octane Fuel, and Doctors Are Jittery." *U.S. News and World Report* (29 April 2007): 58–68.

Singer, L., S. Minnes, E. Short, R. Arendt, K. Farkas, and B. Lewis. "Cognitive Outcomes of Preschool Children with Prenatal Cocaine Exposure." *Journal of the American Medical Association* 291 (2004): 2448–2456.

Smith, P. "Plan Colombia: Ten Years Later." StoptheDrugWar.org. 15 July 2010. Available http://stopthedrugwar.org/chronicle/2010/jul/15/plan_colombia_ten_years_later

Snider, G. "I Thought This Was My Destiny." AskNinaNow.com. 2007. Available http://www.askninanow.com/destiny.htm

Sofuoglu, M., S. Dudish-Poulsen, S. Brown, and D. Hatsukami. "Association of Cocaine Withdrawal Symptoms with More Severe Dependence and Enhanced Subjective Response to Cocaine." *Drug and Alcohol Dependence* 69 (2003): 273–282.

Sprague, J., A. Harrod, and A. Teconchuk. "The Pharmacology and Abuse Potential of Ephedrine." *Pharmacy Times* (May 1998): 72–80.

Stocker, S. "Cocaine Activates Different Brain Regions for Rush Versus Craving." *NIDA Notes* 13 (1999): 7–10.

Substance Abuse and Mental Health Services Administration (SAMHSA). "Medical Aspects of Stimulant Use Disorders." SAMHSA/CSAT Treatment Protocols. 2010. Available http://www.ncbi.nlm.nih.gov/books/NBK26312

Swan, N. "31% of New York Murder Victims Had Cocaine in Their Bodies." *NIDA Notes* 10 (March/April 1995): 4.

Tancer, M., and C. Johanson. "The Effects of Fluoxetine on the Subjective and Physiological Effects of 3,4-Methylenedioxymethamphetamine (MDMA) in Humans." *Psychopharmacology (Berlin)* 189 (2007): 565–573.

The Body. "Crystal Methamphetamine and HIV/AIDS: News and Research." The Body, The Complete HIV/AIDS Resource. November 2010. Available http://www.thebody.com/index/whatis/crystal_meth_news.html

Thesaurus.com. "Freebase." 2010. Available http://thesaurus.com/browse/freebase

Today Health. "Teen Girl Dies of 'Caffeine Toxicity' After Downing 2 Energy Drinks." 21 March 2012. Available http://todayhealth.today.msnbc.msn.com/_news/2012/03/21/10780958-teen-girl-dies-of-caffeine-toxicity-after-downing-2-energy-drinks

Transitions Recovery Program. "Methamphetamine." 2007. Available http://www.drug-rehabcenter.com/methamphetamine.htm

Tuckman, J. "Mexico's Drug Wars: The End of an Exceptionally Bloody Week." Guardian.co.uk. 29 October 2010. Available http://www.guardian.co.uk/world/2010/oct/29/mexico-drug-wars-bloody-week

Turillazzi, E., I. Riezzo, M. Neri, S. Bello, and V. Fineschi. "MDMA Toxicity and Pathological Consequences: A Review About Experimental Data and Autopsy Findings." *Current Pharmaceutical Biotechnology* 11 (2010): 500–509.

Tye, K., L. Tye, J. Cone, E. Hekkelman, P. Janak, and A. Bonci. "Methylphenidate Facilitates Learning-Induced Amygdala Plasticity." *Nature Neuroscience* 13 (2009): 475–481.

United Nations Office on Drugs and Crime. *World Drug Report 2009.* Vienna: United Nations Office on Drugs and Crime, 2009.

University of Florida. "Prenatal Cocaine Exposure Not Linked to Bad Behavior in Kids. University of Florida News. 1 May 2006. Available http://news.ufl.edu/2006/05/01/crack-babies/

U.S. Department of Justice. "Children at Risk." Information Bulletin (July 2002). Product No. 2002-L0424-001.

U.S. Department of Justice. "Methamphetamine." National Drug Threat Assessment (April 2003a). Product No. 2003-Q0317-001: 13–25.

U.S. Department of Justice. "National Drug Threat Assessment 2003." National Drug Intelligence Center (January 2003b). Product No. 2003-Q0317-001: 51–58.

U.S. Department of Justice. "National Methamphetamine Threat Assessment 2010." National Drug Intelligence Center. 2010. Product No. 2010-Q0317-004.

U.S. News and World Report. "Signs of Caffeine Addicton." (17 April 2012). Available http://health.usnews.com/health-news/articles/2012/04/17/signs-of-caffeine-addiction

Van Dyck, C., and R. Byck. "Cocaine." *Scientific American* 246 (1982): 128–141.

Vidaeff, A., and J. Mastrobattista. "In Utero Cocaine Exposure: A Thorny Mix of Science and Mythology." *American Journal of Perinatology* 20 (2003): 165–172.

Volkow, N., L. Chang, G. Wong, J. Fowler, and D. Francesch. "Loss of Dopamine Transporters in Methamphetamine Abusers Recovers with Protracted Abstinence." *Journal of Neuroscience* 21 (2001): 9414–9418.

Volkow, N., and J. Swanson. "Does Childhood Treatment of ADHD with Stimulant Medication Affect Substance Abuse in Adulthood?" *American Journal of Psychiatry* 165 (2008): 553–555.

Voxxi. "Cocaine Trafficking Increased Dramatically In the Dominican Republic." VOXXI. Available http://www.voxxi.com/cocaine-trafficking-increased-caribbean/

Wang, G., N. Volkow, P. Thanos, and J. Fowler. "Similarity Between Obesity and Drug Addiction As Assessed by Neurofunctional Imaging: A Concept Review." *Journal of Addiction Disease* 23 (2004): 39–53.

Washington Times. "Yet Another Warning Against Ephedra." (5 February 2003): A-5.

Weiner, T. "9 Linked to Drug War Found Slain Outside Mexican Border City." *New York Times* (3 April 2003): A-5.

Wheeler, R. "Hooked on Caffeine?" Everyday Health. 2010. Available http://www.everydayhealth.com/addiction/hooked-on-caffeine.aspx

Wilkinson, J. "Headache." In *Handbook of Nonprescription Drugs,* edited by D. Krinsky, 67–86. Washington, DC: American Pharmacists Association, 2012.

Winkel, B. "Real Crack Babies." Treatment Solutions Network, Connections for Recovery. 25 October 2010. Available http://www.treatmentsolutionsnetwork.com/blog/index.php/2010/10/25/real-crack-babies

Woolverton, W., and K. Johnston. "Neurobiology of Cocaine Abuse." *Trends in Pharmacological Sciences* 13 (1992): 193–200.

Wyatt, B. "Agassi Admits Using Crystal Meth." CNN.com. 28 October 2009. Available http://www.cnn.com/2009/SPORT/10/28/tennis.agassi.crystal.meth/index.html

Yui, K., K. Goto, S. Ikemoto, and T. Ishiguro. "Methamphetamine Psychosis: Spontaneous Recurrence of Paranoid-Hallucinating States and Monoamine Neurotransmitter Function." *Journal of Clinical Psychopharmacology* 17 (1997): 34–43.

Zhang, W. "A Benefit–Risk Assessment of Caffeine as an Analgesic Adjuvant." *Drug Safety* 24 (2001): 1127–1142.

Zickler, P. "Methamphetamine, Cocaine Abusers Have Different Patterns of Drug Use, Suffer Different Cognitive Impairments." *NIDA Notes* 16 (December 2001): 11.

© Kondrachov Vladimir/Shutterstock, Inc.

CHAPTER 11

Tobacco

Did You Know?

▶ Approximately 26.5% of the U.S. population age 12 or older reports current (past-month) use of a tobacco product.

▶ Tobacco use is the leading preventable cause of death in the United States.

▶ Tobacco kills approximately 443,000 U.S. citizens each year.

▶ Nicotine is one of thousands of chemicals found in cigarette smoke.

▶ Approximately 3800 young people in the United States will begin smoking today.

▶ Several smoking cessation aids are available, including nicotine gum, patches, nasal sprays, and inhalers. In addition, newer prescription drugs are now used to help with smoking cessation.

Learning Objectives

On completing this chapter you will be able to:

❯ Describe the social and economic costs of smoking in the United States.

❯ Describe the history of tobacco use.

❯ Explain how the quality of leaf tobacco has changed since the mid-1950s.

❯ Describe the pharmacological effects of nicotine.

❯ List several disease states caused by cigarette smoking.

❯ Explain the consequences of environmental tobacco smoke on nonsmokers.

❯ List several reasons individuals smoke.

❯ List several strategies that aid in smoking cessation.

Drugs and Society Online is a great source for additional drugs and society information for both students and instructors. Visit **go.jblearning.com /hanson12** to find a variety of useful tools for learning, thinking, and teaching.

Tobacco Use: Scope of the Problem

#9

Tobacco use is the leading preventable cause of death in the United States, accounting for an estimated 443,000 deaths per year (Centers for Disease Control and Prevention [CDC] 2012c). Another 8.6 million have a serious illness caused by smoking (CDC 2011b). The impact of nicotine addiction in terms of morbidity, mortality, and economic costs to society is staggering. Tobacco use results in an annual cost of $96 billion in medical expenditures and another $97 billion from lost productivity (CDC 2011b). These high costs will likely continue and increase in the future because it is estimated that each day, approximately 3800 people younger than age 18 start smoking, and an estimated 1000 become daily smokers (CDC 2012f).

Although much of this chapter deals with tobacco use in the United States, it is noteworthy that tobacco is used throughout the world and that markets for tobacco sales abroad have expanded in recent years. Tobacco is the single largest cause of preventable death (World Health Organization [WHO] 2013). The World Health Organization (WHO) estimates that tobacco use kills 6 million people each year, of whom 5 million are users or ex-users and more than 600,000 are nonusers exposed to secondhand smoke (WHO 2013).

Current Tobacco Use in the United States

In 2011, 68.2 million Americans, or 26.5% of the population age 12 or older, reported current use of a tobacco product. Among these individuals, 2.1 million smoked tobacco in pipes, 8.2 million used smokeless tobacco, 12.9 million smoked cigars, and 56.8 million smoked cigarettes (Substance Abuse and Mental Health Services Administration [SAMHSA] 2012). Approximately 32.3% of males and 21.1% of females age 12 or older were current users of any tobacco product (SAMHSA 2012).

Of note, rates of past-month tobacco use among 12- to 17-year-olds have declined over the past decade, including a decrease from 15.2% in 2002 to 10.0% in 2011. The rate of past-month cigarette use among 12- to 17-year-olds has also declined, from 13% in 2002 to 7.8% in 2011. However, past-month smokeless tobacco use among youth

The WHO estimates that tobacco kills six million people per year worldwide. Early exposure increases the chance that young people will become regular adult smokers.

remained steady (i.e., 2.0% in 2002 vs. 2.1% in 2011; SAMHSA 2012).

Decreased rates of smoking were not restricted to 12- to 17-year-olds. In fact, cigarette smoking rates have decreased among all adults except those ages 26–34 (see SAMHSA 2013 and references therein). Public policy efforts including cigarette warning labels and increased taxes (see the following discussions) have contributed to these trends.

Current cigarette smoking among individuals age 12 or older by U.S. region is as follows: approximately 24.2% of the population in the Midwest region, 23.2% in the South region, 18.1% in the West region, and 22.2% in the Northeast region. Level of educational attainment was also correlated with cigarette smoking: 33.7% of adults age 18 or older who did not complete high school smoked cigarettes, whereas only 11.7% of college graduates smoked (SAMHSA 2012).

More than 303 billion cigarettes were purchased in the United States in 2010, with three companies responsible for 85% of sales: Philip Morris (46.4%), Reynolds American, Inc. (25.5%), and Lorillard (12.3%; CDC 2012b).

Several investigators have suggested that tobacco can serve as a gateway drug. In other words, its use may lead to the use of other drugs. Although this possibility remains controversial, it is noteworthy that research indicates that cigarette smokers are more likely to use illicit drugs than are nonsmokers. For example, in 2011, among persons age 12 or older, 22.1% of past-month cigarette smokers reported concurrent use of an illicit drug, compared with 4.9% of persons who were not current cigarette smokers. Past-month alcohol use was reported by 66.5% of current cigarette smokers, compared with 47.6% of those who did not use cigarettes in the past month. The association also was found with heavy drinking (15.3% of smokers vs. 3.6% of nonsmokers) and binge drinking (42.5% of current cigarette users vs. 17.0% of current nonusers; SAMHSA 2012).

■ Cigarette Smoking: A Costly Addiction

The past 25 years have been marked by a steady decline in cigarette consumption. Still, an estimated 68.2 million Americans age 12 or older smoke cigarettes (SAMHSA 2012), even though this single behavior will result in death or disability for many of its users.

As noted earlier, tobacco use is responsible for approximately 443,000 deaths each year in the United States (CDC 2012c). This includes approximately 126,000 deaths from ischemic heart disease, 128,900 deaths from lung cancer, 35,300 deaths from other forms of cancer, 92,900 deaths from chronic pulmonary obstructive disease, 15,900 deaths from stroke, and approximately 44,000 deaths from other diagnoses (CDC 2011b) (see **Figure 11.1**). In fact, cigarette smoking is the leading preventable cause of death in the United States (CDC 2011b). More deaths are caused each year by tobacco use than by human immunodeficiency virus (HIV), illegal drug use, murders, alcohol use, suicides, and motor vehicle injuries combined (CDC 2012d).

Overall mortality rates decline the longer ex-smokers abstain from smoking. The mortality

rate for ex-smokers is related to the number of cigarettes they used to smoke per day and the age at which they started to smoke. People who stop smoking at approximately age 30 reduce their risk of dying from smoking-related diseases by more than 90%. Those who quit at approximately age 50 reduce their risk of dying prematurely by 50% (National Cancer Institute [NCI] 2011).

The History of Tobacco Use

Like alcohol, tobacco has a long history of use in the Americas and is indigenous to the United States. In fact, tobacco was one of the New World's contributions to the rest of humanity. The word *tobacco* may have come from *tabacco*, which was a two-pronged tube used by the natives of Central America to take snuff. Columbus reported receiving tobacco leaves from the natives of San Salvador in 1492. However, the native peoples had been smoking the leaves for many centuries before Columbus arrived. Practically all native people—from Paraguay to Quebec—used tobacco. The Mayans regarded tobacco smoke as divine incense that would bring rain in the dry season. The oldest known representation of a smoker is a stone carving from a Mayan temple, which shows a priest puffing on a ceremonial pipe. The Aztecs used tobacco in folk medicine and religious ritual.

Indeed, Native Americans used tobacco in every manner known: smoked as cigars and cigarettes (wrapped in corn husks) and in pipes; as a syrup to be swallowed or applied to the gums; chewed and snuffed; and administered rectally as a ceremonial enema (O'Brien et al. 1992; Schultes 1978).

In the 1600s, Turkey, Russia, and China all imposed death penalties for smoking. In Turkey, smoking was introduced in the 1600s, spread in popularity, and instantly created two camps. On the one hand, poets praised tobacco as one of four elements of the world of pleasure that also included opium, coffee, and wine. On the other hand, priests were violently opposed to this substance. They created the legend that tobacco grew from Mohammed's spittle after he was bitten by a viper, sucked out the venom, and spat.

Murad (Amurath) IV, known as Murad the Cruel, who reigned during 1623–1640, executed many of his subjects caught smoking.

Whenever the Sultan went on his travels or on a military expedition, his halting-places were

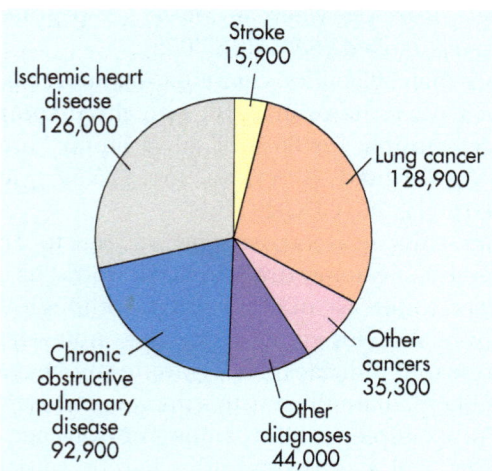

FIGURE 11.1 Annual deaths attributable to cigarette smoking, 2000–2004.

Reproduced from Centers for Disease Control and Prevention (CDC). "Tobacco Use: Targeting the Nation's Leading Killer: At a Glance 2011." Available http://www.cdc.gov/chronicdisease/resources/publications/aag/osh.htm. Accessed 10/31/2013 always distinguished by a terrible increase in the number of executions. Even on the battlefield, he was fond of surprising men in the act of smoking . . . he would punish them by beheading, hanging, quartering, or crushing their hands and feet and leaving them helpless between the lines. . . . Nevertheless, in spite of all the horrors of this lust [smoking] that seemed to increase with age, the passion for smoking still persisted. . . . Even the fear of death was of no avail with the passionate devotees of the habit. (Corti 1931)

The Romanov tsars publicly tortured smokers and exiled them to Siberia. The Chinese decapitated anyone caught dealing in tobacco with the "outer barbarians." Yet smoking continued to grow to epidemic proportions. Despite their opposition to anything foreign, the Chinese became the heaviest smokers in Asia, thus facilitating the later spread of opium smoking. Thus, no nation whose population has learned to use tobacco products has been successful in outlawing use or getting people to stop.

Snuffing first became fashionable in France during the reign of Louis XIII and spread throughout the European aristocracy. Snuffing was regarded as daintier and more elegant than constantly exhaling smoke. Louis XIV, however, detested all forms of tobacco and would not permit its use in his presence. (He would have banned it, but he needed the tax revenue that tobacco brought in.) His sister-in-law, Charlotte of Orleans, was one of the few at court who agreed with him. As she wrote to her sister, "It is better to take no snuff at all than a little; for it is certain that he who takes a little will soon take much, and that is why they call it 'the enchanted herb,' for those who take it are so taken by it that they cannot go without it." Napoleon is said to have used 7 pounds of snuff per month (Corti 1931).

■ Popularity in the Western World

When tobacco reached Europe, it was at first merely a curiosity, but its use spread rapidly. Europeans had no name for the process of inhaling smoke, so they called this "drinking" smoke. Perhaps the first European to inhale tobacco smoke was Rodrig de Jerez, a member of Columbus's crew. He had seen people smoking in Cuba and brought the habit to Portugal. When he smoked in Portugal, his friends, seeing smoke coming from his mouth, believed he was possessed by the devil.

As a result, he was placed in jail for several years (Heimann 1960; O'Brien et al. 1992).

In 1559, the French ambassador to Portugal, Jean Nicot, grew interested in this novel plant and sent one as a gift to Catherine de Medici, Queen of France. The plant was named *Nicotiana tabacum* after him.

The next several hundred years saw a remarkable increase in the use of tobacco. Portuguese sailors smoked it and left tobacco seeds scattered around the world. Over the next 150 years, the Portuguese introduced tobacco to trade with India, Brazil, Japan, China, Arabia, and Africa. Many large tobacco plantations around the world were started by the Portuguese at this time.

An early Christian religious leader, Bishop Bartolome de las Casas (1474–1566), reported that Spanish settlers in Hispaniola (Haiti) smoked rolled tobacco leaves in cigar form like the natives. When the bishop asked about this disgusting habit, the settlers replied that they found it impossible to give up.

As the use of tobacco spread, so did the controversy about whether it was bad or good. Tobacco use inspired the first major drug controversy of global dimensions. As a medicine, tobacco was at first almost universally accepted. Nicholas Monardes, in his description of New World plants (dated 1574), recommended tobacco as an infallible cure for 36 different maladies. It was described as a holy, healing herb—a special remedy sent by God to humans.

Opponents of tobacco use disputed its medical value. They pointed out that tobacco was used in the magic and religion of Native Americans. Tobacco was attacked as an evil plant, an invention of the devil. King James I of England was fanatically opposed to smoking. In an attempt to limit tobacco use, he raised the import tax on tobacco and also sold the right to collect the tax (Austin 1978; O'Brien et al. 1992).

Nevertheless, tobacco use increased. By 1614, the number of tobacco shops in London had mushroomed to more than 7000, and demand for tobacco usually outstripped supply. Tobacco was literally worth its weight in silver; to conserve it, users smoked it in pipes with very small bowls. Use of tobacco grew in other areas of the world as well.

In 1642, Pope Urban VIII issued a formal decree forbidding the use of tobacco in church under penalty of immediate excommunication. This decree was in response to the fact that priests and worshippers had been staining church floors with tobacco juice. One priest in Naples sneezed so hard after taking snuff that he vomited on the altar in full sight of the congregation. In response, Pope Innocent X issued another edict against tobacco use in 1650, but the clergy and the laity continued to take snuff and smoke. Finally, in 1725, Pope Benedict XIII, himself a smoker and "snuff-taker," annulled all previous edicts against tobacco (Austin 1978).

History of Tobacco Use in America

Tobacco played a significant role in the successful colonization of the United States (Langton 1991). In 1610, John Rolfe was sent to Virginia to set up a tobacco industry. At first, the tobacco planted in Virginia was a native species, *Nicotiana rustica*, that was harsh and did not sell well. But in 1612, Rolfe managed to obtain some seeds of the Spanish tobacco species *Nicotiana tabacum*, and by 1613, the success of the tobacco industry and the Virginia colony was ensured.

The history of tobacco smoking in the United States is rich in terms of the tremendous number of laws, rules, regulations, and customs that have arisen around the habit of smoking. Many states have had laws prohibiting the use of tobacco by young people as well as women of any age. In the 1860s, for instance, it was illegal in Florida for anyone younger than the age of 21 to smoke cigarettes. A 20-year-old caught smoking could be taken to court and compelled to reveal his source (the cigarette "pusher"). In Pennsylvania, as in South Carolina, any child not informing on his or her cigarette supplier was a criminal.

Use of spitoons (on the floor at the ends of a table) was considered a preferment in public conduct.

Cigars became popular in the United States in the early 1800s. Cigar manufacturers fought the introduction of cigarettes for many years. They spread rumors that cigarettes contained opium, were made with tobacco from discarded cigar butts, were made with paper made by Chinese lepers, and so on. By about 1920, however, cigarette consumption started to exceed that of cigars.

The introduction of the cigarette-rolling machine in 1883 spurred cigarette consumption because cigarettes became cheaper than cigars. In 2010, more than 303 billion cigarettes were purchased in the United States (CDC 2012b). Noteworthy, total cigarette consumption decreased between 2010 and 2011 by 2.5% (CDC 2012a).

Tobacco Production

Although there are more than 60 species of plants, *Nicotiana tabacum* is the primary species of tobacco cultivated in the United States. Its mature leaves are 1 to 2.5 feet long. The nicotine content ranges from 0.3% to 7%, depending on the variety, leaf position on the stalk (the higher the position, the more nicotine), and growing conditions.

After harvesting and drying, tobacco leaves are shredded, blown clean of foreign matter and stems, remoisturized with glycerine or other chemical agents, and packed in huge tobacco silos. The tobacco is stored for 1 to 2 years to age, during which time the tobacco becomes darker and loses moisture, nicotine, and other volatile substances. When aging has been completed, moisture is again added and the tobacco is blended with other varieties.

There are many types of tobacco, with varying characteristics of harshness, mildness, and flavor. Bright, also called flue-cured or Virginia, has traditionally been among the most common types used in cigarettes. (Flue-cured tobacco is cured with heat transmitted through a flue without exposure to smoke or fumes.) Developed just before the Civil War, this technique made tobacco smoke more readily inhalable.

The amount of leaf tobacco in a cigarette has declined since 1956. There are at least two reasons for this drop. The first reason is the use of reconstituted sheets of tobacco. Parts of the tobacco leaves and stems that were discarded in earlier years are now ground up, combined with many other ingredients to control factors such as moisture, flavor, and color, and then rolled out as a flat, homogenized sheet of reconstituted tobacco. This sheet is shredded and mixed with regular leaf tobacco, thus reducing production costs. Nearly one-fourth of the tobacco in a cigarette comes from tobacco scraps made into reconstituted sheets. (See "Here and Now: What Is in Tobacco Smoke?")

A second technological advance has further reduced the amount of tobacco needed. This process, called puffing, is based on freeze-drying the tobacco and then blowing air or an inert gas, such as carbon dioxide, into it. The gas expands, or puffs up, the plant cells so they take up more space, are lighter, and can absorb additives better. Additives may include extracts of tobacco, as well as nontobacco flavors such as licorice, cocoa, fruit, spices, and floral compositions. (Licorice was first used in tobacco as a preservative around 1830 and became appreciated only later as a sweetener.) Synthetic flavoring compounds also may be used.

In the 1870s, a "cigarette girl" could roll about four cigarettes per minute by hand. When James Duke leased and improved the first cigarette-rolling machine in 1883, he could make about 200 cigarettes per minute. This advance was the last link in the chain of development leading to the modern American blended cigarette. Today's machines make more than 3600 uniform cigarettes per minute.

Tar and nicotine levels in cigarettes have dropped considerably over the past years (Bartecchi, MacKenzie, and Shrier 1995; Palfai and Jankiewicz 1991). Most cigarettes today are low-tar and low-nicotine types. The filter tip, in which the filter is made of cellulose or in some cases charcoal, has also become common; the vast majority of all cigarettes sold currently in the United States have filter tips. The filter does help remove some of the harmful substances in smoke, but most, such as carbon monoxide, pass through into the mouth and lungs. The health consequences of many of the substances found in cigarettes have not been adequately analyzed.

■ Government Regulation

In the early 1960s, attitudes toward tobacco use began to change in the United States. Before this time, tobacco was perceived as being devoid of any negative consequences. After years of study and hundreds of research reports about the effects of smoking, the Advisory Committee to the U.S. Surgeon General reported in 1964 that cigarette smoking is a cause of lung cancer and laryngeal cancer in men, a probable cause of lung cancer in women, and the most important cause of chronic bronchitis. The committee stated, "cigarette smoking is a health hazard of sufficient importance in the United States to warrant appropriate remedial action." In 1965, Congress passed legislation setting up the National Clearinghouse for Smoking and Health. This organization had the responsibility of monitoring, compiling, and reviewing the world's medical literature on the health consequences of smoking.

This clearinghouse published reports in 1967, 1968, and 1969. The statistical evidence presented in 1969 made it difficult for Congress to avoid warning the public that smoking was dangerous to their health. Since November 1, 1970, all cigarette packages and cartons have had to carry this label: "Warning: The Surgeon General Has Determined That Cigarette Smoking Is Dangerous to Your Health." In 1984, Congress enacted legislation requiring cigarette advertisements and packages to post four distinct warnings, which were to be rotated every 3 months.

HERE AND NOW

What Is in Tobacco Smoke?

Tobacco smoke contains chemicals that are harmful to smokers and nonsmokers alike. Of the over 7000 chemicals in tobacco smoke, at least 250 are known to be harmful, including hydrogen cyanide, carbon monoxide, and ammonia. Among these 250 harmful chemicals, more than 69 have been found to be carcinogens. These carcinogens include arsenic, benzene, ethylene oxide, and vinyl chloride. Other suspected carcinogens in tobacco include formaldehyde, benzo[α]pyrene, and toluene.

Data from National Cancer Institute (NCI). "Harms of Smoking and Health Benefits of Quitting." 2011. Available http://www.cancer.gov/cancertopics/factsheet /Tobacco/cessation

Further pressure on Congress prompted laws to be passed that prohibited advertising tobacco on radio and television after January 2, 1971. The intent was to limit the media's ability to make smoking seem glamorous and sophisticated. The loss in revenue to radio and television was enormous.

The 1979 publication *Smoking and Health: A Report of the Surgeon General* gave what was then up-to-date information on research about the effects of tobacco on cardiovascular disease, bronchopulmonary disease, cancer, peptic ulcer, and pregnancy. It also emphasized the increase in smoking by women and girls over the preceding 15 years. The 1981 U.S. Surgeon General's report, *The Changing Cigarette*, gave further information, and the 1985 report, *The Health Consequences of Smoking*, gave research findings showing the relationship among smoking in the workplace, cancer, and chronic lung disease.

Over the years, private insurance companies, as well as state and federal agencies, have paid billions of dollars to cover healthcare costs presumably resulting from diseases caused by tobacco use. A series of lawsuits has forced large tobacco companies to compensate for some of these losses. In a landmark settlement in 1998, 47 states reached an agreement with five major tobacco companies to pay a settlement estimated at exceeding $200 billion. Important features of this "Master Settlement Agreement" include (U.S. Department of Agriculture [USDA] 2001):

- Limitations on advertising
- Ban on cartoon characters in advertising
- Ban on "branded" merchandise
- Limitations on sponsorship of sporting events
- Disbanding of tobacco trade organizations
- Funds designated to support antismoking measures and research to reduce youth smoking

All 50 states have enacted laws that restrict the purchase, possession, and/or use of tobacco products by minors. Although no state has completely banned the sale of tobacco products through vending machines, none allow such sales to minors. In fact, many states have created additional restrictions intended to reduce youth access to vending machines. Some have banned the placement of vending machines in areas accessible to young people and allow their placement only in bars, liquor stores, adult clubs, and other adult-oriented establishments.

Since 1985, numerous other reports on smoking and health by the U.S. Surgeon General have been issued; they invariably repeat the assertions about the devastating effects of cigarette smoking.

In June 2009, President Barack Obama signed legislation that granted the Food and Drug Administration (FDA) the authority to regulate tobacco products. This law, the Family Smoking Prevention and Tobacco Control Act (Tobacco Control Act), put special emphasis on youth because research indicates that most tobacco users become addicted at a young age and when they are too young to understand the risks (FDA 2013d).

The Tobacco Control Act gave the FDA broad authority over tobacco products, including the authority to regulate the manufacture, distribution, and marketing of tobacco products. It restricts smokeless tobacco and cigarette retail sales to youth, requiring proof of age (i.e., older than 18 years) to purchase these tobacco products. Face-to-face sales are also required, with certain exemptions for vending machines in facilities that are available to adults only.

The Tobacco Control Act required bigger, more prominent warning labels for cigarettes and smokeless tobacco products (FDA 2013b). Later, in June 2011, the FDA published a final rule requiring color graphics depicting the negative health consequences of smoking, along with nine new textual warning statements. The final rule was challenged in court by several tobacco companies. In August 2012, the U.S. Court of Appeals for the District of Columbia circuit vacated the rule. The court later denied the government's petition for panel for a rehearing. In a March 2013 statement, the FDA indicated that it will "undertake research to support a new rulemaking consistent with the Tobacco Control Act" (Almasy 2013; FDA 2013c).

Pharmacology of Nicotine

In 1828, **nicotine** was discovered to be one component of tobacco. This alkaloid is one of more than 7000 chemicals found in the smoke from tobacco products such as cigarettes (National Institute on Drug Abuse [NIDA] 2012). When smoked, nicotine enters the lungs and is then absorbed into the

KEY TERM

nicotine
an alkaloid derived from the tobacco plant

bloodstream. When chewed (**tobacco chewing**) or dipped (**snuff dipping**), nicotine is absorbed through the mucous lining of the mouth.

The amount of nicotine absorbed into the body varies according to several factors:

- The exact composition of the tobacco used
- How densely the tobacco is packed in the cigarette and the length of the cigarette smoked
- Whether a filter is used and the characteristics of the filter
- The volume of smoke inhaled
- The number of cigarettes smoked throughout the day

Depending on how tobacco is taken, the rate at which it enters the bloodstream varies widely. Cigarette smoking results in rapid distribution of nicotine throughout the body; it reaches the brain within 10 seconds of inhalation. A typical smoker will take 10 puffs on a cigarette during the 5 minutes that the cigarette is lit. Thus, a person who smokes 1½ packs (30 cigarettes) each day gets 300 "hits" of nicotine to the brain each day (NIDA 2012). In contrast, cigar and pipe smokers typically do not inhale the smoke; nicotine is absorbed more slowly through the lining of the mouth.

■ Effects of Nicotine on the Central Nervous System

Nicotine produces an intense effect on the central nervous system. Research has demonstrated that nicotine activates the brain circuitry in regions responsible for regulating feelings of pleasure. In particular, nicotine increases the release of the neurotransmitter dopamine in the so-called reward or pleasure pathways of the brain. This effect likely contributes to the abuse potential of the stimulant.

The pharmacokinetic properties of nicotine also enhance its abuse potential. Cigarette smoking allows nicotine to enter the brain rapidly, with drug levels peaking within 10 seconds of inhalation. The acute effects of this rapid increase in brain concentration dissipate within a few minutes, causing the smoker to continue to dose frequently throughout the day in an effort to maintain the pleasurable effects of the drug.

■ Other Effects of Nicotine

In addition to its direct effects in the brain, nicotine increases the respiration rate at low dose levels because it stimulates the receptors in the carotid artery (in the neck) that monitor the brain's need for oxygen. It also stimulates the cardiovascular system by releasing epinephrine, which increases coronary blood flow, heart rate, and blood pressure. The effect is to raise the oxygen requirements of the heart muscle. Initially, nicotine stimulates salivary and bronchial secretions; it then inhibits them.

Nicotine has been used as an insecticide, and at higher concentrations it can be extremely toxic. Symptoms of nicotine poisoning include sweating, vomiting, mental confusion, diarrhea, and breathing difficulty. Respiratory failure from the paralysis of muscles usually brings on death. The fatal dose for adults is 60 milligrams. The average smoker takes in 1 to 2 milligrams of nicotine from every cigarette (NIDA 2012). It is virtually impossible to overdose, in part because a smoker feels the effects before any lethal amount can accumulate in the body (Schelling 1992).

Cigarette Smoking

Cigarette smokers not only tend to die at an earlier age than nonsmokers, but also have a higher probability of developing certain diseases, including cardiovascular disease, cancer, bronchopulmonary disease, and other illnesses, which are described in the following sections.

■ Cardiovascular Disease

Overwhelming evidence shows that cigarette smoking increases the risk of cardiovascular disease. Smoking causes coronary heart disease, the leading cause of death in the United States. In fact, compared with nonsmokers, smoking increases the risk of coronary heart disease two to four times. Cigarette smoking also causes aneurysm (a swelling and/or weakening) of the abdominal aorta (a major artery in the body). Smoking also causes reduced circulation, thus putting smokers

KEY TERMS

tobacco chewing
the absorption of nicotine through the mucous lining of the mouth

snuff dipping
placing a pinch of tobacco between the gums and the cheek

at greater risk for developing peripheral vascular disease (CDC 2012d).

■ Cancer

Smoking causes an estimated 80% of all lung cancer deaths in women and 90% in men. Cigarette smoking is a major cause of cancers of the bladder, pancreas, cervix, esophagus, stomach, oral cavity, and kidney. The risk of lung cancer in men who smoke two or more packs per day is 23 times greater than the risk for nonsmokers; the risk for women smokers is approximately 13 times greater than for nonsmokers (CDC 2012d).

■ Bronchopulmonary Disease

Cigarette smoking is the leading cause of bronchopulmonary disease, which includes a host of lung ailments. Cigarette damages the airways and alveoli (small air sacs in the lungs) and causes emphysema and chronic airway obstruction (CDC 2012d). Respiratory infections are more prevalent and more severe among cigarette smokers—particularly heavy smokers—than among nonsmokers.

■ Effects on Pregnancy

In 2011, one in six pregnant women ages 15 to 44 smoked cigarettes in the past month (SAMHSA 2012). Cigarette smoking has several harmful effects besides those described in the previous sections, particularly for pregnant women, including increased risk for stillbirth, preterm delivery, low birth weight, and sudden infant death syndrome (CDC 2012d). Of note, approximately 13% of women report having smoked during their final 3 months of pregnancy (CDC 2013b).

"Light" Cigarettes

Light cigarettes include those with cellulose acetate filters to trap tar, small holes in the filter tip to dilute smoke with air, and pores to allow toxic chemicals to escape. These are no less hazardous than regular cigarettes (National Cancer Institute [NCI] 2010b). Smoking machines indicate that these reduce tar levels, and thus should be of some limited benefit. However, many smokers lose this benefit because they often smoke more cigarettes per day, increase puff number and volume, or block the filter holes with their fingers or lips (see "Here and Now: The Truth About Light Cigarettes").

Electronic Cigarettes

Electronic cigarettes (e-cigarettes) are devices designed to deliver nicotine or other substances to a user as a vapor. These products often resemble cigarettes, cigars, or pipes. For individuals who desire to use e-cigarettes without others noticing, some

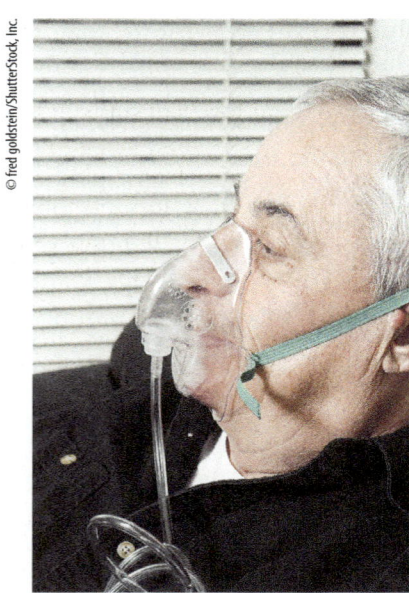

Cigarette smoking is a leading cause of bronchopulmonary disease.

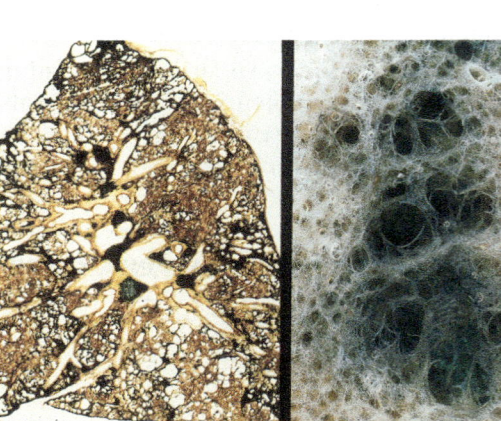

Heavy smoking can severely damage the lungs and cause emphysema. Left, a diseased lung due to smoking. Right, a healthy nonsmoker's lung.

The Truth About Light Cigarettes

Many smokers choose low-tar, mild, or light cigarettes because they believe that these cigarettes may be less harmful to their health than regular or full-flavor cigarettes. Unfortunately, light cigarettes do not reduce the health risks of smoking. The only way to reduce risk to oneself and others is to stop smoking completely. Common questions concerning light cigarettes include the following:

Q. Are light cigarettes less hazardous than regular cigarettes?

A. No. Light cigarettes are no safer than regular cigarettes. According to the National Cancer Institute (NCI), tar exposure from a light cigarette can be just as high as that from a regular cigarette if the smoker takes deeper, longer, or more frequent puffs.

Q. Why would someone smoking a light cigarette take bigger puffs than with a regular cigarette?

A. Features of cigarettes that reduce the yield of machine-measured tar also reduce the yield of nicotine. Thus, smokers may take larger and more frequent puffs, inhale more deeply, or smoke extra cigarettes each day to get enough nicotine to satisfy their craving.

Q. Are machine-measured tar yields misleading?

A. Yes. The ratings cannot be used to predict how much tar a smoker will actually take in because the way the machine smokes a cigarette is not necessarily the same as how an individual smokes. Taking deeper, longer, and more frequent puffs will lead to greater tar exposure.

Q. Do light cigarettes cause cancer?

A. Yes. People who smoke any kind of cigarette are at much greater risk of lung cancer than people who do not smoke.

Data from National Cancer Institute (NCI). "'Light' Cigarettes and Cancer Risk." 2010. Available http://www.cancer.gov/cancertopics/factsheet/Tobacco/light-cigarettes

---

devices are designed to look like pens or USB memory sticks. E-cigarettes are generally composed of a rechargeable, battery-operated heating element, a replaceable cartridge that may contain nicotine (or other chemicals), and an atomizer that, when heated, converts the cartridge into a vapor. The user can then inhale the vapor (FDA 2013a).

The FDA has not evaluated e-cigarettes for effectiveness or safety. However, in limited laboratory studies, the FDA found significant quality issues that indicate that quality control processes used to manufacture e-cigarettes might be substandard. Experts have also suggested that the marketing of products such as e-cigarettes may lead young people to try other tobacco products and may increase nicotine addiction among these individuals (FDA 2013a).

Tobacco Use and Exposure Without Smoking

■ Smokeless Tobacco

Although it is customary to associate the effects of tobacco use with smoking, in fact, millions of nonsmokers experience tobacco effects through their use of smokeless tobacco products. Approximately 3.2% of individuals age 12 or older currently use smokeless tobacco. This represents 6.2% of men and 0.4% of women (SAMHSA 2012). The number of persons age 12 or older who used smokeless tobacco for the first time in the past year was 1.3 million, which was similar to estimates in 2010 (SAMHSA 2012).

There are two main forms of smokeless tobacco in the United States. The first, **chewing tobacco**, comes in the form of loose leaf, a plug, or a twist. The second, **snuff**, is finely ground tobacco that can be moist or dry (NCI 2010c). Most smokeless tobacco users place the product in their cheek or between their cheek and gum. Users suck or chew the tobacco and then spit out the juices. Thus, smokeless tobacco is often called spitting tobacco.

KEY TERMS

chewing tobacco
tobacco leaves shredded and twisted into strands for chewing purposes

snuff
finely ground smokeless tobacco that can be moist or dry

Smokeless tobacco contains powerful chemicals that can injure tissues in the mouth and throat. The following findings have been made regarding smokeless tobacco (NCI 2010c):

- Smokeless tobacco use can lead to nicotine addiction and dependence.
- Smokeless tobacco contains at least 28 cancer-causing agents (carcinogens).
- Smokeless tobacco is strongly associated with leukoplakia—a precancerous lesion of the soft tissues in the mouth that consists of a white patch or plaque.
- Smokeless tobacco increases the risk of developing cancer of the oral cavity and pancreas.

Recently, new smokeless tobacco products have entered the U.S. market including snus (a form of moist snuff) and "dissolvable" products that can take the form of breath mints or strips. These products are available in a range of flavors, which research suggests may make the products more attractive to young adults (Choi et al. 2012). These products can be more appealing than traditional smokeless tobacco products because they do not require spitting and can be used discreetly.

▮ Secondhand Smoke

The health of individuals who neither smoke nor chew is also adversely affected by tobacco, specifically, exposure to **secondhand smoke**—also known as **environmental tobacco smoke (ETS)**—that is inhaled by passive nonsmokers. Secondhand smoke includes a mixture of smoke that comes directly from the lighted tip of a cigarette, cigar, or pipe and smoke that has been exhaled (CDC 2012e). Passive smoking refers to nonsmokers' inhalation of tobacco smoke. Studies of smoking and its effects have directed increased attention to secondhand smoke because smokers and nonsmokers alike breathe in the burning tobacco smoke that pollutes the air. This type of smoke contains hundreds of chemicals, including approximately 70 carcinogens (CDC 2012e).

KEY TERMS

secondhand smoke
smoke released into the air from a lighted cigarette, cigar, or pipe tip and exhaled mainstream smoke

environmental tobacco smoke (ETS)
a term referring to secondhand smoke

Exposure to secondhand smoke has serious health consequences. Secondhand smoke exposure causes an estimated 46,000 heart disease deaths annually in the United States (CDC 2012e). Breathing secondhand smoke has immediate harmful effects on the cardiovascular system of nonsmokers that can increase the risk for heart attack. People who currently have heart disease are at especially high risk. Nonsmokers who are exposed to secondhand smoke at work or home increase their heart disease risk by 25–30% (CDC 2012e).

In addition to increased risk of cardiovascular disease, secondhand smoke causes significant respiratory problems. For example, nonsmokers who are exposed to secondhand smoke at work or home increase their lung cancer risk by 20–30%. As a consequence, secondhand smoke exposure causes an estimated 3400 lung cancer deaths annually among adult nonsmokers in the United States (CDC 2012e).

Of note, pregnant women who are exposed to secondhand smoke have a greater chance of giving birth to a low-birthweight baby (CDC 2013b). Of note, children are particularly vulnerable to secondhand smoke. In children, it contributes to ear infections, more frequent and severe asthma attacks, and an increased risk for sudden infant death syndrome (CDC 2012e).

Reasons for Smoking and the Motivation to Quit

▮ Reasons for Smoking

Nicotine dependency through cigarette smoking is not only one of the most common forms of drug addiction, but also one responsible for numerous deaths. As noted previously, more deaths each year are caused by tobacco use than by HIV, illegal drug use, murders, alcohol use, suicides, and motor vehicle injuries combined (CDC 2012d). Tobacco use continues despite the fact that, since the 1960s, medical research and government assessments have clearly proved that smoking leads to premature death.

If one asks tobacco users why they smoke, their answers are often quite similar:

- It is relaxing.
- It decreases the unpleasant effects of tension, anxiety, and anger.

- It satisfies the craving.
- It is a habit.
- It provides stimulation, increased energy, and arousal.
- It allows the manipulation of objects that have become satisfying habits (the cigarette, pipe, and so on).

In addition,

- Parents and/or siblings smoke.
- A close friend or boyfriend/girlfriend smokes.

Tobacco use fosters dependence for a number of reasons:

- The habit can be rapidly and frequently reinforced by inhaling tobacco smoke.
- The rapid metabolism and clearance of nicotine allow frequent and repeated use, which is encouraged by the rapid onset of withdrawal symptoms.
- Smoking has complex pharmacological effects —both central and peripheral—that may satisfy a variety of the needs of the smoker.
- Some groups offer psychological and social rewards for use, especially the peer groups of young people.
- Smoking patterns can be generalized; that is, the smoker becomes conditioned to smoke with specific activities. For example, some smokers feel the need to smoke after a meal, when driving, and so on.
- Smoking is reinforced by both pharmacological effects and ritual.
- There is no marked performance impairment. In fact, smoking enhances performance in some cases. (Nicotine produces a state of alertness, prevents deterioration of reaction time, and improves learning.)

These reasons may not only explain why people continue to smoke, but also reveal why it is often difficult for them to stop.

Smokers appear to regulate their intake of nicotine. For example, the smoker of a low-nicotine cigarette often smokes more and inhales more deeply. The average one-pack-a-day smoker is estimated to self-administer thousands of pulses (one pulse per inhalation) of nicotine to nicotinic receptors in the brain per year. This rate greatly surpasses the stimulation rate of any other known form of substance abuse. A habit that is reinforced as frequently and easily as smoking is very hard to break.

Other factors responsible for creating the addiction to nicotine follow:

- Cigarettes are readily available.
- No equipment other than a lighter or match is needed.
- Cigarettes are portable and easy to store.
- Cigarettes are legal for individuals over age 18.
- Other rewarding behaviors can occur while smoking (for example, drinking, socializing, and eating).

■ Benefits of Cessation

Individuals who stop smoking greatly reduce their risk for disease and premature death. Although the health benefits are greater for people who stop at earlier ages, cessation is beneficial at all ages. For example, smokers who quit at approximately age 30 reduce their risk of premature death from smoking-related diseases by more than 90%. Individuals who quit at approximately age 50 reduce their risk of dying prematurely by 50% compared with those who continue to smoke. Finally, even those who quit at approximately age 60 or older live longer than those who continue to smoke (NCI 2011). According to the National Cancer Institute (2011), immediate health benefits of quitting smoking are significant and include:

- A return to normalcy of heart rate and blood pressure (which are abnormally high while smoking)
- A decline of carbon monoxide in the blood within hours
- Improved circulation, production of less phlegm, and decreased rate of coughing and wheezing within weeks
- Substantial improvements in lung function within several months

In addition, according to the CDC (2013a), cessation of smoking is associated with the following health benefits, including reducing:

- The risk for lung and other types of cancer
- The risk for coronary heart disease, stroke, and peripheral vascular disease
- Respiratory symptoms such as coughing, wheezing, and shortness of breath
- The risk of developing chronic obstructive pulmonary disease
- The risk for infertility in women
- The risk of having a low-birthweight baby

■ The Motivation to Quit

> Quitting smoking is easy. I've done it a thousand times.
>
> —*Mark Twain*

Approximately 69% of adult smokers report that they want to quit smoking (CDC 2012c), and millions have attempted to do so. When habitual smokers stop smoking on their own, without the use of smoking cessation aids, they may experience a variety of unpleasant withdrawal effects, including craving for tobacco, irritability, restlessness, sleep disturbances, gastrointestinal disturbances, anxiety, and impaired concentration, judgment, and psychomotor performance. The onset of nicotine withdrawal symptoms may occur within hours or days after quitting and may persist from a few days to several months. Frustration over these symptoms leads many people to start smoking again. The intensity of withdrawal effects may be mild, moderate, or severe; it is not always correlated with the amount smoked.

The National Cancer Institute (2010a) has several recommendations of alternative activities that ex-smokers might try as aids to handle the cravings associated with quitting and get through the withdrawal period. These include:

- Reminding oneself that cravings will pass.
- Avoiding situations and activities that one normally associates with smoking.
- Chewing on carrots, pickles, sunflower seeds, apples, celery, or sugarless gum or hard candy as a substitute for smoking so as to keep one's mouth occupied and thus perhaps diminish the psychological craving to smoke.
- Repeatedly taking a deep breath through one's nose and exhaling slowly through one's mouth.

Of note, studies in 2 Canadian and 20 U.S. communities demonstrated that employees who work in environments that implemented smoke-free policies—policies that completely eliminate smoking in indoor public places and work areas—were almost twice as likely to stop smoking than those who worked in settings that permitted smoking everywhere. Further, adolescents who work in smoke-free environments are less likely to become smokers (CDC 2011 and references therein).

In addition to behavioral modifications, several pharmacological interventions are available to aid in smoking cessation. These include nicotine replacement therapy (e.g., nicotine gums, patches, lozenges, inhalers, sprays) and agents such as bupropion (Zyban) and varenicline (Chantix).

NICOTINE GUM

Nicotine gum can be purchased over the counter without a prescription. Chewing the gum allows the rapid absorption of nicotine through the mucous membranes of the mouth. Users chew the gum until noting a peppery taste, and then hold it against the cheek to permit faster absorption. The user will chew on and off for about 20 to 30 minutes.

Significant advantages afforded by nicotine gum are that it is easy to use and allows the user to control the dose of nicotine by controlling the number of pieces chewed each day. Individuals gradually decrease the number of pieces chewed each day, with a goal of complete abstinence from the drug. Side effects of the gum can include a bad taste, throat irritation, nausea (if the gum is swallowed), jaw discomfort (if chewed too rapidly), and racing heartbeat.

NICOTINE PATCHES

Nicotine patches, also known as *transdermal nicotine systems*, are available without a prescription. The patch, which is directly applied and worn on the skin, releases a continuous flow of small doses of nicotine to quell the desire for cigarette-provided nicotine. The method of delivering nicotine to the skin reduces the withdrawal symptoms as the smoker attempts to quit. As the nicotine doses are lowered over a course of weeks, the smoker is

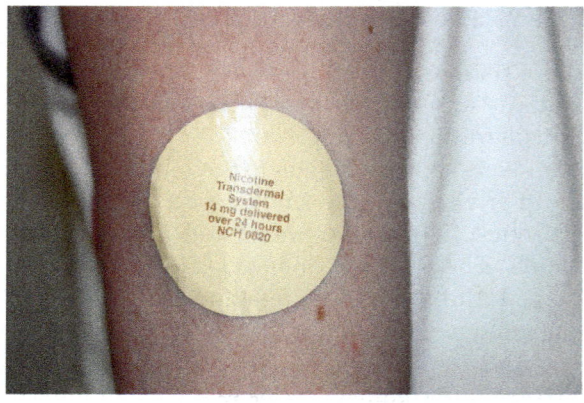

A transdermal patch, an example of a popular therapy for quitting smoking.

weaned away from nicotine. The most common side effects are mild skin irritations such as redness and itching.

NICOTINE NASAL SPRAY, INHALERS, AND LOZENGES

Nicotine nasal sprays rapidly deliver nicotine to the bloodstream as it is absorbed through the membranous lining of the nasal passages. These are easy to use and give immediate relief of withdrawal symptoms. The most common side effects of using the spray include coughing, sinus irritation, runny nose, watery eyes, sneezing, and throat irritation. It is generally not recommended for individuals with asthma, allergies, or other pulmonary problems.

A nicotine inhaler consists of a small plastic tube that contains a nicotine plug. When the user puffs on the inhaler, the plug provides nicotine vapor into the mouth. One advantage to the inhaler is that the action of puffing it mimics some of the behaviors associated with smoking. Side effects associated with its use include coughing and throat irritation.

Nicotine lozenges are alternatives to sprays and inhalers. Like nicotine patches and gums, all three of these items can be purchased without a prescription. Potential side effects can include sore throat and heartburn.

VARENICLINE AND BUPROPION

Varenicline acts at receptors in the brain affected by nicotine. Its common side effects include nausea, constipation, vomiting, difficulty sleeping, and/or strange dreams. Other serious side effects can include changes in behavior, depressed mood, hostility, and suicidal thoughts.

Bupropion also helps patients to abstain from smoking, also by acting at brain nicotine receptors. Noteworthy, this agent is also used as an antidepressant. Its side effects can include dry mouth, headaches, and dizziness. Other serious potential side effects can include changes in behavior, depressed mood, hostility, suicidal thoughts, seizures, and irregular heartbeat.

Smoking Prohibition Versus Smokers' Rights

In response to the banning of smoking from certain public facilities throughout the United States, people who want to continue smoking have formed action groups to press their right to smoke. Although these groups have made some modest gains, the trend toward restricting and banning cigarette smoking remains very strong. Antismoking groups have been highly successful in their own efforts, and restrictions on the sale of cigarettes and tobacco products remain very tight. Further, approximately 47% of Americans live under state or local laws that make workplaces, restaurants, and bars completely smoke-free (CDC 2010).

HERE AND NOW

Taxing Cigarettes and Saving Lives

State and federal excise taxes on cigarettes increased moderately between 1970 and 2011, but cost per pack steeply increased during that time period. In 1970, the average cost and tax per pack were $0.38 and $0.18, respectively. In 2011, the average cost per pack was $5.62, and the average tax per pack was $2.35. According to the U.S. Congressional Budget Office (CBO), a $0.50 increase in tax on cigarettes may have a large impact on public health. The CBO estimated that such a hike in the federal cigarette tax could result in an additional 3 million nonsmokers by 2085 by preventing the initiation of smoking or promoting cessation. This figure includes approximately 200,000 people who would have otherwise died from smoking-related causes before 2085.

Data from Centers for Disease Control and Prevention (CDC). "Trends in State and Federal Cigarette Tax and Retail Price—United States, 1970–2011." 2013. Available http://www.cdc.gov/tobacco/data_statistics/tables/economics/trends/; and U.S. Department of Health and Human Services. "Steep Cigarette Tax Hike Could Save Lives, Money." 2013. Available http://healthfinder.gov/News/Article.aspx?id=671078

LEARNING PORTFOLIO

Key Terms

Discussion Questions

1. If smoking is the most preventable cause of disease and premature death in the United States, why do people continue to smoke?
2. How effective are the health warning labels on cigarette packages?
3. List and define the diseases that cigarette smokers are most likely to contract.
4. What effects do cigarettes have on the fetus?
5. Why is smokeless tobacco perceived as safer than other forms of tobacco?
6. Who is most likely to smoke and why?
7. Why do people who smoke become dependent on tobacco?
8. Assess the major methods for quitting smoking. Which methods are most likely to succeed?
9. Do you think smokers should have the right to smoke in public places? Explain.

Summary

1. Nicotine is a highly addictive substance.
2. Approximately 26.5% of the U.S. population age 12 or older reports current use of a tobacco product.
3. Nicotine is the substance in tobacco that causes dependence. This drug initially stimulates and then depresses the nervous system.
4. The amount of tobacco absorbed varies according to five factors: (a) the exact composition of the tobacco being used, (b) how densely the tobacco is packed in the cigarette and the length of the cigarette smoked, (c) whether a filter is used and the characteristics of the filter, (d) the volume of the smoke inhaled, and (e) the number of cigarettes smoked throughout the day.
5. Cigarette smoking is an addiction that is costly in several ways. For instance, each year approximately 443,000 deaths in the United States are attributed to cigarette smoking.
6. Chewing tobacco and snuff are types of smokeless tobacco products that are commonly referred to as "spitting tobacco." Chewing tobacco consists of tobacco leaves that are shredded and twisted into strands and then either chewed or placed in the cheek between the lower lip and gum. Snuff is finely ground smokeless tobacco that can be moist or dry.
7. Cigarette smokers tend to die at an earlier age than nonsmokers. They also have a greater probability of contracting various illnesses, including types of cancers, chronic bronchitis and

emphysema, diseases of the cardiovascular system, and peptic ulcers. In addition, smoking has adverse effects on pregnancy and may harm the fetus.

References

Almasy, S. "FDA Changes Course on Graphic Warning Labels for Cigarettes." CNN. 13 March 2013.

Austin, G. A. *Perspectives on the History of Psychoactive Substance Use.* Washington, DC: National Institute on Drug Abuse, 1978.

Bartecchi, C. E., T. D. MacKenzie, and R. W. Shrier. "The Global Tobacco Epidemic." *Scientific American* (May 1995): 49.

Centers for Disease Control and Prevention (CDC). "Vital Signs: Tobacco Use: Smoking and Secondhand Smoke." 2010. Available http://www.cdc.gov/VitalSigns/TobaccoUse/SecondhandSmoke/index.html

Centers for Disease Control and Prevention (CDC). "Smoke-Free Policies Reduce Smoking." 2011a. Available http://www.cdc.gov/tobacco/data_statistics/fact_sheets/secondhand_smoke/protection/reduce_smoking/index.htm

Centers for Disease Control and Prevention (CDC). "Tobacco Use: Targeting the Nation's Leading Killer: At a Glance." 2011b. Available http://www.cdc.gov/chronicdisease/resources/publications/aag/pdf/2011/tobacco_aag_2011_508.pdf

Centers for Disease Control and Prevention (CDC). "Drop in Cigarette Consumption Offset by Increases in Other Forms of Smoked Tobacco." 2012a. Available http://www.cdc.gov/media/releases/2012/p0802_tobacco_consumption.html

Centers for Disease Control and Prevention (CDC). "Economic Facts About U.S. Tobacco Production and Use." 2012b. Available http://www.cdc.gov/tobacco/data_statistics/fact_sheets/economics/econ_facts/index.htm

Centers for Disease Control and Prevention (CDC). "Fast Facts." 2012c. Available http://www.cdc.gov/tobacco/data_statistics/fact_sheets/fast_facts/index.htm

Centers for Disease Control and Prevention (CDC). "Health Effects of Cigarette Smoking." 2012d. Available http://www.cdc.gov/tobacco/data_statistics/fact_sheets/health_effects/effects_cig_smoking/

Centers for Disease Control and Prevention (CDC). "Secondhand Smoke (SHS) Facts." 2012e. Available http://www.cdc.gov/tobacco/data_statistics/fact_sheets/secondhand_smoke/general_facts/

Centers for Disease Control and Prevention (CDC). "Youth and Tobacco Use." 2012f. Available http://www.cdc.gov/tobacco/data_statistics/fact_sheets/youth_data/tobacco_use/index.htm

Centers for Disease Control and Prevention (CDC). "Smoking Cessation." 2013a. Available http://www.cdc.gov/tobacco/data_statistics/fact_sheets/cessation/quitting/

Centers for Disease Control and Prevention (CDC). "Tobacco Use and Pregnancy." 2013b. Available http://www.cdc.gov/reproductivehealth/TobaccoUsePregnancy/index.htm

Choi, K., L. Fabian, N. Mottey, A. Corbett, and J. Forster. "Young Adults' Favorable Perceptions of Snus, Dissolvable Tobacco Products, and Electronic Cigarettes: Findings from a Focus Group Study." *American Journal of Public Health* 102(11) (2012): 2088–2093.

Corti, E. C. *A History of Smoking.* London: Harrap and Company, 1931.

Food and Drug Administration (FDA). "E-Cigarettes: Questions and Answers." 2013a. Available http://www.fda.gov/ForConsumers/ConsumerUpdates/ucm225210.htm

Food and Drug Administration (FDA). "Overview of the Family Smoking Prevention and Tobacco Control Act: Consumer Fact Sheet." 2013b. Available http://www.fda.gov/TobaccoProducts/GuidanceComplianceRegulatoryInformation/ucm246129.htm

Food and Drug Administration (FDA). "Tobacco Products: Cigarette Health Warnings." 2013c. Available http://www.fda.gov/TobaccoProducts/Labeling/Labeling/CigaretteWarningLabels/

Food and Drug Administration (FDA). "U.S. Food and Drug Administration Center for Tobacco Products 2009–2010: Inaugural Year in Review." 2013d. Available http://www.fda.gov/downloads/TobaccoProducts/NewsEvents/UCM216374.pdf

Heimann, R. K. *Tobacco and Americans.* New York: McGraw-Hill, 1960.

Langton, P. A. *Drug Use and the Alcohol Dilemma.* Boston: Allyn and Bacon, 1991.

National Cancer Institute (NCI). "How to Handle Withdrawal Symptoms and Triggers When You Decide to Quit Smoking." 2010a. Available http://www.cancer.gov/cancertopics/factsheet/Tobacco/symptoms-triggers-quitting

National Cancer Institute (NCI). "'Light' Cigarettes and Cancer Risk." 2010b. Available http://www.cancer.gov/cancertopics/factsheet/Tobacco/light-cigarettes

National Cancer Institute (NCI). "Smokeless Tobacco and Cancer." 2010c. Available http://www.cancer.gov/cancertopics/factsheet/Tobacco/smokeless

National Cancer Institute (NCI). "Harms of Smoking and Health Benefits of Quitting." 2011. Available http://www.cancer.gov/cancertopics/factsheet/Tobacco/cessation

National Institute on Drug Abuse (NIDA). *Tobacco Addiction.* 2012. NIH Pub. No. 12-4342. Available http://www.drugabuse.gov/sites/default/files/tobaccorrs_v16_0.pdf

O'Brien, R., S. Cohen, G. Evans, and J. Fine. *The Encyclopedia of Drug Abuse*, 2nd ed. New York: Facts on File and Greenspring, 1992.

Palfai, T., and H. Jankiewicz. *Drugs and Human Behavior.* Dubuque, IA: William C. Brown, 1991.

Schelling, T. C. "Addictive Drugs: The Cigarette Experience." *Science* (24 January 1992): 430–433.

Schultes, R. E. "Ethnopharmacological Significance of Psychotropic Drugs of Vegetal Origin." In *Principles of Psychopharmacology*, 2nd ed., edited by W. G. Clark and J. del Guidice, 41–70. New York: Academic Press, 1978.

Substance Abuse and Mental Health Services Administration (SAMHSA). *Results from the 2011 National Survey on Drug Use and Health: Volume I. Summary of National Findings.* NSDUH Series H-44, HHS Pub. No. SMA 12-4713. Rockville, MD: Substance Abuse and Mental Health Services Administration, 2012.

Substance Abuse and Mental Health Services Administration (SAMHSA). "Cigarette Smoking Decreases Among All Adults Except Those Aged 26 to 34." 2013. Available http://www.samhsa.gov/data/spotlight/Spot100-tobacco.pdf

U.S. Department of Agriculture (USDA), Economic Research Service. "Trends in the Cigarette Industry After the Master Settlement Agreement." TBS-250-01, 2001.

World Health Organization (WHO). "Q & A: Tobacco." 2013. Available http://www.who.int/topics/tobacco/qa/en/index.html

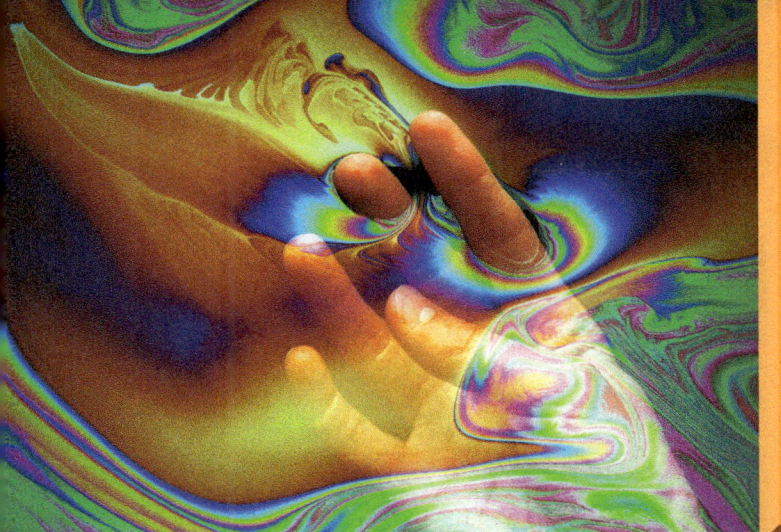
© Elfstrom/iStockphoto.com

CHAPTER 12

Hallucinogens (Psychedelics)

Did You Know?

▶ Hallucinogens were abused by relatively few people in the United States until the social upheaval of the 1960s.

▶ Some hallucinogens—such as LSD—have been used by psychiatrists to assist in psychotherapy with certain patients.

▶ Ecstasy has been tested in FDA-approved clinical trials for its ability to treat PTSD conditions.

▶ Hallucinogens such as LSD do not tend to be physically addicting.

▶ Ketamine has been proposed as a unique antidepressant.

▶ The senses are grossly exaggerated and distorted under the influence of hallucinogens.

▶ Ecstasy abuse increased dramatically from 1996 to 2000 due to its popularity as a "club drug" and its use at "rave" parties. Its use then declined, but it has risen again due to reduced perceived risk by younger populations.

▶ For some users, hallucinogens can cause frightening, nightmarish experiences called *bad trips*.

▶ Phencyclidine (PCP) and ketamine were originally developed as general anesthetics, but because of their ability to cause psychosis their use in humans is either prohibited or very limited.

▶ Abuse of high doses of over-the-counter (OTC) cough medicines that contain dextromethorphan is a problem with young populations and can cause a PCP-like hallucinogenic or psychotic effect.

Learning Objectives

On completing this chapter you will be able to:

❯ Explain why hallucinogens became so popular during the 1960s.

❯ Describe how hallucinogens alter the senses.

❯ Outline how psychedelic, stimulant, and anticholinergic effects are expressed in the three principal types of hallucinogens.

❯ Describe why some psychotherapists believe that using MDMA for their patients may be beneficial.

❯ Explain the reasons for Ecstasy's recent up and down patterns of use.

❯ Explain how hallucinogens differ from other commonly abused drugs in terms of their addicting properties and their ability to cause dependence.

❯ Describe the effects that environment and personality have on the individual's response to hallucinogens.

❯ Explain the term *club drugs* and describe their particular problems.

❯ Characterize how PCP differs from other hallucinogens and why it is so dangerous.

❯ Explain the similarities between PCP and ketamine.

❯ Describe the recreational and legal status of *Salvia divinorum*.

Drugs and Society Online is a great source for additional drugs and society information for both students and instructors. Visit **go.jblearning.com /hanson12** to find a variety of useful tools for learning, thinking, and teaching.

Introduction

The following is a quote regarding caring for someone under the influence of a hallucinogen:

A basic principle in the care of persons who have ingested hallucinogens is calm reassurance. Patients presenting with an acute panic reaction should be placed in a quiet nonthreatening environment with minimal stimuli. Reassure patients that their anxiety is caused by the drug and the effect will wear off in a few hours. Patients that are medically stable but, (i) remain anxious or agitated, (ii) have continued hallucinations, (iii) remain a danger to themselves or others, or (iv) would not be able to care for themselves after several hours of observation, should be admitted to a psychiatric hospital. Patients should be restrained . . . if they are a danger to themselves or others. (Parish 2011)

This quote from an experienced treatment provider illustrates the sensory and emotional distortions that can be caused by using **hallucinogens** or **psychedelics**. The word *psychedelic* comes from the Greek root meaning "mind-revealing." In this chapter, we begin with a brief historical review of the use of hallucinogens, tracing the trend in the United States from the 1960s to today. Next, the nature of hallucinogens and the effects they produce are examined. The rest of the chapter addresses the various types of psychedelic agents—LSD types, phenylethylamines (including Ecstasy), anticholinergics, natural products, and other miscellaneous substances.

The History of Hallucinogen Use

People have known and written about drug-related hallucinations for centuries. Throughout the ages, individuals who saw visions or experienced

Protests against the Vietnam War in the 1960s and 1970s often included the use of hallucinogens.

hallucinations were perceived as being holy or sacred, as receiving divine messages, or possibly as being bewitched and controlled by the devil. There are many indications that medicine men, shamans, witches, oracles, and perhaps mystics and priests of various groups were familiar with drugs and herbs that caused such experiences, which today are known as hallucinogens (National Institute on Drug Abuse [NIDA] 2001).

Before the 1960s, several psychedelic substances, such as mescaline from the peyote cactus, could be obtained from chemical supply houses with no restriction in the United States. Abuse of hallucinogens did not become a major social problem in this country until this decade of racial struggles, the Vietnam War, and violent demonstrations. Many individuals frustrated with the hypocrisy of "the establishment" tried to "turn on and tune in" by using hallucinogens as pharmacological crutches.

Psychedelic drugs became especially popular when some medical professionals, such as then-Harvard psychology professor Timothy Leary, reported that these drugs allowed users to get in touch with themselves and achieve a peaceful inner serenity (Associated Press 1999). At the same time, it became well publicized that the natural psychedelics (such as mescaline and peyote) for many years had been used routinely by some religious organizations of Native Americans for enhancing spiritual experiences. This factor contributed to the mystical, supernatural aura associated with hallucinogenic agents and added to their enticement for the so-called dropout generation.

With widespread use of lysergic acid diethylamide (LSD), it was observed that this and similar drugs may induce a form of psychosis-like schizophrenia (American Psychiatric Association [APA] 2013). The term **psychotomimetic** was coined to describe these compounds; this term means

KEY TERMS

hallucinogens
substances that alter sensory processing in the brain, causing perceptual disturbances, changes in thought processing, and depersonalization

psychedelics
substances that expand or heighten perception and consciousness

psychotomimetics
substances that cause psychosis-like symptoms

"psychosis mimicking" and is still used in medicine today. The basis for the designation is the effects of these drugs, which induce mental states that impair an individual's ability to recognize and respond appropriately to reality.

By the mid-1960s, federal regulatory agencies had become concerned with the misuse of hallucinogens and the potential emotional damage caused by these drugs. Access to hallucinogenic agents was restricted, and laws against their distribution were passed. Despite the problems associated with these psychedelics, some groups demanded that responsible use with therapeutic benefits was possible and that trained clinicians be allowed legal access to these substances.

Peyote is used as a sacramental plant by members of the Native American Church as part of their religious ceremonies.

■ The Native American Church

The hallucinogen peyote plays a central role in the ceremonies of Native Americans who follow a religion that is a combination of Christian doctrine and Native American religious rituals. Members of this church are found as far north as Canada. They believe that God made a special gift of this sacramental plant to them so that they might commune more directly with Him. The first organized peyote church was the First-Born Church of Christ, incorporated in 1914 in Oklahoma. The Native American Church of the United States was chartered in 1918

and is the largest such group at present (approximately 100,000–200,000 members) (Dobner 2010).

Because of the religious beliefs of the members of the Native American Church concerning the powers of peyote, when Congress legislated against its use in 1965, it allowed room for religious use of this psychedelic plant. The American Indian Religious Freedom Act of 1978 was an attempt by Congress to allow the members of the Native American Church access to peyote based on constitutional guarantees of religious freedom. Due to controversy inspired by the original piece of legislation, an amendment to the 1978 act was signed in 1994, which specifically protected the use of

► CASE IN POINT

Peyote and the Rights of Native Americans: How Far Should It Go?

Although federal law protects the rights of Native Americans to use peyote for religious purposes if they are members of the Native American Church, issues remain unresolved. For example, Jonathan Fowler, a member of the Grand Traverse Band of Ottawa and Chippewa Indians, requested a judge allow his 4-year-old son to ingest peyote with him, as part of a religious ritual at the Native American Church of the Morning Star. The boy's mother opposed the request, fearing potential neurological damage to the boy. Although the use of peyote in Native American rituals is legal in all 50 states, the judge ruled against Fowler, stating that the boy could use peyote when he

becomes old enough to comprehend its effects and with permission from both parents. Several Native American congregations who use peyote already have age limitations indicating who can take the substance during religious rites. Another issue relates to members of this church who are not of Indian ancestry. Lawsuits have been filed in federal courts that contend all members of the Native American Church regardless of their ancestry should be allowed to include peyote use as part of their religious practice. This case suggests that in the future, other lawsuits are likely to continue to be tried in court that relate to this practice of religious use of hallucinogenic drugs.

Data from Center for Cognitive Liberty and Ethics. "Court Says No Peyote for Native American Boy." 22 April 2003. Available http://www.cognitiveliberty.org/dll/peyote_boy.html. Accessed March 18, 2011; and Dobner, J. "American Indian Church Sues Feds Over Peyote Use." Native American Times. 20 September 2010. Available http://www.nativetimes.com/index.php?option=com_content&view=article& id=4268:american-indian-church-sues-feds-over-peyote-use&catid=51&Itemid=27. Accessed March 18, 2011.

Timothy Leary advocated the legalization of LSD in the 1960s.

peyote in Native American Church ceremonies. This amendment also prohibits use of peyote for nonreligious purposes (Native American Church 2008). However, despite these efforts by Congress to resolve this issue, controversies continue to arise (see "Case in Point: Peyote and the Rights of Native Americans: How Far Should It Go?").

■ Timothy Leary and the League of Spiritual Discovery

In 1966, 3 years after being fired by Harvard because of his controversial involvement with hallucinogens (Associated Press 1999), Timothy Leary undertook a constitutional strategy intended to retain legitimate access to another hallucinogen, LSD. He began a religion called the League of Spiritual Discovery; LSD was the sacrament. This unorthodox religious orientation to the LSD experience was presented in a manual called *The Psychedelic Experience* (Leary, Metzner, and Alpert 1964), which was based on the *Tibetan Book of the Dead*. It became the "bible" of the psychedelic drug movement.

The movement grew, but most members used street LSD and did not follow Leary's directions. Leary believed that the hallucinogenic experience was only beneficial under proper control and guidance. But most members of this so-called religion

KEY TERM

psychotogenics
substances that initiate psychotic behavior

merely used the organization as a front to gain access to an illegal drug. Federal authorities did not agree with Leary's freedom of religion interpretation and in 1969 convicted him for possession of marijuana and LSD and sentenced him to 20 years in prison (Stone 1991). Before being incarcerated, Leary escaped to Algeria and wandered for a couple of years before being extradited to the United States. He served several years in jail and was released in 1976.

Even in his later years, Leary continued to believe that U.S. citizens should be able to use hallucinogens without government regulation. He died in 1996 at the age of 75 years, revered by some but despised by others (Associated Press 1999; "Many Were Lost" 1996).

Hallucinogen Use Today

Today, the use of hallucinogens (excluding marijuana) is primarily a young-adult phenomenon (Johnston 2013). Although the use rate has not returned to that of the late 1960s and early 1970s (approximately 16%), in high school seniors lifetime use in 2012 was 7.5% (Johnston et al. 2013) (see **Table 12.1**).

The Nature of Hallucinogens

Agreement has not been reached on what constitutes a hallucinogenic agent (O'Brien 2006), for several reasons. First, a variety of seemingly unrelated drug groups can produce hallucinations, delusions, or sensory disturbances under certain conditions. For example, besides the traditional hallucinogens (such as LSD), high doses of anticholinergics, cocaine, amphetamines, and steroids can also cause hallucinations.

In addition, responses to even the traditional hallucinogens can vary tremendously from person to person and from experience to experience (see "Signs & Symptoms: Hallucinogens"). Multiple mechanisms are involved in the actions of these drugs, which contribute to the array of responses that they can cause. These drugs most certainly influence the complex inner workings of the human mind and have been described as psychedelic, **psychotogenic**, or psychotomimetic. The feature of hallucinogens that distinguishes them from other drug groups is their ability to

TABLE 12.1 Trends in the Use of LSD and All Hallucinogens by 8th, 10th, and 12th Graders, 1994–2012

	Used During Lifetime (%)					Used During Year (%)				
	1994	1996	2006	2010	2012	1994	1994	2006	2010	2012
8th Graders										
LSD	3.7	5.1	1.6	1.8	1.3	2.4	3.5	0.9	1.2	0.8
All hallucinogens	4.3	5.9	3.4	3.4	2.8.	2.7	4.1	2.1	2.2	1.6
10th Graders										
LSD	7.2	9.4	2.7	3.0	2.6	5.2	6.9	1.7	1.9	1.7
All hallucinogens	8.1	10.5	6.1	6.1	5.2	5.8	7.8	4.1	4.2	3.5
12th Graders										
LSD	10.5	12.6	3.3	4.0	3.8	6.9	8.8	1.7	2.6	2.4
All hallucinogens	11.4	14.0	8.3	8.6	7.5	7.6	10.1	4.9	5.5	4.8

Data from Johnston, L.D., P. M. O'Malley, J. G. Bachman, and J. E. Schulenberg. *Monitoring the Future: National Survey Results on Drug Use, 2012 Overview, Key Findings on Adolescent Drug Use*. Ann Arbor, MI: Institute for Social Research, University of Michigan, 2013.

alter perception, thought, and feeling in such a manner that does not normally occur except in dreams or during experiences of extreme religious exaltation (NIDA 2009). We examine these characteristics throughout this chapter.

■ Sensory and Psychological Effects

In general, LSD is considered the prototype agent against which other hallucinogens are measured (NIDA 2001). Typical users experience several stages of sensory experiences; they can go through all stages during a single "trip" or, more likely, will pass through only some. These stages are as follows:

1. Heightened, exaggerated senses
2. Loss of control
3. Self-reflection
4. Loss of identity and a sense of cosmic merging

The following illustrations of the stages of the LSD experience are based primarily on an account by Solomon Snyder (1974), a highly regarded neuroscientist (one of the principal discoverers of endorphins), who personally experienced the effects of LSD as a young resident in psychiatry.

ALTERED SENSES

In his encounter with LSD, Snyder used a moderate dose of 100 to 200 micrograms and observed few discernible effects for the first 30 minutes except some mild nausea. After this time had elapsed, objects took on a purplish tinge and appeared to be vaguely outlined. Colors, textures, and lines

SIGNS & SYMPTOMS
Hallucinogens

Possible Signs of Use	Extreme Reactions
Heightened senses	Increased body temperature (MDMA)
Loss of control	Electrolyte imbalance
Loss of identity	Cardiac arrest
Illusions and hallucinations	A nightmare-like trip (LSD)
Altered perception of time and distance	Unable to direct movement, feel pain, or remember

achieved an unexpected richness. Perception was so exaggerated that individual skin pores "stood out and clamored for recognition" (Snyder 1974, p. 42). Objects became distorted; when Snyder focused on his thumb, it began to swell, undulate, and then moved forward in a menacing fashion. Visions filled with distorted imagery occurred when his eyes were closed. The sense of time and distance changed dramatically; "a minute was like an hour, a week was like an eternity, a foot became a mile" (Snyder 1974, p. 43). The present seemed to drag on forever, and the concept of future lost its meaning. The exaggeration of perceptions and feelings gave the sense of more events occurring in a time period, giving the impression of time slowing.

An associated sensation described by Snyder is called **synesthesia**, a crossover phenomenon between senses. For example, sound develops visual dimensions, and vice versa, enabling the user to see sounds and hear colors. These altered sensory experiences are described as a heightened sensory awareness and relate to the first component of the psychedelic state (NIDA 2009).

LOSS OF CONTROL

The second feature of LSD also relates to altered sensory experiences and a loss of control (About .com 2012). The user cannot determine whether the psychedelic trip will be a pleasant, relaxing experience or a "bad trip," with recollections of hidden fears and suppressed anxieties that can precipitate neurotic or psychotic responses. The frightening reactions may persist for a few minutes or several hours and be mildly agitating or extremely disturbing. Some bad trips can include feelings of panic, confusion, suspicion, helplessness, and a total lack of control. The following example illustrates how terrifying a bad trip can be:

> I was having problems breathing [and] my throat was all screwed up. The things that entered my mind were that I was dead and people were saying good-bye, because they

really meant it. I was witnessing my own funeral. I was thinking that I was going to wake either in the back seat of a cop car or in the hospital. *(From Venturelli's files, male, age 19)*

Replays of these frightening experiences can occur at a later time, even though the drug has not been taken again; such recurrences are referred to as **flashbacks** (NIDA 2010) or hallucinogen persisting perception disorder (Halpern and Pope 2003).

It is not clear what determines the nature of the sensory response. Perhaps it relates to the state of anxiety and personality of the user or the nature of his or her surroundings. It is interesting that Timothy Leary tried to teach his "drug disciples" that "turning on correctly means to understand the many levels that are brought into focus; it takes years of discipline, training and discipleship" ("Celebration #1" 1966). He apparently felt that, with experience and training, you could control the sensory effects of the hallucinogens. This is an interesting possibility but has never been well demonstrated.

SELF-REFLECTION

Snyder (1974) made reference to the third component of the psychedelic response in his LSD experience. During the period when sensory effects predominate, self-reflection also occurs. While in this state, Snyder explained, the user "becomes aware of thoughts and feelings long hidden beneath the surface, forgotten and/or repressed" (p. 44). As a psychiatrist, Snyder claimed that this new perspective can lead to valid insights that are useful psychotherapeutic exercises.

Some psychotherapists have used or advocated the use of psychedelics for this purpose since the 1950s, as described many years before by Sigmund Freud, to "make conscious the unconscious" (Snyder 1974, p. 44). Although a case can be made for the psychotherapeutic use of this group of drugs, the Food and Drug Administration (FDA) has not yet approved any of these agents for psychiatric use; it has, however, approved clinical trials to study the psychedelic/stimulant drug Ecstasy (MDMA) to evaluate if it would be useful in the treatment of posttraumatic stress disorder (PTSD). These studies are supported by an organization known as the Multidisciplinary Association for Psychedelic Studies (MAPS) and are speculated to require 10 years at a cost of $15 million to complete. If approved, the intent is to use MDMA as an adjunct to psychotherapy because of its ability to increase feelings of empathy (MAPS 2013). Although considerable

---

KEY TERMS

synesthesia
a subjective sensation or image of a sense other than the one being stimulated, such as an auditory sensation caused by a visual stimulus

flashbacks
recurrences of earlier drug-induced sensory experiences in the absence of the drug

caution is still needed due to the somewhat unpredictable nature of these drugs, other small studies are examining the effects of psychedelic drugs such as psilocybin and LSD to treat emotional problems such as depression in cancer patients, obsessive-compulsive disorder, and end-of-life anxiety. Some of the reported results have been encouraging, but they are very preliminary and still small-scale. There is concern that some of the reported benefits have been exaggerated by scientists-turned-evangelists who are anxious to make these drugs routine therapeutics (Tierney 2010). Only time will tell how, or if, the medical/scientific community will react to the "new science" that is promoted as evidence that psychedelics have an important therapeutic role to play in modern-day medicine. Clearly, this is a controversy that is far from being resolved.

LOSS OF IDENTITY AND COSMIC MERGING

The final features that set the psychedelics apart as unique drugs were described by Snyder (1974) as the "mystical-spiritual aspect of the drug experience." He claimed, "It is indescribable. For how can anyone verbalize a merging of his being with the totality of the universe? How do you put into words the feeling that 'all is one,' 'I am of the all,' 'I am no longer.' One's skin ceases to be a boundary between self and others" (p. 45). Because consumption of hallucinogen-containing plants has often been part of religious ceremonies, it is likely that this sense of cosmic merging and union with all humankind correlates to the exhilaratingly spiritual experiences described by many religious mystics.

The loss of identity and personal boundaries caused by hallucinogens is not viewed as being so spiritually enticing by all. In particular, for individuals who have rigid, highly ordered personalities, the dissolution of a well-organized and well-structured world is terrifying because the drug destroys the individual's emotional support. Such an individual finds that the loss of a separate identity can cause extreme panic and anxiety. During these drug-induced panic states, which in some ways are schizophrenic-like, people have committed suicide and homicide. These tragic reactions are part of the risk of using hallucinogenics and explain some of the FDA's hesitancy to legalize or authorize them for psychotherapeutic use.

■ Mechanisms of Action

As with most drugs, hallucinogens represent the proverbial "double-edged sword." These drugs may cause potentially useful psychiatric effects for many people. However, the variability in positive versus negative responses, coupled with lack of understanding as to what factors are responsible for the variables, suggest that these drugs may be dangerous for some patients and difficult to manage.

Some researchers have suggested that all hallucinogens act at a common central nervous system (CNS) site to exert their psychedelic effects. Although this hypothesis has not been totally disproven, there is little evidence to support it. The fact that so many different types of drugs can cause hallucinogenic effects suggests that multiple mechanisms are likely responsible for their actions.

The most predictable and typical psychedelic experiences are caused by LSD or similar agents. Consequently, these agents have been the primary focus of studies intended to elucidate the nature of hallucinogenic mechanisms. Although LSD has effects at several CNS sites, ranging from the spinal cord to the cortex of the brain, its effects on the neurotransmitter serotonin most likely account for its psychedelic properties (Luscher 2012). That LSD and similar drugs alter serotonin activity has been proven; how they affect this transmitter is not so readily apparent.

Although many experts believe changes in serotonin activity are the basis for the psychedelic properties of most hallucinogens, a case can be made for the involvement of norepinephrine, dopamine, acetylcholine, and perhaps other transmitter systems as well. Only additional research will be able to sort out this complex but important issue.

Types of Hallucinogenic Agents

Due to recent technological developments, understanding of hallucinogens has advanced; even so, the classification of these drugs remains somewhat arbitrary. Many agents produce some of the pharmacological effects of the traditional psychedelics, such as LSD and mescaline.

A second type of hallucinogen includes those agents that have amphetamine-like molecular structures (referred to as phenylethylamines) and possess some stimulant action; this group includes drugs such as DOM (dimethoxymethylamphetamine), MDA (methylenedioxyamphetamine), MDMA (methylenedioxymethamphetamine or Ecstasy), and likely mephedrone (methylmethcathinone). These agents vary in their hallucinogen or stimulant properties. MDA is more like an amphetamine (stimulant), MDMA is more like LSD (hallucinogen), whereas the drug mephedrone has potent properties of both (Hadlock, Webb, and McFadden 2011). In large doses, however, each of the phenylethylamines causes substantial CNS stimulation.

The third major group of hallucinogens comprises the anticholinergic drugs, which block some of the receptors for the neurotransmitter acetylcholine. Almost all drugs that antagonize these receptors cause hallucinations in high doses. Many of these potent anticholinergic hallucinogens are naturally occurring and have been known, used, and abused for millennia.

Albert Hofmann created LSD while trying to synthesize a drug to study psychosis.

■ Traditional Hallucinogens: LSD Types

The LSD-like drugs are considered to be the prototypical hallucinogens and are used as the basis of comparison for other types of agents with psychedelic properties. Included in this group are LSD itself and some hallucinogens derived from plants, such as mescaline from the peyote cactus, psilocybin from mushrooms, dimethyltryptamine (DMT) from seeds, and myristicin from nutmeg. Because LSD is the principal hallucinogen, its origin, history, and properties are discussed in detail, providing a basis for understanding the other psychedelic drugs.

LYSERGIC ACID DIETHYLAMIDE

Lysergic acid diethylamide (LSD) is a relatively new drug, but similar compounds have existed for a long time. For example, accounts from the Middle Ages tell about a strange affliction that caused pregnant women to abort and others to develop strange burning sensations in their extremities. Today, we call this condition **ergotism** and know it is caused by eating grains contaminated by the ergot fungus. This fungus produces compounds related to LSD called the *ergot alkaloids* (Goldstein 1994; NIDA 2007b). Besides the sensory effects, the ergot substances can cause hallucinations, delirium, and psychosis.

In 1938, Albert Hofmann, a scientist for Sandoz Pharmaceutical Laboratories of Basel, Switzerland, worked on a series of ergot compounds in a

search for active chemicals that might be of medical value. Lysergic acid was similar in structure to a compound called nikethamide, a stimulant, and Hofmann tried to create slight chemical modifications that might merit further testing. The result of this effort was the production of lysergic acid diethylamide, or LSD. Hofmann's experience with this new compound gave insight into the effects of this drug (Smith 2008).

Soon after LSD was discovered, the similarity of experiences with this agent to the symptoms of schizophrenia were noted, which prompted researchers to investigate correlations between the two (Weber 2006). The hope was to use LSD as a tool for producing an artificial psychosis to aid in understanding the biochemistry of psychosis (NIDA 2001). Interest in this use of LSD has declined because it is generally accepted that LSD effects differ from natural psychoses.

The use of LSD in psychotherapy has also been tried in connection with the treatment of alcoholism, autism, paranoia, schizophrenia, and various other mental and emotional disorders (Weber 2006). Even though there continues to be advocates for the therapeutic use of LSD (as discussed earlier in this chapter), the administration of LSD for clinical objectives has not been approved for general use because of its limited proven successes, legal aspects, difficulty in obtaining the pure drug, adverse reactions to the drug ("bad trips" can occur under controlled as well as uncontrolled conditions), and rapid tolerance buildup in some patients. However, there has been a recent resurgence in combining low doses of LSD with psychotherapy to treat depression, compulsive disorders, or chronic pain. Researchers conducting small

KEY TERM

ergotism
poisoning by toxic substances from the ergot fungus *Claviceps purpurea*

studies claim that for some patients the drug can be a catalyst to help change perception of problems and make the patient more responsive to the behavioral therapies (Kelland 2010). No one believes that this approach will be a panacea or universally effective, and even the strongest of advocates emphasize that it is important to use only low doses for relatively short periods of time (Ferro 2013; Kelland 2010).

Nonmedical interest in LSD and related drugs began to grow during the 1950s and peaked in the 1960s, when LSD was used by millions of young Americans for chemical escape. On rare occasions, a "bad trip" would cause a user to feel terror and panic; these experiences resulted in well-publicized accidental deaths due to jumping from building tops or running into the pathway of oncoming vehicles (U.S. Department of Justice 1991).

As with other hallucinogens, the use of LSD by teenagers declined somewhat over the 1970s and 1980s but began to rise again in the early 1990s. The reason for this rise was thought to relate to a decline in the perceived dangers of using LSD and an increase in peer approval. However, surveys have demonstrated that recent dramatic drops in LSD use have not been explained (Johnston et al. 2010) (see Table 12.1). Of high school seniors sampled in 1975, 11.3% had used LSD sometime during their life; that number declined to 8.6% in 1992, rebounded to 12.2% in 1999, and tumbled to 4.6% in 2004 and 3.8% in 2012. LSD users are typically college or high school students, white, middle-class, and risk-takers (Johnston 2013).

SYNTHESIS AND ADMINISTRATION

LSD is a complex molecule that requires about 1 week to be synthesized. Because of the sophisticated chemistry necessary for its production, LSD is not manufactured by local illicit laboratories but requires the skills of a trained chemist (U.S. Department of Justice 2002, 2003). Because of LSD's potency, it has been difficult to locate illicit LSD labs; small quantities of LSD are sufficient to satisfy the demand and can be easily transported without detection. The last publicized major LSD lab seizure in the United States was in 2000 when a Drug Enforcement Agency (DEA) raid in Kansas resulted in a temporary 95% decrease in LSD supplies.

The physical properties of LSD are not distinctive. In its purified form, LSD is colorless, odorless, and tasteless. It can be purchased in several forms, including tiny tablets (about one-tenth the size of aspirins, called microdots), capsules, thin squares of gelatin called "window panes," or more

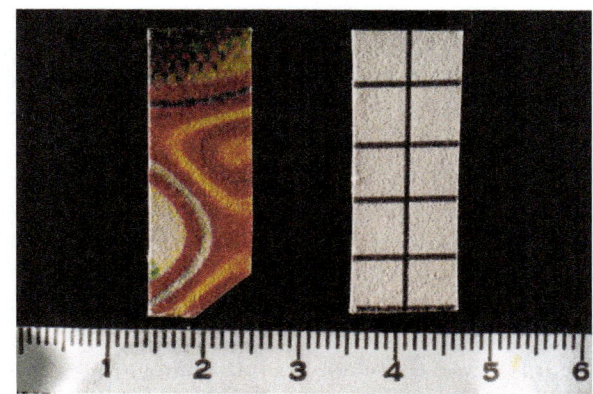

Small quantities of LSD are applied to squares of absorbent blotter paper to be chewed or swallowed.

Courtesy of Orange County Police Department, Florida.

commonly dissolved and applied to paper as "blotter acid" and cut up into 0.25-inch squares for individual dosing (Partnership at DrugFree.org n.d.a.). Each square is swallowed or chewed and represents a single dose. One gram of LSD can provide approximately 10,000 individual doses and be sold on the streets for $10,000–100,000. Although LSD usually is taken by mouth, it is sometimes injected. It costs about $1–10/dose (Freeman 2013).

PHYSIOLOGICAL EFFECTS

Like many hallucinogens, LSD is remarkably potent. The typical dose today is 20 to 30 micrograms, compared with a typical dose of 150 to 300 micrograms in the 1960s. This difference in dose likely explains why today fewer users of LSD are experiencing severe side effects (NIDA 2007b). In monkeys, the lethal dose has been determined to be about 5 milligrams per kilogram of body weight.

When taken orally, LSD is readily absorbed and diffused into all tissues. It passes through the placenta into the fetus and through the blood–brain barrier. The brain receives about 1% of the total dose.

Within the brain, LSD is particularly concentrated in the hypothalamus, the limbic system, and the auditory and visual reflex areas. Electrodes placed in the limbic system show an "electrical storm," or a massive increase in neural activity, which might correlate with the overwhelming flood of sensations and the phenomenon of synesthesia reported by the user (NIDA 2001). LSD also activates the sympathetic nervous system; shortly after the drug is taken, body temperature, heart rate, and blood pressure rise; the person sweats; and the pupils of the eyes dilate. Its effects on the parasympathetic nervous system increase salivation and nausea (NIDA 2007b). These systemic effects do not appear to be related to the hallucinogenic properties of the drug.

The effect of LSD begins within 30 to 90 minutes after ingestion and can last up to 12 hours. Tolerance to the effects of LSD develops more rapidly and lasts longer than tolerance to other hallucinogens (NIDA 2001). Tolerance develops very quickly to repeated doses, probably because of a change in sensitivity of the target cells in the brain rather than a change in its metabolism. Tolerance wears off within a few days after the drug is discontinued. Because there are no withdrawal symptoms, a person does not become physically dependent, but some psychological dependency on LSD can occur (NIDA 2007b).

BEHAVIORAL EFFECTS

Because LSD alters a number of systems in the brain, its behavioral effects are many and variable among individuals (Goldstein 1995; NIDA 2009). The following sections address common CNS responses to this drug.

Creativity and Insight

A question often raised by researchers interested in experimenting with LSD is this: Does LSD help expand the mind, increasing insight and creativity? This question is extremely difficult to answer because no one has ever determined the origin of insight and creativity. Moreover, each of us views these qualities differently.

Subjects under the influence of LSD often express the feeling of being more creative, but creative acts such as drawing and painting are hindered by the motor impairment caused by LSD. The products of artists under the influence of the drug usually prove to be inferior to those produced before the drug experience. Paintings done in LSD creativity studies have been described as reminiscent of "schizophrenic art."

In an often-cited study, creativity, attitude, and anxiety tests on 24 college students found that LSD had no objective effect on creativity, although many of the subjects said they felt they were more creative (McGlothin, Cohen, and McGlothin 1967). This paradox is noted in several studies of LSD use. The subjects believe they have more insight and provide better answers to life's problems, but they do not or cannot demonstrate this increase objectively. Overt behavior is not modified, and these new insights are short-lived unless they are reinforced by modified behavior.

In spite of these results, some researchers still contend that LSD can enhance the creative process.

For example, Oscar Janigar, a psychiatrist at the University of California, Los Angeles, claimed to have determined that LSD does not produce a tangible alteration in the way a painter paints; thus, it does not turn a poor painter into a good one. However, Janigar claimed that LSD does alter the way the painter appraises the world and allows the artist to "plunge into areas where access was restricted by confines of perceptions" and consequently becomes more creative (Tucker 1987, p. 16).

Adverse Psychedelic Effects

It is important to remember that there is no typical pattern of response to LSD. The experience varies for each user as a function of the person's set, or expectations, and setting, or environment, during the experience (Publishers Group 2002). Two of the major negative responses are described as follows (NIDA 2009; Pahnke et al. 1970):

1. The psychotic adverse reaction, or "freakout," is an intense, nightmarish experience. The subject may have complete loss of emotional control and experience paranoid delusions, hallucinations, panic attacks, psychosis, and catatonic seizures. In rare instances, some of these reactions are prolonged, lasting days.

2. The nonpsychotic adverse reaction may involve varying degrees of tension, anxiety, fear, depression, and despair but not as intense a response as the "freakout."

A person with deep psychological problems or a strong need to be in conscious control or one who takes the drug in an unfavorable setting is more likely to have an adverse reaction than a person with a well-integrated personality. Severe LSD behavioral toxicity can be treated with tranquilizers or a sedative like a benzodiazepine.

Perceptual Effects

Because the brain's sensory processing is altered by a hallucinogenic dose of LSD, many kinds of unusual illusions can occur. Some users report seeing shifting geometrical patterns mixed with intense color perception; others observe the movement of stationary objects, such that a speck on the wall appears as a large blinking eye or an unfolding flower. Interpretation of sounds can also be scrambled; a dropped ashtray may become a gun fired at the user, for instance. In some cases, LSD alters perceptions to the extent that people feel they can walk on water or fly through the air. The sensation that the body is distorted and even coming apart is another common effect, especially for novice users.

Courtesy of Dr. Glen Hanson

This head was sculpted by a university student while under the influence of LSD.

Thoughts of suicide and sometimes actual attempts can be caused by use of LSD as well (NIDA 2009).

Many LSD users find their sense of time distorted, such that hours may be perceived as years or an eternity. As discussed earlier, users may also have a distorted perception of their own knowledge or creativity; for instance, they may feel their ideas or work are especially unique, brilliant, or artistic. When analyzed by a person not on LSD or explained after the trip is over, however, these ideas or creations are almost always quite ordinary.

In sum, LSD alters perception such that any sensation can be perceived in the extreme. An experience can be incredibly beautiful and uplifting. However, sometimes the experience can be very unpleasant.

Flashbacks

The flashback is an interesting but poorly understood phenomenon of LSD use. Although usually thought of as being adverse, sometimes flashbacks are pleasant and even referred to as "free trips." During a flashback, sensations caused by previous LSD use return, although the subject is not using the drug at the time.

There are three broad categories of negative LSD-related flashbacks:

1. *"Body trip"*: Recurrence of an unpleasant physical sensation
2. *"Bad mind trip"*: Recurrence of a distressing thought or emotion

3. *Altered visual perception:* The most frequent type of recurrence, consisting of seeing dots, flashes, trails of light, halos, false motion in the peripheral field, and other sensations

Flashbacks are most disturbing because they come on unexpectedly. Some have been reported years after use of LSD; for most people, however, flashbacks usually subside within weeks or months after taking LSD. The duration of a flashback is variable, lasting from a few minutes to several hours (NIDA 2009).

Although the precise mechanism of flashbacks is unknown, physical or psychological stresses and some drugs such as marijuana may trigger these experiences (NIDA 2009). It has been proposed that flashbacks are an especially vivid form of memory that becomes seared into the subconscious mind due to the effects of LSD on the brain's transmitters.

Treatment consists of reassurance that the condition will go away and use of a sedative such as diazepam (Valium), if necessary, to treat the anxiety or panic that can accompany the flashback experience.

GENETIC DAMAGE AND BIRTH DEFECTS

Experiments conducted in the mid-1960s suggested that LSD could cause birth defects, based on the observation that, when LSD was added to a suspension of human white blood cells in a test tube, the chromosomes of these cells were damaged. From this finding, it was proposed that when LSD was consumed by human beings, it could damage the chromosomes of the male sperm or female egg, or the cells of the developing infant. Such damage theoretically could result in congenital defects in offspring (Dishotsky et al. 1971).

Carefully controlled studies conducted after news of LSD's chromosomal effects were made public did not support this hypothesis. Experiments revealed that, in contrast to the test tube findings, there is no chromosomal damage to white blood cells or any other cells when LSD is given to a human being (Dishotsky et al. 1971).

Studies have also shown that there are no carcinogenic or mutagenic effects from using LSD in experimental animals or human beings, with the exception of the fruit fly. (LSD is a mutagen in fruit flies if given in doses that are equivalent to 100,000 times the hallucinogenic dose for people.) Teratogenic effects occur in mice if LSD is given early in pregnancy. LSD may be teratogenic in rhesus monkeys if it is injected in doses (based on body weight) exceeding at least 100 times the usual hallucinogenic dose for humans. In other studies, women who took street LSD, but not those given pure LSD, had a higher rate of spontaneous abortions and births of malformed infants; this finding suggests that contaminants in adulterated LSD were responsible for the fetal effects and not the hallucinogen itself (Dishotsky et al. 1971).

EARLY HUMAN RESEARCH

In the 1950s, the U.S. government—specifically, the Central Intelligence Agency (CIA) and the army—became interested in reports of the effects of mind-altering drugs, including LSD. Unknown to the public at the time, these agencies conducted tests on human beings to learn more about such compounds and determine their usefulness in conducting military and clandestine missions. These activities became public when a biochemist, Frank Olson, killed himself in 1953 after being given a drink laced with LSD. Olson had a severe psychotic reaction and was being treated for the condition when he jumped out of a 10th-story window. His family was told only that he had committed suicide. The connection to LSD was not uncovered until 1975. The court awarded Olson's family $750,000 in damages in 1976.

In 1976, the extent of these studies was revealed; nearly 585 soldiers and 900 civilians had been given LSD in poorly organized experiments in which participants were coerced into taking this drug or not told that they were receiving it. Powerful hallucinogens such as LSD can cause serious psychological damage in some subjects, especially when they are unaware of what is happening (Remsberg 2010; Willing 2007).

The legal consequences of these LSD studies continued for years. As recently as 1987, a New York judge awarded $700,000 to the family of a mental patient who killed himself after having been given LSD without an explanation of the drug's nature. The judge said that there was a "conspiracy of silence" among the army, the Department of Justice, and the New York State Attorney General to conceal events surrounding the death of the subject, Harold Blauer (Government Conspiracy 2010).

MESCALINE (PEYOTE)

Mescaline is one of approximately 30 psychoactive chemicals that have been isolated from the peyote cactus and used for centuries in the Americas (see "Here and Now: Peyote"). One of the first reports on the peyote plant was made by Francisco Hernandez to the court of King Philip II of Spain. King Philip was interested in reports from the earlier Cortés expedition about strange medicines the natives used, and sent Hernandez to collect information about herbs and medicines. Hernandez worked on this project from 1570 to 1575 and reported on the use of more than 1200 plant remedies as well as the existence of many hallucinogenic plants. He was one of the first to record the eating of parts of the peyote cactus and the resulting visions and mental changes.

In the 17th century, Spanish Catholic priests asked their Indian converts to confess to the use of peyote, which they believed was used to conjure up demons. However, nothing stopped its use. By 1760, use of peyote had spread into what is now the United States. Peyote has been confused with another plant, the mescal shrub, which produces dark red beans that contain an extremely toxic alkaloid called *cytisine*. This alkaloid may cause hallucinations, convulsions, and even death. In addition, a mescal liquor is made from the agave

HERE AND NOW

Peyote: An Ancient Indian Way

Members of the Native American Church use the buttons of the hallucinogenic peyote cactus to brew a sacramental tea as sacred to them as the bread and wine of the Christian Eucharist is to Catholics. As described by one member, "Peyote is a gift given to the Indians, but its ways cannot be obtained overnight. It has to be done with sincerity. It becomes part of your way of life. One has to walk that walk." Those who accept this form of worship believe that respectful use of peyote can be a gateway to the realm of the spirit, visions, and guidance. The use of peyote as part of the latest New Age craze is very disturbing to members of this church and is viewed almost as a form of sacrilege.

Data from Mims, B. "Peyote: When the Ancient Indian Way Collides with a New Age Craze." *Salt Lake Tribune* 258 (1 July 1999): A-10; and Native American Church. 2008. Available http://www.nativeamericanchurch.com. Accessed February 17, 2011.

The peyote cactus contains a number of drugs. The best known is mescaline.

cactus. Partly because of misidentification with the toxic mescal beans, the U.S. government outlawed the use of both peyote and mescaline for everyone except members of the Native American Church (Mims 2000). Mescaline has been used for decades by this group as part of their religious sacrament. Research has suggested that long-term religious use of peyote does not have significant psychological effects or cause problems with cognitive performance in Native Americans (Halpern et al. 2005).

Mescaline is the most active drug in peyote; it induces intensified perception of colors and euphoria in the user. However, as Aldous Huxley said in *The Doors of Perception* (1954), his book about his experimentation with mescaline, "Along with the happily transfigured majority of mescaline takers there is a minority that finds in the drug only hell and purgatory." After Huxley related his experiences with mescaline, it was used by an increasing number of people.

PHYSIOLOGICAL EFFECTS
The average dose of mescaline that will cause hallucinations and other physiological effects is from 300 to 600 milligrams. It may take up to 20 peyote (mescal) buttons (ingested orally) to get 600 milligrams of mescaline.

Based on animal studies, scientists estimate that a lethal dosage is 10 to 30 times greater than that which causes behavioral effects in human beings. (About 200 milligrams is the lowest mind-altering dose.) Death in animals results from convulsions and respiratory arrest. Mescaline is perhaps 1000 to 3000 times less potent than LSD and 30 times less potent than another common hallucinogen, psilocybin (Mathias 1993). Psilocybin is discussed later in this chapter.

Mescaline's effects include dilation of the pupils (**mydriasis**), increase in body temperature, anxiety, visual hallucinations, and alteration of body image. The last effect is a type of hallucination in which parts of the body may seem to disappear or to become grossly distorted. Mescaline induces vomiting in many people and some muscular relaxation (sedation). Apparently, there are few aftereffects or drug hangover feelings at low doses. Higher doses of mescaline slow the heart and respiratory rhythm, contract the intestines and the uterus, and cause headache, difficulty in coordination, dry skin with itching, and hypertension (high blood pressure).

Mescaline users report that they lose all awareness of time. As with LSD, the setting for the trip influences the user's reactions. Most mescaline users prefer natural settings, most likely due to the historical association of this drug with Native Americans and their nature-related spiritual experiences (often under the influence of this drug). The visual hallucinations achieved depend on the individual. Colors are at first intensified and may be followed by hallucinations of shades, movements, forms, and events. The senses of smell and taste are enhanced. Some people claim (as with LSD) that they can "hear" colors and "see" sounds, such as the wind. Synesthesia occurs naturally in a small percentage of cases. At low to medium doses, a state of euphoria is reported, often followed by a feeling of anxiety and less frequently by depression. Occasionally, users observe themselves as two people and experience the sensation that the mind and the body are separate entities. A number of people have had cosmic experiences that are profound—almost religious—and in which they discover a sense of unity with all creation. People who have this sensation often believe they have discovered the meaning of existence.

MECHANISM OF ACTION
Within 30 to 120 minutes after ingestion, mescaline reaches a maximum concentration in the brain. The effects may persist for as long as 9 or 10 hours. Hallucinations may last up to 2 hours and are usually affected by the dose level. About half the dose is excreted unchanged after 6 hours and can be recovered in the urine for reuse (if peyote is in short supply). A slow tolerance builds

KEY TERM
mydriasis
pupil dilation

up after repeated use, and there is cross-tolerance to LSD. As with LSD, mescaline intoxication can be alleviated or stopped by taking a dose of chlorpromazine (Thorazine), a tranquilizer, and to a lesser extent by taking diazepam (Valium). Like LSD, mescaline probably exerts much of its hallucinogenic effects by altering serotonin systems (Delgado 2013; NIDA 2009).

Analysis of street samples of mescaline obtained in a number of U.S. cities over the past decade shows that the chemical sold rarely is authentic. Regardless of color or appearance, these street drugs are usually other hallucinogens, such as LSD, 2,6-dimethoxy-4-methylamphetamine (DOM), or PCP. If a person decides to take hallucinogenic street drugs, "let the buyer beware." Not only is the actual content often different and potentially much more toxic than bargained for (they are frequently contaminated), but also the dosage is usually unknown even if the drug is genuine.

PSILOCYBIN

The drug psilocybin has a long and colorful history. Its principal source is the *Psilocybe mexicana* mushroom of the "magic" variety (Goldstein 1994; U.S. Department of Justice 2002). It was first used by some of the early natives of Central America more than 2000 years ago. In Guatemala, statues of mushrooms that date back to 100 BC have been found. The Aztecs later used the mushrooms for ceremonial rites. When the Spaniards came into Mexico in the 1500s, the natives were calling the *Psilocybe mexicana* mushroom "God's flesh." Because of this seeming sacrilege, the natives were harshly treated by the Spanish priests.

Gordon Wasson identified the *Psilocybe mexicana* mushroom in 1955. The active ingredient was extracted in 1958 by Albert Hofmann, who also synthesized LSD. During research, Hofmann wanted to make certain he would feel the effects of the mushroom, so he ate 32 of them, weighing 2.4 grams (a medium dose by Native American standards), and then recorded his hallucinogenic reactions (Burger 1968).

Timothy Leary also tried some psilocybin mushrooms in Mexico in 1960; apparently, the experience influenced him greatly. On his return to Harvard, he carried out a series of experiments using psilocybin with student groups. Leary was careless in experimental procedures and did some work in uncontrolled situations. His actions caused a major administrative upheaval, ending in his departure from Harvard.

One of Leary's questionable studies was the "Good Friday" experiment in which 20 theological students were given either a placebo or psilocybin in a double-blind study (that is, neither the researcher nor the subjects know who gets the placebo or the drug), after which all attended the same 2.5-hour Good Friday service. The experimental group reported mystical experiences, whereas the control group did not (Pahnke and Richards 1966). Leary believed that the experience was of value and that, under proper control and guidance, the hallucinatory experience could be beneficial.

Psilocybin is not very common on the street. Generally, it is administered orally and is eaten either fresh or dried. Accidental poisonings are common for those who mistakenly consume poisonous mushrooms rather than the hallucinogenic variety.

The dried form of these mushrooms contains from 0.2% to 0.5% psilocybin. The hallucinogenic effects produced are quite similar to those of LSD, and there is a cross-tolerance among psilocybin, LSD, and mescaline, suggesting they have similar mechanisms of action. The effects caused by psilocybin vary with the dosage taken. Up to 4 milligrams cause a pleasant experience, relaxation, and some body sensation. In some subjects, higher doses cause considerable perceptual and body image changes, accompanied by hallucinations.

Although psilocybin has been reported to be helpful in the treatment of depression for some people, in extreme cases, psilocybin can cause mental problems and induce the first stages of schizophrenia-like psychosis (NIDA 2001; Unger 2010; Vollenwelder et al. 1998; The Week 2010). Psilocybin stimulates the autonomic nervous system, dilates the pupils, and increases body temperature. There is some evidence that psilocybin is metabolized into psilocin, which is more potent and may be the principal active ingredient. Psilocin is found in mushrooms, albeit in small amounts. Like the other hallucinogens, psilocybin apparently causes no physical dependence (Delgado 2013; NIDA 2009).

TRYPTAMINES

Some compounds related to the tryptamine class of drugs (molecules that resemble the neurotransmitter serotonin) have hallucinogenic properties and can exist naturally in herbs, fungi, and animals or can be synthesized in the laboratory. Some of the newer tryptamines are freely available over

The *Psilocybe* mushroom is the source of the hallucinogens psilocybin and psilocin.

the Internet on websites, but their effects are not well understood. Many, but not all, of these compounds are Schedule I drugs and illegal (DEA 2002b; Gatch et al. 2011). Two examples are discussed in this section.

DIMETHYLTRYPTAMINE

Dimethyltryptamine (DMT) is a short-acting hallucinogen found in the seeds of certain leguminous trees native to the West Indies and parts of South America (Schultes 1978) and is reported to occur naturally in the human body in low quantities (Horgan n.d.). It is also prepared synthetically in illicit laboratories and is reported to have both beneficial and terrifyingly adverse effects (Horgan n.d.). For centuries, the powdered seeds have been used as a snuff called cohoba in pipes and snuffing tubes. Haitian natives claim that, under the influence of the drug, they can communicate with their gods. Its effects occur rapidly and may last less than 1 hour, which has earned it the nickname "the businessman's lunch break" drug (Carollo 2010).

DMT has no effect when taken orally; it is inhaled either as smoke from the burning plant or in vaporized form. DMT is sometimes added to parsley leaves or flakes, tobacco, or marijuana to induce its hallucinogenic effect. The usual dose is 60 to 150 milligrams. In structure and action, it is similar to psilocybin, although it is not as powerful. Like the other hallucinogens discussed, DMT does not cause physical dependence.

FOXY

The synthetic substance chemically named 5-methoxy-N,N-diisopropyltryptamine (Foxy) is a relatively new hallucinogen. This drug has been used at raves and clubs in Arizona, California, New York, and Florida. It was added to the DEA Schedule I

category in 2004. At lower doses, Foxy can cause euphoria; at higher doses, its effects are similar to LSD, causing hallucinations and psychedelic experiences (DEA 2002b).

NUTMEG

High doses of nutmeg can be quite intoxicating, causing symptoms such as drowsiness, stupor, delirium, and sleep. Prison inmates have known about this drug for years, so in most prisons use of spices such as nutmeg is restricted. It is typically young people who experiment with nutmeg to get high, but because of the frequent unpleasant side effects, abusers often end up either in an emergency room or calling a poison control center and usually are not interested in trying nutmeg again. Needless to say, nutmeg is not perceived as a major drug abuse problem by authorities (Conley 2010).

Nutmeg contains 5% to 15% myristica oil, which is responsible for the physical effects. Myristicin (about 4%), which is structurally similar to mescaline, and elemicin are probably the most potent psychoactive ingredients in nutmeg. Myristicin blocks release of serotonin from brain neurons. The exterior covering of the nutmeg seed also contains the hallucinogenic compound myristicin.

Two tablespoons of nutmeg (about 14 grams) taken orally cause a rather unpleasant trip with a dreamlike stage; rapid heartbeat, dry mouth, and thirst are experienced as well. Agitation, apprehension, and a sense of impending doom may last about 12 hours, with a sense of unreality persisting for several days (Claus, Tyler, and Brady 1970; Conley 2010).

■ Phenylethylamine Hallucinogens

The phenylethylamine drugs are chemically related to amphetamines. Phenylethylamines have varying degrees of hallucinogenic and CNS stimulant effects, which are likely related to their ability to release serotonin and dopamine, respectively. Consequently, the phenylethylamines that predominantly release serotonin are dominated by their hallucinogenic action and are more LSD-like, whereas those more inclined to release dopamine are dominated by their stimulant effects and are amphetamine-like.

DIMETHOXYMETHYLAMPHETAMINE

The basic structure of dimethoxymethylamphetamine (DOM or STP) is amphetamine. Nonetheless, it is a fairly powerful hallucinogen that seems to work through mechanisms similar to those found with mescaline and LSD. In fact, the effects of DOM are similar to those caused by a combination of amphetamine and LSD, with the hallucinogenic effects of the drug overpowering the amphetamine-like physiological effects. Like other hallucinogens, DOM is not considered to be particularly addicting, and users experience tolerance with multiple drug exposures (Summit Malibu 2010).

"DESIGNER" AMPHETAMINES

The hybrid actions of "designer amphetamines" as psychedelic stimulants not only make them a particularly fascinating topic for research, but also provide a unique experience described by drug abusers as a "smooth amphetamine" or an **entactogen** (implying that the pleasurable sensation of touch is enhanced). This characterization likely accounts for the popularity of the designer amphetamines (de la Torre et al. 2004; Passie 2012).

3,4-METHYLENEDIOXYAMPHETAMINE

3,4-Methylenedioxyamphetamine (MDA), first synthesized in 1910, is structurally related to both mescaline and amphetamine. Early research found that MDA is an anorexiant (causing loss of appetite) as well as a mood elevator in some persons. Further research has shown that the mode of action of MDA is similar to that of amphetamines. It causes additional release of the neurotransmitters serotonin, dopamine, and norepinephrine (Baggot et al. 2010).

In the past, MDA was used as an adjunct to psychotherapy. In one study, eight volunteers who had previously experienced the effects of LSD under clinical conditions were given 150 milligrams of MDA. Effects of the drug were noted between 40 and 60 minutes following ingestion by all eight subjects. The subjective effects following administration peaked at the end of 90 minutes and persisted for approximately 8 hours. None of the subjects experienced hallucinations, perceptual distortion, or closed-eye imagery, but they reported that the feelings the drug induced had some relationship to those previously experienced with LSD. The subjects found that both drugs induced an intensification of feelings, increased

perceptions of self-insight, and heightened empathy with others during the experience. Most of the subjects also felt an increased sense of aesthetic enjoyment at some point during the intoxication. Seven of the eight subjects said they perceived music as "three-dimensional" (Naranjo, Shulgin, and Sargent 1967).

On the street, MDA has been called the *love drug* because of its effects on the sense of touch and the attitudes of the users. Users often report experiencing a sense of well-being (likely a stimulant effect) and heightened tactile sensations (likely a hallucinogenic effect), and thus increased pleasure through sex and expressions of affection. Those under the influence of MDA frequently focus on interpersonal relationships and demonstrate an overwhelming desire or need to be with or talk to people. Some users say they have a very pleasant "body high"—more sensual than cerebral, and more empathetic than introverted. For these reasons, MDA is sometimes used by persons attending raves, much like MDMA or Ecstasy (Baggott et al. 2010).

The unpleasant side effects most often reported are nausea, periodic tensing of muscles in the neck, tightening of the jaw and grinding of the teeth, and dilation of the pupils. Street doses of MDA range from 100 to 150 milligrams. Serious convulsions and death have resulted from larger doses, but in these cases the quantity of MDA was not accurately measured. Ingestion of 500 milligrams of pure MDA has been shown to cause death. The only reported adverse reaction to moderate doses is a marked physical exhaustion, lasting as long as 2 days (Marquardt, DiStefano, and Ling 1978).

An unpleasant MDA experience should be treated the same as a bad trip with any hallucinogen. The person should be "talked down" (reassured) in a friendly and supportive manner. The use of other drugs is rarely needed, although medical attention may be necessary.

Under the Comprehensive Drug Abuse Prevention and Control Act of 1970, MDA is classified as a Schedule I substance; illegal possession is a serious offense.

METHYLENEDIOXYMETHAMPHETAMINE

Methylenedioxymethamphetamine (MDMA) is a modification of MDA but is thought to have more psychedelic and less stimulant activity (for example, euphoria) than its predecessor. MDMA is also structurally similar to mescaline. This drug has become known as Ecstasy, XTC, and Adam (Zickler 2000).

KEY TERM

entactogen
a drug that enhances the sensation and pleasure of touching

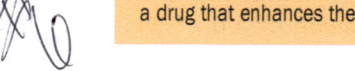

MDMA was synthesized in 1912 to suppress appetite, but due to bizarre side effects it was withdrawn from development until it became widely used in the 1980s (Adam 2006). This designer amphetamine can be produced easily, although the process can be hazardous and the chemicals used for the synthesis are difficult to obtain (DEA 2002a; Friends of Narconon 2010). Although the synthesis can be done by local illicit laboratories (Hyslop 2000), most of the MDMA supplies in this country are smuggled in from outlaw drug laboratories in European countries such as the Netherlands. The unusual psychological effects it produces are part of the reason for its popularity. The drug causes euphoria, increased energy, increased sensitivity to touch, and lowered inhibitions. Many users claim it intensifies emotional feelings without sensory distortion and that it increases empathy and awareness both of the user's body and of the aesthetics of the surroundings (Farley 2000). Some consider MDMA to be an aphrodisiac. Because MDMA lowers defense mechanisms and reduces inhibitions, it has even been used during psychoanalysis (Vastag 2010). In fact, recently there have been reports that an initial FDA-approved clinical trial has demonstrated that MDMA was effective in the treatment of 10 or 12 patients suffering from PTSD (MAPS 2013). Obviously this represents a very small study, and the results must be confirmed by other, much larger clinical trials.

MDMA—popularized in the 1980s by articles in *Newsweek* (Adler 1985), *Time* (Toufexis 1985), and other magazines—recently was again touted on the national newsstands as a drug with euphoric effects, potential therapeutic value, and lack of serious side effects. MDMA is popular with college-age students and young adults (Johnston et al. 2010; Office of National Drug Control Policy [ONDCP] 2008). Because of its effect of enhancing sensations, MDMA has been used as part of a countercultural rave scene, including high-tech music and laser light shows. Observers report that MDMA-linked rave parties are reminiscent of the acid parties of the 1960s and 1970s. The latest cycle of MDMA popularity peaked in 2001 and was being used by 10% of high school seniors (Johnston 2013); however, due to reports of MDMA neurotoxicity and persistent negative side effects, use of this drug decreased dramatically and by 2012 was being used by only 3.8% of high school seniors (Johnston 2013).

Because of the widespread abuse of MDMA, the DEA prohibited its use by formally placing it on the Schedule I list in 1988. At the time of the

Ecstacy is frequently used at "raves" to increase sensory stimulation and the pleasure of touching.

ban, it was estimated that as many as 200 physicians were using the drug in psychotherapy (Greer and Tolbert 1990) and an estimated 30,000 doses per month were being taken for recreational purposes. MDMA is often referred to as a "club drug" because of its frequent use at rave dances, clubs, and bars. It costs 25–50 cents to produce a tablet of Ecstasy in Europe, but on the street that same tablet costs $20–$30 (Scinto 2013). MDMA is usually taken orally, but it is sometimes snorted or even occasionally smoked. After the high starts, it may persist for minutes or even an hour, depending on the person, the purity of the drug, and the environment in which it is taken. When coming down from an MDMA-induced high, people often take small oral doses known as "boosters" to get high again. If they take too many boosters, they become very fatigued the next day. The average dose is about 75 to 150 milligrams; toxic effects have been reported at higher doses. Some statistics suggest that almost 50% of the tablets sold as MDMA actually contain other drugs such as aspirin, caffeine, cocaine, methamphetamine, or pseudoephedrine (Axis n.d.).

There is disagreement as to the possible harmful side effects of MDMA. Use of high doses can cause psychosis and paranoia (NIDA 2010). Some negative physiological responses caused by recreational doses include dilated pupils, dry mouth and throat, clenching and grinding of teeth (resulting in the use of baby pacifiers), muscle aches and stiffness (in 28% of users), fatigue (in 80% of users), insomnia (in 38% of users), agitation, and anxiety. Some of these reactions can be intense and unpredictable. Under some conditions, death can be caused by hyperthermia (elevated body temperature), instability of the autonomic nervous system, underlying cardiovascular problems, or kidney failure (Kaye, Darke, and Duflou 2009; King and Cockery 2010).

Several studies have demonstrated long-term damage to serotonin neurons in the brain following a single high dose of either MDMA or MDA, which may result in impaired memory, diminished ability to process information, and heightened impulsivity (Dean et al. 2013; Kish et al. 2010). Although the behavioral significance of this damage in people is not clear, at the present time caution using this drug is warranted (see "Here and Now: MDMA's Users").

There has been considerable debate as to the addictive properties of MDMA. Some claim this drug is like LSD with little likelihood of causing physical dependence, whereas others claim its properties are likely to be more amphetamine-like and suggest that of those who use MDMA routinely some have developed dependence (NIDA 2010). Part of the difficulty in sorting out this controversy is that most moderate MDMA users also use other drugs, making it difficult to determine which effects are specifically attributable to the MDMA. The potential of MDMA to cause addiction and dependence is likely somewhere between that of amphetamine and LSD. Because of its ability to cause euphoria and release dopamine in the brain, it is very probable that heavy use or administration by smoking or injection can cause significant dependence.

▮ Anticholinergic Hallucinogens

The anticholinergic hallucinogens include naturally occurring alkaloid (bitter organic base) substances that are present in plants and herbs found around the world. These drugs are often mentioned in folklore and in early literature as being added to potions. They are thought to have killed the Roman Emperor Claudius and to have poisoned Hamlet's father. Historically, they have been the favorite drugs used to eliminate inconvenient people (Marken, Stoner, and Bunker 1996). Hallucinogens affecting the cholinergic neurons also have been used by South American Indians for religious ceremonies (Schultes and Hofmann 1980) and were probably used in witchcraft to give the illusion of flying, to prepare sacrificial victims, and even to give some types of marijuana ("superpot") its kick.

The potato family of plants (Solanaceae) contains most of these mind-altering drugs. The following three potent anticholinergic compounds are commonly found in these plants: (1) scopolamine, or hyoscine; (2) hyoscyamine; and (3) atropine. Scopolamine may produce excitement, hallucinations, and delirium even at therapeutic doses. With atropine, doses bordering on toxic levels are usually required to obtain these effects (Schultes and Hofmann 1973). All of these active alkaloid drugs block some acetylcholine receptors.

These alkaloid drugs can be used as ingredients in cold symptom remedies because they have a drying effect and block production of mucus in the nose and throat. They also prevent salivation; therefore, the mouth becomes uncommonly dry and perspiration may stop. Atropine may increase the heart rate by 100% and dilate the pupils markedly, causing inability to focus on nearby objects. Other annoying side effects of these anticholinergic drugs include constipation and difficulty in urinating. These inconveniences tend to discourage excessive abuse of these drugs for their hallucinogenic properties. Usually, people who abuse these anticholinergic compounds are receiving

HERE AND NOW

MDMA's Users

Studies examining regular and novice (first-time) Ecstasy users found that regular users consume, on average, 1.8 MDMA tablets, whereas the novice users take 1.4 MDMA tablets. Both groups report positive moods during activities such as a rave dance. However, days later, both Ecstasy groups often feel significantly depressed, unsociable, unpleasant, and ill-tempered.

Verbal recall is also diminished in MDMA users, who remembered only 60% to 70% of the words recalled by control groups. Those who use Ecstasy regularly have the most difficulty remembering. The heaviest users also report variable acute negative experiences that can include psychotic thoughts, panic attacks, anxiety, and insomnia.

Data from Parrott, A., and J. Lasky. "Ecstasy (MDMA) Effects Upon Mood and Cognition: Before, During, and After a Saturday Night Dance." *Psychopharmacology* 139 (1998): 261–268; and Karlsen, S., O. Spigset, and L. Slordal. "The Dark Side of Ecstasy: Neuropsychiatric Symptoms After Exposure to 3,4-Methylenedioxymethamphetamine." *Basic and Clinical Pharmacology and Toxicology* 102 (2008): 15–24.

the drugs by prescription (Marken et al. 1996; MayoClinic 2010).

Anticholinergics can cause drowsiness by affecting the sleep centers of the brain. At large doses, a condition occurs that is similar to a psychosis, characterized by delirium, loss of attention, mental confusion, and sleepiness (Carlini 1993). Hallucinations may also occur at higher doses. At very high doses, paralysis of the respiratory system may cause death.

Although hundreds of plant species naturally contain anticholinergic substances and consequently can cause psychedelic experiences, only a few of the principal plants are mentioned here.

ATROPA BELLADONNA: THE DEADLY NIGHTSHADE PLANT

Knowledge of *Atropa belladonna* is very old, and its use as a drug is reported in early folklore. The name of the genus, *Atropa*, is the origin for the drug name atropine and indicates the reverence the Greeks had for the plant. Atropos was one of the three Fates in Greek mythology, whose duty it was to cut the thread of life when the time came. This plant has been used for thousands of years by assassins and murderers. In *Tales of the Arabian Nights*, unsuspecting potentates were poisoned with atropine from the deadly nightshade or one of its relatives. Fourteen berries of the deadly nightshade contain enough drug to cause death.

The species name, *belladonna*, means "beautiful woman." In early Rome and Egypt, girls with large pupils were considered attractive and friendly. To create this condition, they would put a few drops of an extract of this plant into their eyes, causing the pupils to dilate (Marken et al. 1996). Belladonna has also enjoyed a reputation as a love potion.

MANDRAGORA OFFICINARUM: THE MANDRAKE

The mandrake contains several active psychedelic alkaloids: hyoscyamine, scopolamine, atropine, and mandragorine. Mandrake has been used as a love potion for centuries but has also been known for its toxic properties. In ancient folk medicine, mandrake was used to treat many ailments in spite of its side effects. It was recommended as a sedative, to relieve nervous conditions, and to relieve pain (Schultes and Hofmann 1980), as portrayed in the 2006 movie *Pan's Labyrinth*.

The root of the mandrake is forked and, viewed with a little imagination, may resemble the human body (as portrayed in the *Harry Potter and the Chamber of Secrets* movie in 2002). Because of this resemblance, it has been credited with human attributes, which gave rise to many superstitions in the Middle Ages about its magical powers. Shakespeare referred to this plant in *Romeo and Juliet*. In her farewell speech, Juliet says, "And shrieks like mandrakes torn out of the earth, that living mortals hearing them run mad."

HYOSCYAMUS NIGER: HENBANE

Henbane is a plant that contains both hyoscyamine and scopolamine. In AD 60, Pliny the Elder spoke of henbane: "For this is certainly known, that if one takes it in drink more than four leaves, it will put him beside himself" (Jones 1956). Henbane was also used in the orgies, or bacchanalias, of the ancient world.

Although rarely used today, henbane has been given medicinally since early times. It was frequently used to cause sleep, although hallucinations often occurred if given in excess. It was likely included in witches' brews and deadly concoctions during the Dark Ages (Schultes and Hofmann 1980).

DATURA STRAMONIUM: JIMSONWEED

The *Datura* genus of the Solanaceae family includes a large number of related plants found worldwide. The principal active drug in this group is scopolamine; there are also several less active alkaloids.

Throughout history, these plants have been used as hallucinogens by many societies. They are mentioned in early Sanskrit and Chinese writings and were revered by the Buddhists. There is also some indication that the priestess (oracle) at the ancient Greek Temple of Apollo at Delphi was under the influence of this type of plant when she made prophecies (Schultes 1970). Before the supposed divine possession, she appeared to have chewed leaves of the sacred laurel. A mystic vapor was also reported to have risen from a fissure in the ground. The sacred laurel may have been one of the *Datura* species, and the vapors may have come from burning these plants.

Jimsonweed gets its name from an incident that took place in 17th-century Jamestown and is a contraction of Jamestown weed. British soldiers ate this weed while trying to capture Nathaniel Bacon, who had made seditious remarks about the

KEY TERM

jimsonweed
a potent hallucinogenic plant

Datura stramonium, or jimsonweed, is a common plant that contains the hallucinogenic drug scopolamine.

king. Jimsonweed is still occasionally consumed by young people who are searching for an inexpensive hallucinogenic experience. Because this wild weed grows in most parts of the United States it is relatively easy to find and is free. This plant has been referred to by names such as angel's trumpet, locoweed, and stinkweed. The hallucinogenic effects from this plant are mainly due to the presence of the two powerful anticholinergic drugs atropine and scopolamine in the roots. Often the person who consumes the jimsonweed in a stew or other brew ends up in the emergency room complaining of hallucinations, confusion, dilated pupils, and rapid heartbeat. Because of the very unpleasant side effects, abuse of jimsonweed is not considered to be a major drug abuse problem, but most emergency rooms will occasionally see an unsuspecting young person who foolishly experiments with jimsonweed for a cheap and natural high and gets much more than expected (MedTox 2010).

■ Other Hallucinogens

Technically, any drug that alters perceptions, thoughts, and feelings in a manner that is not normally experienced except in dreams can be classified as a hallucinogen. Because the brain's sensory

KEY TERM

analogs
drugs with similar structures

input is complex and involves several neurotransmitter systems, drugs with many diverse effects can cause hallucinations (NIDA 2001).

Four agents that do not conveniently fit into the principal categories of hallucinogens are discussed in the following sections.

PHENCYCLIDINE

Phencyclidine (PCP) is considered by many experts as the most dangerous of the hallucinogens (APA 2013; Maier 2003). PCP was developed in the late 1950s as an intravenous anesthetic. Although it was found to be effective, it had serious side effects such as precipitating schizophrenia-like symptoms, which caused it to be discontinued for human use (Farwell 2010; NIDA 2001). Sometimes when people were recovering from PCP anesthesia, they experienced delirium and manic states of excitation lasting 18 hours (APA 2013). PCP is currently a Schedule II drug, legitimately available only as an anesthetic for animals, but it has even been banned from veterinary practice since 1985 because of its high theft rate. Most, if not all, PCP used in the United States today is produced illegally (National Drug Intelligence Center 2004).

Street PCP is mainly synthesized from readily available chemical precursors in clandestine laboratories. Within 24 hours, cooks (the makers of street PCP) can set up a lab, make several gallons of the drug, and destroy the lab before the police can locate them. Liquid PCP is then poured into containers and is ready for shipment (Maier 2003).

PCP first appeared on the street drug scene in 1967 as the *PeaCe Pill*. In 1968, it reappeared in New York as a substance called hog. By 1969, PCP was found under a variety of guises. It was sold as angel dust and sprinkled on parsley for smoking. Today, it is sold on the streets under many different slang names, including *angel dust, supergrass, killer weed, embalming fluid, rocket fuel, wack,* and *ozone,* to mention a few (Partnership at DrugFree.org 2013).

In the late 1960s, PCP began to find its way into a variety of street drugs sold as psychedelics. By 1970, authorities observed that phencyclidine was used widely as a main ingredient in psychedelic preparations. It has been frequently substituted for and sold as LSD, mescaline, marijuana, and cocaine (Maier 2003; National Drug Intelligence Center 2004).

One difficulty in estimating the effects or use patterns of PCP is caused by variance in drug purity. Also, there are about 30 **analogs** of PCP, some of which have appeared on the street. PCP has so many other street names that people may not know they are using it or they may have been deceived when buying what they thought was LSD or mescaline (Dewan 2003). Users may not question the identity of the substances unless they have a bad reaction.

PCP is available as a pure, white crystalline powder; as tablets; or as capsules. However, because it is usually manufactured in makeshift laboratories, it is frequently discolored by contaminants from a tan to brown with a consistency ranging from powder to a gummy mass (U.S. Department of Justice 1991). PCP can be taken orally, smoked, sniffed, or injected (NIDA 2007c). In the late 1960s through the early 1970s, PCP was mostly taken orally, but it is now commonly snorted or applied to dark brown cigarettes, or leafy materials such as parsley, mint, oregano, marijuana, or tobacco, and smoked (U.S. Department of Justice 2003). By smoking PCP, the experienced user is better able to limit his or her dosage to a desired level. After smoking, the subjective effects appear within 1 to 5 minutes and peak within the next 5 to 30 minutes. The high lasts about 4 to 6 hours, followed by a 6- to 24-hour "comedown" (APA 2013).

In the 1979 national drug survey performed by the National Institute on Drug Abuse, about 7% of U.S. high school seniors had used PCP in a 12-month period; however, in 2012, that rate had dropped dramatically to 0.9% (Johnston 2013).

PHYSIOLOGICAL EFFECTS

Although PCP may have hallucinogenic effects, it can cause a host of other physiological actions, including stimulation, depression, anesthesia, and analgesia. The effects of PCP on the CNS vary greatly. At low doses, the most prominent effect is similar to that of alcohol intoxication, with generalized numbness. As the dose of PCP increases, the person becomes even more insensitive and may become fully anesthetized. Large doses can cause coma, convulsions, and death (APA 2013).

The majority of peripheral effects are apparently related to activation of the sympathetic nervous system. Flushing, excess sweating, and a blank stare are common, although the size of the pupils is unaffected. The cardiovascular system reacts by increasing blood pressure and heart rate. Other effects include side-to-side eye movements (called nystagmus), muscular incoordination, double vision, dizziness, nausea, and vomiting (National Drug Intelligence Center 2004). These symptoms occur in many people who take medium to high doses.

PSYCHOLOGICAL EFFECTS

PCP has unpleasant effects most of the time it is used. Why, then, do people use it repeatedly as their drug of choice? *#8*

PCP has the ability to markedly alter the person's subjective feelings; this effect may be reinforcing, even though the alteration is not always positive. Some say use of PCP makes them feel god-like and powerful (Maier 2003). There is an element of risk, not knowing how the trip will turn out. PCP may give the user feelings of strength, power, and invulnerability (NIDA 2007c). Other positive effects include heightened sensitivity to outside stimuli, a sense of stimulation and mood elevation, and dissociation from surroundings. Also, PCP is a social drug; virtually all users report taking it in groups rather than during a solitary experience. PCP also causes serious perceptual distortions. Users cannot accurately interpret the environment or their own emotions and as a result may do what appears to be absurd things such as throwing themselves at moving police cars, mutilating themselves, or assaulting others without provocation (Connections in Recovery 2013).

Chronic users may take PCP in "runs" extending over 2 to 3 days, during which time they do not sleep or eat. In later stages of chronic administration, users may develop outright paranoia, unpredictable violent behavior, and auditory hallucinations (APA 2013; Farwell 2010). Law enforcement officers claim to be more fearful of suspects on PCP than of suspects on other drugs of abuse. Often such people seem to have superhuman strength and are totally irrational and very difficult—even dangerous—to manage (NIDA 2007a, 2007c).

PCP has no equal in its ability to produce brief *#8* psychoses similar to schizophrenia (Jentsch and Roth 1999). The psychoses—induced with moderate doses given to normal, healthy volunteers—last about 2 hours and are characterized by changes in body image, thought disorders, estrangement, autism, and occasionally rigid inability to move (**catatonia**, or catalepsy). Subjects report feeling numb, have great difficulty differentiating between themselves and their surroundings, and complain afterward of feeling extremely isolated and apathetic. They are often violently paranoid during the psychosis (APA 2013; *Medical Letter* 1996).

KEY TERM

catatonia
a condition of physical rigidity, excitement, and stupor

When PCP was given experimentally to hospitalized chronic schizophrenics, it made them much worse not for a few hours but for 6 weeks. PCP is not just another hallucinogen—many authorities view it as much more dangerous than other drugs of abuse (Dewan 2003; Maier 2003).

MEDICAL MANAGEMENT

The diagnosis of a PCP overdose is frequently missed because the symptoms often closely resemble those of an acute schizophrenic episode. Simple, uncomplicated PCP intoxication can be managed with the same techniques used in other psychedelic drug cases. It is important to have a quiet environment, limited contact with an empathic person capable of determining any deterioration in the patient's physical state, protection from self-harm, and the availability of hospital facilities. Talking down is not helpful; the patient is better off isolated from external stimuli as much as possible.

Valium is often used for its sedating effect to prevent injury to self and to staff and also to reduce the chance for severe convulsions. An antipsychotic agent (for example, haloperidol [Haldol]) is frequently administered to make the patient manageable (Jaffe 1990).

The medical management of a comatose or convulsing patient is more difficult. The patient may need external respiratory assistance and external cooling to reduce fever. Blood pressure may have to be reduced to safe levels and convulsions controlled. Restraints and four to five strong hospital aides are often needed to prevent the patient from injuring him- or herself or the medical staff. After the coma lightens, the patient typically becomes delirious, paranoid, and violently assaultive (see "Case in Point: PCP Use Can Mean Violent Trouble").

EFFECTS OF CHRONIC USE

Chronic PCP users may develop a tolerance to the drug; thus, a decrease in behavioral effects and toxicity can occur with frequent administration. Different forms of dependence may occur when tolerance develops. Users may complain of vague cravings after cessation of the drug. In addition, long-term difficulties in memory, speech, and thinking persist for 6 to 12 months in the chronic user (NIDA 2007c). These functional changes are accompanied by personality deficits such as social isolation and states of anxiety, nervousness, and extreme agitation (APA 2013; Farwell 2010).

KETAMINE

Ketamine has been considered a club drug (Cloud 2010). Its annual use in 2012 by high school seniors was 1.5% (Johnston 2013). Almost all persons who abuse ketamine have abused at least three other illicit drugs (Center for Substance Abuse Research [CESAR] 2006), and those who abuse it chronically lose cognitive function and experience a deteriorating sense of well-being (Morgan, Muetzelfeldt, and Curran 2010). Ketamine, like PCP, was originally developed for its general anesthetic properties (AddictionSearch 2010; NIDA 2001). Its effects resemble those of PCP except they are more rapid and less potent (NIDA 2001). Depending on the dose, ketamine can have many effects, ranging from feelings of weightlessness to out-of-body or near-death experiences. Ketamine, often referred to as "Special K," has been abused as a "date rape" drug like other CNS depressants, such as Rohypnol or gamma-hydroxybutyrate (GHB) (NIDA 2001).

▶ **CASE IN POINT**

PCP Use Can Mean Violent Trouble

Although PCP use has fallen out of favor in recent years, occasionally a PCP-precipitated tragedy occurs that reminds us why this drug is considered to be one of the most dangerous of the substances of abuse. In July 2010 the son of the Dallas police chief was shot and killed by a police officer after he had gunned down two innocent bystanders. The medical examiner discovered PCP in his system. Witnesses related that before the senseless rampage, while humming to himself, the young man had stripped to his boxers, a frequent behavior of PCP users because they have the sensation that bugs are crawling all over their skin. Before shooting the two men, the chief's son manifested considerable aggression and paranoia, which is consistent with the fact that PCP users often become violent because they think that someone is trying to kill them. Accounts such as this are reminders of the terrible consequences of abusing this powerful hallucinogen.

Data from Farwell, S. "Though PCP Use Has Been Falling, Drug Can Still Lead to Violent Trouble." *Dallas Morning News.* 9 July 2010. Available http://www .dallasnews.com/sharedcontent/dws/news/localnews/crime/stories/070910dnmetpcp.1cef8c6.html. Accessed March 16, 2011.

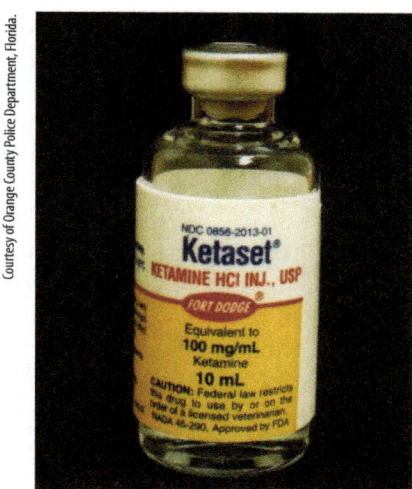

Courtesy of Orange County Police Department, Florida.

Ketamine is frequently used as a general anesthetic for veterinarian procedures.

Abuse of ketamine has been reported in many cities throughout the United States, and the drug is sometimes snorted as a substitute for cocaine. Several deaths have been linked to ketamine overdoses (NIDA 2007a).

Despite its potential as a drug of abuse, recent studies have suggested that it may have some potential as an antidepressant. When given to severely depressed patients in a small clinical trial it resulted in a "robust and rapid (within minutes) antidepressant response." However, it should be pointed out that the improvement was temporary and patients were again depressed 2 weeks after the ketamine treatment (Cloud 2010). The explanation for this effect is being investigated.

DEXTROMETHORPHAN

Dextromethorphan is the active ingredient used in many OTC cough medicines because of its ability to suppress the cough reflex (Delgado 2013; Schumacher 2012). Although harmless in low recommended doses, if consumed in high quantities (approximately 10 times the recommended dose), it can cause some hallucinogenic effects much like PCP and ketamine do, as well as other symptoms such as confusion, numbness, disorientation, and stomach pain (Gresser 2010). The effects of dextromethorphan can vary and have been described

---

PRESCRIPTION FOR ABUSE

Cough Medicine Abuse—Nothing to Be Sneezed At

Although abuse of cough medicine has not been considered serious enough by the FDA or other federal agencies to do anything more than issue warnings, many parents are concerned because cough syrup abuse seems to be on the rise because it is cheap and readily available to almost anyone, including teenagers. It is generally known by young people that high doses of cough medicines that contain the drug dextromethorphan can cause euphoria, some stimulation, and even hallucinations. However, what is not appreciated by many potential young consumers is that high-dose abuse of these products can have serious negative consequences. For example, some of the cough syrups also contain other ingredients such as the analgesic drug acetaminophen (the active ingredient in Tylenol). When consumed in high doses (as would be the case if someone were to ingest 10 times the recommended dose of an acetaminophen-containing cough medicine to achieve a high), the high doses of acetaminophen can do permanent and even fatal damage to the liver. In addition, high doses of dextromethorphan itself cause a dissociative effect (e.g., confusion), loss of

motor control, nausea, dizziness, fever, hypertension, and difficulty breathing. For long-term abusers, dependence on the dextromethorphan can occur, causing significant withdrawal symptoms such as insomnia, dysphoria, and depression. Finally, cough medicine overdoses often are accompanied by alcohol use, resulting in potentially life-threatening interactions such as severe depressed breathing.

© Dana Rothstein/Dreamstime.com

Data from Narconon. "Signs and Symptoms of Dextromethorphan Abuse." Narconon International. 2013. Available http://www.narconon.org/drug-abuse/dextromethorphan-signs-symptoms.html

as ranging from a mild stimulant effect to a complete dissociation from one's body, and they can last for several hours. Abuse of dextromethorphan is typically done by teenagers and is sometimes referred to as "roboing" (CESAR 2005). Recreational use of cough medicines containing this drug reached 5.6% in high school seniors in 2012 (Johnston 2013). This practice of consuming high doses of cough medicine can be extremely dangerous and on occasions even fatal (see "Prescription for Abuse: Cough Medicine Abuse—Nothing to Be Sneezed At"). Most young people who abuse cough medicines are abusing other substances such as marijuana, LSD, or Ecstasy. This surprisingly high rate of abuse for cough medicines has caused some to suggest that these products be removed from shelves and placed behind the pharmacy counters or only be sold to consumers over the age of 18. Although the FDA has considered these strategies, as of yet its advisory panel of medical experts has advised against them (Gresser 2010).

MARIJUANA

In high doses, marijuana use can result in image distortions and hallucinations (Nunez and Gurpegui 2002). Some users claim that marijuana can enhance hearing, vision, and skin sensitivity, although these claims have not been confirmed in controlled laboratory studies.

Although typical marijuana use does not appear to cause severe emotional disorders like the other hallucinogens, some experts suggest it can aggravate underlying mental illness such as depression, schizophrenia, or anxiety (NIDA 2011). Each month, thousands of people seek professional treatment due to marijuana-related problems (Narconon 2007). In contrast to other hallucinogens that have a combination of stimulant and psychedelic effects, high doses of marijuana cause a combination of depression and hallucinations and enhance the appetite (Fleckenstein 2000).

Natural Substances

■ Naturally Occurring Hallucinogens

Many plants contain naturally occurring hallucinogens. As already discussed, examples of such substances include mescaline from the peyote cactus, psilocybin from *Psilocybe* mushrooms, and anticholinergic drugs such as atropine from the deadly nightshade plant, mandrake, or jimsonweed.

Although some of these plants have been used for medicinal purposes for centuries, typically the therapeutic benefit has not been a consequence of the hallucinogenic effects of the substance. For example, anticholinergic drugs usually cause CNS depression and induce sleep; therefore, herbs that contain these drugs have been used as sleep potions. The hallucinogenic properties of some natural products, such as peyote, are viewed as positive by some cultures. As already mentioned, peyote is employed in a religious context as a sacrament for the Native American Church. In the United States today, the hallucinogen-containing natural substances are generally not viewed as therapeutic and are more likely to be used for their mind-altering properties as recreational drugs by adolescents (see "Case in Point: Jimsonweed Toxicity in Maryland"). In 2006 there were almost 1000 reported incidents of poisonings with these hallucinogenic plants, most frequently by kids trying to get high (Leinwand 2006). Some users claim because these are natural rather than synthetic sources of a hallucinogenic episode, that somehow it makes the experience more rewarding and desirable. There is no evidence that the natural-versus-synthetic features of a hallucinogen are responsible for the quality of a drug-induced hallucination. Frequently, consumption of these seeds and weeds causes severe hallucinations, dry mouth, hyperthermia, seizures, and occasionally death (Leinwand 2006; Russell 2010).

SALVIA DIVINORUM

Occasionally, obscure hallucinogenic herbs make their way into the culture of hallucinogenic substance users. This migration has become easier because of the Internet and specialized web sites that provide information (some accurate and much anecdotal) and the means to acquire these typically natural substances. For example, a relatively recent hallucinogenic fad has been the use of the Mexican herb *Salvia divinorum*, a drug that did not reach the United States until the late 1980s (Allday 2007). In 2012 this plant was abused by 4.4% of high school seniors in the United States, a decrease from the rate of use in 2009 (5.7%) (Johnston 2013). This bright, leafy green plant is usually smoked but can also be chewed, crushed, or mixed in a drink (Fernandez 2008). This relatively unknown plant is referred to as "diviner's mint," and although it has become illegal in many states because of its intense hallucinations, "out-of-body" experiences, and short-term memory loss,

►

Jimsonweed Toxicity in Maryland

Jimsonweed is a natural herb with medicinal purposes that include treatment for asthma, muscle spasms, and whooping cough. It also causes a cluster of very annoying and even dangerous side effects. Because of these toxic effects, intentional and unintentional use of jimsonweed can often result in an unexpected visit to an emergency room. For example, six adults of the same family were admitted to a Maryland hospital emergency room suffering from extreme hallucinations, incoherence, dilated pupils (causing blurred vision), a very rapid heartbeat, and, in one case, unconsciousness. The symptoms lasted several hours and the patients remained in the hospital 2–4 days. Follow-up investigations discovered that all of the patients had consumed a meal of homemade stew that included jimsonweed. The preparer of the stew inadvertently included cuttings from a jimsonweed plant outside the kitchen door without a knowledge of the plant's toxic consequences. Such emergency experiences are all too frequent results of ignorance about this natural, but potent, hallucinogen.

Data from Russell, J. "Jimsonweed Poisoning Associated with a Homemade Stew." *Morbidity and Mortality Weekly Report* 59 (2010): 102–104. Available http://www.cdc.gov/mmwr/preview/mmwrhtml/mm5904a3.htm. Accessed March 16, 2011.

the federal government has not yet outlawed this hallucinogenic plant. Promotions for these products include advertising claims such as "The Mazatec people have preserved *Salvia divinorum* and the knowledge surrounding its use for hundreds of years. We are privileged to have them share their sacred herb with us" (Jones 2001, p. A14). The dried herb sells for $10–$60 a hit depending on the quality and purity of the product (Detrick 2010). The substance typically makes the user introverted while "altering the consciousness in unusual ways" (Vince 2006) (see "Here and Now: A Legal High . . . At Least for Now"). This herb can have dramatic effects on perception similar to LSD (Allday 2007), causing hallucinations when chewed or smoked (Leinwand 2003). It typically is not used in social settings and frequently is used only once because for some people the effects can be quite unpleasant, often triggering a lack of coordination and frightening perceptions (Fernandez 2008). Because of its frequent negative consequences, this herb is not viewed as particularly addicting for most people (Detrick 2010; Pienciak 2003). However, some users describe a pleasant experience that is "almost innocent and quaint," with one teenage user describing the effects of salvia as causing "ferris wheels, flying pigs and fairies wearing a green dress" (Fernandez 2008). More recent reports from some scientists researching the active ingredient salvinorum A suggest that this drug may be useful in the treatment of conditions such as depression, stress management, or even drug addiction itself. Much more research needs to be conducted to determine which, if any, of these claims are clinically significant (Memorial Sloan-Kettering Cancer Center 2012).

HERE AND NOW

A Legal High . . . At Least for Now

One user described smoking *Salvia divinorum* he purchased legally at a local health shop near his home. He related an experience unlike any other that gave him a consciousness-expanding journey. His body felt disconnected, resulting in people and objects taking on a cartoonish, surreal, and marvelous appearance. Abruptly the visions ended and the user found himself back in his room with his "sitter" (a person designated to watch the drug user to prevent accidents or harm—this was recommended on the product's package). The user felt awkward and clumsy when talking or trying to stand. Within a couple of minutes his mind felt clear although his body was damp from sweating. The whole experience lasted approximately 5 minutes. The user admits

(continues)

HERE AND NOW

A Legal High . . . At Least for Now (*continued*)

little is known about the adverse effects of salvia and acknowledges the need for additional study. Intriguing descriptions such as this have attracted interest from both young people curious about the effects of this "mysterious" drug and law enforcement agencies wary that abuse of salvia may escalate into a major drug problem. These reactions have been further enhanced by reports of abuse by celebrities such as the pop singer and former child star Miley Cyrus, who has been shown in controversial Internet videos smoking a pipe with salvia while laughing uncontrollably with garbled speech. But as of yet, products containing legal hallucinogenic herbs such as salvia are available in shops throughout most of the United States and around the world without regulation. This is because levels of salvia use appear to be somewhat static, supporting observations that use of this hallucinogen does not appear to be particularly addicting and causes an experience many users are not particularly eager to repeat.

© Aaron Settipane/Dreamstime.com

Data from Vince, G. "Legally High." *New Scientist* (30 September 2006): 40–45; Thier, D. "Salvia Takes Center Stage In Miley Cyrus Bong Video Drama." AOLNews. 13 December 2010. Available http://www.aolnews.com/2010/12/13/salvia-takes-center-stage-in-miley-cyrus-bong-video-drama. Accessed March 16, 2011; and Detrick, B. "Salvia Takes a Starring Role." *New York Times*. 23 December 2010. Available http://www.nytimes.com/2010/12/26/fashion/26noticed.html?_r=1. Accessed March 16, 2011.

LEARNING PORTFOLIO

Discussion Questions

1. Why were substances with hallucinogenic properties used by ancient religions and cults?
2. Would you expect natural hallucinogens such as peyote to have less adverse effects than other hallucinogens? Why or why not?
3. Why would a drug with both stimulant and hallucinogenic effects have peculiar abuse potential, especially to young people?
4. Why do some users find psychedelic experiences terrifying whereas others find them desirable?
5. Do you think the federal government is justified in covering up information about the dangers of hallucinogens to convince people to stop using these drugs? Defend your answer.
6. How do the side effects of LSD compare with those of the CNS stimulants?
7. Why does MDMA have the potential to be popular?
8. Do you think it is all right to research psychedelic drugs such as LSD and MDMA to determine if they have medicinal value? What are the advantages and disadvantages of doing this?
9. Why is PCP more dangerous than LSD?
10. How do PCP and ketamine compare?
11. What is the best way to convince people that hallucinogenic drugs of abuse can be harmful?
12. What is a flashback, and how is it caused?
13. Should *Salvia divinorum* be more tightly controlled by the government?

Key Terms

analogs	390
catatonia	391
entactogen	386
ergotism	378
flashbacks	376
hallucinogens	372
jimsonweed	389
mydriasis	383
psychedelics	372
psychotogenics	374
psychotomimetics	372
synesthesia	376

Summary

1. Many drugs can exert hallucinogenic effects. The principal hallucinogens include LSD types, phenylethylamines, and anticholinergic agents. The four major effects that occur from administering LSD are (a) heightened senses, (b) loss of sensory control, (c) self-reflection or introspection, and (d) loss of identity or sense of cosmic merging.
2. Hallucinogens exaggerate sensory input and cause vivid and unusual visual and auditory effects.
3. The classic hallucinogens, such as LSD, cause predominantly psychedelic effects. Phenylethylamines are related to amphetamines and cause varying combinations of psychedelic and stimulant effects. Anticholinergic drugs also produce psychedelic effects when taken in high doses.

4. One of the prominent effects of hallucinogens is self-reflection. The user becomes aware of thoughts and feelings that had been forgotten or repressed. It is claimed that some experiences help to clarify motives and relationships and cause periods of greater openness. These effects have been promoted by some psychiatrists as providing valid insights useful in psychotherapy, especially for managing conditions such as PTSD, anxiety disorders, and depression.

5. The classic hallucinogens do not cause physical dependence. Although some tolerance can build up to the hallucinogenic effects of drugs such as LSD, withdrawal effects are usually minor.

6. The environment plays a major role in determining the sensory response to hallucinogens. Environments that are warm, comfortable, and hospitable tend to create a pleasant sensory response to the psychedelic effects of these drugs. Threatening, hostile environments are likely to lead to intimidating, frightening "bad trips."

7. In some users, high doses of LSD can cause a terrifying destruction of identity, resulting in panic and severe anxiety that resembles schizophrenia. Another psychological feature commonly associated with LSD is the flashback phenomenon. LSD use can cause recurring, unexpected visual and time distortions that last a few minutes to several hours. Flashbacks can occur months to years after use of the drug.

8. Designer amphetamines such as MDMA (Ecstasy) have been included in the "club drug" phenomenon. MDMA has been used frequently by young people to enhance the sensory experience of raves and the nightclub scene. Although viewed by some as harmless and even therapeutic, evidence of potentially serious negative physiological and neurological consequences suggests that these drugs can be extremely dangerous in high doses and under some conditions.

9. Hallucinogens purchased on the street are often poorly prepared and contaminated with adulterant substances. This practice of cutting the pure drugs with other substances also makes use of street hallucinogens very dangerous.

10. PCP differs from the other traditional hallucinogens in several ways. (a) It is a general anesthetic in high doses. (b) It causes schizophrenia-like psychosis. PCP can produce incredible strength and extreme violent behavior, making users very difficult and dangerous to manage. (c) Management of the severe psychological reactions to PCP requires drug therapy, whereas treatment of other hallucinogens often requires only reassurance, talking down, and supportive therapy. (d) Reactions to overdoses include fever, convulsions, and coma. Ketamine is related to, but less potent than, PCP and shares many of its pharmacological effects.

11. Other substances also abused for their hallucinogenic properties include dextromethorphan, a common OTC anticough medication, and some natural herbs, such as *Salvia divinorum*, that are promoted over the Internet.

References

About.com. "What Are the Effects of LSD?" 12 January 2012. Available http://alcoholism.about.com/cs/lsd/f/lsd_faq04.htm

Adam, D. "Truth About Ecstasy's Unlikely Trip from Lab to Dance Floor." *The Guardian*. 18 August 2006. Available http://guardian.co.uk/uk/2006/aug/18/topstories3.drugsandalcohol

AddictionSearch. "Ketamine Addiction, Abuse and Withdrawal." 2010. Available http://www.addictionsearch.com/treatment_articles/article/ketamine-addiction-abuse-and-withdrawal_23.html

Adler, J. "Getting High on Ecstasy." *Newsweek* (15 April 1985): 15.

Allday, E. "Legal, Intense Hallucinogen Raises Alarms/Salvia Divinorum Produces Short Dreamlike Experience." *San Francisco Chronicle*. 27 June 2007. Available http://www.sfgate.com/health/article/Legal-intense-hallucinogen-raises-alarms-2584286.php

American Psychiatric Association (APA). *Diagnostic and Statistical Manual of Mental Disorders*, 5th ed. (DSM-V). Washington, DC: APA, 2013.

Associated Press. "60s Icon Timothy Leary Cooperated with the FBI." *Salt Lake Tribune* 258 (1 July 1999): A-10.

Axis. "How the Ecstasy Trade Works." Axis Residential Treatment. Available http://www.axisresidentialtreatment.com/ecstasy-abuse/how-the-ecstasy-trade-works/

Baggott, M., J. Siegrist, G. Galloway, L. Robertson, J. Coyle, et al. "Investigating the Mechanisms of Hallucinogen-Induced Visions Using 3,4-Methyleneamphetamine (MDA): A Randomized Controlled Trial in Humans." *PLoS One* 5(12). doi14074.doi10.1371/journal.pone.001407. Available http://www.plosone.org/article/info%3Adoi%2F10.1371%2Fjournal.pone.0014074

Burger, A., ed. "Quotes from Albert Hofmann." *Drugs Affecting the Central Nervous System. Psychotomimetic Agents*, vol. 2. New York: Dekker, 1968.

Carlini, E. "Preliminary Note: Dangerous Use of Anticholinergic Drugs in Brazil." *Drugs and Alcohol Dependence* 32 (1993): 1–7.

Carollo, K. "Georgetown Students Arrested for Manufacturing Illegal Drug in Dorm Room." ABC News. 25 October 2010. Available http://abcnews.go.com/Health/MindMoodNews/georgetown-university-students-busted-illegal-drug-manufacturing/story?id=11963382

"Celebration #1." *New Yorker* 42 (1966): 43.

Center for Cognitive Liberty and Ethics. "Court Says No Peyote for Native American Boy." 22 April 2003. Available http://www.cognitiveliberty.org/dll/peyote_boy.html

Center for Substance Abuse Research (CESAR). "Dextromethorphan (DXM)." 2005. Available http://www.cesar.umd.edu/cesar/drugs/dxm.asp

Center for Substance Abuse Research (CESAR). "Majority of U.S. Youths and Young Adults Who Have Used Club Drugs Have Used 3 or More Types of Illicit Drugs." [FAX] (22 May 2006).

Claus, E. P., V. E. Tyler, and L. R. Brady. *Pharmacognosy*, 6th ed. Philadelphia: Lea & Febiger, 1970.

Cloud, J. "Is Ketamine a Quick Fix for Hard-to-Treat Depression?" *Time* (2 August 2010). Available http://www.time.com/time/health/article/0,8599,2008151,00.html

Conley, M. "Nutmeg Treated as Drug for Hallucinogenic High." ABC World News. 9 December 2010. Available http://abcnews.go.com/Health/large-doses-nutmeg-hallucinogenic-high/story?id=12347815&page=1

Connections in Recovery. "Effects of PCP Abuse." 1 June 2013. Available http://www.connectionsinrecovery.com/2013/06/effects-of-pcp-abuse/

de la Torre, R., M. Farré, P. Roset, S. Abanade, M. Segura, and J. Cami. "Human Pharmacology of MDMA: Pharmacokinetics, Metabolism, and Disposition." *Therapeutic Drug Monitor* 26 (2004): 137–144.

Dean, G., J. Stellplug, A. Burnett, and K. Engebretsen. "2C or Not 2 C: Phenylethylamine Designer Drug Review." *Journal of Medical Toxicology* 9 (2013): 172–178.

Delgado, J. "Intoxication from LSD and Other Common Hallucinogens." UpToDate. 2013. Available http://www.uptodate.com/contents/intoxication-from-lsd-and-other-common-hallucinogens

Detrick, B. "Salvia Takes a Starring Role." *New York Times*. 23 December 2010. Available http://www.nytimes.com/2010/12/26/fashion/26noticed.html?_r=1

Dewan, S. "A Drug Feared in the '70s Is Tied to Suspect in Killing." *New York Times* (6 April 2003).

Dishotsky, N. I., W. D. Loughman, R. E. Mogar, and W. R. Lipscomb. "LSD and Genetic Damage." *Science* 172 (1971): 431–440.

Dobner, J. "American Indian Church Sues Feds Over Peyote Use." *Native American Times*. 20 September 2010. Available http://www.nativetimes.com/index.php?option=com_content&view=article&id=4268:american-indian-church-sues-feds-over-peyote-use&catid=51&Itemid=27

Drug Enforcement Administration (DEA). "September 2002 Highlight." Domestic Strategy. December 2002a. Publication No. DEA-02060.

Drug Enforcement Administration (DEA). "Trippin on Tryptamine." Intelligence Brief. October 2002b. Document No. DEA-02052.

Drug Guide. "PCP." The PartnershipATDrugfree.org (2013). Available www.drugfree.org/drug-guide/pcp

Farley, C. "Rave New World." *Time* 15 (5 June 2000): 69.

Farwell, S. "Though PCP Use Has Been Falling, Drug Can Still Lead to Violent Trouble." *Dallas Morning News*. 9 July 2010. Available http://www.dallasnews.com/sharedcontent/dws/news/localnews/crime/stories/070910dnmetpcp.1cef8c6.html

Fernandez, D. "Salvia Becoming 'Drug du Jour' for Some Teens; Hallucinogenic Herb Salvia Divinorum Causes Concern as Young Adults Use It to Get a Cheap High." WebMD. 26 June 2008. Available http://www.salvia.net/articles.php?id=29

Ferro, S. "Why Doctors Can't Give You LSD (But Maybe They Should)." Popular Science. 16 April 2013. Available http://www.popsci.com/science/article/2013-04/new-science-lsd-therapy?page=1

Fleckenstein, A. "Pharmacological Aspects of Substance Abuse." In *Remington: The Science and Practice of Pharmacy*, 20th ed., edited by A. Gennaro, 1175–1182. Baltimore, MD: Lippincott Williams & Wilkins, 2000.

Freeman, S. "How LSD Works." Howstuffworks. Available http://www.howstuffworks.com/lsd.htm

Friends of Narconon. "Ecstasy/MDMA Manufacturing and Statistics." 2010. Available http://www.friends ofnarconon.org/drug_education/news/latest_news /ecstasy%10mdma_manufacturing_and_statistics

Gatch, M., M. Forster, A. Janow, A. Eshleman, et al. "Abuse Liability Profile of Three Substituted Tryptamine." *Journal of Pharmacology and Experimental Therapeutics* 338 (2011): 280–289.

Goldstein, A. *Addiction: From Biology to Drug Policy.* New York: Freeman, 1994.

Goldstein, F. "Pharmacological Aspects of Substance Abuse." In *Remington's Pharmaceutical Sciences,* 19th ed., edited by A. R. Gennaro, 780–794. Easton, PA: Mack, 1995.

Government Conspiracy. "U.S. Government Research on Psychological and Torture Conspiracy." 18 April 2010. Available http://www.governmentconspiracy.net/tag/mk -ultra/

Greer, G., and R. Tolbert. "The Therapeutic Use of MDMA." In *Ecstasy: The Clinical, Pharmacological and Neurotoxicological Effects of the Drug MDMA,* edited by S. J. Peroutka, 28. Boston: Kluwer, 1990.

Gresser, E. "Cough Syrup As Problem Drug?" AOL News. 25 October 2010. Available http://www.aolnews.com /2010/10/25/opinion-cough-syrup-as-problem-drug

Hadlock, G., K. Webb, L. McFadden, P. Chu, J. Ellis, et al. "4-Methylmethcathinone (Mephedrone): Neuropharmacological Effects of a Designer Stimulant of Abuse." *Journal of Pharmacology and Experimental Therapeutics* 339 (2011): 530–536.

Halpern, J., and H. Pope. "Hallucinogen Persisting Perception Disorder: What Do We Know After 50 Years?" *Drug and Alcohol Dependence* 69 (2003): 109–119.

Halpern, J., A. Sherwood, J. Hudson, D. Yurgelun-Todd, and H. Pope. "Psychological and Cognitive Effects of Long-Term Peyote Use Among Native Americans." *Biological Psychiatry* 58 (2005): 624–631.

Horgan, J. "The Psychedelic Sorcerer." Available http:// www.johnhorgan.org/the_psychedelic_sorcerer_15289 .htm

Huxley, A. *The Doors of Perception.* New York: Harper, 1954.

Hyslop, M. "Townsend Spearheads Campaign to Curb Rising Use of Ecstasy." *Washington Times* (29 September 2000): C-1.

Jaffe, J. "Drug Addiction and Drug Abuse." In *The Pharmacological Basis of Therapeutics,* 8th ed., edited by A. Gilman, T. Rall, A. Nies, and P. Taylor, 522–573. New York: Pergamon, 1990.

Jentsch, J., and R. Roth. "The Neuropsychopharmacology of Phencyclidine: From NMDA Receptor Hypofunction to the Dopamine Hypothesis of Schizophrenia." *Neuropsychopharmacology* 20 (1999): 201–225.

Johnston, L. D. "Monitoring the Future." University of Michigan. 2013. Available http://monitoringthefuture.org

Johnston, L. D., P. M. O'Malley, J. G. Bachman, and J. E. Schulenberg. "Marijuana Use Is Rising; Ecstasy Use Is Beginning to Rise; and Alcohol Use Is Declining Among U.S. Teens." University of Michigan News Service. 14 December 2010. Available http://monitoringthefuture .org/data/10data.html#2010data-drugs

Jones, R. "New Cautions About an Herb That's Hip, Hallucinogenic and Legal." *New York Times* (9 July 2001): A-14.

Jones, W. H. S. *Natural History.* Cambridge, MA: Harvard University Press, 1956.

Karlsen, S., O. Spigset, and L. Slordal. "The Dark Side of Ecstasy: Neuropsychiatric Symptoms After Exposure to 3,4-Methylenedioxymethamphetamine." *Basic and Clinical Pharmacology and Toxicology* 102 (2008): 15–24.

Kaye, S., S. Darke, and J. Duflou. "Methylenedioxymethamphetamine (MDMA)-Related Fatalities in Australia: Demographics, Circumstances, Toxicology and Major Organ Pathology." *Drug and Alcohol Dependence* 104 (2009): 254–261.

Kelland, K. "Scientists Suggest Fresh Look at Psychedelic Drugs." ABC News. 18 August 2010. Available http:// www.commondreams.org/headline/2010/08/18-4

King, L. A., and J. M. Cockery. "An Index of Fatal Toxicity for Drugs of Misuse." *Human Psychopharmacology* 25 (2010): 162–166.

Kish, S., J. Lerch, Y. Furukawa, J. Tong, T. McCluskey, D. Wilkins, et al. "Decreased Cerebral Cortical Serotonin Transporter Binding in Ecstasy Users: A Positron Emission Tomography/[11-C]DASB and Structural Brain Imaging Study." *Brain* 133 (2010): 1779–1797.

Leary, T., R. Metzner, and R. Alpert. *The Psychedelic Experience.* New Hyde Park, NY: University Books, 1964.

Leinwand, D. "Teens, and Now DEA, Are on Trail of Hallucinogenic Herb." *USA Today* (23 June 2003): 1.

Leinwand, D. "Jimson Weed Users Chase High All the Way to the Hospital." *USA Today.* 1 November 2006. Available http://www.usatoday.com/news/nation/2006-11-01 -jimson_x.htm

Luscher, C. "Drugs of Abuse." In *Basic and Clinical Pharmacology,* 12th ed., edited by B. Katzung, 565–580. New York: McGraw-Hill, 2012.

Maier, T. "PCP Is Rearing Its Ugly Head Again." *Insight on the News* (17 February 2003): 4–6.

"Many Were Lost Because of Leary." Letters (to the editor). *USA Today* 14 (3 June 1996): 12-A.

Marken, P., S. Stoner, and M. Bunker. "Anticholinergic Drug Abuse and Misuse." *CNS Drugs* 5 (1996): 190–199.

Marquardt, G. M., V. DiStefano, and L. L. Ling. "Pharmacological Effects of (S)-, and (R)-MDA." In *The Psychopharmacology of Hallucinogens*, edited by R. C. Stillman and R. E. Willette. New York: Pergamon, 1978.

Mathias, R. "NIDA Research Takes a New Look at LSD and Other Hallucinogens." *NIDA Notes* 8 (March/April 1993): 6.

MayoClinic. "Anticholinergics and Antispasmodics (Oral Route, Parenteral Route, Rectal Route, Transdermal Route)." 2010. Available http://www.mayoclinic.com/health/druginformation/DR602315/DSECTION=side-effects

McGlothin, W., S. Cohen, and M. S. McGlothin. "Long-Lasting Effects of LSD on Normals." *Archives of General Psychiatry* 17 (1967): 521–532.

Medical Letter. "Phencyclidine (PCP)." 38 (10 May 1996): 45.

MedTox. "Jimson Weed Poisoning Gives Insight to the Effects Experienced by 'Locoweed' Abusers." *MedTox Journal*, Public Safety Substance Abuse Newsletter. April 2010. Available http://www.medtox.com/Resources/Images/5414.pdf

Mims, B. "Peyote: When the Ancient Indian Way Collides with a New Age Craze." *Salt Lake Tribune* 260 (12 August 2000): C-1.

Morgan, C., L. Muetzelfeldt, and H. Curran. "Consequences of Chronic Ketamine Self-Administration Upon Neurocognitive Function and Psychological Wellbeing: A 1-Year Longitudinal Study." *Addiction* 105 (2010): 121–133.

Multidisciplinary Association for Psychedelic Studies (MAPS). "Research > MDMA-Assisted Psychotherapy." 2013. Available http://www.maps.org/research/mdma/

Naranjo, C., A. T. Shulgin, and T. Sargent. "Evaluation of 3,4 Methylenedioxyamphetamine (MDA) as an Adjunct to Psychotherapy." *Medicina et Pharmacologia Experimentalis* 17 (1967): 359–364.

Narconon. "FAQ About Marijuana." Narconon of Southern California. 2007. Available http://www.addictionca.com/FAQ-marijuana.htm

Narconon International. "Signs and Symptoms of Dextromethorphan Abuse." n.d. Available http://www.narconon.org/drug-abuse/dextromethorphan-signs-symptoms.html

National Drug Intelligence Center. "PCP, Increasing Availability and Abuse." Intelligence Bulletin. 2004. DOJ Document ID No. 2004-L0424-002.

National Institute on Drug Abuse (NIDA). "Hallucinogens and Dissociative Drugs." NIDA Research Report Series. March 2001. NIH Publication No. 01-4209.

National Institute on Drug Abuse (NIDA). "DrugFacts: Club Drugs (GHB, Ketamine, and Rohypnol)." 2007a. Available http://nida.nih.gov/Infofax/clubdrugs.html

National Institute on Drug Abuse (NIDA). "Infofacts. LSD." 2007b. Available http://nida.nih.gov/Infofax/lsd.html

National Institute on Drug Abuse (NIDA). "PCP/Phencyclidine." 2007c. Available http://nida.nih.gov/Infofax/pcp.html

National Institute on Drug Abuse (NIDA). "InfoFacts. Hallucinogens—LSD, Peyote, Psyilocybin, and PCP." 2009. Available http://www.drugabuse.gov/Infofacts/hallucinogens.html

National Institute on Drug Abuse (NIDA). "NIDA InfoFacts: LSD." Education.com. December 2010. Available http://www.education.com/reference/article/Ref_NIDA_InfoFacts_LSD

National Institute on Drug Abuse (NIDA). "Topics in Brief. Marijuana." December 2011. Available http://www.drugabuse.gov/publications/topics-in-brief/marijuana

National Institute on Drug Abuse (NIDA). "DrugFacts: MDMA (Ecstasy or Molly)." December 2013. Available http://drugabuse.gov/infofacts/ecstasy.html

Native American Church. 2008. Available http://www.nativeamericanchurch.com

Nunez, L., and M. Gurpegui. "Cannabis-Induced Psychosis: A Cross-Sectional Comparison with Acute Schizophrenia." *Acta Psychiatrica Scandinavia* 105 (2002): 1173–1178.

O'Brien, C. "Drug Addiction and Drug Abuse." In *The Pharmacological Basis of Therapeutics*, 11th ed., edited by L. Brunton, J. Lazo, and K. Parker, 607–627. New York: McGraw-Hill, 2006.

Office of National Drug Control Policy (ONDCP). "Drug Facts: Club Drugs." January 2008. Available http://webarchive.library.unt.edu/eot2008/20081103232225/http://www.whitehousedrugpolicy.gov/drugfact/club/index.html

Pahnke, W. N., A. A. Kurland, S. Unger, C. Savage, and S. Grof. "The Experimental Use of Psychedelic (LSD) Psychotherapy." In *Hallucinogenic Drug Research: Impact on Science and Society*, edited by J. R. Gamage and E. L. Zerkin. Beloit, WI: Stash, 1970.

Pahnke, W. N., and W. A. Richards. "Implications of LSD and Experimental Mysticism." *Journal of Religion and Health* 5 (1966): 175–208.

Parish, B. "Hallucinogen Use Treatment and Management." Medscape. 2011. Available http://emedicine.medscape.com/article/293752-treatment

Parrott, A., and J. Lasky. "Ecstasy (MDMA) Effects Upon Mood and Cognition: Before, During and After a Saturday Night Dance." *Psychopharmacology* 139 (1998): 261–268.

Partnership at Drugfree.org. "Drug Guide: LSD." n.d.a. Available http://www.drugfree.org/drug-guide/lsd

Partnership at Drugfree.org. "Drug Guide: PCP." n.d.b. Available http://www.drugfree.org/drug-guide/pcp

Passie, T. "Healing with Entactogen: Therapist and Patient Perspective on MDMA-Assisted Group Psychotherapy." Multidisciplinary Association for Psychedelic Studies. 2012. Available http://store.maps.org/np/clients /maps/product.jsp?product=801

Pienciak, R. "DEA Issues Warning for Legal Herb Stronger Than LSD." *Daily News* (NY) (25 July 2003).

Publishers Group. "Street Drugs." Plymouth, MN: Publishers Group, 2002.

Remsberg, R. "Found in the Archives: Military LSD Testing." NPR. 1 December 2010. Available http://www.npr .org/blogs/pictureshow/2010/12/01/131724898/lsd -testing

Russell, J. "Jimsonweed Poisoning Associated with a Homemade Stew." *Morbidity and Mortality Weekly Report.* 2010. Available http://www.faqs.org/periodicals /201002/1971642741.html

Schultes, R. E. "The Plant Kingdom and Hallucinogens (Part III)." *Bulletin on Narcotics* 22 (1970): 25–53.

Schultes, R. E. "Ethnopharmacological Significance of Psychotropic Drugs of Vegetal Origin." In *Principles of Psychopharmacology*, 2nd ed., edited by W. G. Clark and J. del Giudice. New York: Academic Press, 1978.

Schultes, R. E., and A. Hofmann. *The Botany and Chemistry of Hallucinogens.* Springfield, IL: Thomas, 1973.

Schultes, R. E., and A. Hofmann. *The Botany and Chemistry of Hallucinogens*, 2nd ed. Springfield, IL: Thomas, 1980.

Schumacher, M. "Opioid Analgesics & Antagonists." In: *Basic & Clinical Pharmacology*, 12th ed, edited by B. G. Katzung, S. B. Masters, and A. J. Trevor, 543–564. New York: McGraw-Hill Medical, 2012.

Scinto, M. "Inside the Lucrative World of Ecstasy Smuggling." *New York Post.* 28 January 2013. Available http:// www.nypost.com/p/news/opinion/opedcolumnists /riding_the_train_wxKKIdsE4zYejiWxK5AoUO

Sloan-Kettering Cancer Center. "Salvia Divinorum." 2012. Available http://www.mskcc.org/cancer-care/herb /salvia-divinorum

Smith, C. "Albert Hofmann, the Father of LSD, Dies at 102." *New York Times.* 30 April 2008. Available http://www .nytimes.com/2008/04/30/world/europe/30hofmann .html

Snyder, S. H. *Madness and the Brain.* New York: McGraw-Hill, 1974.

Stone, J. "Turn On, Tune In, Boot Up." *Discover* 12 (June 1991): 32–33.

Summit Malibu. "Tryptamine Abuse and Addiction." Summit Malibu. 2010. Available http://www.summitmalibu .com/?s=tryptamine+

Thier, D. "Salvia Takes Center Stage in Miley Cyrus Bong Video Drama." AOLNews. 13 December 2010. Available http://www.aolnews.com/2010/12/13/salvia-takes -center-stage-in-miley-cyrus-bong-video-drama

Tierney, J. "Hallucinogens Have Doctors Tuning in Again." *New York Times.* 11 April 2010. Available http://www.nytimes .com/2010/04/12/science/12psychedelics.html

Toufexis, A. "A Crackdown on Ecstasy." *Time* (10 June 1985): 64.

Tucker, R. "Acid Test." *Omni* (November 1987): 16.

Unger, S. "Mescaline, LSD, Psilocybin and Personality Change." Bluehoney.org. 10 January 2010. Available http://bluehoney.org/2010/01/10/mescaline-lsd -psilocybin-and-personality-change

U.S. Department of Justice. "Let's All Work to Fight Drug Abuse." Pamphlet from DEA published by L.A.W. Publications and distributed with permission by International Drug Education Association, 1991.

U.S. Department of Justice. "Drugs, Youth, and the Internet." Information Bulletin (October 2002). Product No. 2002-L0424-006.

U.S. Department of Justice. "Other Dangerous Drugs, Hallucinogens." National Drug Intelligence Center. 2003. Product No. 2003-Q0317-001.

Vastag, B. "Can the Peace Drug Help Clean Up the War Mess?" *Scientific American.* 20 April 2010. Available http://www.maps.org/media/view/can_the_peace _drug_help_clean_up_the_war_mess

Vince, G. "Legally High." *New Scientist* (30 September 2006): 40–45.

Vollenwelder, F., M. Vollenwelder-Scherpenhuyzen, A. Baber, N. Vogel, and D. Nell. "Psilocybin Induces Schizophrenia-like Psychosis in Human via a Serotonin-2 Agonist Action." *NeuroReport* 9 (1998): 3897–3902.

Weber, B. "Prairie LSD Studies Coined 'Psychedelic.'" *Toronto Star* (6 October 2006): A8.

Week, The. "Medicinal 'Magic Mushrooms': The New Prozac?" 14 April 2010. Available http://theweek.com /article/index/201851/medicinal-magic-mushrooms -the-new-prozac

Willing, R. "Researchers Tested Pot, LSD on Army Volunteers." *USA Today.* 6 April 2007. Available http://www .usatoday.com/news/washington/2007-04-05-army -experiments_N.htm

Zickler, P. "NIDA Launches Initiative to Control Club Drugs." *NIDA Notes* 14 (2000): 1.

© JeremyNathan/iStock/Thinkstock

CHAPTER 13

Marijuana

Did You Know?

▶ George Washington grew marijuana plants at Mount Vernon for medicine and rope making.

▶ Out of 18.1 million past-month illicit drug users in the United States, approximately 10.1 million of them used marijuana. Approximately 80.5% of current illicit drug users use only marijuana (64.3%) or marijuana with other illicit drugs (16.2%).

▶ In some states, marijuana is one of the largest cash-producing crops. "California, for example, produces nearly 40% of the marijuana in the United States, worth an estimated $18.8 billion . . . [and] . . . by far the state's biggest cash crop" (Jenkins 2011).

▶ Marijuana still grows wild in many U.S. states today.

▶ Research shows that many users have difficulty learning and remembering what they have learned when they are "high."

▶ An April [2013] Pew Research Center poll found that ". . .[F]or the first time since the 1960s, most Americans favor legalizing marijuana. The national survey found that 52 percent say marijuana should be made legal while 45 percent say it should not." Pew reported that support for legalizing marijuana has risen 11 points since 2010 (Pew Research Center 2013).

▶ In 2011, 38% of 8th graders, 68% of 10th graders, and 82% of 12th graders reported marijuana as being fairly or very easy to get. It seems clear that marijuana is a highly accessible drug.

▶ The high experienced by using marijuana not only varies according to expectations and the surroundings, but also based on how the drug is taken, whether smoked, inhaled through a vaporizer, or ingested (eaten).

Learning Objectives

On completing this chapter you will be able to:

❭ Explain what marijuana is and why it remains so controversial.

❭ Differentiate between the effects of low and high doses of marijuana.

❭ List and explain the potential effects marijuana use has on the body.

❭ Understand and be able to explain how marijuana use can become psychologically addictive.

❭ Describe how tolerance and dependence affect the response to marijuana and its use.

❭ Explain the medical uses of marijuana.

❭ Explain which age groups are most likely to use marijuana.

❭ Explain the major characteristics of first-time marijuana users.

❭ Explain how the perceived danger of marijuana use has changed with regard to high school seniors and younger age groups.

❭ Differentiate between prior and current beliefs regarding the effects of chronic marijuana use.

Drugs and Society Online is a great source for additional drugs and society information for both students and instructors. Visit **go.jblearning.com /hanson12** to find a variety of useful tools for learning, thinking, and teaching.

Introduction

First interview:

Since I was in college and tried my first hit, I have always been a connoisseur of what we used to call grass, now it's weed or even "the ganja." I first went through a period of using it a lot—it was a different way to get a buzz. Then I got married, and my wife did not like me smoking it, and we had kids, so except for a few occasional puffs from my neighbor, I just about gave it up. Then I got divorced [from my wife] and I married a woman who does not object to me smoking a little weed every now and then, even though she does not do it herself. So sometimes on weekends, I will roll a joint before going to bed and take a few puffs off of it. I know it is illegal, but big deal, who knows about it? I used to watch that program *Cops* and just found it silly when police officers would arrest someone (usually a young kid) for possession. Big bust, I would think. Isn't it silly to charge someone with possession of marijuana? I consider it to be like alcohol and cigarettes. I don't think it should be illegal anymore. I know so many people who do it and there are dozens of people who probably use this drug that I am not even aware of their using it. What happens if two-thirds of our population uses this drug? Are we going to charge and arrest all these people? The whole illegality of it is silly. *(From Venturelli's research files, male restaurant owner, age 48, residing in Reno, Nevada, June 10, 2000)*

Second interview:

My kids know that I still smoke dope, and I know they are used to me doing this since from the day they were born. I never hid this habit of mine. I am now 59, and I never even thought of quitting. You see I started back in the late 60s when I was 17 years old. My wife does not do it as much as I do. Usually a couple of times a week, late at night I go outside on the deck and take a few hits. I don't think it is much different than having a drink. Why I have always done it, so what is the big deal? I have a few friends about my age who do the same thing and we don't bother anyone, we work five and often six days a week at our full time jobs, and only do this away from work,

and as I said only a few times a week. I ask again, what's the big deal? Now society may look down on me, but at this age, I don't give a rat's ass what society thinks. I don't tell anyone about this long-time habit that brings me relief and relaxation and outside of a few friends, my wife, and kids, no one else knows that I do this. As you asked, I really don't care what the law says; I will always do it until I die. It is so natural for me to do this that I don't even think about breaking drug laws. This is a private matter between my family and me. My kids don't smoke dope, and I never thought I would have kids who would not. Especially when I grew up in the 60s everyone I knew smoked dope and I never thought it would change, but today the world is different so I keep to myself with my habits. To me, honestly professor, if marijuana is outlawed and if I wanted to say smoke oregano then they should outlaw oregano. Outlawing a naturally growing plant is just plain stupid. What threat to the world is my smoking weed? I just think this law making marijuana illegal is ridiculous, especially when smoking it is viewed as a violation of law. What a stupid law it is and how effective this law is in that I have smoked dope all my life. *(From Venturelli's research files, male, living in a Midwestern rural area, August 10, 2010)*

Third interview:

We used to have one great big bong and fill it with dope [referring to marijuana], and all of us in someone's fraternity room would each take hits from the bong. Today, it's a different life altogether. I am working three different jobs, one teaching at a junior high school, [one] working at a film production studio, and my third claim to fame is my job as a part-time waiter. . . . I feel that I wasted many nights by just "'smokin," "dopin'," and "drinkin'" back during those college days. I sometimes think that I could have accomplished a lot more if I would not have inhaled so much dope. If I had to do it over again I would not have wasted so much time. *(From Venturelli's research files, male, age 28, August 9, 1996)*

The preceding interviews illustrate contrasting views regarding marijuana usage as a subcultural phenomenon. The first and second interviews present "die-hard" users who refuse to relinquish their use of this drug. These individuals have been using marijuana for many years and they consider it an essential recreational drug. Conversely, the third interviewee expresses some regret over the time "wasted" while becoming intoxicated with marijuana when he could have been pursuing other, more career-oriented activities.

Although marijuana is potentially less addictive than other drugs, such as cocaine, crack, heroin, and barbiturates (to name a few), it remains one of the few drugs that is controversial. (As an example of the controversy that surrounds this drug, see "Here and Now: Legalizing Recreational and Medicinal Marijuana Use.") It is difficult to wade through the emotion, politics, and rigidity found in the writings on marijuana to tease out the objective, clinical reality. In the United States, extreme views go back to the 1930s, when the film *Reefer Madness* portrayed an after-school marijuana "club" for high

HERE AND NOW

Legalizing Recreational and Medicinal Marijuana Use

Recent developments in legalizing recreational and medical marijuana use include the following:

- An April [2013] Pew Research Center poll found that ". . .[F]or the first time since the 1960s, most Americans favor legalizing marijuana. The national survey found that 52 percent say marijuana should be made legal while 45 percent say it should not." Pew reported that support for legalizing marijuana has risen 11 points since 2010 (Pew Research Center 2013).

- "On Tuesday [May 28, 2013], Colorado Gov. John Hickenlooper signed several historic measures to implement marijuana legalization in the state, establishing Colorado as the world's first legal, regulated and taxed marijuana market for adults" (Ferner 2013). Although Governor Hickenlooper is a very vocal opponent of such legalization, he ". . . signed the first bills in history to establish a legal marijuana market as well as starting the development of a regulatory framework for cultivation, distribution, and processing of industrial hemp." (Ferner 2013). At this press conference the governor's chief legal counsel reiterated, ". . . the will of the voters needed to be implemented" (Ferner 2013).

- "The leftwing Party of the Democratic Revolution is preparing legislation that would make it legal to smoke weed in Mexico City, news site Sin Embargo reports. The potentially game-changing legislation, which legislators plan to introduce in September, would allow people to grow marijuana at home, smoke it in designated clubs and carry up to 25 grams. Lawmakers say the bill aims to permit marijuana use for medicinal reasons, but also opens the door to legalizing its recreational use" (Huffington Post 2013). Even ex-president Vicente Fox made public statements endorsing the legalization of marijuana.

- "[Representatives] Barney Frank (D-Mass) and Ron Paul (R-Texas) introduced HR 2306 or the 'Ending Federal Marijuana Prohibition Act of 2011,' Tuesday [June 23, 2011] to end the federal prohibition of marijuana and allow state and local laws to govern its use and regulation. 'We do not believe that the federal government should be involved in prosecuting adults for smoking marijuana,' Frank said. 'I do not think prohibition is ever the effective way to deal with those things'" (Turner 2011). Overall, the bill states that the regulation of marijuana should be decided by states, not the federal government (Turner 2011).

- In Salem, Oregon, "[a] legislative budget committee has signed off on a bill that would legalize medical marijuana dispensaries in Oregon" (*The Republic* and the Associated Press 2013). This bill was approved and sent to the full House for a vote. If passed, the state's 53,000 medical marijuana cardholders would be able to get their medicine (marijuana).

- [Though] "Alaska law currently allows those with a medicinal marijuana prescription to legally grow up to six plants or have up to one ounce marijuana, . . . An Alaska citizens' group is pushing to legalize recreational marijuana, which would make it the third state to do so after Colorado and Washington . . . [While this initiative to legalize marijuana in Alaska has not yet passed, it is] . . . [d]riven by growing public support, . . . [The] Campaign to Regulate Marijuana submitted more than 45,000 signatures Wednesday to Alaska election officials. It needs about 30,000 verified signatures to

(continues)

Legalizing Recreational and Medicinal Marijuana Use (*Continued*)

qualify for the August state ballot. 'The proposed initiative will take marijuana sales out of the underground market and put them in legitimate, taxpaying businesses,' . . . The proposal . . . [expected to be voted on in Alaska is . . .] similar to one passed in Colorado . . . [which] . . . legalizes the growing, buying and consumption of marijuana for adults ages 21 or older. . . . In addition to Colorado and Washington, 18 other states and the District of Columbia allow some legal use of marijuana, primarily for medicinal purposes. Pro-recreational marijuana Initiatives are expected in various states in 2016, including Arizona, California, Maine, Massachusetts, Montana and Nevada, according to Mason Tvert of the Marijuana Policy Project" (Karimi 2014).

Data from Pew Research Center. "Majority Now Supports Legalizing Marijuana." Washington, DC: Pew Research Center (4 April 2013). Available http://www.people-press.org/2013/04/04/majority-now-supports-legalizing-marijuana/; Flores, E. "Group Works to Legalize Marijuana, Others Fight Against It." Tucson, AZ: KVOA.com, 13 June 2013. Available http://www.kvoa.com/news/group-works -to-legalize-marijuana-others-fight-against-it/#_; Ferner, M. "Marijuana Legalization: Colo. Gov. Hickenlooper Signs First Bills in History to Establish a Legal Regulated Pot Market for Adults." *Huffington Post,* posted 28 05 2013 and updated 04 06 2013. Available http://www.huffingtonpost.com/2013/05/28/hickenlooper-signs-colora_n_3346798.html; *Huffington Post.* "Mexico City to Consider Legalizing Marijuana," 18 June 2013. Available http://www.huffingtonpost.com/2013/06/18/mexico-city-marijuana_n_3461671 .html#slide=887952; Turner, C. "Lawmakers: Get Federal Government Out of Marijuana Regulation." *Main Justice,* Washington, DC, 23 June 2011. Available http://www.mainjustice.com/2011/06/23/lawmakers-get-federal-government-out-of-marijuana-regulation/; *The Republic* and the Associated Press. "Ore Legislative Panel Signs Off on Bill Legalizing Medical Marijuana Dispensaries," 19 June 2013. Available http://www.therepublic.com/view/story/f6812ef7a106445f9429b9e01f95e841/OR-XGR–Medical-Marijuana-Dispensaries.

school students in suits and ties who became hallucinatory, homicidal, violent, and suicidal; such symptoms were highly exaggerated. As a complete contradiction, in the same decade, the Rastafarian religion spread among Jamaican agricultural workers, who named marijuana a holy plant.

[In] *Ganja in Jamaica* (Rubin and Comitas 1975) [the book] focused its findings to refute the claim that marijuana users damaged their productive capability. The study found that most rural Jamaicans who smoked ganja (marijuana) were extraordinarily diligent peasants who invested impressive amounts of time and energy in multiple income-bearing schemes every day of the year. Starting before sunrise, they tended livestock and poultry; farmed

gardens; hired out their labor for wages; exchanged goods and services in an indigenous marketing system; maintained churches, self-help associations, political parties, guilds, schools, and households; and sometimes, at night, clandestinely cleared acres of forest to cultivate marijuana. They listened to the radio, watched television, and read newspapers to perform better as citizens in a modern democracy. These active, clear-sighted economic strategists and community builders depended on a heavy daily intake of ganja for nourishment as "brain food," and relied on it specifically to improve production. Adult Jamaican marijuana smokers consumed some six or more large "spliffs" (hand-rolled cigars) of ganja a day, or a few ounces. They also consumed it in teas, tisanes, and tonics. As employers, they preferred to pay their employees ganja rather than money and encouraged its use in the workplace. (Rubin and Comitas 1975, cited in Hamid 1998, p. 61)

Marijuana is a hemp plant that is green, brown, or a gray mixture of dried, shredded leaves, stems, seeds, and flowers. There are two main strains— **Cannabis sativa** and **Cannabis indica**. These two main varieties differ ". . . in their chemical composition, physiological aesthetic, and medical application" (ProCon.org 2012a). *Cannabis sativa* originates from Colombia, Mexico, Jamaica,

KEY TERMS

Cannabis sativa
a biological name of one of two major species of marijuana that originates from Colombia, Mexico, Thailand, and Southeast Asia; generally causes uplifting and energetic feelings and provides pain relief for certain ailments

Cannabis indica
a biological name of one of two major species of marijuana that originates from hash-producing countries (e.g., Afghanistan, Morocco, and Tibet) (ProCon.org 2012a,1); its effects include body relaxation, stress relief, and calmness and serenity (Budfacts.com 2009)

Close-ups of growing marijuana plants of the Cannabis indica strain. This type of marijuana is often used for legal and illegal human consumption as a mind-altering drug.

South Africa, Thailand, and Southeast Asia and generally causes uplifting and energetic feelings, stimulates the appetite, and provides pain relief from certain ailments (Budfacts.com 2009). This strain is grown in hot countries that have higher temperatures. It is a brighter green than the *indica* strain with narrower leaves, and averages over 6 feet tall. *Cannabis indica* originates from hash-producing countries (e.g., Afghanistan, Pakistan, India, Turkey, Morocco, and Tibet) (ProCon.org 2012a), and its effects include body relaxation, stress relief, and calmness and serenity (Budfacts .com 2009). Unlike *Cannabis sativa*, *Cannabis indica* is found in warm countries; the plants are shorter (under 6 feet tall) and a darker green in color with wider leaves (Weedist 2012). The tetrahydrocannabinol (THC) content in the two strains differs; the *indica* strain generally has a lower THC content (Weedist 2012).

Cannabis strains are available across the whole spectrum from pure *sativas* to pure *indicas*, and in every combination in between. From 30% *sativa* – 70% *indica* strains, there are 80%

sativa – 20% *indica* strains, and many, many 50% – 50% combinations, as well as others available. (BudFacts.com 2009)

These two main cannabis family species have been cultivated for thousands of years. When smoked, the dried and crushed leaves, stems, and seeds of cannabis produce sedative and mind-altering effects, which vary according to the potency of the variety of plant used.

Usage in the United States began in the 1920s, rose during the 1960s and 1970s, and fell in every year from 1978 until 1991. From 1991 on, however, usage began to climb. In this chapter, we review the history, past and current usage trends, attitudes, and controversies surrounding marijuana (including the amotivational syndrome and the current debate regarding the legalization of marijuana for medical purposes), and its physiological and behavioral effects on the user.

Marijuana: History and Current Trends

As the rich history in this section will reveal the trends and economic impact of marijuana are noteworthy. Historically, many societies discovered marijuana as a valued crop when marijuana's woody stems known as hemp yielded a fiber that can be made into cloth and rope. The extensive use and economic impact of marijuana continues to the present day exemplified by many states using marijuana as a cash crop. "The annual marijuana crop harvested in the U.S. is now the nation's most valuable, worth more than cultivation of corn and wheat combined, according to an analysis by the former head of the legalization group NORML" (Join Together Staff 2006). Further, *Reuters* reported. . . that public-policy analyst Jon Gettman estimated the value of the U.S. marijuana crop at $35 billion annually, with California, Tennessee, Kentucky, Hawaii and Washington each producing more than $1 billion worth of the illegal drug each year. Gettman estimated the annual California marijuana crop to be worth $13.8 billion" (Join Together Staff 2006). Another report indicates that ". . . marijuana production, . . . [is] . . .at a value of $35.8 billion, exceeds the combined value of corn ($23.3 billion) and wheat ($7.5 billion) (Venkataraman 2006). In looking at one state for example "California produces nearly 40 percent of the marijuana in the U.S.; worth an estimated $18.8 billion . . . [and] . . . by far the state's biggest cash crop" (Jenkins 2011).

▌ Historical Roots of Marijuana

The term *cannabis* comes from the Greek word for hemp. Initially, the Spaniards brought cannabis to the Western Hemisphere as a source of fiber and seeds. For thousands of years, the seeds have been pressed to extract red oil used for medicinal and euphorigenic purposes (Abood and Martin 1992; Iversen 1993). The plant (both male and female) also produces a resin with active ingredients that affect the central nervous system (CNS). Marijuana contains hundreds of chemical compounds, but only a few found in the resin are responsible for producing the euphoric high.

Even the original uses of marijuana remain controversial. Botanists have never been able to trace cannabis to its origins, although some think it originated in Asia. Ancient Chinese documents contain the earliest recorded name of hemp—*ma,* meaning "fiber-producing plant," as well as "valuable" or "endearing." The term *ma* was still used as late as 1930. In the late 1970s, during an archeological dig in Gansu, the seat of Chinese civilization, workers uncovered cannabis seeds stored in an earthen jar.

Ayurvedic documents from 600 BC describe an intoxicating resin from the plant. The fifth-century BC Greek historian Herodotus recorded that the Scythians burned the tops of the plant, producing a narcotic smoke. And a first-century Greek physician wrote that hemp was made into intoxicating cakes, perhaps the forerunners of the marijuana brownies of 1960s fame (Pollan 1998, p. 39).

Other sources report that the first known record of marijuana use is in the *Book of Drugs,* written about 2737 BC by the Chinese Emperor Shen Nung; he prescribed marijuana for treating gout, malaria, gas pains, and absentmindedness. The Chinese apparently had much respect for the plant. They obtained fiber for clothes and medicine from it for thousands of years.

Around 500 BC, another Chinese book of treatments referred to the medical use of marijuana. Nonetheless, the plant got a bad name from the moralists of the day, who claimed that youngsters became wild and disrespectful from the recreational use of *ma*. They called it the "liberator of sin" because, under its influence, the youngsters refused to listen to their elders and did other scandalous things. Although the Chinese recognized *ma*'s medical usefulness, they eventually banned it because of its unpredictable intoxicating effects. Later, because of rampant use, it was legalized again.

India also has a long and varied history of marijuana use. It was an essential part of Indian religious ceremonies for thousands of years. The well-known *Rig Veda* and other chants describe the use of *soma,* which some believe was marijuana. Early writings describe a ritual in which resin was collected from the plants. After fasting and purification, certain men ran naked through the cannabis fields. The clinging resin was scraped off their bodies, and cakes were made from it and used in feasts. For centuries, missionaries in India tried to ban the use of marijuana, but they were never successful, because its use was too heavily ingrained in the culture. From India, the use of marijuana spread throughout Asia, Africa, Europe, and the Americas—English settlers brought it to the U.S. colonies.

Assyrian records dating back to 650 BC refer to a drug called *azulla* that was used for making rope and cloth and was consumed to experience euphoria. The ancient Greeks also knew about marijuana. Galen described the general use of hemp in cakes, which, when eaten in excess, produced narcotic effects. Herodotus described the Scythian custom of burning marijuana seeds and leaves to produce a narcotic smoke in steam baths. It was believed that breathing the smoke from the burning plants would cause frenzied activity. Groups of people stood in the smoke, laughed, and danced as it took effect.

One legend about cannabis is based on the travels of Marco Polo in the 12th century. Marco Polo told of the legendary Hasan Ibn-Sabbah, who terrorized a part of Arabia in the early 1100s. His men were some of the earliest political murderers, and he ordered them to kill under the influence of hashish, a strong, unadulterated cannabis derivative. The cult was called the *hashishiyya,* from which came the word *hashish.* (The word *assassin* may be derived from the name of Sheik Hasan, who was a political leader in the 10th century.) It is unlikely, however, that using hashish can turn people into killers. Experience suggests that people tend to become sleepy and indolent rather than violent after eating or smoking hashish or another of the strong cannabis preparations available in Arabia (Abel 1989).

Napoleon's troops brought hashish to France after their campaign in Egypt at the beginning of the 19th century, despite Napoleon's strict orders to the contrary. By the 1840s, the use of hashish, as well as opium, was widespread in France, and efforts to curb its spread were unsuccessful.

In North America, hemp was planted near Jamestown in 1611 for use in making rope. By 1630, half of the winter clothing at this settlement was made from hemp fibers. There is no evidence that hemp was used medicinally at this time. Hemp was also valuable as a source of fiber for clothing and rope for the Pilgrims at Plymouth. To meet the demand for fiber, a law was passed in Massachusetts in 1639 requiring every household to plant hemp seed. However, it took much manual labor to work the hemp fiber into usable form, resulting in a chronic shortage of fiber for fishnets and the like (Abel 1989).

George Washington cultivated a field of hemp at Mount Vernon, and there is some indication that it was used for medicine as well as for making rope. In his writings, Washington once mentioned that he forgot to separate the male and female plants, a process usually done because the female plant gave more resin if not pollinated.

In the early 1800s, U.S. physicians used marijuana extracts to produce a tonic intended for both medicinal and recreational purposes. This practice changed in 1937 with passage of the Marijuana Tax Act. The Marijuana Tax Act was modeled after the Harrison Act of 1914 in that marijuana was considered a narcotic and subject to the same legal controls as cocaine and the opiates. Like these opiates, marijuana distributors had to register and pay a tax to legally import, buy, or sell this drug (Musto 1999). As a result, the Marijuana Tax Act prohibited the use of this drug as an intoxicant and regulated its use as a medicine.

Most of the abuse of marijuana in the United States during the early part of the 20th century took place near the Mexican border and in the ghetto areas of major cities. Cannabis was mistakenly considered a narcotic, like opium, and legal authorities treated it as such (Abood and Martin 1992). In 1931, Harry Anslinger, who was the first appointed head of the Bureau of Narcotics and later would become responsible for the enforcement of marijuana laws, believed that the problem was slight (Musto 1999). By 1936, however, he claimed that the increase in the use of marijuana was of great national concern (Anslinger and Cooper 1937) (see **Figure 13.1**). Anslinger set up an informational program that ultimately led

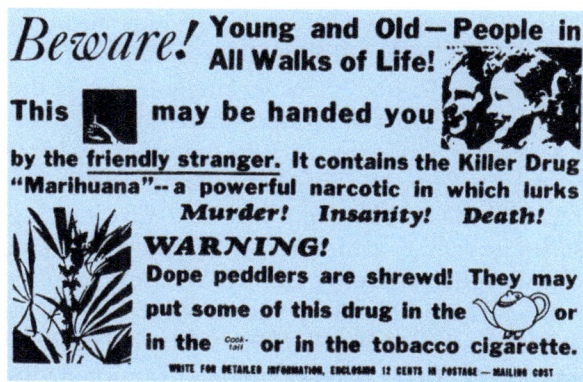

FIGURE 13.1 This antimarijuana poster was distributed by the Federal Bureau of Narcotics in the late 1930s.
Courtesy of Wisconsin Historical Society, WHS-56411.

to the federal law that banned marijuana. The following sensationalized statement was part of Anslinger's campaign to outlaw the drug:

> What about the alleged connection between drugs and sexual pleasure? . . . What is the real relationship between drugs and sex? There isn't any question about marijuana being a sexual stimulant. It has been used throughout the ages for that: in Egypt, for instance. From what we have seen, it is an aphrodisiac, and I believe that the use in colleges today has sexual connotations. (Anslinger and Cooper 1937, p. 19)

In addition, during this time, some usually accurate magazines reported that marijuana was partly responsible for crimes of violence. In 1936, *Scientific American* reported that "marijuana produces a wide variety of symptoms in the user, including hilarity, swooning, and sexual excitement. Combined with intoxicants, it often makes the smoker vicious, with a desire to fight and kill" ("Marijuana Menaces Youth" 1936, p. 151). A famous poster of the day, called "The Assassination of Youth," was effective in molding attitudes against drug use.

Largely because of the media's influence on public opinion, Congress passed the Marijuana Tax Act in 1937. However, because of the discussions and debates before the passage of the 1970 Comprehensive Drug Abuse Prevention and Control Act, which replaced or updated all other laws concerning narcotics and dangerous drugs, the Marijuana Tax Act of 1937 was declared unconstitutional in 1969 because it classified marijuana as a narcotic. Marijuana has not been classified as a narcotic since 1971.

In the early 1900s, marijuana was brought across the U.S. border by Mexican laborers who entered the United States seeking jobs. From the border areas of the United States, recreational use of marijuana spread into mainly the southwestern region of the United States. Such use reached major cities in Texas and surrounding states as well as a number of African American communities in these cities. Heavy users of marijuana included a subpopulation of jazz musicians as well as other "bohemian types" who led more of an unstructured existence in unconventional jobs and occupations (e.g., artists, entertainers, poets, criminals). Thus, before the 1960s, marijuana use was largely confined to small segments of African American urban youth, jazz musicians, and particularly artists and writers who belonged to the 1950s Beat Generation. Use rose tremendously in the 1960s, when it was closely associated with the hippie counterculture, in which marijuana was categorized as a psychedelic (consciousness-expanding) sacrament. It spread into other youth categories during the 1970s, until approximately 1978. In each year from 1978 until 1991, marijuana use fell. After 1991, researchers and prevention specialists were astounded to see a rise in usage among youth.

Marijuana still grows wild in many U.S. states today. Curiously, one reason for the survival of this supply is that, during World War II, the fiber used to make rope (sisal) was hard to import, so the government paid subsidies to farmers who grew hemp. Much of today's crop comes from these same plants. Another reason for the spread of the plants is that, until recently, the seeds were used in birdseed. Leftover seed was discarded in the garbage and thus spread to landfill dumps, where it sprouted. Birdseed containing marijuana seeds is still available, but the seeds are sterilized so that they cannot germinate.

The Indian Hemp Drug Commission Report in the 1890s and the 1930 Panama Canal Zone Report on marijuana stressed that available evidence did not prove marijuana as dangerous as it was popularly thought; these reports were given little publicity, however, and for the most part were disregarded. In 1944, a report was issued by the LaGuardia Committee on Marijuana, which consisted of 31 qualified physicians, psychiatrists, psychologists, pharmacologists, chemists, and sociologists appointed by the New York Academy of Medicine. They stated in one key summary that marijuana was not the killer many thought it to be:

> It was found that marijuana in an effective dose impairs intellectual functioning in general. . . . Marijuana does not change the basic personality structure of the individual. It lessens inhibition and this brings out what is latent in his thoughts and emotions but it does not evoke responses that would otherwise be totally alien to him. . . . Those who have been smoking marijuana for years showed no mental or physical deterioration that may be attributed to the drug. (Solomon 1966, p. 37)

Much of the early research conducted did not consider the potency of marijuana. As a result, findings from various studies are often conflicting and difficult to compare. Because the quality of marijuana varies so greatly, it is impossible to know the amount of drug taken without analyzing the original material and the leftover stub, or "roach." Conditions such as type of seed, soil moisture and fertility, amount of sunlight, and temperature all have an effect on the amounts of active ingredients found in the resulting marijuana plant.

Current Use of Marijuana

The National Survey on Drug Use and Health (NSDUH) reported that among persons age 12 or older, the overall rate of past-month (30 day use of marijuana when surveys were completed) marijuana use in 2011 was 7%; this rate was similar to the rate in 2010, which was 8.9%, and 2009, which was 8.7% (Substance Abuse and Mental Health Services Administration [SAMHSA] 2012). **Figure 13.2** shows that in 2011, out of an estimated 18.1 million Americans age 12 or older who were current users[1] of any type of illicit drugs, the percentage of past-month marijuana users was a staggering 80.5% (64.3% + 16.2%). An estimated 64.3% of current illicit drug users *used only marijuana*, and 16.2% *used marijuana and another illicit drug* (SAMHSA 2012). This leaves a minority of illicit drug users (19.5%, approximately 8 million) who did not use marijuana.

---

[1] *Current drug users* is defined as having used an illicit drug within the month before the National Survey on Drug Use and Health (NSDUH) surveys were taken.

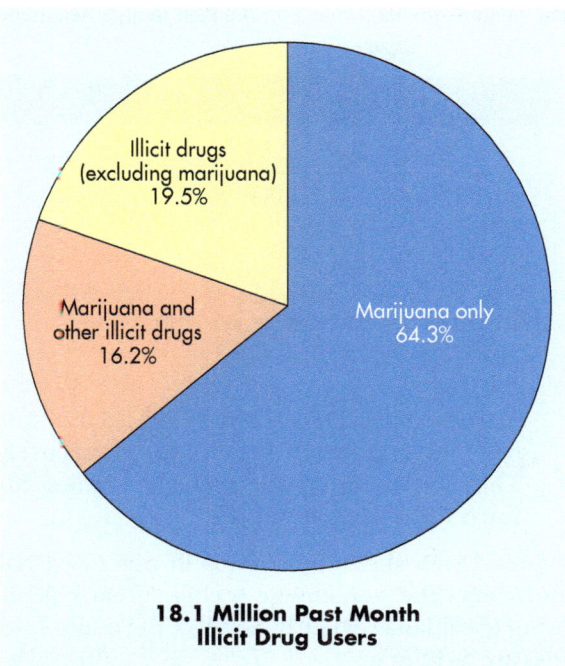

FIGURE 13.2 Types of drugs used in the past month, illicit drug users age 12 or older in 2011.

Data from Substance Abuse and Mental Health Services Administration (SAMHSA). Results from the 2011 National Survey on Drug Use and Health: Detailed Tables. Office of Applied Studies, (HHS Publications No. SMA 12-4713, NSDUH Series H-44)..Rockville, MD 2012.

Other current findings regarding marijuana use are as follows (SAMHSA 2012):

- In 2011, 2.6 million persons had used marijuana for the first time within the past 12 months; this averages to approximately 7200 initiates per day! This estimate was not significantly different from the numbers in 2009 and 2010 (2.4 million for both years), but higher that the estimates in 2002 through 2008 (see **Figure 13.3**).
- In 2011, 1.5 million out of 2.6 million recent marijuana initiates (approximately 58%) were younger than age 18 when they first used the drug.
- Among youth ages 12 to 17, an estimated 6.3% had used marijuana for the first time within the past year, similar to the rate in 2010 (5.9%).
- In 2011, the average age at first marijuana use among recent initiates ages 12 to 49 was 17.5 years. This average was similar to the average age in 2010 (18.4 years) and 2004 through 2008, but was higher than the average ages in 2002, 2003, and 2009.
- In 2011, among recent initiates age 12 or older who initiated marijuana use prior to the age of

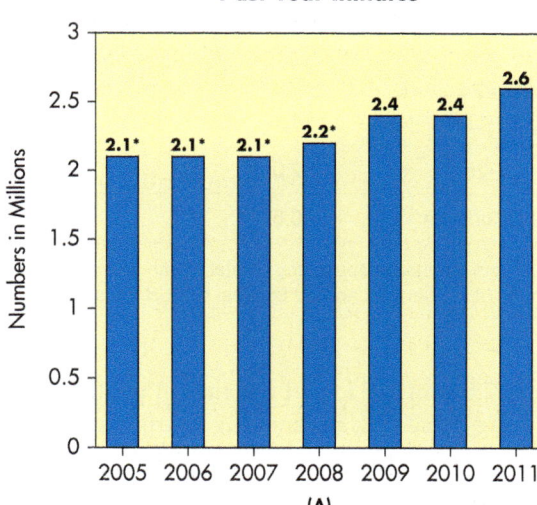

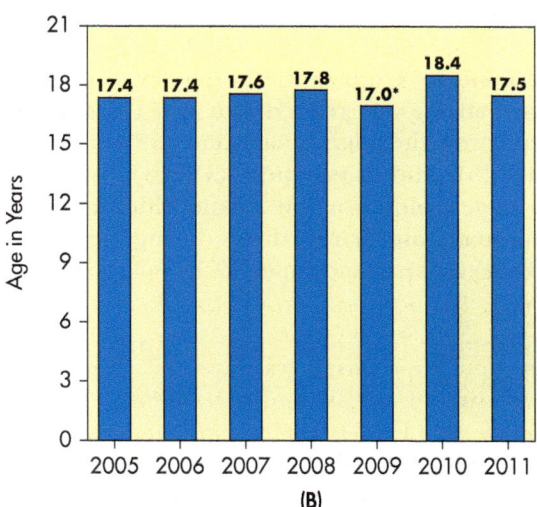

FIGURE 13.3 Past year marijuana Initiates among persons aged 12 or older (A) and mean age at first use of marijuana among past year marijuana Initiates (B) aged 12 to 49: 2005–2011.
+ Difference between this estimate and the 2011 estimate is statistically significant at the .05 level.

Reproduced from Substance Abuse and Mental Health Services Administration (SAMHSA). Results from the 2011 National Survey on Drug Use and Health: Summary of National Findings. NSDUH Series H-44, HHS Publication No. (SMA) 12-4713. Rockville, MD, 2012.

21, the mean age at first use was 16.2 years, which was the same as the mean age in 2010.

- In 2011, the youth marijuana initiation rate—the percentage of those ages 12 to 17 who had not used marijuana prior to the past year—(5.6%) was similar to the rate in 2007 (5.2%).
- The percentage of youth ages 12 to 17 perceiving a great risk in smoking marijuana once a month decreased from 34.4% in 2007 to

TABLE 13.1 Marijuana Use Reported by Americans During Their Lifetime, the Past Year, and the Past Month, According to Age: 2011

Age (Years)	Lifetime (%)	Past Year (%)	Past Month (%)
12–17	17.1	13.9	7.6
18–25	52.0	30.6	18.9
26 or older	46.5	8.8	5.4

Data from Substance Abuse and Mental Health Services Administration (SAMHSA). *Results from the 2011 National Survey on Drug Use and Health: Detailed Tables.* Office of Applied Studies, NSDUH Series H-44, DHHS Publication No. SMA 12-4713. Rockville, MD, 2012.

27.6% in 2011, and the rate of youth perceiving great risk in smoking marijuana once or twice a week also decreased from 54.6% 2007 to 44.8% in 2011. Consistent with decreasing trends in the perceived risk of marijuana use, the prevalence of past-month marijuana use among youth increased between 2007 (6.7%) and 2011 (7.9%).

As **Table 13.1** shows, the frequency of marijuana use is strongly correlated with age. The age group reporting the highest lifetime (52%), past-year (30.6%), and past-month (18.9%) use was 18- to 25-year-olds. For the 26 and older age group, marijuana use sharply drops during the past year (8.8%) and past month (5.4%).

▌ Recent Trends in Use of Marijuana: 8th, 10th, and 12th Graders

Figure 13.4A shows the percentage of 8th-, 10th-, and 12th-grade students who used marijuana in the last 12 months. Some of the major findings are as follows:

- Annual marijuana prevalence peaked among 12th graders in 1979 at 51%.
- Use declined fairly steadily for 13 years, bottoming at 22% in 1992—a decline of more than half.
- In the 1990s a resurgence of marijuana use occurred.
- Annual prevalence rates peaked in 1996 at the 8th-grade level and in 1997 at the 10th- and 12th-grade levels.
- After these peak years, use declined among all three grades through 2006, 2007, and 2008. Since then there has been an upturn in use in all three grades.
- Although not shown in Figure 13.4A, in 2010 there was a significant increase in daily use in all three grades, followed by a nonsignificant

increase in 2011 reaching 1.3%, 3.6%, and 6.6% in grades 8, 10, and 12, respectively. The rate for 12th graders was the highest rate since 1981, when it was 7%.

Figure 13.4B shows the trends in perceived risk and shows the percentage seeing "great risk" in using marijuana regularly. Some of the major findings are as follows:

- The proportion of students seeing great risk from using marijuana regularly fell during the rise in use in the 1970s, and again during the subsequent rise in the 1990s.
- In the 10th and 12th grades, perceived risk declined a year before use rose in the upturn of the 1990s, making perceived risk a leading indicator of change in use. The decline in perceived risk halted in 1996 in 8th and 10th grades; the increases in use ended a year or two later, again making perceived risk a leading indicator.
- From 1996 to 2000, perceived risk held fairly steady and the decline in use in the upper grades stalled.
- After some decline prior to 2002, perceived risk increased in all grades through 2004 as use decreased.
- Perceived risk fell after 2004 in the 8th grade and in 2005 in the 12th grade.
- In 2011, perceived risk continued to decline in grades 10 and 12 and leveled in grade 8.

Figure 13.4C shows the percentage disapproving of using regularly. Some of the major findings are as follows:

- Personal disapproval of trying marijuana use fell considerably among 8th graders between 1991 and 1996 and among 10th and 12th graders between 1992 and 1997—by 17%, 21%, and 19%, respectively—which were intervals of increasing use.

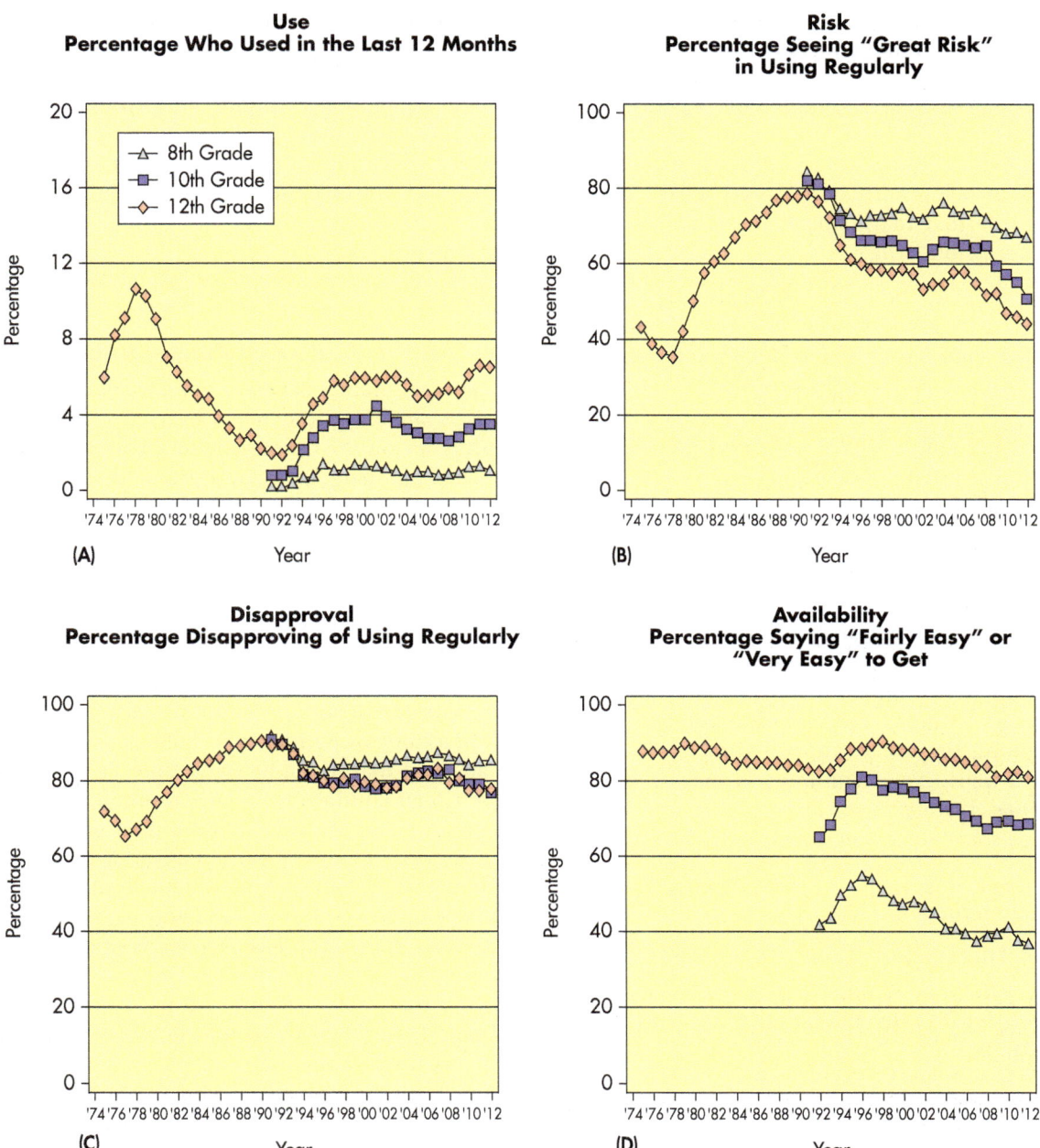

FIGURE 13.4 Marijuana trends: Percentages of marijuana use, risk, disapproval, and availability for 8th-, 10th-, and 12th-grade students.

Data from Johnston, L. D., P. M. O'Malley, J. G. Bachman, and J. E. Schulenberg. *Monitoring the Future: National Survey Results on Drug Use, 2012 Overview, Key Findings on Adolescent Drug Use*, Ann Arbor, MI: Institute for Social Research, University of Michigan, 2013.

- After 1997 there was some modest increase in disapproval among 8th graders, but not much among 10th and 12th graders until 2004, when the lower grades showed increases.
- From 2003 to 2007 (2008 in the case of 10th graders), disapproval increased in all three grades, but has declined some since then as use rose.

Figure 13.4D shows the percentage saying marijuana is "fairly easy" or "very easy" to get. (Availability of marijuana often includes the belief that marijuana is "fairly easy" or "very easy" to get.) Some of the major findings are as follows:

- Ever since the *Monitoring the Future* (MTF) study began in 1975, between 81% and 90%

of 12th graders each year have said that they could get marijuana fairly easily or very easily if they wanted some. (It has been considerably less accessible to younger adolescents.)

- In 2011, 38% of 8th graders, 68% of 10th graders, and 82% of 12th graders reported it as being fairly or very easy to get. It seems clear that marijuana has remained a highly accessible drug.

According to the national *Monitoring the Future* survey, 12th graders' perceived risk of harm from regular marijuana use has declined from 58% of U.S. high school seniors in 2006 to 52% in 2008 and 2009 who thought there was great risk of harm from smoking marijuana (Center for Substance Abuse Research [CESAR] 2010b).

Finally, the following two interviews convey what figures and percentages cannot capture:
First interview:

> What, weed? It's so easy to get. In fact, many times [referring to junior high school] I didn't even have to buy, it would be offered in the morning, at lunchtime, and whenever we get together, even after school it is there. Among the users (and we know each other real well), it's as common as sharing candy. *(From Venturelli's research files, male first-year high school student in a medium-sized town in the Midwest, age 15, June 19, 2000)*

Second interview:

> No, I don't smoke it often, but I know over half my friends smoke it two or three times a week and on weekend nights. It's not unusual for several of my friends to smoke up before partying. I usually take a hit or two, but I wouldn't even do that if it weren't for my friends always having it. *(From Venturelli's research files, male senior in high school in a medium-sized town in the Midwest, age 17, July 16, 2010)*

Marijuana: Is It the Assassin of Youth?

In the late 1930s, the poster "Marijuana: Assassin of Youth" made a clever play on words, bringing up reminders of the Middle Eastern *hashashin* cult, whose terrible exploits were attributed to their use of hashish (marijuana resin). At the time, marijuana was even incorrectly classified

as a narcotic, like opium and morphine. Amotivational syndrome, lassitude, poor driving skills the day after smoking, educational failure, and dependence may not quite add up to "assassination," as wildly exaggerated in *Reefer Madness*. The poster was right, however, in associating use of this drug with young people, among whom marijuana is popular in both local peer groups and broad youth cultures.

▪ Major Factors Affecting Marijuana Use

The mass media, parental role models, perceived risk, availability, and peers have the most direct influence on the development of youth's attitudes regarding drug use. An estimated 8.3 million children—11.9%—live with at least one parent (biological, step-, adoptive, or foster) who had abused or was dependent on alcohol or an illicit drug in the past year (CESAR 2010a). These findings become worrisome when we consider that marijuana is the most frequently used illicit drug and that parental use of marijuana has been found to be a significant influence on teens' use of this drug.

In a study by Kandel et al. (2001), when parents had used marijuana at some time in their lives, their teen children were 40% more likely to have used the drug in their lifetime than teens whose parents had never used marijuana. Moreover, when parents had used marijuana in the past year, their children were twice as likely to have used in the same time period as were teens whose parents had not used in the past year. This same study also found that when parents had used marijuana in the past year, their teen children were more likely to have used marijuana in the past year when compared with the children of parents who had used at some time in their life, but not in the last year. Similarly, parental use of other drugs, such as alcohol, nicotine, and cocaine, was also found to have an impact on their teen children's use of marijuana. More importantly, the perceived risk of use is the most important influence on teen marijuana use. In the Kandel et al. (2001) study, it was found to be five times more important than parental use.

As shown in Figure 13.4A, when comparisons are made among 8th, 10th, and 12th graders, marijuana use rises sharply by 12th grade. One main reason for this is because children in lower grades are less likely to have friends and access to friends who use marijuana (as well as access to other major drugs of abuse). Marijuana has been almost universally available to U.S. high school seniors (from 83% to 90%)

over at least the past 30 years (Johnston et al. 2009) and nearly half of youth ages 12 to 17 reported easy access to marijuana (Johnston et al. 2013).

Beginning several years before age 13 (early adolescence), peers and peer groups begin to exert the most influence (Bauman and Ennett 1996; Greenblatt 1999; Heitzeg 1996; Tudor, Petersen, and Elifson 1987; Venturelli 2000). In fact, even in acquiring the drug, one finding stated that "Marijuana distribution relies primarily on informal dealing through social networks . . ." (CESAR 2007). More than one-half (58%) of household residents who had used marijuana in the past year reported that they most recently obtained their marijuana for free, compared to 39% who reported purchasing it. Nearly all marijuana users (89%) reported getting their most recent acquisition from a friend or relative. Unlike users of more expensive drugs such as cocaine and heroin, the majority of people who used marijuana in the past year (58%) gave away or shared some of their most recent acquisition (CESAR 2007).

Research shows that it is unlikely that an individual will use drugs when his or her peers do not use them. Marijuana use, in particular, is a group-motivated behavior that is strongly affected by peer pressure and influence. In effect, habitual drug users are likely to belong to drug-using groups. In contrast, people who do not use drugs belong to groups in which drug use is perceived as an unacceptable and devious form of social recreation. Learning theory explains how peers can influence one another; drug-using peer members serve as role models, legitimizing use. Peers in such groups are saying, in essence, "It's perfectly normal to use drugs"; in turn, this justifies usage.

A common example of polydrug use (alcohol and marijuana).

In addition to these major factors (the mass media, parental role models, perceived risk, availability, and peer influences), six other factors must be taken into account as influencing drug use:

1. Structural factors, such as age, gender, family background, and religious beliefs.
2. Social and interactional factors, such as the type of interpersonal relationships, friendship cliques, and drug use within the peer group setting.
3. Setting, such as the type of community and neighborhood (physical location where drugs are used).
4. Attitudinal factors, such as personal beliefs and attitudes regarding drug use, and personality factors, such as self-esteem, level of security versus insecurity, and maturation level.
5. Participation in after-school activities is associated with higher levels of academic achievement and self-esteem, as well as lower levels of substance use (SAMHSA 2007b). Regardless of family income, youth ages 12 to 17 who did not participate in any activities had higher rates of past-month cigarette and illicit drug use than those who participated in four, six, seven, or more activities (SAMHSA 2007b).
6. Finally, even the amount of religious involvement affects illicit drug use (which includes marijuana use). In regard to religious involvement and substance use, adults who reported that religious beliefs are a very important part of their lives were less likely to use illicit drugs in the past month than those who reported that religious beliefs are not a very important part of their lives (6.1% vs. 14.3%) (SAMHSA 2007a). Thus, religiosity has been identified in other research as an important protective factor against substance use (Brigham Young University 2008; Kendler, Gardner, and Prescott 1997; National Center on Addiction and Substance Abuse 2001; Wallace, Myers, and Osai 2004).

Keep in mind these factors can easily overlap; they are not separate and distinct. Sociologists have long studied "youth cultures" (Coleman 1961). In the 1970s, sociologists began to examine different subcultures of youth in terms of the behaviors that symbolically represent the group, in which participation in drug use is a ritual that marks off entrance into the group and out of childhood—a rite of passage. Typically, U.S. high school culture includes a leading clique, often associated with team sports, whose members might be called "jocks," and a marginal, deviant, or rebellious group (Eckert 1989). In some cases, the latter group is associated with marijuana use. In the mid-1960s, hippies were perceived as a group whose members were part of a counterculture committed to unconventional values, pacifism, and communalism in addition to psychedelic drugs. By 1970, this name denoted broader segments of youth who adhered merely to hippie styles of clothing and drug use (Buff 1970). By the 1980s, marijuana use was identified with subgroups of youth often called "burnouts." In many communities that were studied by sociologists, burnouts came from all social levels, but were often overrepresented in upper-middle classes, and they were marginal and/or rebellious within the educational system, if not dropouts (Eckert 1989; Gaines 1992). Membership in such marijuana-using subcultures often bonds the youth to ongoing and persistent drug use.

Is Marijuana Really a Gateway Drug?

Gateway drugs (also known as gateway theory, gateway hypothesis, and gateway effect) are drugs that serve as the gate or path that usually precedes the use of illicit drugs, such as tobacco, marijuana, heroin, and LSD. Gateway drugs, or drugs of entry, serve to initiate a novice user into the drug-using world. Although the linkage is not biochemical, common gateway drugs include tobacco, inhalants, alcohol, anabolic steroids, Ritalin, and prescription painkillers (prescription opioid medications) (Benson 2010; National Institute on Drug Abuse [NIDA] 2011).

The claim that marijuana use most often leads to the use of other more serious drugs, such as heroin, remains controversial (Gardner 1992). A Rand press release reported that the gateway theory does not explain the progression to other more addictive drugs; instead, "[t]he people who are predisposed to use drugs and have the opportunity to use drugs *are more likely* than others to use both marijuana and harder drugs. . . . Marijuana typically comes first because it is more available" (Rand Drug Policy Research Center 2002). Thus, instead of assuming that marijuana, alcohol, and other more commonly used drugs are simply gateway drugs responsible for leading to more serious drugs, it is more likely that factors

such as (1) the age when teens have opportunities to use marijuana and other drugs; (2) associated opportunities; and (3) the willingness, mindset, or predisposition to use drugs may be better predictors of the progression from less addictive to more addictive and powerful types of drugs.

For example, the gateway theory cannot explain the fact that although it is true many heroin addicts began drug use with marijuana, it is also true that many, if not most, also used coffee and cigarettes. Millions of marijuana users never go beyond the gateway drugs used. "There are only a few thousand opiate addicts in Great Britain, yet there are millions who have tried cannabis" (Gossop 1987, p. 9).

Nevertheless, the gateway theory may offer a plausible explanation as to why a small percentage of marijuana users progress to hard drugs such as cocaine or heroin. In many cases, it may be unlikely that the use of marijuana as well as other drugs considered to be gateway drugs would be the *principal cause* for progressing to harder and more addictive types of drugs.

Youth who turn to drugs are usually seriously alienated individuals. Thus, progression from marijuana to other drugs is more likely to depend on peer group composition, family relationships, social class, and the age at which drug use begins (Indiana Prevention Resource Center 1996).

It is important to note, however, that many, if not most, young drug users do eventually leave drug-using groups and abandon their drug-using behavior, a process sometimes called maturing out. An example that often typifies maturing out is found in the following interviews:

First interview:

Up until I started my full time job after graduation from college I was smoking weed and at parties using other even worse types of drugs without any hesitation. Even during my senior year in high school I was smoking weed nearly every day and graduated with a B average. But then, once I joined this company I am still working at today, they were drug testing, so I quit everything. I just did not want to risk a good paying job that I liked for drugs. Plus the embarrassment of not passing a drug test, when my dad is a CEO in the company I am working at. Now, I am even a Boy Scout leader and known as the Scout who is totally against any unnecessary drug use. What a change from those younger days! (*From Venturelli's research files, male working for a major corporation in Chicago, age 29, May 12, 2010*)

Second interview:

> I first started with marijuana when I was thirteen. Friends of mine were also smoking cigarettes whenever we got together to smoke weed. It was easy to try cigarettes after smoking weed so at around age 14 or 15 I added cigarettes to my weed smoking. From there and in enjoying the highs alcohol was my next drug of choice. Pills and snorting my best friend's Ritalin crushed into power was added to my favorite drugs. I guess you could say that one led to another, but I never went to snorting coke because it was so expensive and I figured I progressed enough in my drug usage and didn't need to add yet another drug to my drugs of choice. I was 24 when I decided to quit playing around with all these drugs and only drink alcohol occasionally now. *(From Venturelli's research files, male working at a health club in Valparaiso, Indiana, age 29, April 6, 2013)*

Misperceptions of Marijuana Use

In a world in which marijuana can be considered either an assassin or a sacrament, and in which it is associated with membership in prized or despised peer groups, it is not surprising that estimates of its use vary widely and inaccurately. Parents, for example, tend to underestimate their children's use of drugs. Findings from one study indicated that, "only 14% of the parents interviewed thought their children had experimented with marijuana while 38% of the teenagers said they had tried it" (Wren 1996, p. 1). In the same survey, 52% of teenagers reported having been offered drugs, whereas 34% of the parents thought their children might have been offered drugs. Other recent research indicates that parents who more carefully and consistently monitor their children and maintain more open communication are more likely to underestimate their children's risky behavior and ". . . parents of adolescents who perceived themselves as better than average in school performance and who participated in religious services were more likely to underestimate adolescents' substance use . . ." (Hongmei et al. 2006, p. 1).

Interestingly, another report by the former president of the National Center on Addiction and Substance Abuse at Columbia University stated the following with regard to baby boomer parents (parents born between 1946 through 1964):

> Almost half know someone who uses illegal drugs; a third have friends who use marijuana. Almost half expect their children to try illegal drugs, and 65 percent of those who smoked pot regularly when young believe their kids will try drugs . . . almost half of the parents don't think they can have much influence on whether their kids will use drugs. (Califano 1996, p. 19)

Even with regard to users' perceptions of other users, beliefs about marijuana remain distorted. College students tend to have exaggerated misperceptions of use, believing that their peers use marijuana much more than is true (Berkowitz 1991; Johnston et al. 2009; Sorden 2011). For example, at one campus in northern New Jersey, two-thirds of students reported never using marijuana, yet most students polled believed that the average student uses marijuana once per week. Other research also shows a widespread misperception in usage of marijuana. In 2005, in a randomly selected sample of 3639 college students, a large proportion (51%) of undergraduate students overestimated the use of marijuana among their peers on campus (McCabe 2008).

These findings of misperception in the use of marijuana are important because actual marijuana usage remains high for the time being. Recent findings show that marijuana continues to be the most commonly used illicit drug. An estimated 107.8 million Americans age 12 or older have tried marijuana at least once in their lifetime, representing 42% of the U.S. population in that age group. The number of past-year marijuana users in 2011 was approximately 29.7 million (11.5% of the

FIGURE 13.5 Marijuana plant.
© Mitchell Brothers 21st Century Film Group/ShutterStock, Inc.

population age 12 or older), and the number of past-month marijuana users was 18 million (7%) (SAMHSA 2012).

Characteristics of Cannabis

In 1753, Carolus Linnaeus, a Swedish botanist, classified marijuana as *Cannabis sativa* (see **Figure 13.5**). *Cannabis sativa* is a plant that grows readily in many parts of the world. Most botanists agree that there is only one species (*sativa*) and that all the variants (*indica, Americana,* and *Africana*) belong to that species, whereas others believe that the variants are three distinct species (Schultes 1978). *Indica* is considered to have the most potent resin, but climate, soil, and selective plant breeding all influence potency. The world's largest marijuana plant was 39 feet tall, and its woody stem was nearly 3 inches in diameter.

Cannabis is *dioecious*, meaning that there are male and female plants. After the male plant releases its pollen, it usually dies. In any case, even before the male plant dies, cultivators of marijuana often eliminate or remove the male plants before the female plant has been pollinated.

There are more than 421 different chemicals in the cannabis plant, many of which have not yet been identified. Tetrahydrocannabinol, or THC, is the primary mind-altering (psychoactive) agent in marijuana (Abood and Martin 1996; National Institute on Drug Abuse [NIDA] 2009b; Swan 1996) and appears to be important for the reinforcing properties of this substance (Kelly et al. 1994). THC is most highly concentrated in the flowering tops and upper leaves of the female plant. "When crushed or beaten, these flowering tops produce a resin in which the psychoactive ingredient THC is found. The flowering tops, or 'buds' of the female cannabis plant typically have the highest concentrations of THC, followed by

the leaves. Much lower THC levels are found in the stalks and seeds of the cannabis plant and these are of minimal commercial value" (National Cannabis Prevention and Information Centre [NCPIC], 2013).

In cultivated marijuana crops, as mentioned earlier, male plants are eradicated from the growing fields so that they cannot pollinate the female plants. The lack of pollination makes the potency of female plants increase dramatically. **Sinsemilla** (meaning "without seeds" in Spanish) is one of the most potent derivatives of the cannabis plant known in the United States, with an average THC content of 9.6%, but reaching as high as 24%. Sinsemilla is made from the buds of the flowering tops of female plants (NIDA 1998). Other known types that have a high THC content include "hydro" (which means grown in water) "blue berry," and "kind bud."

"The average potency of all marijuana in the US, according to the UMPMC's (University of Mississippi's Potency Monitoring Project) Dec. 2008–Mar. 2009 quarterly report, was 8.52% (5.62% domestic and 9.57% nondomestic). Nondomestic varieties include Jamaican, Colombian, Mexican, and Canadian, which averaged 9.57% THC. Out of 788 domestic and nondomestic samples seized between 2008 and 2009 the average was 8.52% THC (ElSohly 2009, p. 6). "For comparison, the national average of marijuana's THC content in 1978 was 1.37%, in 1988 it was 3.59%, in 1998 4.43%, and in 2008 8.49%" (ProCon 2012b). This dramatic increase in the potency of marijuana results from "[m]ore efficient agriculture—new methods of harvesting and processing marijuana plants—has made pot about 20 times more potent than the marijuana on the street in the 1960s and 1970s, drug treatment experts and law officials say" (Henneberger 1994, p. F-18). Further, the quantities of other, more potent types of marijuana such as *sinsemilla* and hydro are more readily available in illegal drug markets. In addition, recently developed **drug trafficking organizations (DTOs)**—which are complex illegal organizations with highly defined command-and-control structures—produce, transport, and/or distribute large quantities of one or more illicit drugs.

Another finding is that:

Marijuana produced in Mexico remains the most widely available in the United States. High potency marijuana has also entered the U.S. drug market from Canada. Another source for marijuana in the United States is domestically grown marijuana, which includes

KEY TERMS

sinsemilla
meaning without seeds, this marijuana is made from the buds and flowering tops of female plants and is one of the most potent types

drug trafficking organizations (DTOs)
complex organizations with highly defined command-and-control structures that produce, transport, and/or distribute large quantities of one or more illicit drugs

both indoor and outdoor operations. Groups [such as more recently identified drug trafficking organization (DTOs)] operating from Mexico employ a variety of transportation and concealment methods to smuggle marijuana into the United States. Most of the marijuana smuggled into the United States is concealed in vehicles—often in false compartments—or hidden in shipments of legitimate agricultural or industrial products. Marijuana is also smuggled across the border by rail, horse, raft, and backpack. Canada is becoming a source country for indoor-grown, high potency (15% to 25% THC) marijuana destined for the United States. Such indoor-grow operations have become an enormous and lucrative illicit industry, producing a potent form of marijuana that has come to be known as "BC Bud." (ONDCP 2003)

Finally, not only are there many more types of marijuana available today in comparison to twenty years ago from illegal drug markets, but also the types and quality of marijuana seeds for growing marijuana plants have multiplied. One website among many devoted to selling high quality marijuana seeds on the internet is BC Bud Depot in Ontario, Canada, which greets shoppers with the following:

> Welcome to the BC Bud Depot. View our entire seed bank listing here. Along with breeding the world's best marijuana seeds for fast and discreet delivery worldwide, the BC Bud Depot also collaborates with other world renowned breeders to bring you the very best and most comprehensive marijuana seed bank in the world today. Find everything you need here, from CC Bud Depot and Reeferman seeds, to European breeders like T.H. Seeds, Soma, DNA Genetics and Delta-9 Labs. Take a look at our awards cabinet and sign up for our newsletter for amazing monthly specials and limited time offers. (BC Bud Depot n.d.)

Hashish (or hasheesh) is a second derivative of cannabis that contains the purest form of resin. This type of marijuana consists of the sticky resin from the female plant flowers. Domestic samples had an average of 12.14% THC, nondomestic had 7.03% THC, and the average of all samples seized, which includes samples with much higher amounts of THC, was 20.76% THC (ElSohly 2009, p. 6). Historically, hashish users have represented

a somewhat small percentage of the cannabis user population in the United States, whereas in Europe use is much more prevalent. Hashish often is produced in Lebanon, Afghanistan, and Pakistan.

A third derivative of the cannabis plant is ganja, which is produced in India. This preparation consists of the dried tops of female plants. Ganja is also used as a slang term for marijuana (as are pot, herb, weed, grass, boom, Mary Jane, gangster, or chronic). There are more than 200 slang terms for marijuana.

The Behavioral Effects of Marijuana Use

This section will discuss the "high" experienced from marijuana, the subjective euphoric effects of this drug, how the use of marijuana affects driving performance and critical-thinking skills, and the amotivational syndrome that appears to be a characteristic effect of marijuana use.

■ The High

The widely held belief of the 1930s that marijuana was a destructive assassin of youth is no longer considered valid for casual or occasional users of this drug. In most individuals, low to moderate doses of cannabis produce euphoria and a pleasant state of relaxation (Goldstein 1994). What are the common effects experienced from marijuana use? After a few delayed moments of forcibly holding the smoke in the lungs, most users suddenly experience the high. In this state of euphoria, the user experiences a dry mouth, elevated heartbeat, and some loss of coordination and balance, coupled with slower reaction times and a feeling of euphoria (mild to elevated intoxication). Blood vessels in the eyes expand, which accounts for reddening of the eyes. Some people experience slightly elevated blood pressure, which can double the normal heart rate. These effects can become intensified when other drugs,

KEY TERM

hashish
contains the purest form of resin from the female plant flowers. Domestic samples had an average of 12.14% THC, nondomestic had 7.03% THC, and the average of all samples seized, which includes samples with much higher amounts of THC, was 20.76%.

such as LSD and/or psychedelic ("magic") mushrooms, are combined with the marijuana.

The state of euphoria that results from the high is usually mild and short-lived; a typical high from one joint may last from 2 to 3 hours. Subjectively, the user experiences altered perception of space and time, impaired memory of recent events, and impaired physical coordination (Abood and Martin 1992). (More of these subjective effects are discussed at length in the next section.) An occasional high is not usually hazardous unless the person attempts to drive a car, operate heavy machinery, fly a plane, or function in similar ways requiring coordination, good reflexes, or quick judgment (Nahas and Latour 1992). Even low doses of marijuana alter perception, such as being able to judge the speed of an approaching vehicle or how much to slow down on an exit ramp.

> In trying to describe the high, it's not like an alcohol high. In an alcohol high, you are a lot more uncoordinated if drinking a lot. With weed, it's like reality changes—you add a lot more bass so-to-speak to what you see, hear, think, and feel. The reality is tempered with some distortion that to me and many others is pleasurable. You know how you feel after three or four very strong drinks [referring to alcoholic beverages]. Well take two more of those drinks and then look around the room you are in. Now, the difference between alcohol and weed is that you can walk to the bathroom quite well while under the influence of weed, while with alcohol you walk carefully so that no one notices that you are just about drunk. Weed is a mind high while alcohol is more of a body high. (Venturelli's research files, female professionally employed and residing in San Francisco, age 23, May 19, 2000)

Three additional interviews attempted to compare the high from marijuana with the effects of alcohol.

First interview:

> The marijuana high is also not nearly as harsh on the body. Being high doesn't give you that painful hangover as alcohol does. The actual high is very functional; I tend to do some of my best work (after burning a "dubbie") in that state [of mind]. It is part of the lifestyle of marijuana. [In contrast], alcohol makes me (and most people I know) very unproductive when the "buzz" is reached. (From Venturelli's research files, "Lectus Ferberger," male

> undergraduate student at a Midwestern university, age 21, August 10, 2000)

Second interview with the same person a day later:

> There seems to be a small misconception about the effects of marijuana and alcohol. For me, anyway, in looking at the physical "buzz" you get from alcohol, it is very physically disabling. You get drunk and stumble around, your lips loosen up, and you say things that you would not normally say. I find that marijuana has more of a calming effect. It makes you relaxed, a little more perceptive to some stimuli, and obviously less perceptive to other stimuli. It is a light feeling, but not overwhelming to the equilibrium. (From Venturelli's research files, same student as above, August 11, 2000)

Third interview:

> I can't drink much, because I feel the effects of alcohol more than the average person. I also don't like the effects of being high on alcohol. I feel very loopy and uncoordinated. Then, the next morning after drinking the night before is very unpleasant for me with headaches and sometimes even nausea. This is why I like to smoke weed. With weed you don't have all the impairment, the sick feelings, and you don't wake all messed up. I also have great conversations with people who are high on marijuana and find myself in a good mood while high. Also with regard to impairment, I would never drive under the influence of alcohol, but with marijuana, I have no problem driving. I even had a police officer stop me one night when my tail light was out on one side while on weed, and he never detected my marijuana high. He just wrote me a warning notice. Now, if it were alcohol, he probably would have become suspicious. Everyone is different, and this is my take on comparing these two drugs. (From Venturelli's research files, female student at a Midwestern university, age 22, September 9, 2010)

An acute dose of cannabis can produce adverse reactions, ranging from mild anxiety to panic and paranoia in some users. These reactions occur most frequently in individuals who are under stress or who are anxious, depressed, or borderline schizophrenic (Nahas and Latour 1992). Such effects also may be seen in normal users who accidentally take much more than they feel they can handle.

Extreme reactions can also occur because of ingesting marijuana treated (or "laced") with such things as opium, PCP, or other additives. Based on limited evidence from survey studies, mild or often adverse reactions are experienced on one or more occasions by more than one-half of regular users; they are mainly self-treated and usually go unreported (see "Signs and Symptoms: Specific Indicators of Marijuana Use").

■ Subjective Euphoric Effects

Subjective euphoric effects associated with marijuana use refer to the ongoing social and psychological experiences incurred while intoxicated by marijuana. These effects of intoxication include both the user's altered state of consciousness and his or her perceptions. Subjective effects in experienced users include a general sense of relaxation and tranquility, coupled with heightened sensitivity to sound, taste, and emotionality. For inexperienced users the subjective effects can vary from very similar experiences that experienced users have to some anxiety from anticipation of the effects. Often, it depends on the set (state of mind and mood) and setting (surroundings where the drug is taken, which includes the people in the immediate environment when the drug is consumed). Some users report occasional similarities to the typical hallucinogenic high, emphasizing much less intensity. How closely the marijuana high resembles a hallucinogenic high depends on the amount of THC absorbed from marijuana. For example, higher amounts of THC found in more potent plants of marijuana, like *sinsemilla*, hydro, and kind bud, more clearly mimic a hallucinogenic high. These effects are especially evident when considering the extent to which the senses of hearing, vision, sound, and taste are distorted by use of highly potent forms of marijuana. Other reported most potent varieties of marijuana include Rock Star, OG Kush, Jean Guy, Berry Kush, M39, Purple Kush, Chocolate Thai, Cannatonic, Pink Jush, and Mango Kush (Mernagh 2011).

Some marijuana users become very attached to these euphoric effects (in search of reexperiencing these effects). Such users often pride themselves on their extensive knowledge of this drug and maintain interest in discussing past experiences of "when I was really high" or "let me tell you about that night we smoked hydro. . . ." Devotees stay current with developments in the marijuana field by avidly reading monthly issues of magazines

devoted to marijuana (the art of marijuana use) and frequently scan the Internet for information and conversations in chat rooms about the best varieties of marijuana, best growing techniques, announcements of hemp festivals, advice, and information regarding current laws, fines, and other information. A vivid example of such an enthusiast is recalled in the following observation:

This author recalls visiting a neighbor one evening and noticing that one of the visitors sat very quietly with a pleasant smile while several intense conversations were occurring. I recall noticing this student in that he sat very quietly appearing somewhat distant and occasionally displaying several facial gestures in either approval or disapproval of comments and suggestions during the ongoing conversations. After approximately one hour during my visit, while others continued having multiple conversations, I directed my attention to this "quiet" individual with some introductory comments. He made minimal responses in the conversation. As others were discussing multiple topics, several of the guests began talking about drug use. Immediately, this quiet and reserved individual became very lively and began talking about the best types of marijuana on campus. Within several minutes, I literally saw a transformation in his involvement with the ongoing conversation. He was incessantly talking about marijuana and dominated the conversation with his many insights about the drug. I realized, prior to the topic of drug use and marijuana, he probably did not have much interest in the other topics. However, when we "hit" what appeared to be an interesting topic, which was a passion for marijuana use, an intensive amount of enthusiasm emerged. Clearly, this former "quiet young man" had transformed and clearly appeared to be quite a connoisseur about the varieties and the subjective euphoric effects of marijuana. By his overall conversational enthusiasm, he appeared quite content in letting us know how much he knew about this topic—and it was an extensive amount of knowledge. (*Observation from*

KEY TERM

subjective euphoric effects
ongoing social and psychological experiences incurred while intoxicated with marijuana

SIGNS & SYMPTOMS
Specific Indicators of Marijuana Use

A sweet odor similar to burnt rope in room, on clothes, and so on.

Roach: The small butt end of a marijuana cigarette.

Joint: Looks like a hand-rolled cigarette; usually the ends are twisted or crimped.

Roach clips: Holders for the roach could be any number of common items such as paper clips, bobby pins, or hemostats. They also could be of a store-bought variety in a number of shapes and disguises.

Herb/marijuana grinder: Usually a round device in which solid marijuana is placed that can grind the bud into fine bits so that marijuana joints or blunts can be made.

© iStock/Thinkstock

Seeds or leaves in pockets or possession.

Plastic baggies, either with some amount of marijuana inside the baggie or an empty baggie often found in pant or shirt pockets.

Rolling papers or pipes, usually hidden somewhere.

Eye drops: For disguising red eyes.

Excessive use of incense, room deodorizers, or breath fresheners.

Devices for storing the substance, such as film canisters, boxes or cans, a dugout (containing a one hitter device), pill bottles (fully formed buds of marijuana or high-end strains may be distributed in pill bottles to protect their shape and size).

Eating binges: An after effect for some marijuana users.

Appearance of intoxication, yet no smell of alcohol.

Excessive laughter.

Initial use (first hour): Animated behavior (loud or excessive talking).

Hours later: Fatigue or drowsiness.

Venturelli visiting a neighbor's home in a small Midwestern town, June 9, 2010)

Why is marijuana so attractive to many individuals? One quote from an interview illustrates the extensive psychological and social reinforcement experienced by marijuana users:

It's the high that I particularly like. Everything becomes mellower. Everyday tensions are released or submerged by more inner-like experiences. I can review the day and how happy or miserable I feel. Actually, when I am thinking and I am high on grass, I always feel that my thoughts are profound. You think from another perspective, one that numbs the more reality-based everyday strains. On the other hand, there are moments when this drug affects your mood and channels it [in] different ways. You have moments when you either feel sad, happy, angry (in a more contemplative way), or worried. These moods are both good and bad. If for the moment you feel good, then your mood is positive. If you feel down, your mood is negative in a particular way. If I am with friends and we are all sharing the bong or joint or pipe, we laugh a lot together. It's a type of drug that makes you more jovial, more introspective, and friendly, gregarious. . . . *(From Venturelli's research files, male personnel manager, age 40, August 20, 1996)*

As documented, marijuana enthusiasts have a strong attachment to their passionate feelings surrounding the use of marijuana. Psychologists believe the drug user becomes attached and habituated to the drug largely through the reinforcement of pleasurable feelings. If these subjective euphoric experiences were to become largely negative, attachment to and repeated use of this drug would cease. Thus, the theory of differential association applies. This theory, developed by Edwin Sutherland in 1939 and revised in 1947, attempts to explain delinquent behavior. Sociologists define the term **differential association** as the process by which individuals become socialized into the perceptions and values of a group. Differential association can apply to drug use. In using this drug, the *camaraderie*, the conversations and banter that often occur among friends, is often perceived as fun activity. It can include the perception that marijuana relieves boredom or stress, or is the perfect drug for just hanging out, chilling, partying, and getting high together. Specifically, the definition of differential association can include the behavioral satisfaction derived from friends who use marijuana. In this situation, getting high with others is the positive reward that solidifies the user to his or her friends and the drug.

■ Driving Performance

Evidence shows that the ability to perform complex tasks, such as driving, can be impaired while under the influence of marijuana (Couper and Logan 2004; Goldstein 1994; Mathias 1996; TheWeek.com 2010). Research indicates that "Cannabis consumption impairs motor coordination, reaction time, sensory perceptions and glare recovery" (Teen Challenge 2000, p. 1). This effect has been demonstrated in laboratory assessments of driving-related skills such as eye–hand coordination and reaction time, in driver simulator studies, in test course performance, and in actual street driving situations (Chait and Pierri 1992; Couper and Logan 2004; Mathias 1996; Teen Challenge 2000). Other research summarizes the key impairments with driving under the influence of marijuana as deficiencies in "attentiveness, vigilance, perception of time and speed, and use of acquired knowledge . . ." (Sewell, Poling, and Sofuoglu 2009).

Another study tested the effects of known amounts of marijuana, alcohol, or both on driving. The subjects drove a course rigged with various traffic problems. There was a definite deterioration in driving skills among those who had used either drug, but the greatest deterioration was observed in subjects who had taken both. In another test, 59 subjects smoked marijuana until they were intoxicated and then were given sobriety tests on the roadside by highway patrol officers. Overall, 94% of the subjects did not pass the test 90 minutes after smoking, and 60% failed at 150 minutes, even though the blood THC was much lower at this time (Hollister 1986). Other studies on driving show this same inability to drive for as long as 12 to 24 hours after marijuana use.

A more recent study detailing results from driving performance found that the short-term effects of marijuana use include problems with memory and learning, distorted perception, difficulty in thinking and problem-solving, and loss of coordination (NHTSA 2004). Heavy users may have increased difficulty sustaining attention, shifting attention to meet the demands of changes in the environment, and registering, processing, and using information. In general, laboratory performance studies indicate that sensory functions are not highly impaired, but perceptual functions are significantly affected. The ability to concentrate and maintain attention is decreased during marijuana use, and impairment of hand–eye coordination is dose-related over a wide range of dosages. Impairment in retention time and tracking, subjective sleepiness, distortion of time and distance, vigilance, and loss of coordination in divided attention tasks have been reported. Note, however, that subjects can often "pull themselves together" to concentrate on simple tasks for brief periods of time. However, significant performance impairments are usually observed for at least 1–2 hours following marijuana use, and residual effects have been reported for up to 24 hours (Couper and Logan 2004, p. 1; see also NIDA 2010b).

Another, slightly less critical study of city driving

. . . showed that drivers who drank alcohol overestimated their performance quality [often by speeding and overconfidence] whereas those

KEY TERM

differential association
process by which individuals become socialized into the perceptions and values of a group

who smoked marijuana under-estimated it [slower speed and more cautious driving]. . . . Drivers under the influence of marijuana retain insight in their performance and will compensate where they can, for example, by slowing down or increasing effort. As a consequence, THC's adverse effects on driving performance appear relatively small. Still we can easily imagine situations where the influence of marijuana smoking might have an exceedingly dangerous effect; i.e., emergency situations which put high demands on the driver's information processing capacity, prolonged monotonous driving, and after THC has been taken with other drugs, especially alcohol. (U.S. Department of Transportation 1993)

More recent research reported by the Drug Enforcement Administration indicates that:

- "... over 3000 fatally-injured drivers in Australia showed that when marijuana was present in the blood of the driver they were much more likely to be at fault for the accident. And the higher the THC concentration, the more likely they were to be culpable" (DEA 2013, p. 43).
- "A study in the *British Medical Journal* on the consequences of cannabis impaired driving found that drivers who consume cannabis within three hours of driving are nearly twice as likely to cause a vehicle collision as those who are not under the influence of drugs or alcohol" (DEA 2013, p. 41).
- "A study in the *Epidemiologic Reviews* by researchers from Columbia University found that drivers who get behind the wheel after smoking pot run more than twice the risk of getting into an accident" (DEA 2013, p. 42).
- "In 2009, marijuana was the most prevalent drug found in this population—approximately 28 percent of fatally injured drivers who tested positive tested positive for marijuana" (DEA 2013, p. 42).

Other surveys conducted by Mothers Against Drunk Driving (MADD) and the Liberty Mutual

insurance company revealed that many teenagers (41%) were not concerned about driving after taking drugs. Another interesting report pointing to the severity of teens driving under the influence stated that in 2007, the State of Maryland Adolescent Survey indicated that 11.1% of the state's licensed adolescent drivers reported driving under the influence of marijuana on three or more occasions, and 10% reported driving while using a drug other than marijuana (not including alcohol) (NIDA 2010b).

Drugged driving is defined as operating a motor vehicle with a measurable quantity (or quantities) of a legal and/or an illegal drug in the driver's body, which most often results in impaired driving. Medical data indicate a connection between drugged driving and accidents—a study of patients in a shock trauma unit who had been in collisions revealed that 15% of those who had been driving a car or motorcycle had been smoking marijuana, and another 17% had both THC and alcohol in their blood. In 2009, an estimated 12% of persons age 12 or older (30.2 million persons) drove under the influence of alcohol at least once in the past year (NIDA 2010b) and another major study found that 33% of fatally injured drivers with known test results tested positive for at least one drug (Dupont 2011).

Research conducted by the University of Auckland, New Zealand, proves the link between marijuana use and car accidents. The research found that habitual cannabis users were 9.5 times more likely to be involved in crashes, with 5.6% of people who had crashed having taken the drug, compared to 0.5% of the control group (Blows et al. 2005).

A study published by researchers at the University of Maryland Medical Center Shock Trauma Center indicates that during a 90-day study, about half of the drivers admitted to the shock trauma center tested positive for drugs other than alcohol. Additionally, one in four drivers admitted to the shock trauma unit tested positive for marijuana.

This population-based case–control study indicates that habitual use of marijuana is strongly associated with car crash injury. The nature of the relationship between marijuana use and risk-taking is unclear and needs further research. The prevalence of marijuana use in this driving population was low, and acute use was associated with habitual marijuana use, suggesting that intervention strategies may be more effective if they are targeted towards high use groups. (Blows et al. 2005, p. 605)

KEY TERM

drugged driving
operating a motor vehicle with a measurable quantity or quantities of a legal and/or an illegal drug in the driver's body, which most often results in impaired driving

One notable interview presents us with a negative experience regarding use of marijuana and driving experiences:

> One time I smoked some real strong dope at my friend's house, then had to drive back home, which was 2 miles in one direction. I remember wigging out [panicking] in trying to get home. There were moments when I did not know where I was until I would see the next marker of my neighborhood. I remember having seconds of panic because I did not know where I was; then suddenly, I would notice a neighborhood restaurant or some other marker that said I was right around my neighborhood. I took smaller streets on the way home and even took a longer way home because I was freaking out about the cops— what if one would spot me? This was bogus thinking because how the hell would anyone suddenly spot me while driving home? Well, that's an example of wigging out on weed. But, I still don't think that even that time I would be getting into an accident. I was so freaked out that I was extra careful not to speed, pass stop signs, or violate any law for fear of being seen. If anything, I drive slower when I am really high, not more dangerously. (*From Venturelli's research files, male college student in a Midwestern town, age 20, July 19, 2000*)

In contrast to this student's beliefs, scientific research indicates that some perceptual or other performance deficits resulting from marijuana use may persist for some time after the high, and users who attempt to drive, fly, operate heavy machinery, perform surgery, and so on may not recognize their impairment because they do not feel intoxicated. States such as California have established testing procedures to detect the presence of THC in urine or blood samples from apparently intoxicated drivers.

If the use of marijuana becomes more socially acceptable (or perhaps even legal) and penalties for simple possession become more lenient, it is likely that individuals will feel less inclined to hide their drug use. Unfortunately, it follows that these individuals may also be more inclined to drive while high, endangering themselves and others.

∎ Critical Thinking Skills

Marijuana has been found to have a negative impact on critical thinking skills. Recent research

by NIDA shows that heavy marijuana use impairs critical skills related to attention, memory, and learning. Another study showed that even alertness, coordination, and reaction time were impaired by marijuana usage (Couper and Logan 2004; National Clearinghouse on Alcohol and Drug Information [NCADI] 1998; NIDA 2010a). Impairment from marijuana continues even after discontinuing use of the drug for at least 24 hours (Brown and Massaro 1996).

In the same study, researchers compared 65 heavy users (using approximately every other day) with light users (using once or twice per week). Heavy users made more mistakes and had greater difficulty sustaining attention, shifting attention to meet the demands of challenges in the environment, and registering, processing, and using information (Brown and Massaro 1996; Fuller 2008; Norton 2009) compared with light users. In addition, heavy users had greater difficulty completing the tests, which specifically measured aspects of attention, memory, and learning, such as intellectual functioning, abstraction ability, attention span, verbal fluency, and learning and recalling abilities (Brown and Massaro 1996; Teen Challenge 2000). One researcher stated, "If you could get heavy users to learn an item, then they could remember it; the problem was getting them to learn it in the first place" (Brown and Massaro 1996, p. 3). The researchers surmised that marijuana alters brain activity because residues of the drug persist in the brain or because a withdrawal syndrome follows the euphoric effects of the marijuana.

In another study, researchers tested the cognitive functioning of 65 marijuana-using college students. Residual impairments were seen in the 24 hours after use in terms of sustaining attention, shifting attention, and hence in registering, organizing, and using information (NIDA 2010a; Pope and Yurgulen-Todd 1996). This study, which was undertaken during the 1990s, is significant because it was carefully controlled. The unresolved question is whether these memory impairments are short term or long term. These noteworthy findings complement many other similar findings that identified protracted cognitive impairment among heavy users of marijuana (Fuller 2008; NCADI 1998; Norton 2009).

∎ Amotivational Syndrome

The so-called **amotivational syndrome** (sometimes referred to as antimotivational syndrome) is a flashpoint of controversy about marijuana, although not as newsworthy as that regarding medical legalization. Amotivational syndrome refers to a belief that heavy use of marijuana causes a lack of motivation or "impaired desire" and reduced productivity. Specifically, users show apathy, poor short-term memory, difficulty in concentration, and a lingering disinterest in pursuing goals (Abood and Martin 1992; Right Diagnosis 2010).

In the past, this syndrome received considerable attention. People who are high, or stoned, lack the desire to perform hard work and are not interested in doing difficult tasks. There is some evidence of this behavior in regular marijuana users (Nahas and Latour 1992). Overall, although not solely the result of cannabis use, chronic users have lower grades in school, are more likely to be absent from classes, and are likely not to complete assignments and to drop out of school (Hardcastle 2007; Henneberger 1994; Liska 1997). In terms of age, the earlier someone begins smoking marijuana, coupled with heavier use, the more likely the amotivational characteristics will prevail and the more difficult it will be to cease using this drug.

Although the effects of marijuana per se are somewhat responsible for creating this syndrome, other factors contribute as well. For instance, is the lack of motivation caused by the drug itself or is it that poorly motivated people begin using marijuana, which then further exacerbates their

Typical effects of amotivational syndrome.

KEY TERM

amotivational syndrome
a controversial syndrome whose proponents claim that heavy use of marijuana causes a lack of motivation and reduced productivity

lack of motivation? Surveys show that a sizable number of marijuana users and their peer groups tend to be alienated from society and are likely to be classified as nonconformists and/or rebellious youth. They may, in fact, select to emphasize pleasure and nonconformity rather than goal-directed behavior. Another challenge to the concept of amotivational syndrome argues that the lack of motivation may simply be due to the effects of marijuana while under its influence and not any type of longer term or unique syndrome (Iverson 2005; Johns 2001).

Advocates of marijuana legalization stress data that tend to debunk research on amotivational syndrome. One institute that supports legalization, the Lindesmith Center, published a study asserting that college students who are users have higher grades than nonusers (Zimmer and Morgan 1997). How can we account for the discrepancies between this study and others, not to mention the clinical experiences of students, who often report academic repercussions of heavy use? One factor in the explanation is sociocultural:

> In the New York–New Jersey metro region, there are "druggy" schools and "drinking" schools. The "druggy" schools are more upper-middle class, liberal arts schools, artsy types, latter-day hippies, etc. The boozer campuses are filled with blue-collar and lower-middle-class kids—sometimes big fraternity schools. Frontloading at basketball games, comas after pledge parties. . . . Not as good educational backgrounds as the artsy potheads, who went to better schools, private schools, read a lot, or heard a lot at dinner before college, so they get by with their profs. However, the potheads ratchet down into easier majors, and they get crummier grades as they get into regular use. (*Interview with Pearl Mott for a prevention newsletter, prevention specialist, Drug Prevention Programs in Higher Education, Washington, DC, October 1994*)

A second methodological factor complicating drug research among such students is simply that academic failures stay in "F" categories for only one or two semesters. Many then disappear from statistics entirely, via academic attrition.

A more serious challenge to the notion of amotivational syndrome comes from the same ethnographic research that was mentioned at the beginning of this chapter. The most well-known of these investigations was carried out by Vera Rubin and Labros Comitas, as reported in their book *Ganja in Jamaica* (1975). Follow-up studies were done in

Jamaica (Dreher 1982; Hamid 1998) and Costa Rica (Carter 1980; Pollan 1998). None of these works found that chronic use impaired occupational or other functioning; in fact, the main point of the Jamaican studies was that users defined this drug as helpful and motivating for work—a "motivational syndrome." This work is often cited to counter amotivational syndrome claims. By this logic, dropping out of the rat race is a cultural posture, with marijuana being secondary to, or, at most, reinforcing the drift away from a mainstream lifestyle.

The Jamaican and Costa Rican subjects, however, were not observed engaging in an academic, cognitively complex, or rapid reflex activity, nor were they found in occupations that were competitive and striving for mobility. Rather, these subjects were involved in repetitive, physical labor involving sugar-cane cutting. In such a context, marijuana drug use functions to provide a pleasant stimulation that counters the monotony and physical discomfort of such labor.

When studies in other cultures contradict the American notion of amotivational syndrome, we are left to be cautious in making a direct assumption that marijuana use *per se* leads to such a syndrome, especially given that one strain of marijuana, *indica*, causes sedation, whereas the other strain, *sativa*, causes stimulation. More than likely, if we agree that the amotivational syndrome does manifest itself in marijuana users, it may be a direct result of a particular strain of marijuana. As discussed previously, it is important to keep in mind that *Cannabis indica* remarkably differs from *Cannabis sativa*. Also, there is great likelihood that in Jamaica, the stimulation caused by *Cannabis sativa* (which is a native variety of marijuana in Jamaica) may explain why these sugar-cane field workers under the effects of this particular strain of marijuana are able to work long hours. (For additional information on how marijuana affects personality, see "Case in Point: A Letter to an Editor: No Valid Reason to Ban Marijuana.")

to calm or to relieve symptoms of an illness. At the heart of this controversy is the use of an illicit drug for medical purposes. However, the desire to use cannabis in this fashion is nothing new. Between 1840 and 1900, European and American medical journals published more than 100 articles on the therapeutic use of the drug known then as *Cannabis indica* (or Indian hemp) and now as marijuana. It was recommended as an appetite stimulant, muscle relaxant, analgesic, hypnotic, and anticonvulsant. As late as 1913, Sir William Osler recommended it as the most satisfactory remedy for migraines (Grinspoon and Bakalar 1995).

Marijuana was used to treat a variety of human ills in folk and formal medicine for thousands of years in South Africa, Turkey, South America, and Egypt as well as such Asian countries as India, Malaysia, Myanmar, and Siam. Thus, marijuana, known as *cannabis* back then, has a 5000-year medical history that came to an abrupt end in the United States by passage of the Marijuana Tax Act of 1937. When the Marijuana Tax Act became law, marijuana was legally classified as a narcotic, and at that time medical use of this substance effectively ceased. Only in the past 2 decades has there been organized renewed interest in possible medical uses for cannabis. Because of potential clinical uses for marijuana, enforcement of laws prohibiting the use of this substance has been very controversial (see "Holding the Line: Despite Federal Drug Laws Prohibiting the Cultivation, Possession, Use, and the Sale of Marijuana, States Sanction *Cannabis* Buyer's Clubs").

Marijuana has been shown to be effective in the treatment of certain types of medical conditions. However, because medicines exist that are at least as effective and without abuse potential, (such as legally approved **Marinol** (dronabinol), none of these applications is currently approved by the Food and Drug Administration (FDA). According to researchers (Abood and Martin 1992; Consroe and

Therapeutic Uses and the Controversy over Medical Marijuana Use

Although the use of marijuana for medical purposes is far more accepted than it was 7 years ago, the controversy about the medical uses of marijuana remains. Basically, **medical marijuana** use involves using cannabis, primarily THC, as a drug

KEY TERMS

medical marijuana
use of the THC in cannabis as a drug to calm or to relieve symptoms of an illness

Marinol
FDA-approved synthesized THC in capsule form (dronabinol); primarily used to treat nausea and vomiting, prescribed to people diagnosed with acquired immune deficiency syndrome (AIDS)

► **CASE IN POINT**

A Letter to an Editor: No Valid Reason to Ban Marijuana

An Associated Press release printed in the *Kentucky Enquirer* had the head of the White House Office of Drug Control Policy, Gil Kerlikowske, President Obama's Drug Czar, extolling the necessity of continuing the prohibition of marijuana. The reasons he cites for continuing the 70-year war on marijuana smokers are a clear indication that history is correct in judging marijuana prohibition as one of the greatest policy failures in the history of the federal government. The letter is as follows:

Those who support prohibition started in 1933 at the end of alcohol prohibition to shift all the bad outcomes of alcohol use to marijuana. The films and newspaper stories of the day claimed that using marijuana leads to violence, murder, and insanity. Think of the movie, "Reefer Madness." Cut to the present and the Drug Czar is reduced to claiming that marijuana causes lung cancer, and that marijuana use is the cause of a significant amount of traffic accidents. The lung cancer, marijuana connection is a myth that grows out of the fact that tobacco smoking causes lung cancer therefore marijuana smoking should too. With this in mind, the Government originally supported the work of Dr. Donald Tashkin. His study on marijuana smoking and head, neck, and lung cancer was expected to be a slam-dunk for the Government. The problem is that the results of Dr. Tashkin's and other studies is that the opposite is true. Dr. Tashkin's study showed that people who regularly use marijuana get head, neck, and lung cancer at the same rate as people who do not smoke at all. He reported that marijuana seemed to have an anti-cancer effect and acted as a cancer preventer. One would think medical researchers would be all over this like "stink on poopy" looking for a cancer cure, but the forces of prohibition continue to block research, even though compassion for one's fellow men and the saving of lives would indicate the opposite.

Mr. Kerlikowske's claim about marijuana being the cause of a significant amount of traffic accidents is a "fact" that he must have pulled out of a lower opening. There is no data to support this. Again, what studies have been done on this angle do not support his claim. Studies have found that marijuana smokers get into accidents as often as those who do not use marijuana. Think about it! I returned to Northern Kentucky in 1996. I watch local news at least once a day and read the paper every day.

In the 14 years since 1996, I have seen only one report of a marijuana caused traffic accident. If I remember right, a young man had blown through an intersection and someone was killed in the resulting accident. The local media reported that the driver had been smoking marijuana and that was the cause of the accident. A follow up report later claimed the driver was texting when he blew the intersection. You have to ask yourself that if there are so many marijuana caused accidents, where are all the marijuana accident stories, arrests, trials, and incarcerations.

Marijuana prohibition is an idea that has lived long past the point of being something that is "good" for America. Marijuana use is not as Reagan said that it's the greatest threat faced by America. The end of the federal ban on marijuana is long overdue. It has no basis in science or logic, costs billions of tax dollars, and causes more harm than good. At a time when Americans need jobs and economic growth, we are shooting ourselves in the foot by continuing to suppress the marijuana/hemp industry, an industry that could go a long way in creating jobs and economic activity worth billions of dollars.

Msgt Thomas Vance, USAF Ret., Alexandria

Questions to Consider

1. What is your initial reaction to this letter?

2. Like the firmly established link between lung cancer and smoking tobacco, do you think a similar argument can be made between smoking marijuana and lung cancer? What are the reasons for your answer?

3. Do you think the "forces of prohibition" are masking potential benefits of using marijuana, as the writer claims? Explain.

4. What is your opinion about using marijuana and driving? Do you think drivers under the influence are adversely affected by the effects of this drug? Explain.

5. How do you generally feel about marijuana drug users?

6. How much of a threat to society is marijuana use? Should marijuana be decriminalized? If yes, why? Should it remain illegal? If so, what penalties should apply and why?

Reproduced from Cincinnati.com. Letters to the Editor, "No Valid Reason to Ban Marijuana." *The Enquirer.* 9 August 2010. Available http://cincinnati.com /blogs/letters/2010/08/09/no-valid-reason-to-ban-marijuana. Accessed February 17, 2011.

HOLDING THE LINE

Despite Federal Drug Laws Prohibiting the Cultivation, Possession, Use, and Sale of Marijuana, States Sanction *Cannabis* Buyer's Clubs

Currently 21 states plus the District of Columbia (DC) are medical marijuana states. The 21 states are Alaska, Arizona, California, Colorado, Connecticut, Delaware, Hawaii, Illinois, Maine, Maryland, Massachusetts, Michigan, Montana, Nevada, New Hampshire, New Jersey, New Mexico, Oregon, Rhode Island, Vermont, and Washington (ProCon.org 2013). Out of approximately 311.5 million total population in these states and Washington, DC, a rough estimate of 2,421,069 people are registered as medical marijuana patients (ProCon.org 2012c).

Why should medically ill patients, those afflicted with acquired immune deficiency syndrome (AIDS) and AIDS wasting, lack of appetite, nausea, arthritis, hepatitis C, migraines, multiple sclerosis, muscle spasms, chronic pain, glaucoma, and other illnesses (such as posttraumatic stress disorder [PTSD], depression, or bipolar disorder) or those suffering the deleterious effects of chemotherapy and/or radiation not be able to legally purchase marijuana if they find relief from the effects of their illnesses? The first *cannabis* buyers club began in 1996, when the voting citizens of Marin County, California, passed ". . . Proposition 215, which authorized the use of medical marijuana . . . for those who have a doctor's recommendation" (*Cannabis News* 2002). The main problem facing this club in Marin County, and all the other *cannabis* buyers' clubs throughout the United States, is that although these 20 states and DC have legalized such enterprises, they continue to violate federal drug laws, causing a conflict between federal and state law. At times, the clubs can be ordered closed by a superior court judge, resulting in federal agents raiding the clubs, confiscating the marijuana, and arresting the owners and operators of these establishments.

To date, this cyclical pattern of raids and arrests by federal officials is repetitive and ongoing because of this rift between state and federal laws. The clubs are for either profit or nonprofit organizations whose sole intent is to distribute marijuana for medicinal purposes when prescribed by a licensed physician. Many of the buyers (known as patients) report relief and satisfaction from their use of marijuana. For example, a man by the name of Clay Shinn, 46, was diagnosed with AIDS in 1992. At the time of his interview, he had been going to the Marin Alliance's Cannabis Buyers Club for 5 years. "It's made a major difference in my life," he said. After taking his [AIDS] medication morning, afternoon, and evening, he said, "I was always getting nauseated . . . I could set my watch by it. I hate it. God, it's awful. Now I don't barf

(continues)

Despite Federal Drug Laws Prohibiting the Cultivation, Possession, Use, and Sale of Marijuana, States Sanction *Cannabis* Buyer's Clubs (*continued*)

anymore" (*Cannabis News* 2002). Another interviewee, who is an arthritic, HIV-positive cabaret performer, said, "After I leave here . . . I won't feel my pain" (Goldberg 1996). Another man, the club's director, reiterated that, "'You have to be sick or dying' . . . If you are, with a doctor's note to prove that you have AIDS or cancer or another condition with symptoms that marijuana is known to alleviate, Mr. Peron [the club's director] is willing to sell some relief" (Goldberg, 1996). Finally, Dennis Peron, the founder of the San Francisco Buyers' Club, stated that "We have over four hundred senior citizens that come here for arthritis, glaucoma, pain, etc. We have an old woman trapped in her wheelchair, day in and day out. Marijuana makes her feel a little bit better. I don't require a letter of diagnosis for people sixty-five or

older—things wear out—or for people who are blind or deaf, as they say it helps their other senses" (Fuhrman 1995).

What are your views regarding the prescribed use of marijuana, especially when these clubs or cooperatives provide seriously ill patients with a safe and reliable source of medical cannabis information and patient support? Would you support a cannabis buyers club or cooperative in your community? What are your views regarding federal laws that prohibit such establishments while states pass laws allowing these establishments to legally operate? How do you think this current problem of the illegality on the federal level should be resolved? Finally, how do you think this dilemma will be resolved in your lifetime?

Data from *Cannabis News*. "Medical Pot War Rages On." *Marin Independent Journal*, (1 July 2002). Available http://cannabisnews.com /news/13/thread13278.shtml; Goldberg, C. "Marijuana Club Helps Those in Pain." *New York Times* (26 February 1996). Available http://query.nytimes.com/gst/fullpage.html?res=9C06E6DF1139F936A15751C0A960958260&sec=&spon=&pagewanted=all; Fuhrman, R. A. "Cannabis Buyers' Club Flourishes in 'Frisco." San Francisco: Cannabis Buyers' Club, 1995; ProCon.org. "How Many People in the United State Use Medical Marijuana?" Santa Monica: CA, 2013. Available http://medicalmarijuana .procon.org/view.answers.php?questionID=001199

In November 2010, Arizona began to issue cards that allow the users to purchase marijuana for medicinal purposes.

Sandyk 1992; Iversen 1993; ProCon.org 2012a) and proponents for the medical uses of marijuana, the potential uses are as listed in the following sections.

KEY TERM

glaucoma
potentially blinding eye disease causing continual and increasing intraocular pressure

■ Reduction in Intraocular (Eye) Pressure

Marijuana lowers glaucoma-associated intraocular pressure, even though it does not cure the condition or reverse blindness (Goldstein 1995; Green 2006; NIDA 2010c). **Glaucoma** is the second leading cause of blindness, and is caused by uncontrollable eye pressure (Julian 1994; National Eye Institute 2010).

■ Antiasthmatic Effect

Some research indicates that short-term smoking of marijuana improves breathing for asthma patients. Marijuana smoke dilates the lungs' air passages (bronchodilation). Other findings also show, however, that the lung-irritating properties of marijuana smoke seem to offset its benefits. The adverse effects of marijuana smoke remain controversial (NIDA 2006, 2010c). Regardless, marijuana may still prove useful when other drugs are not effective because of a different mode of action in causing bronchodilation.

Another study made a distinction between short-term and long-term marijuana smoking, emphasizing a distinction. "Short-term exposure to marijuana is associated with bronchodilation, . . . [however]. . . . Physiologic data were inconclusive regarding an association between long-term marijuana smoking and airflow obstruction measures. Long-term marijuana smoking is associated with increased respiratory symptoms suggestive of obstructive lung disease" (Barclay and Vega 2007).

Muscle-Relaxant Effect

Some studies indicate that muscle spasms are relieved when patients with muscle disorders, such as multiple sclerosis, use marijuana. "Scientifically, there is basis for the use of cannabis in the treatment of muscle spasms. Cannabis' key medicinal ingredients, tetrahydrocannabinol (THC) and cannabidiol (CBD), have been shown to have beneficial effects in the treatment of muscle spasms and spasticity" (Medical Marijuana Education Center 2012). Another finding indicates "Many patients report that medical cannabis is effective in relieving their muscle spasms. Medical cannabis may also be effective in alleviating uncontrollable and debilitating muscle tremors. Some patients with severe spasticity report that medical cannabis is the only treatment that allows them to function" (Medical Marijuana Education Center 2012).

Antiseizure Effect

Marijuana has both convulsing and anticonvulsant properties and has been considered for use in preventing seizures associated with epilepsy. In animal experimentation, the cannabinoids reduced or increased seizure activities, depending on how the experiments were conducted. One or more of the marijuana components may be useful in combination with other standard antiseizure medication.

Antidepressant Effect

Cannabis and the synthetic cannabinoid synhexyl have been used successfully in Great Britain as a specific euphoriant for the treatment of depression.

Analgesic Effect

Published testimonials have reported that marijuana can relieve the intense pain (Green 2006) associated with migraine and chronic headaches or inflammation (Grinspoon and Bakalar 1995).

"Survey data indicates that the use of cannabis is common in chronic pain populations and several recent clinical trials indicate that inhaled marijuana can significantly alleviate neuropathic pain" (Cone et al. 2008, p. 532; Gardner 2010; Green 2006; National Organization for the Reform of Marijuana Laws [NORML] 2013). In South Africa, native women smoke cannabis to dull the pain of childbirth (Hamid 1998; Solomon 1966). The pain-relieving potency of marijuana has not been carefully studied and compared with other analgesics, such as narcotics or aspirin-type drugs.

Antinauseant

Marijuana can relieve the nausea that accompanies chemotherapy for cancer treatment (NIDA 2010c; Robson 2001).

Appetite Stimulant

Marijuana is also a powerful appetite stimulant (NIDA 2010c; NORML n.d.). The stimulant effects on appetite are seen as useful for patients with human immunodeficiency virus (HIV), the AIDS wasting syndrome, or dementia, as well as those with eating disorders (NORML n.d.; Sewester 1993).

Short-Term Dangers of Smoking Marijuana

According to Brown University's health education web site (Brown University Health Education 2007), discomforts associated with smoking marijuana include dry mouth, dry eyes, increased heart rate, and visible signs of intoxication such as bloodshot eyes and puffy eyelids. Other problems during intoxication include:

- Impaired short-term memory and ability to learn (NIDA 2010c).
- Difficulty thinking and problem solving (NIDA 2010c).
- Anxiety attacks or feelings of paranoia.
- Impaired muscle coordination and judgment.
- Impairment of driving skills. Studies show that it impairs braking time, attention to traffic signals, and other driving behaviors.
- Cardiac problems for people with heart disease or high blood pressure because marijuana increases the heart rate (Brown University 2007; NIDA 2010c).
- Psychotic episodes (NIDA 2010c).

Long-Term Consequences of Smoking Marijuana

Long-term consequences, lasting longer than intoxication, and cumulative effects of chronic abuse of smoking marijuana include:

- *Respiratory problems:* Many of these are the same as for cigarette smokers. Persistent coughing, symptoms of bronchitis, and more frequent chest colds are possible symptoms from the 400-plus chemicals (some carcinogenic) in marijuana smoke. "Researchers report that marijuana cigarettes release five times as much carbon monoxide into the bloodstream and three times as much tar into the lungs of smokers as tobacco cigarettes" (Marijuana-Detox.com 2008; NIDA 2010c).

- *Memory and learning:* Regular marijuana use compromises the ability to learn and to remember information by impairing the ability to focus, sustain, and shift attention. One study also found that long-term use reduces the ability to organize and integrate complex information. Marijuana impairs short-term memory and decreases motivation to accomplish tasks, even after the high is over.

- *Fertility:* Long-term marijuana use suppresses the production of hormones that help regulate the reproductive system. For men, this can cause decreased sperm counts, and very heavy users can experience erectile dysfunction. Women may experience irregular periods from heavy marijuana use.

- *Marijuana can also be addictive:* More studies are finding that marijuana has addictive properties. "Contrary to common belief, marijuana is addictive. Estimates from research suggest that about 9 percent of users become addicted to marijuana; this number increases among those who start young (to about 17 percent, or 1 in 6) and among daily users (to 25–50 percent)" (NIDA 2012). Both animal and human studies show physical and psychological withdrawal symptoms from marijuana, including irritability, restlessness, insomnia, nausea, and intense dreams. Tolerance to marijuana also builds up rapidly. Heavy users need eight times higher doses to get the same effects as infrequent users. For a small percentage of people who use it, long-term marijuana use can lead to addiction (NIDA 2010c). It is estimated that 10% to 14% of users will become heavily dependent. More than 120,000 people in the United States seek treatment for marijuana addiction every year (Brown University 2007). Why would abusers go to treatment centers if this drug were not addictive? Finally, ". . . marijuana addiction is also linked to a withdrawal syndrome similar to that of nicotine withdrawal, which can make it difficult to quit. People trying to quit report irritability, sleeping difficulties, craving, and anxiety" (NIDA 2010c, p. 7).

All of these reasons have either been disputed or shown to be exaggerated claims by proponents who are in favor of allowing marijuana to be medically used. Proponents for medical use argue that "its illegality [marijuana] . . . imposes much anxiety and expense on suffering people, forces them to bargain with illicit drug dealers, and exposes them to the threat of criminal prosecution" (Grinspoon and Bakalar 1995, p. 1876). For a list of states currently allowing the use of marijuana for medical purposes, see the "Holding the Line" feature earlier in this chapter.

The Physiological Effects of Marijuana Use

Although the literature on marijuana use repeatedly states that "in 5,000 years of medical and nonmedical use, marijuana has not caused a single overdose death" (Grinspoon and Bakalar 1995, p. 1875), the effects of marijuana use should not be overlooked. We begin by examining the effects of marijuana on the lungs.

When marijuana smoke is inhaled into the lungs, THC, the psychoactive ingredient, leaves the blood rapidly through metabolism and efficient uptake into the tissues. THC and its metabolites tend to bind to proteins in the blood and remain stored for long periods in body fat. Five days after a single dosage of THC, 20% remains stored, whereas 20% of its metabolites remain in the blood (Indiana Prevention Resource Center 1996; Kryger 1995). Complete elimination of a single dose can take up to 30 days. Measurable levels of THC in blood from chronic users can often be detected for several days or even weeks after their last marijuana cigarette (joint).

In smokers, lung absorption and transport of THC to the brain are rapid; THC reaches the brain within as little as 14 seconds after inhalation. Marijuana is metabolized more efficiently

through smoking than via intravenous injection or oral ingestion. Smoking is also three to five times more potent than these two methods (Jones 1980; Kaplan and Whitmire 1995; Kryger 1995). Other findings that compare the amounts of marijuana with tobacco conclude, "three to four joints a day is about as harmful to your lungs as smoking a pack of cigarettes a day" (Reaney 2000, p. 1).

Some effects of cannabis described in the following sections are unquestionably toxic in that they can either directly or indirectly produce adverse health effects. Other effects may be beneficial in treating some medical conditions. The use of marijuana, THC, and synthetic cannabinoids, either alone or in combination with other drugs, continues to be discussed and investigated for treating pain, inflammation, glaucoma, nausea, and muscle spasms (Iversen 1993; NIDA 2010c).

■ Effects on the Brain

As THC enters the brain, it causes the user to feel euphoric—or high—by acting on the brain's reward system, which is made up of regions that govern the response to pleasurable things like sex and chocolate, as well as to most drugs of abuse. THC activates the reward system in the same way that nearly all drugs of abuse do: by stimulating brain cells to release the chemical dopamine (NIDA 2010c). THC affects the nerve cells in the part of the brain where memories are formed. This makes it hard for the user to recall recent events (such as what happened a few minutes ago). It is hard to learn while high—a working short-term memory is required for learning and performing tasks that call for more than one or two steps (NIDA 2007, 2010c).

Among a group of long-time heavy marijuana users in Costa Rica, researchers found that the people had great trouble when asked to recall a short list of words (a standard test of memory). People in that study group also found it very hard to focus their attention on the tests given to them.

As people age, they normally lose nerve cells in a region of the brain that is important for remembering events. Chronic exposure to THC may hasten the age-related loss of these nerve cells. In one study, researchers found that rats exposed to THC every day for 8 months (about one-third of their lifespan) showed a loss of brain cells comparable to rats that were twice their age. It is not known whether a similar effect occurs in humans. Researchers are still learning about the many ways that marijuana could affect the brain (NIDA 2007).

When someone smokes marijuana, THC stimulates the cannabinoid receptors (CBRs) artificially, disrupting function of the natural, or endogenous, cannabinoids. An overstimulation of these receptors in key brain areas produces the marijuana high, as well as having other effects on mental processes. Over time, this overstimulation can alter the function of CBRs, which, along with other changes in the brain, can lead to addiction and to withdrawal symptoms when drug use stops (NIDA 2010c).

■ Effects on the Central Nervous System

The primary effects of marijuana—specifically, of THC—are on CNS functions. The precise CNS effects of consuming marijuana or administering THC can vary according to the expectations of the user, the social setting, the route of administration, and previous experiences (Abood and Martin 1992; Jaffe 1990). Smoking a marijuana cigarette can alter mood, coordination, memory, and self-perception. Usually, such exposure causes some euphoria, a sense of well-being, and relaxation. Marijuana smokers often claim heightened sensory awareness and **altered perceptions** (particularly a slowing of time), symptoms associated with hunger (the **munchies**), and a dry mouth (Hubbard, Franco, and Onaivi 1999; Swan 1994). High doses of THC or greater exposure to marijuana can cause hallucinations, delusions, and paranoia (American Psychiatric Association [APA] 1994; Goldstein 1995; Hubbard et al. 1999; NIDA 2007). Some users describe anxiety after high-dose exposure. Due to the availability and widespread use of marijuana, psychiatric emergencies from marijuana overdose are becoming somewhat common. Long-term, chronic users often show decreased interest in personal appearance or goals (part of the amotivational syndrome discussed earlier in this chapter) as well as an inability to concentrate, make appropriate decisions, and recall information from short-term memory (Abood and Martin 1992; Block 1996).

The precise classification of THC is uncertain because the responses to marijuana are highly

KEY TERMS

altered perceptions
changes in the interpretation of stimuli resulting from marijuana

munchies
hunger experienced while under the effects of marijuana

#15

variable and appear to have elements of all three major groups of drugs of abuse. Consequently, marijuana use can cause euphoria and paranoia (like stimulants), drowsiness and sedation (like depressants), and hallucinations (like psychedelics). It is possible that THC alters several receptor or transmitter systems in the brain; this action would account for its diverse and somewhat unpredictable effects.

The dramatic discovery of a specific receptor site in the brain for THC, called the *cannabinoid* receptor (mentioned earlier), suggests that a selective endogenous marijuana system exists in the brain and is activated by THC when marijuana is consumed (Hudson 1990; NIDA 2007). Some researchers speculate that an endogenous fatty acid–like substance called *anandamide* naturally works at these marijuana sites; efforts are being made to characterize this substance, which is a neurotransmitter (Iversen 1993; NIDA 2010c). It is possible that, from this discovery, a group of new therapeutic agents will be developed that can selectively interact with the marijuana receptors, resulting in medical benefits without the side effects that generally accompany marijuana use (Iversen 1993; Swan 1993).

▪ Effects on the Respiratory System: Smoking Marijuana

Marijuana is often smoked like tobacco and, like tobacco, it can cause damage to the lungs (Adams and Martin 1996; Consroe and Sandyk 1992; NIDA 2010c). When smoking tobacco, nearly 70% of the total suspended particles in the smoke are retained in the lungs. Because marijuana smoke is inhaled more deeply than tobacco smoke, even more tar residues may be retained with its use.

Smoke is a mixture of tiny particles suspended in gas, mostly carbon monoxide. These solid particles combine to form a residue called tar. Cannabis produces more tar (as much as 50% more) than an equivalent weight of tobacco and is smoked in a way that increases the accumulation of tar (Jones 1980).

More than 140 chemicals have been identified in marijuana smoke and tar. A few are proven carcinogens; many others have not yet been tested for carcinogenicity. The carcinogen benzopyrene, for example, is 70% more abundant in marijuana smoke than in tobacco smoke. When cannabis tar is applied to the skin of experimental animals, it causes precancerous lesions similar to those caused by tobacco tar. Similarly, whenever isolated lung tissue is exposed to these same tars, precancerous changes result (Hollister 1986; Jones 1980; Turner 1980).

Special white blood cells in living lung tissue—alveolar macrophages—play a role in removing debris from the lungs. When exposed to smoke from cannabis, these cells are less able to remove bacteria and other foreign debris.

Smoking only a few marijuana cigarettes a day for 6 to 8 weeks can significantly impair pulmonary function. Laboratory and clinical evidence often indicate that heavy use of marijuana causes cellular changes, and those heavy users have a higher incidence of such respiratory problems as laryngitis, pharyngitis, bronchitis, asthma-like conditions, cough, hoarseness, and dry throat (Goldstein 1995; Hollister 1986). Some reports emphasize the potential damage to pulmonary function that can occur from chronic marijuana use (NIDA 1991). Evidence suggests that many 20-year-old smokers of both hashish and tobacco have lung damage comparable to that found in heavy tobacco smokers older than 40 years of age. It is believed that the tar from tobacco and marijuana has damaging effects, but it is not known whether smokers who use both products suffer synergistic or additive effects (Hollister 1986; Jones 1980).

▪ Effects on the Respiratory System: Vaporizing Marijuana

As just presented, the evidence shows that smoking marijuana clearly appears to be hazardous to the respiratory system, having the most negative impact on the lungs. A newer method of use, known as vaporizing marijuana, is slowly increasing among users, even though one major study of 6883 people surveyed showed that "only 152 participants (2.2%) reported vaporizing as their primary method for cannabis use" (Earleywine and Smucker Barnwell 2007, p. 3).

Cannabis smoke contains gaseous and particulate matter with the potential to create symptoms of respiratory problems. Although cannabis creates fewer problems than cigarette smoking, increasing its safety has the potential to improve quality of life. One step toward increasing the safety of cannabis involves the use of vaporizers. Vaporizers heat cannabis to temperatures that release cannabinoids in a fine mist without creating the toxins associated with combustion. Although vaporizers are not common knowledge in popular culture, a recent photograph of one appeared in the *New England Journal of Medicine,* and information about the machine is becoming more available. A vaporizer has the potential to increase the safety of cannabis use, but data from human users appear only rarely (Earleywine and Smucker Barnwell 2007, p. 2).

The results from the study quoted earlier in this section "suggest that the respiratory effects of cannabis can decrease with the use of a vaporizer. The data reveal that respiratory symptoms like cough, phlegm, and tightness in the chest increase with cigarette use and cannabis use, but are less severe among users of a vaporizer" (Earleywine and Smucker Barnwell 2007, p. 3).

The cost of a vaporizer unit can usually run several hundred dollars and above. Using a vaporizer for marijuana use may decrease respiratory problems; however, other hazards continue to exist. Users who replace smoking marijuana with vaporizing marijuana continue to run the risk of marijuana dependence (addiction); impaired driving skills; and cognitive, mainly short-term memory impairment. Also, users often mix smoking with vaporizing, resulting in increased usage. Thus, although pulmonary damage is likely to be minimized when using a vaporizer, other deleterious consequences from marijuana use are continued and even increased.

■ Effects on the Cardiovascular System

In human beings, cannabis causes both *vasodilation* (enlarged blood vessels) and an increase in heart rate related to the amount of THC consumed (Abood and Martin 1992; NIDA 2000, 2010c). The vasodilation is responsible for the reddening of the eyes often seen in marijuana smokers. In physically healthy users, these effects, as well as slight changes in heart rhythm, are transitory and do not appear to be significant. In patients with heart disease, however, the increased oxygen requirement due to the accelerated heart rate may have serious consequences. The effect of cannabis on people with heart rhythm irregularities is not known. Because of vasodilation caused by marijuana use, abnormally low blood pressure can occur when standing. In addition, if a user stands up quickly after smoking, a feeling of lightheadedness or fainting may result. Chronic administration of large doses of THC to healthy volunteers shows that tolerance develops to the increase in heart rate and vasodilation.

People with cardiovascular problems seem to be at an increased risk when smoking marijuana (Hollister 1986; NIDA 2010c). Marijuana products also bind hemoglobin, limiting the amount of oxygen that can be carried to the heart tissue. In a few cases, this deficiency could trigger heart attacks in

A demonstration of a marijuana vaporizer.

susceptible people (Palfai and Jankiewicz 1991). The National Academy of Sciences' Institute of Medicine recommends that people with cardiovascular disease avoid marijuana use because there are still many unanswered questions about its effects on the cardiovascular system.

■ Effects on Sexual Performance and Reproduction

Drugs may interfere with sexual performance and reproduction in several ways (Hanson 2011). They may alter sexual behavior, affect fertility, damage the chromosomes of germ cells in the male or female, or adversely affect fetal growth and development.

The Indian Hemp Commission (Taylor 1963, 1966), which wrote the first scientific report on cannabis, commented that it had a sexually stimulating effect, like alcohol. However, the report also said that cannabis was used by Asian Indian ascetics to destroy the sexual appetite. This apparent discrepancy may be a dose-related effect. Used occasionally over the short term, marijuana may act as an **aphrodisiac** by decreasing CNS inhibitions. In addition, the altered perception of time under the influence of the drug could make the pleasurable sensations appear to last longer than they actually do.

Marijuana affects the sympathetic nervous system, increasing vasodilation in the genitals and delaying ejaculation. High doses over a period of time lead to depression of libido and impotence—possibly due to the decreased amount

KEY TERM

aphrodisiac
a compound that is believed to be the cause of sexual arousal

of testosterone, the male sex hormone. "Some research has found a relationship between long-term use of marijuana . . . [and] increased erectile dysfunction" (Silverberg 2007).

Cannabis has several effects on semen (Cadena 2007). The total number of sperm cells and the concentration of sperm per unit volume are decreased during ejaculation (Cadena 2007). Moreover, there is an increase in the proportion of sperm with abnormal appearance and reduced motility. These qualities are usually associated with lower fertility and a higher probability of producing an abnormal embryo should fertilization take place.

Despite these effects, there are no documented reports of children with birth defects in which the abnormality was linked to the father's smoking marijuana. It is possible that damaged sperm cells are incapable of fertilization (so that only normal sperm cells reach the egg) or that the abnormal sperm appearance is meaningless in terms of predicting birth defects. When marijuana use stops, the quality of sperm gradually returns to normal over several months.

"Heavy marijuana use in women has been associated with inhibiting ovulation, and marijuana use during pregnancy can have a variety of harmful developmental effects on the fetus including neurobehavioral and physical abnormalities, as well as increasing the chance of a premature birth" (Silverberg 2007). Less reliable data are available on the effects of cannabis on female libido, sexual response (ability to respond to sexual stimulation with vaginal lubrication and orgasm), and fertile reproductive (menstrual) cycles (Consroe and Sandyk 1992; Grinspoon 1987). Data from the Reproductive Biology Research Foundation show that chronic smoking of cannabis (at least three times per week for the preceding 6 months) adversely affects the female reproductive cycle. Results with women were correlated with work in rhesus monkeys; it was found that THC blocks ovulation (due to effects on female sex hormones).

Data on the effects of marijuana use during pregnancy and lactation are inconclusive. Some evidence suggests that the use of this drug by pregnant women can result in intrauterine growth retardation, which is characterized by increased fetal mortality, prolonged labor, low-birth-weight babies (Foley 2007), and behavioral abnormalities in newborns (Fernandez-Ruiz et al. 1992; Nahas and Latour 1992; Roffman and George 1988). THC and other cannabinoids pass through the blood–placenta barrier and concentrate in the fetus's fatty tissue, including its brain. Ethical considerations prevent duplication of the experiment in humans.

Women who smoke marijuana during pregnancy also often use other drugs—such as alcohol, tobacco, and cocaine—that are known to have adverse effects on the developing fetus. Because multiple drugs are used, it is difficult to isolate the specific effects of marijuana during pregnancy. Like many other substances, THC is taken up by the mammary glands in lactating women and is excreted in the breast milk. Effects of marijuana in the breast milk on human infants have not been determined (Christina 1994; Murphy and Bartke 1992).

In studies on mice and rats (but not humans), the addition of THC to pregnant animals lowered litter size, increased fetal reabsorption, and increased the number of reproductive abnormalities in the surviving offspring (Dewey 1986). The offspring of the drug-treated animal mothers had reduced fertility and more testicular abnormalities. The dose of cannabinoids used in these studies was higher than that used by humans. Clearly, pregnant women should be advised against using marijuana, even though there are few direct data on its prenatal effects in humans (Dewey 1986; Foley 2007; Murphy and Bartke 1992).

▪ Tolerance and Dependence

It has been known for many years that tolerance to some effects of cannabis builds rapidly in animals—namely, the drug effect becomes less intense with repeated administration. Frequent use of high doses of marijuana or THC in humans produces similar tolerance. For example, increasingly higher doses must be given to obtain the same intensity of subjective effects and increased heart rate that occur initially with small doses (Abood and Martin 1992; NIDA 2010c).

Frequent high doses of THC also can produce mild physical dependence. Healthy subjects who smoke several joints a day or who are given comparable amounts of THC orally experience irritability, sleep disturbances, weight loss, loss of appetite, sweating, and gastrointestinal upsets when drug use is stopped abruptly. However, not all subjects experience this mild form of withdrawal.

It is much easier to show psychological dependence in heavy users of marijuana (Abood and

Martin 1992; Hollister 1986; NIDA 2010c). Psychological dependence involves an attachment to the euphoric effects of the THC content in marijuana and may include craving for the drug. The subjective psychological effects of marijuana intoxication include a heightened sensitivity to and distortion of sight, smell, taste, and sound; mood alteration; and diminished reaction time.

DIAGNOSIS: CANNABIS DEPENDENCE

In general, outright cannabis addiction, with obsessive drug-seeking and compulsive drug-taking behavior, is relatively rare with low-THC cannabis. Contributing to this is the fact that the less potent forms of marijuana are most readily available in the United States, resulting in most chronic users in this country having little problem controlling or eliminating their cannabis habit if they so desire.

The Diagnostic and Statistical Manual of Mental Disorders, *(DSM-5)* recognizes a diagnosis of cannabis dependence. It is characterized by compulsive use and spending hours per day acquiring and using the substance. Compulsive users persist in their use despite knowledge of physical problems (for example, chronic cough related to smoking) or psychological problems (for example, excessive sedation resulting from repeated use of high doses) (APA 2013).

■ Chronic Use

Research on chronic use of marijuana (repeated daily use of this drug) in the 1970s indicated the possibility of three types of damage: (1) chromosomal damage (Stenchever, Kunysz, and Allen 1974), (2) cerebral atrophy (shrinking of the brain) (Campbell et al. 1971), and (3) lowered capacity of white blood cells to fight disease (Suciu-Foca, Armand, and Morishima 1974). These findings have all been contradicted or refuted by subsequent research. The only finding that appears very credible is that heavy use of this drug impairs lung capacity (Bloodworth 1987; Henneberger 1994; Kaplan and Whitmire 1995; NIDA 2010c; Oliwenstein 1988; Swan 1994).

Other evidence indicates that chronic, heavy use of cannabis can lead to unforeseen calamities in some users (see "Case in Point: Chronic Marijuana Use").

We have pointed out that marijuana produces a variety of psychoactive effects. One of those effects is sedation of unwanted emotional states such as anxiety, which are inevitable given the conflicts and turmoil of living in our fast-paced society today. As with the chronic use of any psychoactive drug that produces sedating effects, normal emotional and psychosocial development can be arrested by heavy marijuana consumption. For example, a youth who is usually high at a party avoids the anxieties and embarrassments of introspective and critical interpersonal interactions but instead will be interested in thrill-seeking behavior, such as romantic and sexual involvements, experimentation with and heavy use of other drugs, and other types of more daring experiences.

From years of research with this drug, we find that heavy and chronic use of marijuana can very easily compromise cognitive functions, such as short-term memory, concentration, moderately taxing problem solving, and even spiritual growth and development. Often, the more serious costs in using this drug are that the individual acquires a poor record for development and advancement of learning, as is often expected in educational settings (schools, colleges, trade schools, and universities). Another cost that is more serious is the retardation in emotional development. Such types of development are often obscured by being high all the time. Further, in such chronic use cases, much time is wasted seeking the pleasures and sometimes the longed-for thrills derived from the habitual use of marijuana.

The amotivational syndrome, in fact, can be deconstructed into the sedation, depression, and cognitive impairment discussed throughout this chapter. The user who is experiencing a subjective euphoric effect, enjoying the presence and social reinforcement of peers, feeling no pain, and remaining cognitively unfocused finds it difficult to intellectually grasp the learned experiences from such developmental delays. Although many do mature out of use, this step may occur only after years of development have slipped away, never to be regained. Sometimes treatment interventions are necessary to get the subject into a drug-free state and reunited with non–drug-using peer groups.

In concluding this chapter, we note that the history of this drug indicates that usage and availability will remain widespread despite all the efforts to eradicate its existence. Despite all the prevention efforts to date, marijuana remains the most popular illicit drug, topped only by alcohol and tobacco, which are licit drugs.

► **CASE IN POINT**

Chronic Marijuana Use

The following comments show how marijuana use can become a disturbing habit:

I guess you could say it was peer pressure. Back in 1969, I was a sophomore in college, and everyone was smoking "dope." The Vietnam War was in progress, and most students on college campuses were heavily involved in the drug scene. I first started smoking marijuana when my closest friends did. I was taught by other students who already knew how to enjoy the effects of "pot."

I recall that one of my fellow students used to supply me with "nickel bags," and many users nicknamed him "God." How did he get such a name? Because he sold some very potent marijuana that at times caused us to hallucinate.

I used pot nearly every day for about a year and a half, and hardly an evening would pass without smoking dope and listening to music. Smoking marijuana became as common as drinking alcohol. I used it in the same manner a person has a cocktail after a long day. At first, I liked the effects of being "high," but later I became so accustomed to the stuff that life appeared boring without it.

After graduating, my college friends went their separate ways, and I stopped using marijuana for a few years. A year later, in graduate school, a neighborhood friend reintroduced me to the pleasure of smoking pot. I began to use it again but not as often. Whenever I experienced some pressure, I would use a little to relax.

After finishing my degree, I found myself employed at an institution that at times was boring. Again, I started using pot at night to relax, and somehow it got out of control. I used to smoke a little before work and sometimes during lunch. I thought all was well until one day I got fired because someone accused me of being high on the job.

Soon afterward, I came to the realization that the use of marijuana can be very insidious. It has a way of becoming psychologically addictive, and you don't even realize it. When I was high, I thought that no one knew, and that I was even more effective with others. Little did I know, I was dead wrong and fooling no one. *(From Venturelli's research files, male, age 39, May 1990)*

In May 2013, this same interviewee, now 62 years of age, was asked if he had any additional remarks about the interview he gave in May 1990. He said the following:

How time flies! Now it's been 23 years since I was interviewed. I can say that as a very recent retired man I still occasionally dabble in pot smoking and still enjoy it. I did quit for many years, but about nine years ago, a lifelong friend of mine was visiting and I asked him to get me some so we could "fire one up after a long time." We did that and it was nothing but memory lane while we were smoking it. We had a good time talking and laughing about things we did during those as you say [referring to the interviewer] days of chronic marijuana use.

What I really like about the pot these days is that you have real quality and really powerful stuff. Several puffs and you can get really stoned. My friend picked up some blueberry marijuana and it was really powerful. I only had a few puffs during the first few hours I tried it with him and I was really high. Very potent stuff for sure. Thank God we did not have this stuff when I was doing it a lot in my younger days. I think I really would have been totally addicted. Back when I was young, we had stuff that was effective in achieving a buzz but not feeling it so strongly as the stuff my friend brought me. Get this: he got it from his grandchild when he told him to get him some because he was visiting me.

I want to emphasize, I only smoke marijuana about once or twice a month now and I am very careful to not like it too much because as I said in my first interview back in 1990, I really had a problem years ago. It's real good today and think that there must be a lot more addiction to this drug today in comparison to when I was young when we did not have such potent stuff. *(Second interview with same interviewee on May 12, 2013, from Venturelli's research files, male, age 62)*

Second interview with same interviewee on May 12, 2013, from Venturelli's research files, male, age 62.

LEARNING PORTFOLIO

Discussion Questions

1. What are the pharmacological, sociological, and psychological reasons why the very young continue to use marijuana at alarming rates despite the illegality of usage?

2. Do you believe that prosecution for marijuana possession should be more or less rigid than it currently is? Why?

3. Debate whether marijuana use adversely affects driving capabilities.

4. Either directly interview or imagine interviews of several users and nonusers of marijuana. How do you think they would answer the question of whether their critical thinking skills are adversely affected by this drug?

5. Among marijuana users, do you believe that the amotivational syndrome exists as a syndrome? Interview several users and try to either add to the characteristics of this syndrome from your interviews or modify the syndrome as discussed in this chapter.

6. In light of the information in "Holding the Line," do you believe the sale of marijuana for medical and/or for recreational purposes will ever be completely legalized at the state and federal levels in all 50 states? Why or why not for medical, and why or why not for recreational purposes?

7. What is your reaction to legalizing marijuana as a controlled substance like alcohol and tobacco products? Give reasons either for or against legalization.

8. Do you believe consistent use of marijuana changes personality? If so, how?

9. Summarize how marijuana affects the brain, CNS, respiratory system, cardiovascular system, and sexual performance and reproduction.

10. Debate how much family upbringing and attachment to a religion affect later drug use.

11. From reading this chapter, try to explain why most heroin users have used marijuana, whereas the vast majority of marijuana users never advance to such highly addictive drugs.

12. Explain how a user of cannabis might develop psychological dependence.

13. Do you believe that use of marijuana is more or less harmful than use of tobacco products? Should they be regulated differently?

14. Why do you think that in 2012 such a high percentage of 12th graders (approximately 52%) do not perceive *regular use* of marijuana as harmful (Johnston et al. 2013)?

Key Terms

Summary

1. Marijuana consists of the dried and crushed leaves, flowers, stems, and seeds of the *Cannabis sativa* plant. Tetrahydrocannabinol (THC) is the primary mind-altering (psychoactive) ingredient in marijuana. There are two main strains—*Cannabis sativa* and *Cannabis indica*. These two main varieties differ ". . . in their chemical composition, physiological aesthetic, and medical application" (ProCon.org 2012a). *Cannabis sativa* originates from Colombia, Mexico, Jamaica, South Africa, Thailand, and Southeast Asia and generally causes uplifting and energetic feelings, stimulates the appetite, and provides pain relief from certain ailments (Budfacts.com 2009). This strain is grown in hot countries that have higher temperatures. It is a brighter green than the *indica* strain with narrower leaves, and averages over 6 feet tall. *Cannabis indica* originates from hash-producing countries (e.g., Afghanistan, Pakistan, India, Turkey, Morocco, and Tibet) (ProCon.org 2012a), and its effects include body relaxation, stress relief, and calmness and serenity (Budfacts.com 2009). Unlike *Cannabis sativa*, *Cannabis indica* is found in warm countries; the plants are shorter (under 6 feet tall) and a darker green in color with wider leaves (Weedist 2012). The THC content in the two strains differs; the *indica* strain generally has a lower THC content (Weedist 2012).

2. Marijuana remains very controversial for the following reasons: (a) a high percentage of the U.S. population uses this drug; (b) it remains illegal in most states; (c) 20 states and the District of Columbia have legalized the sale of marijuana for medical purposes, although the use and sale of marijuana in these states remains illegal at the federal level; (d) marijuana accounts for a large number of arrests for simple possession; (e) it is one of the least addictive-type drugs; and (f) most marijuana users do not graduate to other, more addictive illicit drugs.

3. The effects of marijuana can vary according to expectations and surroundings. At low doses, such as when smoked or ingested (eaten), the *Cannabis indica* strain often has a sedative effect. At higher doses, it can produce hallucinations and delusions.

4. As with tobacco, heavy use of marijuana can impair pulmonary function, cause chronic respiratory diseases (such as bronchitis and asthma), and promote lung cancer. Marijuana causes vasodilation and a compensatory increase in heart rate. The effects of marijuana on sexual performance and reproduction are controversial. Some studies have indicated this substance enhances sexual arousal.

5. Tolerance to the CNS and cardiovascular effects of marijuana develops rapidly with repeated use. Although physical dependence and associated withdrawal are minor, psychological dependence can be significant in chronic, heavy users.

6. The active ingredient in marijuana, THC, has been used for treating a variety of seemingly unrelated medical conditions. This drug is indicated for treatment of nausea and vomiting in cancer patients receiving chemotherapy and for treatment of anorexia (lack of appetite) in AIDS patients. Other potential therapeutic uses for THC include relief of intraocular pressure associated with glaucoma, as an antiasthmatic drug, for muscle relaxation, as prevention for some types of seizures, as an antidepressant, and as an analgesic to relieve migraines and other types of pain.

7. The age groups most likely to use marijuana are the following: (a) highest lifetime use, adults between 18 and 25 years of age (52%), and (b) highest past-year (30.6%) and past-month (18.9%) use, 18- to 25-year-olds. There is a sharp drop in past-year and past-month use in the 26 and older age group.

8. In 2011, 2.6 million persons had used marijuana for the first time within the past 12 months; this averages to approximately 7200 initiates per day. In 2011, 1.5 million (approximately 58%) out of 2.6 million recent marijuana initiates were younger than age 18 when they first used the drug. Also in 2011, the average age at first marijuana use among recent initiates ages 12 to 49 was 17.5

years. The percentage of youth ages 12 to 17 indicating great risk in smoking marijuana once a month decreased from 34.4% in 2007 to 27.6% in 2011, and the rate of youth perceiving great risk in smoking marijuana once or twice a week also decreased from 54.6% in 2007 to 44.8% in 2011. It seems clear that marijuana has remained a highly accessible drug. In 2011, 38% of 8th graders, 68% of 10th graders, and 82% of 12th graders reported it as being fairly or very easy to get.

9. A study in the *Epidemiologic Reviews* by researchers from Columbia University found that drivers who get behind the wheel after smoking pot run more than twice the risk of getting into an accident (DEA 2013, p. 42). In 2009, marijuana was the most prevalent drug found in this population—approximately 28 percent of fatally injured drivers who tested positive tested positive for marijuana (DEA 2013, p. 42). Other surveys conducted by MADD and the Liberty Mutual insurance company revealed that many teenagers (41%) were not concerned about driving after taking drugs. Medical data indicate a connection between drugged driving and accidents—patients in a shock-trauma unit who had been in collisions revealed that 15% of those who had been driving a car or motorcycle had been smoking marijuana and another 17% had both THC and alcohol in their blood. Another significant and notable study revealed the link between smoking marijuana and car accidents. Habitual marijuana users (used every day) were 9.5 times more likely to be involved in crashes, with 5.6% of people who had crashed having taken the drug, compared to 0.5% of the control group. This study revealed that habitual use of marijuana is strongly associated with car crash injury.

10. Currently 20 states plus the District of Columbia (DC) are medical marijuana states. The 20 states are Alaska, Arizona, California, Colorado, Connecticut, Delaware, Hawaii, Illinois, Maine, Maryland, Massachusetts, Michigan, Montana, Nevada, New Hampshire, New Jersey, New Mexico, Oregon, Rhode Island, Vermont, and Washington (ProCon.org 2013). Out of approximately 311.5 million total population in these states and Washington, DC, a rough estimate of 2,421,069 people are registered as medical marijuana patients (ProCon.org 2012c).

11. Legalization of the medical use of marijuana entails permitting physicians to prescribe marijuana for medical problems, with the idea that terminally ill as well as other types of sick patients could be given the option of smoking marijuana as opposed to taking the already-approved Marinol (dronabinol), an FDA-approved version of THC in capsule form.

References

Abel, E. L. *Marijuana: The First Twelve Thousand Years*. New York: Plenum, 1989.

Abood, M., and B. Martin. "Neurobiology of Marijuana Abuse." *Trends in Pharmacological Sciences* 13 (May 1992): 201–206.

Abood, M. E., and B. R. Martin. "Molecular Neurobiology of the Cannabinoid Receptor." *International Review of Neurobiology* 39 (May 1996): 197–219.

Adams, I. B., and B. R. Martin. "Cannabis: Pharmacology and Toxicology in Animals and Humans." *Addiction* 91 (1996): 1585–1614.

American Psychiatric Association (APA). *Diagnostic and Statistical Manual of Mental Disorders*, 4th ed. [DSM-IV]. Washington, DC: APA, 1994.

American Psychiatric Association (APA). "Substance-Related and Addictive Disorders." In *Diagnostic and Statistical Manual of Mental Disorders, DSM-5,* Fifth Edition. Arlington, VA: APA, 2013.

Anslinger, H. J., and C. R. Cooper. "Marijuana: Assassin of Youth." *American Magazine* 124 (July 1937): 19–20, 150–153.

Barclay, L., and C. Vega. "Marijuana Use Linked to Bronchodilation and Respiratory Symptoms." Medscape Medical News. 19 February 2007. Available http://www.medscape.org/viewarticle/552405

Bauman, K. E., and S. T. Ennett. "On the Importance of Peer Influence for Adolescent Drug Use: Commonly Neglected Considerations." *Addiction* 91 (February 1996): 185–198.

BC Bud Depot. "Welcome to the BC Bud Depot." Available https://www.bcbuddepot.com

Benson, J. "Prescription Painkillers Now Gateway Drugs to Hard Drug Use." Natural News.com. 30 August 2010. Available http://www.naturalnews.com/029606_prescription_opioids_gateway_drugs.html

Berkowitz, A. "Following Imaginary Peers: How Norm Misperceptions Influence Student Substance Abuse." In *Project Direction*, edited by G. Lindsay and G. Rulf, 12–15 (Module No. 2). Muncie, IN: Ball State University, 1991.

Block, R. I. "Does Heavy Marijuana Use Impair Human Cognition and Brain Function?" *Journal of the American Medical Association* 275 (1996): 560–561.

Bloodworth, R. C. "Major Problems Associated with Marijuana Use." *Psychiatric Medicine* 3 (1987): 173–184.

Blows, S., R. Q. Ivers, J. Connor, S. Ameratunga, M. Woodward, and R. Norton. "Marijuana Use and Car Crash Injury." *Society for the Study of Addiction* 100 (2005): 605–611.

Brigham Young University. "News Release: National Study Finds Religiosity Curbs Teen Marijuana Use by Half." 1 October 2008. Available http://news.byu.edu/archive08-oct-religiosity.aspx

Brown, M. W., and S. Massaro. *Attention and Memory Impaired in Heavy Users of Marijuana*. Rockville, MD: NIDA, 20 February 1996.

Brown University Health Education. "Marijuana." 2007. Available http://brown.edu/Student_Services/Health_Services/Health_Education/alcohol,_tobacco,_&_other_drugs/marijuana.php

BudFacts.com. "Types of Medical Marijuana." 26 June 2009. Available http://budfacts.com/126/types-of-medical-marijuana/

Buff, J. "Greasers, Dopers, and Hippies: Three Responses to the Adult World." In *The White Majority*, edited by L. Howe, 60–70. New York: Random House, 1970.

Cadena, C. "Marijuana Promotes Relaxation in Sexual Activity but Depresses Libido." Yahoo! Voices. 13 November 2007. Available http://www.associatedcontent.com/article/443811/marijuana_promotes_relaxation_in_sexual.html

Califano, J. A. "Dangerous Indifference to Drugs." *Washington Post* (23 September 1996): A-19.

Campbell, A. G., M. Evans, J. L. Thomson, and M. J. Williams. "Cerebral Atrophy in Young Cannabis Smokers." *Lancet* 19 (1971): 1219–1225.

Carter, E. *Cannabis in Costa Rica*. Philadelphia, PA: Institute for the Study of Human Issues, 1980.

Center for Substance Abuse Research (CESAR). "Marijuana Distribution Relies Primarily on Generosity of Friends and Family." CESAR FAX 16 (19 March 2007). Available http://www.cesar.umd.edu/cesar/cesarfax/vol16/16-11.pdf

Center for Substance Abuse Research (CESAR). "More than One in Ten Children in the U.S. Live with Substance-Abusing or Substance-Dependent Parent." CESAR FAX 18. (11 May 2010a). Available http://www.cesar.umd.edu/cesar/cesarfax/vol18/18-18.pdf

Center for Substance Abuse Research (CESAR). "U.S. High School Seniors' Perception of Harm from Regular Marijuana Use Decreasing." CESAR FAX 19 (19 January 2010b). Available http://www.cesar.umd.edu/cesar/cesarfax/vol19/19-02.pdf

Chait, L., and J. Pierri. "Effect of Smoked Marijuana on Human Performance: A Critical Review." In *Marijuana/Cannabinoids, Neurobiology and Neurophysiology*, edited by L. Murphy and A. Bartke, 387–424. Boca Raton, FL: CRC Press, 1992.

Christina, D. *Marijuana: Personality and Behavior*. Tempe, AZ: Do It Now, 1994.

Cincinnati.com. "Letters to the Editor: No Valid Reason to Ban Marijuana." *Enquirer*. 9 August 2010. Available http://cincinnati.com/blogs/letters/2010/08/09/no-valid-reason-to-ban-marijuana

Coleman, J. S. *The Adolescent Society*. New York: Free Press of Glencoe, 1961.

Cone, E. J., Y. H. Kaplan, D. L. Black, T. Robert, and F. Moser. "Urine Drug Testing of Chronic Pain Patients: Licit and Illicit Drug Patterns." *Journal of Analytic Toxicology* 32 (2008): 532–543.

Consroe, P., and R. Sandyk. "Potential Role of Cannabinoids for Therapy of Neurological Disorders." In *Marijuana/Cannabinoids, Neurobiology and Neurophysiology*, edited by L. Murphy and A. Bartke, 459–524. Boca Raton, FL: CRC Press, 1992.

Couper, F. J., and B. K. Logan. *Cannabis/Marijuana (Δ^9 Tetrahydro-cannabinol, THC)*. Drugs and Human Performance Fact Sheets. Washington, DC: National Highway Traffic Safety Administration, March 2004.

Dewey, W. L. "Cannabinoid Pharmacology." *Pharmacological Reviews* 38 (1986): 48–50.

Dreher, M. C. *Working Men and Ganja: Marijuana Use in Rural Jamaica*. Philadelphia, PA: Institute for the Study of Human Issues, 1982.

Drug Enforcement Administration. (DEA). "The DEA Position on Marijuana." Washington, DC: Drug Enforcement Administration, April 2013. Available http://www.justice.gov/dea/docs/marijuana_position_2011.pdf

Dupont, R. L. "Drugged Driving Research: A White Paper." Rockville, MD: Institute for Behavior and Health, Inc. Drugged Driving Committee. 31 March 2011. Available http://www.whitehouse.gov/sites/default/files/ondcp/issues-content/drugged-driving/nida_dd_paper.pdf

Earleywine M., and S. Smucker Barnwell. "Decreased Respiratory Symptoms in Cannabis Users Who Vaporize." *Harm Reduction Journal* 4 (16 April 2007): 1–6.

Eckert, P. *Jocks and Burnouts: Social Categories and Identity in the High School*. New York: Teachers College, Columbia University, 1989.

ElSohly, M. *Quarterly Report: Potency Monitoring Projected, Report 104, December 16, 2008 thru March 15, 2009.* National Institute on Drug Abuse (NIDA). Oxford, MS: National Center for Natural Products Research, Research Institute of Pharmaceutical Sciences, School of Pharmacy, University of Mississippi, 2009.

Fernandez-Ruiz, J., F. Rodriguez de Fonseca, M. Navarro, and J. Ramos. "Maternal Cannabinoid Exposure and Brain Development: Changes in the Ontogeny of Dopaminergic Neurons." In *Marijuana/Cannabinoids, Neurobiology and Neurophysiology*, edited by L. Murphy and A. Bartke, 118–164. Boca Raton, FL: CRC Press, 1992.

Flores, E. "Group Works to Legalize Marijuana, Others Fight Against It." KVOA.com. 13 June 2013. Available http://www.kvoa.com/news/group-works-to-legalize-marijuana-others-fight-against-it/#_

Foley, M. R. "Drug Use During Pregnancy." *Merck Manuals Online Edition*. Whitehouse Station, NJ: Merck & Co, 2007. Available http://www.merck.com/mmhe/sec22/ch259/ch259a.html

Fuhrman, R. A. *Cannabis Buyers' Club Flourishes in "Frisco."* San Francisco: Cannabis Buyers' Club, 1995.

Fuller, D. "Adolescent Brain Function Adversely Affected By Marijuana Use." Medical News Today. October 2008. Available http://www.medicalnewstoday.com/articles/125443.php

Gaines, G. *Teenage Wasteland: Suburbia's Dead-End Kids.* New York: Harper Perennial, 1992.

Gardner, A. "Study: Smoking Pot May Ease Chronic Pain." CNN.com, Health Magazine. 30 August 2010. Available http://www.cnn.com/2010/HEALTH/08/30/health.pot.reduce.pain/index.html

Gardner, E. "Cannabinoid Interaction with Brain Reward Systems: The Neurobiological Basis of Cannabinoid Abuse." In *Marijuana/Cannabinoids, Neurobiology and Neurophysiology*, edited by L. Murphy and A. Bartke, 275–335. Boca Raton, FL: CRC Press, 1992.

Goldberg, C. "Marijuana Club Helps Those in Pain." *New York Times*. 25 February 1996. Available http://www.nytimes.com/1996/02/25/us/marijuana-club-helps-those-in-pain.html?ref=carey_goldberg

Goldstein, A. *Addiction from Biology to Drug Policy*. New York: Freeman, 1994.

Goldstein, F. "Pharmacological Aspects of Substance Abuse." *Remington's Pharmaceutical Sciences*, 19th ed. Easton, PA: Mack, 1995.

Gossop, M. *Living with Drugs*, 2nd ed. Aldershot, England: Wildwood House, 1987.

Green, C. A. "Gender and Use of Substance Abuse Treatment Services." *Alcohol Research and Health* 29 (2006): 55–62.

Greenblatt, J. C. *Adolescent Self-Reported Behaviors and Their Association with Marijuana Use*. Office of Applied Studies (OAS), Substance Abuse and Mental Health Services Administration (SAMHSA). Rockville, MD: National Clearinghouse for Alcohol and Drug Information, July 1999.

Grinspoon, L. "Marijuana." *Harvard Medical School Mental Health Letter* 4 (November 1987): 1–4.

Grinspoon, L., and J. B. Bakalar. "Commentary, Marijuana as Medicine: A Plea for Reconsideration." *Journal of the American Medical Association* 273 (1995): 1875–1876.

Hamid, A. *Drugs in America: Sociology, Economics, and Politics*. Gaithersburg, MD: Aspen, 1998.

Hanson, D. "Sex, Drugs, and . . . Sex: Pharmaceuticals and Sexual Performance." Addiction Inbox, The Science of Substance Abuse. 28 July 2011. Available http://addiction-dirkh.blogspot.com/2010/09/sex-drugs-and-sex.html

Hardcastle, M. "Marijuana Use Can Threaten Teen's Academic Success." About.com. 15 March 2007. Available http://teenadvice.about.com/od/marijuanause/a/marijana1.htm

Heitzeg, N. *Deviance: Rulemakers and Rulebreakers*. St. Paul, MN: West Publishing, 1996.

Henneberger, M. "Pot Surges Back, It's Like a Whole New World." *New York Times* (6 February 1994): C19.

Hollister, L. E. "Health Aspects of Cannabis." *Pharmacological Reviews* 38 (1986): 39–42.

Hongmei, Y., B. Stanton, L. Cottrel, L. Kaljee, J. Galbraith, et al. "Parental Awareness of Adolescent Risk Involvement: Implications of Overestimates and Underestimates." *Journal of Adolescent Health* 39 (September 2006): 353–361.

Hubbard, J. R., S. E. Franco, and E. S. Onaivi. "Marijuana: Medical Implications." *American Family Physician* 283 (1999): 231–240.

Hudson, R. "Researchers Identify Gene That Triggers Marijuana's 'High.'" *Wall Street Journal* (9 August 1990): B2.

Indiana Prevention Resource Center. *Factline on: Marijuana*. Bloomington, IN: Indiana Prevention Resource Center, 1996.

Iversen, L. "Medicinal Use of Marijuana." *Nature* 365 (1993): 12–13.

Iverson, L. "Long-Term Effects of Exposure to Cannabis." *Current Opinion in Pharmacology* 5 (2005): 69–72.

Jaffe, J. H. "Drug Addiction and Drug Abuse." In *The Pharmacological Basis of Therapeutics*, 8th ed., edited by A. Gilman, T. Rall, A. Nies, and P. Taylor, 522–575. New York: Pergamon, 1990.

Jenkins, M. "Ganjanomics: Bringing Humboldt's Shadow Economy into the Light." *High Country News*. 8 August 2011. Available http://www.hcn.org/issues/43.13/ganjanomics-bringing-humbolts-shadow-economy-into-the-light?gclid=CODc-56K-bcCFe9cMgodihMAmg

Johns, A. "Psychiatric Effects of Cannabis." *British Journal of Psychiatry* 178 (2001): 116–122.

Johnston, L. D., P. M. O'Malley, J. G. Bachman, and J. E. Schulenberg. *Monitoring the Future: National Survey Results on Drug Use*. Bethesda, MD: National Institute on Drug Abuse, 2009.

Johnston, L. D., P. M. O'Malley, J. G. Bachman, and J. E. Schulenberg. *Monitoring the Future: National Survey Results on Drug Use, 1975-2012: Volume I, Secondary School Students*. Ann Arbor, MI: Institute for Social Research, University of Michigan, 2013.

Join Together Staff. "Biggest U.S. Cash Crop: Marijuana." New York, NY: The Partnership at Drugree.org, (19 December 2006). Available http://www.drugfree.org/join-together/drugs/biggest-us-cash-crop

Jones, R. T. "Human Effects: An Overview." In *Marijuana Research Findings: 1980*. NIDA Research Monograph No. 31. Washington, DC: National Institute on Drug Abuse, 1980.

Julian, B. S. "alt.hemp Cannabis/Marijuana FAQ." University of Massachusetts at Amherst. 1994. Available http://www.faqs.org/faqs/drugs/hemp-marijuana

Kandel, D. B., P. C. Griesler, G. Lee, M. Davies, and C. Shaffsan. *Parental Influences on Adolescent Marijuana Use and the Baby Boom Generation: Findings from the 1995–1996 National Household Surveys on Drug Abuse*. Rockville, MD: Substance Abuse and Mental Health Services Administration, 2001.

Kaplan, L. F., and R. Whitmire. "Pot—It's Potent, Prevalent and Preventable." *Salt Lake Tribune* 250 (21 May 1995): 9.

Kelly, T., R. Foltin, C. Enurian, and M. Fischman. "Effects of THC on Marijuana Smoking, Drug Choice and Verbal Report of Drug Liking." *Journal of Experimental Analysis of Behavior* 61 (1994): 203–211.

Kendler, K. S., C. O. Gardner, and C. A. Prescott. "Religion, Psychopathology, and Substance Use and Abuse: A Multimeasure, Genetic-Epidemiologic Study." *American Journal of Psychiatry* 154 (1997): 322–329.

Kryger, A. H. "Preventive Medicine Clinic of Monterey: Marijuana Mental Disturbances." Virtual Hospital Home Page. 24 October 1995. Available http://vh.radiology.uiowa.edu

Liska, K. *Drugs and the Human Body*, 5th ed. Upper Saddle River, NJ: Prentice Hall, 1997.

MarijuanaDetox.com. "Marijuana Detox." 2008. Available http://www.marijuana-detox.com/m-facts.htm

"Marijuana Menaces Youth." *Scientific American* 154 (1936): 151.

Mathias, R. "Marijuana Impairs Driving-Related Skills and Workplace Performance." *NIDA Notes* 11 (January/February 1996): 6.

McCabe, S. E. "Misperceptions of Nonmedical Prescription Drug Use: A Web Survey of College Students." *Addictive Behavior* 33 (May 2008): 713–724.

Medical Marijuana Education Center. "Medical Cannabis and Muscle Spasms." Centric Wellness. 3 July 2012. Available http://medicalmarijuanaeducationcenter.com/2012/07/03/medical-cannabis-and-muscle-spams/

Mernagh, M. "Top 10 Best Marijuana Strains 2001 As Chosen by Google." 13 December 2011. Available http://www.mernagh.ca/top-10-best-marijuana-strains-2011-as-chosen-by-google/

Murphy, L., and A. Bartke. "Effects of THC on Pregnancy, Puberty, and the Neuroendocrine System." In *Marijuana/Cannabinoids, Neurobiology and Neurophysiology*, edited by L. Murphy and A. Bartke, 539. Boca Raton, FL: CRC Press, 1992.

Musto, D. F. *The American Disease: Origins of Narcotic Control*, 3rd ed. New York: Oxford University Press, 1999.

Nahas, G., and C. Latour. "The Human Toxicity of Marijuana." *Medical Journal of Australia* 156 (1992): 495–497.

National Cannabis Prevention and Information Centre (NCPIC). "Cannabis Potency." 1 April 2013. Available http://ncpic.org.au/ncpic/publications/factsheets/article/cannabis-potency

National Center on Addiction and Substance Abuse at Columbia University. "Casa Report: Spirituality and Religion Reduce Risk of Substance Abuse." 2001. Available http://www.casacolumbia.org/absolutenm/templates/PressReleases.aspx?articleid=115&zoneid=48

National Clearinghouse on Alcohol and Drug Information (NCADI). *Marijuana: Facts Parents Need to Know. Quick Screen, At Home Drug Test*. Rockville, MD: National Clearinghouse on Alcohol and Drug Information, November 1998.

National Eye Institute. *Facts About Glaucoma*. Bethesda, MD: U.S. Department of Health and Human Services (USDHHS) and National Institutes of Health (NIH), 2010.

National Highway Traffic Safety Administration (NHTSA). "Cannabis/Marijuana." In *Drugs and Human Performance Fact* Sheets, edited by F. J. Couper and B. K Logan. Washington, DC: National Highway Traffic Safety Administration, 2004.

National Institute on Drug Abuse (NIDA). *Drug Abuse and Drug Abuse Research*. DHHS Pub. No. 91-1704. Washington, DC: U.S. Department of Health and Human Services, 1991.

National Institute on Drug Abuse (NIDA). *Marijuana: Facts Parents Need to Know*. NIH Pub. No. 95-4037. Rockville, MD: National Clearinghouse on Alcohol and Drug Information, 1998.

National Institute on Drug Abuse (NIDA). *DrugFacts: Marijuana*. Bethesda, MD: U.S. Department of Health and Human Services, 29 March 2000. Available http://www.nica.nih.gov/infofax/marijuana.html

National Institute on Drug Abuse (NIDA). *Marijuana Smoking Is Associated with a Spectrum of Respiratory Disorders*. Bethesda, MD: National Institute on Drug Abuse (NIDA) and National Institutes of Health (NIH), 21 October 2006.

National Institute on Drug Abuse (NIDA). *Marijuana: Facts Parents Need to Know*. Bethesda, MD: National Institute on Drug Abuse (NIDA) and National Institutes of Health (NIH), August 2007.

National Institute on Drug Abuse (NIDA). *InfoFacts: Marijuana*. Bethesda, MD: National Institute on Drug Abuse (NIDA) and National Institutes of Health (NIH), 2009b.

National Institute on Drug Abuse (NIDA). "Does Marijuana Use Affect Driving?" Bethesda, MD: National Institute on Drug Abuse, December 2010a. Available http://www.drugabuse.gov/publications/marijuana-abuse/does-marijuana-use-affect-driving

National Institute on Drug Abuse (NIDA). "DrugFacts: Drugged Driving." Bethesda, MD: National Institute on Drug Abuse, December 2010b. Available http://www.drugabuse.gov/publications/drugfacts/drugged-driving

National Institute on Drug Abuse (NIDA). "Research Report Series: Marijuana Abuse." Bethesda, MD: U.S. Department of Health and Human Services (USDHHS) and National Institutes of Health (NIH), September 2010c. Available http://www.drugabuse.gov/PDF/RRMarijuana.pdf

National Institute on Drug Abuse (NIDA). "NIH Study Examines Nicotine as a Gateway Drug." NIH News, National Institutes of Health. Bethesda, MD: U.S. Department of Health and Human Services (USDHHS). 2 November 2011. Available http://www.nih.gov/news/health/nov2011/nida-02.htm

National Institute on Drug Abuse (NIDA). "Drug Facts: Marijuana." Bethesda, MD: National Institute on Drug Abuse, December 2012.

National Organization for the Reform of Marijuana Laws (NORML). "Chronic Pain." 30 January 2013. http://norml.org/library/item/chronic-pain

National Organization for the Reform of Marijuana Laws (NORML). "Medical Use." n.d. Available http://norml.org/marijuana/medical

New York Times. "U.S. Marijuana is Getting More Potent and More Dangerous, Study Contends." (12 June 2008). Available http://www.nytimes.com/2008/06/12/world/americas/12iht-pot.1.13656558.html

Norton, A. "Address Client Myths About Marijuana: Professionals Can Counteract Mixed Messages in Society That Impede Healing." *Addiction Professional* 4 (July/August 2009): 32–34.

Office of National Drug Control Policy (ONDCP). "Drug Facts: Marijuana." 2003. Washington, DC: Office of National Drug Control, 2003.

Oliwenstein, L. "The Perils of Pot." *Discover* 9 (1988): 18.

Palfai, T., and H. Jankiewicz. *Drugs and Human Behavior*. Dubuque, IA: William C. Brown, 1991.

Pew Research Center. "Majority Now Supports Legalizing Marijuana." Washington, DC: Pew Research Center (4 April 2013). Available http://www.people-press.org/2013/04/04/majority-now-supports-legalizing-marijuana/

Pollan, M. "Medical Marijuana: Can It Help You? Should It Be Legal? A Report from California." *Herbs for Health* (March/April 1998): 38–50.

Pope, H. G., Jr., and D. Yurgulen-Todd. "The Residual Cognitive Effects of Heavy Marijuana Use in College Students." *Journal of the American Medical Association* 275 (1996): 521–527.

ProCon.org. "Medical Marijuana: What Are the Differences Between Cannabis Indica and Cannabis Sativa, and How Do They Vary in Their Potential Medical Utility?" (11 June 2012a) Available http://medicalmarijuana.procon.org/view.answers.php?questionID=000638#answer-id-011092

ProCon.org. "Is Marijuana Significantly More Potent Now Than in the Past?" (7 February 2012b). Available http://medicalmarijuana.procon.org/view.answers.php?questionID=000336

ProCon.org. "How Many People in the United States Use Medical Marijuana?" (31 December 2012c). Available http://medicalmarijuana.procon.org/view.answers.php?questionID=001199

ProCon.org. "20 Legal Medical Marijuana States and DC." 2013. Available http://medicalmarijuana.procon.org/view.resource.php?resourceID=000881

Rand Drug Policy Research Center. "Rand Releases Study on Marijuana 'Gateway Effect.'" Press Release. 26 December 2002. Available http://www.jointogether.org

Reaney, P. "Getting High May Not Be So Harmless After All." Reuters Limited. (20 March 2000).

Right Diagnosis. "Amotivational Syndrome." Health Grades Inc. August 2010. Available http://www.wrongdiagnosis.com/a/amotivational_syndrome/intro.htm#whatis

Robson, P. "Therapeutic Aspects of Cannabis and Cannabinoids." *British Journal of Psychiatry* 178 (2001): 107–115.

Roffman, R. A., and W. H. George. "Cannabis Abuse." In *Assessment of Addictive Behaviors*, edited by D. M. Donovan and G. A. Marlatt, 78–86. New York: Guilford, 1988.

Rubin, V., and L. Comitas. *Ganja in Jamaica: A Medical Anthropological Study of Chronic Marijuana Use*. Paris: Mouton, 1975.

Schultes, R. E. "Ethnopharmacological Significance of Psychotropic Drugs of Vegetal Origin." *Principles of Psychopharmacology*, 2nd ed., edited by W. G. Clark and J. del Giudice. New York: Academic Press, 1978.

Sewell. R. A., J. Poling, and M. Sofuoglu. "The Effect of Cannabis Compared with Alcohol on Driving." *American Journal of Addictions* 18 (2009): 185–193. Available http://www.ncbi.nlm.nih.gov/pmc/articles/PMC2722956/

Sewester, S. *Drug Facts and Comparisons*. St. Louis, MO: Kluwer, 1993, 259h–259k.

Silverberg, C. "Sex and Marijuana." About.com Sexuality. 5 July 2007. Available http://sexuality.about.com/od/sex_and_drugs/a/marijuana_sex.htm

Solomon, D., ed. *The Marihuana Papers*. New York: New American Library, 1966.

Sorden, S. "The Promise of Social Norming." *John's Addiction* (7 October 2011). Available http://johnsaddiction.com/911-social-norming-drinking/

Stenchever, M. A., T. J. Kunysz, and M. A. Allen. "Chromosome Breakage in Users of Marijuana." *American Journal of Obstetrics and Gynecology* 118 (January 1974): 106–113.

Substance Abuse and Mental Health Services Administration (SAMHSA), Office of Applied Studies. "The NHSDA Report. Religious Involvement and Substance Use Among Adults." 23 March 2007a. Available http://www.oas.samhsa.gov

Substance Abuse and Mental Health Services Administration (SAMHSA), Office of Applied Studies. "The NHSDA Report. Youth Activities, Substance Use, and Family Income." 19 April 2007b. Available http://www.oas.samhsa.gov

Substance Abuse and Mental Health Services Administration (SAMHSA), Office of Applied Studies. *Results from the 2011 National Survey on Drug Use and Health: Detailed Tables*. HHS Pub. No. SMA 12-4713, NSDUH Series H-44. Rockville, MD: Author, 2012.

Suciu-Foca, N., J. P. Armand, and A. Morishima. "Inhibition of Cellular Immunity in Marijuana Smokers." *Science* 183 (1974): 419–420.

Swan, N. "Researchers Make Pivotal Marijuana and Heroin Discoveries." *NIDA Notes* 8 (10 September 1993): 1.

Swan, N. "A Look at Marijuana's Harmful Effects." *NIDA Notes* 9 (February/March 1994): 3–4.

Swan, N. "Facts About Marijuana and Marijuana Abuse." *NIDA Notes* 11 (March/April 1996): 15.

Taylor, N. *Narcotics: Nature's Dangerous Gifts*. New York: Dell, 1963.

Taylor, N. "The Pleasant Assassin: The Story of Marijuana." In *The Marihuana Papers*, edited by D. Solomon. New York: Signet Books, 1966.

Teen Challenge. *Drugs: Frequently Asked Questions*. South Australia: Pragin Press, 2000.

TheWeek.com. "Do Marijuana and Driving Mix?" 7 June 2010. Available http://theweek.com/article/index/203778/do-marijuana-and-driving-mix

Tudor, C. G., D. M. Petersen, and K. W. Elifson. "An Examination of the Relationships Between Peer and Parental Influences and Adolescent Drug Use." In *Chemical Dependencies: Patterns, Costs, and Consequences*, edited by C. D. Chambers, J. A. Inciardi, D. M. Petersen, H. A. Siegal, and O. Z. White. Athens, OH: Ohio University Press, 1987.

Turner, C. E. "Chemistry and Metabolism." In *Marijuana Research Findings: 1980*. NIDA Research Monograph No. 31. Washington, DC: National Institute on Drug Abuse, 1980.

U.S. Department of Transportation. *Marijuana and Actual Driving Performance: Effects of THC on Driving Performance*. DOT HS 808 078. Washington, DC: National Highway Traffic Safety Administration (NHTSA), November 1993.

Venkataraman, N. "Marijuana Called Top U.S. Cash Crop." ABC News Internet Ventures (18 December 2006). Available http://abcnews.go.com/Business/story?id=2735017

Venturelli, P. J. "Drugs in Schools: Myths and Reality." In *The Annals of the American Academy of Political and Social Science*, edited by W. Hinkle and S. Henry, 72–87. Thousand Oaks, CA: Sage Publications, January 2000.

Wallace, J. M., V. L. Myers, and E. R. Osai. *Faith Matters: Race/Ethnicity, Religion and Substance Use*. Baltimore, MD: Annie E. Casey Foundation, 2004.

Weedist. "Cannabis 101: Differences Between Sativa and Indica Marijuana." 17 August 2012. Available http://www.weedist.com/2012/08/differences-between-sativa-and-indica-marijuana/

Wingett Sanchez, Y. "Arizona Recreational Marijuana Use Initiative Launched." azcentral.com. 12 June 2013. Available http://www.azcentral.com/news/politics/articles/20130612personal-experience-spurs-effort-legalize-pot-recreational-use.html

Wren, C. S. "Youth Marijuana Use Rises." Themes of the Times, *New York Times* (20 February 1996): 1.

Zimmer, L., and J. P. Morgan. *Marijuana Myths, Marijuana Facts: A Review of the Scientific Evidence*. New York: Lindesmith Center, 1997.

CHAPTER 14

Inhalants

© Marmaduke St. John/Alamy

Did You Know?

▶ More than 1000 different commercial and household products are abused commonly in the United States.

▶ Ordinary household products are misused as inhalants: glues/adhesives, nail polish remover, gasoline, paint thinner, spray paint, butane lighter fluid, propane gas, typewriter correction fluid, household cleaners, cooking sprays, deodorants, whipping cream aerosols, marking pens, and air conditioning coolants.

▶ Inhalant abuse is typically a problem of adolescents and teenagers. By the time children reach 8th grade, 11.8% will have misused inhalants.

▶ Each year, young people in this country die of inhalant abuse or suffer severe consequences, including permanent brain damage and damage to the heart, kidneys, and liver.

▶ Inhalant abusers can die suddenly and without warning even first-time abusers have died from sniffing nhalants.

Learning Objectives

On completing this chapter you will be able to:

❯ Understand that inhalant use is not harmless and that even one-time use could lead to sudden sniffing death syndrome.

❯ List the household and commercial products that are most often abused as inhalants.

❯ Describe the principal means of using household and commercial products as inhalants.

❯ Identify signs of abuse.

❯ Examine the current patterns of abuse among various groups.

❯ List the dangers of inhalant abuse.

Drugs and Society Online is a great source for additional drugs and society information for both students and instructors. Visit **go.jblearning.com /hanson12** to find a variety of useful tools for learning, thinking, and teaching.

Introduction

Inhalants are **volatile** substances that elicit psychological or physiological changes when introduced into the body via the lungs. They are rarely administered by any other route. Most cause intoxicating and/or **euphorigenic** effects. Many of these substances were never intended to be used by humans as drugs; consequently, they are not often thought of as having abuse potential. However, abuse of inhalants is a serious public health problem; according to data obtained from the National Institute on Drug Abuse (NIDA)-sponsored *Monitoring the Future* study, 11.8% of 8th graders have misused an inhalant at least once in their lifetime. Among 10th and 12th graders, lifetime reported use was 9.9% and 7.9%, respectively (Johnston et al. 2013). This frequency of inhalant abuse among 8th graders surpasses the frequency of abuse of such highly publicized drugs as cocaine (1.9%) and amphetamines (4.5%), and approaches that of marijuana/hashish (15.2%) in this age group (Johnston et al. 2013). Noteworthy, in 2011, of the estimated 3.1 million individuals age 12 or older who used illicit drugs for the first time within the past 12 months, 7.5% reported inhalants as their first illicit drug (Substance Abuse and Mental Health Services Administration [SAMHSA] 2012b). The average age of first use of inhalants was 16.4 years (SAMHSA, 2012b).

A widespread misconception is that inhalant abuse is a harmless phase that occurs commonly during normal childhood and teenage development and as such is not worthy of significant concern because young people will grow out of it without experiencing harm. On the contrary, numerous adolescents and teenagers in the United States die or are seriously injured each year as a result of inhalant abuse. Even first-time users may die from **sudden sniffing death syndrome (SSDS)**, a condition characterized by serious cardiac **arrhythmia** occurring during or immediately after inhaling. Accurate statistics regarding the number of inhalant-associated deaths and injuries each year are unavailable, in part because medical examiners often attribute deaths from inhalant use to suicide, suffocation, or accidents. Nevertheless, every year young people in the United States die from inhalant abuse, and many more suffer severe consequences such as damage to the brain, heart, kidneys, and liver (U.S. Consumer Product Safety Commission, n.d.).

Most inhalants are household or commercial products composed of several different chemicals. These compounds can act alone or synergistically to exert toxic effects. The potential of these agents to cause harm is compounded by the high concentrations of these substances absorbed in the body by inhalation and the tendency for these often lipid-rich (oily or fatty) substances to be retained in lipid-containing vital organs. Another important consideration is that the users are often developmentally immature and as such can be more susceptible to the toxic effects of inhalants. The summation of these factors makes inhalants dangerous substances of abuse.

History of Inhalants

The modern era of inhalant abuse can be traced to 1776, when British chemist Joseph Priestley synthesized nitrous oxide (Kennedy and Longnecker 1990), a colorless gas with a slightly sweet odor and no noticeable taste. Roughly 20 years later, he and Humphry Davy suggested correctly that the gas might be useful as an anesthetic, and experiments were conducted to test this possibility.

Dentists contributed greatly to the introduction of nitrous oxide as an anesthetic. At a stage show in the 1840s, Horace Wells, a dentist, noticed that one of the persons involved in the show injured himself while under the influence of nitrous oxide yet felt no pain. Wells was so impressed by this anesthetic effect that he subsequently allowed his own tooth to be extracted while under the influence of the gas. His experiment was a success; Wells did not experience pain. He went on to attempt to demonstrate his discovery at Massachusetts General Hospital in Boston; unfortunately, the patient cried out during the procedure and the experiment was deemed unsuccessful (Kennedy and Longnecker 1990). Nevertheless, word of this demonstration and others like it spread, ultimately leading to the use of nitrous oxide and other volatile anesthetics as legitimate medical therapy.

KEY TERMS

volatile
readily evaporated at low temperatures

euphorigenic
having the ability to cause feelings of pleasure and well-being

arrhythmia
an irregular heartbeat

Over the years, it was discovered that many chemicals, in addition to nitrous oxide, could be inhaled so as to alter psychological function. Such abuse of inhalants came to public attention in the 1950s when the news media reported that young people were getting high from sniffing glue. The term *glue sniffing* is still used today, but it is often used to describe inhalation of many products besides glue. In fact, more than 1000 different products are currently misused as inhalants (U.S. Consumer Product Safety Commission n.d.). These chemicals are not regulated like other drugs of abuse; hence, they are readily available to young people. This category of drugs can be classified into three major groups: volatile substances, anesthetics, and nitrites.

Types of Inhalants

■ Volatile Substances

Over the past 50 years, the number of products containing volatile substances has increased substantially. This category of agents includes aerosols (e.g., spray paints, hair sprays, deodorants, vegetable oil sprays), art or office supplies (e.g., correction fluids, felt-tip marker fluids), adhesives (e.g., airplane and other glues), fuels (e.g., propane, gasoline), and industrial or household solvents (e.g., nail polish remover, paint thinners, dry-cleaning fluids). Some volatile substances exist as gases (e.g., nitrous oxide, the propellant in whipping cream cans), whereas others are liquids that vaporize at room temperature (e.g., gasoline). In some cases, the abuser inhales vapors directly from their original containers (called *sniffing* or *snorting*). Still others inhale volatile solvents from plastic bags (called *bagging*) or from old rags or bandannas soaked in the solvent fluid and held over the mouth (called *huffing*).

Acute effects of the volatile chemicals that are commonly abused include initial nausea with some irritation of airways causing coughing and sneezing. Low doses often bring a brief feeling of lightheadedness, mild stimulation followed by a loss of control, lack of coordination, and disorientation accompanied by dizziness and possible hallucinations. In some instances, higher doses can produce relaxation, sleep, or even coma. If inhalation is continued, dangerous **hypoxia** may occur and cause brain damage or death. In other cases, SSDS can occur. Other potential toxic consequences of inhaling such substances include hypertension and damage to the cardiac muscle, peripheral nerves, brain, and kidneys. In addition, chronic users of inhalants frequently lose their appetite, are continually tired, and experience nosebleeds. If use of inhalants persists, some of the damage may become irreversible (see "Here and Now: Chronic Solvent Abuse, Brain Abnormalities, and Cognitive Deficits").

AEROSOLS

Chemicals associated with aerosol sprays are popular among young inhalant abusers. They include spray paints, deodorant and hair sprays, vegetable oil sprays for cooking, and fabric protector sprays (National Institute on Drug Abuse [NIDA] 2012). Aerosol sprays are often abused not because of the effects produced by their principal ingredients, but rather because of the effects of their propellant gases. Inhalation of aerosol preparations can be dangerous because these devices are capable of generating very high concentrations of the inhaled chemicals, much greater than those released more slowly from liquid products.

TOLUENE

Toluene is a chemical found in some glues, paints, thinners, nail polishes, and typewriter correction fluid. It is a principal ingredient in "Texas shoe shine" (a shoe spray; NIDA 2012). Toluene is detectable in the arterial blood within 10 seconds of inhalation exposure (National Highway Traffic Safety Administration [NHTSA] n.d.). Because this molecule is highly lipid-soluble, the brain, heart, and liver rapidly absorb it. Accordingly, toluene abuse can cause brain damage. Other damage can include impaired cognition and gait disturbances. Loss of coordination, equilibrium, hearing, and vision can also occur. Liver and kidney damage have also been reported (NIDA 2012). Of note, at least one study indicates that toluene activates dopaminergic activity in the brain (NIDA 2012). The dopamine system is important for the rewarding effects of nearly all drugs of abuse.

KEY TERM

hypoxia
a state of oxygen deficiency

HERE AND NOW

Chronic Solvent Abuse, Brain Abnormalities, and Cognitive Deficits

Chronic inhalant abuse has long been associated with neurological damage and cognitive abnormalities that can range from mild impairment to severe dementia. In fact, the severity of these problems can be greater than for drugs often considered by the general population as being more harmful. For example, a 2002 report published by Neil Rosenberg of the University of Colorado Health Sciences Center found that chronic solvent abusers performed worse than chronic users of other drugs (especially cocaine and alcohol) on tests of working memory and executive function. In this study, abusers inhaled primarily vapors from spray paint containing toluene, and averaged more than 10 years of abuse. More than half of the group reported near-daily inhalant intoxication.

According to Rosenberg,

the extensive neurological damage and cognitive impairments we found among chronic solvent abusers in our study could limit their ability to control their behavior and perceive problems associated with their substance abuse. . . . Some of the

brain damage and cognitive deficits seen in both primary inhalant and cocaine abusers in the study could stem from the heavy use of alcohol that was common among both groups. . . . However, the diffuse white matter changes and abnormalities found in the thalamus have not been seen in alcohol abusers and are clearly from solvent abuse.

© AbleStock

Data from Mathias, R. "Chronic Solvent Abusers Have More Brain Abnormalities and Cognitive Impairments Than Cocaine Abusers." *NIDA Notes* 17 (4). (November 2002). Available http://archives.drugabuse.gov/NIDA_notes/NNVol17N4/Chronic.html. Accessed February 17, 2011; and Rosenberg, N. L., J. Grigsby, J. Dreisbach, D. Busenbark, and P. Grisby. "Neuropsychologic Impairment and MRI Abnormalities with Chronic Solvent Abuse." *Journal of Clinical Toxicology* 40 (2002): 21–34.

BUTANE AND PROPANE

Butane and propane are found commonly in hair and paint sprays and lighter fluid. Serious burn injuries (because of flammability) and SSDS have resulted from their abuse (NIDA 2012).

GASOLINE

Because of its widespread availability, young people, often in rural settings, sometimes abuse gasoline. Gasoline is a mixture of volatile chemicals, including toluene, benzene, and triorthocresyl phosphate (TCP). Because it is a mixture of chemicals, the intentional inhalation of gasoline can be especially dangerous. Benzene is an organic compound that causes impaired immunologic function, bone marrow injury, increased risk of leukemia, and reproductive system toxicity (NIDA 2012). TCP is a fuel additive that causes degeneration of motor neurons (Scatterday n.d.). Furthermore, gasoline is highly flammable; as with butane and propane,

fires and serious burn injuries have resulted when gasoline inhalation has been combined with smoking of marijuana, tobacco, or other drugs.

FREON

Freon and other related agents are used in a number of products including refrigerators, air conditioners, and airbrushes. Their inhalation can cause not only serious liver damage, but also SSDS (NIDA 2012). Inhaling these agents also poses other dangers; freeze injuries can occur when individuals inhaling freon lose consciousness, leaving unprotected skin in close proximity to cold. In one serious, but rare, case, a 16-year-old male attempted to get high by inhaling airbrush propellant. The patient lost consciousness. When he awoke, he discovered that his tongue and lips were frozen and that he had suffered serious burns on his larynx, vocal cords, trachea, bronchi, and esophagus (Kuspis and Krenzelok 1999).

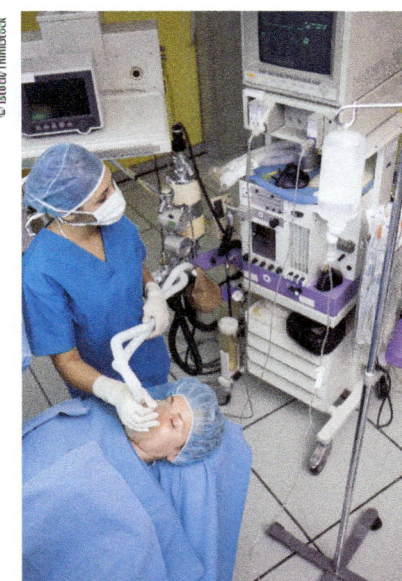

Anesthetics are an example of an inhalant.

Anesthetics ~~#30 NITRous OX.DB~~

When used properly, other forms of inhalants with abuse potential are important therapeutic agents. Included in this category are anesthetics such as ether, chloroform, halothane, and nitrous oxide. Only nitrous oxide is available widely enough to be a significant abuse concern. Nitrous oxide is a colorless gas that is used for minor outpatient procedures in offices of both physicians and dentists. It is often referred to as "laughing gas" because it can cause giggling and laughter in the patient receiving it. It is also found in products used in cars to boost octane levels (NIDA 2012). Because it is readily accessible, health professionals themselves or their staff are most likely to abuse nitrous oxide.

In addition to being found in a clinical setting, nitrous oxide can also be sold in large balloons from which the gas is released and inhaled for its mind-altering effects. It is also found in small cylindrical cartridges used as charges for whipped cream dispensers. These cylinders and other plastic containers filled with nitrous oxide are referred to as "whippets." Although significant abuse problems of nitrous oxide are infrequent, there are occasional reports of severe hypoxia (i.e., a lack of oxygen) or death due to acute overdoses. Nitrous oxide can also cause loss of sensation, limb spasms, altered perception and motor coordination, blackouts resulting from blood pressure changes, and reduced cardiac function (NIDA 2012).

Nitrites

Nitrites are chemicals that cause vasodilation. Owing to this property, the prototype of this group, amyl nitrite, has been used in the past to treat angina. Nitrites have been abused most commonly as sexual enhancers. Nitrites were first abused in the 1960s when ampules of the compound were available over the counter (OTC). The ampules were popped between the fingers (hence, the name "poppers") and held to the nostrils for inhalation.

Although the use of nitrites is now prohibited by the Consumer Product Safety Commission, they can still be obtained in small bottles labeled as "video head cleaner," "room odorizer," "leather cleaner," or "liquid aroma" (NIDA 2012). The use of amyl, and the related butyl, nitrite has decreased dramatically from an annual use among 12th graders of 6.5% in 1979 to only 0.9% in 2009; since then, the *Monitoring the Future* study (MTF; an ongoing series of national surveys of American adolescents and adults that has provided important data concerning drug usage for over 30 years; Johnston et al. 2013) has ceased to monitor usage because of this low prevalence.

Legislation

Inhalants of abuse are generally not regulated as controlled substances. However, at least 26 states have enacted laws regulating inhalant and aerosol sales and/or abuse (National Conference of State Legislatures, 2010).

Current Patterns and Signs of Abuse

Inhalants, particularly gases and aerosols, are often among the first drugs that young children misuse. The inhalants are popular for several reasons:

- They are legally obtained.
- They are readily available in most households and workplaces.
- They are inexpensive.
- They are easy to conceal.
- Most users are uninformed about the potential dangers.

In addition, inhalation is popular because it causes feelings of intoxication and euphoria much more

TABLE 14.1 Inhalant Use Among 8th, 10th, and 12th Graders

	8th Graders (%)			10th Graders (%)			12th Graders (%)		
	2010	2011	2012	2010	2011	2012	2010	2011	2012
Lifetime	14.5	13.1	11.8	12.0	10.1	9.9	9.0	8.1	7.9
Annual	8.1	7.0	6.2	5.7	4.5	4.1	3.6	3.2	2.9
30-day	3.6	3.2	2.7	2.0	1.7	1.4	1.4	1.0	0.9

Data from Johnston, L. D., P. M. O'Malley, J. G. Bachman, and J. E. Schulenberg. *Monitoring the Future: National Survey Results on Drug Use, 1975–2012. Volume I: Secondary School Students.* Ann Arbor, MI: Institute for Social Research, The University of Michigan, Ann Arbor, 2013.

rapidly than does the consumption of agents such as alcohol.

Adolescent and Teenage Usage

Adolescents most commonly use inhalants, with usage decreasing as students grow older. For example, according to the 2009 Monitoring the Future study (Johnston et al. 2013), 2.7% of 8th graders reported using inhalants within the past month, whereas only 1.4% of 10th graders and 0.9% of high school seniors reported a similar pattern of use (see **Table 14.1**). By comparison, in 2012, past-month use among college students was 0.2%. One reason for this age difference is that older individuals often view use of inhalants with disdain and consider it unsophisticated and a "kid's habit."

Lifetime inhalant use among 12th graders in 2012 was 7.9%, compared with 9.9% among 10th graders. Of considerable concern are reports that inhalant abuse can begin in very young children (Spiller and Krenzelok 1997). Researchers and poison information centers have described cases of 2- to 6-year-old children inhaling gasoline vapors. Imitation of older siblings or neighbors often accounts for this initial exposure. Hence, education efforts should be directed at very young children as well as adolescents and their parents.

Gender, Race, Socioeconomics, and Abuse

According to the 2011 National Survey on Drug Use and Health, a greater percentage of men (0.9%) than women (0.5%) age 12 or older have used an inhalant during the past year. However, that gender difference is diminishing, as evidenced by recent findings that rates of past-year inhalant use were greater among females (3.5%) than males (3.1%) ages 12 to 17. Nine percent of American Indian or Alaskan Natives ages 12–17 have abused an inhalant at least once. White, non-Hispanic; Hispanic; black or African American; and Asian individuals ages 12 to 17 abused inhalants at least once in their lifetime at rates of 6.9%, 8.6%, 7.5%, and 7.1%, respectively (SAMHSA 2012a).

Signs of Inhalant Abuse

Individuals under the influence of inhalants are often uncoordinated and disoriented and appear drunken, as if having consumed alcohol. Red and watery eyes, slurred speech, nausea, headaches, and nosebleeds are also common. Rashes around the nose and mouth or unexplained paint on the hands and mouth can be signs of inhalant abuse. Other signs include smelling a chemical odor in the room or in unusual containers (e.g., soda cans, plastic bags), finding cans of aerosol whipped cream that will not foam, or discovering air conditioners that do not work. In addition, children who are frequent users of inhalants have the following characteristics:

- Often collect an unusual assortment of chemicals (such as glues, paints, thinners and solvents, nail polish, liquid eraser, and cleaning fluids) in bedrooms or with belongings
- Have breath that occasionally smells of solvents
- Often have the sniffles similar to a cold but without other symptoms of the ailment
- Appear drunk for short periods of time (15 to 60 minutes) but recover quickly
- Do not do well in school and are often unkempt

Other signs of inhalant abuse can include the following:

- Sitting with a pen or marker near nose
- Constantly smelling clothing sleeves

- Hiding rags, clothes, or empty containers of the potentially abused products in closets, boxes, and other places
- Possessing chemical-soaked rags, bags, or socks
- Abusable household items missing

Dangers of Inhalant Abuse

The dangers of inhalant abuse stretch beyond simply the direct physical damage to the heart, lungs, liver, and brain. Other dangers can include death by choking on their own vomit or by fatal injury from accidents, including car crashes (NIDA 2012).

Use of inhalants by pregnant women also may put newborns at risk of developmental deficits. Although it is not yet possible to link prenatal exposure to specific inhalants with a specific birth defect, case reports have documented developmental abnormalities in offspring of mothers who chronically abuse inhalants (NIDA 2012).

According to NIDA (2012), many individuals who have abused inhalants for prolonged periods over many days report a strong need to continue inhalant use. A mild withdrawal syndrome and compulsive use can occur with long-term inhalant abuse.

A recent survey of 43,000 U.S. adults indicates that inhalant users, on average, initiate use of alcohol, cigarettes, and almost all other drugs at younger ages than those who don't abuse inhalants. Further, these individuals display a higher lifetime prevalence of substance use disorders, including prescription drug abuse, when compared with substance abusers without a history of inhalant use (NIDA 2012).

Of note, between 2006 and 2008, nearly 1 in 20 adolescents with at least one of four respiratory conditions (asthma, bronchitis, pneumonia, or sinusitis) also reported past-year use of an inhalant. This is significant because inhalant use may exacerbate existing medical conditions, including respiratory conditions. Still, adolescents with respiratory conditions are no less likely to use inhalants than those in the general population. Thus, continuing efforts are needed to educate individuals about the health risks of inhalant abuse (SAMHSA 2010).

LEARNING PORTFOLIO

Key Terms

Discussion Questions

1. Name the three types of inhalants and list examples of each type. List the dangerous side effects associated with the misuse of each type of inhalant.
2. Why are inhalants widely abused?
3. What is sudden sniffing death syndrome?
4. What chemical properties of inhalants make these agents particularly dangerous?
5. Who is most likely to abuse inhalants?
6. List several signs of inhalant abuse.
7. List several dangers of inhalant abuse other than the direct physical damage done by the chemical itself.

Summary

1. Inhalants are volatile substances that cause intoxicating and /or euphorigenic effects. Most were never intended to be used as drugs and are not often thought of as having abuse potential. However, inhalant abuse is a serious public health problem. Hundreds of adolescents and teenagers in the United States die or are seriously injured each year as a result of inhalant abuse. Even first-time users can die from a condition referred to as sudden sniffing death syndrome (SSDS).
2. Most inhalants are household or commercial products composed of several different fat-soluble chemicals that can act alone or synergistically to exert toxic effects. These agents can be classified into three groups: volatile substances, anesthetics, and nitrites.
3. Volatile substances include aerosols, adhesives, fuels, and household solvents. Abusers inhale vapors directly from their original containers (called sniffing or snorting), from plastic bags (called bagging), or from old rags or bandannas soaked in the solvent fluid and held over the mouth (called huffing). Abuse of these agents can cause damage to the liver, brain, kidneys, and immune system as well as SSDS.
4. Anesthetics include ether, chloroform, halothane, and nitrous oxide. When used properly, these forms of inhalants are important therapeutic agents; however, their misuse can cause severe hypoxia and death.
5. Inhalants are popular because they are legally obtained, readily available, inexpensive, and easy to conceal.
6. Inhalant abuse is typically a problem of adolescents and teenagers.
7. Signs of inhalant abuse include a drunken appearance, watery eyes, nausea, headaches, and nosebleeds. Rashes around the

nose and mouth or unexplained paint on the hands and mouth can be signs of inhalant abuse. Other signs can include smelling a chemical odor in the room or in unusual containers (e.g., soda cans, plastic bags), finding cans of aerosol whipped cream that will not foam, or discovering air conditioners that do not work.

References

Johnston, L. D., P. M. O'Malley, J. G. Bachman, and J. E. Schulenberg. *Monitoring the Future: National Survey Results on Drug Use, 1975–2012. Volume I: Secondary School Students.* Ann Arbor, MI: Institute for Social Research, University of Michigan, Ann Arbor, 2013.

Kennedy, S. K., and D. E. Longnecker. "History and Principles of Anesthesiology." In *The Pharmacological Basis of Therapeutics,* edited by A. G. Gilman, T. W. Rall, A. S. Nies, and P. Taylor, 269. New York: Pergamon Press, 1990.

Kuspis, D. A., and E. P. Krenzelok. "Oral Frostbite Injury from Intentional Abuse of a Fluorinated Hydrocarbon." *Journal of Toxicology and Clinical Toxicology* 37 (1999): 873–875.

Mathias, R. "Chronic Solvent Abusers Have More Brain Abnormalities and Cognitive Impairments Than Cocaine Abusers." *NIDA Notes.* 17 (4). (November 2002). Available http://archives.drugabuse.gov/NIDA_Notes/NNVol17N4/Chronic.html

National Conference of State Legislatures "Youth Use of Inhalants and Aerosols—State Laws 2010. 2010. Available http://www.ncsl.org/issues-research/human-services/youth-use-of-inhalants-and-aerosols-state-laws-201.aspx

National Highway Traffic Safety Administration (NHTSA). "Drug and Human Performance Fact Sheets: Toluene." Available http://www.nhtsa.gov/people/injury/research/job185drugs/toluene.htm

National Institute on Drug Abuse (NIDA). *Research Report Series: Inhalant Abuse.* NIH Pub. No. 12-3818. July 2012. Available http://www.drugabuse.gov/publications/research-reports/inhalant-abuse

Rosenberg, N. L., J. Grigsby, J. Dreisbach, D. Busenbark, and P. Grigsby. "Neuropsychologic Impairment and MRI Abnormalities with Chronic Solvent Abuse." *Journal of Clinical Toxicology* 40 (2002): 21–34.

Scatterday, R. "Commonly Abused Products and Chemical Effects." Available http://www.inhalants.org/scatter.htm

Spiller, H. A., and E. P. Krenzelok. "Epidemiology of Inhalant Abuse Reported to Two Regional Poison Centers." *Clinical Toxicology* 35 (1997): 167–173.

Substance Abuse and Mental Health Service Administration (SAMHSA). "Adolescent Inhalant Use and Selected Respiratory Conditions." 2010. Available http://oas.samhsa.gov/2k10/175/175RespiratoryCond.htm

Substance Abuse and Mental Health Services Administration (SAMHSA). *Results from the 2011 National Survey on Drug Use and Health: Detailed Tables.* Rockville, MD: 2012a.

Substance Abuse and Mental Health Services Administration (SAMHSA). *Results from the 2011 National Survey on Drug Use and Health: Volume I. Summary of National Findings.* NSDUH Series H-44, HHS Pub. No. SMA 12-4713. Rockville, MD: 2012b.

U.S. Consumer Product Safety Commission. "A Parent's Guide to Preventing Inhalant Abuse." Document #389. Available http://www.cpsc.gov/cpscpub/pubs/389gph.html

CHAPTER 15

Over-the-Counter, Prescription, and Herbal Drugs

© DNY59/iStockphoto.com

Did You Know?

▶ More than 700 of the current over-the-counter (OTC) drug products were available only by prescription 30 years ago.

▶ Pharmacists can provide useful counseling in selecting appropriate OTC products.

▶ Careless, excessive use of some OTC medications can cause addiction, physical dependence, tolerance, and withdrawal symptoms.

▶ When used together, prescription drugs or drugs of abuse can interact with OTC or herbal drugs in a dangerous and sometimes even lethal manner.

▶ Most herbal (natural) remedies are very popular products that, despite containing drugs, are available without a prescription and by law are excluded from routine OTC regulation by the FDA.

▶ More people die in the United States from adverse reactions to legal medications than succumb to all illegal drug use.

▶ There are more than 40 deaths from prescription pain killers every day in the United States.

▶ One-fifth of college students take prescription drugs to either get high or enhance their academic performance.

▶ Most generic drugs are as effective as, but substantially less expensive than, their proprietary counterparts.

Drugs and Society Online is a great source for additional drugs and society information for both students and instructors. Visit **go.jblearning.com /hanson12** to find a variety of useful tools for learning, thinking, and teaching.

Learning Objectives

On completing this chapter you will be able to:

❯ Outline the general differences between prescription and nonprescription drugs.

❯ Explain why the Food and Drug Administration (FDA) occasionally switches prescription drugs to over-the-counter (OTC) status.

❯ Describe potential abuse problems with OTC, prescription, and herbal drugs.

❯ Identify some of the drugs that have been switched to OTC.

❯ Discuss the potential problems of making more effective OTC drugs available to the public for self-care.

❯ Describe the type of information that is included on the labels of nonprescription medicines.

❯ Discuss the rules for safe use of nonprescription drugs.

❯ Determine the difference between herbal products and OTC medications.

❯ Explain why the FDA has removed ephedrine and ephedra from its list of approved OTC products.

❯ Compare problems of abuse/addiction of illicit and prescription drugs and explain why prescription abuse has become so widespread.

❯ Discuss the type of information that should be communicated between doctor and patient to avoid unnecessary drug side effects.

❯ Explain how prescription drugs should be disposed of properly.

❯ Explain the advantages and disadvantages of generic and proprietary drugs.

❯ Explain which prescription drugs are most likely to be abused and why.

Introduction

Drug costs approach 15% of overall health spending in the United States (Kaiser Family Foundation [KFF] 2010), and medication errors kill a person every day and injure approximately 1.3 million people annually by errors in prescribing, dispensing, or taking these products (Food and Drug Administration [FDA] 2009). Over-the-counter (OTC) and prescription drugs have been viewed differently by the public since these classifications were formally established by the Durham–Humphrey Amendment of 1951. In general, we view OTC medications as less effective, relatively free from side effects, and rarely abused; in contrast, we often consider prescription drugs as much more potent, typically used for more serious medical conditions, and frequently dangerous. However, distinctions between prescription and nonprescription drugs, which at one time appeared to be obvious, have become blurred by changes in public demand and federal policies. Because of escalating health costs and a growing interest in self-care, people today want access to effective medications, and governmental agencies such as the Food and Drug Administration (FDA) are responding to their demands. Consequently, the FDA has been involved in switching some 90 effective and relatively safe prescription medications to OTC status. In fact, more than 700 drug products sold OTC today were available only by prescription 30 years ago (Henderson 2012). It is estimated that these switches have saved consumers $13 billion (Henderson 2012). It is likely that in the future, other drugs will be removed from behind the pharmacist's counter and made available for public access as nonprescription medications. These changes emphasize the somewhat arbitrary nature of classifying drugs as prescription and OTC and remind us that similar care should be taken with all medications to achieve maximal benefit and minimal risk.

In this chapter, we begin by discussing OTC (nonprescription) drugs. The first topic encompasses policies regarding OTC drug regulation and is followed by a discussion of safe self-care with nonprescription drug products. Explanations of some of the most common medications in this category, including herbal (natural) remedies, conclude the section on OTC drugs. The second part of this chapter gives a general overview of prescription drugs. The consequences of misusing prescription drugs, as well as ways for you to avoid such problems, are discussed. A brief presentation of some of the most commonly prescribed drugs ends the chapter.

OTC Drugs

Each year people in the United States spend more than $18 billion on drug products that are purchased OTC, at a savings of $17 billion in health-care costs annually. Today, more than 100,000 different OTC products including more than 1000 active ingredients are available to treat everything from age spots to halitosis; they account for 60% of the annual drug purchases in this country (Henderson 2012). An estimated 60% of the population routinely self-medicate with these drug products (Henderson 2012). Some of the 80 major drug classes currently approved for OTC status are shown in **Table 15.1**.

OTC remedies are nonprescription drugs that may be obtained and used without the supervision of a physician or other health professional. Nevertheless, for some people, certain OTC products can be dangerous when used alone or in combination with other drugs. Although some OTC drugs are very beneficial in the self-treatment of minor to moderate uncomplicated health problems, others are of questionable therapeutic value, and their usefulness is often misrepresented by manufacturers.

■ Abuse of OTC Drugs

A couple of high school students from Oregon became extremely ill from overdosing on multiple boxes of cold and cough OTC products that they had shoplifted while ditching school. The students were found stumbling around in an alley near their school, disoriented and lethargic. A local secondary education official implied that the practice was routine and referred to by the local kids as "popping Skittles" because the cold medicine capsules are multicolored. Although, the consequences of abusing OTC drugs can be substantial, relatively speaking the occurrence rate is low; however, there are some notable exceptions such as cough medicines and decongestants (Martinez 2007).

Because these drugs are usually available on demand, perceived as being exceptionally safe, and poorly understood by the general public, their abuse patterns differ somewhat from those seen with the so-called hard-core drugs of abuse;

TABLE 15.1 Some Major Drug Classes Approved by the FDA for OTC Status

Drug Class	Effects
Analgesics and anti-inflammatories	Relieve pain, fever, and inflammation
Cold remedies	Relieve cold symptoms
Antihistamines and allergy products	Relieve allergy symptoms
Stimulants	Diminish fatigue and drowsiness
Sedatives and sleep aids	Promote sleep
Antacids	Relieve indigestion from rebound activity
Laxatives	Relieve self-limiting constipation
Antidiarrheals	Relieve minor, self-limiting diarrhea
Gastric secretion blockers	Relieve heartburn
Topical antimicrobials	Treat skin infections
Bronchodilators and antiasthmatics	Assist breathing
Dentifrices and dental products	Promote oral hygiene
Acne medications	Treat and prevent acne
Sunburn treatments and sunscreens	Treat and prevent skin damage from ultraviolet rays
Dandruff and athlete's foot medications	Treat and prevent specific skin conditions
Contraceptives and vaginal products	Prevent pregnancy and treat vaginal infections
Ophthalmics	Promote eye hygiene and treat eye infections
Vitamins and minerals	Provide diet supplements
Antiperspirants	Promote body hygiene
Hair growth stimulators	Promote hair growth

Data from Henderson, M. "Self-Care and Nonprescription Pharmacotherapy." In *Handbook of Nonprescription Drugs*, 17th ed., edited by D. Krinsky et al., 3–36. Washington, DC: American Pharmacists Association, 2012.

nevertheless, they can be equally harmful. Even though the OTC products generally have a greater margin of safety than their prescription counterparts, issues of abuse need to be considered. For example, many OTC drugs, when misused, can cause physical and psychological dependence. Nonprescription products that can be severely habit-forming include nasal and ophthalmic (eye) decongestants, laxatives, antihistamines, sleep aids, and antacids. Of particular abuse concern are OTC stimulants, such as ephedrine, that can be severely toxic by themselves or can be used as precursors to the synthesis of the extremely addicting and dangerous amphetamines. In fact, because of these concerns, the FDA ruled that ephedrine no longer can be included in OTC or herbal products, and most states require that cold products

containing amphetamine precursors be safeguarded behind the counter (Cunningham 2012).

Because use of OTC products is unrestricted, the patterns of abuse are impossible to determine accurately. However, these products are more likely to be abused by members of the unsuspecting general public who inadvertently become dependent due to excessive self-medication than by hard-core drug addicts who obtain the most potent drugs of abuse by illicit means.

▮ Federal Regulation of OTC Drugs

In the United States, the FDA is responsible for regulating OTC drugs through the Center for Drug Evaluation and Research (CDER). Under the direction of the FDA, the active ingredients in

OTC drugs have been, and continue to be, evaluated and classified according to their effectiveness and safety (Henderson 2012).

The FDA has attempted to make even more drugs available to the general public by switching some frequently used and safe prescription medications to OTC status. This policy is in response to public demand to have access to effective drugs for self-medication and has resulted in approximately 90 successful switches, leading to hundreds of new OTC products (Henderson 2012). This policy helps to cut medical costs by eliminating the need for costly visits to healthcare providers for treatment of minor, self-limiting ailments (Henderson 2012). A few of the more notable drugs that have been switched from prescription to nonprescription status since 1985 (Henderson 2012) are naproxen (analgesic, anti-inflammatory: Aleve); hydrocortisone (anti-inflammatory steroid: Cortaid); loperamide (antidiarrheal: Imodium); miconazole (antifungal: Monistat 7); cimetidine (heartburn medication: Tagamet); increased-strength minoxidil (hair growth stimulant: Rogaine); nicotine patch (smoking cessation aid: Nicotrol); orlistat (weight loss: Alli); lansoprazole (gastric acid reducer: Prevacid); diphenhydramine (sleep aid: Sominex); levonorgestrel (contraception: Plan B); and cetirizine (allergy: Zyrtec).

A major concern of health professionals is that reclassification of safe prescription drugs to OTC status will result in overuse or misuse of these agents. The reclassified drugs may tempt individuals to self-medicate rather than seek medical care for potentially serious health problems or encourage the use of multiple drugs at the same time, increasing the likelihood of dangerous interactions (Henderson 2012).

However, because there has been no evidence of significant problems, it is likely that effective and safe prescription drugs will continue to be made available OTC, although the rate of switching prescription drugs to OTC status does appear to be slowing.

■ OTC Drugs and Self-Care

Of the approximately 3.5 billion health problems treated in the United States annually, almost 2 billion can be treated with an OTC drug. This fact demonstrates that the public frequently engages in medical self-care with OTC products. Self-care with nonprescription medications occurs because we decide that we have a health problem that can

be adequately self-medicated without involving a health professional. Proper self-care assumes that the individual has made a correct diagnosis of the health problem and is informed enough to select the appropriate OTC product. If done correctly, self-care with OTC medications can provide significant relief from minor, self-limiting health problems at minimal cost. However, a lack of understanding about the nature of the OTC products—what they can and cannot do—and their potential side effects can result in harmful misuse. For this reason, it is important that those who consume OTC medications be fully aware of their proper use. This goal usually can be achieved by reading product labels carefully and asking questions of health professionals such as pharmacists and physicians (Henderson 2012).

OTC LABELS

Information about proper use of OTC medications is required to be cited on the drug label and is regulated by the FDA. Required label information includes (1) approved uses of the product, (2) detailed instructions on safe and effective use, and (3) cautions or warnings to those at greatest risk when taking the medication. FDA regulations require that this information be readily intelligible to the lay public and easily read (Henderson 2012) (see **Figure 15.1**). Many consumers experience adverse side effects because they either choose to ignore the warnings on OTC labels or simply do not bother to read them. For example, as previously mentioned, excessive or inappropriate use of some nonprescription drugs can cause drug dependence; consequently, people who are always dropping medication in the eyes "to get the red out" or popping antacids like dessert after every meal are likely dependent. They continue to use OTC products to avoid unpleasant eye redness or stomach acidity, which are likely withdrawal consequences of excessive use of these medications.

RULES FOR PROPER OTC DRUG USE

The OTC marketplace for drugs operates differently than does its prescription counterpart. The use of OTC drugs is not restricted, and consumers are responsible for making correct decisions about these products. Thus, to a large degree, the consumer sets policy and determines use patterns.

Because there are no formal controls over the use of OTC drugs, abuse often occurs. In extreme situations, the abuse of OTC medication can be very troublesome, even causing structural damage

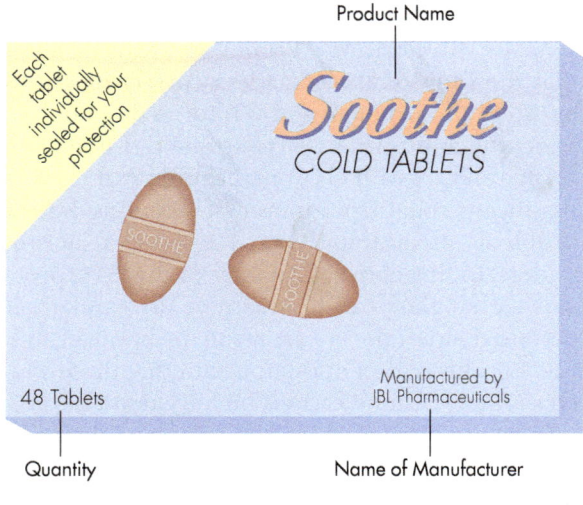

FIGURE 15.1 OTC Label. Certain information must appear on the labels of an OTC medicinal product.

to the body and, on rare occasions, death. Proper education about the pharmacological features of these agents is necessary if consumers are to make intelligent and informed decisions about OTC drug use. To reduce the incidence of problems, the following rules should be observed when using nonprescription products (Center for Drug Evaluation and Research [CDER] 2002):

- Always know what you are taking. Identify the active ingredients in the product.
- Know the effects. Be sure you know both the desired and potential undesired effects of each active ingredient.

KEY TERM

salicylates
aspirin-like drugs

- Read and heed the warnings and cautions. The warnings are not intended to scare but to protect.
- Do not use OTC drug products for more than 1 to 2 weeks. If the problem being treated persists beyond this time, consult a health professional.
- Be particularly cautious if you are also taking prescription or herbal drugs. Serious interactions between OTC drugs and these medications frequently occur. If you have a question, be sure to find out the answer.
- If you have questions, ask a pharmacist. Pharmacists are excellent sources of information about OTC drugs. They possess up-to-date knowledge of OTC products and can assist consumers in selecting correct medications for their health needs. Ask them to help you.
- Most importantly: If you don't need it, don't use it!

■ Types of OTC Drugs

It is impossible to provide a detailed description of the hundreds of active ingredients approved by the FDA for OTC distribution; however, the following includes a brief discussion of the most common OTC drugs available in the United States.

INTERNAL ANALGESICS

We spend more than $2 billion on internal (taken by mouth) analgesics, the largest sales category of OTC drugs in the United States (Henderson 2012). Most of the money is for **salicylates** (aspirin products: Anacin, Bayer), acetaminophen (Tylenol, Datril, Pamprin, Panadol), ibuprofen (Advil, Nuprin), and ibuprofen-like drugs such as naproxen (Aleve) (Wilkinson 2012). The compositions of common OTC internal analgesics are given in **Table 15.2**.

THERAPEUTIC CONSIDERATIONS

The internal analgesic products are effective in treating several common ailments (Feret 2012; Olenak 2012; Wilkinson 2012).

- *Analgesic action:* The OTC analgesics effectively relieve mild to moderate somatic pain associated with musculoskeletal structures such as bones, skin, teeth, joints, and ligaments. Pains that are relieved by the use of these drugs include headaches, toothaches, earaches, and muscle strains. In contrast, these drugs are not effective in the treatment of severe pain

TABLE 15.2 Compositions of OTC Internal Analgesics (Dose per Unit)

Product	Aspirin (mg)	Acetaminophen (mg)	Ibuprofen (mg)	Other
Bayer Aspirin	325	–	–	–
Ecotrin	325	–	–	Coated tablet
Tylenol, Children's	–	80	–	–
Advil	–	–	200	–
Motrin IB	–	–	200	–
Motrin, Children's	–	–	100	–
Aleve	–	–	–	Naproxen (220 mg)

Data from Wilkinson, J. "Headache." In *Handbook of Nonprescription Drugs,* 17th ed., edited by D. Krinsky et al., 67–86. Washington, DC: American Pharmacists Association, 2012.

or pain associated with internal organs, such as the heart, stomach, and intestines.

- *Anti-inflammatory effects:* Use of high doses (two to three times the analgesic dose) of the salicylates and ibuprofen relieves the symptoms of inflammation such as those associated with arthritis. In contrast, even high doses of acetaminophen have little **anti-inflammatory** action. Because of this anti-inflammatory effect, these drugs are frequently compared with a group of natural, very potent anti-inflammatory compounds, the steroids. To distinguish drugs such as the salicylates and ibuprofen from steroids, these drugs are often called **nonsteroidal anti-inflammatory drugs (NSAIDs)**.

- *Antipyretic effects:* The OTC analgesics, such as aspirin and acetaminophen, reduce fever but do not alter normal body temperature. Such drugs are called **antipyretics**. The frequent use of these drugs to eliminate fevers is very controversial. Some clinicians believe that low-grade fever may be a defense mechanism that helps destroy infecting microorganisms such as bacteria and viruses; thus, interfering with fevers may hamper the body's ability to rid itself of infection-causing microorganisms. Because no serious problems are associated with fevers of 102°F or less, they are probably better left unmedicated.
- *Side effects:* When selecting an OTC analgesic drug for relief of pain, inflammation, or fever, possible side effects should be considered. Although salicylates such as aspirin are frequently used, they can cause problems for both children and adults (see "Signs & Symptoms: Common Side Effects of OTC NSAIDs"). Because of their side effects, salicylates are not recommended for (1) children, because of the potential for **Reye's syndrome**; (2) people suffering from gastrointestinal problems, such as ulcers; or (3) people with bleeding problems, who are taking anticlot medication, who are scheduled for surgery, or who are near term in pregnancy, because salicylates interfere with blood clotting and prolong bleeding.

For minor aches and pains, acetaminophen substitutes adequately for salicylates, has no effect on blood clotting, and does not cause stomach irritation. In addition, acetaminophen does not influence the occurrence of Reye's syndrome, a potentially deadly complication of colds, flu, and chicken pox in children up to the age of 18 years who are using salicylates (Wilkinson 2012). However, even acetaminophen, if used in high

KEY TERMS

anti-inflammatory
relieves symptoms of inflammation

nonsteroidal anti-inflammatory drugs (NSAIDs)
anti-inflammatory drugs that do not have steroid properties

antipyretics
drugs that reduce fevers

Reye's syndrome
potentially fatal complication of colds, flu, or chicken pox in children

SIGNS & SYMPTOMS
Common Side Effects of OTC NSAIDs

Drugs	System Affected	Side Effects
Salicylates (aspirin-like)	Gastrointestinal	Can cause irritation, bleeding; aggravate ulcers
	Blood	Interfere with clotting; prolong bleeding
	Ears	Chronic high doses cause ringing (tinnitus) and hearing loss
	Pediatric	Can cause Reye's syndrome
Acetaminophen	Liver	High acute doses or chronic exposure can cause severe damage
Ibuprofen (includes other, newer NSAIDs)	Gastrointestinal	Similar to salicylates but less severe
	Blood	Similar to salicylates but less severe
	Kidneys	Damage in elderly or those with existing kidney disease

Data from Wilkinson, J. "Headache." In *Handbook of Nonprescription Drugs*, 17th ed., edited by D. Krinsky et al., 67–86. Washington, DC: American Pharmacists Association, 2012.

doses, can have serious health consequences. Concern that excessive use of acetaminophen can cause permanent and even fatal liver damage has caused the FDA to put out warnings to consumers of acetaminophen-containing products to avoid the use of high doses of this drug (Wilkinson 2012).

CAFFEINE AND OTHER ADDITIVES

A number of OTC analgesic products contain caffeine. Caffeine may relieve the negative element of pain due to its stimulant effect, which may be perceived as pleasant and energizing. The combination of caffeine with OTC analgesics may enhance pain relief (Wilkinson 2012) and be especially useful in treating vascular headaches because of the vasoconstrictive properties on cerebral blood vessels caused by this stimulant. In most OTC analgesic products—for example, Anacin or Excedrin—the amount of caffeine is less than that found in one-fourth to one-half cup of coffee (about 30 milligrams/tablet). Other ingredients—such as antacids, antihistamines, and decongestants—sometimes included in OTC pain-relieving products have little or no analgesic action and usually add little to the therapeutic value of the medication. A recent development for OTC analgesic products was FDA permission to advertise pain-relieving products effective in the relief of migraine headaches. Although these products have been found to provide relief from minor migraine headaches, they do not contain any new breakthrough drugs; these products contain previously available ingredients, such as aspirin, ibuprofen, and caffeine, just in higher doses (e.g., Migraine Extra Strength Excedrin).

COLD, ALLERGY, AND COUGH REMEDIES

More than 50% of the population routinely use OTC medicines to treat cold symptoms (Consumer Healthcare Products Association 2010). The incidence of the common cold varies with age. Children between 1 and 5 years are most susceptible; each child averages 6 to 12 respiratory illnesses per year, most of which are common colds. Individuals 25 to 30 years old average about six respiratory illnesses a year, and older adults average two or three. The declining incidence of colds with age is owing to the immunity that occurs after each infection with a cold virus; thus, if reinfected with the same virus, the microorganism is rapidly destroyed by the body's defense system and the full-blown symptoms of a cold do not occur (Scolaro 2012).

Most colds have similar general symptoms. In the first stage, the throat and nose are dry and scratchy; in the second stage, secretions accumulate in the air passages, nose, throat, and bronchial tubes. The second stage is marked by continuous sneezing, nasal obstruction, sore throat, coughing, and nasal discharge. There may be watering

TABLE 15.3 Compositions of Common OTC Cold and Allergy Products (Dose per Tablet)

Product	Sympathomimetic (mg or %)	Analgesic (mg)
Afrin	Oxymetazoline (0.05%)	—
Alka-Selzer Plus	Phenylephrine (7.8)	Aspirin (325)
Tylenol Cold	Pseudoephedrine (5)	Acetaminophen (325)
Aleve-D Sinus	Pseudoephedrine (120)	Naproxen (220)

Data from Scolaro, K. "Disorders Related to Colds and Allergies." In *Handbook of Nonprescription Drugs*, 17th ed., edited by D. Krinsky et al., 180–204. Washington, DC: American Pharmacists Association, 2012.

and redness of the eyes and pain in the face (particularly near the sinuses) and ears. One of the most bothersome symptoms of the common cold is the congestion of the mucous membranes of the nasal passages, due in part to capillary dilation, which causes these blood vessels to enlarge and become more permeable. Such vascular changes allow fluids to escape, resulting in drainage and also inflammation due to fluid-swollen tissues (Scolaro 2012).

There has been a growing problem of young people abusing these OTC products. Recent surveys suggest that up to 5.6% of high school seniors have used cough medicine with dextromethorphan to get high (Johnston 2013). This practice is sometimes referred to as *robo-tripping* or *skittling*. Common side effects include confusion, dizziness, excessive sweating, stomach pain, numbness, and blurred vision (Martinez 2007).

DECONGESTANTS

The cold and allergy products we use are principally formulated with such drugs as decongestants (sympathomimetics), antihistamines (chlorpheniramine and pheniramine), and analgesics (aspirin, acetaminophen, and naproxen). **Table 15.3** lists the ingredients found in many common OTC cold and allergy products.

Antihistamines reduce congestion caused by allergies, but their effectiveness in the treatment of virus-induced colds is controversial. In high doses, the anticholinergic action of antihistamines also decreases mucus secretion, relieving the runny nose; however, this action is probably insignificant at the lower recommended doses of OTC preparations (Scolaro 2012). An anticholinergic drying action may actually be harmful because it can lead to a serious coughing response. Due to anticholinergic effects, antihistamines also may cause dizziness, drowsiness, impaired judgment, constipation, and dry mouth; they sometimes

are abused because of psychedelic effects resulting from high-dose consumption. Because of the limited usefulness and the side effects of antihistamines for treating colds, decongestant products without such agents are usually preferred for these viral infections. In contrast, antihistamines are very useful in relieving allergy-related congestion and symptoms.

The sympathomimetic drugs used as decongestants cause nasal membranes to shrink because of their vasoconstrictive effect, which reduces the congestion caused by both colds and allergies. Such drugs can be used in the form of sprays or drops (topical decongestants) or systemically (oral decongestants) (see **Table 15.4**). FDA-approved sympathomimetics include pseudoephedrine, phenylephrine (probably the most effective topical), and oxymetazoline (Scolaro 2012). A substantial problem associated with the sympathomimetic decongestant ingredients in cold medicines is that they can easily be chemically converted into methamphetamine. For this reason the federal government passed the Combat Methamphetamine Epidemic Acts of 2005 and 2010, which require these decongestant products to be kept behind the counter and records to be

TABLE 15.4 Compositions of OTC Topical Decongestants (Drug Concentrations)

Product	Sympathomimetic
Afrin	Oxymetazoline (0.05%)
Neo-Synephrine	Phenylephrine (0.5%)
Vicks Sinex	Oxymetazoline (0.05%)

Data from Scolaro, K. "Disorders Related to Colds and Allergies." In *Handbook of Nonprescription Drugs*, 17th ed., edited by D. Krinsky et al., 180–204. Washington, DC: American Pharmacists Association, 2012.

The common cold accounts for 20% of all acute illnesses in the United States.

kept of those who purchase these medications (see "Here and Now: Fighting the 'Common Cold' Pills"). In addition to the federal laws, many states have also passed their own statutes to regulate the sale of precursors used to make methamphetamine. The control varies from state to state, and many of these local laws are more rigid than the federal regulations (Rickert 2012).

Someone using decongestant nasal sprays frequently can experience **congestion rebound** due to tissue dependence. After using a nasal spray regularly for longer than the recommended period of time, the nasal membranes adjust to the effect of the vasoconstrictor and become very congested when the drug is not present. One can become hooked and use the spray more and more with less and less relief until one's tissues no longer respond and the sinus passages become almost completely obstructed (Scolaro 2012). Allergists

frequently see new patients who are addicted to nasal decongestant sprays and are desperate for relief from congestion. This problem can be prevented by using nasal sprays sparingly and for no longer than the recommended time.

Orally ingested sympathomimetic drugs give less relief from congestion than the topical medications but are less likely to cause rebound effects. In contrast, systemic administration of these drugs is more likely to cause cardiovascular problems (that is, stimulate the heart, cause arrhythmia, increase blood pressure, and cause stroke).

ANTITUSSIVES

Other drugs used to relieve the common cold are intended to treat coughing. The cough reflex helps clear the lower respiratory tract of foreign matter, particularly in the later stages of a cold. There are two types of cough: productive and nonproductive. A *productive cough* removes mucus secretions and foreign matter so that breathing becomes easier and the infection clears up. A *nonproductive, or dry, cough* causes throat irritation; this type of cough is of little cleansing value. Some types of cough suppressant (antitussive) medication are useful for treating a nonproductive cough but should not be used to suppress a productive cough (Tietze 2012).

Two kinds of OTC preparations are available to treat coughing:

- **Antitussives**—such as codeine, dextromethorphan, and diphenhydramine (an antihistamine)—that act on the central nervous system (CNS) to raise the threshold of the cough-coordinating center, thereby reducing the frequency and intensity of a cough
- **Expectorants**—such as guaifenesin and terpin hydrate—which theoretically (but not very effectively) increase and thin the fluids of the respiratory tract in an attempt to soothe the irritated respiratory tract membranes and decrease the thickness of the accumulated secretions so that coughing becomes more productive

Table 15.5 lists commonly used OTC antitussives and their compositions. Often, the tickling sensation in the throat that triggers a cough can be eased by sucking on a cough drop or hard candy, which stimulates saliva flow to soothe the irritated membranes. Unless the cough is severe, sour hard candy often works just as well as more expensive cough lozenges.

KEY TERMS

congestion rebound

withdrawal from excessive use of a decongestant, resulting in congestion

antitussives

drugs that block the coughing reflex

expectorants

substances that stimulate mucus secretion and diminish mucus viscosity

HERE AND NOW

Fighting the "Common Cold" Pills

It is becoming harder and harder to get those pills we all buy to fight the common cold. This problem is not because drugs like Sudafed are themselves particularly addicting; rather, the concern arises because of what they can become, and this is leading to the imposition of tighter controls on these popular decongestants. Because ingredients in OTC cold medicines, such as pseudoephedrine, can easily be converted into methamphetamine, these products have been bought in large quantities to be used in makeshift meth labs across the country. As a result, law enforcement agencies and even Congress itself have pointed out these drugs' potential dangers. Besides requiring that these OTC products be kept behind the counter in pharmacies, there have been attempts to pass local and national legislation to limit purchases of these drugs to about 9 grams (roughly 300 pills) in a 30-day period. This quantity of pseudoephedrine can be turned into approximately 25 doses of methamphetamine. Such restrictions have made it difficult, although not impossible, for small neighborhood meth labs to cook their dangerous brew. However, as the local "mom-and-pop" domestic producers have been significantly curtailed, Mexican drug cartels have filled the gap with large

© Reuters/STR/Landov

quantities of methamphetamine manufactured in Mexico and smuggled across the border. The cartels are using dummy corporations and false labeling to bring ordinary cold, flu, and allergy medicines into Mexico from China, India, and Bangladesh and converting the ingredients from these common decongestants into large quantities of methamphetamine for illicit sale. Despite efforts by both the Mexican and U.S. governments, these trafficking groups are very resilient, keeping ahead of the law, and have become the primary source for illegal U.S. methamphetamine.

Data from Reuters Health. "Bill Would Restrict Cold Pills to Fight 'Meth.'" 27 January 2005; and Booth, W., and A. O'Connor. "Mexican Cartels Emerge as Top Source for U.S. Meth." *Washington Post.* 28 November 2010. Available http://www.washingtonpost.com/wp-dyn/content/article/2010/11/23/AR2010112303703.html?sid=ST2010112303730. Accessed March 29, 2011.

TABLE 15.5 Compositions of Common OTC Antitussives

Product	Antitussive	Expectorant
Delsym	Dextromethorphan	—
Humibid	—	Guaifenesin
Vicks Cough Drops	—	Guaifenesin
Robitussin DM Cough	Dextromethorphan	Guaifenesin

Data from Scolaro, K. "Disorders Related to Colds and Allergies." In *Handbook of Nonprescription Drugs*, 17th ed., edited by D. Krinsky et al., 180–204. Washington, DC: American Pharmacists Association, 2012.

Cough remedies, like other medications, have a psychological value. Many patients with respiratory tract infections claim they cough less after using cough remedies, even when it is objectively demonstrated that the remedies reduce neither the frequency nor the intensity of the cough. Cough remedies work in part by reducing patients' anxiety about the cough and causing them to believe that their cough is lessening. If one believes in the remedy, one often can get as much relief from a simple, inexpensive product as from the most sophisticated and costly one. If a cough does not ease in a few days, one should consult a doctor (Tietze 2012).

As mentioned earlier, abuse of antitussive products by teenagers is a significant problem in some regions of this country. This abuse likely relates to the fact that in high doses the antitussive ingredient dextromethorphan can have a phencyclidine (PCP)–like effect (see "Here and Now: The Dextromethorphan Trip"). Up to 10% of young people use high doses of antitussives that contain dextromethorphan to get high (Colliver 2011; Leong 2010). Even though possession of cough medicines is not controlled, the National Institute on Drug Abuse advises parents to control access to cough and cold medications at home to prevent this potential problem (Mitchell 2010).

WHAT REALLY WORKS?

With all the advances in medicine today, there is still no cure for the common cold. In most cases, the best treatment is plenty of rest, increased fluid intake to prevent dehydration and to facilitate productive coughing, humidification of the air if it is dry, gargling with diluted salt water (2 teaspoons per quart), an analgesic to relieve the accompanying headache or muscle ache, and perhaps an occasional decongestant if nasal stuffiness is unbearable. Allergy symptoms, in contrast, are best relieved by antihistamines.

SLEEP AIDS

In 1995, an estimated 49% of the U.S. population experienced insomnia (the inability to fall asleep or stay asleep) at least 5 nights each month (Gill 1999). About 1% of the adult population routinely self-medicate their insomnia with OTC sleep aids that are advertised as inducing a "safe and restful sleep." Described as nonbarbiturate and non–habit forming, these low-potency products are frequently misused (Kirkwood and Melton 2012).

HERE AND NOW

The Dextromethorphan Trip

Dextromethorphan is the antitussive ingredient frequently found in nonprescription cough medicine. Because of pharmacological properties that resemble those of PCP, OTC cough medicines are sometimes abused by teenagers. One such person, who had consumed almost an entire bottle of a popular anticough product, described his experience. He related that the effects of the drug hit first with lightheadedness and slight disorientation. After 1 hour, the disorientation became severe. He explained that it felt as though he were outside of himself looking in. The hallucinations were somewhat subtle with things appearing grainy and distorted. He found that breathing was sometimes constricted, as though he were wearing a tight shirt collar. Then came hot flashes, which caused him to turn on a fan to cool down. He found walking was difficult, and time became distorted. The trip lasted 1 to 2 hours for the strong effects, but it seemed to continue forever. This person was an experienced user of acid (LSD) and mushrooms, but he had never been on a trip as scary as the one with the cough medicine. Several times he thought he was going to die. He found that coming down took a while. He decided that he would never do "dex" (dextromethorphan) again. Because of such side effects, these antitussive products are not considered to be especially addicting, although in 2008 there were about 8000 visits to emergency departments in the United States due to abuse of these OTC medications, a number almost twice that reported in 2004. Despite concern for this trend, for now the FDA has decided not to restrict dextromethorphan-containing OTC antitussive products as prescription medicines. A panel of medical experts recommended against such an action because they felt that the reduced availability of these cough medicines would do more harm than good.

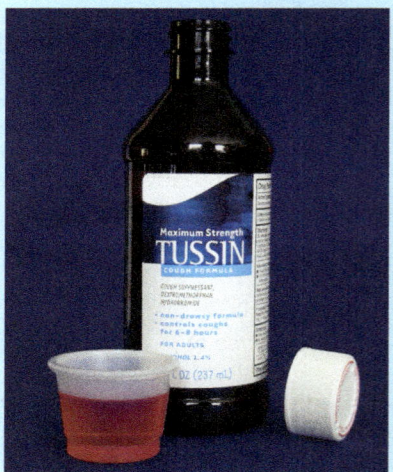

Data from Allen, J. "Over-the-Counter Cough Medicines Escape FDA Restrictions." ABC Good Morning America. 14 September 2010. Available http://abcnews.go .com/Health/Wellness/dextromethorphan-ingredient-robitussin-cough-medicines-escapes-fda-restrictions/story?id=11638160. Accessed March 16, 2011.

For example, the parents of a young child were traveling cross-country. They knew the trip would be long and the child would likely grow tired and cranky. To keep the child quiet and manageable, the parents used Benadryl, an allergy medication, which contains an antihistamine to cause sedation (personal communication to Hanson 2010). Use of these products in young children is inappropriate and can be dangerous because their response is unpredictable. The drugs commonly used in OTC sleep aids are antihistamines, particularly diphenhydramine (Kirkwood and Melton 2012). Although antihistamines have been classified as OTC category I sleep aid ingredients, their usefulness in treating significant sleep disorders is highly questionable (Kirkwood and Melton 2012). At best some people who suffer mild, temporary sleep disturbances caused by problems such as physical discomfort, short-term disruption in daily routines (such as jet lag), and extreme emotional upset might experience temporary relief. However, even for those few who initially benefit from these agents, tolerance develops within 4 days. For long-term sleep problems, OTC sleep aids are of no therapeutic value and are rarely recommended by health professionals. Actually, their placebo benefit is likely more significant than their actual pharmacological benefit. Usually counseling and psychotherapy are more effective approaches for resolving chronic insomnia than OTC or even prescription sleep aid drugs (Kirkwood and Melton 2012).

Because antihistamines are CNS depressants, in low doses they can cause sedation and antianxiety action. Although in the past, some OTC products containing antihistamines were promoted for their relaxing effects (e.g., Quietworld, Compoz), currently, no sedatives are approved for OTC marketing. The FDA decided that the earlier products relieved anxiety by causing drowsiness, so, in fact, they were not legitimate sedatives. Because of this ruling, medications that are promoted as antianxiety products are no longer available without a prescription. However, antihistamines have been added to an array of other OTC drug products marketed for the purpose of causing relaxation or promoting sleep; such products include analgesics (e.g., Excedrin PM), cold medicines (e.g., Tylenol Cold Multisymptom Nighttime), Midol Complete, and many others (Kirkwood and Melton 2012; Scolaro 2012; Shimp 2012). The rationale for such combinations is questionable, and their therapeutic value unsubstantiated.

MELATONIN

The hormone melatonin is currently being used by millions to induce sleep or to help the body's natural clock readjust after the effects of jet lag. Melatonin was referred to as the "all-natural nightcap of the 1990s." Although most users of this hormone want assistance in falling asleep, some people claim that melatonin also slows the aging process, stimulates the immune system, and enhances the sex drive. Melatonin is a naturally occurring hormone, also found in some foods. Under the 1994 Dietary Supplement and Education Act, melatonin is considered a dietary supplement and is not regulated by the FDA. Despite the popularity of melatonin products, the efficacy of supplemental melatonin as a sleep aid or to help with jet lag is not proven (McQueen and Orr 2012). Products containing melatonin should be used cautiously, if at all (van den Heuval et al. 2005).

STIMULANTS

Some OTC drugs are promoted as stay-awake (e.g., NoDoz) or energy-promoting (e.g., Vivarin) products (Kirkwood and Melton 2012). In general, these medications contain high doses of caffeine (100–200 milligrams per tablet). Although it is true that CNS stimulation by ingesting significant doses of caffeine can increase the state of alertness during periods of drowsiness, the repeated use of such an approach is highly suspect.

For example, college students sometimes rely on such products to repeatedly enhance mental endurance during cramming sessions for examinations. In fact, at one western U.S. university, the back page of a quarterly class schedule, printed and distributed by the university, included a full-page advertisement for the OTC stimulant Vivarin with the caption, "Exam Survival Kit." The implications of such promotions are obvious and disturbing. Due to the objections of the faculty, the advertisement was not run again at the university.

Routine use of stay-awake or energy-promoting products to enhance performance at work or in school can lead to dependence, resulting in withdrawal when the person stops using the drug. Most health professionals agree that there are more effective and safer ways to deal with fatigue and drowsiness—for example, managing time efficiently and getting plenty of rest (Kirkwood and Melton 2012).

SYMPATHOMIMETICS

Mild OTC sympathomimetics have been marketed as safe stimulants and as legal alternatives to cocaine and other illicit stimulants. The principal ingredients found in the mild stimulants are drugs such as phenylephrine and caffeine. The same drugs are also found in OTC decongestants and diet aids (Miller and Bartels 2012; Scolaro 2012). Ephedrine, a naturally occurring stimulant (i.e., from the ephedra plant), and phenylpropanol-amine were withdrawn from OTC use due to their potential toxicity on the cardiovascular system (Miller and Bartels 2012).

Although much less potent than amphetamines, when used in high doses, the OTC stimulants can cause anxiety, restlessness, throbbing headaches, breathing problems, and tachycardia (rapid heartbeat). There have been reports of death due to heart arrhythmia, cerebral hemorrhaging, and strokes, as discussed earlier from excessive ephedrine use.

GASTROINTESTINAL MEDICATIONS

The gastrointestinal (GI) system consists principally of the esophagus, stomach, and intestines and is responsible for the absorption of nutrients and water into the body, as well as the elimination of body wastes. The function of the GI system can be altered by changes in eating habits, stress, infection, and diseases such as ulcers and cancers. Such problems may affect appetite, cause discomfort or pain, result in nausea and vomiting, and alter the formation and passage of stools from the intestines.

A variety of OTC medications is available to treat GI disorders such as indigestion (antacids), heartburn (gastric secretion blockers), constipation (laxatives), and diarrhea (antidiarrheals) (Zweber and Berardi 2012). However, before individuals self-medicate with nonprescription drugs, they should be certain that the cause of their GI problem is minor, is self-limiting, and does not require professional care. Because antacids are the most frequently used of the GI nonprescription drugs, they are discussed next.

ANTACIDS AND ANTIHEARTBURN MEDICATION

More than $1 billion is spent annually on antacid preparations that claim to give relief from heartburn and indigestion caused by excessive eating or

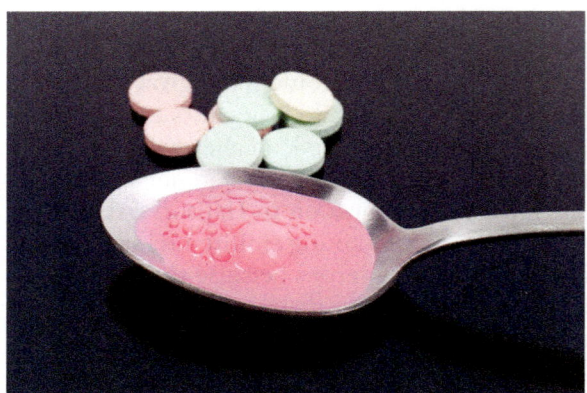

More than $1 billion is spent each year on antacid products such as this in the United States.

drinking and to provide long-term treatment of chronic peptic ulcer disease. It is estimated that as much as 50% of the population has had one or more attacks of **gastritis**, often referred to as "acid indigestion, heartburn, upset stomach, and sour or acid stomach." These attacks are often due to acid rebound, occurring 1 to 2 hours after eating; by this time, the stomach contents have passed into the small intestine, leaving the gastric acids to irritate or damage the lining of the empty stomach. Heartburn, or gastroesophageal reflux, occurs after exposure of the lower esophagus to these very irritating gastric chemicals.

Some cases of severe, chronic acid indigestion may progress to peptic ulcer disease. Peptic ulcers (open sores) most frequently affect the duodenum (first part of the intestine) and the stomach. Although this condition is serious, it can be treated effectively with antacids, which are often combined with drugs available OTC or by prescription such as cimetidine (Tagamet), ranitidine (Zantac), and famotidine (Pepcid). A person with acute, severe stomach pain; chronic gastritis; blood in the stools (common ulcer symptoms); diarrhea; or vomiting should see a physician promptly and should not attempt to self-medicate with OTC antacids (Zweber and Berardi 2012).

Most bouts of acid rebound, however, are associated with overeating or consuming irritating foods or drinks; these self-limiting cases can usually be managed safely with OTC antacids (such as sodium bicarbonate, calcium carbonate, aluminum salts, and magnesium salts). Because of their alkaline (opposite of acidic) nature, the nonprescription products neutralize gastric acids and give relief.

Generally speaking, OTC antacid preparations are safe for occasional use at low recommended doses, but excessive use can cause serious problems.

KEY TERM

gastritis
inflammation or irritation of the gut

In addition, all antacids can interact with other drugs; they may alter the GI absorption or renal elimination of other medications. For example, some antacids inhibit the absorption of tetracycline antibiotics; thus, these products should not be taken at the same time. Consequently, patients using prescription drugs should consult with their physicians before taking OTC antacids (Zweber and Berardi 2012).

Heartburn can be treated effectively with low doses of Tagamet, Zantac, or Pepcid. These drugs were switched to OTC status in the mid-1990s and help reduce gastric secretions (Zweber and Berardi 2012).

DIET AIDS

In U.S. society, being slim and trim are prerequisites to being attractive. It is estimated that approximately 34% of the people in the United States are obese (body fat in excess of 20% of normal) and 50% are overweight (Stobbe 2011). Being obese has been linked to cardiovascular disease, some cancers, diabetes, chronic fatigue, and an array of aches and pains, not to mention psychological disorders such as depression (Miller and Bartels 2012). Popular remedies for losing weight often include fad diets advertised in supermarket journals, expensive weight loss programs, or both prescription and OTC diet aids.

Using drugs as diet aids is highly controversial (Miller and Bartels 2012). Most experts view them as useless or even dangerous. These drugs are supposed to depress the appetite, which helps users maintain low-calorie diets. The most effective of these agents are called **anorexiants**. Potent anorexiants, such as amphetamine-like drugs (including the once-popular diet aid, Phen-fen), can cause dangerous side effects and are available only by prescription. The appetite suppression effects of prescription anorexiants are usually temporary, after which tolerance often builds. Thus, even prescription diet aid drugs are usually effective for only a short period. There are no wonder drugs to help the obese lose weight permanently.

The most potent and most frequently used OTC diet aid ingredients were the sympathomimetic drugs phenylpropanolamine and ephedrine, but several years ago the FDA removed both drugs from all OTC products (About.com 2010). The current OTC diet aids are minimally effective and of no value in the treatment of significant obesity; they typically contain high doses of caffeine and sometimes natural ingredients such as "bitter orange,"

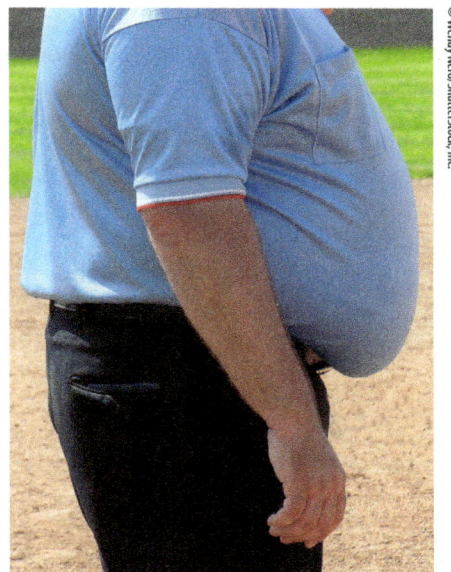

Approximately 25% to 30% of the people in the United States are obese and 50% are overweight.

which contains the mild sympathomimetic, synephrine. Despite their minimal value, frequent use of high doses of the OTC diet aid products is a common practice by weight-conscious female high school and college students. As one college sophomore who routinely carried a package of Dexatrim in her purse said, "Popping two or three of these before an important date helps me to eat like a bird and appear more petite" (personal communication to Hanson). Interestingly, this same woman also occasionally induced vomiting after eating because of her fear that she was gaining weight. Such weight-management practices are extremely worrisome and may be part of strategies of young people suffering from eating disorders such as anorexia and bulimia (Life Challenges 2010).

SKIN PRODUCTS

Because the skin is so accessible and readily visible, most people are sensitive about its appearance. These cosmetic concerns are motivated by attempts to look good and preserve youth. Almost 5% of the population in the United States have a chronic skin problem; many others suffer from seasonal or acute skin disorders (Scott and

KEY TERM

anorexiants
drugs that suppress the activity of the brain's appetite center, causing reduced food intake

Martin 2006). Only a few of the most commonly used products are mentioned here: acne medications, sun products, and basic first-aid products.

ACNE MEDICATIONS

Acne is the most common skin disorder that affects adolescents (Foster and Coffrey 2012) and typically occurs during puberty in response to the secretion of the male hormone androgen (both males and females have this hormone; Foster and Coffrey 2012). Acne is usually chronic inflammation caused by bacteria trapped in plugged sebaceous (oil) glands and hair follicles. This condition consists of whiteheads, pimples, nodules, and, in more severe cases, pustules, cysts, and abscesses. Moderate to severe acne can cause unsightly scarring on the face, back, chest, and arms and should be treated aggressively by a dermatologist with drugs such as antibiotics (tetracycline) and potent **keratolytics**, such as Retin-A (retinoic acid) or vitamin A, or Accutane (isotretinoin). Usually, minor to moderate acne does not cause scarring or permanent skin damage and often can be safely self-medicated with OTC acne medications (Foster and Coffrey 2012).

Several nonprescription approaches to treating mild acne are available, including the following:

- *Sebum removal:* Oil and fatty chemicals (sebum) can accumulate on the skin and plug the sebaceous glands and hair follicles. Use of OTC products such as alcohol wipes (e.g., Stri-Dex) can help remove such accumulations.
- *Peeling agents:* The FDA found several keratolytic agents safe and effective for treatment of minor acne: benzoyl peroxide (Oxy 10 Daily Wash), salicylic acid (Neutrogena Rapid Defense), resorcinol, and sulfur (DDF Sulfur), alone or in combination. These drugs help to prevent acne eruption by causing the **keratin layer** of the skin to peel or by killing the bacteria that cause inflammation associated with acne. If multiple concentrations of a keratolytic are available, it is better to start

with a lower concentration and move up to the higher one, allowing the skin to become accustomed to the caustic action of these products. The initial exposure may worsen the appearance of acne temporarily; however, with continual use, the acne usually improves.

SUN PRODUCTS

The damaging effects of sun exposure on the skin have been well publicized in recent years. It is now clear that the ultraviolet (UV) rays associated with sunlight have several adverse effects on the skin. It has been demonstrated that almost 2 million cases of skin cancer each year occur in the United States, most of which are a direct consequence of exposure to UV rays, which causes cumulative skin damage throughout our lives (Crosby and O'Neal 2012).

The majority of cases will be cancers of skin cells called basal cell or squamous cell carcinomas (Crosby and O'Neal 2012). These cancers usually are easily removed by minor surgery, and patients have a good prognosis for recovery. About 0.5% of the population will suffer a much more deadly 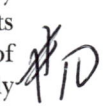 form of skin cancer called *melanoma*. Melanomas are cancers of the pigment-forming cells of the skin, called *melanocytes*, and spread rapidly from the skin throughout the body, causing death in 20% to 25% of patients (Crosby and O'Neal 2012). Almost 10,000 deaths occur from skin cancer each year, most of which are melanomas (Crosby and O'Neal 2012).

Another long-term concern related to UV exposure is premature aging. Skin frequently exposed to UV rays, such as during routine tanning, experiences deterioration associated with the aging process. Elastin and collagen fibers are damaged, causing a loss of pliability and elasticity in the skin and resulting in a leathery, wrinkled appearance (Crosby and O'Neal 2012).

Because of these damaging effects of sun exposure, an array of protective sunscreen products is available OTC. Most sunscreens are formulated to screen out the shorter UVB rays. Due to their deep penetration in the skin, the longer UVA rays likely contribute to melanoma as well as chronic skin damage, causing skin to wrinkle, sag, and lose tone; consequently, many of the newer sunscreens block the UVA rays as well (Crosby and O'Neal 2012).

The protection afforded by sunscreens is designated by an **SPF (sun protection factor) number**. This designation tells users the relative length of time they can stay in the sun before burning, and includes ratings of 2 to 11 (minimum), 12 to 30

KEY TERMS

keratolytics
caustic agents that cause the keratin skin layer to peel

keratin layer
outermost protective layer of the skin

SPF (sun protection factor) number
designation to indicate a product's ability to screen ultraviolet rays

(moderate), and greater than 30 (high) (Crosby and O'Neal 2012). For example, proper application of a product with an SPF of 10 allows users to remain in the sun without burning 10 times longer than if it was not applied. It is important to remember that the SPF designation does not indicate protection against UVA rays. Although there currently is no convenient rating system to assess UVA screening, products with SPF ratings of 15 or greater usually offer some protection against the longer UV radiation. In addition, a compound called avobenzone appears to offer the fullest protection against UVA rays (Crosby and O'Neal 2012). Because the natural pigment in the skin affords some UV protection, people with fair complexions (less skin pigmentation) require products with higher SPF numbers than do dark-skinned people.

People who want complete protection from UVB exposure can use OTC sunblockers, which prevent any tanning. Sunscreen ingredients in high concentrations essentially become sunblockers. In addition, an opaque zinc oxide ointment is a highly effective and inexpensive sun-blocking product and is available OTC.

SKIN FIRST-AID PRODUCTS

A variety of unrelated OTC drugs are available as first-aid products for the self-treatment of minor skin problems, such as burns, sunburns, and wounds (Bernard 2012). Included in this category of agents are the following products:

- Local anesthetics, such as benzocaine (e.g., Dermoplast) to relieve the discomfort and pain of burns or trauma
- Antibiotics and antiseptics, such as bacitracin (Polysporin), neomycin (Neosporin), betadine, and tincture of iodine to treat or prevent skin infections
- Antihistamines (Benadryl) or corticosteroids (hydrocortisone [Cortaid]) to relieve itching or inflammation associated with skin rashes, allergies, or insect bites

These first-aid skin products can be effective when used properly. In general, side effects to such topical products are few and minor when they occur.

■ OTC Herbal (Natural) Products

There are over 5000 brands of herbal medicines currently available in the United States and other countries with approximately 1000 active ingredients (National Library of Medicine 2010). Fish oil,

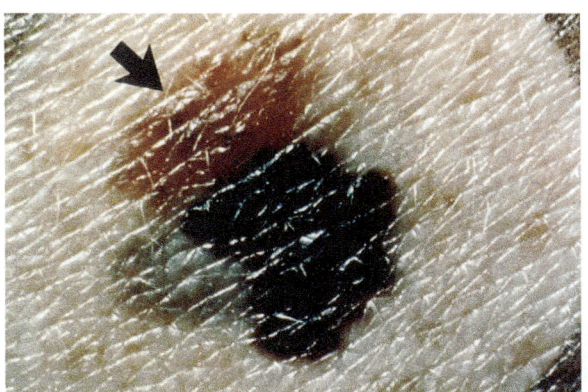

This skin cancer is melanoma and is caused by excessive exposure to ultraviolet light.

glucosamine, echinacea, flaxseed products, and ginseng are the most frequently used by adults (McQueen and Orr 2012). Herbal products are a unique category of OTC remedies that account for almost $5 billion a year in U.S. sales (Nutraceuticals World 2011). They are unique because, despite the presence of active ingredients, there is little or no federal regulation due to a 1994 law, supported by the dietary supplement industry, called the Dietary Supplement Health and Education Act (National Library of Medicine 2010). This law requires the government to demonstrate that substances in the herbal products are harmful before such products can be removed from the market; the burden of proof lies with the FDA, not the manufacturer (Rickert 2012).

This act also (1) makes the manufacturer responsible for its product's safety; (2) explains how product literature is used for product promotion; and (3) describes what can be included on labels. Due to these regulations, manufacturers cannot use terms such as *diagnose, treat, prevent,* or *cure* to describe their herbal products. Companies can, however, make claims about affecting body function. For example, manufacturers of glucosamine cannot claim their product helps cure arthritis, but they can say products with glucosamine help the joints function better (National Library of Medicine 2010). Because of the lack of regulation, these products often are not scientifically tested, and they vary considerably in both the quantity and quality of active ingredients (National Library of Medicine 2010). Herbal products have been viewed with considerable skepticism by many experts who argue that "assertions, speculation and testimonials do not substitute for evidence" when it comes to establishing the value of a drug (McQueen and Orr 2012).

Herbal products have become very popular and widely accepted.

In the past few years, some changes in attitude toward herbal products have occurred. More people, including a few traditional health professionals, believe that some herbs may be useful in the treatment of minor health problems (McQueen and Orr 2012). However, physicians are typically not taught about herbal medicines in medical school and are generally perceived as being ignorant about herbal products and knowing little about their therapeutic value or their ability to interact with prescribed drugs (Medical News Today 2010). Despite greater acceptance, the fact that most people who use herbs to treat medical conditions still consider prescription drugs to be considerably more effective suggests there exists persistent skepticism regarding these products, even among consumers (Lampert 2013).

Frequent uses of herbal products include treatment of anxiety, chronic fatigue, arthritis, and digestive problems (McQueen and Orr 2012). Another common use of these natural products is to elevate mood. The most popular herbs for these purposes are St. John's wort, S-adenosylmethionine (SAM-e), and kava kava (Hume and Strong 2006; Williams et al. 2005) (see "Here and Now: Herbal Options"). It is generally thought that although these products do have some effect in the treatment of minor to moderate depression and anxiety, there is no evidence they elevate a normal, undisturbed mood or that they are particularly effective against severe mood disturbances (National Center for Complementary and Alternative Medicine [NCCAM] 2013). A major risk of self-administering these remedies for mood disorders is that some of the people self-treating their depression are severely emotionally unstable. Overall, depression leads to approximately 20,000 suicides in this country each year. Another considerable problem of self-medicating with herbal products for mood disorders is the lack of standardization for these substances. A recent survey revealed that the actual amount of active SAM-e per pill in products claiming to contain 200 mg of active ingredient ranged from 80 to 250 mg. For these reasons, it is almost universally recommended that patients with serious emotional disturbances, especially depression, be diagnosed by a mental health professional even though some of these professionals may find use of the natural products to be acceptable for treatment of mild emotional problems.

HERE AND NOW

Herbal Options

With the increasing popularity of herbal products, an array of choices has become available for dealing with many common, usually self-limiting health problems. The following is a list of some of the most popular of these medicinal herbs.

Echinacea

Common Claim: Stimulates immune system and helps fight infections.

Common Use: Reduce cold symptoms and help accelerate recovery.

Effectiveness: May shorten the duration of a cold, but does not prevent it; however, even this is controversial.

Concerns: Relatively well tolerated, but fatigue and sleepiness occasionally occur.

Garlic

Common Claim: Inhibits production of cholesterol and reduces blood sugar.

Common Use: Treat diabetes and prevent cardiovascular disease.

Effectiveness: Most studies do not find garlic effective against serious diseases.

Concerns: Mild stomach discomfort and possible interaction with blood-thinning (anticlotting) prescription drugs occur.

Ginkgo Biloba

Common Claim: Improves memory.

Common Use: Often promoted to enhance memory for patients with Alzheimer's disease.

Effectiveness: At best helps to prevent some mental decline in Alzheimer's patients but does not appear to reverse memory loss or help normal or age-related memory losses.

Concerns: Can interact with blood-thinning medications such as aspirin.

Glucosamine and Chondroitin

Common Claim: Contributes to joint strength.

Common Use: Relieve the discomfort of arthritis.

Effectiveness: Provides moderate relief from the pain of arthritis and may help to slow progress of the disease.

Concerns: May interact with blood thinners and adversely affect adult-onset diabetes.

Saw Palmetto

Common Claim: Relieves discomforts associated with prostate gland.

Common Use: Shrink enlarged prostate and facilitate urination.

Effectiveness: Provides relief for most men within a month of use.

Concerns: Well tolerated by most men.

SAM-e

Common Claim: Helps regulate brain transmitters such as dopamine.

Common Use: Relieve symptoms of depression.

Effectiveness: Some evidence that it relieves moderate depression.

Concerns: Side effects are typically mild, such as stomach upset, insomnia, and nervousness. Can be very expensive, ranging from $55 to $260 per month.

St. John's Wort

Common Claim: Elevates mood.

Common Use: Treat mild to moderate depression.

Effectiveness: Appears to relieve some cases of mild depression for the short term.

Concerns: Recent alert from the FDA warns about interactions with numerous medications, such as birth-control pills and other antidepressants.

Ginseng

Common Claim: Increases energy.

Common Use: Treat fatigue and enhance performance.

Effectiveness: There may be some mild stimulation, but there is no evidence of enhanced performance.

Concerns: Well tolerated for the most part, although there are some reports of minor addiction.

Data from McQueen, C., and K. Orr. "Natural Products." In *Handbook of Nonprescription Drugs*, 17th ed., edited by D. Krinsky, 967–1006. Washington, DC: American Pharmacists Association, 2012; and National Center for Complementary and Alternative Medicine (NCCAM). "Herbs at a Glance." 10 June 2013. Available http://nccam.nih.gov/health/herbsataglance.htm

Other concerns with herbal products include the possibility of interaction with other OTC and prescription medications, especially in the elderly population (NCCAM 2013). This is becoming more problematic as the routine use of herbs becomes common, especially because unscrupulous manufacturers may deceive customers into thinking that these products are perfectly safe and do not really contain any drugs but "only natural ingredients." Products containing herbs such as garlic, ginkgo biloba, and ginseng have been shown to interact with some drugs (Fugh-Berman 2000). A notable example of drug interactions has been reported with St. John's wort and kava, which increase the metabolism and inactivate drugs used to treat heart failure, asthma, infections, or blood clots (Fugh-Berman 2000; McQueen and Orr 2012).

Finally, lack of regulation has encouraged such a lackadaisical attitude concerning herbs that their use has been trivialized to the extent that they and their associated active drugs are now being included in foods and marketed in both health-food stores and supermarkets. Recent snacks, cereals, and beverages spiked with medicinal herbs include ginseng ginger ale, kava kava corn chips, echinacea fruit drinks, and ginkgo biloba chocolate bars. These products, sometimes referred to as "functional foods," are typically packaged in colorful containers with cartoon figures that are likely to appeal to kids and accompanied by subtle suggestive promotions implying that they can "support emotional and mental balance." The exact quantities of herbal substances added to such food and snack products and their actual effects (if any) are difficult to monitor. Although concerned, regulatory agencies are uncertain as to how to deal with the potential problems associated with this marketing strategy (Brophy and Schardt 2010).

HERBALS AND ABUSE

Despite the lack of governmental control, drugs found naturally in plants or herbs can have serious side effects or can be abused. In fact, some of the most powerful substances of abuse are extracted from plants, including drugs such as cocaine (*Erythroxylum coca*), marijuana (*Cannabis sativa*), peyote (*Lophophora williamsii*), and tobacco (*Nicotiana tabacum*). These substances are mentioned to emphasize the point that being associated with herbs and natural products does not exclude a drug from being abused. Of concern in this section are unregulated herbal products and their potential for abuse and addiction. As a general rule, if a substance (including a natural product) elevates mood, causes a feeling of energy, or brings on a feeling of relaxation and relief from stress, it likely has potential for abuse. Based on these principles, the herbal products most likely to be abused include those containing ma huang, ginseng, kava kava, and ephedrine (NCCAM 2013). Of course, with addiction typically comes high-quantity use and a greater chance of serious side effects. Even though serious abuse of herbal products is possible, it does not occur frequently and, when it does occur, it is generally relatively easy to treat.

Prescription Drugs

The Durham–Humphrey Amendment of 1951 established the criteria that are still used today to determine whether a drug should be used only under the direction of a licensed health professional, such as a physician. According to this piece of legislation, drugs are controlled with prescriptions if they are (1) habit-forming, (2) not safe for self-medication, (3) intended to treat ailments that require the supervision of a health professional, or (4) new and without an established safe track record (Katzung 2012a). Currently more than 10,000 prescription products are sold in the United States, representing approximately 1500 different drugs, with 20 to 50 new medications approved each year by the FDA (Borgsdorf 2007; Drugs.com 2013a). In 2009, 3.9 billion drug prescriptions were written at a cost of about $300 billion; this cost was expected to rise soon to $400 billion

(Bartholow 2010; KFF 2010). With statistics like these it is not surprising that the United States leads the world in prescription drug consumption on a per capita basis (Hanson 2010).

Because of their specialized training, physicians, dentists, and, under certain conditions, podiatrists, physician assistants, nurse practitioners, pharmacists, and optometrists are granted drug-prescribing privileges. The health professionals who write prescriptions are expected to accurately diagnose medical conditions requiring therapy, consider the benefits and risks of drug treatment for the patient, and identify the best drug and safest manner of administering it. The responsibility of the health professional does not conclude with the writing of a prescription; in many ways, it only just begins. Professional monitoring to ensure proper drug use and to evaluate the patient's response is crucial for successful therapy.

■ Prescription Drug Abuse

Daniel had been sober for 1 ½ years, and his parents thought he had finally got his addiction to painkiller prescription drugs under control after multiple attempts at treatment. But for no apparent reason, his drug problems all came back and spiraled out of control. Daniel, a well-liked former hockey player, died at his best friend's house after overdosing on OxyContin and cocaine. "We heard that he had told his girlfriend that he wanted to start again and turn his life around, and that night he overdosed," said his mother (Thomas 2010).

In many places, abuse of prescription drugs is a greater problem than use of illicit drugs. This is supported by the following:

- The overall cost of prescription painkiller abuse is $70 billion per year (O'Toole 2012).
- There are more than 40 deaths caused by prescription painkillers every day in the United States (Stack 2013).
- More accidental deaths occur from medication overdoses than from car crashes (Biekiempis 2012; Kerlikowske 2012).
- In the past decade, death from overdoses of prescription drugs increased five-fold in women (Waseem 2013). (See "Here and Now: Celebrity Death and Prescription Abuse.")
- There has been a four-fold increase in admissions for treatment of persons addicted to prescription drugs (Stetka and McCance-Katz 2012; Thomas 2010).

Celebrity Death and Prescription Abuse

Whitney Houston has been added to an ever-increasing list of celebrities whose lives have been ended prematurely due to an "accidental" prescription drug overdose. It was reported that the 48-year-old singer was being medicated for anxiety and depression with several prescription drugs including the CNS depressant Xanax. In addition, Houston had been drinking heavily the night before she was discovered dead in her Beverly Hilton Hotel bathtub with her head submerged in water. This combination of a sedative/hypnotic drug and alcohol can have a fatal outcome under some conditions, which appears to be the case with this celebrity. In addition to her celebrity status, it has been suggested that Whitney Houston's gender may also have contributed to her vulnerability to drug addiction–related problems. It is thought that women may develop drug and alcohol dependence quicker, may tend to have serious consequences sooner, may be less likely to seek treatment, and may have greater problems with relapses than men.

Data from Walton, A. "Whitney Houston's Death: Why Addiction Is Harder on Women." *Forbes.* 16 February 2012. Available http://www.forbes.com/sites/alicegwalton/2012/02/16/whitney-houstons-death-why-addiction-is-harder-on-women; Hsu, C. "Whitney Houston's Death Highlights the Growing Trend of Celebrity Death By Prescription-Drug Abuse." *Medical Daily.* 13 February 2012. Available http://www.medicaldaily.com/news/20120213/9103/celebrities-prescription-drugs-whitney-houston-xanax-alcohol-michael-jackson-heath-ledger-ann.htm; and Moyer, W. "Deadly Duo: Mixing Alcohol and Prescription Drugs Can Result in Addiction or Accidental Death." *Scientific American.* 24 February 2012. Available http://www.scientificamerican.com/article.cfm?id=mixing-alcohol-prescription-drugs-result-addiction-accidental-death

- An average of 5500 people per day use prescription painkillers nonmedically for the first time (Stack 2012).
- There has been a doubling of emergency department visits for nonmedical use of prescription opioid analgesics (Quest Diagnostics 2010); specifically, in 2004, 627,000 persons went to emergency rooms due to problems with pharmaceutical drugs, compared to 1.2 million in 2009 (Goodnough 2011).
- It is estimated that one-fifth of U.S. college students are taking prescription drugs to either get high or enhance their academic performance (Freundlich 2010).
- Nearly 70% of those who misuse prescription painkillers obtain their drugs from friends or relatives (free, paid for, or stolen), and not from a legitimate prescriber (Stack 2012).
- In the United States, we prescribe enough opioid narcotics each year to medicate every adult around the clock for 1 month (Stack 2012).

The three classes of prescription drugs most likely to be abused, in order of their abuse frequency, are narcotic analgesics, CNS depressants, and stimulants (used to treat obesity and attention-deficit hyperactivity disorder [ADHD]). Particularly troubling is what appears to be an exploding epidemic of abusing prescription narcotic painkilling drugs such as OxyContin and Vicodin (Freundlich 2010; Johnston 2013). Headlines announcing a celebrity seeking treatment for dependence on, or even death because of, these drugs are becoming disturbingly routine (Waseem 2013). In fact, as mentioned earlier, abuse of prescription narcotics appears to be the leading problem with prescription drugs (Waseem 2013). Often young people abuse a combination of these prescribed drugs, and their sources include the medicine cabinets in their parents' or friends' homes or the Internet from "web pharmacies" that do not require legitimate prescriptions (Thomas 2010). This is a problem with youth and adults from all backgrounds

(Kaus 2010). For example, Wade Juracek, mayor of the town of Gregory, personally became acquainted with the dangers of prescription drugs. While taking painkillers to treat an intestinal inflammatory disease, Wade developed an addiction to narcotic analgesics that caused him to ingest up to 100 Vicodin pills daily. His dependence led to numerous illegal activities and his conviction on three felony counts that included drug theft, misrepresentation, and prescription forgery. After getting clean and sober, Wade shared his story with many audiences to help educate about the unexpected nature of prescription addictions. Wade tells others, "I think when people think of an addict, they think of some junkie lying in the streets or somebody shooting up. It can happen to anybody. There are lawyers, doctors, pastors, and priests that struggle (with this problem)" (Kaus 2010).

In order to deal with this escalating problem, it is important to determine why nonmedical prescription drug abuse occurs. Although there are many general and personal explanations for why a person takes medications that were not prescribed for them, the most frequent are as follows (Health Day News 2012; McCabe, Boyd, and Teter 2009):

- Thirteen percent abuse the prescription drugs for recreation, usually to get high or to try to feel better.
- Thirty-nine percent try to self-medicate a pre-existing medical/emotional problem with someone else's prescription medication (e.g., use a benzodiazepine to relieve anxiety).
- Forty-eight percent have elements of both explanations 1 and 2.
- Prescription abuse can be part of a bigger picture of substance abuse that includes the abuse of other drugs (both licit and illicit). One drug may be used to either embellish or relieve withdrawal from another drug of abuse (e.g., benzodiazepines taken to relieve the withdrawal from alcohol) (DiGravio 2010).

HERE AND NOW

Pharm Parties and Russian Roulette

One expression of prescription abuse is seen with high school students who bring samples of prescription drugs from home and dump them into a common bowl. The teens then grab a handful and pop them into their mouths like trail mix and swallow. The objective is to try to produce bizarre feelings and unusual highs. The mixtures often include medications such as antidepressants, stimulants, sleeping pills, antianxiety drugs, and narcotic pain relievers. One doctor described the activity as "Russian roulette," only with pills instead of bullets. The source of the drugs is often parents' or grandparents' medicine cabinets that frequently are filled with years of drug accumulation. For example, one 15-year-old said he wanted to be "cool" and told his friends that he could get some Percocets out of his stepdad's bottle. He explained that his stepdad had undergone many surgeries, so he had a lot of pills. The young man explained that the pills went down quick and the smooth buzz was free and everyone thought it was safe. Soon other friends joined the group and each would bring medicines from their own homes—a little Vicodin here, some OxyContin there, usually with

some whiskey and vodka to wash it down. As word got around, other friends joined the "cool" group and more prescription drugs were pooled and the activity had escalated into a "pharm party." Although at first everything seemed innocent and fun, the group soon learned that use of high quantities and mixed assortments of drugs that belong to someone else can be disastrous and even deadly.

Data from WIXT/WSYR, TV ABC 9. "Pharm Parties. Popping Prescriptions." Syracuse. 18 May 2007; Fagan, K. "'Pharma Parties: A Troubling Trend Among Youths." *San Francisco Chronicle.* 16 March 2010. Available http://www.sfgate.com/bayarea/article/Pharma-parties-a-troubling-trend-among-youths-3270176.php. Accessed March 29, 2011; and Valley, J. " 'Pharm Parties,' Designer Drugs Among Trends for High Schoolers." *Las Vegas Sun.* 19 April 2012. Available http://www.lasvegassun.com/news/2012/apr/19/pharm-parties-designer-drugs-among-trends-high-sch/#axzz2XuZw4jK2

Dealing with suspected abuse of prescription medication can pose a difficult management problem for physicians and pharmacists. It has become such a major issue that some third-party payers (that is, health insurance companies) have implemented tight monitoring procedures. Those who try to fraudulently obtain controlled substances with valid and invalid prescriptions include persons from all walks of life.

In the United States, young people frequently abuse prescription drugs. One trend is called "pharm parties," where high school students get together and try to get high on a mixture of prescription drugs followed by a chaser of alcohol (Valley 2012) (see "Here and Now: Pharm Parties and Russian Roulette"). However, young people rarely obtain the drugs by theft, fraud, or doctor shopping, although occasionally unscrupulous doctors will write prescriptions without questions for money (Reavy 2007). Instead, they usually obtain their prescription drugs from peers, friends, or family members or sometimes purchase them from rogue Internet pharmacies (Stack 2012). In some areas, the problem is so severe that high schools have implemented programs to prevent such sharing.

Abusers of prescription drugs often have multiple addictions, including dependence on caffeine, alcohol, or nicotine. In addition, once a pharmacy is recognized as an easy target, word spreads and other abusers often begin to frequent the same store. Signs of patients with drug-seeking behavior include the following:

- Use of altered or forged prescriptions
- Claims that a prescription has been lost and a physician is unavailable for confirmation
- Frequent visits to emergency rooms or clinics for poorly defined health problems
- Visits made to a pharmacy late in the day, on weekends, or just before closing
- Alteration of doses on a legitimate prescription
- Loud, abusive, and insulting behavior
- Use of several names
- Being particularly knowledgeable about drugs

Prescription Abuse and Pregnancy

It has been said that babies born to mothers addicted to prescription drugs have become the youngest victims of the prescription abuse epidemic. In excess of 13,000 babies are born annually who are physically dependent on the prescription analgesics to which their mothers were addicted (Olian 2012). This disturbing outcome includes a newborn who within days after birth, for no apparent reason, experienced vomiting with diarrhea, extreme irritability and shaking, inability to sleep, trouble eating, and frequent shrieking from pain. Infants such as this are manifesting withdrawal symptoms caused by their in utero exposure to the drugs (usually prescription narcotics) the mother consumed in large quantities during pregnancy (Olian 2012). Although these infants are sometimes described as addicted to their mothers' drugs, this is inaccurate. Their bodies have become physically dependent on the substances the newborns were exposed to during development; after birth their bodies are abruptly removed from drug exposure and thrown into a withdrawal reaction. These drug-dependent babies should remain in the hospital for weeks or months while they are gradually weaned from the drug on which they are physically dependent. These babies put a tremendous financial strain on our healthcare systems, costing an average of about $50,000 per child. As stated by a maternal–fetal medicine specialist, "They are the innocent victims. They had no control over it and yet they suffer tremendously for it" (Olian 2012).

Necessary Drug Information for Healthcare Providers

Many unnecessary side effects and delays in proper care are caused by poor communication between the health professional and the patient or by a doctor's lack of knowledge concerning the patient's medical history when a drug is prescribed. The smaller a drug's margin of safety (the difference between therapeutic and toxic doses), the more critical it becomes that the doctor has all relevant information regarding the patient's medical needs and vulnerabilities. The following is a brief overview of principles to help ensure that the health professional has the necessary information to properly prescribe and manage drug use for the patient.

Doctor–patient communication must be reciprocal. We tend to think that patients listen while doctors talk when it comes to deciding on the best medication for treatment. To ensure a proper diagnosis, precise and complete information from the patient is also essential. In fact, if a doctor is to select the best and safest drug for a patient, he or she needs to know everything possible about the medical problems to be treated. In addition, the patient should provide the doctor with a complete medical and drug history, particularly if there has been a problem with the patient's cardiovascular system,

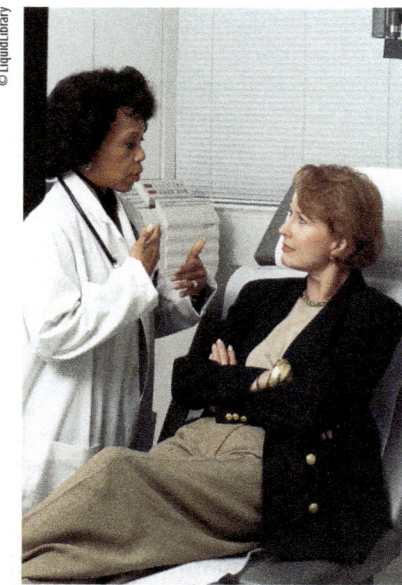

In order to maximize benefit and minimize risk, there must be proper doctor–patient communication.

kidneys, liver, or mental functions. Other information that should be shared with the doctor includes previous drug reactions as well as a complete list of drugs routinely being used, including prescription, nonprescription, and herbal products. In this regard, more and more states are establishing database systems that include up-to-date information concerning prescription drug histories that allow monitoring of what has been prescribed and dispensed to individual patients. Currently, most states have passed legislation authorizing, and in some cases mandating, such programs, but making these databases real-time can be extremely expensive and must adequately address issues such as patient confidentiality (Small 2013). However, it is hoped that eventually there will be a nationwide program that allows pharmacies, doctors, and other medical personnel to contribute to and access information from the prescription drug history of their patients in order to avoid dangerous and unnecessary prescribing practices and to be aware of potential prescription abuse problems (Risling 2010).

The patient needs to be educated about proper drug use. If the doctor does not volunteer this information, the patient should insist on answers to the following questions:

- *What is being treated?* This question does not require a long, unintelligible scientific answer. It should include an easy-to-understand explanation of the medical problem.

- *What is the desired outcome?* The patient should know why the drug is prescribed and what the drug treatment is intended to accomplish. It is difficult for the patient to become involved in therapy if he or she is not aware of its objectives.

- *What are the possible side effects of the drug?* This answer does not necessitate an exhaustive list of every adverse reaction ever recorded in the medical literature; however, it is important to realize that adverse drug reactions to prescription drugs are very common. In the United States, more people die from adverse reactions to legal medications than succumb to all illegal drug use. It is estimated that approximately 20,000 people die while another 2.1 million are seriously injured in this country each year from reactions to legal medications (Whitney 2007). In general, if adverse reactions occur in more than 1% of users, this should be mentioned to the patient. In addition, the patient should be made aware of ways to minimize the occurrence of side effects (e.g., an irritating drug should not be taken on an empty stomach, to minimize nausea) as well as what to do if a side effect occurs (e.g., if a rash occurs, call the doctor immediately).

- *How should the drug be taken to minimize problems and maximize benefits?* This answer should include details on how much, how often, and how long the drug should be taken.

- *How should the drug be disposed of?* This should include a discussion of the facts concerning proper and safe elimination of prescription drugs (see "Here and Now: Do Not Flush! Do Not Pour!").

Although it is a health professional's legal and professional obligation to communicate this information, patients frequently leave the doctor's office with a prescription that gives them legal permission to use a drug but without the knowledge of how to use it properly. Because of this all-too-common problem, pharmacists have been mandated by legislation referred to as the Omnibus Budget Reconciliation Act of 1990 to provide the necessary information to patients on proper drug use (Warholak-Juarez et al. 2000; Zak 1993) (see "Here and Now: OBRA '90"). Patients should be encouraged to ask questions of those who write and fill prescriptions.

HERE AND NOW

Do Not Flush! Do Not Pour!

Most of us have prescription drugs we no longer need sitting in our medicine cabinets or in other unsecured places. Often these medications have long passed their recommended expiration dates or intended use, but due to ignorance or neglect they become forgotten and a potential risk to an inquisitive child, to someone who is tempted to use them for medical purposes other than those for which they were prescribed, or to someone who is desperately looking to steal drugs to satisfy a substance abuse problem. To avoid these undesirable outcomes, along with water pollution, it is important for patients to be educated about the proper use and disposal of their prescription drugs. For safe management of prescription drugs, the following guidelines should be observed:

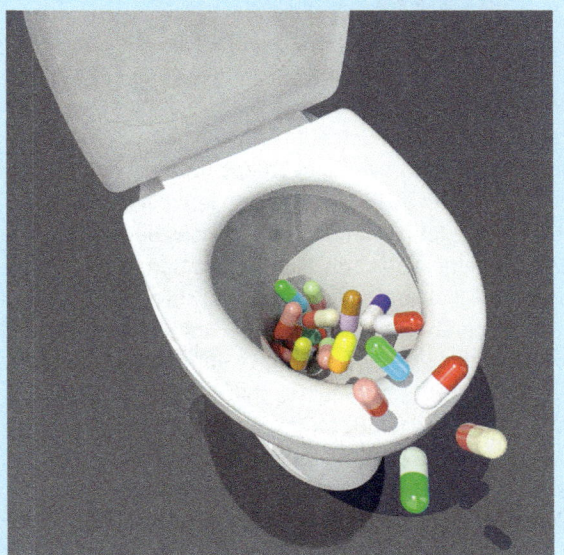

© Fabio Berti/ShutterStock, Inc.

- *Don't flush unused prescription drugs down the toilet or pour them down the drain.* Some drugs that are disposed of in our sewers end up in our water systems, causing pollution and damaging the environment. This is not a desirable method of disposing of prescription substances.

- *Don't throw unused prescription drugs into the garbage.* Because abuse of some of the prescription drugs such as opioid painkillers is very common, often persons with substance abuse problems check the garbage cans of acquaintances and strangers alike for unused drugs that satisfy their intense cravings.

- *Prescription drugs still being used should be safely secured.* Keeping in mind the potential danger and abuse of many prescription drugs, it is important that these substances be stored in a secure place that can be locked and is inaccessible to children and unintended users.

- *Disposal of unused prescription drugs at approved permanent collection sites is preferred.* There are typically steel-mounted metal drug disposal bins at approved law enforcement stations or offices. The prescription drugs can be anonymously deposited in the bins for frequent removal by law enforcement officers and then transferred to special facilities for incineration.

- *Prescription medicines can be safely disposed of at home.* If there is not access to a permanent collection site, safe disposal at home can be achieved by mixing all unused drugs with an undesirable substance such as coffee grounds, moist unused cat litter, or spoiled food and putting it into a sealable plastic bag. The bag should be wrapped with duct tape or placed in a solid container. If the medications are solid, water should be added to dissolve them before mixing. The container should then be thrown away on the day of garbage collection. When disposing of the drug container, be sure all identifying personal information has been removed or destroyed.

Data from Use Only As Directed. "Safe Disposal: Learn the Facts." Utah State Division of Substance Abuse 24 June 2013. Available http://www.useonlyasdirected.org/safe-disposal

HERE AND NOW

OBRA '90: The Evolving Role of Pharmacists in Drug Management

In 1990, the U.S. Congress passed section 4401 of the Omnibus Budget Reconciliation Act (commonly referred to as OBRA '90), which substantially altered the role of pharmacists in drug management. This act designated the pharmacist as the key player in improving the quality of drug care for patients in this country. Because OBRA '90 is federal legislation, it can require drug-related services for Medicare patients only; however, most states have recognized that similar services should be made available to all patients and have enacted legislation to that end. OBRA '90 requires pharmacists to conduct a drug use review (DUR) for each prescription to improve the outcome of drug therapy and reduce adverse side effects. The DUR program describes four basic professional services that a pharmacist must render whenever a drug prescription is filled:

1. Prescriptions and patients' records must be screened to avoid problems caused by drug duplications, adverse drug–drug interactions, medical complications, incorrect drug doses, and incorrect duration of drug treatment.

2. Patients should be counseled regarding the following:
   - How to safely and effectively administer the drug
   - Common adverse effects and interactions with other drugs, food, and so forth
   - How to avoid problems with the drug
   - How to monitor the progress of drug therapy
   - How to store the drug properly
   - Whether a refill is intended
   - What to do if a dose is missed

3. Patient profiles, including information on disease, a list of medications, and the pharmacist's comments relevant to drug therapy, must be maintained. This information should be stored in computer files for future reference.

4. Documentation must record if the patient refuses consultation from the pharmacist, or if a potential drug therapy problem is identified and the patient is warned.

Note: In 2013 the OBRA '90 act was still being enforced.

Data from Abood, R. "OBRA '90: Implementation and Enforcement." *NABP U.S. Pharmacists, State Boards—A Continuing Education Series*. Park Ridge, IL: National Association of Pharmacy, 1992.

■ Drug Selection: Generic Versus Proprietary

Although it is the primary responsibility of the doctor or healthcare provider to decide which drug is most suitable for a treatment, often an inexpensive choice can be as effective and safe as a more costly option. This statement frequently is true when choosing between generic and proprietary drugs. The term **generic** refers to the common name of a drug that is not subject to trademark rights; in contrast, **proprietary** denotes medications marketed under specific brand names. For example, diazepam is the generic designation for the proprietary name Valium. Often, the most common proprietary name associated with a drug is the name given when it is initially released for marketing. Because such drugs are almost always covered by patent restrictions for several years when first sold to the public, they become identified with their first proprietary names. After the patent lapses, the same drug often is also marketed by its less-known generic designation (Stoppler and Hecht 2010).

Because the pharmaceutical companies that market the generic products usually have not invested in the discovery or development of the drug, they often charge much less for their version of the medication. This situation contrasts with that of the original drug manufacturer, which may have invested as much as $0.5–$1 billion for research and development. Even though the generic product frequently is less expensive, because of FDA regulations the quality is not inferior to the related

KEY TERMS

generic
official, nonpatented, nonproprietary name of a drug

proprietary
brand or trademark name that is registered with the U.S. Patent Office

proprietary drug; thus, substitution of generic for proprietary products usually does not compromise therapy (Stoppler and Hecht 2010).

Because of reduced cost, generic products have become very popular. Currently, generic drugs account for approximately 80% of prescriptions dispensed (Stone 2013), up from 57% in 2004, and they account for $74 billion in annual sales (Bartholow 2010). Due to the great demand, all states have laws that govern the use and substitution of generic drugs; unfortunately, the laws are not all the same. Some states have positive laws that require pharmacists to substitute a generic product unless the physician gives specific instructions not to do so. Other states have negative laws that forbid substitution without the physician's permission. Some physicians use convenient prescription forms with "May" or "May Not" substitution boxes that can be checked when the prescription is filled out.

■ Common Categories of Prescription Drugs

Of the approximately 10,000 different prescription drugs available in the United States, the top 50 drugs in sales account for almost 30% of all new and refilled prescriptions (RxList 2010). As an example, a list of the 25 top-selling prescription drugs for the first quarter of 2013 is shown in **Table 15.6**. The following includes a brief discussion of some of the more popular prescription drug groups used in the United States. This list is not intended to be all-inclusive, but gives only a sampling of common prescription products.

ANALGESICS

The prescription analgesics consist mainly of narcotic and NSAID types. The narcotic analgesics most often dispensed to patients by prescription are (1) codeine and hydrocodone (e.g., Lortab,

TABLE 15.6 The Top 25 Prescription Drugs by U.S. Sales: 2013, First Quarter

Rank	Proprietary Name	Generic Name	Principal Clinical Use
1	Abilify	Aripiprazole	Antipsychotic
2	Nexium	Esomeprazole	Relieve ulcers
3	Cymbalta	Duloxetine	Antianxiety
4	Crestor	Rosuvastatin	Reduce cholesterol
5	Advair Diskus	Corticosteroid	Treat asthma
6	Humira	Adalimumab	Reduces swelling
7	Enbrel	Etanercept	Treat autoimmune disorders
8	Remicade	Infliximab	Treat rheumatoid arthritis
9	Copaxone	Glatiramer	Treat multiple sclerosis
10	Neulasta	Pegfilgrastim	Stimulate bone marrow
11	Rituxan	Rituximab	Suppress immune response
12	Spiriva	Tiotropium	Treat emphysema
13	Atripla	Drug combination	Treat HIV/AIDS
14	Januvia	Sitagliptin	Treat type 2 diabetes
15	OxyContin	Oxycodone	Relieve pain
16	Avastin	Bevacizumab	Treat cancer
17	Lantus Solostar	Human insulin (long-lasting)	Treat diabetes
18	Lantus	Human insulin	Treat diabetes

(continues)

TABLE 15.6 The Top 25 Prescription Drugs by U.S. Sales: 2013, First Quarter (*continued*)

Rank	Proprietary Name	Generic Name	Principal Clinical Use
19	Lyrica	Gabapentin	Treat pain (e.g., fibromyalgia)
20	Diovan	Valsartan + hydrochlorothiazide	Treat hypertension
21	Truvada	Emtricitabine and tenofovir	Prevent HIV/AIDS
22	Celebrex	Celecoxib	Relieve pain
23	Epogen	Epoetin alpha	Produce red blood cells, treat anemia
24	Herceptin	Trastuzumab	Treat breast cancer
25	Namenda	Memantine	Treat moderate to severe Alzheimer's disease

Data from Drugs.com. "U.S. Pharmaceutical Sales - Q1, 2013." 3 July 2013. Available http://www.drugs.com/stats/top100/sales

Vicodin), (2) the moderate-potency agents pentazocine (e.g., Talwin) and oxycodone (e.g., Percodan), and (3) the high-potency drug morphine. All narcotic analgesics are scheduled drugs because of their abuse potential and are effective against most types of pain. The narcotic analgesic products are often combined with aspirin or acetaminophen (e.g., Lortab and Vicodin are combinations of hydrocodone and acetaminophen) to enhance their pain-relieving actions. These are the most likely prescription drugs to be abused and can cause severe substance dependence and can devastate lives when not managed properly (see "Case in Point: Pain Killer Addiction: A Game-Changer"). Unfortunately, because of concern about abuse of the prescription painkillers, many patients with legitimate pain symptoms are inadequately treated to relieve their extreme discomfort for fear by the prescribers that they may be contributing to the development of a narcotic addict (Stack 2012).

The NSAIDs constitute the other major group of analgesics available by prescription. The pharmacology of these drugs is very similar to that of the OTC compound ibuprofen, discussed earlier in this chapter. These medications are used to relieve inflammatory conditions such as arthritis and are effective in relieving minor to moderate musculoskeletal pain (pain associated with body structures such as muscles, ligaments, bones, teeth, and skin). These drugs have no abuse potential and are not scheduled; several are also available OTC (see the discussion of OTC analgesics). Their principal adverse side effects include stomach irritation, kidney damage, tinnitus (ringing in the ears), dizziness, and swelling from fluid retention. Most prescription NSAIDs have similar pharmacological and side effects. Included

in the group of prescription NSAIDs are ibuprofen (e.g., Motrin), naproxen (e.g., Anaprox), indomethacin (e.g., Indocin), sulindac (e.g., Clinoril), mefenamic acid (e.g., Ponstel), tolmetin (e.g., Tolectin), piroxicam (e.g., Feldene), and ketoprofen (e.g., Orudis) (Furst 2012).

ANTIBIOTICS

Drugs referred to by the layperson as "antibiotics" are more accurately described by the term *antibacterials*, although the more common term will be used here. For the most part, antibiotics are effective in treating infections caused by microorganisms classified as bacteria. Bacterial infections can occur anywhere in the body, resulting in tissue damage, loss of function, and, if untreated, ultimately death. Even though bacterial infections continue to be the most common serious diseases in the United States and throughout the world today, the vast majority of these can be cured with antibiotic treatment.

There are currently close to 100 different antibiotic drugs, which differ from one another in (1) whether they kill bacteria (bactericidal) or stop their growth (bacteriostatic), and (2) the species of bacteria that are sensitive to their antibacterial action (Deck 2012). Antibiotics that are effective against many species of bacteria are classified as broad-spectrum types, whereas those antibiotics that are relatively selective and effective against only a few species of bacteria are considered narrow-spectrum drugs.

Although most antibiotics are well tolerated by patients, they can cause very serious side effects, especially if not used properly. For example, the penicillins have a very wide margin of safety for

► **CASE IN POINT**

Pain Killer Addiction: A Game-Changer

Ray Lucas is a former NFL quarterback who played for the Patriots, Jets, Dolphins, and Ravens. After retiring from playing football in 2003, he became an Emmy-award-winning studio analyst for SportsNet New York. While outwardly living the glamorous dream of a professional sports figure with a wonderful wife and three daughters, internally Lucas struggled through a secret nightmare: he had become seriously addicted to prescription painkillers that he had started using to treat severe football-related neck injuries. Lucas relates that he was "popping pills like candy," up to 800 a month, trying to figure out what went wrong. He describes episodes of depression associated with his drug abuse that led to thoughts of suicide and even attempts to end his life by overdosing on his medication or driving his car off of the George Washington bridge. Finally, after seeking and receiving help, Lucas was able to control his addiction and put his life back together. When asked to sum up his experience he said, "I still

have a lot of pain that I deal with, but I relish in the fact that sometimes you've got to walk through hell to get to heaven."

Data from Associated Press. "Former QB Lucas Hopes His Tale Helps Other Addicts." Samachar.com. 3 May 2012. Available http://www.samachar.com /former-qb-lucas-hopes-his-tale-helps-other-addicts-mfdvMQbhcch.html

most patients, but 5% to 10% of the population are allergic to these drugs, and life-threatening reactions can occur in sensitized patients if penicillins are used.

The most common groups of antibiotics include penicillins (e.g., amoxicillin [Amoxil, Augmentin, and Trimox]), cephalosporins (e.g., cephalexin), fluoroquinolones (e.g., ciprofloxacin [Cipro]), tetracyclines (e.g., minocycline [Minocin]), aminoglycosides (e.g., streptomycin), sulfonamides (e.g., sulfamethoxazole [Bactrim and Septra]), and macrolides (e.g., erythromycin [E-Mycin]).

ANTIDEPRESSANTS

Severe depression is characterized by diminished interest or pleasure in normal activities accompanied by feelings of fatigue, pessimism, and guilt as well as sleep and appetite disturbances and suicidal desires (American Psychiatric Association 2013). Major depression afflicts approximately 6% to 7% of the population at any one time, and it is estimated that about 23% of the population will become severely depressed during their life (Beck and Alford 2009). This high prevalence makes

depression the most common psychiatric disorder. According to the American Psychiatric Association's (2013) classification in the *Diagnostic and Statistical Manual of Mental Disorders*, fifth edition, several types of depression exist, based on their origin:

- *Endogenous major depression:* A genetic disorder that can occur spontaneously and is due to transmitter imbalances in the brain.
- *Depression associated with bipolar mood disorder:* That is, manic-depressive disorder.
- *Drug-induced depression:* The depressive symptoms are associated with the ingestion, injection, or inhalation of a substance (e.g., drug abuse, toxin, psychotropic medication, or other medication), and the symptoms persist beyond the expected length of physiological effects, intoxication, or withdrawal period. The relevant depressive disorder should have developed during or within 1 month after use of the depression-inducing substance.
- *Reactive depression:* The most common form of depression, which is a response to situations of grief, personal loss, illness, or other very stressful situations.

Antidepressant medication is typically used to treat endogenous major depression, although on occasion these drugs are used to treat other forms of depression if they are resistant to conventional therapy (Beck and Alford 2009).

Several groups of prescription antidepressant medications are approved for use in the United States (DeBatista 2012). The most commonly used category is the **tricyclic antidepressants**. Included in this group are drugs such as amitriptyline (e.g., Elavil), imipramine (e.g., Tofranil), and nortriptyline (e.g., Pamelor). Although usually well tolerated, the tricyclic antidepressants can cause annoying side effects due to their anticholinergic activity. These adverse reactions include drowsiness, dry mouth, blurred vision, and constipation. Tolerance to these side effects usually develops with continued use.

The second group of drugs used to treat depression is referred to as the **monoamine oxidase inhibitors (MAOIs)**. Historically, these agents have been backup drugs for the tricyclic antidepressants. Because of their annoying and sometimes dangerous side effects as well as problems interacting with other drugs or even food, the MAOIs have become less popular with clinicians. These drugs can have deadly interactions with many of the stimulants of abuse such as methamphetamine, cocaine, and Ecstasy. Drugs belonging to this group include phenelzine (Nardil) and tranylcypromine (Parnate).

Agents from a third, somewhat disparate, group of antidepressants that are safer and have fewer side effects than the tricyclic or MAOI antidepressants are very popular. They include fluoxetine (Prozac), sertraline (Zoloft), paroxetine (Paxil), fluvoxamine (Luvox), bupropion (Wellbutrin), trazodone (Desyrel), and duloxetine (Cymbalta). Although the side effects and margin of safety of these groups of antidepressants may differ, in general they all appear to have similar therapeutic benefits. Of this third group of antidepressants, Prozac is the best known and used to be the most frequently prescribed antidepressant; in 2003 it was the 11th most frequently prescribed drug in the United States. However, by 2009 it had been replaced by other antidepressants such as Lexapro (escitalopram) (Bartholow 2010). Although most commonly used to treat depression, Prozac has also been prescribed by physicians to treat more than 30 other conditions ranging from drug addiction (although not found to be generally effective) to kleptomania. The vast majority of these uses are not proven to be effective nor are they approved by the FDA.

ANTIDIABETIC DRUGS

Diabetes mellitus is likely the leading metabolic endocrine disease in this country; it afflicts approximately 26 million people in the United States, 19 million diagnosed and 7 million undiagnosed (American Diabetes Association [ADA] 2011). Of the 25 top-selling prescription drugs, 3 are for the treatment of diabetes (see Table 15.6). It is the result of insufficient or ineffective activity of insulin, a hormone secreted from the pancreas (ADA 2011). Due to the lack of insulin, untreated diabetics have severe problems with cellular and systemic metabolism and elevated blood sugar (called **hyperglycemia**). The two major types of diabetes are type 1 and type 2. **Type 1 diabetes** is caused by total destruction of the insulin-producing cells in the pancreas and usually begins in juveniles, although it occasionally begins during adulthood. In contrast, **type 2 diabetes**, which used to be called adult-onset diabetes, typically occurs after age 40 and is frequently associated with obesity. Recently, however, because severe obesity is occurring more often in younger persons (about 17% of Americans), an epidemic of type 2 diabetes has erupted in adolescents (ADA 2011), making the term *adult-onset diabetes* less meaningful. In type 2 diabetes, the pancreas is able to produce insulin, but insulin receptors no longer respond normally to this hormone (Seeringer et al. 2010). In both types of diabetes mellitus, drugs are administered to restore proper insulin function.

KEY TERMS

tricyclic antidepressants
most commonly used group of drugs to treat severe depression

monoamine oxidase inhibitors (MAOIs)
drugs used to treat severe depression

diabetes mellitus
disease caused by elevated blood sugar due to insufficient insulin

hyperglycemia
elevated blood sugar

type 1 diabetes
disease associated with complete loss of insulin-producing cells in the pancreas

type 2 diabetes
disease usually associated with obesity; does not involve a loss of insulin-producing cells

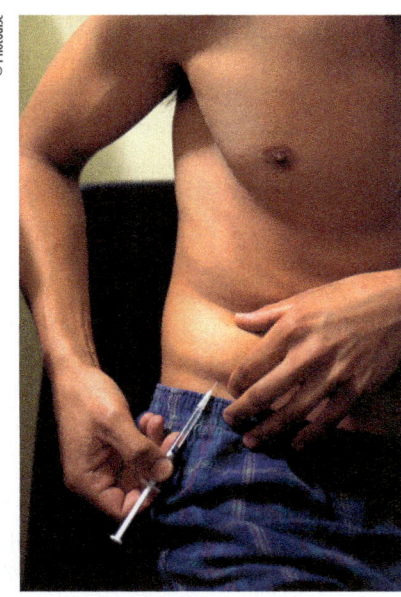

Insulin is self-administered by diabetic patients in subcutaneous injections.

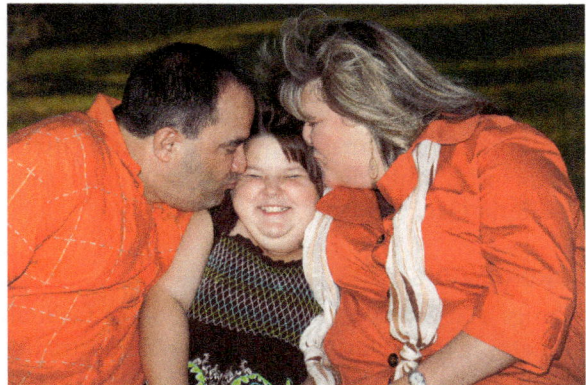

Obesity in young children has reached epidemic status and is causing type 2 diabetes to occur at a younger age.

Because of the inability to produce or release insulin in the type 1 diabetic, these patients are universally treated with subcutaneous injections of insulin one to three times per day, depending on their needs. Usually the levels of sugar (glucose) in the blood are evaluated to determine the effectiveness of treatment. Insulin products are characterized by their onset of action (either rapid or delayed onset) and duration (short to long) (Kennedy 2012).

The strategy for treating type 2 diabetics is somewhat different. For many of these patients, the symptoms of diabetes and problems of insufficient insulin function subside with proper diet, weight, and exercise management. If an appropriate change in lifestyle does not correct the diabetes-associated problems, drugs called **oral hypoglycemics** (meaning they are taken by mouth and lower blood sugar) are often prescribed. These drugs, which stimulate the release of additional insulin from the pancreas, include popular drugs such as rosiglitazone (Avandia). Recently, however, there have been concerns that although these drugs are effective in controlling glucose levels, some of them might increase the incidence of cardiovascular disease (Kennedy 2012). If the diabetic symptoms are not adequately controlled with the oral hypoglycemic drugs, type 2 diabetics are treated with insulin injections, as are type 1 patients. There has been substantial improvement in the treatment of diabetes in the past few years due to new, more selective and effective drugs that control glucose blood levels (Kennedy 2012).

ANTIULCER DRUGS

Peptic ulcers are sores that recur in the lining of the lower stomach (gastric ulcer) or most often in the upper portion of the small intestine (duodenal ulcer). It is apparent that secretions of gastric acids and digestive enzymes are necessary for ulcer development. Because gastric secretions are involved in developing peptic ulcers, several drug types are useful in ulcer treatment.

Antacids help to relieve acute discomfort due to ulcers by neutralizing gastric acidity. These drugs are discussed in greater detail in the OTC section of this chapter. Prescription drugs that block gastric secretion have been the mainstay of ulcer treatment. Because the endogenous chemical histamine is important in regulating gastric secretions, drugs that selectively block the activity of gastric histamine (called H_2 blockers) substantially reduce secretion of gastric acids and digestive enzymes. The very popular drugs cimetidine (Tagamet), ranitidine (Zantac), and famotidine (Pepcid) function in this manner. Because Tagamet, Zantac, and Pepcid are used so frequently, they have been switched to OTC status by the FDA—not to treat ulcers but to relieve heartburn (esophageal reflux) (FamilyDoctor 2010).

KEY TERMS

oral hypoglycemics
drugs taken by mouth to treat type 2 diabetes

peptic ulcers
open sores that occur in the stomach or upper segment of the small intestine

Although the exact causes of peptic ulcers are not completely understood, it is widely accepted that the bacteria *Helicobacter pylori* play a role. Because of the involvement of these microorganisms, most clinicians treat patients with recurring ulcers with multiple antibiotics to eliminate these bacteria (McQuaid 2012).

BRONCHODILATORS

Drugs that widen air passages (bronchi) facilitate breathing in patients with air passage constriction or obstruction. Such drugs are called **bronchodilators** and are particularly useful in relieving respiratory difficulty associated with asthma. Asthmatic patients frequently experience bouts of intense coughing, shortness of breath, tightness in the chest, and wheezing resulting in breathing difficulties. Many of the symptoms of asthma are due to an increased sensitivity of the airways to irritating substances and can result in serious asthma attacks that are life threatening if not treated promptly (Mayo Clinic 2010). Two major categories of bronchodilators are the sympathomimetics known as **beta-adrenergic stimulants**—for example, isoproterenol (e.g., Isuprel) and albuterol (e.g., Proventil, Ventolin)—and xanthines (caffeine-like drugs) such as theophylline and its derivatives. These drugs relax the muscles of the air passages, cause bronchodilation, and facilitate breathing (National Heart Lung and Blood Institute [NHLBI] 2010b). In the early 1990s, some bronchial dilator medications were switched to OTC status, such as Bronkaid Mist and Primatene Mist. These contain relatively low amounts of epinephrine and are safe and effective when used for mild, intermittent disease. Typically these OTC medications should not be used by patients with cardiovascular disease (Medicinenet 2013) and may dangerously interact with sympathomimetic stimulants of abuse such as cocaine and the amphetamines.

CARDIOVASCULAR DRUGS

Cardiovascular disease has been the number one cause of death in the United States for the past several decades. Consequently, of the 25 top-selling drugs in this country, 3 are medications for diseases related to the cardiovascular system (see Table 15.6). The following are brief discussions of the major categories of cardiovascular drugs (NHLBI 2010a).

ANTIHYPERTENSIVE AGENTS

It is estimated that about 29% of U.S. adults have **hypertension** (persistent elevated high blood pressure) (Benowitz 2012). Because hypertension can result in serious damage to the heart, kidneys, and brain, this condition needs to be treated aggressively. Treatment should consist of changes in lifestyle, including exercise and diet, but usually also requires drug therapy. Two of the principal classes of antihypertensive agents are diuretics and direct vasodilators (Benowitz 2012):

1. *Diuretics* lower blood pressure by eliminating sodium and excess water from the body. Included in this category is hydrochlorothiazide.
2. *Direct vasodilators* reduce blood pressure by relaxing the muscles in the walls of blood vessels that cause vasoconstriction, thereby dilating the blood vessels and decreasing their resistance to the flow of blood. Drugs included in this category are calcium-channel blockers (diltiazem [Cardizem], verapamil [Calan], nifedipine [Procardia]); inhibitors of the enzyme that synthesizes the vasoconstricting hormone, angiotensin II (enalapril [Vasotec]); and drugs that block the vasoconstricting action of the sympathetic nervous system (clonidine [Catapres] and prazosin [Minipress]).

ANTIANGINAL AGENTS

When the heart is deprived of sufficient blood (a condition called **ischemia**), the oxygen requirements of the cardiac muscle are not met and the breakdown of chemicals caused by the continual activity of the heart results in pain; this viselike chest pain is called **angina pectoris**. The most

---

KEY TERMS

bronchodilators
drugs that widen air passages

beta-adrenergic stimulants
drugs that stimulate a subtype of adrenaline and noradrenaline receptors

hypertension
elevated blood pressure

ischemia
tissue deprived of sufficient blood and oxygen

angina pectoris
severe chest pain usually caused by a deficiency of blood to the heart muscle

frequent cause of angina is obstruction of the coronary vessels (Katzung 2012c). Angina pectoris frequently occurs in patients with hypertension; left untreated, the underlying blockage of coronary vessels can result in heart attacks. All the drugs used to relieve or prevent angina decrease the oxygen deficit of the heart either by decreasing the amount of work required of the heart during normal functioning or by increasing the blood supply to the heart (Katzung 2012c). The three types of drugs prescribed for treating angina pectoris are (Katzung 2012c): (1) calcium-channel blockers (e.g., verapamil [Calan], diltiazem [Cardizem]); (2) nitrates and nitrites (e.g., amylnitrite [Vaporate], nitroglycerin [Transderm-Nitro]); and (3) blockers of the sympathetic nervous system, specifically classified as beta-adrenergic blockers (e.g., atenolol [Tenormin], propranolol [Inderal]).

DRUGS TO TREAT CONGESTIVE HEART FAILURE

When the cardiac muscle is unable to pump sufficient blood to satisfy the oxygen needs of the body, congestive heart failure occurs. This condition causes an enlarged heart, decreased ability to exercise, shortness of breath, and accumulation of fluid (edema) in the lungs and limbs (Katzung 2012b). The principal treatment for congestive heart failure consists of drugs that improve the heart's efficiency, such as digoxin (Lanoxin) (Katzung 2012b).

Drugs that cause vasodilation are also sometimes used successfully to reduce the work required of the heart as it pumps blood through the body. Among the drugs causing vasodilation are those already discussed in conjunction with other heart conditions such as hypertension and angina pectoris (e.g., enalapril [Vasotec]).

CHOLESTEROL- AND LIPID-LOWERING DRUGS

Cholesterol and some types of fatty (lipid) molecules can accumulate in the walls of arteries and narrow the openings of these blood vessels. Such arterial changes cause hypertension, heart attacks, strokes, and heart failure and are the leading cause of death in the United States, costing about $316 billion annually (Centers for Disease Control and Prevention [CDC] 2010). These health problems can often be avoided by adopting a lifestyle that includes a low-fat and low-cholesterol diet combined with regular, appropriate exercise (Malloy and Kane 2012). However, sometimes lifestyle changes are insufficient; in such cases, cholesterol-lowering drugs can be used to prevent the damaging changes in blood vessel walls. The drugs most often used include lovastatin (Mevacor), cholestyramine (Questran), and niacin (vitamin B_3) (Malloy and Kane 2012).

HORMONE-RELATED DRUGS

Hormones are released from endocrine (ductless) glands and are important in regulating metabolism, growth, tissue repair, reproduction, and other vital functions. When there is a deficiency or excess of specific hormones, body functions can be impaired, causing abnormal growth, imbalance in metabolism, disease, and often death. Hormones, or hormone-like substances, are sometimes administered as drugs to compensate for an endocrine deficiency and to restore normal function. This is the case for (1) insulin used to treat diabetes (see the earlier discussion for more details), (2) levothyroxine (Synthroid, an artificial thyroid hormone) to treat hypothyroidism (insufficient activity of the thyroid gland), and (3) conjugated estrogens (Premarin) to relieve the symptoms caused by estrogen deficiency during menopause.

Hormones also can be administered as drugs to alter normal body processes. Thus, drugs containing the female hormones, estrogen and progesterone (norethindrone, ethinyl estradiol [Ortho Novum]), can be used as contraceptives to alter the female reproductive cycles and prevent pregnancy. Another example involves drugs related to corticosteroids (hormones from the cortex of the adrenal glands), which are often prescribed because of their immune-suppressing effects. In high doses, the corticosteroid drugs (e.g., triamcinolone [Kenalog]) reduce symptoms of inflammation and are used to treat severe forms of inflammatory diseases, such as arthritis (Schimmer and Parker 2006). Finally,

KEY TERMS

congestive heart failure
the heart is unable to pump sufficient blood for the body's needs

edema
swollen tissue due to an accumulation of fluid

hypothyroidism
thyroid gland does not produce sufficient hormone

hormone-linked drugs such as etanercept (Enbrel), which depress the important immune mediator, tissue necrosis factor (TNF), have also become very popular for suppressing serious inflammatory diseases such as arthritis (see Table 15.6).

SEDATIVE-HYPNOTIC AGENTS

About 12.5% of U.S. adults use sedative-hypnotics annually, and 2% use them daily (Sola 2010). Some popular sleeping medications include Ambien (zolpidem), Lunesta (eszopiclone), Rozerem (ramelteon), Sona (carisoprodol), and Silenor (doxepin) (Trevor and Way 2012; WebMD 2010). If one is not careful, these drugs can be used excessively for reducing stress and aiding sleep, leading to addictions and adverse consequences. Benzodiazepines commonly prescribed for these purposes are clonazepam (Klonopin) and lorazepam (Ativan) (Charney, Mihic, and Harris 2006; Trevor and Way 2012).

STIMULANTS

One of the most common uses for prescription stimulants is the treatment of attention deficit hyperactivity disorder (ADHD). This neurobehavioral disorder is the most common mental health problem in children, affecting approximately 7–9% of all school-aged children (CDC 2013). Of those children diagnosed with ADHD, the majority will continue to manifest associated impairment into adolescence and even adulthood (National Institute of Mental Health [NIMH] 2010). The most frequent treatment for ADHD includes stimulants such as methylphenidate (Ritalin) and amphetamine (Adderall), which have been proven to improve attention while controlling impulsivity and disruptive behaviors. Of some concern is a dramatic increase in stimulant prescriptions for ADHD treatment and whether they are the best drug choice for treating ADHD patients (Awad 2013). This rise in ADHD-related medication use has corresponded with a disturbing increase in the use of these stimulants without prescriptions. It has been estimated that approximately 21 million people age 12 or older in the United States are prescribed these stimulants annually, and in 2012 these drugs were abused by approximately 7% of high school seniors, many of whom are not the legal recipients of the prescriptions (Johnston 2013).

Perhaps the most troubling issue is the trend for college students to abuse these short-acting stimulants to enhance performance during studying to prepare for examinations or stay awake to party well into the night (Awad 2013). Another common reason for this group to abuse these drugs is to lose weight due to their appetite-suppressing actions. It is likely that the increase of stimulant abuse by college students reflects an assumption that these agents must be safe or they would not be prescribed by physicians. Due to this growing problem, there is a major effort by scientists and drug companies to develop nonaddicting medications to treat ADHD.

DRUGS TO TREAT HIV

In the top-25 list of prescription drugs (see Table 15.6), medications to treat and to prevent HIV infection are included. Of relevance to our discussion on prescription drugs are recent advances in pharmacological management of this disease. Although no cure for HIV or immunization against this virus is available yet, some drug therapies can delay the onset or dramatically slow the progression of this infection. The first drugs to be used effectively in AIDS therapy were the transcriptase inhibitors such as zidovudine (AZT) and stavudine (Zerit), which block a unique enzyme essential for HIV replication (Flexner 2006). Another group of anti-AIDS drugs called the protease inhibitors prevent HIV maturation; they include aquinavir (Fortovase). The protease inhibitors are particularly effective when used in combination with the transcriptase inhibitor drugs (Flexner 2006). Most current strategies for AIDS therapy include drug combinations based on issues such as viral susceptibility, drug toxicity, drug metabolism, drug interaction potential, and medical conditions of the patient. There are more than 20 approved anti-HIV drugs from 6 different mechanistic classes that can be used to design combination-drug treatments. These include drug categories such as the transcriptase inhibitors, protease inhibitors, fusion inhibitors, and CCR5 antagonists. Strategies for more effective drug treatments are continually being developed (AIDSinfo 2009; Safrin 2012). Research suggests that if done properly, antiviral treatment is more than 80% effective in suppressing the symptoms of AIDS and preventing death (Marconi et al. 2010).

PRESCRIPTION FOR ABUSE

Invitation for Prescription Abuse

Michael was polite, clean-cut, and a typical white-collar professional. To consider him a drug addict would be unthinkable. And yet, Michael would be the first to admit his drug addiction on prescription medication is as strong and debilitating as an addiction to illegal drugs such as cocaine and heroin. Michael became extremely skilled in his ability to feign back pain in a doctor's office or emergency room so he could walk away with a prescription for potent narcotic painkillers. When asked if he drove himself to the office, Michael would always say no, so he could also get an injection of the potent narcotic Demerol. If he had difficulty getting a medication from legitimate or forged prescriptions, Michael would steal pills from easy targets in the suburbs. For example, at garage sales he would ask to use the bathroom, and unsuspecting homeowners would nicely open their houses to him and leave him unsupervised. People trying to sell their house would usually invite him in as a prospective buyer, and, as he looked around unattended, he would sneak into a bathroom or bedroom and rifle through medicine cabinets and dresser drawers for drugs to satisfy his cravings. Michael tells of one experience when he went to an open house pretending to be an interested buyer. When the owner wasn't looking, Michael slipped into a bedroom and snatched a large bottle of Vicodin and an unfilled prescription next to a wheelchair

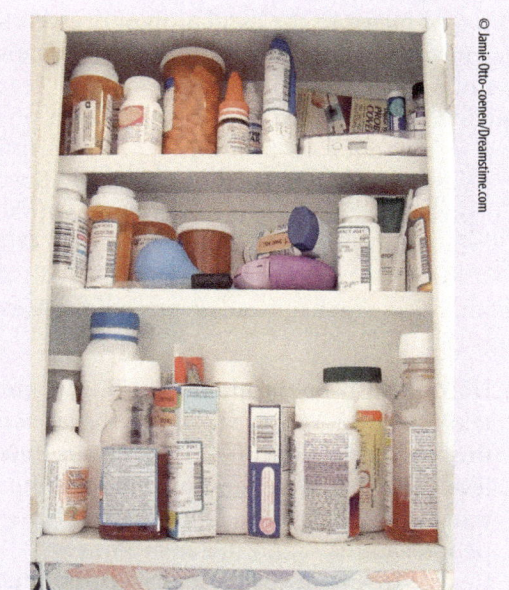

and crutches. At the peak of his addiction, Michael was consuming up to 120 narcotic painkillers a day. Michael explains that using large quantities of these prescriptions was not all that difficult. He claims that "doctors and psychiatrists would hand out drugs like candy" and people were so unsuspecting that it was easy to take unsecured prescription drugs from bathrooms and bedrooms.

Data from Sotonoff, J. "Addiction Began with Prescription Drugs He Got from Your Homes." *Chicago Daily Herald*. 26 July 2010. Available http://www.dailyherald .com/story/?id=396310. Accessed March 16, 2011.

Common Principles of Drug Use

Probably the most effective way to teach people not to use drugs improperly is to help them understand how to use drugs correctly. This goal can be achieved by educating the drug-using public about prescription, OTC, and herbal drug products. If people can appreciate the difference between the benefits of therapeutic drug use and the negative consequences of drug misuse or abuse, they will be more likely to use medications in a cautious and thoughtful manner. To reach this level of understanding, patients must be able to communicate freely with health professionals. Before prescription or OTC drugs are purchased and used, patients should have all questions answered about the therapeutic objective, the most effective mode of administration, and side effects. Education about proper drug use greatly diminishes drug-related problems and unnecessary health costs.

To minimize problems, before using any drug product, the patient should be able to answer the following questions:

- Why am I using this drug?
- How should I be taking this drug?
- What are the active ingredients in this drug product?

- What are the most likely side effects of this drug?
- How long should this drug be used?
- How should this drug be disposed of?

A major factor in the escalation of prescription drug misuse is that excess unused medications are not dealt with appropriately and are readily available to those who would abuse them or use them in a dangerous fashion (see "Prescription for Abuse: Invitation for Prescription Abuse"). This problem can be prevented by complying with the following guidelines from the Office of National Drug Control Policy (ONDCP) that explain how to manage and dispose of these extra drugs (Smith 2010):

- Do not flush medications. The Environmental Protection Agency (EPA) has declared that flushing drugs down the toilet results in high levels of many medications in community water supplies, causing health problems for people, animals, and the environment.
- Realize that many of these prescription medications are in high demand on the Internet and street, are often sold for a considerable amount of money, and can be very tempting to young people. Consequently, teens frequently raid home medicine cabinets to use these drugs for "pharm parties," where the pills are mixed together and shared or sold to friends and acquaintances. For these reasons, all prescription drugs should be stored in a secure (even locked) place (*Alcoholism & Drug Abuse Weekly* 2010).
- Do not dispose of your medications or their containers with labels in the trash. The bright labels of these bottles are highly visible in garbage cans and landfills and contain important personal information that can be used to steal your identity.
- The FDA recommends placing unused prescription medications into a plastic bag with moist coffee grounds or cat litter before disposing of the pills/tablets in the garbage. The moisture from the coffee grounds or cat litter will help dissolve the capsules, pills, or tablets, making them unusable.
- Many communities have secured drop-off boxes that are attended by certified law-enforcement personnel. Medications left in these boxes are collected by authorized personnel and properly disposed of. Locations of these drop-off containers can usually be determined by checking with local police.

LEARNING PORTFOLIO

Discussion Questions

1. Why are some prescription drugs appropriate for switching to OTC status?
2. What should the FDA use as a standard of safety when evaluating OTC and prescription drugs?
3. What role should the pharmacist play in providing information about OTC and prescription drugs to patients?
4. What type of formal training should be required before a health professional is allowed to prescribe drugs?
5. What kinds of questions should be asked by a health professional to ensure that a patient has sufficient understanding concerning a drug to use it properly and safely?
6. What are the basic rules for using OTC drugs properly?
7. Why is abuse of prescription drugs such a common problem?
8. Why are the opioid painkillers the most frequently abused of the prescription drugs?
9. How should users of prescription drugs handle their medications to prevent their abuse by others?
10. Why are some people more likely to abuse prescription drugs than illegal substances?
11. Even though some antibiotics have a wide margin of safety, currently there is no systemic antibiotic available OTC. Why is the FDA not willing to make some of these drugs available on a nonprescription basis?
12. Should herbal remedies be required to be safe and effective by the FDA like other OTC drug products?
13. What role, if any, should the FDA have in regulating herbal products?

Summary

1. Prescription drugs are available only by recommendation of an authorized health professional, such as a physician. Nonprescription (OTC) drugs are available on request and do not require approval by a health professional. In general, OTC medications are safer than their prescription counterparts, but often less effective.
2. The switching policy of the FDA is an attempt to make available more effective medications to the general public on a nonprescription basis. This policy has been implemented in response to the interest in self-treatment by the public and in an attempt to reduce healthcare costs.
3. Drugs switched by the FDA to OTC status include ulcer medications, such as cimetidine (Tagamet) and ranitidine (Zantac); medications for asthma and allergies; the contraceptive

Key Terms

levonorgestrel (Plan B); and the weight loss drug orlistat (Ally).

4. Potential problems caused by making more effective drugs available OTC include overuse and inappropriate use, leading to dependence and other undesirable side effects. For example, these more effective drugs could encourage self-treatment of medical problems that usually require professional care.

5. Information on OTC product labels is crucial for proper use of these drugs and thus is regulated by the FDA. Product labels must list the active ingredients and their quantities in the product. Labels must also provide instructions for safe and effective treatment with the drug as well as cautions and warnings.

6. Many herbal products contain active drugs and have become very popular. The lack of regulation makes these remedies difficult to assess for either efficacy or safety.

7. Although OTC drug products can be useful for treatment of many minor to moderate, self-limiting medical problems, when used without proper precautions, they can cause problems.

8. The principal drug groups available OTC are used in the treatment of common, minor medical problems and include analgesics, cold remedies, allergy products, mild stimulants, sleep aids, antacids, laxatives, antidiarrheals, antiasthmatics, acne medications, sunscreens, contraceptives, and nutrients.

9. For drugs to be prescribed properly, patients need to provide complete and accurate information about their medical condition and medical history to their physicians. In turn, providers need to communicate to patients what is being treated, why the drug is being used, how it should be used for maximum benefit, and what potential side effects can occur.

10. Proprietary drug names can be used legally only by the drug company that has trademark rights. Often, the original proprietary name becomes the popular name associated with the drug. Because the pharmaceutical company that develops a drug is trying to recover its investment, a newly marketed proprietary drug is expensive. Once the patent rights expire, other drug companies can also market the drug but under a different name; often, the common, generic name is used because it cannot be trademarked. The generic drugs are less expensive because the manufacturers do not need to recover any significant investment. The FDA requires the less expensive generic drug to be as effective and safe as the proprietary counterpart.

11. Of the approximately 1500 different prescription drugs currently available in the United States, the most commonly prescribed groups are analgesics, antibiotics, antidepressants, drugs used for diabetes, antiulcer drugs, antiepileptic drugs, bronchodilators, drugs used to treat cardiovascular diseases, hormone-related drugs, and sedative-hypnotics.

12. Abuse of prescription drugs is a serious problem in the United States. Some patients try to persuade clinicians or pharmacists to make prescription medications available by using deceit or intimidation. Legal drugs obtained in this manner are often used to relieve drug dependence or to reduce withdrawal symptoms from illicit substances. Those who abuse prescription drugs often abuse other substances as well such as alcohol, tobacco, or even illicit drugs.

13. To help reduce prescription abuse, those who use these drugs legitimately should make sure their medications are securely stored and that unused prescriptions are disposed of properly.

References

Abood, R. "OBRA '90: Implementation and Enforcement." *NABP U.S. Pharmacists, State Boards—A Continuing Education Series.* Park Ridge, IL: National Association of Pharmacy, 1992.

About.com. "Urban Legends: Phenylpropanolamine Recall." 2010. Available http://urbanlegends.about.com/library /blppa.htm

AIDSinfo. "Guidelines for the Use of Antiretroviral Agents in HIV-1-Infected Adults and Adolescents." December 2009; updated 2013. Available http://aidsinfo.nih.gov/contentfiles/AdultandAdolescentGL.pdf

Alcoholism & Drug Abuse Weekly. "Only Federal Prevention Message About Prescription Drugs: Lock Up or Throw Out." 15 March 2010. Available http://onlinelibrary.wiley.com/doi/10.1002/adaw.20225/abstract

Allen, J. "Over-the-Counter Cough Medicines Escape FDA Restrictions." *ABC Good Morning America.* 14 September 2010. Available http://abcnews.go.com/Health/Wellness/dextromethorphan-ingredient-robutussin-cough-medicines-escapes-fda-restrictions/story?id=11638160

American Diabetes Association (ADA). "Diabetes Basics: Diabetes Statistics." 2011. Available http://www.diabetes.org/diabetes-basics/diabetes-statistics/

American Psychiatric Association. "Depressive Disorders." In *Diagnostic and Statistical Manual of Mental Disorders,* 5th ed., 155–188. Washington, DC: American Psychiatric Association, 2013.

Associated Press. "Former QB Lucas Hopes His Tale Helps Other Addicts." Samachar.com. 3 May 2012. Available http://www.samachar.com/former-qb-lucas-hopes-his-tale-helps-other-addicts-mfdvMQbhcch.html

Awad, S. "ADHD Medication Stimulates Controversy." Technician Online. 17 April 2013. Available http://www.technicianonline.com/article_c5a144c6-a004-11e2-9ff0-0019bb30f31a.html

Bartholow, M. "Top 200 Prescription Drugs of 2009." *Pharmacy Times.* 11 May 2010. Available http://www.pharmacytimes.com/issue/pharmacy/2010/May2010/RxFocusTopDrugs-0510

Beck, A., and B. Alford. *Depression Causes and Treatment,* 2nd ed. Philadelphia: University of Pennsylvania Press, 2009.

Benowitz, N. "Antihypertensive Agents." In *Basic and Clinical Pharmacology,* 12th ed, edited by B. Katzung, 169–191. New York: McGraw-Hill, 2012.

Bernard, D. "Minor Burns, Sunburn and Wounds." In *Handbook of Nonprescription Drugs,* 17th ed., edited by D. Krinsky et al., 735–755. Washington, DC: American Pharmacists Association, 2012.

Biekiempis, V. "America's Prescription Addiction Suggests a Sick Nation." *The Guardian.* 2012. Available http://www.guardian.co.uk/commentisfree/2012/apr/09/america-prescription-drug-addiction

Booth, W., and A. O'Connor. "Mexican Cartels Emerge as Top Source for U.S. Meth." *Washington Post.* 28 November 2010. Available http://www.washingtonpost.com/wp-dyn/content/article/2010/11/23/AR2010112303703.html?sid=ST2010112303730

Borgsdorf, L. "Preface." In *Drug Facts and Comparisons,* edited by L. Borgsdorf, et al., xi. St. Louis: Wolters & Kluwar, 2007.

Brophy, B., and D. Schardt. "Functional Foods." HighBeam Research. 2011. Available http://www.highbeam.com/doc/1G1-54271809.html

Center for Drug Evaluation and Research (CDER). "Over-the-Counter Medicine: What's Right for You?" Food and Drug Administration. February 2002. Available http://www.fda.gov/cder

Centers for Disease Control and Prevention (CDC). "Heart Disease Facts." 2010. Available http://www.cdc.gov/heartdisease/facts.htm

Centers for Disease Control and Prevention (CDC). "Attention-Deficit/Hyperactivity Disorder (ADHD) Data and Statistics." 13 May 2013. Available http://www.cdc.gov/ncbddd/adhd/data.html

Charney, D., S. Mihic, and R. Harris. "Hypnotics and Sedatives." In *The Pharmacological Basis of Therapeutics,* 11th ed., edited by L. Brunton, J. Lazo, and K. Parker, 401–427. New York: McGraw-Hill, 2006.

Colliver, V. "Curbing Cough Medicine Abuse Target of Calif. Law." SF Gater. 28 December 2011. Available http://www.sfgate.com/cgi-bin/article.cgi?f=/c/a/2011/12/28/MNQE1MAS92.DTL&type=science

Consumer Healthcare Products Association. "White Paper on the Benefits of OTC Medicines in the United States." 2010. Available http://www.yourhealthathand.org/images/uploads/r_6842.pdf

Crosby, K., and O'Neal, K. "Prevention of Sun-Induced Skin Disorders." In *Handbook of Nonprescription Drugs,* 17th ed., edited by D. Krinsky et al., 707–722. Washington, DC: American Pharmacists Association, 2012.

Cunningham, J. K., R. C. Callaghan, D. Tong, L. M. Liu, H. Y. Li, and W. J. Lattyak. "Changing Over-the-Counter Ephedrine and Pseudoephedrine Products to Prescription Only: Impacts on Methamphetamine Clandestine Laboratory Seizures." *Drug and Alcohol Dependency* 126 (2012): 55–64.

DeBatista, C. "Antidepressant Agents." In *Basic and Clinical Pharmacology,* 12th ed., edited by B. Katzung, 521–541. New York: McGraw-Hill Medical, 2012.

Deck, D. "Section VIII: Chemotherapeutic Drugs." In *Basic and Clinical Pharmacology,* 12th ed., edited by B. Katzung, 789–1000. New York: McGraw-Hill Medical, 2012.

DiGravio, G. "In a Primary Care Setting Researchers Define Traits Associated with Prescription Drug Disorders." Medical News Today. 17 May 2010. Available http://www.medicalnewstoday.com/articles/188891.php

Drugs.com. "New Drug Approvals." 2013a. Available http://www.drugs.com/newdrugs.htmlDrugs.com.

Drugs.com. "U.S. Pharmaceutical Sales - Q1, 2013." 3 July 2013b. Available http://www.drugs.com/stats/top100/sales

FamilyDoctor. "What Is Heartburn?" 2010. Available http://familydoctor.org/online/famdocen/home/common/digestive/disorders/087.html

Feret, B. "Fever." In *Handbook of Nonprescription Drugs*, 17th ed., edited by D. Krinsky et al., 87–100. Washington, DC: American Association of Pharmacists, 2012.

Flexner, C. "Antiretroviral Agents and Treatment of HIV Infection." In *The Pharmacological Basis of Therapeutics*, 11th ed., edited by L. Brunton, J. Lazo, and K. Parker, 1273–1314. New York: McGraw-Hill, 2006.

Food and Drug Administration (FDA). "Medication Error Reports." 2009. Available http://www.fda.gov/Drugs/DrugSafety/MedicationErrors/ucm080629.htm

Food and Drug Administration (FDA). "Rx-to-OTC Switch List." 2010. Available http://www.fda.gov/AboutFDA/CentersOffices/OfficeofMedicalProductsandTobacco/CDER/ucm106378.htm

Foster, K., and C. Coffrey. "Acne." In *Handbook of Nonprescription Drugs*, 17th ed., edited by D. Krinsky et al., 693–722. Washington, DC: American Pharmacists Association, 2012.

Freundlich, N. "Illicit Drugs on Campus Are Increasingly the Rx Variety." Taking Note. 13 July 2010. Available http://takingnote.tcf.org/2010/07/illicit-drugs-on-campus-are-increasingly-the-rx-variety.html

Fugh-Berman, A. "Herb–Drug Interactions." *Lancet* 355 (2000): 134–138.

Furst, D. "Nonsteroidal Antiinflammatory Drugs, Disease-Modifying Antirheumatic Drugs, Nonopioid Analgesics, and Drugs Used in Gout." In *Basic and Clinical Pharmacology*, 12th ed., edited by B. Katzung, 635–657. New York: McGraw-Hill Medical, 2012.

Gill, M. "The Pharmacist's Role in Sleep Disorders." *Pharmacy Times* (August 1999): 103–116.

Goodnough, A. "Prescription Drug Abuse Sends More People to the Hospital." *New York Times*. 5 January 2011. Available http://www.nytimes.com/2011/01/06/health/06drugs.html

Hanson, D. "U.S. Leads World in Prescription Drug Use." Addiction Inbox. 28 July 2010. Available http://addiction-dirkh.blogspot.com/2010/07/us-leads-world-in-prescription-drug-use.html

Health Day News. "More Mental Health Woes in College Kids Who Abuse Prescription Drugs." *US News and World Report*. 19 June 2012. Available http://health.usnews.com/health-news/news/articles/2012/06/19/more-mental-health-woes-in-college-kids-who-abuse-prescription-drugs

Henderson, M. "Self-Care and Nonprescription Pharmaco-therapy." In *Handbook of Nonprescription Drugs*, 17th ed., edited by D. Krinsky et al., 3–36. Washington, DC: American Pharmacists Association, 2012.

Hsu, C. "Whitney Houston's Death Highlights the Growing Trend of Celebrity Death by Prescription-Drug Abuse." Medical Daily. 13 February 2012. Available http://www.medicaldaily.com/news/20120213/9103/celebrities-prescription-drugs-whitney-houston-xanax-alcohol-michael-jackson-heath-ledger-ann.htm

Hume, A., and K. Strong. "Botanical Medicines." In *Handbook of Nonprescription Drugs*, 15th ed., edited by I. Bernardi, 1103–1136. Washington, DC: American Pharmacists Association, 2006.

Johnston, L. "Monitoring the Future." 2013. Available http://monitoringthefuture.org

Kaiser Family Foundation. "Prescription Drug Trends." May 2010. Available http://www.kff.org/rxdrugs/upload/3057-08.pdf

Katzung, B. "Development and Regulation of Drugs." In *Basic and Clinical Pharmacology*, 12th ed., edited by B. Katzung, 69–77. New York: McGraw-Hill Medical, 2012a.

Katzung, B. "Drugs Used in Heart Failure." In *Basic and Clinical Pharmacology*, 12th ed., edited by B. Katzung, 211–225. New York: McGraw-Hill Medical, 2012b.

Katzung, B. "Vasodilators and the Treatment of Angina Pectoris." In *Basic and Clinical Pharmacology*, 12th ed., edited by B. Katzung, 193–210. New York: McGraw-Hill Medical, 2012c.

Kaus, A. "A 'Trendy and Popular' Problem." *Daily Republic*. 15 May 2010. Available https://secure.forumcomm.com/?publisher_ID=4&article_id=43079&CFID=283784732&CFTOKEN=52166350

Kennedy, M. "Pancreatic Hormones and Antidiabetes Drugs." In *Basic and Clinical Pharmacology*, 12th ed., edited by B. Katzung, 743–768. New York: McGraw-Hill Medical, 2012.

Kerlikowske, G. "Setting the Record Straight: Responding to the Prescription Drug Abuse Epidemic." Huffington Post. 22 March 2012. Available http://www.huffingtonpost.com/r-gil-kerlikowske/prescription-drug-abuse_b_1365785.html

Kirkwood, C., and S. Melton. "Insomnia, Drowsiness, and Fatigue." In *Handbook of Nonprescription Drugs*, 17th ed., edited by D. Krinsky et al., 867–883. Washington, DC: American Pharmacists Association, 2012.

Lampert, P. "Consumer Skepticism Growing Regarding 'All Natural' Food Claims." PR Newswire. 14 May 2013. Available http://www.prnewswire.com/news-releases

/consumer-skepticism-growing-regarding-all-natural-food-claims-207362511.html

Leong, K. "The Dangers of Dextromethorphan Abuse." Associated Content. 9 March 2010. Available http://voices.yahoo.com/the-dangers-dextromethorphan-abuse-5549597.html

Life Challenges. "Anorexia and Bulimia—Serious Consequences." 2010. Available http://www.allaboutlifechallenges.org/anorexia-bulimia.htm

Malloy, M., and J. Kane. "Agents Used in Dyslipidemia." In *Basic and Clinical Pharmacology*, 12th ed., edited by B. Katzung, 619–633. New York: McGraw-Hill Medical, 2012.

Marconi, V., G. Grandits, A. Weintrob, H. Chun, M. Landrum, A. Ganesan, et al. "Outcomes of Highly Active Antiretroviral Therapy in the Context of Universal Access to Healthcare: The U.S. Military HIV Natural History Study." *AIDS Research and Therapy* 7 (2010): 14.

Martinez, B. "Study Shows Teens Using Prescription, OTC Drugs to Get High." Defiance Crescent News. 16 January 2007. Available http://www.crescent-news.com/news/article/1486152

Mayo Clinic. "Asthma: Symptoms." 27 May 2010. Available http://www.mayoclinic.com/health/asthma/DS00021/DSECTION=symptoms

McCabe, S., C. Boyd, and C. Teter. "Subtypes of Nonmedical Prescription Drug Misuse." *Drug and Alcohol Dependence* 102 (2009): 63–70.

McQuaid, K. "Drugs Used in the Treatment of Gastrointestinal Diseases." In *Basic and Clinical Pharmacology*, 12th ed., edited by B. Katzung, 1081–1114. New York: McGraw-Hill Medical, 2012.

McQueen, C., and R. Orr. "Natural Products." In *Handbook of Nonprescription Drugs*, 17th ed., edited by D. Krinsky et al., 967–1006. Washington, DC: American Pharmacists Association, 2012.

Medical News Today. "Are Doctors Knowledgeable About Herbal Medicines?" Medical News Today. 2010. Available http://www.medicalnewstoday.com/articles/184716.php

MedicineNet. "Asthma: Over-the Counter Treatment." 2013. Available http://www.medicinenet.com/asthma_over_the_counter_treatment/article.htm

Miller, S., and C. Bartels. "Overweight and Obesity." In *Handbook of Nonprescription Drugs*, 17th ed., edited by D. Krinsky et al., 488–505. Washington, DC: American Pharmacists Association, 2012.

Mitchell, D. "Is Your Child Abusing Cough and Cold Medications?" EmaxHealth.com. 2010. Available http://www.emaxhealth.com/1275/your-child-abusing-cough-and-cold-medications

Moyer, W. "Deadly Duo: Mixing Alcohol and Prescription Drugs Can Result in Addiction or Accidental Death." *Scientific American*. 24 February 2012. Available http://www.scientificamerican.com/article.cfm?id=mixing-alcohol-prescription-drugs-result-addiction-accidental-death

National Center for Complementary and Alternative Medicine (NCCAM). "Herbs at a Glance." 10 June 2013. Available http://nccam.nih.gov/health/herbsataglance.htm

National Heart, Lung, and Blood Institute (NHLBI). "Heart and Vascular Information." 2010a. Available http://www.nhlbi.nih.gov/health/public/heart/index.htm

National Heart, Lung, and Blood Institute (NHLBI). "What's New/Highlights." 2010b. Available http://hp2010.nhlbihin.net/as_frameset.htm

National Institute of Mental Health (NIMH). "Attention Deficit Hyperactivity Disorder (ADHD)." 2010. Available http://www.nimh.nih.gov/health/publications/attention-deficit-hyperactivity-disorder/complete-index.shtml

National Library of Medicine. "Dietary Supplement Labels Database." 2010. Available http://www.dsld.nlm.nih.gov/dsld/

Nutraceuticals World. "Herbal Supplement Sales Increase to $5 Billion in Sales in the U.S." 2011. Available http://www.nutraceuticalsworld.com/contents/view/24313

Olenak, J. "Musculoskeletal Injuries and Disorders." In *Handbook of Nonprescription Drugs*, 17th ed., edited by D. Krinsky et al., 101–117. Washington, DC: American Pharmacists Association, 2012.

Olian, K. "Prescription Drug Addiction Among Women Becoming 'Monstrous Tidal Wave.'" NBC News. 5 July 2012. Available http://rockcenter.nbcnews.com/_news/2012/07/05/12570381-prescription-drug-addiction-among-pregnant-women-becoming-monstrous-tidal-wave?lite

O'Toole, J. "How Prescription Drug Abuse Costs You Money." CNN. 24 February 2012. Available http://money.cnn.com/2012/02/22/news/economy/prescription_drug_abuse/index.htm

Quest Diagnostics. "U.S. Worker Use of Prescription Opiates Climbing, Shows Quest Diagnostics Drug Testing Index." 2 September 2010. Available http://newsroom.questdiagnostics.com/index.php?s=30649&item=94682

Reavy, P. "Murray Doctor Arrested—Called the Drug 'Candyman.'" *Deseret News* 157 (2007): A1.

Reuters Health. "Bill Would Restrict Cold Pills to Fight 'Meth.'" 27 January 2005. Available http://naturalsolutionsradio.com/blog/natural-solutions-radio/bill-would-restrict-cold-pills-fight-meth

Rickert, E. "Legal and Regulatory Issues in Self-Care Pharmacy Practice." In *Handbook of Nonprescription Drugs*,

17th ed., edited by D. Krinsky et al., 53–64. Washington, DC: American Pharmacists Association, 2012.

Risling, G. "State Databases Blocking 'Doctor Shoppers.'" *Washington Post*. 16 May 2010. Available http://www .highbeam.com/doc/1P2-22027753.html

RxList. "Top 200 Drugs." 2010. Available http://www.rxlist .com/script/main/hp.asp

Safrin, S. "Antiviral Agents." In *Basic and Clinical Pharmacology*, 12th ed., edited by B. Katzung, 861–889. New York: McGraw-Hill Medical, 2012.

Schimmer, B., and K. Parker. "Adrenocorticotropic Steroids and Their Synthetic Analogs: Inhibitors of the Synthesis and Actions of Adrenocortical Hormones." In *The Pharmacological Basis of Therapeutics*, 11th ed., edited by L. Brunton, J. Lazo, and K. Parker, 1587–1612. New York: McGraw-Hill, 2006.

Scolaro, K. "Disorders Related to Colds and Allergies." In *Handbook of Nonprescription Drugs*, 17th ed., edited by D. Krinsky et al., 180–204. Washington, DC: American Pharmacists Association, 2012.

Scott, S., and R. Martin. "Atopic Dermatitis and Dry Skin." In *Handbook of Nonprescription Drugs*, 15th ed., edited by I. Bernardi, 711–728. Washington, DC: American Pharmacists Association, 2006.

Seeringer, A., S. Parmar, A. Fischer, B. Altissimo, L. Zondler, E. Lebedeva, et al. "Genetic Variants of the Insulin Receptor Substrate-1 Are Influencing Therapeutic Efficacy of Oral Antidiabetics." *Diabetes, Obesity and Metabolism* 12 (2010): 1106–1112.

Shimp, L. "Disorders Related to Menstruation." In *Handbook of Nonprescription Drugs*, 17th ed., edited by D. Krinsky et al., 139–158. Washington, DC: American Pharmacists Association, 2012.

Small, J. "Funds to Run Out for Database That Monitors Prescription Drug Usage." 89.3 KPCC Southern California Public Radio. 15 April 2013. Available http://www.scpr .org/news/2013/04/15/36829/funds-to-run-out-for -database-that-monitors-prescr/

Smith, E. "Proper Disposal of Prescription Medication or Prescription Drugs." Suite101.com. 14 November 2010. Available http://www.suite101.com/content/proper-disposal -of-prescription-medication-or-prescription-drugs -a308788

Sola, C. "Sedative, Hypnotic, Anxiolytic Use Disorders." Emedicine from WebMD. 2010. Available http://emedicine .medscape.com/article/290585-overview

Stack, S. "Prescription Abuse Laws Can Create a No-Win Situation for Doctors." American Medical News. 13 August 2012.

Available http://www.amednews.com/article/20120813 /opinion/308139962/5/

Stetka, B., and E. McCance-Katz. "Two New Resources to Curb Prescription Drug Abuse." Medscape. 8 May 2012. Available http://www.medscape.com/viewarticle /763209

Stobbe, M. "Study: US Has Much Higher Obesity Rate Than Canada." Phys.Org. 2 March 2011. Available http:// phys.org/news/2011-03-higher-obesity-canada.html

Stone, K. "Top Generic Drug Companies." About.com Pharma. 2013. Available http://pharma.about.com /od/Generics/a/Top-Generic-Drug-Companies.htm

Stoppler, M., and B. Hecht. "Generic Drugs, Are They as Good as Brand Names?" MedicineNet.com. 29 December 2010. Available http://www.medicinenet.com/script /main/art.asp?articlekey=46204

Thomas, M. "Prescription Drug Abuse Is Fastest-Growing Drug Problem in Country." *Chicago Sun-Times*. 26 December 2010. Available http://www.suntimes.com/news /metro/2989811-418/drug-prescription-abuse-daniel -drugs.html

Tietze, K. "Cough." In *Handbook of Nonprescription Drugs*, 17th ed., edited by D. Krinsky et al., 205–216. Washington, DC: American Pharmacists Association, 2012.

Trevor, A., and W. Way. "Sedative-Hypnotic Drugs." In *Basic and Clinical Pharmacology*, 12th ed., edited by B. Katzung, 373–385. New York: McGraw-Hill Medical, 2012.

Valley, J. "'Pharm Parties,' Designer Drugs Among Trends for High Schoolers." *Las Vegas Sun*. 19 April 2012. Available http://www.lasvegassun.com/news/2012/apr/19 /pharm-parties-designer-drugs-among-trends-high -sch/#axzz2XuZw4jK2

van den Heuval, C., S. Ferguson, M. Macchiand, and D. Dawson. "Melatonin as a Hypnotic: Con." *Sleep Medicine Review* 9 (2005): 71–80.

Walton, A. "Whitney Houston's Death: Why Addiction Is Harder on Women." *Forbes*. 16 February 2012. Available http://www.forbes.com/sites/alicegwalton/2012/02 /16/whitney-houstons-death-why-addiction-is-harder -on-women

Warholak-Juarez, T., M. Rupp, T. Salazar, and S. Foster. "Effect of Patient Information on the Quality of Pharmacists' Drug Use Review Decisions." *Journal of American Pharmaceutical Association* 40 (2000): 500–508.

Waseem, F. "Drug Overdose Deaths Spike Among Middle-Aged Women." *USA Today*. 3 July 2013. Available http:// www.usatoday.com/story/news/nation/2013/07/02 /drug-overdose-deaths-women/2483169/

WebMD. "Drugs to Treat Insomnia." 2010. Available http://www.webmd.com/sleep-disorders/guide/insomnia-medications

Whitney, M. "Prescription Drug Deaths Skyrocket 68 Percent over Five Years as Americans Swallow More Pills." NewsTarget.com. 14 September 2007. Available http://www.naturalnews.com/021635_prescription_drug_deaths_the_FDA.html

Wilkinson, J. "Headache." In *Handbook of Nonprescription Drugs*, 17th ed., edited by D. Krinsky et al., 67–86. Washington, DC: American Pharmacists Association, 2012.

Williams, A., C. Girard, D. Jui, A. Sabina, and D. Katz. "SAMe as Treatment for Depression: A Systemic Review." *Clinical Investigation of Medicine* 28 (2005): 132–139.

WIXT/WSYR, TV ABC 9. "Pharm Parties. Popping Prescriptions." Syracuse (18 May 2007).

Zak, J. "OBRA '90 and DUR." *American Druggist* (October 1993): 57.

Zweber, A., and R. Berardi. "Heartburn and Dyspepsia." In *Handbook of Nonprescription Drugs*, 17th ed., edited by D. Krinsky et al., 221–235. Washington, DC: American Pharmacists Association, 2012.

CHAPTER 16

Drug Use in Subcultures of Special Populations

© Deco Images/Alamy

Did You Know?

- ▶ Athletes are much more likely than other subculture groups to take drugs that enhance physical attributes.
- ▶ In the United States, approximately 500,000 teenagers use steroids and 52,000 children (12 and younger) use anabolic steroids.
- ▶ In general, compared with men, women are more likely to become addicted to tobacco.
- ▶ In comparison to men, women are more reluctant to seek substance abuse treatment.
- ▶ Approximately 70% of women in drug abuse treatment report histories of physical and sexual abuse, with victimization beginning before 11 years of age and occurring repeatedly.
- ▶ The major reasons adolescents use drugs are to cope with boredom, unpleasant feelings, emotions, and stress or to relieve depression and reduce tension and alienation.
- ▶ Prescription drugs are the drugs of choice among 12- to 13-year-olds.
- ▶ Street gangs, outlaw motorcycle gangs, and prison gangs are the primary distributors of illegal drugs in the United States.
- ▶ Alcohol use is implicated in one-third to two-thirds of sexual assaults and acquaintance or date rape cases among teens and college students.
- ▶ The amount and proportion of alcohol consumed by college students varies depending on where they live.
- ▶ AIDS is a common killer, second only to cancer and heart disease for women. It is the third most deadly disease for women in the United States.
- ▶ An HIV-infected individual may not manifest symptoms of AIDS for as many as 10 to 12 years after the initial infection.

Drugs and Society Online is a great source for additional drugs and society information for both students and instructors. Visit **go.jblearning.com /hanson12** to find a variety of useful tools for learning, thinking, and teaching.

Learning Objectives

On completing this chapter you will be able to:

- ❯ Know which drugs are most likely to be abused by athletes and why.
- ❯ Describe the use of drug testing in athletic competitions.
- ❯ Determine where anabolic steroids come from.
- ❯ Describe the purpose and goals of the Adolescents Training and Learning to Avoid Steroids (ATLAS) prevention program.
- ❯ Explain two major ways women's history differs from men's history with regard to drug abuse.
- ❯ Explain the major reasons why adolescents use substances of abuse.
- ❯ Explain which types of parents are more likely to raise drug-abusing adolescents.
- ❯ List which types of drugs adolescents are most likely to abuse.
- ❯ List two major findings from research regarding drug use by college students.
- ❯ Know what club drugs are and how they are used.
- ❯ Explain how drug abuse contributes to the spread of AIDS.
- ❯ Know the key statistics regarding AIDS.
- ❯ List the major strategies to prevent contracting HIV infection.
- ❯ Know how the use of alcohol and other drugs are presented in popular movies and songs.
- ❯ Understand how Internet access can lead to drug use and abuse.

Introduction

Although similarities appear in the patterns of addiction among drug users, the development of initial use and eventual abuse varies from individual to individual. When attempting to understand common patterns and causes of drug use, examining the subcultures of special populations provides a better grasp of commonalities within such groups. A **subculture** is defined as a special population or subgroup whose members share similar values, attitudes, and patterns of related behaviors that differ from those of other subcultures within the larger population. Even though many subcultures are often so broad and diverse that not all members may be consciously aware of one another, from an **outsider's perspective** they qualify as subcultures because they share similar behavior patterns. For example, racial and ethnic, gender, age, and drug subcultures are often very large across the United States, and most members of such subcultures are not aware of one another. However, in looking at them from the outside (an outsider's perspective), they have patterns of behavior that are similar. An **insider's perspective** refers to viewing the subculture from the inside, as the members of this subculture are experiencing ongoing activity within their group. For example, a group of adolescents using drugs from a particular locality in a city or town and divorced women meeting to discuss coping with separation and being single qualify as distinct subcultures. Although both insiders' and outsiders' perspectives may include similar behavior patterns, the inside and outside perspectives differ. An insider's perspective looks at the group and its behavior from the inside and an outsider's perspective is looking at the group and its behavior from the outside.

When defining a subculture, some sociologists refer to it as a "world within a world." Subcultures create and provide their members with lifestyle patterns that are observable, fairly consistent, and interwoven. For example, viewing a drug-using group as a subculture offers a way to look for more generalized and distinctive patterns of drug use. In looking at this example of a subculture of drug users, we can begin by examining why individuals within various subcultures might initially turn to drugs. The two types of forces that affect members of a subculture are internal and external forces, both of which affect these individuals' drug use behavior.

Internal subcultural forces include the following:

- Shared in-group attitudes about people who do and do not use drugs (drug users versus nonusers)
- Compatibility with other members of the peer group (often peer members share complementary personality traits)
- Shared attitudes favorable to drug use despite conventional society's view that such behavior is deviant
- Addiction to drugs or, at minimum, habitual drug usage
- A common secrecy about drug use (who you can and cannot trust in knowing about your drug usage)

External subcultural forces include the following:

- Preoccupation with law enforcement while procuring the drugs and while under the effects of illicit drugs
- A desire to identify other users and dealers of illicit drugs, such as verifying the dependability of the drug dealer (who best to deal drugs with and who has the best quality drugs)
- Constant preoccupation regarding drug supply and when to keep in touch with drug dealer(s) and concern about acquiring a new supply of their drug of choice
- Some preoccupation with being observed using or acting "high" in public, at work, at school, or at a social function where drug use would be perceived as deviant social behavior

To further understand how similar patterns of drug use and/or abuse occur, in this chapter we look at drug use and users from both outsiders' and insiders' perspectives, from the vantage point of the members belonging to a distinct subculture

KEY TERMS

subculture
subgroup within the population whose members share similar values and patterns of related behaviors that differ from other subcultures and the larger population

outsider's perspective
viewing a group or subculture from outside the group and viewing the group and its members as an observer; looking "in" at the members

insider's perspective
viewing a group or subculture from inside the group; seeing members as they perceive themselves

and how they are perceived by society. This chapter examines drug use and potential abuse in the following seven drug-using subcultures:

1. Athletes/those involved in sports
2. Women
3. Adolescents
4. College students
5. HIV and AIDS carriers
6. A certain percentage of professional actors, actresses, and music celebrities
7. Internet users who are seeking and purchasing illicit drugs

Athletes and Drug Abuse

Drug abuse has been reported since the Greeks started the Olympics in 776 BC. It was then reported that certain substances were ingested by competitors in an attempt to gain some ground against fellow competitors (Lajis 2007).

Using performance-enhancing drugs for increased athletic ability is known as **doping** National Institute on Drug Abuse [NIDA] 2009.

Doping in sport is the deliberate or inadvertent use by an athlete of a substance or method banned by the International Olympic Committee (IOC). FIMS [International Federation of Sports Medicine] supports the prohibition of doping to protect athletes from the:

- unfair advantage, which may be gained by those athletes who use banned substances or methods to enhance performance,
- possible harmful side effects, which some substances or methods can produce. (Technische Univeristät München n.d.)

In the past, reports revealed that "'Doping' among world-class competitors is rampant . . . and the governing bodies of individual sports, as well as the International Olympic Committee, turn a blind eye" (Begley et al. 1999, p. 49). The reasons boil down to winning in sports, especially when millisecond differences exist between gold

KEY TERM

doping
the use of performance-enhancing drugs to increase athletic ability

and silver medals. The differences between the two medals "can amount to millions in endorsement contract and appearance fees" (Begley et al. 1999, p. 49), and apparently the world of professional sports and "drugs [performance-enhancing drugs] go together like socks and sweat" (Begley et al. 1999, p. 49). Charles Yesalis, an epidemiologist at Pennsylvania State University at University Park, stated that

> Elite athletes stay away from traditional anabolic steroids. They use testosterone creams or gels, which dramatically reduce the chance of being caught, in conjunction with insulin or insulin-like growth factor,. . . . The supplement industry has exploded since the passage of the Dietary Supplement Health and Education Act in 1994. . . . Anyone can buy substances like testosterone, human-growth hormone (HGH), and insulin-like growth factor over the Internet. One site requires a doctor's prescription, but will sell one to any customer for $100 or someone can just walk down to the local GNC, like Mr. Jackson's teammates at Florida State. There, one can buy muscle-building steroid "precursors" like androstenedione and creatine monohydrage. "Andro" is banned by the [World Anti-Doping Agency (WADA 2009)] and the National Collegiate Athletic Association and other sports governing bodies, but it's legal to buy. They're not as effective as older anabolic steroids, but they do provide some benefits. . . . The law allows stores to sell vitamins, herbal remedies, and other supplements over-the-counter. (Suggs 2003, p. 36)

More recently however, findings indicate that since ". . . 2007, anti-doping agencies introduced the concept of a "biological passport," a record of the substances found normally in an athlete's blood and urine, created by repeated sampling over time. By comparing the results of a blood test administered right before a competition to the passport, officials can determine if an athlete has been using EPO or other performance-enhancing drugs" (Harris 2013). As a result, the use of muscle-building steroid "precursors" like androstenedione and creatine monohydrage are now detectable in drug testing.

Another finding as to why athletes want to take performance-enhancing substances lists three important reasons: (1) inadvertent (or allegedly inadvertent) consumption of any pharmaceutical medicine that is banned from commercial competition, either because the ingredients or manufacturing method are kept secret or because it is protected by trademark or copyright (also known as a **proprietary medicine**); (2) "deliberate consumption for misuse as a recreational drug"; and (3) "deliberate consumption to enhance performance" (Docherty 2008, p. 606). To further our understanding of why athletes are willing to risk using these drugs, it is necessary to further explore their mind-set.

To excel in athletic competition is admirable. Most high school, college, amateur, and professional athletes participate in sports for the opportunity to pit their abilities against those of their peers, and to experience the satisfaction that comes from playing to their potential. Others do so to satisfy a desire for recognition and fame. Unfortunately, that creates some athletes who are determined to win at any cost. And, they may use that determination to justify the use of anabolic steroids, despite evidence that these drugs can inflict irreversible physical harm and have significant side effects (New York State Department of Health 2010).

Young athletes receive exaggerated attention and prestige in almost every university, college, high school, and junior high school in the United States. Pressure to excel or be the best is placed on athletes by parents, peers, teachers, coaches, school administrators, the media, and the surrounding community. The importance of sports is frequently distorted and even used by some to evaluate the quality of educational institutions (Lawn 1984; New York State Department of Health 2010) or the quality of living conditions in a city. Athletic success can determine the level of financial support these institutions receive from local and state governments, alumni, and other private donors; thus, winning in athletics often translates into fiscal stability and institutional prosperity.

For the athlete, success in sports means psychological rewards such as the admiration of peers, school officials, family, and the community. In addition, athletic success can mean financial rewards such as scholarships, paid living expenses in college, advertising endorsement opportunities, and, for a few, incredible salaries as professional athletes. With the rewards of winning, athletes have to deal with the added pressures of not winning: "What will people think of me if I lose?" "When I lose, I let everybody down." "Losing shows that I am not as good as everyone thinks." These pressures on young, immature athletes can result in poor coping

responses. Being better than competitors, no matter the cost, becomes the driving motivation, and doing one's best is no longer sufficient. Such attitudes may lead to serious risk-taking behavior in an attempt to develop an advantage over the competition; this situation can include using drugs to improve performance.

The Canadian sprinter Ben Johnson, once known as the fastest human in history, was banned for life from competitive running in March 1993 (Begley et al. 1999; Hoberman and Yesalis 1995). Five years earlier, at the 1988 Seoul Olympics, Johnson was stripped of a world record for the 100-meter dash and forfeited the gold medal when his urine tested positive for steroids. Because of the first incident, Johnson was suspended from competition for 2 years. However, in 1992, the 31-year-old sprinter was attempting a comeback, with speeds that approached his world record times. In January 1993, a routine urine test determined Johnson was again using steroids to enhance his athletic performance (Ferrente 1993).

Another incident involving the use of steroids that ended in shocking tragedy was the case of wrestler Chris Benoit's double murder–suicide. Evidence proved that the pro wrestler asphyxiated his son and wife before he hanged himself in a basement weight room using a cord from one of the weight machines (ESPN.com 2007). "Steroids were among the prescription medications found by investigators going through . . . Benoit's house" (Donaldson-Evans 2007). "Anabolic steroids affect neurochemicals in the brain. . . . It's those neurochemical changes that cause the extreme anger. . . . Officials found many different prescription medications—including prescription anabolic steroids—inside the house . . ." (Donaldson-Evans 2007).

In another story, "eighty-three players have been suspended under baseball's controversial new steroids policy" (Anonymous, as told by Penn

KEY TERMS

proprietary medicine
pharmaceutical medicine that is protected from commercial competition because the ingredients or manufacturing method is kept secret or because it is protected by trademark or copyright

ergogenic
drugs that enhance athletic performance

2005, p. 292). "Guys did steroids because it was easy to get away with." Several other noteworthy and revealing quotes from this report are: "So many people were doing it that it didn't feel like cheating. If anything, it felt like leveling the field. . . . I juiced because I love playing more than anything else in the world, and I would have pretty much done anything to keep my career going" (Anonymous 2005, p. 297). Widely publicized incidents such as these concerning illicit use of so-called **ergogenic** (performance-enhancing) drugs by professional and amateur athletes have created intense interest in the problems of drug abuse in sports (Begley et al. 1999; Merchant 1992) (see "Point/Counterpoint: How the 'Juice' Was and Is Flowing in Baseball").

A more recent case of steroid use in professional sports involves Alexander Emmanuel "Alex" Rodriguez. Rodriguez (born in 1975) is currently a U.S. Major League Baseball player for the New York Yankees. He is considered one of the youngest best players in baseball history, and in 2007, he signed a 10-year, $252 million contract (Britannica.com 2010).

The Slugger [Rodriguez] who might someday become baseball's all-time home run king remembered more details about performance-enhancing drugs Tuesday, saying his cousin repeatedly injected him from 2001–03 with a mysterious substance from the Dominican Republic. 'I didn't think they were steroids' the New York Yankees star said. Later, he admitted, 'I knew we weren't taking Tic Tacs.' (Blum 2009, p. A11)

It was at this press conference that Rodriguez made ". . . his second public attempt to explain a 2003 positive drug test while with Texas . . . while his cousin persuaded him to use 'boli'—a substance he said the cousin obtained without a prescription and without consulting doctors or trainers" (Blum 2009, p. A11).

Finally, one of the most recent cases that was particularly shocking was that of Lance Armstrong, who, because of doping, was stripped of his record-holding *seven* Tour de France titles that he received from 1999 to 2005. Armstrong stated that in order to be a record holder, doping is needed to win (Leicester 2013). In the same recent news article, Armstrong also stated, ". . . his life has been ruined by the U.S. Anti-Doping Agency investigation that exposed as lies his years of denials that he and his teammates doped" (Leicester 2013).

▶ POINT/COUNTERPOINT

How the "Juice" Was and Is Flowing in Baseball

We embrace instant gratification in the United States. We are a society that embraces "bigger, faster, stronger" and winning at all costs (Dvorchak 2005). This concept now applies to professional sports with a devious outcome. A sampling from news sources reveals the following:

- Jose Canseco, a Major League Baseball player for the Oakland Athletics and Texas Rangers (among other teams), wrote a tell-all book titled *Juiced*, in which he exposed not only the rampant use of performance-enhancing substances in baseball. . . . A steroid devotee since the age of 20, Conseco goes beyond admitting his own usage . . . [to claiming that] he often injected [Mark] McGwire while they were teammates. . . . According to Conseco, steroids and human growth hormone gave McGwire and Sammy Sosa (whose own usage was 'so obvious, it was a joke') the strength, stamina, regenerative ability, and confidence they needed for [the] record setting home run duels often credited with restoring baseball's popularity after the 1994 strike" (Amazon.com 2005).

- "[S]everal star athletes, including New York Yankees slugger Jason Giambi, have reportedly told a federal grand jury investigating the [Balco] lab that they used illegal steroids, prompting Congress to hold hearings on the testing policies of all the major sports leagues" (Coile 2005).

- "Seattle Mariners minor-league outfielder Jamal Strong was suspended for 10 days . . . making him the fourth player to test positive under Major League Baseball's new policy on performance-enhancing drugs" (Associated Press 2005).

- "McGwire's shameful refusal to answer questions about his alleged steroid use before a congressional committee and Bonds' unbelievable claim that he did not know that substances rubbed into his body were steroids clearly suggest deceit and dishonesty" (Eilek 2005).

- "Performance enhancing drugs (PEDs) have once again taken a toll on the professional sports world with yesterday's suspensions of 13 Major League Baseball players, including Alex Rodriguez–the highest paid player in professional baseball" (Woemer 2013).

- "Rodriguez was suspended in August for an unprecedented 211 games for his connection to the now defunct Biogenesis anti-aging clinic linked to providing 14 players with performance enhancing drugs. His suspension came since he violated the joint drug agreement and the collective bargaining agreement. A-Rod had the harshest punishment of all the players as Ryan Braun received a 65-game ban while the other 12 players each accepted and served 50-game suspensions" (Smollins 2013).

- "According to Ken Rosenthal, Major League Baseball has suspended 12 players in relation to the Biogenesis case.. . . [Biogenesis case occurred in 2013 involving a recent defunct clinic, Biogenesis of America, provided performance-enhancing drugs ("PEDs") to MLB players]. . . Nelson Cruz, Jhonny Peralta, Antonio Bastardo, Jordany Valdespin, Everth Cabrera, Francisco Cervelli, Jesus Montero, Sergio Escalona, Fautino De Los Santos, Cesar Puello, Fernando Martinez, and Jordan Norberto will all be suspended. All 12 players have accepted their 50-game suspensions" (TheScore.com 2013).

Questions to Consider

1. Are professional sports players entitled to claim records set if they were on drugs during their successful career? If they are entitled to their accomplishments regardless of their drug usage, how would it affect non–drug-using players? Is it fair to the sport and to the fans supporting the players? If they are not entitled to their accomplishments under drugged conditions, what should the penalty be?

2. Should all players in professional sports be continuously tested for drugs? Should this policy extend to both high school and college sports players? If so, what should the penalties for drug violations be? If high school and college sports players should not be tested for drugs, why not?

3. What if we find clear evidence that some currently admired major sports figures who scored big-time records in the past were using steroids or other performance-enhancing drugs while setting new and impressive records? Should anything be done about such evidence? If so, what penalties should the athletes receive? If not, why should we let them remain unblemished?

4. Are the real victims of this tragedy America's youth? Have athletes such as McGwire, Bonds, and Rodriguez betrayed the young people who admire and emulate them? Do you think America's youth are affected by their drug use in professional sports?

5. Does this scandal about professional sports and drug use suggest anything about the findings by the Centers for Disease Control and Prevention that steroid use among high school students more than doubled from 1991 to 2003?

Data from Amazon.com. "Editorial Reviews." Available http://www.amazon.com/exec/obidos/asin/0060746408/ref=bxgy. Accessed February 17, 2011; Associated Press. "Strong Suspended for Performance-Enhancing Drugs." Sports ESPN. (26 April 2005). Available http://sports.espn.go.com/mlb/news/story?id=2046762. Accessed April 18, 2011; Coile, Z. "House Bill Seeks to Toughen Steroid Rules: Athletes in All Leagues Would Be Held to the Strict Standards Used in Olympics." *San Francisco Chronicle,* Washington Bureau. (27 April 2005): 1–2; Dvorchak, R. "Former Steeler Courson Outlines Solutions for Steroid Use." Post-Gazette.com. (27 April 2005). Available http://blackandgoldworld.blogspot.com/2005/04/robert-dvorchak-courson-outlines.html. Accessed February 17, 2011; Eilek, R. "Pro Sports Keep Heads in Sand on Steroids." *U~T San Diego.* (17 April 2005). Available http://www.utsandiego.com/news/2005/Apr/17/pro-sports-keep-heads-in-sand-on-steroids/2/. Accessed February 17, 2011; and Health Reuters and Yahoo! News. "Anti-steroid Rules Proposed for U.S. Pro Sports." (27 April 2005); Woemer, A. "MLB Players' Use of Performance Enhancing Drugs Comes with Serious Health Risks." FoxNews.com, (6 August 2013). Available http://www.foxnews.com/health/2013/08/06/mlb-players-use-performance-enhancing-drugs-comes-with-serious-health-risks/; Smollins, M. "Alex Rodriguez Biogenesis Case: MLB CEO Rob Manfred Calls A-Rod Career 'Sad and Tarnished,' Claims Rodriguez PED Use 'Longer Than Any Other Player.'" *Sports World News* (Sportswn.Com) (1 November 2013). Available http://www.sportsworldnews.com/articles/6205/20131101/alex-rodriguez-biogenesis-case-mlb-ceo-rob-manfred-calls-a-rod-career-sad-tarnished-claims-rodriguez-ped-use-longer-than-any-other-player.htm; UIC College of Pharmacy. "Anabolic Steroids: An Overview." Chicago, IL: University of Illinois at Chicago (UIC), (2005). Available https://www.uic.edu/pharmacy/services/di/methamphetamine.htm

■ Laws Intended to Stop the Use of Performance-Enhancing Drugs in Professional Sports

In 2003, the **World Anti-Doping Code** was approved and remained in effect from January 1, 2004, to December 31, 2008. This code is the core document that provides the framework for harmonized antidoping policies, rules, and regulations within sport organizations and among public authorities.

The code consultation process, which was revised in April 2006, was similar to that used in the original drafting of the document between 2001 and 2003. The process included three stages of consultation, and culminated at the Third World Conference on Doping in Sport, which was held in November 2007. The revised code was endorsed by delegates at the World Conference on November 17, 2007, and unanimously adopted by the World Anti-Doping Agency's (WADA's) Foundation Board (WADA 2009).

This code has proven to be a very powerful and effective tool in the harmonization of antidoping efforts worldwide since it came into force on January 1, 2004 (WADA 2009). In January 2009, the code's key principles and elements, along with several changes, were reapproved by WADA's Foundation Board for implementation. In addition, governments and sports leagues have shown overwhelming support in adopting the code and have supported the growing body of jurisprudence from the Court of Arbitration for Sport (CAS) that furthers the code's tenets.

The major changes in the 2009 code include "... firmness and fairness" (WADA 2009) so that what is already in place strengthens the prevention of doping in sport. There also are provisions for increased sanctions, greater flexibility (the accused athlete has the option to provide evidence that the substance used was not intended to enhance performance), clear listing and definition of specified substances violating the rules, incentives to come forward and report personal usage or use by other athletes of performance-enhancing drugs, financial sanctions (including clearly specified periods

of ineligibility), and WADA's right to appeal to a Court of Sport Arbitration (WADA 2009).

■ Drugs Used by Athletes

A very memorable interview:

> Yes, the steroids I used certainly made me get bigger. I was going out for football and I had just made the team, so I kept using them and the results were phenomenal. Now, 2 years later, I won't be graduating. Several months ago, they removed a tumor on my liver, but they didn't get all the cancer. I am going home at the end of this semester. My parents want me to stay with them for the time I have left. When I go, I only have one wish—I want to die big and always be known as Big Jim. *(From Venturelli's research files, male, age 20, December 13, 1996)*

Studies have shown that athletes are less likely than nonathletes to use other drugs of abuse such as marijuana, alcohol, barbiturates, cocaine, and hallucinogens (Hoberman and Yesalis 1995; Substance Abuse and Mental Health Services Administration [SAMHSA] 2007). However, athletes are much more likely than other populations to take drugs that enhance (physically or psychologically) or are thought to enhance competitive performance; these drugs include stimulants such as amphetamines and cocaine and an array of drugs with presumed ergogenic effects, such as anabolic steroids (Bell 1987; National Institute on Drug Abuse [NIDA] 2006b). Some of the major drugs abused by athletes are listed in **Table 16.1**, along with their desired effects. The sections that follow discuss the drugs that are most frequently self-administered by athletes in an effort to improve their competitive performance.

ANABOLIC STEROIDS

Anabolic steroids consist of a group of natural and synthetic drugs that are chemically similar to cholesterol and related to the male hormone testosterone (Guide4living.com 2005; Lukas 1993) and its artificial derivatives. Steroids are used for treatment of certain diseases such as specific types of anemia, some breast cancers, and testosterone deficiency. Although illegal when taken for nonmedical purposes, steroids have been illegally used by both athletes and nonathletes since the late 1950s to improve athletic ability and physical appearance because steroids have performance-enhancing

TABLE 16.1 Partial List of Ergogenic Substances* and Expected Effects

Drugs	Expected Results
Amino acids	Stimulate natural production of growth hormone
Amphetamines and cocaine	Increase strength, alertness, and endurance
Anabolic steroids	Increase muscle mass and strength
Asthma medication	Improve breathing
B-complex vitamins	Enhance body metabolism and increase energy
Beta-blockers	Reduce hand tremor and stimulate growth hormone
Caffeine	Reduce fatigue
Chromium	Enhance carbohydrate metabolism
Ephedrine	Improve breathing
Furosemide	Mask steroid use and enable rapid weight loss
Methylphenidate	Enhance alertness and endurance
Over-the-counter decongestants	Increase endurance and energy
Thyroid hormone	Enhance metabolism

*Ergogenic drugs are substances that are used to enhance athletic performance.

Reproduced from Harlan, R., and M. Garcia. "Neurobiology of Androgen Abuse." *Drugs of Abuse and Neurobiology,* edited by R. Watson, 185–201. Boca Raton, FL: CRC Press, 1992.

and bodybuilding properties. Steroids are taken orally or injected into the muscles. Although males and females both use steroids, males have higher rates of use (NIDA 2009; SAMHSA 1999b).

Naturally occurring male hormones, or androgens, are produced by the testes in males. These hormones are essential for normal growth and development of male sex organs as well as secondary sex characteristics such as muscular development, male hair patterns, voice changes, and fat distribution. The androgens are also necessary for appropriate growth spurts during adolescence (Olin 1994). The principal accepted therapeutic use for androgens is for hormone replacement in males with abnormally functioning testes. In such cases, the androgens are administered before puberty and for prolonged periods during puberty to stimulate proper male development (Olin 1994).

THE MAJOR REASONS FOR THE ABUSE OF ANABOLIC STEROIDS

In light of a finding on the sources of banned substances in sports it was reported that "Athletes may obtain banned medicines from physicians, pharmacists, retail outlets, health and lifestyle magazines, gymnasiums, coaches, family members, fellow athletes, the Internet and the black market" (The Athlete.org 2011). The major reason for the use and abuse of anabolic steroids is that they are used by many athletes to improve athletic performance (Burke and Davis 1992; NIDA 2006b). Under some conditions, androgen-like drugs can increase muscle mass and strength; for this reason, they are referred to as anabolic (able to stimulate the conversion of nutrients into tissue) steroids (because chemically, they are similar to the steroids produced in the adrenal glands).

Another reason for taking steroids is to increase their muscle size or to reduce their body fat (NIDA 2006b). Others who abuse steroids in order to boost their muscle size have experienced physical or sexual abuse. In one series of interviews with male weightlifters, 25% who abused steroids reported memories of childhood physical or sexual abuse. Similarly, female weightlifters who had been raped were found to be twice as likely to report use of anabolic steroids or another purported muscle-building drug, compared with those women who had not been raped. Moreover, almost all of those who had been raped reported that they markedly increased their bodybuilding activities after the attack (NIDA 2006b). Finally, regarding adolescent steroid abuse, it is part of a pattern of high-risk behaviors. Such steroid-abusing adolescents have been found to take risks such as drinking and driving, carrying a gun, driving a motorcycle without a helmet, and abusing other illicit drugs. In conclusion, conditions such as **muscle dysmorphia** (a behavioral syndrome that causes individuals to have a distorted image

KEY TERM

muscle dysmorphia
behavioral syndrome that causes men to have a distorted image of their bodies, perceiving themselves as looking small and weak, even when they may be large and muscular; women with this condition think they look fat and flabby, even though they may actually be lean and muscular

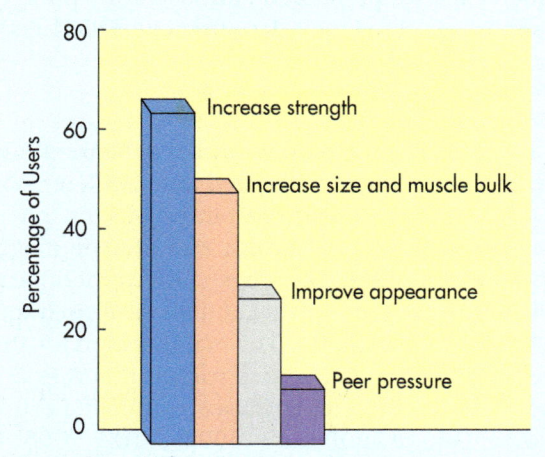

FIGURE 16.1 Reasons for nonmedical steroid use by college students.

Reproduced with permission from Harlan, R., and M. Garcia. "Neurobiology of Androgen Abuse," *Drugs of Abuse and Neurobiology*, edited by R. Watson, 186, Boca Raton, FL: CRC Press, 1992.

of their bodies, perceiving themselves as looking small and weak, even when they may be large and muscular), a history of physical or sexual abuse, or a history of engaging in high-risk behaviors have all been associated with an increased risk of initiating or continuing steroid abuse.

A study from *The American Journal of Sports Medicine* reported that the number of anabolic steroid users in the United States is estimated at approximately 3 million people. This number has dramatically increased from 1991 where data from the *National Household Survey on Drug Abuse* demonstrated the number of anabolic steroid users in the United States to be more than 1 million. The *National Household Survey on Drug Abuse*, reports a similar finding stating that 1,084,000 adult Americans admitted using steroids at one point or another (e-Steroid.com 2013) (see **Figure 16.1**). The most commonly abused steroids are in two categories: oral and injectable steroids. Oral steroids include:

- Anadrol (oxymetholone)
- Oxandrin (oxandrolone)
- Dianabol (methandrostenolone)
- Winstrol (stanozolol)

Injectable steroids include:

- Deca-Durabolin (nandrolone decanoate)
- Durabolin (nandrolone phenylpropionate)
- Depo-Testosterone (testosterone cypionate)
- Equipoise (boldenone undecylenate)
- Tetrahydrogestrinone (THG)

A 2009 study funded by the National Institute on Drug Abuse (NIDA) found that only 1.3% of 8th and 10th graders and 2.2% of 12th graders had used steroids at least once in their lifetimes (NIDA 2010). "A more recent study shows that about five percent of middle and high school students have used anabolic steroids to put on muscle, and that as many as one-third of boys and one-fifth of girls have used protein powder or shakes. Between five and 10 percent admitted to using non-steroid muscle-enhancing substances like creatine" (Alvarez 2012). "A 2001 NCAA survey found that usage of stimulants, including ephedrine and amphetamines, and anabolic steroids had risen slightly since 1997. Between 3% and 4% of athletes surveyed admitted using stimulants, and 1.4% admitted using steroids" (Suggs 2003). Also realize that these percentages are much lower than actual usage rates because athletes are inclined to hide drug usage for fear of jeopardizing their eligibility to play sports as well as other more personal reasons having to do with image in the eyes of others. Further, in the United States, approximately 500,000 adolescents use steroids, and 52,000 children use anabolic steroids; "a study in the journal *Pediatrics* . . . found that 2.7% of Massachusetts middle-school athletes were using steroids" (Begley et al. 1999, p. 54). Another source indicates that males are more likely to use and abuse steroids than are females (Johnston et al. 2006). In a much larger nationwide study, in 2005, annual use rates were 1.2%, 1.8%, and 2.6% for boys in grades 8, 10, and 12, respectively, compared with 0.9%, 0.7%, and 0.4% for girls in those grades (Johnston et al. 2006). Encouraging results indicate that steroid use among adolescents in 8th, 10th, and 12th grade is significantly lower than in previous years (Johnston et al. 2006). Competition for scholarships and entry into professional sports are major factors that influence young athletes to use steroids (Scott, Wagner, and Barlow 1996).

Although the vast majority of anabolic steroid users are male, women involved in bodybuilding and strength and endurance sports also abuse these drugs. In another study, among seniors in high school, 3.2% of the males reported steroid use in the past year compared with 1.1% of the females. These statistics are much lower among 19- to 32-year-olds—0.4%, with males accounting for all steroid use (Johnston et al. 2004).

The first report of use of anabolic steroids to improve athletic performance was in 1954 by the Russian weightlifting team. These drugs'

Besides risking their health, athletes who choose to dope should remember that they are role models. Seventy-three percent of youth want to be like a famous athlete; 53% of youth say it is common for famous athletes to use banned substances to get ahead.

performance-enhancing advantages were quickly recognized by other athletes, and it has been estimated that as many as 90% of the competitors in the 1960 Olympic Games used some form of steroid (Toronto 1992). Because of the widespread misuse and associated problems with the use of these drugs, in the United States anabolic steroids were classified as Schedule III controlled drugs in 1991 (Merchant 1992).

Due to federal regulations, individuals convicted of a first offense of trafficking with anabolic steroids can be sentenced to a maximum prison term of 5 years and a $250,000 fine. For a second offense, the prison term can increase to 10 years with a $500,000 fine. Even possession of illicitly obtained anabolic steroids can result in a 1-year term with at least a $1000 fine (U.S. Department of Justice 1991–1992).

PATTERNS OF ABUSE

Geographical factors appear to have little to do with the use of anabolic steroids among athletes. In both inner city and suburban schools, all are equally attracted to these drugs. However, some athletes are more inclined to abuse anabolic steroids than others. For example, football players have the highest rate of abuse; in a survey conducted by the National Collegiate Athletic Association (NCAA) of 11 NCAA colleges and universities, 9% of football players self-reported, whereas track and field athletes have the lowest rate of abuse (4% reported) (National Institutes of Health [NIH] and NIDA 1998). A more recent study by the World Anti-Doping Agency (WADA) looked at blood samples taken between 2003 and 2008 across all professional sports; it found the following (Burn-Murdoch 2012):

- Of the 26 sports included in the 2012 Games, the worst offender in terms of the rate of findings per sample (averaged across all eight years) is cycling, 3.71%.
- The second highest rate—3.05%—was found among boxers. Badminton had the lowest rate of usage-indication findings per sample, at 0.87%.
- Footballers were the most tested athletes in terms of the total number of samples (30,398), followed by athletics (competitive running, jumping, throwing, and walking) (25,013), cycling (21,427), and aquatics (13,138).

Another study using a more indirect method of interviewing found rates three times higher than the percentages just reported. In addition, the likelihood of abusing these drugs increases as the level of competition increases. Usage rates were approximately 14% in NCAA Division I athletes and 30% to 75% in professional athletes (Lukas 1993). In general, usage patterns for anabolic steroids vary considerably according to athletes' motivation, the level of competition, the type of sport, and the pressure for winning.

The pattern usually consists of self-administering doses that are 1 to 100 times greater than dosages used for legitimate medical conditions (U.S. Department of Justice 2004). Users take nonmedical anabolic-androgenic steroids in cycles, which are periods of use lasting 6 to 12 weeks or longer. **Stacking** these drugs means taking two or more types of steroids, which is common. The use of different steroids taken singly but in sequence is called **cycling**. To avoid developing tolerance to a particular steroid (**plateauing**), athletes often stagger the various drugs, sometimes taking them in overlapping patterns or alternately. Users often

KEY TERMS

stacking
use of several types of steroids at the same time

cycling
use of different types of steroids singly but in sequence

plateauing
developing tolerance to the effects of anabolic steroids

move from a low daily dose at the beginning of a cycle to a higher dose, then reduce their use toward the end of the cycle (**pyramiding**). To combat the unwanted side effects of steroids, such as severe skin rashes and development of irreversible masculine traits in women, as well as sudden anger and explosive physical aggressiveness (known as "roid rage" in men), other drugs such as diuretics, antiestrogens, human chorionic gonadotropin, and antiacne medication are often taken concurrently. This pattern of use is referred to by users as an **array**. In general, power athletes prefer stacking, whereas bodybuilders prefer cycling. (See **Table 16.2**, which lists classes of drugs banned by the NCAA, drugs and procedures subject to restrictions, and some examples of NCAA banned substances in each drug class.)

Because steroid use has been prohibited by all legitimate sporting organizations, urine testing just before the athletic event has become commonplace (Lukas 1993). Steroid-using athletes attempt to avoid detection by trying to fool the tests. These highly questionable strategies include the following (Lukas 1993; Merchant 1992):

- Using the steroid only during training for the athletic events, but discontinuing its use several weeks before the competition to allow the drug to disappear from the body. Because oral steroids are cleared from the body faster than the injectable types, they are usually discontinued 2 to 4 weeks prior to competition, and the injection steroids are stopped 3 to 6 weeks before competition.
- Taking drugs, such as probenecid, that block the excretion of steroids in the urine. Probenecid is often used in an attempt to mask (cover up) anabolic steroids when drug tests are taken. Probenecid "[d]ecreases entry of steroids into the urine" (U.S. Department of Justice 2004). Current drug testing can detect the use of these drugs.
- Adding adulterant chemicals to the urine, such as Drano, Clorox, ammonia, or eye drops in order to invalidate the tests.

KEY TERMS

pyramiding
moving from a low daily dose at the beginning of the cycle to a higher dose, then reducing use toward the end of the cycle

array
use of other drugs while taking anabolic steroids to avoid possible side effects

Some of the most recent types of drugs that athletes use, even though they are all banned by WADA, are listed in **Table 16.3**. This table summarizes the 2013 list of prohibited performance-enhancing substances banned by the World Anti-Doping Code—International Standard.

EFFECTS OF ANABOLIC STEROIDS

Low to moderate doses of anabolic steroids have little effect on the strength or athletic skills of the average adult. However, when high doses are used by athletes during intense training programs, these drugs cause significant gains in lean body mass (i.e., muscle) and strength while decreasing fat (Lukas 1993). Because most of these effects are transient and will disappear when steroid use is stopped, athletes feel compelled to continue using them and become psychologically hooked (Toronto 1992). The drugs are most likely to benefit athletes in contact and strength sports in which increased muscle mass provides an advantage, such as weightlifting and football; anabolic steroids are less likely to benefit athletes involved in sports requiring dexterity and agility, such as baseball or tennis.

The risks associated with anabolic steroids are not completely understood. Most certainly, the higher the doses and the longer the use, the greater the potential damage these drugs can do to the body. Some of the adverse effects thought to occur with heavy steroid use (10 to 30 times the doses used therapeutically) include the following:

- Increased bad blood cholesterol levels, which could eventually clog arteries and cause heart attacks and strokes (National Clearinghouse for Alcohol and Drug Information [NCADI] 1999)
- Increased risk of liver disorders, such as jaundice and tumors (Lukas 1993)
- Psychological side effects, including irritability, outbursts of anger, mania, psychosis, and major depression
- Possible psychological and physical dependence with continual use of high doses, resulting in withdrawal symptoms, such as steroid craving (52%), fatigue (43%), depression (41%), restlessness (29%), loss of appetite (24%), insomnia (20%), diminished sex drive (20%), and headaches (20%) (Lukas 1993)
- Alterations in reproductive systems and sex hormones, causing changes in gender-related characteristics (Burke and Davis

TABLE 16.2 NCAA (National Collegiate Athletic Association) Banned Drug List

---

The NCAA bans the following classes of drugs:

a. Stimulants
b. Anabolic Agents
c. Alcohol and Beta Blockers (banned for rifle only)
d. Diuretics and Other Masking Agents
e. Street Drugs
f. Peptide Hormones and Analogues
g. Anti-Estrogens
h. Beta-2 Agonists

Note: Any substance chemically related to these classes is also banned.

The institution and the student-athlete shall be held accountable for all drugs within the banned drug class regardless of whether they have been specifically identified.

Drugs and Procedures Subject to Restrictions:

a. Blood Doping.
b. Local Anesthetics (under some conditions).
c. Manipulation of Urine Samples.
d. Beta-2 Agonists permitted only by prescription and inhalation.
e. Caffeine if concentrations in urine exceed 15 micrograms/ml.

Note: *There is no complete list of banned drug examples!*

Check with your athletics department staff before you consume any medication or supplement.

Some Examples of NCAA Banned Substances in Each Drug Class

Stimulants: amphetamine (Adderall); caffeine (guarana); cocaine; ephedrine; fenfluramine (Fen); methamphetamine; methylphenidate (Ritalin); phentermine (Phen); synephrine (bitter orange); etc.
    exceptions: phenylephrine and pseudoephedrine are not banned.

Anabolic Agents: (sometimes listed as a chemical formula, such as 3,6,17-androstenetrione) boldenone; clenbuterol; DHEA; nandrolone; stanozolol; testosterone; methasterone; androstenedione; norandrostenedione; methandienone; etiocholanolone; trenbolone; etc.

Alcohol and Beta Blockers (banned for rifle only): alcohol; atenolol; metoprolol; nadolol; pindolol; propranolol; timolol; etc.

Diuretics (water pills) and Other Masking Agents: bumetanide; chlorothiazide; furosemide; hydrochlorothiazide; probenecid; spironolactone (canrenone); triameterene; trichlormethiazide; etc.

Street Drugs: heroin; marijuana; tetrahydrocannabinol (THC)—no other substances are classified as NCAA street drugs.

Peptide Hormones and Analogues: growth hormone (hGH); human chorionic gonadotropin (hCG); erythropoietin (EPO); etc.

Anti-Estrogens: anastrozole; tamoxifen; formestane; 3,17-dioxo-etiochol-1,4,6 -triene (ATD), etc.

Beta-2 Agonists: bambuterol; formoterol; salbutamol; salmeterol; etc.

Any substance that is chemically related to the class of banned drugs is also banned (unless otherwise noted).

TABLE 16.3 Extract from The 2013 List of Prohibited Substances and Methods*

Substances and Methods Prohibited at All Times (In- and Out-of-Competition)

Non-Approved Substances: Any pharmacological substance which is not addressed by any of the subsequent sections of the List and with no current approval by any governmental regulatory health authority for human therapeutic use (e.g., drugs under pre-clinical or clinical development or discontinued, designer drugs, substances approved only for veterinary use) is prohibited at all times.

Anabolic Androgenic Steroids (AAS)

Exogenous[1]–(e.g., 1-androstenediol; 1-androstenedione); bolandiol, bolasterone, boldenone, calusterone, clostebol, danazol)

(continues)

TABLE 16.3 Extract from The 2013 List of Prohibited Substances and Methods* (*continued*)

Endogenous[2] (AAS when administered exogenously)–(e.g., androstenediol; androstenedione, dihydrotestosterone, prasterone, dehydroepiandrosterone, DHEA, testosterone)

Other Anabolic Agents, including but not limited to: Clenbuterol, selective androgen receptor modulators (SARMs), tibolone, zeranol, zilpaterol.

Peptide Hormones, Growth Factors and Related Substances (Erythropoiesis-Stimulating Agents [e.g. erythropoietin (EPO), darbepoetin (dEPO), hypoxia-inducible factor (HIF) stabilizers, methoxy polyethylene glycol-epoetin beta (CERA), peginesatide (Hematide)]

Chorionic Gonadotrophin (CG) and Luteinizing Hormone (LH) in males

Corticotrophins

Growth Hormone (GH), Insulin-like Growth Factor-1 (IGF-1), Fibroblast Growth Factors (FGFs), Hepatocyte Growth Factor (HGF), Mechano Growth Factors (MGFs), Platelet-Derived Growth Factor (PDGF), etc.

Beta-2 Agonists–(e.g., all beta-2 agonists, including all optical isomers where relevant, are prohibited except inhaled salbutamol [maximum 1600 micrograms over 24 hours], inhaled formoterol [maximum delivered dose 54 micrograms over 24 hours] and salmeterol when taken by inhalation in accordance with the manufacturers' recommended therapeutic regimen)

Hormone and Metabolic Modulators–(e.g., aromatase inhibitors, selective estrogen receptor modulators (SERMs), other anti-estrogenic substances, agents modifying myostatin function(s), metabolic modulators)

Diuretics and Other Masking Agents–(e.g., diuretics, desmopressin, plasma expanders)

Diuretics (e.g., acetazolamide, amiloride, bumetanide, canrenone, chlorthalidone, etacrynic acid, furosemide)

Manipulation of Blood and Blood Components–(e.g., administration or reintroduction of any quantity of autologous, homologous or heterologous blood or red blood cell products of any origin into the circulatory system; artificially enhancing the uptake, transport or delivery of oxygen; any form of intravascular manipulation of the blood or blood components by physical or chemical means)

Chemical and Physical Manipulation–(e.g., includes tampering with blood samples and intraveneous infusion and/or injections)

Gene Doping–(e.g., transfer of polymer, nucleic acids or nucletic acid analogues and the use of normal or genetically modified cells)

Substances and Methods Prohibited In-Competition

Stimulants–Non-specified stimulant (e.g., adrafinil, amfepramone, amiphenazole, amphetamine, amphetaminil, benfluorex) and specified stimulants (e.g., adrenaline,[3] cathine,[4] ephedrine,[5] etamivan, etilefrine, fenbutrazate)

Narcotics–(e.g., buprenorphine, dextromoramide, diamorphine (heroin), fentanyl and its derivatives, hydromorphone, methadone, morphine, oxycodone)

Cannabinoids–(e.g. cannabis, hashish, marijuana) or synthetic delta 9-tetrahydrocannabinol (THC) and cannabimimetics (e.g., "Spice," JWH018, JWH073, HU-210)

Glucocorticosteroids–are prohibited when administered oral, intravenous, intramuscular or rectal routes.

Substances Prohibited in Particular Sports

Alcohol–(ethanol) is prohibited *In-Competition* only in the following sports. Detection will be conducted by analysis of breath and/ or blood. The doping violation threshold (haematological values) is 0.10 g/L. [aeronautic (FAI), archery (FITA), automobile (FIA), karate (WKF), motorcycling (FIM), and powerboating (UIM)]

Beta-Blockers–is prohibited in the following sports archery (FITA) (also prohibited Out-of-Competition) automobile (FIA), billiards (all disciplines) (WCBS), darts (WDF), golf (IGF), shooting (ISSF, IPC) (also prohibited Out-of-Competition), skiing/snowboarding (FIS) in ski jumping, freestyle aerials/halfpipe and snowboard halfpipe/big air.

Beta blockers (e.g., cebutolol, alprenolol, atenolol, betaxolol, bisoprolol, bunolol, carteolol, carvedilol, celiprolol, esmolol)

[1] "exogenous" refers to a substance which is not ordinarily capable of being produced by the body naturally.
[2] "endogenous" refers to a substance which is capable of being produced by the body naturally.
[3] Local administration (e.g. nasal, ophthalmologic) of Adrenaline or co-administration with local anesthetic agents is not prohibited.
[4] Cathine is prohibited when its concentration in urine is greater than 5 micrograms per milliliter.
[5] Each of ephedrine and methylephedrine is prohibited when its concentration in urine is greater than 10 micrograms per milliliter.

*This table was extracted from The 2013 Prohibited List – World Anti-Doping Agency's (WADA) International Standard, identifying substances and methods prohibited in-competition, out-of-competition, and in particular sports. The complete list is available at http://www.wada-ama.org/Documents/World_Anti-Doping_Program/WADP-Prohibited-list/2013/WADA-Prohibited-List-2013-EN.pdf. Please note that the Prohibited List is updated annually and the most current edition can be found on WADA's website at http://list.wada-ama.org.

1992): breast enlargement in males, breast reduction and bodily hair growth in females, infertility in both genders, and changes in genitalia—atrophy (shrinkage) of the penis and testicles in males and enlargement of external genitalia in females (Street, Antonio, and Cudlipp 1996)

- Changes in skin and hair in both genders: increased incidence and severity of acne, male pattern baldness, and increased body hair (Burke and Davis 1992)
- Persistent unpleasant breath odor (NCADI 1999)
- Swelling of the feet or lower limbs (NCADI 1999)
- Other changes, including stunted growth in adolescents, deepening of voice in females, and water retention, causing bloating (Burke and Davis 1992; Street et al. 1996)

SOURCES OF STEROIDS

Where do the anabolic steroids come from? About 50% of the anabolic steroids used in the United States are prescribed by doctors; the other 50% are obtained from the black market. Black market sources of steroids include drugs diverted from legitimate channels, smuggled from foreign countries—including Brazil, Italy, Mexico, Great Britain, Portugal, France, and Peru (NIDA 1996)—that are designated for veterinarian use, or inactive counterfeits (U.S. Department of Justice 1991–1992). A primary source for steroids in the United States is the Baja, California, area of Mexico (Yesalis and Cowart 1998). The steroids are manufactured in Mexico City and shipped to pharmacies in the Baja region. Some health food stores and mail-order firms also offer products with names similar to the prescription anabolic steroids, such as Dynabdin, Metrobolin, and Diostero. These sham steroids contain only vitamins, amino acids, or micronutrients (Merchant 1992; NIDA 2006b).

Most steroids used for nonmedical purposes are obtained illegally. A major federal report indicates that sources of illicit steroids fall into three rough categories: (1) smuggled steroids manufactured licitly or illicitly abroad, (2) drugs legally manufactured in this country and diverted to illicit sales at various places in the distribution chain, and (3) drugs clandestinely produced domestically. Small minorities of users obtain their drugs by prescription. Actual doses are often difficult to estimate because the product may

have been produced in an uncontrolled laboratory with unknown quality control, may have been intended for veterinary use with its human equivalent doses not known, or may be counterfeit (NIH and NIDA 1998). Another source noted that the majority of young people report that steroids are easily available through their friends and coaches (McCaffrey 1999).

STIMULANT USE AMONG ATHLETES

There are often reports in the media of football, basketball, or baseball players who have tested positive in a drug-screening evaluation or who have been suspended from competition due to drug abuse. In 1986, reports of cocaine-related deaths of sports figures included basketball star Len Bias and professional football player Don Rogers. Perhaps such sports tragedies helped convince some U.S. youth of the dangers of stimulant abuse and contributed to the decline in drug abuse in the late 1980s (Johnston et al. 1993). Clearly, no one—not even an athlete—is immune from the risks of these drugs (see "Case in Point: When Drugs Enter the Boxing Ring").

Amphetamines and cocaine are abused to improve athletic skills (McDonald 1995). However, it is not clear if stimulants actually enhance athletic performance or merely the athlete's perception of performance. Many athletes believe these drugs promote quickness, enhance endurance, delay fatigue, increase self-confidence and aggression, and mask pain (Hoberman and Yesalis 1995). In fact, some studies have shown that stimulants can improve some aspects of athletic performance, especially in the presence of fatigue (NIDA 1996).

Although some athletes would never consider using the hard stimulants, such as cocaine and amphetamines, milder stimulants that are legal and available over-the-counter (OTC) may be thought to be acceptable. Such stimulants include caffeine and OTC decongestants (for example, phenylpropanolamine and phenylephrine). These drugs can be a double-edged sword for the athlete. Their use can reduce fatigue, give a sense of energy, and even mask pain. Nevertheless, in high doses, especially when combined, they can cause nervousness, tremors, and restlessness; impair concentration; accelerate dehydration; and interfere with sleep ("OTC Drugs and Athletes" 1992). Some athletic competitions limit permissible blood levels of caffeine and do not allow the use of OTC stimulants such as decongestant drugs.

▶ CASE IN POINT

When Drugs Enter the Boxing Ring

When Oliver McCall entered the boxing ring to fight for the heavyweight championship on February 7, 1997, he was not alone. With him came the specter of years of drug abuse. Just 7 weeks before, McCall had been arrested for swinging a Christmas tree around a hotel lobby while in a drug-induced haze. A few years earlier, he was found in a crack house after having been mugged by a fellow addict, to whom he lost the $1.5 million check he had carried with him in a sock to buy drugs. These events were just two of many drug-related occurrences on his record. His most recent arrest, however, had been followed by a drug treatment program, which he attended daily.

But something went wrong the night of February 7. After having announced to a friend, "I want my title. I'm fighting for my life," McCall seemed to want to get knocked out. In the third round, in the middle of the ring, in front of a packed audience, he listlessly walked around as his opponent, Lennox Lewis, threw punches at him. McCall dodged and bobbed his head, yet refused to fight back. After the fourth round, McCall stood alone, away from his corner, sobbing uncontrollably, seemingly having a nervous breakdown in front of a worldwide cable television audience. Fifty-five seconds into the fifth round, referee Mills Lane stopped the fight. Lewis was the winner. McCall, in more ways than one, was not.

Although drugs have been an unwelcome part of sports in recent years, there are few cases where the consequences became more publicly evident. Here was a great contradiction for the world to see: Lennox Lewis, the athlete who had never been knocked down, and Oliver McCall, the man floored by the pain and drugs in his life. McCall's trainer, George Benton, said, "It was hard to watch, but it could be the best thing that ever happened to the human race. Now a father can tell his kids, 'You see what you saw on T.V.? You see what happens on drugs?' It was a hell of a lesson."

Data from Eskenazi, G. "McCall Tries to Explain Bizarre Action." *New York Times.* (9 February 1997). Available http://www.nytimes.com/1997/02/09/sports/mccall-tries-to-explain-bizarre-actions.html?scp=4&sq=oliver%20mccall&st=cse. Accessed April 18, 2011.

MISCELLANEOUS ERGOGENIC DRUGS

Most athletic organizations have banned the use of anabolic steroids and stimulants and are using more effective screening procedures to detect offenders. A result of this clampdown has been the search for alternative performance-enhancing drugs by athletes who feel a need for such pharmacological assistance. The following are brief discussions of a few of these substitute ergogenic substances.

CLENBUTEROL

At the 1992 Olympic Games in Barcelona, Spain, at least four athletes, including German world sprint champion Katrina Krabbe, were disqualified from competition for using the drug clenbuterol to enhance their athletic performance (Merchant 1992). Not legally available in the United States, this drug is known as "Doper's Delight" and is supposed to improve breathing and increase strength. Currently, most athletic urine examinations test for it.

ERYTHROPOIETIN

Clinically, erythropoietin is a drug used to treat patients with anemia (Kennedy 2000). Because it stimulates the production of red blood cells (the oxygen-carrying cells in the blood), it is thought that this drug enhances oxygen use and produces additional energy. Erythropoietin was being used as a substitute for blood doping, when it was undetectable (today it is detectable). *Blood doping* is when athletes attempt to increase their number of red blood cells by reinfusing some of their own blood (which has been stored) before an athletic event.

Erythropoietin (EPO) can now be detected through testing and in the past it was reported to be used by athletes engaged in endurance activities such as long-distance cycling. "EPO has its dangers. EPO injections thicken the blood, which increases the strain on the heart. This is particularly dangerous when the heart rate slows down, such as during sleep. The increased thickness, or viscosity, of the blood increases the risk of blood clots, heart attacks, and strokes" (Quinn 2011).

HUMAN GROWTH FACTOR AND HUMAN GROWTH HORMONE

Athletes sometimes abuse two types of hormones: **human growth factor (HGF)** and its designer drug synthetic version, **human growth hormone (HGH)**. HGH also is referred to simply as GH (growth hormone). HGF, also known as *somatotropin*, is a hormone naturally secreted by the pituitary gland at the base of the brain that helps to achieve normal growth potential of muscles, bones, and internal organs. Some athletes claim that release of natural HGF can be simulated by using drugs such as levodopa (used to treat Parkinson's disease), clonidine (used to treat hypertension), and amino acids. Athletes use commercially prepared HGH because it cannot be distinguished from naturally occurring HGF (Kennedy 2000).

Use of this hormone by athletes is limited, however, by its high cost. The benefits of HGF to athletic performance are very controversial, although the potential side effects are substantial, including abnormal growth patterns (called acromegaly), diabetes, thyroid gland problems, heart disease, and loss of sex drive (Merchant 1992).

The synthetic HGH is available in the form of a structured steroid-type analog sold in vials; this product is used to build muscle tissue, with corresponding decreases in body fat, without exercise (McDonald 1995). HGH is probably the most potent anabolic agent ever discovered, but it is also one of the most expensive. In fact, HGH is so expensive that until the mid-1990s, "its use in the United States was confined to pediatric endocrinologists who used it to treat undersized children" (McDonald 1995, p. C1). To date, tests are capable of detecting HGH in the blood (WebMD.com 2008). In addition, the side effects of this drug remain largely unknown. As a result, this drug is highly vulnerable to abuse.

BETA (β)-ADRENERGIC BLOCKERS

The β-adrenergic blockers are drugs that affect the cardiovascular system and are frequently used to treat hypertension. They have been used in sports because they reduce heart rate and signs of nervousness, which in turn quiets hand tremors. Consequently, these drugs are most likely to be used by individuals participating in sports that require steady hands, such as competitive shooting. The use of these drugs is prohibited by most athletic organizations (Kennedy 2000; Merchant 1992).

GAMMA-HYDROXYBUTYRATE

The substance gamma-hydroxybutyrate (GHB) is found naturally in the brain and has been used in England to treat insomnia. Athletes and bodybuilders have used GHB to increase muscle mass and strength (Kennedy 2000). Although the actual effects of the compound are not known, it has been reported to cause euphoria and increase the release of growth hormone. Acute poisoning with GHB has occurred, causing hospitalization; other adverse effects can include headaches, nausea, vomiting, muscle jerking, and even short-term coma, though full recovery has been universal ("Bodybuilding Drug" 1992; "Multistate Outbreak" 1994). Prolonged use may cause withdrawal (insomnia, anxiety, and tremor). GHB is especially dangerous when combined with central nervous system (CNS) stimulants such as amphetamines and cocaine (U.S. Department of Justice 2004).

▪ Prevention and Treatment

If the problem of drug abuse among athletes is to be dealt with effectively, sports programs must be designed to discourage inappropriate drug use and assist athletes who have developed drug abuse problems. Coaches and administrators should make it clear to sports participants that substance abuse will never give an athlete a competitive advantage in their programs and will not be tolerated. The **Adolescents Training and Learning to Avoid Steroids (ATLAS) program**, which was developed by Dr. Linn Goldberg of Oregon Health Sciences at the University of Portland, is one of the most successful prevention programs for steroid abuse.

The Adolescent[s] Training and Learning to Avoid Steroids Program (ATLAS) was designed to lower the use of anabolic steroids among high school athletes. The program combined

KEY TERMS

human growth factor (HGF)
a hormone that stimulates normal growth

human growth hormone (HGH)
a designer drug synthetic version of HGF; also referred to as simply GH (growth hormone)

Adolescents Training and Learning to Avoid Steroids (ATLAS) program
an anabolic abuse prevention educational program that empowers student athletes to make the right choices about steroid use

classroom and weight-training sessions, to teach students about strength training, nutrition, and risk factors for steroid use. Overall, the ATLAS program was found to reduce the use of steroids. (Child Trends 2009)

Athletes, coaches, and team leaders are trained to educate team members about the effects of anabolic steroid abuse. Because adolescents already know that anabolic steroids build muscles and can increase athletic abilities, both desirable and adverse effects of steroid use are taught. Research has shown that information about anabolic steroids that fails to acknowledge potential benefits creates a credibility gap that can make youth distrustful of the prevention program. The program consists of three components—classroom, weight training, and parent information—to "give the student athletes the knowledge and skills to resist steroid use and achieve their athletic goals in more effective, healthier ways" (Goldberg et al. 1996, p. 1555):

1. The classroom component consists of football coaches and student leaders conducting highly interactive sessions that explore the effects of steroids, the elements of sports nutrition, and strength training alternatives to steroid use. In this setting, while the coaches introduce topics and act as leaders, the students are exploring and learning from one another (Goldberg et al. 1996).

2. In the weight-training component, research staff members conduct seven hands-on sessions that teach the students proper weight-training techniques (Goldberg et al. 1996).

3. The parent information component consists of discussions and information sessions with parents. The staff provides nutrition guidelines and seeks compliance while stressing the very best nutrition for the athletes and their families. Parents become more vigilant against steroid use and learn to enjoy well-balanced, nutritious meals (Goldberg et al. 1996).

Briefly summarized, results indicate that the students who participated in this program in comparison with the control group (a group of students not participating in the program) showed they (1) knew more about proper exercise, (2) had a clear understanding of the dangers of using steroids and had become much more sensitized to the harmful effects of such drugs, (3) held more unfavorable views of others' use of anabolic steroids, and (4) were more likely to avoid unhealthy eating (such as frequenting fast-food restaurants) (Child Trends 2009; Goldberg et al. 1996).

Drug Use Among Women

Until recently, little was known about the patterns of female drug abuse. In general, most clinical drug abuse research, including treatment and rehabilitation outcomes, was either conducted in male populations and the results were extrapolated to women or the research was done in general populations with little regard to gender influences (About.com 2007a; Dicker and Leighton 1994; Klee and Jackson 2002; Lin 1994; NIDA 2006a; U.S. Department of Health and Human Services (USDHHS) and NIDA 1999). Most researchers considered drug abuse to be a male problem. Today, the research focusing on women and drug use is better, but a greater amount of study is still needed. Even today, scientists performing even basic research with animals generally prefer male animal models to avoid the hormonal complexities of female animals. However, a growing concern for the importance of unique emotional, social, biochemical, and hormonal features in females has caused researchers to acknowledge the importance of gender differences.

■ Women Are More Concerned About Drug Use than Men

Women express greater initial concerns about drug use than men, although "most recent studies suggest that gender either has no effect on treatment initiation, or, if it has an effect, women are more likely than men to initiate treatment" (Green 2006, p. 6). When asked whether drug abuse is a greater problem now than 5 years earlier, 51% of women and 42% of men answered "yes" (Drug Strategies 1998). When asked whether drug use is a big concern among youth, 58% of women and 48% of men answered "yes" (Drug Strategies 1998). Further, 58% of women and 50% of men thought it was wrong to reduce prevention funds while increasing prison funds (Drug Strategies 1998). One reason for this discrepancy may be that women traditionally have been primary caregivers; therefore, they feel more responsible about issues that can plague their communities and their families and often feel the need to be more vocal and be in positions that maintain harmony within the family setting (Green 2006). Women also generally express more concerns about safety issues than men because they are more likely to be victims of violent crimes, such as muggings or sexual assaults.

■ Patterns of Drug Use: Comparing Females with Males

Recent surveys comparing male and female drug use patterns confirm that differences exist among the licit and illicit drug-using populations. **Table 16.4** compares annual female and male drug use among respondents ages 19 to 30. The research findings in this table indicate the following gender-related differences in drug use (Johnston et al. 2012):

- Overall, females consistently use fewer licit and illicit drugs (31% of females versus 37% of males use illicit drugs).
- The most common types of abused drugs (in descending order) for females were: alcohol (83.1%), flavored alcoholic beverages (60.2%), binge drinking (five or more drinks in a row in last 2 weeks (29%), any illicit drug (31.3%), cigarettes (27.8%), marijuana (26.3%), and any illicit drug other than marijuana (15.6%).
- Males have higher annual prevalence rates for nearly all illicit drugs—with ratios of two times greater or more for synthetic marijuana, hallucinogens, LSD, hallucinogens other than LSD, Salvia, heroin, heroin with a needle, methamphetamine, crystal methamphetamine (ice), and steroids (see Table 16.4).
- Females (60.2%) have a much greater tendency to drink flavored alcoholic beverages than males (46.5%), and females are slightly

TABLE 16.4   Annual Percentage Use of Various Types of Drugs by Gender Among Respondents of Modal, Age 19–30*

	Males	Females	Totals
Alcohol	84.7	83.1	83.8
Flavored alcoholic beverages	46.5	60.2	54.6
Five or more drinks in a row in last 2 weeks	45.4	29.0	35.5
Any illicit drug (non medical use)	36.6	31.3	33.3
Cigarettes	35.9	27.8	31.0
Marijuana	34.1	26.3	29.4
Any illicit drug other than marijuana	19.2	15.6	17.0
Narcotics other than heroin**	8.6	7.2	7.7
Amphetamines, adjusted**	7.7	5.8	6.6
Tranquilizers**	6.3	5.4	5.8
Other cocaine	4.1	7.4	5.4
Cocaine	6.4	3.3	4.5
Sedatives (barbiturates)**	5.7	3.0	4.1
MDMA (Ecstasy)	3.8	3.1	3.4
Hallucinogens	5.3	2.2	3.4
Hallucinogens other than LSD	4.7	1.7	2.9
LSD	2.6	0.9	1.6
Inhalants	1.1	0.6	0.8
Methamphetamines	0.8	0.4	0.6
Crack	0.7	0.5	0.6

(continues)

TABLE 16.4 Annual Percentage Use of Various Types of Drugs by Gender Among Respondents of Modal, Age 19–30* (*continued*)

	Males	Females	Totals
Crystal methamphetamine (ice)	0.7	0.3	0.4
Heroin	0.7	0.3	0.4
PCP	0.2	0.3	0.3
Heroin (with a needle)	0.5	0.2	0.3
Steroids	0.3	0.1	0.2
Heroin (without a needle)	0.1	0.2	0.2

*Drugs listed below are rank ordered from highest to lowest by usage in the totals column).

**Nonprescription use.

Data from Johnston, L. D., P. M. O'Malley, J. G Bachman, and J. E Schulenberg. *Monitoring the Future: National Survey Results on Drug Use, 1975–2011. Volume II: College Students and Adults Ages 19–50.* Ann Arbor, MI: Institute for Social Research, the University of Michigan, 2012.

more likely to use other cocaine than males (7.4% vs. 4.1%), as well as PCP (0.3% vs. 0.2%) and heroin without a needle (0.2% vs. 0.1%).

- All three measures of cocaine (cocaine, other cocaine, and crack) showed higher rates of use by males than females (19- to 30-year-olds).
- Other large gender differences among 19- to 30-year-olds are found in daily marijuana use (8.0% for males vs. 4.2% for females, not shown in table), daily alcohol use (8.0% vs. 3.4%, not shown in table), and occasions of drinking five or more drinks in a row in the prior 2 weeks (45% vs. 29%). The gender difference in occasions of drinking five or more drinks in a row is larger among young adults than among 12th graders, where it is 26% for males versus 18% for females.
- Ecstasy (MDMA) use is slightly higher among males than among females in the young adult sample overall, with annual prevalence of 3.8% and 3.1%, respectively.
- Annual prevalence of use of narcotics other than heroin outside of medical supervision shows only limited gender differences: 8.6% for males and 7.2% for females. Use of Vicodin, one of the most widely used drugs in the class, is 7.0% and 6.8%, respectively. The gender difference for OxyContin is 3.5% for males vs. 2.2% for females.
- The use of amphetamines is a little higher among males than among females, with annual prevalence of 7.7% and 5.8%, respectively.
- Males are also more likely to smoke cigarettes than females (35.9% for males versus 27.8% for females).

- Steroid use among young adults is much more prevalent among males than females, as is true for 12th graders. Among 12th graders, 1.8% of males report steroid use in the past year versus 0.5% of females. These statistics are much lower among 19- to 30-year-olds, but use by males remains higher (0.3% for males vs. 0.1% for females)

Recent findings regarding gender differences among 8th, 10th, and 12th grade students are:

- Annual marijuana use is higher among males than among females, and daily marijuana use is roughly two to three times as high among males.
- Males have considerably higher prevalence rates than females on most other illicit drugs, too—at least by 12th grade. The annual prevalence rates for 12th-grade males, compared to 12th-grade females, are more than twice as high for hallucinogens other than LSD, crack, other cocaine, heroin, OxyContin, Vicodin, amphetamines, Adderall, methamphetamine, and Rohypnol. The use of inhalants, tranquilizers, alcohol, and flavored alcoholic beverages is slightly higher among females in those grades. Alcohol used to the point of being drunk is slightly higher among females in 8th grade and among males in 10th grade (Johnston et al. 2013).

Additional findings among older adults and gender differences indicate that:

To date, there is extensive evidence of the differences between women and men regarding substance use. Epidemiological studies show that even though women are less likely to initiate drug use than men, they start earlier and are more susceptible to develop an addiction. Women are also more vulnerable to drug-related pathologies, such as liver and cardiovascular diseases, and are more exposed to sexual and physical abuse and violence and to sexually transmitted diseases. At the same time studies of gender differences in drug treatment show that reasons why women and men seek help are often dissimilar, and that psychological, biological and social gender differences are important factors for the success of diverse types of treatment and for retention into treatment (UNICRI 2013,1)

Although some similarities appear between genders in drug usage rates for specific types of drugs, the general differences in the prevalence rates for females and males compel researchers to look for explanations so that we can better understand and deal with gender-related drug abuse problems.

■ Female Roles, Seeking Treatment, and Drug Addiction

Women are expected to take on more responsibilities than in my mother's day. Not only are we expected to work like men, but we also take care of the house, worry about the children, and get dinner on the table. If the house needs cleaning, everyone looks at the woman of the house. Men still have these expectations. I know things are changing with more equality between the sexes, but real equality of responsibilities has yet to occur. After everyone gets to bed on weekdays, I have a few drinks in order to calm me down before I go to bed. *(From Venturelli's research files, female employed full-time, age 43, June 30, 1996)*

Another interview revealed the following:

My boyfriend does vacuum when I ask, but not much else. Of course, if his boss is coming to visit, then he appears concerned about cleaning the house. How many times is he fast asleep and I am having some hard liquor and a few puffs from a joint after cleaning everything before we get up the next morning. I used to complain but he does not really care about the housework, so I compensate by getting buzzed before going to sleep.

(From Venturelli's research files, female employed part-time, age 29, 1997)

Recent research indicates that most people who have a substance use problem do not receive treatment. In comparing men with women, women are at a greater disadvantage for receiving substance abuse treatment.

In 2006, 7.4 million women aged 18 or older needed treatment for a substance abuse disorder involving alcohol or illicit drugs, but only 822,000 (11.2%) received treatment. . . . Of the women aged 18 to 49 who needed substance abuse treatment in the past year, 5.5% felt they needed treatment but did not receive it, and 84.2% neither received treatment nor perceived a need for it. (NSDUH 2007)

The reasons why women ages 18 to 49 who needed treatment did not receive it (and the percentage for each reason) were as follows (NSDUH 2007; SAMHSA 2010):

- Not ready to stop using (36%)
- Cost/insurance barriers (34%)
- Social stigma (29%)
- Did not feel need for treatment/could handle the problem without treatment (15.5%)
- Did not know where to go for treatment (13.2%)
- Did not have the time (4.7%)
- Treatment would not help (2.7%)
- Other access barriers (15.7%)

To appreciate the impact of drug abuse on women and the reasons why they are more reluctant to seek substance abuse treatment, it is necessary to understand the uniqueness of female roles in our society. Relative to drug abuse problems, women today are often judged by a double standard. Women suffering from drug addictions are often perceived less tolerantly than comparably addicted men (Erickson and Murray 1989). Because of these social biases, women are afraid of being condemned and are less likely to seek professional help for their own personal drug abuse problems; they also are more likely to report feeling shame or embarrassment because they are in substance abuse treatment (Green 2006). In addition, family, friends, and associates are less inclined to provide drug-dependent women with important emotional support (Klee and Jackson 2002; NSDUH 2007; USDHHS and NIDA 1999).

The image of the alcoholic woman has always been that of one who is boisterous, flirtatious, effusive, and, sometimes, loudmouthed. This may be the person she might become on occasion, but more often she is secluded in the privacy of her apartment or home after getting the kids off to school or having just come home from the office, classroom, or business. She is shy, reclusive to a point, alienated, retrospective, and lacking in self-esteem. Later in her drinking, she may become self-pitying, resentful, and even childishly cruel because of alcohol usage (Kirkpatrick 1999; Verhaak et al. 2010).

Due to their unique socioeconomic and family roles, women are especially vulnerable to emotional disruptions resulting from divorce, loneliness, and professional failures. Studies suggest that such stresses aggravate tendencies for women to abuse alcohol and other substances (Brady and Ashley 2005; Kirkpatrick 1999; Korolenko and Donskih 1990). More specifically, "women drink from a feeling of inadequacy and from a need for love, the kind of love not found within a sexual relationship but, rather, a love that is deeper and more primal" (Kirkpatrick 1999, p. 1; Verhaak et al. 2010).

In addition, drug addiction can occur in some women as a result of domestic adversities. Consequently, there is a high prevalence of drug dependence in women who are victims of sexual and/ or physical abuse (Ladwig and Anderson 1989). "Approximately 70% of women in drug abuse treatment report histories of physical and sexual abuse, with victimization beginning before 11 years of age and occurring repeatedly" (SAMHSA 1999a, p. 1). These physical and emotional traumas result in, or are precursors to, factors leading to drug abuse, such as low self-esteem, self-condemnation, anxiety and personal conflicts, dysfunctional dependencies, and overwhelming feelings of guilt (Kirkpatrick 1999; Verhaak et al. 2010). In addition, because of the crucial nurturing roles women hold, drug abuse problems can be particularly damaging to family stability.

Another unique role for women in drug abuse situations is that of a spouse, significant other, or mother to a drug addict. Often, in both traditional and nontraditional family relationships, women are expected to be nurturing, understanding, and willing to sacrifice to preserve the family integrity. If a family member becomes afflicted by drug dependence, the wife or mother is viewed as a failure. In other words, if the woman had maintained a good home and conducted her domestic chores properly, the family member would not have been driven to drugs (Green 2006; Klee and Jackson 2002; USDHHS and NIDA 1999).

Despite the disruption and considerable stress caused by drug addiction in the home, women continue to bear the burden of raising children, performing domestic chores, and keeping the family together. In addition, women in such circumstances are frequently put at great physical risk. The risk is from an addicted spouse who becomes abusive to his partner or from exposure to sexually transmitted infections, such as HIV or hepatitis, transmitted by a careless infected partner. The anxiety and frustrations resulting from these stressful circumstances can encourage women themselves to become dependent as they seek emotional relief by using drugs.

▪ Women's Response to Drugs

Research continues to lag regarding how women respond to substances of abuse. Although matters are slowly changing, the trend in drug abuse studies is still to avoid female populations; the effects of the drugs in men are still extrapolated to women. Even when drug abuse research is conducted on women, frequently the woman's response is not of primary concern; the objective is to determine the effects on a fetus during pregnancy or an infant during nursing (Klee and Jackson 2002; NSDUH 2007; USDHHS and NIDA 1999).

Although it generally can be assumed that the physiological and drug responses of men and women are similar, some distinctions should be recognized. For example, one study compared the risk for lung cancer in men and women after a lifetime of cigarette smoking. It was found that female smokers were twice as likely to get lung cancer as males who had smoked an identical number of cigarettes in their lifetimes ("Women Smokers" 1994). Another study indicated that women are *three* times more likely to contract lung cancer than men when smoking the same amount of cigarettes (Kirkpatrick 1999). These differences clearly indicate that cigarette smoking is far more dangerous for women than for men. Finally, women's unique response to drugs includes a finding discovered by researchers at the University of California at San Francisco that women respond to a class of painkillers called kappa-opioids, which are ineffective in men (*Science Daily* 2000).

DRUG ABUSE AND REPRODUCTION

A very important physiological distinction that sets women apart from men in terms of taking drugs is their ability to bear children. Because of this unique function, men and women have different endocrine (hormone) systems, organs, and structures, and women have varied drug responses according to their reproductive state. The unique features of women have a substantial impact on the response to drug abuse in the presence and absence of pregnancy.

Drug abuse patterns can influence the outcome of pregnancy even if they occur before a woman becomes pregnant. For example, women who are addicted to heroin are more likely to have poor health, including chronic infections, poor nutrition, and sexually transmitted infections such as human immunodeficiency virus (HIV), which can damage the offspring if pregnancy occurs. If substances are abused during pregnancy, they may directly affect the fetus and adversely alter its growth and development. The incidence of substance abuse during pregnancy is not known precisely, but undoubtedly hundreds of thousands of children have been exposed to drugs in utero. The effects of individual drugs of abuse taken during pregnancy are not discussed in depth in this chapter, but several specific observations merit reiteration here:

- Cocaine is a substantial threat for both the pregnant woman and the fetus. Although a number of specific claims for the fetal effects of cocaine are controversial, several observations appear legitimate: Cocaine use increases the likelihood of miscarriage when used during pregnancy; cocaine use in the late stages of pregnancy can cause cardiovascular or CNS complications in the baby at birth and immediately thereafter; and due to its vasoconstrictor effects, cocaine may deprive the fetal brain of oxygen, resulting in strokes and permanent physical and mental damage to the child.
- The impact of alcohol consumption during pregnancy has been well documented and publicized (Mathias 1995). When alcohol is consumed by the mother, it crosses the placenta, but the effect of this drug on the fetus is highly variable and depends on the quantity of alcohol consumed, timing of exposure, maternal drug metabolism, maternal state of health, and presence of other drugs. A particularly alarming consequence of high alcohol intake during pregnancy is an aggregate of physical and mental defects called fetal alcohol syndrome (FAS). Characteristics of this syndrome include low birth weight, abnormal facial features, mental retardation, and retarded sensorimotor development. In addition to its direct effects on the

fetus, alcohol has played a major role in many unwanted pregnancies or has resulted in women's exposure to sexually transmitted infections. As a CNS depressant, alcohol impairs judgment and reason and, in turn, encourages sexual risk taking that normally would not occur. The results are all too frequently tragic for women (SAMHSA 1999a).

- Tobacco use, primarily smoking, during pregnancy is an avoidable health hazard in the United States. In 2002, smoking during pregnancy was reported by 11.4% of all women giving birth in the United States, a decrease of 38% from 1990, when 18.4% reported (CDC 2004d). However, in 2002, the percentage of maternal smokers aged 15–19 years (16.7%) was the same as that for women aged 20–24 years, with the highest percentage observed among women aged 18–19 years (18.2%). Some experts suggest smoking cigarettes during pregnancy may pose a greater risk to the fetus than taking cocaine. Tobacco use by pregnant women may interfere with blood flow to the fetus, deprive it of oxygen and nutrition, and disrupt development of its organs—particularly the brain. Smoking harms many aspects and every phase of reproduction. Despite having greater increased knowledge of the adverse health effects of smoking during pregnancy, many pregnant women and girls continue to smoke (estimates range from 12% to 22%). It is estimated that only 18% to 25% quit smoking once they become pregnant (CDC 2004d).
- Also of significant concern is the possibility that exposure of nonsmoking pregnant women to secondhand tobacco smoke may be damaging to the fetus.
- Other drugs of abuse that have been associated with abnormal fetal development when used during pregnancy include barbiturates, benzodiazepines, amphetamines, marijuana, lysergic acid diethylamide (LSD), and even caffeine when consumed in high doses.

Clearly, women should be strongly urged to avoid all substances of abuse, especially during pregnancy.

WOMEN AND ALCOHOL

Alcohol is the drug most widely used and abused by women in the United States. According to the 2005 National Household Survey on Drug Abuse, among women age 12 or older, 45.9% used alcohol in the past month and 15.2% reported binge drinking (SAMHSA 2007). Alcohol abuse is also a major problem for women on college campuses, even though male college students are more likely than their female counterparts to use alcohol on a daily basis.

As a rule, women are less likely than men to develop severe alcohol dependence; thus, only 25% of the alcoholics in the United States are female. Women are also likely to initiate their drinking patterns later in life than men (Green 2006; Klee and Jackson 2002; USDHHS and NIDA 1999). "Women are older than men are when they begin drinking to intoxication, but once they develop a pattern of regular intoxication, they: [E]ncounter drinking-related problems more quickly than men and lose control over their drinking more quickly than men" (Green 2006). Interesting ethnic patterns of alcohol consumption have been reported in females, with black and white women manifesting similar drinking patterns. Although the proportions are similar, black women are more likely to completely abstain from alcohol than white women are.

Women who are dependent on alcohol are usually judged more harshly than men with similar difficulties. Alcoholic males are more likely to be excused because their drinking problems are often perceived as being caused by frustrating work conditions, family demands, economic pressures, or so-called nagging wives and children. In contrast, women with drinking problems are often perceived as spoiled or pampered, weak, deviant, or immoral. Such stigmas cause women to experience more guilt and anxiety about their alcohol dependence and discourage them from admitting their drug problems and seeking professional help (Kirkpatrick 1999).

The principal reasons for excessive alcohol consumption in women range from loneliness, boredom, and domestic stress in the housewife drinker to financial problems, sexual harassment, lack of challenge, discrimination, and powerlessness in the career woman. Depression is often associated with alcohol problems in women, although it is not clear whether this condition is a cause or an effect of the excessive use.

WOMEN'S PHYSIOLOGICAL RESPONSES TO ALCOHOL

Health consequences for excessive alcohol consumption appear to be more severe for women than for men. For example, alcoholic women are more likely to suffer premature death than alcoholic men. In addition, liver disease is more common and occurs at a younger age in female drinkers than in male alcoholics. In general, higher morbidity rates are experienced by alcoholic women than by their male counterparts.

Several explanations have been suggested for the higher rate of adverse effects seen in female alcoholics. Their higher blood alcohol concentrations may be due to a smaller blood volume and more rapid absorption into the bloodstream after drinking. Alternatively, slower alcohol metabolism in the stomach and liver might cause more alcohol to reach the brain and other organs as well as prolong exposure to the drug following consumption (Goldstein 1995). Studies have shown that for a woman of average size, one alcoholic drink has effects equivalent to two drinks in an average-size man.

DEALING WITH WOMEN'S ALCOHOL PROBLEMS

Alcoholic consumption varies considerably in women, ranging from total abstinence or an occasional drink to daily intake of large amounts of alcohol. Clearly, much is yet to be learned about the cause of some women's excessive drinking and dependence on alcohol. The role of genetic factors in predisposing women to alcohol-related problems is still unclear. The environment is certainly a major factor contributing to excessive alcohol consumption in women. It is well established that depression, stress, and trauma encourage alcohol consumption because of the antianxiety and amnesic properties of this drug. Because of unreasonable societal expectations and numerous socioeconomic disadvantages, women are especially vulnerable to the emotional upheavals that encourage excessive alcohol consumption.

As with all drug dependence problems, prevention is the preferred solution to alcohol abuse by women. Alcohol usually becomes problematic when it is no longer used occasionally to enhance social events but used daily to deal with personal problems. Such alcohol dependence can best be avoided by using constructive techniques to manage stress and frustrations. Because of unique female roles and society's expectations, women especially need to learn to be assertive with family members, associates in the workplace (including bosses), and other contacts in their daily routines. By expecting and demanding equitable treatment and consideration in personal and professional activities, stress and anxiety can often be reduced. Education, career training, and development of communication abilities can be particularly important in establishing a sense of self-worth. With these skills and confidence, women are better able to manage problems associated with their lives and less likely to resort to drugs for an escape.

WOMEN AND PRESCRIPTION DRUGS

Women are more likely than men to suffer depression, anxiety, and panic attacks (About.com 2006); be unable to express anger; be victims of physical and sexual abuse; and be subject to overwhelming guilt feelings (Kirkpatrick 1999). Consequently, they are also more likely to take and become addicted to the prescription drugs used in treating these disorders. Because these drugs are used as part of psychiatric therapy and under the supervision of a physician, drug dependence frequently is not recognized and may be ignored for months or even years. This type of legitimate drug abuse occurs most often in elderly women and includes the use of sedatives, antidepressants, and antianxiety medications. A recent study found that one in four women older than age 60 takes at least one of these drugs daily and that some of them develop serious drug problems (Drug Strategies 1998). Excessive use of these drugs by older women results in side effects such as insomnia, mood fluctuations, and disruption of cognitive and motor functions that can substantially compromise the quality of life.

■ Treatment of Drug Dependence in Women

As previously discussed, women are less likely than men to seek treatment for, and rehabilitation from, drug dependence (Kirkpatrick 1999; SAMHSA 2010). Possible reasons for their reluctance are as follows:

- In more traditional families, women have unique roles with high expectations. They are expected to assume demanding and ongoing responsibilities, such as motherhood, child rearing, and family maintenance, that cannot be postponed and often cannot be delegated, even temporarily, to others. Consequently, many women feel that they are too essential for the well-being of other family members to leave the home and seek time-consuming treatment for drug abuse problems.
- Drug treatment centers often are not very well designed to handle the unique health requirements of females—thus, women face more

obstacles. These obstacles involve barriers to treatment entry, treatment engagement, and long-term recovery (About.com 2007b; NIDA 1999). Women have been shown to have greater health needs than men due to more frequent respiratory, genitourinary (associated with the sex and urinary organs), and circulatory problems. If drug treatment centers are not capable of providing the necessary physical care, women are less likely to participate in associated drug abuse programs.

- Women are also more likely to relapse when their romantic partners are substance users (Rubin, Stout, and Longabaugh 1996).
- Drug-dependent women are more inclined to be unemployed than their male counterparts and more likely to be receiving public support. The implications of this difference are twofold. First, because concerns about one's job often motivate drug-dependent workers to seek treatment, this issue is less likely to be a factor in unemployed women. Second, without the financial security of a job, unemployed women may feel that good treatment for their drug problems is unaffordable.

The unique female requirements must be recognized and considered if women are to receive adequate treatment for drug dependence. Some considerations on how to achieve this objective include the following: (1) availability of female-sensitive services; (2) nonpunitive and noncoercive treatment that incorporates supportive behavior change approaches; and (3) treatment for a wide range of medical problems, mental disorders, and psychosocial problems (NIDA 1999). The role of motherhood needs to be used in a positive manner in drug treatment strategies. For most women, motherhood is viewed with high regard and linked to self-esteem. Approximately 90% of female drug abusers are in their childbearing years, and many have family responsibilities. Consequently, treatment approaches need to be tailored to allow women to fulfill their domestic responsibilities and satisfy their maternal obligations.

Women dependent on drugs often lack important coping skills. Because even today, many women lead restricted, almost isolated lives that focus entirely on domestic responsibilities, they face limited alternatives for dealing with stressful situations. Under these restrictive circumstances, the use of drugs to cope with anxieties and frustrations is very appealing. To enhance their ability to cope, drug-dependent women need to develop communication and assertiveness skills. Further, they need to be encouraged to control situations rather than allowing themselves to be controlled by the situation. Specific techniques that have proven useful in coping management are exercise (particularly relaxation types), relaxing visual imagery, personal hobbies, and outside interests that require active participation. Many drug-dependent women require experiences that divert their attention from the source of their frustrations while affording them an opportunity to succeed and develop a sense of self-worth.

Finally, one research study found that the most effective treatment for women included a mutually supportive therapeutic environment that addressed the following issues: psychopathology (such as depression), a woman's role as mother, interpersonal relationships, and the need for parenting education. Another study found that cocaine-using women whose children were living with them during residential treatment remained in the treatment programs significantly longer than women whose children were not living with them at the facility. Thus, having the children in the treatment facility provides opportunities to assess and meet women's needs, which in turn affects the women's prognosis (About.com 2007b; NIDA 1999).

■ Prevention of Drug Dependence in Women

The best treatment for drug addiction is prevention. To help prevent drug problems in women, as opposed to men, socioeconomic disadvantages need to be recognized as factors that make women more vulnerable to drug dependence, especially dependence on prescription medication. Women need to learn that nondrug approaches are often more desirable for dealing with situational problems than prescribed medications. For example, for older women suffering loneliness, isolation, or depression, it is better to encourage participation in outside interests, such as hobbies and service activities. In addition, social support and concern should be encouraged from family, friends, and neighbors. Such nonmedicinal approaches are preferred over prescribing sedatives and hypnotics to cope with emotional distresses. Similarly, medical conditions such as obesity, constipation, or insomnia should be treated by changing lifestyle, eating, and exercise habits rather than using drug "bandage therapy."

When women are prescribed drugs, they should ask about the associated risks, especially as they relate to drug abuse potential. Frequently, drug dependency develops insidiously and is not recognized by either the patient or the attending physician until it is already firmly established. If a woman taking medication is aware of the potential for becoming dependent and is instructed on how to avoid its occurrence, the problems of dependence and abuse can frequently be averted.

Drug Use in Adolescent Subcultures

I love waking up in the morning and smoking a nice fat joint. I live above the garage now, and my mom lives across the yard from the garage. This is a great living arrangement! I go to my room a few hours before crashing on many school nights, get high, drink some vodka that my older brother buys for me, then finally crash. In the morning, I always wake myself up so my mom stays away from my room, and my hide-away stash box is always locked. I roll me a joint and get a little high before I greet mom in the morning for a quick breakfast. I think she gets high too, but if I ask her and she says "no," what if she then asks me and gets all suspicious and shit? Besides, my Uncle Prentice always gets high with me, so I still think my mom really does not care about smoking weed. In fact, I know she is more worried about me drinking and driving than my friend "Mary Jane" [nickname for marijuana]. That's just my private life and no one needs to know. *(From Venturelli's research files, male residing in Chicago, age 18, July 10, 2000)*

From ages 13 through 18, adolescents are more likely to experience heightened psychological, social, and biological changes (Office of the Surgeon General 2007). Often, such internal and external changes are manifested by emotional outbursts. Why do such changes and urges arise? The adolescent's body is stretching, growing, and sometimes appearing out of control due to the hormonal changes of puberty.

Adolescents are uncertain and confused about not knowing who or what they are becoming. They often are confused as to their worth to family, peers, society, and even to themselves (Kantrowitz and

Wingert 1999). Adding to the frustration of growing up, the cultural status of adolescents is poorly defined. They find themselves trapped in a "no man's land" between the acceptance, simplicity, and security of childhood, and the stress, complexities, expectations, independence, and responsibilities of adulthood. Not only do adolescents have difficulty deciding who and what they are, but adults are equally unsure as to how to deal with these transitional human beings. Although the grown-up world tries to push adolescents out of the secure nest of childhood, it is not willing to bestow the full membership and rights of adulthood upon them (Johnson, Hoffmann, and Gerstein 1996; Kantrowitz and Wingert 1999).

Because of their uniquely rapid development, several developmental issues are particularly important to evolving adolescents (Elmen and Offer 1993; Johnson, Hoffman, and Gerstein 1996; Kantrowitz and Wingert 1999; Office of the Surgeon General 2007; Von Der Haar 2005):

- Discovering and understanding their distinctive identities
- "Feeling awkward or strange about one's self and one's body" (American Academy of Child and Adolescent Psychiatry 2006)
- Forming more intimate and caring relationships with others
- Conflicts with parents over the need for independence
- Increased interest in sexuality and concern with heterosexual versus homosexual identities
- "Experimentation with sex and drugs (cigarettes, alcohol, and marijuana)" (American Academy of Child and Adolescent Psychiatry 2006)
- Establishing a sense of autonomy
- Coming to terms with the hormone-related feelings of puberty and expressing their sexuality
- Learning to become productive contributors to society
- Feeling alone and alienated

Due to all of this developmental confusion, "normal" behavior for the adolescent is difficult to define precisely. Experts generally agree that persistent low self-esteem, depression, feelings of alienation, and other emotional disturbances can be troublesome for teenagers (Von Der Haar 2005). Most adolescents are relatively well adjusted and are able to cope with **sociobiological changes**.

Emotionally stable adolescents relate well to family and peers and function productively within their schools, neighborhoods, and communities. The majority of adolescents experience transient problems, which they are able to resolve, but some become deeply disturbed and are unable to grow out of their problems without counseling and therapy (see also Jayson 2007). Those adolescents who are unable or unwilling to ask for assistance often turn to destructive devices, such as drugs or violence (Kantrowitz and Wingert 1999), for relief from their emotional dilemmas.

■ Consequences of Underage Drug Use

Some of the well-known consequences of underage drug use by adolescents are (Office of the Surgeon General 2007):

- Alcohol poses a greater risk than any other drug, including marijuana, to the largest number of teens, largely because of alcohol's availability.
- Underage alcohol use is the major cause of death from injuries among young people. Each year approximately 5000 people under the age of 21 die as a result of underage drinking; this includes about 1900 deaths from motor vehicle crashes, 1600 as a result of homicides, and 300 from suicide as well as hundreds from other injuries such as falls, burns, and drowning.
- Alcohol use increases the risk of carrying out, or being a victim of, a physical or sexual assault.
- Underage alcohol use can affect the body in many ways. The effects of alcohol and other drug use ranges from hangovers to death from alcohol and/or other drug abuse.
- Alcohol and other drugs can lead to other problems such as bad grades in school and run-ins with the law.
- Alcohol and other drugs affect how well a young person judges risk and makes sound decisions, such as driving while under the influence and riding with a driver under the influence.

KEY TERM

sociobiological changes
the belief that biological forces (largely genes) have a direct influence on the root causes of social psychological behavior

- Alcohol and other drugs play a role in risky sexual activity, which can increase the chance of teen pregnancy and sexually transmitted infections (STIs), including HIV.
- Alcohol can harm the growing brain. (Current research clearly shows that the brain continually develops from birth through the teen years into the mid-20s.)

▪ Why Adolescents Use Drugs

Although there is no such thing as a typical substance-abusing adolescent, certain physiological, psychological, and sociological factors are often associated with drug problems in this subculture (Johnson, Hoffman, and Gerstein 1996; Johnston et al. 2009a). In looking at an array of explanations regarding why adolescents use drugs, one study by Columbia University's National Center on Addiction and Substance Abuse found that children ages 12 to 17 who are frequently bored are 50% more likely to smoke, drink, get drunk, and use illegal drugs. In addition, kids with $25 or more a week in spending money are nearly twice as likely to smoke, drink, or use drugs as children with less money. Anxiety is another risk factor. The study found that youngsters who said they're highly stressed are twice as likely as low-stress kids to smoke, drink, or use drugs (Associated Press 2003).

It is important to remember that not all drug use by adolescents means therapy is necessary or even desirable. More traditional proven and accepted explanations stress that most excessive drug use that often leads to abuse by adolescents results from the desire to experience new behaviors and sensations, a passing fancy of maturation, an attempt to relieve peer pressure, feelings of alienation, or an inclination to enhance a social setting with chemistry (Jayson 2007; Kantrowitz and Wingert 1999). Most of these adolescent users will not go on to develop problematic dependence on drugs and, for the most part, should be watched but not aggressively confronted or treated. The adolescents who usually have significant difficulty with drug use are those who turn to drugs for extended support as coping devices and become drug reliant because they are unable to find alternative, less destructive solutions to their problems. Several major factors can contribute to serious drug dependence in adolescents (Archambault 1992; Johnson, Hoffman, and Gerstein 1996; Walsh and Shenkman 1992).

Research indicates that the most important factor influencing drug use among adolescents is peer drug use (Bahr, Marcos, and Maughan 1995; Focus Adolescent Services 2008; Jayson 2007; Kandel 1980; NIDA 1999; Swadi 1992; Winters 1997). Other primary factors that can either increase or decrease drug use include how teens perceive the risk in the use of drugs, perceived social approval, and perceived availability of drugs (CRC Health Group 2007).

Consequently, eventual transition to heavier substance use also directly correlates with peer use (Steinberg, Fletcher, and Darling 1994). Conversely, individuals whose peer groups do not use or abuse drugs are less likely to use drugs themselves (Venturelli 2000). Research has identified a correlation between strong family bonds and non–drug-using peer groups (NIDA 1999). "Adolescents with higher [stronger] family bonds are less likely than adolescents with lower [weaker] bonds to have close friends who use drugs" (Bahr et al. 1995, p. 466). In addition, family bonding is highly correlated with educational commitment. In essence, family bonding influences choice of friends and educational goals and aspirations (Bahr et al. 1995). Three noteworthy differences exist between male and female adolescents: (1) males demonstrate a stronger association between educational achievement and family bonds; (2) among females, peer drug use is negatively associated with family bonds, so peer drug use and family bonds are not likely to influence the use of licit and illicit drugs by females; and (3) the impact of age on peer drug use (the younger the age, the more vulnerable to peer pressure) and on the amount of alcohol consumed can be predicted with slightly greater accuracy for males than females (Teen Challenge 2000).

Many adolescents use drugs to help cope with boredom, unpleasant feelings, emotions, and stress or to relieve depression, reduce tension, and reduce alienation (Teen Challenge 2000). Psychological differences among adolescents who are frequent drug users, experimenters, and abstainers often can be traced to early childhood, the quality of parenting in their homes, and their home environment. It has been suggested that certain types of parents are more likely to raise children at high risk for substance abuse (Archambault 1992). Children from families where a parent or caregiver is suffering from alcohol abuse often suffer from guilt, anxiety, embarrassment, inability to have close relationships, confusion, anger, and depression (American Academy of Child and Adolescent Psychiatry 2011).

For example, an alcoholic adolescent usually has at least one parent of the following types:

- *Alcoholic:* This parent serves as a negative role model for the adolescent. The child sees the parent dealing with problems by consuming drugs. Even though drinking alcohol is not illegal for adults, it sends the message that drugs can solve problems. The guilt-ridden alcoholic parent is unable to provide the child with a loving, supportive relationship. In addition, the presence of the alcoholic parent is often disruptive or abusive to the family and creates fear or embarrassment in the child.

- *Nonconsuming and condemning:* This type of parent not only chooses to abstain from drinking, but also is very judgmental about drinkers and condemns them for their behavior. Such persons, who are often referred to as teetotalers, have a rigid, moralistic approach to life. Their black-and-white attitudes frequently prove inadequate and unforgiving in an imperfect, gray world. Children in these families can feel inferior and guilty when they are unable to live up to parental expectations, and they may resort to drugs to cope with their frustrations.

- *Overly demanding:* This type of parent forces unrealistic expectations on his or her children. These parents often live vicariously through their children and require sons and daughters to pursue endeavors in which the parents were unable to succeed. Particular emphasis may be placed on achievements in athletics, academics, or career selections. Even though the parents' efforts may be well intended, the children get the message that their parents are more concerned about what they are than who they are. These parents frequently encourage sibling rivalries to enhance performance, but such competitions always yield a loser.

- *Overly protective:* These types of parents do not give their children a chance to develop a sense of self-worth and independence. Because the parents deprive their children of the opportunities to learn how to master their abilities within their surroundings, the children are not able to develop confidence and a positive self-image. Such children are frequently unsure about who they are and what they are capable of achieving. Parents who use children to satisfy their own ego needs or who are trying to convince themselves that they really do like their children tend to be overly protective.

The principal influence for learned behavior is usually the home; therefore, several other family-related variables can significantly affect adolescents' decision to start, maintain, or cease a drug habit (Kinney 2000; Lawson and Lawson 1992). For example, adolescents usually learn their attitudes about drug use from family models. In other words, what are the drug-consuming patterns of parents and siblings? Adolescents are more likely to develop drug problems if other members of the family (1) are excessive in their drug (legal or illegal) consumption, (2) approve of the use of illicit drugs, or (3) use drugs as a problem-solving strategy.

Sociological factors that damage self-image can also encourage adolescent drug use. Feelings of rejection may cause poor relationships with family members, peers, school personnel, or coworkers. Ethnic differences sometimes contribute to a poor self-image because people of minority races or cultures are frequently socially excluded and are sometimes viewed as being inferior and undesirable by the majority population. This type of negative message is very difficult for adolescents to deal with. Sometimes, to ensure acceptance, adolescents adopt the attitudes and behaviors of their affiliated groups. If a peer group, or a gang, views drug use as cool, desirable, or even necessary, members (or those desiring membership) feel compelled to conform and become involved in drugs.

■ Patterns of Drug Use in Adolescent Families

Growing minorities of younger teenagers are exposed to drug use within their own families. One study reported that "20% of . . . 600 teens in drug treatment in New York, Texas, Florida and California said they have shared drugs other than alcohol with their parents, and that about 5% of the teens actually were introduced to drugs—usually marijuana—by their moms and dads" (Leinwand 2000, p. 1). In 1999, Partnership for a Drug-Free America reported similar alarming findings (Leinwand 2000).

Years ago, alcohol may have been shared between parents and their children in a low percentage of cases; however, today there are parents who either have been or are currently using illicit drugs and they appear to be influencing their children in the use of these drugs. Currently, this occurs in a small minority of families; nevertheless, it remains shocking.

Jason, 17, a recovering addict from an upper-middle-class family in Simi Valley, California, says he wishes his father had been more of a parent and less of a buddy when it came to marijuana. "[Jason] made his drug purchase: a $5 bag of pot. Jason says his father walked by his room's open door as he was stashing it in a dresser drawer. [His father then] '. . . told about his marijuana use,' Jason says. 'We went into his [dad's] office, and he had a (water pipe) and we got high together.' [Jason reports that at the time, he] '. . . thought it was sooo cool'" (Leinwand 2000, p. 2).

In another example, La'kiesha, 15, of southern California, is the third generation of a family in which members have become addicted to drugs. La'kiesha said her grandmother smoked pot regularly and gave her a few puffs when she was 5 years old to settle her down before bedtime (Leinwand 2000).

Other recent findings of drug use in families reveal "One in five drug abusers in some treatment programs in the United States received their first taste of these illegal substances from their parents, usually before the age of 18. . ." (Livni 2013). This same survey from 70 Phoenix House drug treatment programs in the United States also showed that drug treatment candidates completing the survey ". . . are 19 times more likely to have been introduced to illicit drugs by a family member than a professional drug dealer, according to Penn, Schoen, and Berland Associates, the national research firm in New York that conducted the study. Twenty percent obtained the drugs from the parents, and of these 6 percent even used heroin with them" (Livni 2013).

∎ Current Changes in Teen Drug Use Cause Concern

Recent surveys regarding drug use patterns found that by 12th grade (seniors in high school), approximately 69.4% of the teens had used alcohol, approximately 40% had used cigarettes, approximately 45% had used marijuana, and 7.9% had used inhalants in 2012. (See **Table 16.5**, which details 8th, 10th, and 12th graders' use of drugs from 2009 through 2012.)

In addition, there are now more new users (age 12 or older) of prescription drugs than any other illegal drug—even marijuana. Teens are turning away from street drugs and the stigma that goes along with using them, and abusing prescription drugs to get the same type of high. Many young people are under the false notion that prescription

and OTC drugs are medically safer, when in fact, they can be just as dangerous and addictive as street drugs (NEAHIN 2013).

In a press conference, White House drug czar John Walters stated "The drug dealer is us . . ." (*USA Today* 2007). What the national drug policy director was alluding to was that ". . . many teenagers are obtaining drugs over the Internet, getting them free from their family members, friends, or taking them from other people's medicine cabinet . . ." and that ". . . 2.1 million teenagers abused prescription drugs in 2005" (*USA Today* 2007). A recent report found that

> Every day in the United States, an average of 2,000 teenagers use prescription drugs without a doctor's guidance for the first time. Among youth who are 12 to 17 years old, 2.8% reported past-month nonmedical use of prescription medications. According to the 2012 Monitoring the Future survey, prescription and over-the-counter drugs are among the most commonly abused drugs by 12th graders, after alcohol, marijuana, synthetic marijuana (e.g., "Spice"), and tobacco. Youth who abuse prescription medications are also more likely to report use of other drugs. (NIDA for Teens 2013)

The three most common sources for obtaining prescription drugs were: "given for free by a friend or relative," which was stated by approximately 51% of adolescents; "bought from a friend or relative," which was stated by approximately 35% of adolescents; and "taking the drug from a friend or relative without asking," which was reported by approximately 12% of adolescents. Surprisingly, only 2% of adolescents "bought prescription drugs on the Internet" (Johnston et al. 2009a). Clearly, the informal network of family and friends is a major source of these drugs for adolescents.

Another source indicates that although teen marijuana use declined from 30.1% to 25.8% from 2002 to 2006, use of OxyContin rose among 12th graders (Johnston et al. 2006). Between 2002 and 2005, annual prevalence increased almost 40% among 12th graders, to 5.5%. Considering the addictive potential of this drug, this rate seems quite high for them to have attained. Another, more recent finding is that

> . . . a significant proportion of 12th graders have used one or more of these drugs [referring to prescription drugs like amphetamines, sedatives (barbiturates), and tranquilizers] . . .

TABLE 16.5 Drug Use Among 8th, 10th, and 12th Graders*

	8th Graders				10th Graders				12th Graders			
	2009	2010	2011	2012	2009	2010	2011	2012	2009	2010	2011	2012
Any illicit drug												
Lifetime	19.9	21.4	20.1	18.5	36.0	37.0	37.7	36.8	46.7	48.2	49.1	49.0
Annual	14.5	16.0	14.7	13.4	29.4	30.2	31.1	30.1	36.5	38.3	40.0	39.7
30-day	8.1	9.5	8.5	7.7	17.8	18.5	19.2	18.6	23.3	23.8	25.2	25.2
Alcohol												
Lifetime	36.6	35.8	33.1	29.5	59.1	58.2	56.0	54.0	72.3	71.0	70.0	69.4
Annual	30.3	29.3	26.9	23.6	52.8	52.1	49.8	48.5	66.2	65.2	63.5	63.5
30-day	14.9	13.8	12.7	11.0	30.4	28.9	27.2	27.6	43.5	41.2	40.0	41.5
Cigarettes (Any Use)												
Lifetime	20.1	20.0	18.4	15.5	32.7	33.0	30.4	27.7	43.6	42.2	40.0	39.5
Annual**	–	–	–	–	–	–	–	–	–	–	–	–
30-day	6.5	7.1	6.1	4.9	13.1	13.6	11.8	10.8	20.1	19.2	18.7	17.1
Marijuana/Hashish												
Lifetime	15.7	17.3	16.4	15.2	32.3	33.4	34.5	33.8	42.0	43.8	45.5	45.2
Annual	11.8	13.7	12.5	11.4	26.7	27.5	28.8	28.0	32.8	34.8	36.4	36.4
30-day	6.5	8.0	7.2	6.5	15.9	16.7	17.6	17.0	20.6	21.4	22.6	22.9
Inhalants												
Lifetime	14.9	14.5	13.1	11.8	12.3	12.0	10.1	9.9	9.5	9.0	8.1	7.9
Annual	8.1	8.1	7.0	6.2	6.1	5.7	4.5	4.1	3.4	3.6	3.2	2.9
30-day	3.8	3.6	3.2	2.7	2.2	2.0	1.7	1.4	1.2	1.4	1.0	0.9
Amphetamines												
Lifetime	6.0	5.7	5.2	4.5	10.3	10.6	9.0	8.9	9.9	11.1	12.2	12.0
Annual	4.1	3.9	3.5	2.9	7.1	7.6	6.6	6.5	6.6	7.4	8.2	7.9
30-day	1.9	1.8	1.8	1.3	3.3	3.1	3.1	2.8	3.0	3.7	3.7	3.3
Hallucinogens												
Lifetime	3.0	3.4	3.3	2.8	6.1	6.1	6.0	5.2	7.4	8.6	8.3	7.5
Annual	1.9	1.8	1.8	1.3	4.1	3.5	3.5	3.0	4.7	4.8	4.3	4.0
30-day	0.9	1.0	1.0	0.6	1.4	1.6	1.4	1.2	1.6	1.9	1.6	1.6
Cocaine												
Lifetime	2.6	2.6	2.2	1.9	4.6	3.7	3.3	3.3	6.0	5.5	5.2	4.9
Annual	1.6	1.6	1.4	1.2	2.7	2.2	1.9	2.0	3.4	2.9	2.9	2.7
30-day	0.8	0.6	0.8	0.5	0.9	0.9	0.7	0.8	1.3	1.3	1.1	1.1

(continues)

TABLE 16.5 Drug Use Among 8th, 10th, and 12th Graders* (*continued*)

	8th Graders				10th Graders				12th Graders			
	2009	2010	2011	2012	2009	2010	2011	2012	2009	2010	2011	2012
Crack												
Lifetime	1.7	1.5	1.5	1.0	2.1	1.8	1.6	1.4	2.4	2.4	1.9	2.1
Annual	1.1	1.0	0.9	0.6	1.2	1.0	0.9	0.8	1.3	1.4	1.0	1.2
30-day	0.5	0.4	0.5	0.3	0.4	0.5	0.4	0.4	0.6	0.7	0.5	0.6
Steroids												
Lifetime	1.3	1.1	1.2	1.2	1.3	1.6	1.4	1.3	2.2	2.0	1.8	1.8
Annual	0.8	0.5	0.7	0.6	0.8	1.0	0.9	0.8	1.5	1.5	1.2	1.3
30-day	0.4	0.3	0.4	0.3	0.5	0.5	0.5	0.4	1.0	1.1	0.7	0.9
Heroin												
Lifetime	1.3	1.3	1.2	0.8	1.5	1.3	1.2	1.1	1.2	1.6	1.4	1.1
Annual	0.7	0.8	0.7	0.5	0.9	0.8	0.8	0.6	0.7	0.9	0.8	0.6
30-day	0.4	0.4	0.4	0.2	0.4	0.4	0.4	0.4	0.4	0.4	0.4	0.3

*Data show the percentages of 8th, 10th, and 12th graders who used both licit and illicit types of drugs in 2009, 2010, 2011, and 2012.
**Not available at time of printing.

Data from Johnston, L. D., P. M. O'Malley, J. G. Bachman, J. E. Schulenberg. *Monitoring the Future: National Survey Results on Drug Use, Overview of Key Findings on Adolescent Drug Use: 2012.* Ann Arbor, MI: Institute for Social Research, The University of Michigan, 2013.

without a doctor's order—21.5%, 15.4%, and 7.2% for lifetime, annual, and 30-day prevalence, respectively, in 2008. Rates have fallen somewhat in recent years, but significant numbers of teens are still misusing prescription drugs. (Johnston et al. 2009a)

Finally, "Teens are also abusing stimulants like Adderall and anti-anxiety drugs like Xanax because they are readily available and perceived as safer than street drugs," says White House drug czar Walters (*USA Today* 2007). The extent of naiveté is best illustrated by the interview of one female in Indiana, as stated in the *Daily News*, Muncie, on November 6, 2006: "It's not like I'm taking cocaine or crack—it's OK, these are pharmaceutical drugs made by professionals who know what they are doing" (National Youth Anti-Drug Media Campaign 2007). Another study found that

> The classes of prescription drugs most commonly abused are: opioid pain relievers, such as Vicodin or Oxycontin; stimulants for treating Attention Deficit Hyperactivity Disorder (ADHD), such as Adderall, Concerta, or Ritalin; and central nervous system (CNS) depressants for relieving anxiety, such as Valium or Xanax. The most commonly abused OTC

drugs are cough and cold remedies containing dextromethorphan. (NIDA 2013)

The use of prescription-type drugs by high numbers of young people is of special concern. In looking at past-year initiates (new users), the following findings are noteworthy regarding teen prescription drug abuse (Office of National Drug Control Policy [ONDCP] 2008, unless indicated otherwise):

- In 2010, 10.1% of youth ages 12 to 17 were current illicit drug users, with 7.4% current users of marijuana and 3.0% current nonmedical users of psychotherapeutic drugs (SAMHSA 2011). Nonmedical use of prescription drugs among youth and young adults in 2010 was the second most prevalent illicit drug use category, with marijuana being first.
- In the past, opiate overdoses were almost always due to heroin use; now opiate overdoses are increasingly due to abuse of prescription painkillers (SAHMSA 2011).
- In 2006, more than 2.1 million teens abused prescription drugs.
- In 2011, an average of 35% of 8th, 10th, and 12th graders used an illicit drug during their lifetime.

- Every day, 2500 youth (12–17 years old) abuse a prescription pain reliever for the very first time.
- One-third of all new abusers of prescription drugs in 2006 were 12- to 17-year-olds.
- Three percent of teens (12–17 years old) reported current abuse of prescription drugs in 2006, following only marijuana (7%) and well ahead of cocaine (0.4%), Ecstasy (0.3%), meth (0.2%), and heroin (0.1%).
- Prescription drugs are the drug of choice among 12- to 13-year-olds.
- Among teens, 13 is the mean age of first non-prescribed use of sedatives and stimulants. Sixty percent of teens (12–17 years old) who have abused prescription painkillers first tried them before age 15 (Wu, Pilowsky, and Patkar 2007).
- Among teens who have abused painkillers, nearly one-fifth (18%) used them at least weekly in the past year (Wu et al. 2007).
- The prescription drugs most commonly abused by teens are painkillers, powerful narcotics prescribed to treat pain; depressants, such as sleeping pills or antianxiety drugs; and stimulants, mainly prescribed to treat attention deficit hyperactivity disorder (ADHD).
- Pain relievers like Vicodin and OxyContin are the prescription drugs most commonly abused by teens.
- Among 12th graders, past-year abuse of OxyContin increased 30% between 2002 and 2007.
- Past-year abuse of Vicodin is particularly high among 8th, 10th, and 12th graders, with nearly 1 in 10 high school seniors reporting taking it in the past year without a doctor's approval.

Teens also are abusing some over-the-counter (OTC) drugs, primarily cough and cold remedies that contain dextromethorphan (DXM), a cough suppressant, to get high. Products with DXM include NyQuil, Coricidin, and Robitussin, among others. This type of drug abuse is a particular concern, given the easy access teens have to these products. Teens who abuse prescription or OTC drugs may be abusing other substances as well. Sometimes they abuse prescription and OTC drugs together with alcohol or other drugs, which can lead to dangerous consequences, including death. Teens are abusing prescription drugs because they are widely available, free or inexpensive, and they believe they are not as risky as street drugs. The majority of teens who abuse these products say they get them for free, usually from friends and relatives, and often without their knowledge. Because these drugs are so readily available, teens

who otherwise would not touch street drugs might abuse prescription drugs (ONDCP 2008).

Two licit drugs plaguing early and mid-teens are cigarettes and alcohol. Alcohol use is more widespread than use of any of the illicit drugs. Almost three out of every four 12th-grade students (72%) have at least tried alcohol, and over two-fifths (43%) are current drinkers. Even among 8th graders, the proportion of students who reported some alcohol use in their lifetime is nearly two-fifths (39%), and a sixth (16%) are current (past–30-day) drinkers. Of greater concern than just any use of alcohol is its use to the point of inebriation: 18% of 8th graders, 37% of 10th graders, and 54.2% of 12th graders said they have been drunk at least once in their lifetime. Like alcohol, use of cigarettes is generally more widespread than use of any of the illicit drugs. Almost half (45%) of 12th graders reported having tried cigarettes at some time, and one-fifth (20%) had smoked at least some in the prior 30 days. Daily use of cigarettes in the 30 days prior to being surveyed was considerably higher than daily use of marijuana or alcohol (Johnston et al. 2012).

■ Adolescent Versus Adult Drug Abuse

Adolescent patterns of drug abuse are very different from drug use patterns in adults (Moss et al. 1994). The uniqueness of adolescent drug abuse means that drug-dependent teenagers usually are not successfully treated with adult-directed therapy. For example, compared with adults who abuse drugs, drug-using adolescents are (1) more likely to be involved in criminal activity, and at earlier ages; (2) more likely to have other members of the family who abuse drugs; (3) more likely to be associated with a dysfunctional family that engages in emotional and/or physical abuse of its members; and (4) more likely to begin drug use because of curiosity or peer pressure (Bahr et al. 1995; Daily 1992b; Hoshino 1992; Steinberg et al. 1994; Teen Challenge 2000). Such differences need to be considered when developing adolescent-targeted treatment programs.

■ Consequences and Coincidental Problems

Researchers have concluded that the problem of adolescent drug use is a symptom and not a cause of personal social maladjustment. Even so, because of the pharmacological actions of drugs, routine use can contribute to school and social failures, unintended injuries (usually automobile-related), criminal and violent behavior, sexual risk taking, depression, and suicide (Curry and Spergel 1997).

It is important to realize that, because serious drug abuse is usually the result of emotional instability, consequences of the underlying disorders may be expressed with chemical dependence, making diagnosis and treatment more difficult. The undesirable coincidental problems may include self-destruction, risk taking, abuse, or negative group behaviors. Some of these adolescent problems and their relationship to drug abuse are discussed in the following sections.

ADOLESCENT SUICIDE

Current research shows that although no cause-and-effect relationship exists between use of alcohol and/or other drugs and suicide, such drugs are often contributing factors (About.com 2005; Minnesota Institute of Public Health 1995). Adolescents are particularly vulnerable to suicide actions; in fact, white males between 14 and 20 years old are the most likely to commit suicide in the United States (Daily 1992b). Further, the teenage suicide rate has doubled since 1980 (Siegel and Senna 1997; Siegel and Welsh 2009). "Suicides among young people continue to be a serious problem. Each year in the U.S., thousands of teenagers commit suicide. Suicide is the third leading cause of death for 15-to-24-year-olds, and the sixth leading cause of death for 5-to-14-year-olds" (American Academy of Child and Adolescent Psychiatry 2004). Twenty percent to 36% of suicide victims have a history of alcohol abuse or were drinking shortly before their suicide. Some experts have described severe chemical dependence as a form of slow, drug-related suicide. For clinicians, every case of serious drug addiction conceals a suicidal individual because all drug abuse inevitably constitutes a game of life and death very similar to "Russian roulette," which comes back into fashion at certain times and under certain circumstances (Bergeret 1981).

Clearly, many teenagers who abuse alcohol and other drugs possess a self-destructive attitude (About.com 2005), as this quote from an online chat with Dr. David Shaffer, a teen suicide expert, demonstrates: "[T]wo-thirds of all suicides amongst boys occur in boys who are abusing alcohol or other drugs; so the link between suicide and alcohol and certain drugs, like cocaine and Ecstasy and other stimulant drugs, is a very close one" (Schaefer et al. 1993, p. 39). According to Shaffer, adolescents who attempt suicide are more likely to

(1) have disciplinary problems, then abuse alcohol and feel even more depressed; (2) be very anxious and not display any bad behavior problems; or (3) have a perfectionist attitude and never be satisfied with their outcomes. Nearly all suffer from depression before their suicide attempts. Females generally differ from males in that they are prone to even greater amounts of depression with fewer cases of alcohol or other drug abuse. Finally, another study based on extensive survey data suggests that ". . . between 12 and 25 percent of school age youth consider suicide or make plans to commit suicide . . . [and that]. . . the rate of youth suicide is on an upward path, tripling between 1950 and 1990." This research also states that alcohol and drug use increases the likelihood of suicidal thoughts and attempts (Bussing-Burks 2013).

Besides posing a direct health threat because of their physiological effects, drugs of abuse can precipitate suicide attempts due to their pharmacological impact. A number of studies have found a very high correlation between acute suicidal behavior and drug use (About.com 2005; Buckstein et al. 1993). One report noted that adolescent alcoholics have a suicide rate 58 times greater than the national average. In another study, 30% of adolescent alcoholics had made suicide attempts, although 92% admitted to a history of having suicidal thoughts (Daily 1992b). It has been speculated that the incidence of suicide in drug-consuming adolescents is high because both types of behavior are the consequence of an inability to develop fundamental adult attributes of confidence, self-esteem, and independence. When drug use does not make up for their need for these characteristics, the resulting frustrations are intensified and ultimately played out in the suicide act.

Most adolescents experiment with drugs for reasons not related to antisocial or deviant behavior but rather due to curiosity, desire for recreation, boredom, peer pressure, desire to gain new insights and experiences, or urge to heighten social interactions. These adolescents are not likely to engage in self-destructive behavior. In addition, adolescents from "healthy" family environments are not likely to attempt suicide. Specifically, Daily (1992b) stated that the families least likely to have suicidal members are those that:

- Express love and show mutual concern
- Are tolerant of differences and overlook failings
- Encourage the development of self-confidence and self-expression

- Have parents who assume strong leadership roles but are not autocratic
- Have interaction characterized by humor and good-natured teasing
- Are able to serve as a source of joy and happiness to their members

Suicide is more likely to be attempted by those adolescents who turn to alcohol and other drugs to help them cope with serious emotional and personality conflicts and frustrations. These susceptible teenagers represent approximately 5% of the adolescent population (Beschner and Friedman 1985; Siegel and Senna 1997; Siegel and Welsh 2009). Wright (1985) found that four features significantly contribute to the likelihood of suicidal thought in high school students:

1. Parents with interpersonal conflicts who often use an adolescent child with drug problems as the scapegoat for family problems
2. Fathers who have poor, and often confrontational, relationships with their children
3. Parents who are viewed by their adolescent children as being emotionally unstable, usually suffering from perpetual anger and depression
4. A sense of frustration, desperation, and inability to resolve personal and emotional difficulties through traditional means

Clearly, it is important to identify those adolescents who are at risk for suicide and to provide immediate care and appropriate emotional support.

SEXUAL VIOLENCE AND DRUGS

Alcohol use has been closely associated with almost every type of sexual abuse in which the adolescent is victimized. "For the perpetrator, being under the influence may remove both physical and psychological inhibitors which keep people from acting out violently. They may also use alcohol or drugs as an excuse for criminal behavior" (Wisconsin Coalition Against Sexual Assault [WCASA] 1997, p. 13). For example, alcohol is by far the most significant factor in date, acquaintance, and gang rapes involving teenagers (Office of the Surgeon General 2007; Parrot 1988; Prendergast 1994). The evidence for alcohol involvement in incest is particularly overwhelming. Approximately 4 million children in the United States live in incestuous homes with alcoholic parents. In addition, 42% of drug-abusing female adolescents have been victims of sexual abuse (Daily 1992a). It is estimated

that almost half of the offenders consume alcohol before molesting a child and at least one-third of the perpetrators are chronic alcoholics (Baltieri and de Andrad 2008, p. 77). Finally, 85% of child molesters were sexually abused themselves as children, usually at the same age as their victims, and the vast majority of these molesters abused drugs as adolescents (Daily 1992a).

These very disturbing associations illustrate the relationship between drugs and violent sexual behavior both in terms of initiating the act and because of the act. The effects of such sexual violence are devastating and far-reaching. Thus, incest victims are more likely than the general population to abuse drugs as adolescents and to engage in antisocial delinquency, prostitution, depression, and suicide (Daily 1992a).

GANGS AND DRUGS

The very disturbing involvement of adolescents in gangs and gang-related activities and violence is a social phenomenon that first became widely recognized in the 1950s and 1960s. Hollywood, for example, introduced America to the problems of adolescent gangs in the classic movies *Blackboard Jungle* and *West Side Story*. Although the basis for gang involvement has not changed over the years, the levels of violence and public concern have increased dramatically. Many communities consider gang-related problems to be their number one social issue. Access to sophisticated weaponry and greater mobility have drawn unsuspecting neighborhoods and innocent bystanders into the often-violent clashes of **intragang** and **intergang** warfare. Individuals and communities have been reacting angrily to this growing menace. To deal effectively with the threats of gang-initiated violence and crime, however, it is important to understand why gangs form, what their objectives are, how they are structured, and how to discourage adolescent involvement.

Children often join gangs because they are neglected by their parents, lack positive role models, and fail to receive adequate adult supervision. Other motivations for joining a gang include peer

KEY TERMS

intragang
between members of the same gang

intergang
between members of different gangs

pressure, low self-esteem, and the perceived easy acquisition of money from gang-related drug dealing and other criminal activities.

In comparison to traditional, formal youth organizations, juvenile gangs may appear disorganized. Research shows, however, that verbal rules, policies, customs, and hierarchies of command are rigidly observed within the gang. Thus, common values and attitudes exist:

- Gang membership is usually defined in socioeconomic, racial, and ethnic terms, and adolescents involved have similar backgrounds.
- Gang members are distinguished by a distinctive and well-defined dress code. Violation of this code by members, or mimicking of the dress code by non–gang members, can result in ostracism, ridicule, physical abuse, and violence.
- Leadership and seniority within the gang are defined by vested time in belonging to the gang, age, loyalty, and demonstrated delinquent cleverness (often related to drug dealing and other crimes).
- Gang members use gang slang to ensure camaraderie and group loyalty.

Although a stable home life does not ensure that an adolescent will not become involved with gang-related activity, a strong family environment and guidance from respected parents and guardians are clearly deterrents (Lale 1992). Many gang members are children from dysfunctional, broken, or single-parent homes. Many parents are aware of their children's gang involvement but they lack the skill, confidence, and authority to deter the gang or curtail drug involvement of their teenagers. To make matters worse, ineffective parents often discourage or even interfere with involvement by outside authorities due to misdirected loyalty to their children and/or to avoid embarrassment to their family and community.

Because troubled adolescents are often estranged from their families, they are particularly influenced by their peer groups. These teenagers are most likely to associate with groups whose members have similar backgrounds and problems and who make them feel accepted. Because of this vulnerability, adolescents may become involved with local gangs. In summary, gangs offer the following:

- Fellowship and camaraderie
- Identity and recognition
- Membership and belonging
- Family substitution and role models

- Security and protection
- Diversion and excitement
- Friendships and structure
- Money and financial gain for relatively little effort
- Ability to live the crazy life (*vida loca*) (Sanders 1994; Shelden, Tracy, and Brown 2001) or *locura* (craziness) (Shelden et al. 2004)

In the United States, estimates of the total number of existing gangs vary widely. There are at least 21,500 gangs and more than 731,000 active gang members in the United States. Gangs conduct criminal activity in all 50 states and the U.S. territories. Although most gang activity is concentrated in major urban areas, gangs also are proliferating in rural and suburban areas of the country as gang members flee increasing law enforcement pressure in urban areas or seek more lucrative drug markets. This proliferation in nonurban areas increasingly is accompanied by violence and is threatening society in general (National Drug Intelligence Center [NDIC] 2009).

For example, in Chicago, estimates have ranged from 12,000 to 120,000 gang members. Two additional and more recent findings report that "[a] round 70 gangs operate in Chicago, with more than 100 thousand members among them (Lamberson 2009). A second finding indicates that:

> In 2009, about 20 percent of students ages 12–18 reported that gangs were present at their school during the school year. This was a decrease from the 23 percent of students who reported a gang presence in 2007. A higher percentage of students from urban schools (31 percent) reported a gang presence at their school in 2009 than students from suburban and rural schools (17 percent and 16 percent, respectively). (National Center for Education Statistics 2011)

Spergel (1990) provided the following percentages of those who are reportedly in gangs within a particular school population in the Chicago area: "... 5% of the elementary school youths, 10% of all high school youths, 20% of those in special school programs, and, more alarmingly perhaps, 35% of those between 16 and 19 years of age who have dropped out of school" (Shelden et al. 2004, p. 29). Keep in mind that these data are for just one city.

Street gangs, outlaw motorcycle gangs (OMGs), and prison gangs in prisons are the primary distributors of illegal drugs in the United States. Gangs also smuggle drugs into the United States and produce and transport drugs within the country supplying most major drug dealers.

Street gang members convert powdered cocaine into crack cocaine and produce most of the phencyclidine (PCP) available in the United States. Gangs, primarily OMGs, also produce marijuana and methamphetamine. In addition, gangs increasingly are involved in smuggling large quantities of cocaine and marijuana and lesser quantities of heroin, methamphetamine, and MDMA (also known as Ecstasy) into the United States from foreign sources of supply. Gangs primarily transport and distribute powdered cocaine, crack cocaine, heroin, marijuana, methamphetamine, MDMA, and PCP in the United States.

Located throughout the country, street gangs vary in size, composition, and structure. Large, nationally affiliated street gangs pose the greatest threat because they smuggle, produce, transport, and distribute large quantities of illicit drugs throughout the country and are extremely violent. Local street gangs in rural, suburban, and urban areas pose a growing threat (NDIC 2009).

Another recent survey claims that 27% of public school students ages 12 to 17 attend schools that are both gang and drug infested. That means 5.7 million students attend schools that are both gang and drug dominated. Nearly 50% of all public school students report drug use or sales on school grounds (Funk 2010). Research shows that teenage gangs are becoming major players in the drug trade (Siegel and Senna 1997; Siegel and Welsh 2009). Two of the largest gangs in Los Angeles, the Bloods and the Crips, are examples of this trend. Estimated membership in these two gangs exceeds 20,000. In the past, organized crime families maintained a monopoly on the Asian heroin market. Today, youth gangs have entered this trade, for two reasons: (1) recent efforts and successes in prosecuting top mob bosses by criminal justice officials have created opportunities for new players, and (2) demand has grown for cocaine and synthetic drugs that are produced locally in many U.S. cities. In Los Angeles and most major large cities, drug-dealing gangs maintain "rock houses" or "stash houses" (where crack cocaine is used and sold) that serve as selling and distribution centers for hard drugs. The crack cocaine found in these rock houses is often supplied or run by gang members (Siegel and Senna 1997; Siegel and Welsh 2009).

To a lesser extent, other, less violent gangs with smaller memberships are also involved in drug dealing. Research shows that the media may exaggerate the percentage of gangs involved in drug dealing. In the past, citywide drug dealing by tightly organized "super" gangs appeared to be on the decline and was being superseded by the activities of loosely organized, neighborhood-based groups (Siegel and Senna 1997). In the past, the main reason for this shift was that federal and state law enforcement of drug laws have forced drug dealers to become "flexible, informal organizations [rather] than rigid vertically organized gangs with . . . [leaders] . . . who are far removed from day-to-day action [on the street]" (Siegel and Senna 1997, p. 409). Other past findings were that

"[l]arge trafficking organizations dominate the illicit drug market. These groups include the "families" of America's La Cosa Nostra, as well as an array of more recently identified crime groups such as the Sicilian "Mafia," outlaw motorcycle gangs and groups based in the Nigerian and Colombian communities.... Organized crime groups involved in drug trafficking, however, share a central feature with other organized crime groups in that they consist of a core criminal group and a specialized criminal support designed to facilitate illicit activity. (Gonzales et. al 1986, 71)

More recently, Levitt's and Venkatesh's research involving criminal gangs in Chicago revealed that the gang's turf they studied

". . . for most of the time period examined is a twelve-square block area bordered by major thoroughfares on all sides. Most of the drug-dealing is conducted along the edges of the territory on or near one of the major streets. The gang sells perhaps 30 percent of the drugs to those living within the twelve-block area—most of the remaining purchasers come from a relatively limited geographic range. In this particular area, few buyers come from the suburbs" (Levitt and Venkatesh 2000, 763).

Drug use and gang-related activities are often linked, but the relationship is highly variable (Curry and Spergel 1997; Fagan 1990). Clearly, problems with drugs exist without gangs, and gang-related activities can occur despite the absence of drugs; however, because they have common etiologies, their occurrences are often intertwined. Most adolescents who are associated with gangs are knowledgeable about drugs. Many gang members have experimented with drugs, much like other adolescents their age. However, the hard-core gang members are more likely to be engaged not only in drug use, but also in drug dealing as a source of revenue to support the gang-related activities (Lale 1992; Siegel and Senna 1997). The types of drugs used and their significance and functions vary from gang to gang (Fagan 1990; Siegel and Senna 1997). For example, many Latino gangs do not profit from drug trafficking but are primarily interested in using hard-core drugs such as heroin and PCP. In contrast, African American gangs tend to be more interested in the illicit commercial value of drugs and often engage in dealing crack and other cocaine forms.

PREVENTING ADOLESCENT GANG INVOLVEMENT

The most effective way to prevent adolescent gang involvement is to identify, at an early age, those children at risk and provide them with lifestyle alternatives. Important components of such strategies are as follows:

- Encourage parental awareness of gangs and teach parents how to address problems in their own families that may encourage gang involvement.
- Provide teenagers with alternative participation in organizations or groups that satisfy their needs for camaraderie, participation, and emotional security in a constructive way. These groups can be organized around athletics, school activities, career development, or service rendering.
- Help children to develop coping skills that will enable them to deal with the frustration and stress in their personal lives.
- Educate children about gang-related problems and help them understand that, like drugs, young people who join gangs create more problems for themselves, and gang membership is not a solution to their personal or family problems.

■ Prevention, Intervention, and Treatment of Adolescent Drug Problems

As with most health problems, the sooner drug abuse is identified in the adolescent, the greater the likelihood that the problem can be resolved. It can be difficult to recognize signs of drug abuse in teenagers because their behavior can be erratic and unpredictable even under the best of circumstances. In fact, many of the behavioral patterns

that occur coincidentally with drug problems are also present when drugs are not a problem. However, frequent occurrence or clustering of these behaviors may indicate the presence of substance abuse. The behaviors that can be warning signs include the following (Archambault 1992):

- Abruptly changing their circle of friends
- Experiencing major mood swings
- Continually challenging rules and regulations
- Overreacting to frustrations
- Being particularly submissive to peer pressures
- Sleeping excessively
- Keeping very late hours
- Withdrawing from family involvement
- Letting personal hygiene deteriorate
- Becoming isolated
- Engaging in unusual selling of possessions
- Manipulating family members
- Becoming abusive toward other members of the family
- Frequently coming home at night high

PREVENTION OF ADOLESCENT DRUG ABUSE

Logically, the best treatment for drug abuse is to prevent the problem from starting. This approach, referred to as **primary prevention**, typically has been viewed as total abstinence from drug use. Informational scare tactics are frequently used as a component of primary prevention strategies. These messages often focus on a dangerous (although in some cases rare) potential side effect and present the warning against drug use in a graphic and frightening fashion. Although this approach may scare naive adolescents away from drugs, many adolescents today, especially if they are experienced, question the validity of the scare tactics and ignore the message.

Another form of primary prevention is to encourage adolescents to become involved in formal groups, such as structured clubs or organizations, in an effort to reduce the likelihood of substance abuse (Howard 1992). Group memberships can help adolescents develop a sense of belonging and contributing to a productive, desirable objective. This involvement can also provide the adolescent with the strength to resist undesirable peer pressures. In contrast, belonging to informal groups such as gangs— groups with loose structures and ill-defined, often antisocial objectives—can lead to participation in poorly chaperoned parties, excessive sexual involvement, and nonproductive activities. Adolescent members of such poorly defined

KEY TERM

primary prevention
prevention of using any drug use

organizations tend to drink alcohol at an earlier age and are more likely to use other substances of abuse.

Some experts claim that primary prevention against drug use is unrealistic for many adolescents. They believe that no strategy is likely to stop adolescents from experimenting with alcohol or other drugs of abuse, especially if these substances are part of their home environment (e.g., if alcohol or tobacco is routinely used) and are viewed as normal, acceptable, and even expected behaviors (Howard 1992). For these adolescents, it is important to recognize when drug use moves from experimentation or a social exercise to early stages of a problem and to prevent serious dependence from developing. This approach, referred to as **secondary prevention**, consists of (1) teaching adolescents about the early signs of abuse, (2) teaching adolescents how to assist peers and family members with drug problems, and (3) teaching adolescents how and where help is available for people with drug problems (Archambault 1992). Regardless of the prevention approach used, adolescents need to understand that drugs are never the solution for emotional difficulties, nor are they useful for long-term coping.

TREATMENT OF ADOLESCENT DRUG ABUSE

To provide appropriate treatment for adolescent drug abuse, the severity of the problem must be ascertained. The criteria for such assessments include the following:

- Differentiating between abuse and normal adolescent experimentation with drugs
- Distinguishing between minor abuse and severe dependency on drugs
- Distinguishing among behavioral problems resulting from (1) general behavioral disorders, such as juvenile delinquency; (2) mental retardation; and (3) drugs of abuse

There is no single best approach for treating adolescent substance abuse. Occasionally, the troubled adolescent is admitted to a clinic and treated on an inpatient basis. The inpatient approach is very expensive and creates a temporary artificial environment that may be of limited value in preparing adolescents for the problems to be faced in their real homes and neighborhoods. However, the advantage of an inpatient approach is that adolescents can be managed better and their behavior can be more tightly monitored and controlled (Hoshino 1992). A more practical and routine treatment approach is to allow adolescents to

remain in their natural environment and to provide the necessary life skills to be successful at home, in school, and in the community. For example, adolescents being treated for drug dependence should be helped with:

- Schoolwork, so that appropriate progress toward high school graduation occurs
- Career skills, so that adolescents can become self-reliant and learn to care for themselves and others
- Family problems and learning to communicate and resolve conflicts

If therapy is to be successful, it is important to improve the environment of the drug-abusing adolescent. This aspect of treatment includes disassociation of the adolescent from groups (such as gangs) or surroundings that encourage drug use and promoting association with healthy and supportive groups (such as a nurturing family) and experiences (such as athletics and school activities). Although desirable, such separation is not always possible, especially if the family and home environment are factors that encourage abuse; the likelihood of therapeutic success is substantially diminished under these circumstances.

Often, therapeutic objectives are facilitated by positive reinforcement that encourages life changes that eliminate access to and use of drugs. This goal frequently can be achieved by association with peers who have similar drug and social problems but are motivated to make positive changes in their life. Group sessions with such peers are held under the supervision of a trained therapist and consist of members sharing problems and solutions (Hoshino 1992). Some other options include holistic therapies such as acupuncture, homeotherapy, massage therapy, aromatherapy, yoga, nutrition therapy, and many more alternatives that were once marginalized by the medical profession (Apostolides 1996).

Another useful approach is to discourage use of drugs by reducing their reinforcing effects. This result can sometimes be achieved by substituting a stronger positive or negative reinforcer. For example, if adolescents use drugs because they believe these substances cause good feelings and

KEY TERM

secondary prevention
preventing casual and/or recreational drug use from advancing to drug dependence

help them cope with emotional problems, it may be necessary to replace the drug-taking behavior with other activities that make the adolescent feel good without the drug (such as participation in sports or recreational activities). Negative reinforcers, such as parental discovery and punishment or police apprehension, may discourage drug use by teenagers who are willing to conform and respect authorities; however, negative approaches are ineffective deterrents for nonconforming, rebellious adolescents. Negative reinforcers also do not tend to discourage adolescent use of substances that are more socially acceptable, such as alcohol, tobacco, and even marijuana (Howard 1992).

Regardless of the treatment approach, adolescents must meet several basic objectives if therapy for their drug dependence is to be successful (Daily 1992b):

- Realize that drugs do not solve problems—they only make the problems worse.
- Understand why they turned to drugs in the first place.
- Be convinced that abandoning drugs grants them greater independence and control over their own lives.
- Understand that drug abuse is a symptom of underlying problems that need to be resolved.

■ **Summary of Adolescent Drug Abuse**

Drug abuse by adolescents is particularly problematic in the United States. The teenage years are filled with experimentation, searching, confusion, rebellion, poor self-image, and insecurity. These attributes, if not managed properly, can cause inappropriate coping and lead to problems such as drug dependence, gang involvement, violence, criminal behavior, and suicide. Clearly, early detection of severe underlying emotional problems and application of effective early preventive therapy are important for proper management. Approaches to treatment of drug abuse problems must be individualized because each adolescent is a unique product of physiological, psychological, and environmental factors.

Almost as important as early intervention for adolescent drug abuse problems is recognizing when treatment is unnecessary. We should not be too quick to label all young drug users as antisocial and emotionally unstable. In most cases, teenagers who have used drugs are merely experimenting with new emotions or exercising their newfound freedom. In such situations, nonintervention is

usually better than therapeutic meddling. For the most part, if adolescents are given the opportunity, they will work through their own feelings, conflicts, and attitudes about substance abuse, and they will develop a responsible philosophy concerning the use of these drugs.

Drug Use in College Student Subcultures

This section focuses on college undergraduate use of alcohol, with additional emphasis on the use and abuse of illicit drugs by college students currently attending institutions of higher education.

Table 16.6 compares trends in the annual use of various types of licit and illicit drugs by full-time college students with annual usage by others who are the same age (1 to 4 years beyond high school) but are not attending college. Overall, Table 16.6 shows the following noteworthy prevalence trends (Johnston et al. 2012):

- In 2011, college students were modestly higher in annual and 30-day use of alcohol than the noncollege group; the difference was largest in the 30-day rate (64% vs. 56%) (not shown in Table 16.6).
- College students had a higher prevalence of occasions of heavy drinking (five or more drinks in a row in the past two weeks)—36% versus 32% among their age peers (not shown in this table). Indeed, 4 in every 10 college students (40%) report having been drunk in the prior 30 days, compared to 36% of the noncollege respondents. The groups do not differ much in rates of daily drinking (not shown in Table 16.6), at 3.8% versus 4.9%. In high school, college-bound students, especially in earlier grades, were far less likely to drink alcohol at any level compared to their non-college-bound peers; thus, the relative and absolute increases in alcohol use among college students in the first few years following high school are quite striking.
- Full-time college students were slightly less likely to use any illicit drugs in 2011 than others (36% vs. 39%) and annual prevalence of any illicit drug other than marijuana (16.8% vs. 19.4%).
- Annual marijuana use was somewhat similar among college students and high school graduates of the same age that were not in

TABLE 16.6 Annual Prevalence of Drug Use, 2011 Full-Time College Students Versus Others, 1 to 4 Years Beyond High School*

	Full-Time College Students	Others
Any illicit drug**	36.3	39.9
Any illicit drug** other than marijuana	16.8	19.4
Alcohol	77.4	75.8
Marijuana	33.2	36.8
Cigarettes	25.8	42.6
Amphetamines[+]	9.3	7.8
Ritalin	2.3	2.0
Methamphetamine	0.2	0.7
Crystal Methamphetamine (Ice)	0.1	1.0
Synthetic Marijuana	8.5	15.5
Other Narcotics[+]	6.2	10.2
OxyContin	2.4	4.2
Vicodin	5.8	8.9
MDMA (Ecstasy)	4.2	5.7
Tranquilizers	4.2	7.2
Hallucinogens	4.1	6.4
LSD	2.0	3.8
Cocaine	3.3	5.5
Crack	0.3	1.0
Sedatives[+] (barbiturates)	1.7	4.8
Inhalants	0.9	1.7
Ketamine	0.6	1.4
Heroin	0.1	0.8
GHBs	0.1	0.6

*All full-time college entries, except for the first two percentage entries are college from highest to lowest.

**Use of any illicit drug includes use of marijuana, halluciinogens, cocaine, or heroin, or any use of other narcotics, amphetamines, sedatives (barbiturates), or tranquilizers not under a doctor's orders.

[+]Only drug use that was not under a doctor's orders is included here.

Data from Johnston, L. D., P. M. O'Malley, J. G. Bachman, and J. E. Schulenberg. *Monitoring the Future, National Survey Results on Drug Use, 1975–2011. Volume II: College Students and Adults Ages 19-50.* Ann Arbor, MI: Institute for Social Research, The University of Michigan, 2012.

college (33.2% vs. 36.8%). However, the rate of current daily marijuana use (not shown in this table) was lower among college students than among their out-of-school counterparts (19.4% vs. 24.0%).

- It is clear that use of a number of illicit drugs other than marijuana tends to be distinctly higher among those not in college. (Such differences would likely be larger if the noncollege group included high school dropouts.) In fact, in 2011, several drugs showed annual use rates for noncollege respondents that were two or more times those for college students, including Salvia, crack cocaine, heroin, heroin without a needle, Provigil, methamphetamine, crystal methamphetamine (ice), sedatives (barbiturates), GHB, and ketamine.

- In 2011, significant proportions of both the noncollege group (10.2%) and college students (6.2%) reported use of narcotics other than heroin without medical supervision in the past year. With respect to specific drugs in this class, OxyContin was used by 4.2% of the noncollege group and 2.4% of college students; the corresponding numbers for Vicodin were 8.9% and 5.8%, respectively.

- Amphetamines were the only illicit drugs with higher college than noncollege rates of use. Annual prevalence of amphetamine use among college students was 9.3% in 2011, compared to 7.8% in the noncollege group. Adderall use specifically was somewhat higher among college students (9.8%) than among noncollege respondents (7.0%), as was the case for the 2 years prior to this study. The higher use by college students is very likely because this amphetamine drug, intended for the treatment of attention deficit hyperactivity disorder (ADHD), is sometimes used by students to stay awake and alert in order to complete course work and to study for exams. Ritalin, another drug prescribed for ADHD, is slightly higher among college students (2.3% annual prevalence vs. 2.0% for noncollege), but had much lower usage rates than for Adderall.

- Though not shown in Table 16.6, in comparing male and female college students with noncollege peers, the findings indicate that among college students males tend to use most substances, licit and illicit, more than their female counterparts, with the greatest proportional differences occurring for various hallucinogens. Compared with college females and with noncollege peers, college males are also more frequent users of alcohol and marijuana, and more likely to use Adderall outside of medical supervision.

In summary, the noncollege segment is generally more drug-involved than the college student segment. This pattern is a continuation of the high school scenario in which those without college plans are more likely to use drugs. The only substance that college students are significantly and substantially more likely to be users of is alcohol (particularly getting drunk and binge drinking), and this difference emerges primarily after high school.

Table 16.7 shows yearly trends in drug use among U.S. college students from 2008 through 2011 (Johnston et al. 2012). This table details the percentages of college students who used drugs in the past 12 months before the surveys were administered. The main finding is that the overall use of any illicit drugs remained fairly constant from 2008 to 2011—approximately 35.6%, when averaging the 4 years of surveying. The following list shows those drugs as either declining in usage, holding steady in usage, or decreasing in usage.

Drugs declining in use from 2008 to 2011 (from slight declines to more moderate declines):

- Alcohol
- Cigarettes
- Hallucinogens
- Methamphetamine
- Cocaine
- Sedatives (barbiturates)
- Inhalants
- Heroin

Drugs holding relatively steady from 2008 to 2011:

- Any illicit drug
- Any illicit drug other than marijuana
- Marijuana
- LSD
- Adderall
- Crystal methamphetamine (ice)
- Crack
- Narcotics (other than heroin)
- OxyContin
- Vicodin
- Tranquilizers

Drugs increasing in use from 2008 to 2011 (from very slight increases to more moderate increases):

- MDMA (Ecstasy)
- Amphetamines
- Ritalin
- Ketamine

▌ Reasons for College Students' Drug Use

Figure 16.2A shows the primary reasons why a sample survey of 48,650 male and female college students used alcohol and other drugs (38% were male and 62% were female). The major reasons cited in this sample survey were (1) breaks the ice (74.4%), (2) enhances social activity (74.4%), (3) gives people something to do (71.7%), (4) gives people something to talk about (66.5%), (5) allows people to have more fun (63.1%), (6) facilitates connection with peers (61.7%), (7) facilitates male bonding (60.1%), (8) facilitates sexual opportunity (53.0%), (9) facilitates female bonding (51.7%), and (10) makes it easier to deal with stress (43.9%) (Southern Illinois University Carbondale [SIUC]/ Core Institute 2013, p. 5) (see **Figure 16.2B**). Though not shown in this figure, this same survey revealed the following regarding alcohol (SIUC/ Core Institute 2013, p. 1):

- 81.4% of the students consumed alcohol in the past year ("annual prevalence").
- 69.0% of the students consumed alcohol in the past 30 days ("30-day prevalence").
- 63.4% of underage students (younger than 21) consumed alcohol in the previous 30 days.
- 44.8% of students reported binge drinking in the previous two weeks. (A binge is defined as consuming 5 or more drinks in one sitting.)

Key findings on the use of illegal drugs included the following (SIUC/Core Institute 2013, p. 1):

- 32.0% of the students have used marijuana in the past year ("annual prevalence").
- 18.7% of the students are current marijuana users ("30-day prevalence").
- 11.8% of the students have used an illegal drug other than marijuana in the past year ("annual prevalence").
- 6.4% of the students are current users of illegal drugs other than marijuana ("30-day prevalence")

The most frequently reported illegal drugs used in the past 30 days were (SIUC/Core Institute 2013, p. 1):

- 18.7% marijuana (pot, hash, hash oil)
- 3.4% amphetamines (diet pills, speed)
- 2.0% cocaine (crack, rock, freebase)

TABLE 16.7 Trends in Annual Use of Drugs Among College Students 1 to 4 Years Beyond High School (Percentage Who Used in the Past 12 Months Except as Noted)

	2008	2009	2010	2011
Approximate weighted N	1270	1320	1260	1230
Any illicit drug*	35.2	36.0	35.0	36.3
Any illicit drug other than marijuana*	15.3	16.9	17.1	16.8
Alcohol	82.1	79.4	78.6	77.4
Cigarettes	30.0	29.9	28.1	25.8
Marijuana	32.3	32.8	32.7	33.2
Hallucinogens	4.4	4.7	4.9	4.1
LSD	2.6	2.0	2.1	2.0
MDMA (Ecstasy)	3.7	3.1	4.3	4.2
Amphetamines+	5.7	7.5	9.0	9.3
Ritalin	3.2	1.7	1.9	2.3
Adderall	—	10.2	9.0	9.8
Provigil	—	—	—	0.2
Methamphetamine	0.5	0.3	0.4	0.2
Crystal Methamphetamine (ice)	0.1	0.1	0.5	0.1
Cocaine	4.4	4.2	3.5	3.3
Crack	0.5	0.3	0.4	0.3
Narcotics (other than Heroin)	6.5	7.6	7.2	6.2
OxyContin	3.6	5.0	2.3	2.4
Vicodin	6.7	8.4	4.9	5.8
Tranquilizers	5.0	5.4	4.9	4.2
Sedatives (barbiturates)+	3.7	3.1	2.5	1.7
Inhalants	1.1	1.2	1.7	0.9
Heroin	0.3	0.4	0.2	0.1
GHB	0.2	--	0.1	0.1
Ketamine	0.4	0.1	0.7	0.6

*Use of any illicit drug includes any use of marijuana, hallucinogens, cocaine, or heroin, or any use of other narcotics, amphetamines, sedatives (barbiturates), or tranquilizers not under a doctor's orders.

+Only drug use that was not under a doctor's orders is included here.

— no data available

Data from Johnston, L.D., P. M. O'Malley, J. G. Bachman, and J. E. Schulenberg. *Monitoring the Future: National Survey Results on Drug Use, 1975-2012, Volume II: College Students and Adults 19-50.* Ann Arbor, MI: Institute for Social Research, The University of Michigan, 2013.

Demographically, approximately 83.1% of the students taking this survey were between the ages of 18 and 22, and 94.5% were full-time students. Approximately 28.5% were freshmen, 24.3% were sophomores, 21.5% were juniors, 20.1% were seniors, 4.5% were graduates, and 1.1% were other.

In addition, 45.1% lived off campus, and 94.5% were full-time students. There is a very good likelihood that these results regarding college students' use of alcohol and other drugs are fairly similar on other larger state campuses in the United States.

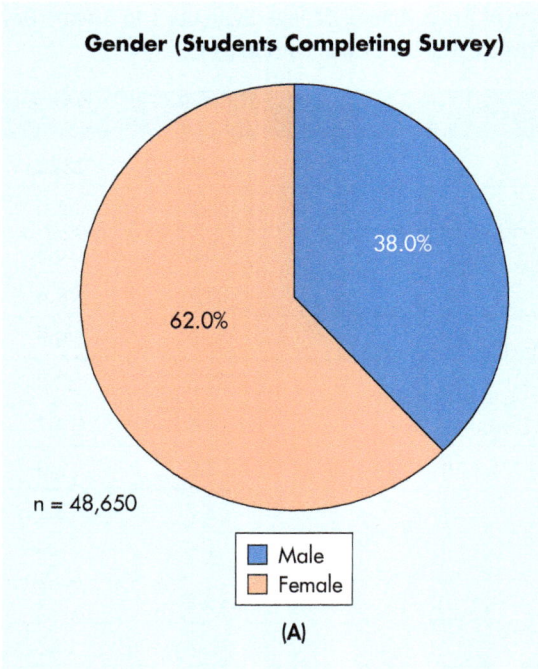

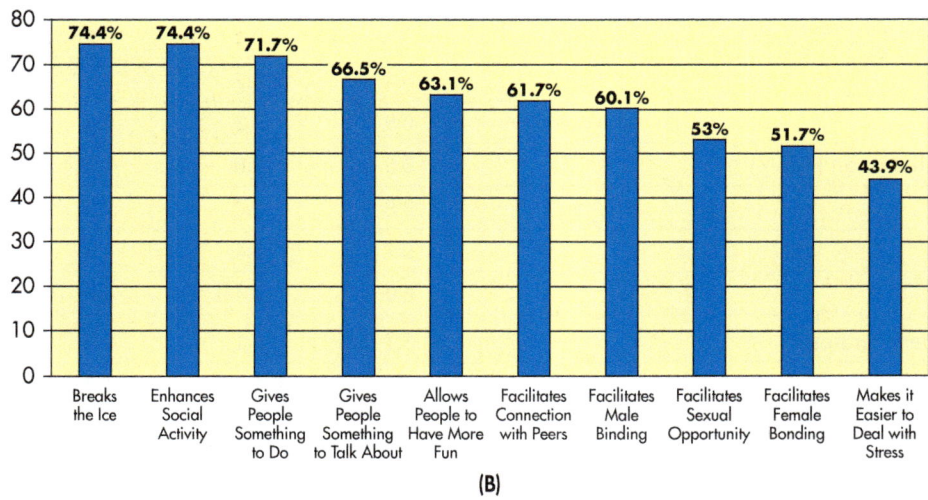

FIGURE 16.2 Sample of major reasons for using alcohol and other drugs.

Adapted from Southern Illinois University/Core Institute, Carbondale, IL: 2011 Annual Reference Group, Core Alcohol and Drug Survey Long Form - Form 194, Executive Summary, August 23, 2013, p. 5.

▮ Additional Noteworthy Findings Regarding Drug Use by College Students

The following sections describe the most recent significant studies and findings regarding the use of drugs by college students.

PATTERNS OF ALCOHOL AND OTHER DRUG USE

Research reviews of undergraduates' substance use and abuse and the prevalence patterns of alcohol and other drug use found that the most popular substance used by undergraduates is alcohol (Leinwand 2007b). "Nearly half of America's 5.4 million full-time college students abuse drugs or drink alcohol on binges at least once a month, according to a new study that portrays substance and alcohol abuse as an increasingly urgent problem on campuses across the nation" (Leinwand 2007b). While college students are drinking more alcohol on college campuses than similar aged peers not attending college, reports are that binge drinking has declined in the last decade. "In 2002, the binge drinking rate among 18–24 year olds was 41.0% compared with 39.1%. Among part-time college students and others not in college, the rate decreased from 38.9 to 35.4% during the same time period" (Stewart 2013, p. 2–3).

Common heavy drinking settings include:

- Fraternity parties
- Drinking in conjunction with athletic events
- Drinking in residence halls
- Drinking in off-campus housing areas with a high proportion of students
- Drinking in bars adjacent to campus (Stewart 2013, 3).

Other results showed that alcohol use was associated with serious and acute problems such as alcoholism, poor academic performance, drinking and driving, and criminalistic behavior (e.g., driving while intoxicated, vandalism, violence) (CSPINET.org 2007).

College students vary greatly in their use of alcohol and their beliefs about its positive and negative effects. Studies show that two major drinking patterns appear dominant among college students: (1) drinking related to impulsivity, disinhibition, and sensation-seeking and (2) drinking to manage negative emotional states, such as depression (National Institute on Alcohol Abuse and Alcoholism [NIAAA] 2005a).

Summarized in the following list are other significant findings regarding alcohol and other drug use:

- *High risk drinking:* Studies show that about 43% of all students report drinking in a high-risk manner at some point in their college career. Twenty percent of students report drinking in a high-risk manner often (Gloucester County College 2013).
- *Poor grades:* College students who received grades of D or below were more likely than those with higher grades to have used cigarettes, alcohol, or illicit drugs during the past month (SAMHSA 2011).
- *Death:* Each year, 1825 college students between the ages of 18 and 24 die from alcohol-related unintentional injuries, including motor vehicle crashes (Hingson, Zha, and Weitzman 2009; NIAAA 2005a).
- *Injury:* Each year, 599,000 students between the ages of 18 and 24 are unintentionally injured under the influence of alcohol (Hingson et al. 2009; NIAAA 2005a).

- *Assault:* Each year, 696,000 students between the ages of 18 and 24 are assaulted by another student who has been drinking (Hingson et al. 2009; NIAAA 2005b).
- *Sexual abuse:* Each year, 97,000 students between the ages of 18 and 24 are victims of alcohol-related sexual assault or date rape (Hingson et al. 2009; NIAAA 2005b). Researchers estimate that alcohol use is implicated in one-third to two-thirds of sexual assault and acquaintance or date rape cases among teens and college students.
- *Unsafe sex:* Each year, 400,000 students between the ages of 18 and 24 have unprotected sex, and more than 100,000 students between the ages of 18 and 24 report having been too intoxicated to know if they consented to having sex (NIAAA 2005a).
- *Academic problems:* About 25% of college students report academic consequences of their drinking including missing class, falling behind, doing poorly on exams or papers, and receiving lower grades overall (NIAAA 2005a).
- *Health problems/suicide attempts:* More than 150,000 students develop an alcohol-related health problem each year (Hingson et al. 2009), and between 1.2% and 1.5% of students indicate that they tried to commit suicide within the past year due to drinking or drug use (NIAAA 2005a).
- *Drunk driving:* Each year, 3,360,000 students between the ages of 18 and 24 drive under the influence of alcohol (Hingson et al. 2009; NIAAA 2005a).
- *Vandalism:* About 11% of college student drinkers report that they have damaged property while under the influence of alcohol (SAMHSA 2011).
- *Property damage:* More than 25% of administrators from schools with relatively low drinking levels and over 50% from schools with high drinking levels say their campuses have a "moderate" or "major" problem with alcohol-related property damage (SAMHSA 2011).
- *Police involvement:* About 5% of 4-year college students are involved with the police or campus security as a result of their drinking (Wechsler et al. 2002), and 110,000 students between the ages of 18 and 24 are arrested each year for an alcohol-related violation such as public drunkenness or driving under the influence (SAMHSA 2011).

- *Alcohol abuse and dependence:* In the past 12 months, 31% of college students met criteria for a diagnosis of alcohol abuse and 6% for a diagnosis of alcohol dependence, according to questionnaire-based self-reports about their drinking (NIAAA 2005a).
- *Binge drinking:* Young adults ages 18 to 25 are most likely to binge or drink heavily; 54% of the drinkers in this age group binge and about one in four are heavy drinkers (SAMHSA 2011).
- *Victimization:* About four in ten violent crimes against college students were committed by offenders who were perceived by victims to be using drugs or alcohol (NCVRW Resource Guide 2007).
- The amount and proportion of alcohol consumed by college students varies depending on where they live. Drinking rates are highest in fraternities and sororities, followed by on-campus housing (e.g., dormitories, residence halls). Students who live independently off-site (e.g., in apartments) drink less, and commuting students who live with their families drink the least (NIAAA 2005b).

PREDICTING DRUG USE FOR FIRST-YEAR COLLEGE STUDENTS

One of the best predictors of drug use for first-year college students was drug use during a typical month in the senior year of high school. Overall, college students responding to a questionnaire were found to use marijuana less frequently than they did in high school. Further, alcohol use increased early in the college years. Although the frequency of alcohol use increased, the number of times that college students got drunk did not rise. Most of these students found new friends in college with whom they got drunk. Alcohol and drug use depended on the choice of new college friends (Leibsohn 1994).

Another more recent finding includes personality dispositions to risky behavior as a predictor of first-year college drinking. Research findings from 418 first-year U.S. college students at the University of Kentucky reveal that students with a preponderance of sensation-seeking predispositions (risk taking) are more likely to drink more frequently, consume greater quantities of alcohol, and experience negative outcomes from drinking than students scoring significantly lower on the UPPS-R Impulsive Behavior Scale, the positive urgency measure (PUM), and the Drinking Styles Questionnaire (DSQ). Sensation-seeking students experience more lack of control (dyscontrol) stemming from extreme positive mood swings and

it is during these times that alcohol consumption rapidly increases (Cyders et al. 2009).

DORMITORIES FOR NON-DRUG-USING STUDENTS

In 1988, Rutgers University was one of the first universities to create a dormitory for students who are recovering addicts and who want to stay away from the alcohol-charged atmosphere of conventional dormitories. The dormitory at Rutgers maintains strict rules and careful management (Witham 1995). Other universities offer similar variations for on-campus living. In 1989, the University of Michigan opened a substance-free housing facility and set aside 500 dormitory spaces; 1200 students applied for these spaces (Belsie 1995). More recent findings indicate that "[N]ow that substance-free housing is commonplace, a handful of campuses, including Rutgers, have gone [even] further, offering 'recovery' housing for students who have been in treatment for addiction" (Lewin 2005). Today, substance-free housing has become a nationwide choice. This type of housing is found "... at dozens of campuses nationwide, from huge state universities like the University of Michigan to Ivy League schools like Dartmouth and small liberal arts colleges like Vassar" (Lewin 2005). For example,

> ... a junior at Earlham College who asked that his name not be used ... [said] "When I got to college, I didn't want to have to worry about having all that stuff in my face [in reference to having to live with drunk and drugged students in the dorm]. I've been in wellness housing my whole time here. I could handle normal housing now, but I like the people I live with, and there's a very good atmosphere." (Lewin 2005)

Further, on some campuses, large numbers of entering freshmen prefer substance-free living accommodations, mainly dormitories as well as other types of housing. "At Dartmouth, for example, about 400 of the 1075 incoming freshmen requested it, compared with only about 200 of the 2200 sophomores, juniors and seniors who live on campus" (Lewin 2005).

REMAINING POPULARITY OF CERTAIN TYPES OF "SOFTER" DRUGS

Marijuana and psilocybin mushrooms are two types of illicit recreational drugs whose popularity appeared to grow in the 1990s and to date remain popular on most college campuses. Referred to as "soft drugs," these substances are commonly used on most college campuses (Ravid 1995).

I know my older brothers told me that when they were at this same college I am now attending "shrooms" [referring to psilocybin mushrooms] were not that easy to get and the better types of weed were very infrequent back seven years ago. Well, today it's really different! Even at this smaller university it's all a matter of finding the right dude to hook you up. I have a hook-up that always has blueberry, which is a small percentage *Sativa* and nearly all *Indica*. He is in partnership with a friend in Michigan who grows only this kind. It is expensive but oh is it worth it. You certainly don't need much like the other stuff that is weaker. It is awesome stuff. The "shrooms" are not as frequent and several times I had to go to another friend's campus to get them. *(From Venturelli's research files, male attending a smaller comprehensive university in the Midwest, age 22, June 12, 2013)*

Nationwide surveys studying yearly drug use averages from 1984 through 1999 showed a steady, progressive increase in the use of hallucinogens, which include psilocybin mushrooms, Ecstasy, and LSD. In 1984 (the first year of the survey), 3.7% of college students used LSD; in 1999, 5.4% used this same drug. Similarly, in 1984, 6.2% used hallucinogens (excluding LSD) and in 1999, 7.8% used these same hallucinogenic-type drugs (Johnston et al. 2000a, 2000b). Updated findings show hallucinogen use has been dropping, from 7.4% in 2003 to 5.1% in 2008. One noteworthy finding is that the use of LSD slightly increased from 2007 (1.3%) to 2008 (2.6%) (a 1.3% increase over a 2-year period) (Johnston et al. 2009b). Concerning college students' use of MDMA (Ecstasy), the annual use was 9.1% in 2000, 4.4% in 2003, dropping to 2.2% in 2007, then rising to 3.7% in 2008 (an increase of 1.6% over a 2-year period) (Johnston et al. 2009b). More recently, the annual prevalence of LSD remains fairly low among college students in 2012. In 2012 annual prevalence is 1.9% among college students, 2.2% in the noncollege group (after a significant 1.6 percentage-point decrease in 2012), and 2.4% among 12th graders (Johnston et al. 2013). The use of Ecstasy (MDMA) by college students stands at 5.8% in 2012, up from 2.2% in 2007. Both the college and noncollege groups showed some increase by 2012, to 5.8% and 5.4%, respectively, while the 12th graders remained about the same, at 3.8%. While none of these groups has usage rates comparable to what they were in 2001, all three have shown some resurgence in use in recent years (Johnston et al. 2013).

ROHYPNOL AND DATE RAPE

Rohypnol, also known as the "date-rape drug," is one of six drugs referred to as *club drugs*. The other club drugs are MDMA (Ecstasy), gamma-hydroxybutyrate (GHB), ketamine, methamphetamine, and LSD. Club drugs are used by individuals at all-night dance parties such as raves or trances, dance clubs, and bars. All of these drugs are colorless, tasteless, and odorless. They can be added unobtrusively to beverages by individuals who may want to intoxicate or sedate others (NIDA 2000). In cases of sexual assault or rape, the small white Rohypnol pills are slipped into a person's drink, causing the person to black out and have no memories of events that occurred while he or she was under the influence of the drug. A minority of undergraduates also use the drug to intensify the effects of marijuana and alcohol. One problem with identifying whether this drug has been given to an unwilling recipient is that Rohypnol can be detected only for 60 hours after ingestion (Lively 1996).

Rohypnol (flunitrazepam) belongs to a class of drugs known as benzodiazepines (such as Valium and Xanax). Although this drug is not approved for prescription use in the United States, it is approved and used in more than 60 countries as a treatment for insomnia, as a sedative, and as a presurgery anesthetic (NIDA 2000).

■ Recommendations for Reducing Drug Use and Abuse on College Campuses

There is an elevated risk of increased drug use and abuse when students move to a college campus. Approaches to minimize increased drug use include the following (Ross and Dejong 2008, p. 3):

- *Alcohol-free options:* ". . . offer and promote social, recreational, extracurricular, and public service options that do not include alcohol and other drugs."
- *Normative environment:* ". . . create a social, academic, and residential environment that supports health-promoting norms."
- *Alcohol availability:* ". . . limit alcohol availability both on and off campus."

KEY TERM

Rohypnol
the "date-rape drug," used on some college campuses

- *Alcohol marketing and promotion:* ". . . restrict marketing and promotion of alcohol beverages both on and off campus."
- *Policy development and enforcement:* ". . . develop and enforce campus policies and enforce local, state, and federal laws, and make sure everyone knows what the policies are."

HIV and AIDS

Acquired immune deficiency syndrome (AIDS) came to the attention of medical authorities in the United States on June 4, 1981, in a newsletter from the Centers for Disease Control and Prevention (CDC) in Atlanta, Georgia (Zuger 2000). Human immunodeficiency virus (HIV), the virus that causes AIDS, was not discovered until 1983. Current findings reveal the following (AIDS.gov 2012a):

- Estimates are that throughout the world 33.4 million people are currently living with HIV /AIDS.
- More than 25 million people have died of AIDS worldwide since the first cases were reported in 1981.
- In 2008, 2 million people died due to HIV/ AIDS, and another 2.7 million were newly infected.
- Although cases have been reported in all regions of the world, almost all those living with HIV (97%) reside in low- and middle-income countries, particularly in sub-Saharan Africa.
- According to the World Health Organization (WHO), most people living with HIV or at risk for HIV do not have access to prevention, care, and treatment, and there is still no cure.
- The HIV epidemic not only affects the health of individuals, but also impacts households, communities, and the development and economic growth of nations. Many of the countries hardest hit by HIV also suffer from other infectious diseases, food insecurity, and other serious problems.
- Despite these challenges, there have been successes and promising signs. New global efforts have been mounted to address the epidemic, particularly in the last decade. Prevention has helped to reduce HIV prevalence rates in a small but growing number of countries, and new HIV infections are believed to be on the decline. In addition, the number of people with HIV receiving treatment in resource-poor

countries has increased 10-fold since 2002, reaching an estimated 4 million by 2008.

In the United States, "CDC [the Centers for Disease Control and Prevention] estimates that 1,148,200 persons aged 13 years and older are living with HIV infection, including 207,600 (18.1%) who are unaware of their infection" (CDC 2013b). Looking at risk groups in the United States, the major findings are (CDC 2013a):

Gay, bisexual, and other men who have sex with men (MSM) of all races and ethnicities remain the population most profoundly affected by HIV.

- In 2010, the estimated number of new HIV infections among MSM was 29,800, a significant 12% increase from the 26,700 new infections among MSM in 2008.
- Although MSM represent about 4% of the male population in the United States, in 2010, MSM accounted for 78% of new HIV infections among males and 63% of all new infections. MSM accounted for 52% of all people living with HIV infection in 2009, the most recent year these data are available.
- In 2010, white MSM continued to account for the largest number of new HIV infections (11,200), by transmission category, followed closely by black MSM (10,600).
- The estimated number of new HIV infections was greatest among MSM in the youngest age group. In 2010, the greatest number of new HIV infections (4,800) among MSM occurred in young black/African American MSM aged 13–24. Young black MSM accounted for 45% of new HIV infections among black MSM and 55% of new HIV infections among young MSM overall.
- Since the epidemic began, an estimated 302,148 MSM with an AIDS diagnosis have died, including an estimated 5,909 in 2010.

Heterosexuals and injection drug users also continue to be affected by HIV.

- Heterosexuals accounted for 25% of estimated new HIV infections in 2010 and 27% of people living with HIV infection in 2009.
- Since the epidemic began, almost 85,000 persons with an AIDS diagnosis, infected through heterosexual sex, have died, included an estimated 4,003 in 2010.
- New HIV infections among women are primarily attributed to heterosexual contact

(84% in 2010) or injection drug use (16% in 2010). Women accounted for 20% of estimated new HIV infections in 2010 and 24% of those living with HIV infection in 2009. The 9,500 new infections among women in 2010 reflect a significant 21% decrease from the 12,000 new infections that occurred among this group in 2008.

- Injection drug users represented 8% of new HIV infections in 2010 and 16% of those living with HIV in 2009.
- Since the epidemic began, nearly 182,000 injection drug users with an AIDS diagnosis have died, including an estimated 4,218 in 2010.

By Race/Ethnicity

Blacks/African Americans continue to experience the most severe burden of HIV, compared with other races and ethnicities.

- Blacks represent approximately 12% of the U.S. population, but accounted for an estimated 44% of new HIV infections in 2010. They also accounted for 44% of people living with HIV infection in 2009.
- Since the epidemic began, more than 260,800 blacks with an AIDS diagnosis have died, including an estimated 7,678 in 2010.
- Unless the course of the epidemic changes, at some point in their lifetime, an estimated 1 in 16 black men and 1 in 32 black women will be diagnosed with HIV infection.

Hispanics/Latinos are also disproportionately affected by HIV.

- Hispanics/Latinos represented 16% of the population but accounted for 21% of new HIV infections in 2010. Hispanics/Latinos accounted for 19% of people living with HIV infection in 2009.
- Disparities persist in the estimated rate of new HIV infections in Hispanics/Latinos. In 2010, the rate of new HIV infections for Latino males was 2.9 times that for white males, and the rate of new infections for Latinas was 4.2 times that for white females.
- Since the epidemic began, more than 96,200 Hispanics/Latinos with an AIDS diagnosis have died, including 2,370 in 2010.

With regard to estimated new HIV infections in the United States in 2010, the most affected subpopulations were (CDC 2013b):

- White males who have sex with other men (MSM), 11,200 cases
- Black males having sex with other men (MSM), 10,600 cases
- Hispanic/Latino males having sex with other men (MSM), 6,700 cases
- Black heterosexual women, 5,300 cases
- Black heterosexual men, 2,700 cases
- White heterosexual women, 1,300 cases
- Hispanic/Latino heterosexual women, 1,200 cases
- Black males IDUs (injection drug users), 1,100 cases
- Black females IDUs (injection drug users), 850 cases

In comparing the years 2005 and 2011 regarding HIV and AIDS statistics in major regions of the world, the most significant regional statistics regarding adults and children newly infected and living with HIV and those who died from AIDS-related causes are as follows (United Nations Programme on HIV/AIDS [UNAIDS] 2012, p. 12):

- "The number of people dying from AIDS-related causes in sub-Saharan Africa declined by 32% from 2005 to 2011, although the region still accounted for 70% of all the people dying from AIDS in 2011."
- "The Caribbean (48%) and Oceania (41%) experienced significant declines in AIDS-related deaths between 2005 and 2011."
- "More modest declines occurred during the same period in Latin America (10%), Asia (4%) and Western and Central Europe and North America (1%)."
- "Two other regions, however, experienced significant increases in mortality from AIDS—Eastern Europe and Central Asia (21%) and the Middle East and North Africa (17%)."

The following shows the regional statistics for adults and children living with HIV/AIDS at the end of 2011 (from highest to lowest) (UNAIDS 2012):

- Sub-Saharan Africa had 23.5 million adults and children living with HIV and had 1.2 million AIDS-related deaths in adults and children.
- South and South-East Asia had 4 million adults and children living with HIV/AIDS and had 250,000 AIDS-related deaths in adults and children.

- Latin America had 1.4 million adults and children living with HIV/AIDS and 54,000 AIDS-related deaths in adults and children.
- North America had 1.4 million adults and children living with HIV/AIDS and 21,000 AIDS-related deaths in adults and children.
- Eastern Europe and Central Asia had 1.4 million adults and children living with HIV/AIDS and 92,000 AIDS-related deaths in adults and children.
- Western and Central Europe had 900,000 adults and children living with HIV/AIDS and 7000 AIDS-related deaths in adults and children.
- East Asia had 830,000 adults and children living with HIV/AIDS and 59,000 AIDS-related deaths in adults and children.
- The Middle East and North Africa had 300,000 adults and children living with HIV and had 23,000 AIDS-related deaths in adults and children.
- The Caribbean had 230,000 adults and children living with HIV/AIDS and 10,000 AIDS-related deaths in adults and children.
- Oceania had 53,000 adults and children living with HIV/AIDS and 1300 AIDS-related deaths in adults and children.

UNAIDS reports the following regarding worldwide totals of adults and children with HIV/AIDS in 2011 (UNAIDS 2012):

- There was an *increase* worldwide in adults and children living with HIV, from 29.4 million in 2001 to 34 million in 2011.
- The total number of adults and children newly infected with HIV *decreased* from 3.2 million in 2001 to 2.5 million in 2011 (good news).
- The percentage of total HIV adult prevalence for those ages 15–49 years *remained the same* throughout the world in 2001 (0.8%) and 2011 (0.8%).
- The total number of AIDS-related deaths among adults and children *decreased* from 2005 (2.3 million) to 2011 (1.8 million) (good news).

Finally, UNAIDS also reports that:

The number of people dying from AIDS-related causes began to decline in the mid-2000s because of scaled-up antiretroviral therapy and the steady decline in HIV incidence since the peak in 1997. In 2011, this decline continued, with evidence that the drop in the number of people dying from AIDS-related causes

is accelerating in several countries (UNAIDS 2012, p. 12).

▌Major U.S. Statistics and Trends in Specific Populations Living with HIV/AIDS

In the United States, the following are significant findings regarding this disease (CDC 2013a):

- Currently, 1.1 million people are living with HIV in the United States (an estimated 1,148,200 adults and adolescents), and nearly one in five of those (18%) are unaware of their infections.
- Despite increases in the total number of people living with HIV in the United States in recent years, the annual number of new infections has remained relatively stable overall. However, HIV infections continue at far too high a level, with approximately 50,000 Americans becoming newly infected with HIV each year.
- More than 15,000 people with AIDS still die each year in the United States.

Heavily Affected Populations
. . . Heterosexuals and injection drug users also continue to be affected by HIV:

- Individuals infected through heterosexual contact account for 25% of annual new HIV infections and 27% of people living with HIV.
- Injection drug users represent 9% of annual new HIV infections and 16% of those living with HIV.

By Race/Ethnicity
. . . Among racial/ethnic groups, African Americans face the most severe burden of HIV and AIDS in the nation:

- While blacks represent approximately 14% of the U.S. population, the latest CDC estimates show that they account for almost half of all new infections in the United States each year (44%) as well as almost half of all people living with HIV (44%).
- At some point in their lives, approximately one in 16 black men will be diagnosed with HIV, as will one in 32 black women.
- The rate of new HIV infections for black men is more than six times as high as that of white men, and more than two times that of Hispanic men and of black women.

- Comparing 2008 to 2010, new HIV infections among black women decreased 21% (from 7,700 to 6,100); however, black women account for the vast majority (64%) of all new infections among women overall and the HIV incidence rate for black women remains 20 times as high as that of white women, and almost five times that of Hispanic women.
- HIV infections among blacks overall have been roughly stable in recent years.

. . . Latinos are also disproportionately impacted:

- Hispanics represent approximately 16% of the population and the latest CDC estimates show that they account for 19% of people living with HIV in the United States, as well as 21% of new infections each year.
- At some point in their lives, approximately one in 36 Hispanic men will be diagnosed with HIV, as will one in 106 Hispanic women.
- The rate of new HIV infections among Hispanic men is almost three times that of white men, and the rate among Hispanic women is more than four times that of white women.
- HIV infections among Hispanics overall have been roughly stable in recent years.

▪ The Nature of HIV Infection and Related Symptoms

AIDS, which is caused by HIV, is a disease in which the body's immune system breaks down and is unable to fight off certain infections, known as "opportunistic infections," and other illnesses that take advantage of a weakened immune system.

In the early stage of HIV infection, often referred to as the *HIV syndrome*, the symptoms can include the following (TreatHIVNow 2013):

- Fever
- Headache
- Feeling very tired
- Swollen lymph glands
- Sore throat
- Skin rash

Be aware that many of these symptoms can also be symptoms of mononucleosis (mono), other sexually transmitted infections (STIs), or viral hepatitis. Only an HIV test can determine if a person displaying any combination of these symptoms has contracted HIV. Symptoms for HIV as it advances and worsens include the following (AIDS.gov 2012b; TreatHIVNow 2013):

- Swollen lymph glands
- Diarrhea that is frequent or ongoing
- Frequent high fevers (over 100°F)
- Shaking chills
- Shortness of breath
- Blurred and distorted vision
- Unplanned or rapid weight loss
- Feeling very tired
- Ulcerated skin in the mouth
- Soaking night sweats
- Cough
- Headaches
- Skin rashes or bumps

When a person is infected with HIV, the virus enters the body and lives and multiplies primarily in the white blood cells (see **Figure 16.3**). These immune cells normally protect us from disease. The hallmark of HIV infection is the progressive loss of a specific type of immune cells called T-helper or CD4+ cells.

As the virus grows, it damages or kills CD4+ and other cells, weakening the immune system and leaving the individual vulnerable to numerous opportunistic infections and other illnesses, ranging from pneumonia to cancer. The CDC defines someone as having a clinical diagnosis of AIDS if he or she has tested positive for HIV and has one or both of these conditions (Schernoff and Smith 2001):

- The person has experienced one or more AIDS-related infections or illnesses.
- The number of CD4+ cells has reached or fallen below 200 per cubic millimeter of blood (a measurement known as a T-cell count).

As mentioned previously, the immune systems of HIV-positive individuals become severely compromised as important immune cells called CD4+ helper T lymphocytes and macrophages are destroyed. Because these immune cells are crucial in identifying and eliminating infection-causing microorganisms such as bacteria, fungi, and viruses, their deficiency substantially increases the likelihood and severity of infectious diseases. Progression of the disease brings weight loss, infections in the throat (thrush) and skin (shingles), and other opportunistic infections and/or cancer (e.g., Kaposi's sarcoma). Infections become increasingly difficult to control with medication, and consequently severe opportunistic infections, such as pneumonia, meningitis, hepatitis, and tuberculosis,

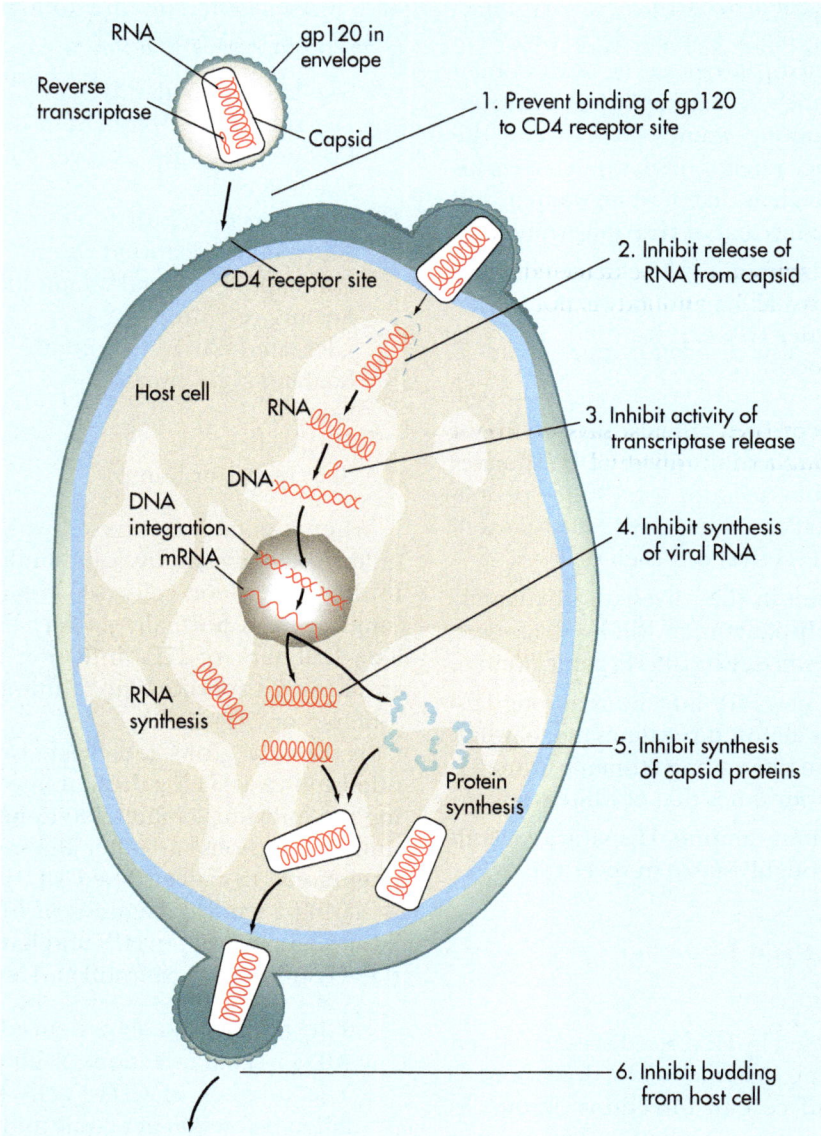

FIGURE 16.3 Disrupting the assembly line, HIV survives by invading white blood cells and turning them into virus factories. There are six possible approaches for developing anti-HIV therapies by interfering with the replication of HIV.

occur and eventually lead to death. The likelihood of introducing these opportunistic infections into the body increases in patients who are injection drug users because they often share injection equipment, such as needles and syringes that are contaminated with disease-causing microorganisms.

An HIV-infected individual may not manifest symptoms of AIDS for as many as 10 to 12 years after the initial infection. Although the HIV-infected individual may experience no symptoms, he or she is highly contagious.

After an individual has become infected, he or she may have a brief flu-like illness, usually within 6 to 12 weeks. It is not known what determines the length of the latency period, when symptoms are not present. The asymptomatic period eventually ends, however, and signs of immune disorder appear.

▮ Diagnosis and Treatment

It is crucial that HIV-infected people be aware of their condition to avoid activities that might transmit the infection to others. Testing for the presence of infection has been available since 1985 and is done by determining whether the body is producing antibodies against HIV. Further, since 1996, newspapers, magazines, radio, and television have been advertising a take-at-home HIV antibody test. (These advertisements are not as widely publicized today, but the test can readily be found on the Internet.) The presence of these specific antibodies indicates HIV infection. If an individual is infected, it takes 6 to 12 weeks after the HIV exposure before the body produces enough antibodies to be detected in currently available tests. If the antibody is not present within 6 months after HIV exposure, it is likely that infection did not occur (Pietroski 1993).

Although the tests for HIV infection are reliable, false negatives (i.e., the test says no HIV is present even though the individual is infected) and false positives (i.e., the test says the individual is infected even though no HIV is present) occur in 1 out of 30,000 tests. Because testing positive for HIV is currently perceived as eventually life-threatening and is a highly emotional diagnosis, great effort is made to ensure confidentiality of the test results. The blood specimens to be tested are coded, and the personnel conducting the tests are not allowed to divulge the results to anyone but the individual who was tested. The issue of confidentiality is very controversial, however. It often is difficult to decide who has the right to know when HIV has been detected (see "Point/Counterpoint: Who Should Know the Results of Your HIV Test If You Test Positive?").

▶ POINT/COUNTERPOINT

Who Should Know the Results of Your HIV Test If You Test Positive?

Most people would probably want to keep such results private, but would your opinion about HIV-positive people keeping their results confidential change in the following circumstances:

- You require first aid after a serious auto accident and the emergency medical technician assisting is HIV positive?
- Your doctor is HIV positive?
- Your dentist is HIV positive?
- Your manicurist is HIV positive?
- Your massage therapist is HIV positive?
- Your severely handicapped daughter's elementary school teacher is HIV positive?
- Your lover is HIV positive?
- Your tattoo artist is HIV positive?
- Your jeweler who is about to pierce your daughter's ears is HIV positive?
- Your boxing partner is HIV positive?
- Your jail cellmate is HIV positive?

Arguments for not disclosing HIV-positive results to anyone other than the person undergoing HIV screening are that reporting such results to others would (1) cause many people not to take the test for fear of disclosure to others; (2) possibly cause loss of employment (if the results require mandatory reporting to supervisors or managers); (3) unnecessarily stigmatize the HIV-positive person, exposing an infected person to social ostracism and gossip and potentially creating fear and panic in others; and (4) potentially destroy a partner or marriage relationship if the significant other or spouse is notified.

Arguments for mandatory disclosure to others potentially affected by the results of this disease include (1) to protect domestic or marital partners, (2) to protect others from HIV-positive workers who could infect them (such as surgeons who are involved in invasive bodily care or procedures), and (3) to honor the public's right to know of the threat of contracting this terminal disease.

Currently, employers cannot legally terminate a worker for being HIV positive. In cases of direct potential threat to the public, an HIV-positive worker can be reassigned to a different position. Also, in most cases, employers cannot legally inquire about HIV test results. An exception to this is the military and prison, where mandatory testing is required. What is your opinion about this issue?

The sooner an HIV-positive person begins drug treatment, the more effective the treatment may be. Knowing this, should HIV-positive individuals be required to inform past sexual partners and people with whom they have shared needles so that these people can be tested (known as "partner notification" or "contact tracing")?

If an HIV-positive surgeon is going to operate on you, your mother, your father, or your child, do you have the right to know? What are the rights of the HIV-positive individual versus the rights of the public?

After a positive HIV diagnosis, the best way to lengthen one's life is to immediately begin drug treatments. The first prescription drug treatment for AIDS, AZT, was introduced in 1987. In 1996, **protease inhibitors** came on the market. When combined with AZT and other drugs, protease inhibitors resulted in miraculous remissions of desperately ill AIDS patients (Zuger 2000). Further, it appears that with such drug combinations, HIV blood levels in newly infected patients remain at exceedingly low levels (Zuger 2000). Although the drug combinations do not rid the body of infected cells, results indicate that HIV infections could become as manageable as diabetes (Crowley 1996).

Today, people in the United States and other developed countries can use a number of drugs to treat HIV infection and AIDS. Some of these are designed to treat the opportunistic infections and illnesses that affect people with HIV/AIDS. In addition, several types of drugs seek to prevent HIV from reproducing and destroying the body's immune system. Reverse transcriptase inhibitors attach to an HIV enzyme called reverse transcriptase. "There are two major categories of reverse transcriptase inhibitors: nucleoside/nucleotide reverse transcriptase inhibitors (NRTIs) and non-nucleoside reverse transcriptase inhibitors (NNRTIs)" (EBSCO 2013). The NRTIs and NNRTIs include the following drugs (EBSCO 2013):

- Combivir (lamivudine and zidovudine [AZT])
- Emtriva (emtricitabine)
- Epivir (lamivudine)
- Epzicom (abacavir and lamivudine)
- Hivid (zalcitabine)
- Rescriptor (delavirdine)
- Retrovir (AZT and zidovudine)
- Trizivir (abacavir, lamivudine, and zidovudine)
- Truvada (emtricitabine and tenofovir)
- Videx (didanosine)
- Viramune (nevirapine)
- Viread (tenofovir)
- Zerit (stavudine)
- Ziagen (abacavir)

Medications used to treat HIV infection (antiretroviral drugs) help many people with HIV to lower the levels of virus in their blood (viral load) to undetectable levels. Effective treatment with these medications (antiretroviral therapy [ART]) may decrease the chance that an infected person will transmit HIV to others

through sex. However, the risk of spreading infection is still not zero, which means that persons with HIV who are taking ART, or persons who are in a relationship with someone who has HIV and is taking ART, should still use proven prevention methods, such as condoms. (CDC 2010d)

Many HIV patients are taking several of these drugs in combination, a regimen known as **highly active antiretroviral therapy (HAART)**. When successful, combinations or "cocktail" therapy can reduce the level of HIV in the bloodstream to very low—even undetectable—levels and sometimes enable the body's CD4+ immune cells to rebound to normal levels (amfAR 2001, pp. 6–9). Less than 15 years ago the drug regimen was difficult:

> I take the famous drug "cocktail" and have to wake myself up in the middle of the night around 4 in the morning, then go back to sleep. I am used to it. I know it is a pain in the neck, but I think that despite this, the side effects can even be worse at times. I really don't want to go into it; it's depressing. The bright side: I am still alive after 9 years since diagnosed with AIDS; I am not dead yet. *(From Venturelli's research files, male bartender in Chicago, age 52, May 18, 2000)*

An update regarding the treatment of HIV/AIDS reveals that:

> It wasn't until 1995, with the development of a second class of anti-HIV drugs, that we began to make real progress in controlling the pandemic. These drugs target the HIV protease, an enzyme involved in processing HIV proteins into their functional forms. Today, 20 out of the 21 USDA-approved antiretroviral drugs target either the reverse transcriptase or the viral protease. With the introduction of multiple antiretroviral therapies, clinicians began a treatment regime known as HAART (Highly Active Antiretroviral Therapy) that involves

KEY TERMS

protease inhibitors
a major breakthrough class of drugs used to treat HIV infected individuals

highly active antiretroviral therapy (HAART)
more recent types of medications used to treat HIV/AIDS infected individuals

combinations of 3–4 drugs at once. Despite the fact that there might be viruses resistant to one drug, they can still be suppressed by one of the other drugs being used. Just as the probability of getting struck by lightning twice in a row is much lower than getting struck once, the probability of finding a virus resistant to multiple drugs is much lower than being resistant to one. By reducing the probability of resistance, HAART was finally able to increase patient lifespan by suppressing viral replication and curbing immune cell loss. Although HAART has been very successful in preventing those infected with HIV from progressing to AIDS, it is not a cure, thus making prevention of new HIV cases a critical component of the strategy against HIV/AIDS. (Clark 2010)

As a therapy regimen, HAART results in a dramatic reduction in the incidence of AIDS and death in individuals infected with HIV (MyDNA .com 2005). Less than 15 years ago, patients took approximately 37 pills per day; a few years later it was a 14-pill-a-day regimen. Today, in the majority of cases, only three pills have to be taken each day (Scripps Howard News Service 2003). The pills must be taken regularly each day to ensure effective therapy. The cost of the cocktail was $2000 to $3000 per month. Another source estimated the annual cost of care is about $10,000 to $15,000 per year (AVERT.org 2011). In a recent review of the cost of 24 major HIV medications by this author, the average yearly cost was approximately $8000 for each of the medications taken. If, for example, three types of HIV drugs are required then the average amount is approximately $24,000 per year. Note, however, this approximate cost can *vary significantly* depending on what combinations of the 28 major HIV drugs are prescribed on a daily basis. For example, in 2008 Aptivus cost $1071 monthly whereas another HIV drug, Videx and Videx EC, cost $368 monthly (Diaz-Linares et al. 2008). Another recent estimate indicates that "[m]onthly HIV treatment regimens range from $2,000 to $5,000—much of it for drugs. With the life expectancy for HIV patients increasing, the lifetime cost of treatment in today's terms is estimated at more than half-million dollars (Aguirre 2012).

Recently, a new class of medicines known as integrase inhibitors was discovered that are very efficient in controlling HIV (Chong 2006). "Integrase inhibitors prevent HIV, or human immunodeficiency virus, from replicating by blocking its ability to patch its DNA onto cells" (Chong 2006, p. A9). When combined with two other drugs, tenoflovir and lamivudine, it appears promising. Used as part of a drug cocktail, "the amount of HIV in 90% of patients . . . [was reduced to] . . . undetectable levels in 24 weeks" (Chong 2006, p. A9).

Newer AIDS drugs include "[e]ntry inhibitors that work by preventing HIV from entering healthy CD4 cells (T-cells) in the body" (AIDS-MEDS 2011). Entry inhibitors (including fusion inhibitors) ". . .work differently than many of the approved anti-HIV drugs—the protease inhibitors (PIs), the nucleoside reverse transcriptase inhibitors (NRTIs), and the non-nucleoside reverse transcriptase inhibitors (NNRTIs)—which are active against HIV after it has infected a CD4 cell" (AIDSMEDS 2011). "Entry/fusion inhibitors... stops the virus from entering cells. Two drugs in this class have been approved by the Food and Drug Administration (FDA): maraviroc, an entry inhibitor, and enfuvirtide, a fusion inhibitor" (amfAR 2010). "Integrase inhibitors prevent an HIV enzyme called integrase from inserting HIV's genetic information into the virus's target cell. To date, only one integrase inhibitor, reltegravir, has been approved by the FDA" (amfAR 2010).

Because these newer drugs halt the progression of HIV to AIDS, the rate of new AIDS cases fell 25% by 1998 (Zuger 2000). Today, there is approximately a 70% survival rate for those on daily medication (CDC 2010d).

Unfortunately, many health insurance companies continue to actively issue restrictive amendments on their policies that cap reimbursement for such expensive drug therapies. As a result, infected individuals with extensive debt obligations and patients without health insurance are often unable to afford the latest drug therapy.

A successful prognosis for HIV infection and AIDS relies on three factors: (1) initiation of a drug regimen as soon as possible after an HIV-positive diagnosis, (2) strict adherence to medical advice and treatment, and (3) maintenance of a healthy diet without drug use or abuse in order to avoid taxing the immune system.

▪ Who Is at Risk for AIDS?

Although anyone can become infected with HIV, its routes of transmission are limited to blood, semen, vaginal fluid, and possibly some other body fluids (Grinspoon 1994). Before the advent of AZT, mothers were more likely to pass the virus to their children prenatally or through breast milk. HIV is a virus that is not likely to survive outside of the body. Consequently, it is not spread by casual contact, such as by shaking hands, touching, hugging, or kissing (although "deep" kissing with an infected person is not recommended). In addition, it is not spread through food or water, by sharing cups or glasses, by coughing and sneezing, or by using common toilets. It is not spread by mosquitoes or other insects.

The following populations are at greatest risk for contracting AIDS:

- Men with a history of having had multiple homosexual or bisexual partners. Men who have sex with men (MSM) account for more than half of all new HIV infections in the United States each year (53%), as well as nearly half of people living with HIV (48%) (CDC 2010a). Although new HIV infections have declined among both heterosexuals and injection drug users, infections among MSM have been steadily increasing since the early 1990s (CDC 2010a).
- Injecting drug users and their sexual partners.
- Heterosexuals with multiple partners.
- Infants born to HIV-infected women (approximately 10% of all HIV-positive mothers have HIV-positive babies).
- People who receive contaminated blood products, such as for transfusions or treatment of blood disorders. (Blood banks have improved the screening of their blood supplies in the last decade.)

See **Figure 16.4** and **Figure 16.5** for a detailed breakdown of categories of U.S. AIDS cases by type of HIV exposure for men and women.

Figure 16.4 shows that approximately 63% of men with AIDS reported sex with men, and another approximately 8% of people reported injection drug use. An estimated 3% of cases were attributed to male-to-male sexual contact and injection drug use, 25% were attributed to heterosexual contact, and other risk exposures accounted for the remaining 1% of cases. Figure 16.5 shows that 25% of women with AIDS attributed their exposure to heterosexual contact, 73% attributed their exposure to injection drug use, and 2% reported another type of exposure.

■ AIDS and Drugs of Abuse

The AIDS epidemic is closely associated with drug abuse problems. As mentioned earlier, individuals addicted to illicit drugs are currently the second largest risk group for contracting AIDS. At the end of 2010, an estimated 25% of adults and adolescents

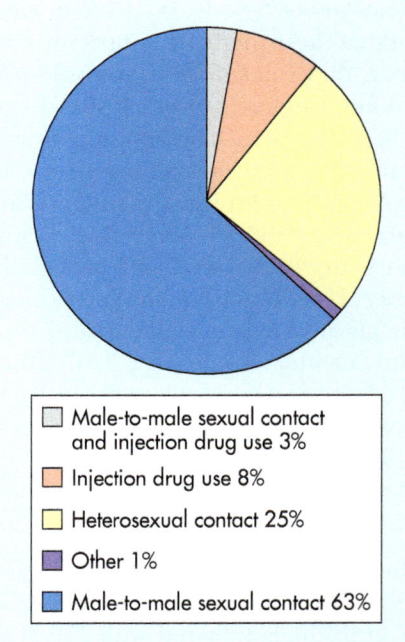

Male-to-male sexual contact and injection drug use 3%

Injection drug use 8%

Heterosexual contact 25%

Other 1%

Male-to-male sexual contact 63%

FIGURE 16.4 Estimated new HIV infections, 2010, by transmission category.

Data from Centers for Disease Control and Prevention (CDC). HIV/AIDS Statistics and Surveillance Report, 2010. Atlanta, GA: U.S. Department of Health and Human Services, 2013.

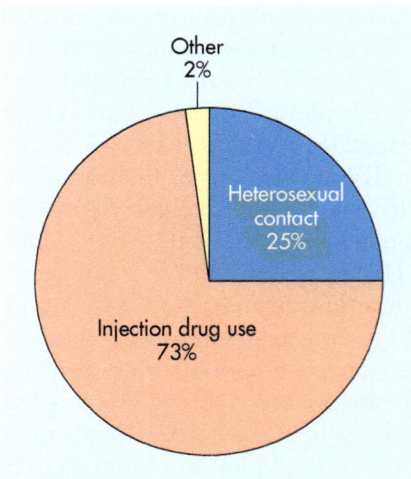

Other 2%

Heterosexual contact 25%

Injection drug use 73%

FIGURE 16.5 Approximate percentages of AIDS cases in adult women, by risk exposure, 2010.

Data from Centers for Disease Control and Prevention (CDC). HIV/AIDS Surveillance Report, 2010. Atlanta, GA: U.S. Department of Health and Human Services, 2013.

aged 13 years or older living with a diagnosis of HIV in the United States were women. In 2010, women accounted for an estimated 9,500, or 20%, of the estimated 47,500 new HIV infections in the United States. Most of these (8,000, or 84%) were from heterosexual contact with a person known to have, or to be a high risk for, HIV infection (CDC 2013d). AIDS in women is particularly linked to drug abuse.

A substantial number of HIV infections among women are attributable to injection drug and other substance use—either directly, through sharing drug injection equipment contaminated with HIV, or indirectly, through engaging in high-risk behaviors like unprotected sex, while under the influence of drugs or alcohol (CDC 2013e). Several reasons account for the high incidence of this deadly infection in the drug-abusing population.

INTRAVENOUS DRUGS

Intravenous drug use has become the most important factor in the spread of AIDS in the United States. "Drugs can be taken in a variety of ways including drinking, smoking, snorting, and rubbing, but it is the injection of drugs that creates the biggest risk of HIV transmission" (AVERT .org 2013). Among severely addicted populations, intravenous drug use is often undertaken with little regard to hygiene, and injection paraphernalia such as needles, syringes, and cotton are frequently shared with other drug addicts (Millstein 1993). Sharing HIV-contaminated injection equipment can easily result in the transmission of this virus. The likelihood of an intravenous drug user contracting AIDS is directly correlated with (1) the frequency of drug injections, (2) the number of partners with whom injection equipment is shared, (3) the frequency of needle sharing, and (4) the frequency of injections in locations where there are high AIDS infection rates, such as in shooting galleries or crack houses (Booth, Watters, and Chitwood 1993).

CRACK

Use of drugs such as crack (Ciba Foundation 1992) and alcohol (Colthurst 1993) tends to compromise judgment and encourage high-risk activities such as injection drug use or sexual risk taking (Beard and Kunsman 1993; Inciardi, Lockwood, and Pottieger 1993). In particular, the use of crack has been associated with high rates of HIV infection (Campsmith, Nakashima, and Jones 2000). Further, another study found that "[i]n poor, inner-city communities young smokers of crack cocaine, particularly women who have sex in exchange for money or drugs, are at a high risk for HIV infection. Crack use promotes the heterosexual transmission of HIV" (Edlin et al. 1994). Crack addicts often exchange sex for drugs or money to purchase drugs (Inciardi et al. 1993; Mathias 1993). These dangerous activities frequently occur in populations with an already high rate of HIV infection. Once infected, almost half of crack users continue to use sex to obtain their drugs and become a source of HIV infection for others (Diaz and Chu 1993).

■ Youth and AIDS

The Centers for Disease Control and Prevention (2008) reports that young people in the United States are at persistent risk for HIV infection. This risk is especially notable for youth of minority races and ethnicities. Continual HIV prevention outreach and education efforts, including programs on abstinence and on delaying the initiation of sex, are required as new generations replace the generations that benefited from earlier prevention strategies. Unless otherwise noted, this section defines youth, or young people, as persons who are 13–24 years of age.

In 2011, adolescent males (13–19 years of age) and young adult males (20–24 years of age) who were diagnosed with AIDS contracted the disease in the following ways (CDC 2013c):

- Male-to-male sexual contact: 91.8%
- Heterosexual contact: 4%
- Male-to-male sexual contact and injection drug use: 2.7%
- Injection drug use (IDU): 1.5%

Regarding race and ethnicity, this group was composed of the following (CDC 2013b):

- Sixty-two percent of males and 64% of females were black/African American.
- Nineteen percent of males and 18% of females were Hispanic/Latino.
- Sixteen percent of males and 14% of females were white.
- Two percent of males and 2% of females were from multiple races.

Other important findings include the following (CDC 2010b):

- An estimated 4,883 young people received a diagnosis of HIV infection or AIDS, representing about 13% of the persons given a diagnosis during that year.
- HIV infection progressed to AIDS more slowly among young people than among all other persons with a diagnosis of HIV infection. The following are the proportions of persons in whom HIV infection did not progress to AIDS within 12 months after diagnosis of HIV infection:
  - 81% of persons ages 15–24
  - 70% of persons ages 13–14
  - 61% of all persons

- African Americans were disproportionately affected by HIV infection, accounting for 55% of all HIV infections reported among all other persons ages 13–24.

- Young men who have sex with men (MSM), especially those of minority races or ethnicities, were at high risk for HIV infection. In the seven cities that participated in the CDC's Young Men's Survey during 1994–1998, 14% of African American MSM and 7% of Hispanic MSM ages 15–22 were infected with HIV.

- During 2001–2004, in the 33 states with long-term, confidential name-based HIV reporting, 62% of the 17,824 persons 13–24 years of age given a diagnosis of HIV/AIDS were male, and 38% were female.

- "It is estimated that 50% of all new HIV infections are among young people (about 7,000 young people become infected every day), and that 30% of the 40 million people living with HIV/AIDS are in the 15–24 age group" (World Health Organization [WHO] 2005). Equally serious is the fact that "[T]he vast majority of young people who are HIV positive do not know that they are infected, and few young people who are engaging in sex know the HIV status of their partners" (WHO 2005).

- Approximately 68,600 young people ages 13–24 years were living with HIV infection at the end of 2008; of those, nearly 60% did not know they were infected (CDC 2010c).

- Young people in the United States use alcohol, tobacco, and other drugs at high rates. Both casual and chronic substance users are more likely to engage in high-risk behaviors, such as unprotected sex, when they are under the influence of drugs or alcohol. Runaways and other homeless people are at high risk for HIV infection if they are exchanging sex for drugs or money (CDC 2007).

- Approximately two-thirds of AIDS cases among adolescent and young adult women were attributed to heterosexual contact as the mode of exposure to HIV. Cases among 13- to 19-year-old women were less likely to be attributed to injection drug use (19%) than were cases among 20- to 24-year-old women (29%).

- Most 13- to 19-year-old females reported contracting HIV followed by AIDS through heterosexual contact (66%), injection drug use (19%), and other/not identified causes (15%) (CDC 2004a).

- A recent United Nations AIDS (UNAIDS) report estimated that throughout the world,

"one-third of those living with AIDS are aged 15–24" (MSNBC 2004). Further, most of these individuals who contract HIV do not even know they have the disease.

- HIV infection is spreading rapidly among younger urban gay men who are too young to recall the beginning of the AIDS epidemic two decades ago.

- Nearly half of the roughly 40,000 Americans who become newly infected with HIV each year are younger than the age of 25. Approximately 25% of the people now living with HIV in this country became infected when they were teenagers. More importantly, many young people also use drugs and alcohol, which can increase the likelihood that they will engage in high-risk sexual behavior.

- Adolescents who are most vulnerable to HIV infection include those who are homeless or runaways, juvenile offenders, and school dropouts.

- Worldwide, sexual intercourse is by far the most common mode of HIV transmission. In the United States, however, as many as half of all new HIV infections are associated either directly or indirectly with injection drug use (i.e., using HIV-contaminated needles to inject drugs or having sexual contact with an HIV-infected drug user) (amFAR 2010).

Three of the principal ways adolescents become infected with HIV are as follows: (1) high-risk sexual activity (unprotected sexual intercourse is reported by more than half of adolescents by the age of 17 years); (2) injection of substances of abuse; and (3) sex with multiple partners (CDC 2004b, 2004c, 2010b; Schaefer et al. 1993). Clearly, young people must be better educated about HIV, its transmission, and potential consequences before this epidemic becomes even more disastrous in adolescents.

■ What to Do About HIV and AIDS

Yep, I live with it [being HIV positive] and my partner is HIV negative. We are pretty careful with sex. The drugs they have today are really effective. Luckily I did not contract HIV until two years ago before I met my current partner. I had older friends who did not make it twelve years ago while others I knew had this disease and were able to survive until the medication became a lot more effective. I do give presentations about having HIV/AIDS to organizations that have a majority of their members who are either gay or bisexual. I figure, why not do some good for the world and help others understand that safe sex is the only way to have sex. I have written pamphlets on safe sex from an insider's perspective and give out these pamphlets and other written material each time I make a presentation. *(From Venturelli's research files, male pharmacist, age 29, June 10, 2013)*

To date, the combination of various types of protease inhibitors and antiretroviral therapy medications is the most promising treatment for remaining relatively healthy with HIV. Although protease inhibitors do not completely rid the body of HIV antibodies, this category of drugs is usually successful in holding the virus at low levels in the bloodstream. The current lack of a permanent cure makes prevention the most important element in dealing with the AIDS problem. There are two main strategies for preventing HIV:

- People should be encouraged to adopt safer sexual behavior. Some of the steps to help achieve this include (1) avoiding multiple sex partners, especially if they are strangers or only casual acquaintances; (2) avoiding risk-taking sexual behavior that may allow HIV transmission, such as unprotected vaginal, oral, and anal intercourse; and (3) encouraging individuals who choose to continue high-risk sexual behaviors to use condoms or insist that their sexual partner use a condom.
- Drug abusers should be educated about their risk of contracting AIDS. They should be encouraged to reduce their risk by (1) abstaining from injecting drugs, (2) not sharing injection paraphernalia or always using clean needles (if available through needle exchange programs), (3) not sharing drugs with groups with high rates of HIV infection such as those in shooting galleries or crack houses, and (4) disinfecting the equipment (cleaning and boiling equipment for at least 15 minutes) between uses if they continue to share injection equipment.

One of the major difficulties in controlling the AIDS epidemic is identifying where preventive efforts should be focused. Because of limited resources, it is impossible to personally educate everyone in this country about HIV and AIDS. Consequently, our most intense efforts must be targeted at populations, neighborhoods, and areas

with particularly high HIV infection rates. At the end of 2010, the South accounted for 45% of the estimated 33,015 new AIDS diagnoses in the 50 states and the District of Columbia, followed by the Northeast (24%), the West (19%), and the Midwest (13%). In 2010, the Northeast reported the highest rate of new AIDS diagnoses (14.2%/100,000), followed by the South (13.0%/100,000), the West (8.8%/100,000), and the Midwest (6.3%/100,000) and most HIV and AIDS are generally concentrated in urban areas in the United States (CDC 2013f).

It has also been proposed that AIDS prevention efforts particularly be focused on younger gay men and injection drug users who have multiple sex partners in the high-density AIDS neighborhoods found in many large metropolitan cities throughout the United States. Even with this focused approach, no one should be fooled into thinking that the HIV/AIDS problem will be eliminated. Everyone should approach potential sexual partners with some degree of caution, especially because the carrier of HIV may be unaware of infection or be reluctant to admit being a carrier for fear of abandonment. One thing is evident: If any doubt exists, we strongly recommend both partners being tested several times in a row before engaging in potentially life-threatening sexual contact.

The Entertainment Industry and Drug Use

Musicians sing about guzzling liquor and movie stars puff cigarettes and take drugs on the big screen. However, federal officials ask: Where is the unglamorous side of substance use—like hangovers, slurred speech, or trouble with the law (*News Tribune* 1999)? Drug use has a tendency to be displayed or fueled (depending on your perspective) by popular culture. In this section, we discuss three important genres of popular culture—movies, music, and the Internet—as one electronic subculture that depicts and promotes drug use.

At the Lollapalooza music festival held in July 1997 in an amphitheater in Massachusetts, the mostly white, suburban teen crowd cheered wildly when rap group Cypress Hill pushed a 6-foot-tall bong, or water pipe, onstage. The group sold 5 million copies of its first two albums, one of which included songs titled "Legalize It," "Hits from the Bong," and "I Wanna Get High" (Winters 1997).

In a research study for Columbia's Center on Addiction and Substance Abuse, 76% of 12- to

17-year-olds indicated that the entertainment industry encourages illegal drug use. One 16-year-old daily marijuana user said, "All I know is that almost every song you listen to says something about [drug use]. It puts it into your mind constantly. . . .When you see the celebrities doing it, it makes it seem okay" (Winters 1997, p. 41).

About 20 years ago, the rock and rap music industries experienced a heroin epidemic. Although many other rock stars before Kurt Cobain used and abused drugs, Cobain's struggle with heroin and his 1994 suicide appear to have glamorized the use of this drug. "The number of top alternative bands that have been linked to heroin through a member's overdose, arrest, admitted use, or recovery is staggering: Nirvana, Hole, Smashing Pumpkins, Everclear, Blind Melon, Skinny Puppy, 7 Year Bitch, Red Hot Chili Peppers, Stone Temple Pilots, Breeders, Alice in Chains, Sublime, Sex Pistols, Porno for Pyros, and Depeche Mode" (Schoemer 1996, p. 50). Together these bands have sold more than 60 million albums—"that's a heck of a lot of white, middle-class kids in the heartland" (Schoemer 1996, p. 50).

Despite such excessive drug use and glamorization of drug use in the past, more recent findings reveal that "[s]ince the 1970s, addiction has become something which the music industry has, in the main, been happy to see swept under the carpet. Perhaps partly because the drug of choice during the "great rave explosion" of the late 1980s and 1990s was Ecstasy, which is not considered physically addictive, the last few decades have been short on songs about addiction. There is a sizeable tranche celebrating drug indulgence, from bands like Happy Mondays, Black Grape, and Primal Scream, but the only one I can recall confronting the possibility of addiction is Oasis's "Morning Glory", which deals with the need for artificial energy in ambivalent fashion. . ." (The Independent 2013). More recent reports regarding drug use in the music industry show change. Past president of CBS Records International and CBS Records reiterates that "[i]n the '80s, drug use was more prevalent, . . .[t]oday, it's more spotty" (Paoletta 2004). Reasons cited for this change in drug use include growing awareness of the numbers of tragic drug overdoses and deaths of past musicians coupled with increasing pressures, demands, and "cut-throat" competition to remain musically successful. "Today, there is a lot more demand for an artist's time," says Flom, who has been sober since 1987. "Artists must perform at the top of their game at all times." Further, "'artists on drugs can definitely slow down the promotional process,'" Warner Bros. senior VP Liz Rosenberg says. "'In the publicity world, this has a very strong impact.'" (Paoletta 2004). Finally, more so today, "in the ever-changing addiction scene, alcohol is a continuing problem. But doctors and counselors say such prescription painkillers as Vicodin and OxyContin have eclipsed street drugs (cocaine, heroin) during the past five years" (Paoletta 2004).

How pervasive is drug use in today's popular movies and music? Research indicates that there is much substance abuse in popular movies and music. Studies revealed that 98% of movies reviewed depicted illicit drugs, alcohol, tobacco, or OTC and prescription medicines. Alcohol and tobacco appeared in more than 90% of movies, and illicit drugs appeared in 22%. About one-fourth (26%) of the movies that depicted illicit drugs contained explicit, graphic portrayals of their preparation and/or ingestion. Substance use was almost never a central theme, and very few movies ever specified motivations for use. Less than one-half (49%) of the movies portrayed short-term consequences of substance use, and about 12% depicted long-term consequences. Of the 669 adult major characters featured in the 200 movies studied, 5% used illicit drugs, 25% smoked tobacco, and 65% consumed alcohol. At least two major characters used illicit drugs in 12% of the movies, tobacco in 44%, and alcohol in 85% (ONDCP 1999).

One recent list of 10 top drinking movies included *Barfly* (1987), *Dazed and Confused* (1993), *Animal House* (1978), *The Thin Man* (1934), *Old School* (2003), *Arthur* (1981), *The Hangover* (2009), *The Lost Weekend* (1945), *The Big Lebowski* (1998), and *Who's Afraid of Virginia Woolf* (1966) (Goodykoontz 2011). In all of these movies, which spanned the 20th and 21st centuries, "[l]ots of people drink lots of alcohol . . ." (Goodykoontz 2011). A good number of these movies remain popular with movie buffs. Another news article discussing cocaine use on film sets noted that author Bob Woodward, who with Carl Bernstein first chronicled the Watergate scandal that brought down President Nixon, wrote a ". . . detailed biography of [John] Belushi (*Wired: The Short Life and Fast Times of John Belushi*), [and] 'lots of cocaine' was used on set both by some of the actors and members of the production team. Then, when the film came to be released, the mostly negative reviews couldn't help making indirect references to drugs" (Brown 2013).

Snoop Dogg consuming a drug. Do such pictures have any effect on viewers?

The following summarizes the main findings from a study conducted by the Office of National Drug Control Policy (1999) regarding substance use in both movies and songs

- Alcohol appeared in 93% of the movies and 17% of the songs; tobacco appeared in 89% of the movies but only 3% of the songs.
- "About one-third of hit songs—including three-quarters of rap songs—have some form of explicit reference to drug, alcohol or tobacco use . . ." (Yahoo! News 2008).
- Alcohol use was associated with wealth or luxury in 34% of the movies in which it appeared, with sexual activity in 19%, and with crime or violence in 37%.
- Alcohol use was associated with wealth or luxury in 24% of the songs in which it was referenced, with sexual activity in 3%, and with crime or violence in 13%.
- In movies depicting illicit drugs, marijuana appeared most frequently (51%), followed by powder cocaine (33%); hallucinogens, heroin or other opiates, and miscellaneous others (each 12%); and crack cocaine (2%).
- In songs referring to illicit drugs, marijuana appeared most frequently (63%), followed by crack cocaine (15%); powder cocaine (10%); and hallucinogens, heroin or other opiates, and miscellaneous others (4% each).

These findings clearly indicate that both movies and songs continue to reflect widespread use of alcohol and other drugs in our culture. Furthermore, their influence on the public viewing audiences continues to have an impact on values and attitudes about the use and/or abuse of drugs. One executive director of a Washington, D.C., area youth group, said, "It's becoming increasingly difficult to administer our preventive drug programs because the youth culture has changed in a manner that a lot more of popular music idolizes the use of marijuana and hallucinogens and that has a profound effect on young people" (Haywood 1996, p. 14).

Another top administrator at the Center for Substance Abuse Prevention of the Substance Abuse and Mental Health Services Administration agreed, "Our pop culture is sending a lot of pro-drug messages" (Haywood 1996). In addition to these observations, the major findings noted earlier with regard to substance use in movies and songs support the amount of alcohol and other drugs used in these two major types of electronic and audio media.

Promoters of Drug Use: The Internet

As of 2013, 85% of American adults ages 18 and older use the Internet or email (Zickuhr 2013) and 72% of online adults use social networking sites, 18% use Twitter, and 6% use reddit. (Brenner 2013). There is no question that prodrug messages and detailed information are readily available over the Internet. The Internet maintains a unique subculture of drug enthusiasts. Drug use information found online includes how to roll super-joints, bake marijuana-laced brownies, grow "magic" psilocybin mushrooms, and create formulas for making amphetamine-like drugs; where to purchase the latest equipment for indoor growing of marijuana; and where to obtain catalogs that offer drug paraphernalia for sale. Similarly, magazines such as *High Times* and *Hemp Times* claim growing numbers of subscribers. These magazines devote most of their articles, features, advice columns, hemp festival information, and advertisements to the pleasures of drug consumption. Further, chat rooms devoted to finding, growing, purchasing, and making drug substances are growing in popularity. Those who don't use illicit drugs are often oblivious to the chat rooms and exchange of information found on the Internet.

"The Internet is great at proliferating this sort of [drug] information almost faster than law enforcement can really keep track of it," says Robert J. Bell, a coordinator inside the DEA's synthetic drug department. Once the recipe makes its way online, anyone with the financial means can order chemicals in bulk, usually from China and Southeast Asia. (Vargas-Cooper 2012, p. 64)

A more recent and alarming occurrence is the boom in illicit drug sales online. Prescription drugs are being sold without a prescription over the Internet. Often solicitations are in the form of spam (unsolicited emails), including multiple offers each day. The International Narcotics Control Board (INCB) reported recently, "90% of online drug sales take place without a medical prescription" (Join Together Online and BBC News 2005). The INCB said, "The illicit trade over the Internet has been identified as one of the major sources for prescription medicines abused by children and adolescents in certain countries such as the United States."

Billions of [doses of] controlled substances— some of them highly potent drugs such as oxycodone, equivalent to morphine, and fentanyl, which is many times stronger than morphine [as well as Viagra, Xanax, and Oxy-Contin (to name a few)]—are being sold by unlicensed Internet pharmacies. (Join Together Online and BBC News 2005)

Another report indicated that

Despite new efforts to regulate Internet pharmacies, 85% of sites selling controlled drugs do not require a prescription. Most orders filled by the 365 Internet pharmacies examined were for controlled substances, especially benzodiazepines like Xanax and Valium, according to the report by the National Center on Addiction and Substance Abuse at Columbia University in New York. (Seetharaman 2008)

In addition, *USA Today* reported that "... more than 10 million online messages written by teens in the past year shows they regularly chat about drinking alcohol, smoking pot, partying and hooking up" (Leinwand 2007a). "Many of the teens who posted messages about drugs or alcohol often traded information about using illicit substances without getting hurt or caught. Some teens debated drug legalization and the drinking age. Other teens recounted their partying experiences, including sexual liaisons while drunk or high" (Leinwand 2007a).

SOCIAL NETWORKING MOTIVATING DRUG USE

A new form of peer pressure has emerged. Peer pressure has been defined as collective human behavior where the norms of a group persuade and motivate naive group members to seek and act out certain forms of behavior in order to achieve peer acceptance and approval. There now appears to be an additional form of peer pressure to recreationally use drugs. The National Center on Addiction and Substance Abuse at Columbia University ". . . surveyed 12-to-17 year olds asking whether they spent any time on social media sites, finding that 70 percent of the teens they surveyed do use the sites. The survey also found that 40 percent of all teens have seen pictures on those sites of kids drinking or using drugs and that half of those teens were not yet teens—they were 13 years old or younger" (Reuters and Fox News Network 2011).

Teens who regularly use Facebook and MySpace are much more likely than social network avoiders to drink, smoke and use marijuana. One possible reason for that, the report concluded, is that teens that use social media are likely to see images of their peers drinking or using drugs. A large body of research has shown the influence of peer pressure on teen substance abuse, and this could well be the new frontier. (Keilman 2012)

It appears that drug use is now linked to Facebook and MySpace as the link is made between electronic media and peer pressure.

IS THIS THE BIRTH OF ONLINE ILLICIT DRUG PURCHASING?

An alarming new underground web site called Silk Road came into existence in February 2011.

Silk Road, a digital black market that sits just below most Internet users' purview, does resemble something from a cyberpunk novel. Through a combination of anonymity technology and a sophisticated user-feedback system, Silk Road makes buying and selling illegal drugs as easy as buying used electronics—and seemingly as safe. It's Amazon—if Amazon sold mind-altering chemicals.

...

Here is just a small selection of the 340 items available for purchase on Silk Road by anyone, right now: a gram of Afghani hash; 1/8th ounce of "sour 13" weed; 14 grams of Ecstasy; 0.1 grams tar heroin. A listing for "Avatar" LSD includes a picture of blotter paper with big blue faces from the James Cameron movie on it. The sellers are located all over the world, a large portion from the U.S. and Canada.

. . .

Sellers feel comfortable openly trading hardcore drugs because the real identities of those involved in Silk Road transactions are utterly obscured. If the authorities wanted to ID Silk Road's users with computer forensics, they'd have nowhere to look. TOR (a specialized Internet browser) masks a user's tracks on the site. The site urges sellers to "creatively disguise" their shipments and vacuum seal any drugs that could be detected through smell. As for transactions, Silk Road doesn't accept credit cards, PayPal, or any other form of payment that can be traced or blocked. The only money good here is Bitcoins. (Chen 2011)

On October 2, 2013, after almost 3 years in operation as an Amazon-like marketplace for the purchase of illicit drugs over the Internet, Silk Road's alleged administrator, Ross Ulbricht, was arrested in California. The Federal Bureau of Investigation (FBI) shut down the online drug marketplace and seized billions of dollars in Bitcoins (the currency used for purchasing drugs on Silk Road) (Franceschi-Bicchierai 2013). Although this particular web site was eliminated by law enforcement officials, this author immediately envisioned the possibility that other types of illicit online drug marketplaces may emerge throughout the world in the years ahead given the very extensive amount of money and profits confiscated by the FBI's successful sting operation. The following confirms this prediction:

Maybe it should be no big surprise, but hours after Silk Road was shut down, Web users were flocking to online forums with one question: "Where can I buy my drugs now?" The answer? Take your pick. Sites with names like Sheep Marketplace, Black Market Reloaded and Deep Bay were just some of the ones being mentioned as possibilities. (Goss 2013)

Another report after the Silk Road web site was shut down claimed the following:

One Silk Road moderator, Libertas, posted a long, heartfelt letter to the community urging them to go on. "We have the power to fight these agents of oppression, to fight the governments that task them with that oppression, and with the fires that Silk Road has stoked in our hearts and minds we must do just that," he wrote. "No doubt we will all regroup elsewhere, and I look forward to seeing all of you again, still free and still engaging in free trade without government interference into your personal affairs." (Jeffries 2013)

It appears that in the end, Silk Road may have become a symbolic blueprint fueling other Internet drug mass marketplaces.

Clearly, the Internet is a more recent source for marketing illicit drugs for anyone having access to computers, and this audience includes younger teens and adults. Legal suppliers appear to be fueling the trade by providing their products to unlicensed Internet pharmacies that then sell these legally restricted types of drugs (Join Together Online and BBC News 2005). The potential impact of acquiring illicit drugs from Internet sites was emphasized by a journalist warning that we should "Forget the drug dealer on the corner, teens are increasingly turning to the Internet to get high" (Fiore 2008).

Although the Internet serves as an immensely valuable medium for learning, conducting business, communicating, and making information available, it is also used by a growing number of drug users as a forum for exchanging and learning about the latest information and techniques of drug consumption. Individuals who use the Internet for this type of information should be particularly wary because it is difficult, if not impossible, for harmful myths and fallacies posted on the web to be regulated.

LEARNING PORTFOLIO

Key Terms

Discussion Questions

1. What are two strengths and two weaknesses of studying subcultures from (a) an insider's perspective and (b) an outsider's perspective?
2. What are the principal drugs abused by athletes?
3. What are the principal effects and side effects of steroids?
4. What factors encourage drug use by athletes?
5. From the world of steroid abusers, define and give an example of the following terms: *stacking, cycling, plateauing, pyramiding,* and *array.*
6. Argue both for and against drug testing in sports.
7. What types of penalties do you think should be used against athletes who abuse drugs?
8. Review the ATLAS steroid prevention program. Can you improve its methods for lessening steroid use among adolescents? How effective do you think this program would be at your college or university?
9. List the reasons why women are more concerned about drug use and abuse than men. Can you add several reasons not mentioned in this chapter?
10. Do you believe that drug prevention programs should be created uniquely for males and females? Support your answer.
11. What factors in the unique female roles encourage the use of substances of abuse?
12. Should pregnant women who abuse drugs be punished? Why or why not?
13. Why are women who have been or are being sexually abused more likely to become addicted to drugs?
14. Why are adolescents especially vulnerable to drug abuse problems?
15. List and explain three reasons why you think adolescents from upper-middle-class socioeconomic backgrounds become drug abusers.
16. What types of parents are most likely to have children who develop drug abuse problems?
17. How do adolescent drug abuse patterns differ from those in adults?
18. In what way are drugs of abuse associated with juvenile gang activity?
19. Should all adolescents who use drugs of abuse be treated for drug dependence? Explain your answer.
20. Do you think that it is realistic to expect drug abusers to change their habits to prevent the spread of AIDS? Why or why not?
21. John was caught by city police growing psilocybin (hallucinogenic) mushrooms in his off-campus college apartment. Should John be punished by his college or university in addition to

the punishment that will be meted out by the criminal justice system? Why or why not?

22. What if you discover that your roommate is HIV positive? How would you handle this situation?

23. Do you think that the excessive use of alcohol and other drugs in movies influences viewers? Further, are people who enjoy rap or rock music affected by the lyrics that refer to drug use and/or abuse? Why or why not?

24. Do you believe that drug information found on the Internet, such as in chat rooms devoted to the use of certain drugs (e.g., where to purchase equipment for growing marijuana, OTC stimulant pills, and the spores of psilocybin mushrooms), promotes drug use? Why or why not?

Summary

1. The most common drugs abused by athletes are the ergogenic (performance-enhancing) substances. They include the anabolic steroids, for building muscle mass and strength, and the CNS stimulants, to achieve energy, quickness, and endurance.

2. Drug testing is conducted for most professional athletic competitions and usually includes screens for steroids and stimulants. Unlike years ago, nearly all performance-enhancing drugs are now detectable. Even though athletes often go to great lengths to avoid detection, it is virtually impossible to mask usage drug tests.

3. About 50% of the anabolic steroids used in the United States are prescribed by doctors; the other 50% are obtained from the black market. Black market steroids include drugs diverted from legitimate channels smuggled from foreign countries—for example, Brazil, Italy, Mexico, Great Britain, Portugal, France, and Peru—designated for veterinarian use, or inactive counterfeits.

4. The ATLAS prevention program uses athletes, coaches, and team leaders who are trained to educate team members about the effects of anabolic steroid abuse. They emphasize both desirable and adverse effects of steroid use. Presenting a balanced perspective is stressed because adolescents know very well how anabolic steroids build muscles and can increase athletic abilities.

5. In general, women are more likely than men to (a) be concerned about drugs and drug use; (b) believe in drug prevention programs, such as needle exchange and testing reckless drivers for drug use; and (c) speak with their children about drug use (Drug Strategies 1998).

6. There is a high prevalence of drug dependence in women who are victims of sexual and/or physical abuse. Approximately 70% of women in drug abuse treatment report histories of physical abuse, with victimization beginning at 11 years of age and occurring repeatedly. Further, women and men have different endocrine (hormone) systems, organs, and structures, and women's responses to drugs vary according to their reproductive states.

7. For women to receive adequate treatment for drug dependence, certain considerations must be met: (a) availability of female-sensitive services, (b) nonpunitive and noncoercive treatment that incorporates supportive behavior change approaches, and (c) treatment for a wide range of medical problems, mental disorders, and psychosocial problems.

8. Most adolescents who use substances of abuse are going through normal psychosocial development and will not develop problematic dependence on these drugs. The adolescent users who have difficulty with drugs often lack coping skills to deal with their problems, have dysfunctional families, possess poor self-images, and/or feel socially and emotionally insecure.

9. Parents who are most likely to raise drug-abusing adolescents are (a) drug abusers, (b) non–drug-using coupled with being constantly condemning, (c) overly demanding, (d) overly protective, or (e) unable to communicate effectively with their children.

10. The substances adolescents are most likely to abuse are alcohol, cigarettes, inhalants, marijuana, LSD, Ecstasy, and prescription stimulants. High-frequency use is most likely to occur with cigarettes, alcohol, and marijuana.

11. Research continues to show that the most important factor influencing drug use among adolescents is peer drug use.

12. People who become gang members were often neglected by their parents, lacked positive role models, and failed to receive adequate adult supervision. Other motivations for joining a gang include peer pressure, low self-esteem, and perceived easy acquisition of money from gang-related drug dealing and other criminal activities.

13. The major reasons cited by college students for their use of drugs were: (a) breaks the ice, (b) enhances social activity, (c) gives people something to do, (d) gives people something to talk about, (e) allows people to have more fun, (f) facilitates connection with peers, (g) facilitates male bonding, (h) facilitates sexual opportunities, and (i) facilitates female bonding.

14. Two interesting findings from research regarding drug use by college student subcultures are that (a) the best predictor of drug use for first-year college students is drug use during a typical month in the senior year of high school, and (b) usually recreational drug use does not begin in college but has already been established in high school. Another more recent finding includes personality dispositions to risky behavior as a predictor of first-year college drinking (mainly impulsivity and sensation-seeking types of students).

15. Club drugs include MDMA (Ecstasy), GHB, Rohypnol, ketamine, methamphetamine, and LSD. The phrase "club drug" is derived from the use of these drugs at all-night dance parties such as raves or trances, dance clubs, and bars. All these drugs are colorless, tasteless, and odorless. Individuals who want to intoxicate, sedate, and later sexually take advantage of others can add them unobtrusively to beverages.

16. Estimated new HIV infections in 2010 by transmission category are: male-to-male sexual contact (63%), heterosexual contact (25%), injection drug use (8%), male-to-male sexual contact and injection drug use (3%), and other causes (not specified) (1%).

17. Currently, 1.1 million people are living with HIV in the United States (an estimated 1,148,200 adults and adolescents), and nearly one in five of those (18%) are unaware of their infections. Despite increases in the total number of people living with HIV in the United States in recent years, the annual number of new infections has remained relatively stable overall. However, HIV infections continue at far too high a level, with approximately 50,000 Americans becoming newly infected with HIV each year. More than 15,000 people with AIDS still die each year in the United States.

18. Major ways to prevent contracting HIV include (a) engaging in safe (protected) sexual behavior, (b) avoiding use of contaminated drug paraphernalia and especially use of intravenous drugs, (c) avoiding use of drugs in groups with high rates of HIV infection, and (d) frankly discussing past sexual histories with potential sexual partners and, if in any doubt, having potential partners be tested for HIV several times in a row.

19. The extent of alcohol and drug use in movies and songs is startling. One study found that 98% of movies reviewed depicted illicit drugs, alcohol, tobacco, or OTC/prescription medicines. In this same detailed study, alcohol appeared in 93% of the movies and in 17% of the songs; tobacco appeared in 89% of movies but only 3% of songs. The lyrics of 63% of rap songs versus about 10% of the lyrics in other categories had substance references.

20. More recent reports regarding drug use in the music industry show change. Reasons cited for this change in drug use include growing awareness of the numbers of tragic

drug overdoses and deaths of past musicians coupled with increasing pressures, demands, and "cut-throat" competition to remain musically successful.

21. New media influences contribute to drug use. An underground web site called Silk Road came into existence in February 2011. It was like an eBay or Amazon in the world of drug purchasing over the Internet. It was shut down by the FBI in 2013.

22. The Internet is considered to be the latest burgeoning source of information about using illicit drugs.

References

About.com. "Alcoholism: Sex, Drug Use Increase Teen Depression, Suicide." 9 April 2005. Available http://alcoholism.about.com/od/tipsforparents/a/blnida050408.htm

About.com. "Alcohol and Hormones." Alcohol Alerts from the National Institute on Alcohol Abuse and Alcoholism (NIAAA). 2006. Available http://alcoholism.about.com/cs/alerts/1/binaa26.htm

About.com. "Alcohol and Women." Alcohol Alerts from the National Institute on Alcohol Abuse and Alcoholism (NIAAA). June 2007a. Available http://alcoholism.about.com/cs/alerts/1/binaa10.htm

About.com. "Alcoholism and Substance Abuse." Alcohol Alerts from the National Institute on Alcohol Abuse and Alcoholism (NIAAA). June 2007b. Available http://alcoholism.about.com/cs/alerts/1/blnaa10.htm

Aguirre, J. C. "Cost of Treatment Still a Challenge for HIV Patients in U.S." NPR (National Public Radio) Shop. 27 July 2012. Available http://www.npr.org/blogs/health/2012/07/27/157499134/cost-of-treatment-still-a-challenge-for-hiv-patients-in-u-s

AIDSMEDS. "Entry Inhibitors (including Fusion Inhibitors)." Smart + Strong, CDM Publishing LLC, 16 September 2011. Available http://www.aidsmeds.com/archive/EIs_1627.shtml

AIDS.gov. "Global Statistics: The Global HIV/AIDS Crisis Today." U.S. Department of Health and Human Services. 6 June 2012a. Available http://aids.gov/hiv-aids-basics/hiv-aids-101/global-statistics/index.html

AIDS.gov. "HIV/AIDS 101: Signs and Symptoms." U.S. Department of Health and Human Services. 6 June 2012b. Available http://aids.gov/hiv-aids-basics/hiv-aids-101/signs-and-symptoms/

Alvarez, M. "A Dangerous Trend: Kids and Teens Using Steroids." Fox News Network. 19 November 2012. Available http://www.foxnews.com/health/2012/11/19/dangerous-trend-kids-and-teens-using-steroids/

American Academy of Child and Adolescent Psychiatry. *Facts for Families: Teen Suicide.* Washington, DC: American Academy of Child Adolescent Psychiatry, 2004. Available http://www.aacap.org/cs/root/facts_for_families/teen_ suicide

American Academy of Child and Adolescent Psychiatry. *Facts for Families: Normal Adolescent Development.* Number 57. Washington, DC: American Academy of Child and Adolescent Psychiatry, 2006.

American Academy of Child and Adolescent Psychiatry. *Teens: Alcohol and Other Drugs.* Number 3. Washington, DC: American Academy of Child and Adolescent Psychiatry, 2011.

American Foundation for AIDS Research (amfAR). *Facts About HIV/AIDS, 2001.* New York: Body Health Resources Corporation, 2001.

American Foundation for AIDS Research (amfAR). *Facts for Life: What You and the People You Care About Need to Know About HIV/AIDS.* New York: amfAR AIDS Research, 2010.

Anonymous, as told by Penn, N. "Confession: Why I Juiced." *Gentleman's Quarterly* (September 2005): 292–297.

Apostolides, M. "How to Quit the Holistic Way." *Psychology Today* 29 (September/October 1996): 30–43, 75–76.

Archambault, D. "Adolescence, a Physiological, Cultural and Psychological No Man's Land." In *Adolescent Substance Abuse, Etiology, Treatment and Prevention,* edited by G. Lawson and A. Lawson, 11–28. Gaithersburg, MD: Aspen, 1992.

Associated Press. "Boredom, Stress, Money Linked to Drug Abuse." *Chesterton/Valparaiso Post Tribune* (20 August 2003): A1, A8.

AVERT.org. "AIDS, Drug Prices and Generic Drugs." 2011. Available http://www.avert.org/generic.htm

AVERT.org. "Injecting Drug Users and HIV/AIDS." 2013. Available http://www.avert.org/hiv-injecting-drug-users.htm

Bahr, S. J., A. C. Marcos, and S. L. Maughan. "Family, Educational and Peer Influences on Alcohol Use of Female and Male Adolescents." *Journal of Studies on Alcohol* 56 (1995): 457–469.

Baltieri, D. A., and A. G. de Andrad. "Alcohol and Drug Consumption and Sexual Impulsivity Among Sexual Offenders." In *Sexual Offenders: Management, Treatment and Bibliography,* edited by J. V. Fenner, 73–96. New York: Nova Science, 2008.

Beard, B., and V. Kunsman. "A Cause for Concern: Alcohol-Induced Risky Sex on College Campuses." *Prevention Pipeline* 6 (September–October 1993): 24.

Begley, S., and M. Brant with C. Dickey, K. Helmstaedt, R. Nordland, and T. Hayden. "The Real Scandal." *Newsweek* 133 (15 February 1999): 48–54.

Bell, J. "Athletes' Use and Abuse of Drugs." *The Physician and Sports Medicine* 15 (March 1987): 99–108.

Belsie, L. "Temperance Movement Hits College Dorms." *Christian Science Monitor* 87 (30 August 1995): 1, 2.

Bergeret, J. *Young People, Drugs . . . and Others.* Rockville, MD: United Nations Office for Drug Control and Crime Prevention (UN/ODCCP), 1 January 1981.

Beschner, G., and A. Friedman. "Treatment of Adolescent Drug Abusers." *International Journal of the Addictions* 20 (1985): 977–993.

Blum, R. "Rodriguez: 'Amateur Hour.'" *Post-Tribune*, Nation/World (18 February 2009): A11.

"Bodybuilding Drug Yields 'High.'" *Pharmacy Times* (June 1992): 14.

Booth, R., J. Watters, and D. Chitwood. "HIV Risk-Related Sex Behaviors Among Injection Drug Users, Crack Smokers, and Injection Drug Users Who Smoke Crack." *American Journal of Public Health* 83 (1993): 1144–1148.

Brady, T. M., and O. S. Ashley, Eds. *Women in Substance Abuse Treatment: Results from the Alcohol and Drug Services Study (ADSS).* DHHS Pub. No. SMA 04–3968, Analytic Series A–26. Rockville, MD: Substance Abuse and Mental Health Services Administration, Office of Applied Studies, 2005.

Brenner, J. "Pew Internet: Social Networking (full detail)." Pew Internet & American Life Project, 5 August 2013. Available http://pewinternet.org/Commentary/2012/March/Pew-Internet-Social-Networking-full-detail.aspx

Brown, A. M. "Drug Use on Film Sets—You'd Be Amazed by How Much of It Goes On." *The Telegraph.* 22 July 2013. Available http://blogs.telegraph.co.uk/news/andrewmcfbrown/100021797/drug-use-on-film-sets-%E2%80%93-youd-be-amazed-by-how-much-of-it-goes-it-on/

Britannica.com. "Alex Rodriguez." Encyclopedia Britannica Online. 31 October 2010. Available http://www.britannica.com/EBchecked/topic/914723/Alex-Rodriguez

Buckstein, D., D. Brent, J. Perper, G. Moritz, M. Baugher, J. Schweers, et al. "Risk Factors for Completed Suicide Among Adolescents with a Lifetime History of Substance Abuse: A Case-Control Study." *Acta Psychiatrica Scandinavia* 88 (1993): 403–408.

Burke, C., and S. Davis. "Anabolic Steroid Abuse." *Pharmacy Times* (June 1992): 35–40.

Burn-Murdoch, J. "Doping in Olympic Events: How Does Each Sport Compare?" Guardian News and Media Limited. 4 July 2012. Available http://www.guardian.co.uk/sport/datablog/2012/jul/04/olympics-2012-athletics

Bussing-Burks, M. "Alcohol and Drug Use Increases Suicidal Behaviors." National Bureau of Economic Research. 9 July 2013. Available http://www.nber.org/digest/aug02/w8810.html

Campsmith, M. L., A. K. Nakashima, and J. L. Jones. "Association Between Crack Cocaine Use and High-Risk Sexual Behaviors After HIV Diagnosis." *Journal of Acquired Immune Deficiency Syndrome (JAIDS)* 25 (1 October 2000): 192–198.

Center for Science in the Public Interest (cspinet.org). "College Students and Alcohol Use." Center for Science in the Public Interest, August 2007. Available http://cspinet.org/booze/FactSheets/0311CollegeStudents.pdf

Centers for Disease Control and Prevention (CDC). *Estimated AIDS Cases Among Female Adolescents and Young Adults by Exposure Category, Diagnosed through 2002, United States.* Washington, DC: National Center for HIV, STD, and TB Prevention, Divisions of HIV/AIDS Prevention Surveillance Branch, 2004a.

Centers for Disease Control and Prevention (CDC). *Estimated AIDS Cases Among Male Adolescents and Young Adults by Exposure Category, Diagnosed Through 2002, United States.* Washington, DC: National Center for HIV, STD, and TB Prevention, Divisions of HIV/AIDS Prevention Surveillance Branch, 2004b.

Centers for Disease Control and Prevention (CDC). *HIV/AIDS Surveillance Report, 2003.* Vol. 15. Atlanta, GA: U.S. Department of Health and Human Services, CDC, 2004c.

Centers for Disease Control and Prevention (CDC). "Smoking During Pregnancy-United States, 1990–2003." *Morbidity and Mortality Weekly Report* (MMWR), Vol. 53. Atlanta, GA: U.S. Department of Health and Human Services, CDC, 7 October 2004d.

Centers for Disease Control and Prevention (CDC). "HIV/AIDS Among Youth." The Body Health Resources Corporation. 2007. Available http://www.thebody.com/content/art17110.html

Centers for Disease Control and Prevention (CDC). *HIV/AIDS Among Youth.* Atlanta, GA: Division of HIV/AIDS Prevention, National Center for HIV/AIDS, Viral Hepatitis, STD, and TB Prevention, 2008.

Centers for Disease Control and Prevention (CDC). *HIV and AIDS in America: A Snapshot.* Atlanta, GA: Division of HIV/AIDS Prevention, National Center for HIV/AIDS, Viral Hepatitis, STD, and TB Prevention, 2010a.

Centers for Disease Control and Prevention (CDC). *HIV in the United States.* Atlanta, GA: Divisions of HIV/AIDS Prevention, National Center for HIV/AIDS, Viral Hepatitis, STD, and TB Prevention, 2010b.

Centers for Disease Control and Prevention (CDC). *HIV /AIDS and Women.* Atlanta, GA: Division of HIV/AIDS Prevention, National Center for HIV/AIDS, Viral Hepatitis, STD, and TB Prevention, 2010c.

Centers for Disease Control and Prevention (CDC). *Questions and Answers on the Use of HIV Medications to Help Prevent the Transmission of HIV.* Atlanta, GA: Division of HIV/AIDS Prevention, National Center for HIV/AIDS, Viral Hepatitis, STD, and TB Prevention, 2010d.

Centers for Disease Control and Prevention (CDC). *CDC Fact Sheet, HIV and AIDS in America: A Snapshot.* Atlanta, GA: Division of HIV/AIDS Prevention, National Center for HIV/AIDS, Viral Hepatitis, STD, and TB Prevention, 2013a.

Centers for Disease Control and Prevention (CDC). "HIV in the United States: At a Glance." Division of HIV/AIDS Prevention. 23 April 2013b. Available http://www.cdc .gov/hiv/statistics/basics/ataglance.html

Centers for Disease Control and Prevention (CDC). "HIV Surveillance in Adolescents and Young Adults (through 2011)." National Center for HIV/AIDS, Viral Hepatitis, STD, and TB Prevention, Division of HIV/AIDS Prevention, 11 June 2013c.

Centers for Disease Control and Prevention (CDC). "HIV Among Women." National Center for HIV/AIDS, Viral Hepatitis, STD, and TB Prevention, Division of HIV /AIDS Prevention, March 2013d. Available http://www .cdc.gov/hiv/pdf/risk_women.pdf

Centers for Disease Control and Prevention (CDC). "HIV Among Women: Fact Sheet." National Center for HIV /AIDS, Viral Hepatitis, STD, and TB Prevention, Division of HIV/AIDS Prevention, 3 July 2013e. Available http:// www.cdc.gov/hiv/risk/gender/women/facts/index .html

Centers for Disease Control and Prevention (CDC). "HIV and AIDS in the United States by Geographic Distribution." National Center for HIV/AIDS, Viral Hepatitis, STD, and TB Prevention, Division of HIV/AIDS Prevention, 23 April 2013f. Available http://www.cdc.gov/hiv /statistics/basics/geographicdistribution.html

Chen, A. "The Underground Website Where You Can Buy Any Drug Imaginable." Kotaku. 1 June 2011. Available http://kotaku.com/the-underground-website-where -you-can-buy-any-drug-imag-30818160

Child Trends. "Adolescents Training and Learning to Avoid Steroids Program (ATLAS)." 2009. Available http://www.childtrends.org/lifecourse/programs /AvoidSteroids.htm

Chong, J-R. "Study Casts Positive Light on AIDS Drug." *Los Angeles Times,* reported in *Post Tribune* [Merrillville, IN] (13 August 2006): A9.

Ciba Foundation. "AIDS and HIV Infection in Cocaine Users." In *Cocaine: Scientific and Social Dimensions,* edited by G. Block and J. Whelan, 181–194. New York: Wiley, 1992.

Clark, E. *HIV Progress and Prevention.* Boston, MA: Science in the News (SITN), Harvard Graduate School of Arts and Sciences, 2010.

Colthurst, T. "HIV and Alcohol Impairment: Reducing Risks." *Prevention Pipeline* 6 (July–August 1993): 24.

CRC Health Group. "Factors of Teen Drug Use." 2007. Available http://www.adolescent-substance-abuse.com

Crowley, G. "Targeting a Deadly Scrap of Genetic Code." *Newsweek* (2 December 1996): 68–69.

Curry, D. G., and I. A. Spergel. "Gang Homicide, Delinquency, and Community." In *Gangs and Gang Behavior,* edited by G. L. Mays, 314–336. Chicago, IL: Nelson-Hall, 1997.

Cyders, M. A., K. Flory, S. Rainer, and G. T. Smith. "The Role of Personality Dispositions to Risky Behavior in Predicting First-Year College Drinking." *Addiction* 104 (2009): 193–202.

Daily, S. "Alcohol, Incest, and Adolescence." In *Adolescent Substance Abuse, Etiology, Treatment and Prevention,* edited by G. Lawson and A. Lawson, 251–266. Gaithersburg, MD: Aspen, 1992a.

Daily, S. "Suicide Solution: The Relationship of Alcohol and Drug Abuse to Adolescent Suicide." In *Adolescent Substance Abuse, Etiology, Treatment and Prevention,* edited by G. Lawson and A. Lawson, 233–250. Gaithersburg, MD: Aspen, 1992b.

Diaz, T., and S. Chu. "Crack Cocaine Use and Sexual Behavior Among People with AIDS." *Journal of the American Medical Association* 269 (1993): 2845–2846.

Diaz-Linares, M., E. Vázquez, J. Gallant, and M. Delaney. "12th Annual HIV Drug Guide." Positively Aware. January/February 2008. Available http://positivelyaware .com/2008/08_01/drug_guide.html

Dicker, M., and E. A. Leighton. "Trends in the U.S. Prevalence of Drug-Using Parturient Women and Drug-Affected Newborns, 1979 Through 1990." *American Journal of Public Health* 84 (1994): 1433.

Docherty, J. R. "Pharmacology of Stimulants Prohibited by the World Anti-Doping Agency (WADA)." *British Journal of Pharmacology* 154 (2008): 606–622.

Donaldson-Evans, C. "Wrestler Chris Benoit Double Murder-Suicide: Was It 'Roid Rage'?" FoxNews.com. 27 June 2007.

Available http://www.foxnews.com/printer_friendly _story/0,3566,286834,00.html

Drug Strategies. "Drug Use and Attitudes." In *Keeping Score*, Washington, DC: Drug Strategies, 4-10, 1998. Available http://www.drugstrategies.com/pdf/ks_1998.pdf

EBSCO. "Reverse Transcriptase Inhibitors." 2013. Available https://healthlibrary.epnet.com/GetContent.aspx? token=e0498803-7f62-4563-8d47-5fe33da65dd4&chunkiid =111797

Edlin, B. R., K. L. Irwin, S. Faruque, C. B. McCoy, C. Word, Y. Serrano, et al. "Intersecting Epidemics—Crack Cocaine Use and HIV Infection among Inner-City Young Adults. Multicenter Crack Cocaine and HIV Infection Study Team." *New England Journal of Medicine* 331 (24 November 1994): 1422–1427.

Elmen, J., and D. Offer. "Normality, Turmoil and Adolescence." In *Handbook of Clinical Research and Practice with Adolescents*, edited by P. Tolan and B. Cohler, 5–19. New York: Wiley, 1993.

Erickson, P. G., and G. F. Murray. "Sex Differences in Cocaine Use and Experiences: A Double Standard Revived?" *American Journal of Drug and Alcohol Abuse* 15 (1989): 135–152.

ESPN.com. "Steroids Discovered in Probe Slayings, Suicide." 27 July 2007. Available http://sports.espn.go.com /espn/news/story?id=2917133

e-Steroid.com. "Steroid Statistics." (2 November 2013). Available http://www.e-steroid.com/steroid-articles/steroid -statistics.html

Fagan, J. "Social Processes of Delinquency and Drug Use Among Urban Gangs." In *Gangs in America*, edited by C. R. Huff, 183–213. Newbury Park, CA: Sage, 1990.

Ferrente, R. "Ben Johnson Retires from Running After Positive Test." Morning Edition on National Public Radio (8 March 1993).

Fiore, M. "Using the Internet to Get High." FoxNews.com. 9 September 2008. Available http://www.foxnews.com /story/0,2933,419582,00.html

Fischer, J. S. "Searching for That Ounce of Prevention: Promising Strategies for an AIDS Vaccine." *U.S. News and World Report* (17 July 2000).

Focus Adolescent Services. "Your Teen's Friends: Peer Influence and Peer Relationships." *InFocus Newsletter.* Available http://focusas.com/PeerInfluence.html

Franceschi-Bicchierai, L. "The Silk Road Online Drug Marketplace by the Numbers." Mashable. 4 October 2013. Available http://mashable.com/2013/10/04/silk-road- by-the-numbers/

MyFoxNY.com. 19 August 2010. Available http://www .freerepublic.com/tag/crime/index?more=8492611

Glave, J. "Betty Ford Got Help, But Addiction Stalks Thousands of Women." *Salt Lake Tribune* 248 (3 June 1994): A-1.

Gloucester County College. "Crime Prevention and Safety: Alcohol and Drug Abuse on Campus." Gloucester County Educational Campus—Safety & Security, 2013. Available http://www.gccnj.edu/security/crime_prevention _safety/alcohol_and_drug_abuse.cfm

Goldberg, L., D. Elliot, G. N. Clarke, D. P. MacKinnon, E. Moe, L. Zoref, et al. "Effects of a Multidimensional Anabolic Steroid Prevention Intervention: The Adolescents Training and Learning to Avoid Steroids (ATLAS) Program." *Journal of the American Medical Association* 276 (1996): 1555–1562.

Goldstein, F. "Pharmacological Aspects of Substance Abuse." In *Remington's Pharmaceutical Sciences*, 19th ed., edited by A. R. Genaro and M. Easton, 780–794, 1995.

Gonzales, M., K McEnery, T. Sheehan, and S. Mellody. *America's Habit: Drug Abuse, Drug Trafficking, and Organized Crime*. Washington, DC: President's Commission on Organized Crime, 1986.

Goodykoontz, B. "'Big Lebowski,' 'Animal House' Make List of 10 Top Drinking Movies." *Chicago Sun-Times.* 27 October 2011. Available http://www.suntimes.com /entertainment/movies/8442007-421/big-lebowski -arthur-animal-house-among-top-drinking-movies-ever -made.html

Goss, D. "Web's Black Market Peddles Drugs, Guns and More." CNN Tech. 4 October 2013. Available at http:// www.cnn.com/2013/10/04/tech/web/internet-black -market/index.html

Green, C. A. *Gender and Use of Substance Abuse Treatment Services*. Bethesda, MD: NIAAA, 2006: 1–12.

Grinspoon, L. "AIDS and Mental Health—Part 1." *Harvard Mental Health Letter* 10 (January 1994): 1–4.

Guide4Living.com. "Steroid Abuse and Addiction." 2005. Available http://www.guide4living.com/drugabuse /steroids.htm

Harlan, R., and M. Garcia. "Neurobiology of Androgen Abuse." In *Drugs of Abuse*, edited by R. Watson, 185–201. Boca Raton, FL: CRC Press, 1992.

Harris, W. "10 Performance-enhancing Drugs That Aren't Steroids." Science: howstuffworks. Atlanta, GA: Discovery Communications LLC. (2013). Available http:// science.howstuffworks.com/10-performance-enhancing -drugs.htm

Haywood, R. L. "Why More Young People Are Using Drugs." *Jet* 90 (9 September 1996).

Hingson, R. W., W. Zha, and E. R. Weitzman. "Magnitude of and Trends in Alcohol-Related Mortality and Morbidity Among U.S. College Students Ages 18–24, 1998–2005."

Journal of Studies on Alcohol and Drugs, Suppl. No. 16 (2009): 12–20.

Hoberman, J. M., and C. E. Yesalis. "The History of Synthetic Testosterone." *Scientific American* (February 1995).

Hoshino, J. "Assessment of Adolescent Substance Abuse." In *Adolescent Substance Abuse, Etiology, Treatment and Prevention,* edited by G. Lawson and A. Lawson, 87–104. Gaithersburg, MD: Aspen, 1992.

Howard, M. "Adolescent Substance Abuse: A Social Learning Theory Perspective." In *Adolescent Substance Abuse, Etiology, Treatment and Prevention,* edited by G. Lawson and A. Lawson, 29–40. Gaithersburg, MD: Aspen, 1992.

Inciardi, J. A., D. Lockwood, and A. E. Pottieger. *Women and Crack-Cocaine.* New York: Macmillan, 1993.

Jayson, S. "Expert: Risky Teen Behavior Is All in the Brain." USAToday.com. 5 April 2007. Available http://www.usatoday.com/news/health/2007-04-04-teen-brain_N.htm

Jeffries, A. "After Silk Road's Demise, Online Drug Dealing Moves to New Sites." The Verge. 4 October 2013. Available http://www.theverge.com/2013/10/4/4799770/drug-dealers-set-up-mini-silk-roads-after-federal-bust

Johnson, R. A., J. P. Hoffmann, and D. R. Gerstein. The Relationship Between Family Structure and Adolescent Substance Use. Rockville, MD: SAMHSA, Office of Applied Studies, July 1996.

Johnston, L. D., P. M. O'Malley, and J. G. Bachman. *National Survey Results from the Monitoring the Future Study, 1975–1992.* Rockville, MD: National Institute on Drug Abuse, 1993.

Johnson, R. A., J. P. Hoffmann, and D. R. Gerstein. *The Relationship Between Family Structure and Adolescent Substance Use.* Rockville, MD: SAMHSA, Office of Applied Studies, July 1996.

Johnston, L. D., P. M. O'Malley, and J. G. Bachman. *National Survey Results from the Monitoring the Future Study, 1975–1994.* Rockville, MD: National Institute on Drug Abuse, 1996.

Johnston, L. D., P. O'Malley, and J. G. Bachman. *The Monitoring the Future National Results on Adolescent Drug Use: Overview of Key Findings, 1999.* Ann Arbor, MI: The University of Michigan Institute for Social Research and Bethesda, MD: National Institute on Drug Abuse, U.S. Department of Human Services, National Institutes of Health, 2000a.

Johnston, L. D., P. O'Malley, and J. G. Bachman. *National Survey Results on Drug Use from the Monitoring the Future Study, 1975–1999. Vol. 2, College Students and Young Adults.* U.S. Department of Health and Human Services (USDHHS), National Institute on Drug Abuse (NIDA). Washington, DC: U.S. Government Printing Office, 2000b.

Johnston, L. D., P. M. O'Malley, J. G. Bachman, and J. E. Schulenberg. *Monitoring the Future: National Survey Results on Drug Use, 1975–2003. Volume I: Secondary School Students.* Bethesda, MD: National Institute on Drug Abuse, 2004.

Johnston, L. D., P. M. O'Malley, J. G. Bachman, and J. E. Schulenberg. *Monitoring the Future: National Results on Adolescent Drug Use.* Bethesda, MD: National Institute on Drug Abuse, 2006.

Johnston, L. D., P. M. O'Malley, J. G. Bachman, and J. E. Schulenberg. *Monitoring the Future: National Results on Adolescent Drug Use 1975–2008. Volume I: Secondary School Students 2008.* Bethesda, MD: National Institute on Drug Abuse, 2009a.

Johnston, L. D., P. M. O'Malley, J. G. Bachman, and J. E. Schulenberg. *Monitoring the Future: National Results on Adolescent Drug Use 1975–2008. Volume II: College Students and Adults 19–50.* Bethesda, MD: National Institute on Drug Abuse, 2009b.

Johnston, L. D., P. M. O'Malley, J. G. Bachman, and J. E. Schulenberg. *Monitoring the Future: National Survey Results on Drug Use, 1975–2011. Volume II: College Students and Adults 19–50.* Ann Arbor, MI: Institute for Social Research, the University of Michigan, 2012.

Johnston, L. D., P. M. O'Malley, J. G. Bachman, and J. E. Schulenberg. *Monitoring the Future: National Survey Results on Drug Use, 1975–2012. Volume I, Secondary School Students.* Ann Arbor, MI: Institute for Social Research, the University of Michigan, 2013.

Join Together Online and BBC (British Broadcasting Company) News. *Illicit Drug Sales Booming Online.* Boston, MA: Boston University School of Public Health, 2005.

Kandel, D. B. "Drug and Drinking Behavior Among Youth." *Annual Review of Sociology* 6 (1980): 235–285.

Kantrowitz, B., and P. Wingert. "Beyond Littleton: How Well Do You Know Your Kid?" *Newsweek* (10 May 1999).

Keilman, J. "Dangers of Facebook for Teens." Soberinfo. 25 August 2012. Available http://www.soberinfo.com/news/2011/08/dangers-of-facebook-for-teens.html

Kennedy, M. C. "Newer Drugs Used to Enhance Sporting Performance." *Medical Journal of Australia* 273 (2000): 314–317.

Kinney, J. *Loosening the Grip,* 6th ed. Boston: McGraw-Hill, 2000.

Kirkpatrick, J. *The Woman Alcoholic.* Quakertown, PA: Women for Sobriety, 1999.

Klee, H., and M. Jackson. *Drug Misuse and Motherhood.* New York: Routledge, 2002.

Kolata, G. "Targeting Urged in Attack on AIDS." *New York Times* 142 (7 March 1993): 1.

Korolenko, C. P., and T. A. Donskih. "Addictive Behavior in Women: A Theoretical Perspective." *Drugs and Society* 4 (1990): 39–65.

Ladwig, G. B., and M. D. Anderson. "Substance Abuse in Women: Relationship Between Chemical Dependency of Women and Past Reports of Physical and/or Sexual Abuse." *International Journal of the Addictions* 24 (1989): 739–754.

Lajis, R. H. "Steroids: The Next Drug Problem." 2007. Available http://www.cedu.niu.edu/~shumow/itt/doc /Steroid Abuse.pdf

Lale, T. "Gangs and Drugs." In *Adolescent Substance Abuse, Etiology, Treatment and Prevention*, edited by G. Lawson and A. Lawson, 267–281. Gaithersburg, MD: Aspen, 1992.

Lamberson, H. "Gangs in Chicago." The Chicago Maroon. Chicago: University of Chicago, (2 December 2009). Available http://chicagomaroon.com/2009/12/02/gangs -in-chicago/

Lawn, J. *Team Up for Drug Prevention with America's Young Athletes.* Washington, DC: Drug Enforcement Administration, U.S. Department of Justice, 1984.

Lawson, G., and A. Lawson, "Etiology." In *Adolescent Substance Abuse, Etiology, Treatment and Prevention*, edited by G. Lawson and A. Lawson, 1–10. Gaithersburg, MD: Aspen, 1992.

Leibsohn, J. "The Relationship Between Drug and Alcohol Use and Peer Group Associations of College Freshmen as They Transition from High School." *Journal of Drug Education* 24 (1994): 177–192.

Leicester, J. "Lance Armstrong Considers Himself Tour de France Record-Holder Still, Believes Doping Needed to Win." Huff Post: Sports. 28 June 2013. Available http:// www.huffingtonpost.com/2013/06/28/lance-arm-strong-tour-de-france_n_3515081.html

Leinwand, D. "20% Say They Used Drugs with Their Mom or Dad. Among Reasons: Boomer Culture and Misguided Attempts to Bond." *USA Today.* (27 August 2000).

Leinwand, D. "Study: Drug Chat Pervasive Online—Teens Use Internet to Share Stories, Get How-To Advice." *USA Today.* 2007a. Available http://www.usatoday.com /printedition/news/20070619/a_online19.art.htm

Leinwand. D. "College Drug Use, Binge Drinking Rise." *USA Today,* 15 March 2007b. Available http://usatoday30 .usatoday.com/news/nation/2007-03-15-college-drug -use_N.htm

Levitt, D. and S. A. Venkatesh. "An Economic Analysis of A Drug-Selling Gang's Finances." *The Quarterly Journal of Economics,* 115 (2000): 755–789.

Lewin, T. "Does it Work? Substance-Free Dorms—Clean Living on Campus." *The New York Times.* 6 November 2005. Available http://www.nytimes.com/2005/11/06 /education/edlife/work.html

Lin, A. Y. F. "Should Women Be Included in Clinical Trials?" *Pharmacy Times* 10 (November 1994): 27.

Lively, K. "The 'Date-Rape Drug': Colleges Worry about Reports of Growing Use of Rohypnol, a Sedative." *Chronicle of Higher Education* 42 (28 June 1996): A–29.

Livni, E. "Some Parents Introduce Kids to Drugs." ABC News, New York, (24 August 2013). Available http:// abcnews.go.com/Health/story?id=118024

Lukas, S. "Urine Testing for Anabolic-Androgenic Steroids." *Trends in Pharmacological Sciences* 14 (1993): 61–68.

Mathias, R. "Sex-for-Crack Phenomenon Poses Risk for Spread of AIDS in Heterosexuals." *NIDA Notes* 8 (May /June 1993): 8–11.

Mathias, R. "NIDA Survey Provides First National Data on Drug Use During Pregnancy." *NIDA Notes* 10 (January /February 1995): 6–7.

McCaffrey, B. R. "McCaffrey Announces Strategy to Fight Drug Use in Sports." *Daily Washington File* (21 October 1999).

McDonald, M. "Fast, Strong, Dead?" *Salt Lake Tribune* 250 (22 June 1995): C1, C8.

Merchant, W. "Medications and Athletes." *American Druggist* (October 1992): 6–14.

Millstein, R. *Community Alert Bulletin.* Rockville, MD: National Institute on Drug Abuse, U.S. Department of Health and Human Services, 25 March 1993.

Minnesota Institute of Public Health. *Alcohol and Other Drugs and Suicide.* Mounds View, MN: Chemical Health Division, Minnesota Department of Human Services, Spring 1995.

Moss, H., L. Kirisci, H. Gordon, and R. Tarter. "A Neuropsychological Profile of Adolescent Alcoholics." *Alcoholism: Clinical and Experimental Research* 18 (1994): 159–163.

MSNBC. "AIDS Outruns Efforts to Combat It, Says U.N. Report: New HIV Infections Hit Record High Last Year." Health News. 2004. Available http://www.msnbc.msn .com/ID/5377027

"Multistate Outbreak of Poisonings Associated with Illicit Use of GHB." *Prevention Pipeline* 7 (May–June 1994): 95, 96.

MyDNA.com. *News Center: HAART Therapy Slows Progression to AIDS.* Washington, DC: American Medical Association, 2005.

National Center for Education Statistics. "Indicators of School Crime and Safety: 2011: Indicator 8: Students' Reports of Gangs at School." Washington, DC: U. S. Department of Education, Institute of Education Sciences, and National Center for Education Statistics,

2011. Available http://nces.ed.gov/programs/crimein-dicators/crimeindicators2011/ind_08.asp

National Clearinghouse for Alcohol and Drug Information (NCADI). *Drugs of Abuse.* Rockville, MD: Substance Abuse and Mental Health Services Administration, 1999.

National Crime Victims' Rights Week Resource Guide (NCVRW Resource Guide). "Campus Crime." Victim Services: Office of Victim & Survivor Rights and Services, 2007. Available http://www.cdcr.ca.gov/victim_services/crime_and_victimization_stats.html

National Drug Intelligence Center (NDIC). *Drugs and Gangs: Fast Facts, Questions and Answers.* Washington, DC: National Drug Intelligence Center, 2009.

National Education Association and Health Information Network (NEAHIN). *RX for Understanding: Preventing Prescription Drug Abuse.* 2013. Available http://www.gadoe.org/Curriculum-Instruction-and-Assessment/Curriculum-and-Instruction/Documents/Prescription%20Drug%20Abuse%20Prevention%20Program_Grades%209-12%20Lesson%20Plans.pdf

National Institute on Alcohol and Alcoholism (NIAAA). "High-Risk Drinking in College: What We Know and What We Need to Learn." College Drinking—Changing the Culture. 2005a. Available http://www.collegedrinkingprevention.gov/niaaacollegematerials/panel01/execsum_01.aspx

National Institute on Alcohol and Alcoholism (NIAAA). "Living Arrangements." College Drinking—Changing the Culture. 2005b. Available http://www.collegedrinkingprevention.gov/NIAAACollegeMaterials/TaskForce/Factors_01.asp

National Institute on Drug Abuse (NIDA). *Anabolic Steroid Abuse.* Capsule 43. Rockville, MD: NIDA, 1996.

National Institute on Drug Abuse (NIDA). *Drug Abuse and Addiction Research: The Sixth Triennial Report to Congress.* Rockville, MD: U.S. Department of Health and Human Services, 1999.

National Institute on Drug Abuse (NIDA). "Club Drugs: Community Alert Bulletin." *NIDA Notes* 14 (30 March 2000).

National Institute on Drug Abuse (NIDA). *NewsScan for October 13, 2006—Women and Substance Abuse Issue.* Bethesda, MD: NIDA and the National Institutes of Health (NIH), 2006a.

National Institute on Drug Abuse (NIDA). *Research Report Series—Anabolic Steroid Abuse.* Bethesda, MD: U.S. Government Printing Office, 2006b.

National Institute on Drug Abuse (NIDA). *NIDA InfoFacts: Steroids (Anabolic-Androgenic).* Bethesda, MD: NIDA and National Institutes of Health (NIH), 2009.

National Institute on Drug Abuse (NIDA). "Monitoring the Future: Data Tables and Figures." December 2010. Available http://monitoringthefuture.org/data/09data/pr09t1.pdf

National Institute on Drug Abuse (NIDA). *DrugFacts: Prescription and Over-the-Counter Medications.* Bethesda, MD: National Institute on Drug Abuse, May 2013.

National Institute on Drug Abuse (NIDA) for teens. "Drug Facts: Prescription Drugs." 26 June 2013. Available http://teens.drugabuse.gov/drug-facts/prescription-drugs

National Institutes of Health (NIH) and National Institute on Drug Abuse (NIDA). *Drug Abuse and Drug Abuse Research: Executive Summary.* Rockville, MD: Substance Abuse and Mental Health Services Administration, 1998.

National Survey on Drug Use and Health (NSDUH). *The NSDUH Report: Substance Use Treatment among Women of Childbearing Age.* Research Triangle Park, NC: Office of Applied Studies (OAS), Substance Abuse and Mental Health Services Administration (SAMHSA) and RTI International, 4 October 2007.

National Youth Anti-Drug Media Campaign. "The 411 on Rx Drugs." 2007. Available http://www.theantidrug.com/drug_info/prescription_411.asp

New York State Department of Health. "Anabolic Steroids and Sports: Winning at Any Cost." 2010. Available http://www.health.state.ny.us/publications/1210

News Tribune. "Alcohol, Tobacco or Drugs Used in 98% of Popular Movies." (29 April 1999): 7–8, 14.

Office of National Drug Control Policy (ONDCP). *Substance Use in Popular Movies and Music. Media Campaign, Campaign Publications.* Rockville, MD: ONDCP Drugs and Crime Clearinghouse, 1999.

Office of National Drug Control Policy (ONDCP). *Prescription for Danger.* Rockville, MD: ONDCP, January 2008.

Office of the Surgeon General. "Surgeon General's Call to Action to Prevent and Reduce Underage Drinking." U.S. Department of Health and Human Services (DHHS). 2007. Available http://www.surgeongeneral.gov/topics/underagedrinking/familyguide.pdf

Olin, B. R. *Drug Facts and Comparisons.* St. Louis, MO: Kluwer, 1994, 109–109c.

"OTC Drugs and Athletes." *Pharmacy Times* (June 1992): 16.

Paoletta, M. "Music Industry Coming to Grips with Addiction." *Today,* 21 May 2004. Available http://www.today.com/id/5033438#.Un8j5JSEayW

Parrot, A. *Date Rape and Acquaintance Rape.* New York: Rosen, 1988.

Pietroski, N. "Counseling HIV/AIDS Patients." *American Druggist* (August 1993): 50–56.

Prendergast, M. L. "Substance Use and Abuse Among College Students: A Review of Recent Literature." *Journal of American College Health* 43 (1994): 99–113.

Quinn. E. "EPO and Blood Doping in Sports." About.com. May 23, 2011. Available http://sportsmedicine.about .com/od/performanceenhancingdrugs/a/EPO.htm

Ravid, J. "The Hard-Core Curriculum." *Rolling Stone* 719 (19 October 1995): 99.

Reuters and Fox News Network. "Facebook Linked to Teenage Drinking, Drug Use." 24 August 2011. Available http:// www.foxnews.com/tech/2011/08/24/report-links-social -networking-sites-to-teenage-drinking-drug-use/

Ross, V., and W. Dejong. *Alcohol and Other Drug Abuse Among First-Year College Students.* Newton, MA: Higher Education Center for Alcohol and Other Drug Abuse and Violence Prevention, March 2008: 1–8.

Rubin, A., R. L. Stout, and R. Longabaugh. "Gender Differences in Relapse Situations." *Addiction* 91 (Suppl.) (1996): S111–S120.

Sanders, W. B. *Gangbangs and Drive-bys.* New York: Aldine De Gruyter, 1994.

Schaefer, M. A., J. F. Hilton, M. Ekstrand, and J. Keogh. "Relationship Between Drug Use and Sexual Behaviors and the Occurrence of Sexually Transmitted Diseases Among High-Risk Male Youth." *Sexually Transmitted Diseases* 20 (November–December 1993): 39–47.

Schernoff, M., and R. A. Smith. "HIV Treatments: A History of Scientific Advance." *Body Positive* XIV (July 2001): 1–7.

Schoemer, K. "Rockers, Models and the New Allure of Heroin." *Newsweek* (26 August 1996): 24–36.

Science Daily. "Pain Drug Reveals What Most Already Know—Men's and Women's Brains Are Simply Different." 15 March 2000. Available http://www.sciencedaily.com /releases/2000/03/000315075845.htm

Scott, D. M., J. C. Wagner, and T. W. Barlow. "Anabolic Steroids Use Among Adolescents in Nebraska Schools." *American Journal of Health-System Pharmacy* 53 (1996): 2068–2072.

Scripps Howard News Service. "AIDS Fear: Complacency: Infection Rate Is on Rise for First Time Since 1994." *Post-Tribune* (21 August 2003): A-10.

Seetharaman, D. "Study: Addictive Drugs Easily Ordered Online." Thomson Reuters. 9 July 2008. Available http://www.usatoday.com/news/health/2008-07-09 -online-pharmacies_N.htm

Shelden, R. G., S. Tracy, and W. Brown. *Youth Gangs in American Society.* Belmont, CA: Wadsworth/Thomson Learning, 2001.

Shelden, R. G., S. K. Tracy, and W. B. Brown. *Youth Gangs in American Society,* 3rd ed. Belmont, CA: Wadsworth /Thomson Learning, 2004.

Siegel, L., and J. Senna. *Juvenile Delinquency,* 6th ed. St. Paul, MN: West, 1997.

Siegel, L. J., and B. C. Welsh. *Juvenile Delinquency: Theory, Practice, and Law,* 10th ed. Belmont, CA: Wadsworth, Cengage Learning, 2009.

Southern Illinois University Carbondale/Core Institute. "2011 Annual Reference Group, Core Alcohol and Drug Survey Long Form—Form 194, Executive Summary." 23 April 2013. Available http://core.siu.edu /pdfs/report11.pdf

Spergel, I. A. *Youth Gangs: Problem and Response.* Chicago, IL: University of Chicago, School of Social Service Administration, 1990.

Steinberg, L., A. Fletcher, and N. Darling. "Parental Monitoring and Peer Influences on Adolescent Substance Use." *Pediatrics* 93 (1994): 1060–1064.

Street, C., J. Antonio, and D. Cudlipp. "Androgen Use by Athletes: A Reevaluation of the Health Risks." *Canadian Journal of Applied Physiology* 2 (1996): 421–440.

Stewart, K. "Facts and Myths about College Drinking: A Serious Problem with Serious Solutions." Berkeley, CA: Prevention Research Center, (May 2013, 1–8). Available http://resources.prev.org/documents/FactsMyths CollegeDrinking.pdf

Substance Abuse and Mental Health Services Administration (SAMHSA). *Making the Connection Between Substance Abuse and HIV/AIDS Prevention for Women of Color and Youth.* Rockville, MD: U.S. Department of Health and Human Services, 1999a.

Substance Abuse and Mental Health Services Administration (SAMHSA). *Tips for Teens: About Steroids. Center for Substance Abuse Prevention.* Rockville, MD: U.S. Department of Health and Human Services, 1999b.

Substance Abuse and Mental Health Services Administration (SAMHSA), Office of Applied Studies. *National Household Survey on Drug Abuse, The NHSDA Report. Team Sports Participation and Substance Use Among Youths.* Rockville, MD: SAMHSA, 17 March 2007.

Substance Abuse and Mental Health Services Administration (SAMHSA), Office of Applied Studies (OAS). *The TEDS (Treatment Episode Data Set) Report: Trends in Adult Female Substance Abuse Treatment Admissions Reporting Primary Alcohol Abuse: 1992 to 2007.* Rockville, MD, U.S. Department of Health and Human Services, 7 January 2010.

Substance Abuse and Mental Health Services Administration (SAMHSA). *Results from the 2010 National Survey* on Drug Use and Health: Summary of National Findings. NSDUH Series H-41, HHS Pub. No. (SMA) 11-4658. Rockville, MD: SAMHSA, 2011.

Suggs, W. "Deadly Fuel: As Supplements and Steroids Tempt and Endanger More Athletes, What Are Colleges Doing?" *Chronicle of Higher Education* 49 (14 March 2003): A36–A38.

Swadi, H. "Relative Risk Factors in Detecting Adolescent Drug Abuse." *Drug and Alcohol Dependence* 29 (1992): 253–254.

Technische Univerisität München. «Doping Definition.» Available http://www.doping-prevention.sp.tum.de /doping-in-general/doping-definition.html

Teen Challenge. *Drugs: Frequently Asked Questions.* South Australia: Pragin Press, 2000.

The Athlete.org. "The Athlete: Doping in Sports - A Deadly Game." (2011). Available http://www.theathlete.org /doping-in-sport.htm

The Independent. "Music and Drugs - It's a Hard Habit to Break." London, United Kingdom (UK): Independent .co.uk, 10 November 2013. Available http://www .independent.co.uk/arts-entertainment/music/features /music-and-drugs--its-a-hard-habit-to-break-2327654 .html

TheScore.com. "MLB Suspends 12 Players in Biogenesis Case." TheScore, (5 August 2013). Available http://www .thescore.com/home/articles/1246300-mlb-suspends -12-players-in-biogenesis-case

Toronto, R. "Young Athletes Who Use 'Enhancing' Steroids Risk Severe Physical Consequences." *Salt Lake Tribune* 244 (6 July 1992): C-5.

TreatHIVNow. "Signs and Symptoms." 2013. Available http://www.treathivnow.com/hiv-facts/hiv-signs-and -symptoms

United Nations Programme on HIV/AIDS (UNAIDS). *Global Report: UNAIDS Report on the Global Aids Epidemic 2012.* Geneva, Switzerland: UNAIDS, 2012: 14–15. Available http://www.unaids.org/en/media/unaids/contentassets /documents/epidemiology/2012/gr2012/20121120 _UNAIDS_Global_Report_2012_en.pdf

U.S. Department of Health and Human Services (USD-HHS), National Institute on Drug Abuse (NIDA). *Drug Abuse and Addiction Research: The Sixth Triennial Report to Congress. NIDA Research Priorities and Highlights, Role of Research: Women's Health and Gender Differences.* Washington, DC: U.S. Government Printing Office, 1999.

U.S. Department of Justice (DOJ). *Anabolic Steroids and You.* Washington, DC: Demand Reduction Section, Drug Enforcement Administration, 1991–1992.

U.S. Department of Justice (DOJ). *Steroid Abuse in Today's Society.* Washington, DC: Drug Enforcement Administration (DEA). 2004. Available http://www.deadiversion. usdoj.gov/pubs/brochures/steroids/professionals/

United Nations Interregional Crime and Justice Research Institute (UNICRI). "Dawn: Promoting Gender-Based Drug Prevention and Recovery." Geneva 10, Switzerland: United Nations Interregional Crime and justice Research Institute, 2013.

USA Today. "Teen Prescription Drug Abuse Reportedly Holding Steady." Associated Press. 14 February 2007. Available http://www.usatoday.com/news/health/2007-02-14-teens-rxdrugs_x.htm?csp=34

Vargas-Cooper, N. "Bath Salts." *Spin* (July/August 2012): 58–64, 94.

Venturelli, P. J. "Drugs in Schools: Myths and Reality." In *The Annals of the American Academy of Political and Social Science*, edited by W. H. Hinkle and S. Henry, (567) 72–87. Thousand Oaks, CA: Sage, January 2000.

Verhaak, C. M., A. M. E. Lintsen, A. W. M. Evers, and D. D. M. Braat. "Who Is at Risk of Emotional Problems and How Do You Know? Screening of Women Going for IVF Treatment." *Human Reproduction* 25 (2010): 1234–1240.

Von Der Haar, C. M. *Social Psychology: A Sociological Perspective.* Upper Saddle River, NJ: Pearson Education, 2005.

Walsh, F., and M. Shenkman. "Family Context of Adolescence." In *Adolescent Substance Abuse, Etiology, Treatment and Prevention,* edited by G. Lawson and A. Lawson, 149–171. Gaithersburg, MD: Aspen, 1992.

WebMD.com. "Information and Resources: Growth Hormone." 14 August 2008. Available http://www.webmd .com/a-to-z-guides/growth-hormone

Wechsler, H., J. E. Lee, M. Kuo, M. Seibring, T. F. Nelson, and H. P. Lee. "Trends in College Binge Drinking During a Period of Increased Prevention Efforts: Findings from Four Harvard School of Public Health Study Surveys, 1993–2001." *Journal of American College Health* 50 (2002): 203–217.

Winters, P. A. *Teen Addiction.* San Diego, CA: Greenhaven Press, 1997.

Wisconsin Coalition Against Sexual Assault (WCASA). *Sexual Violence and Sexual Abuse.* Madison, WI: WCASA, 1997.

Witham, D. "Recovery in the Dorm: Rutgers University's Special Housing for Addicted Students." *Chronicle of Higher Education* 42 (10 November 1995): A-33.

"Women Smokers Run High Risk for Lung Cancer." *Prevention Pipeline* 7 (May–June 1994): 7.

World Anti-Doping Agency (WADA). Questions and Answers on 2009 World Anti-Doping Code. Montreal (Quebec), Canada: WADA, 2009. Available http://www.wada-ama.org/en/Resources/Qand-A/Why-is-it-important-to-combat-doping-in-sport

World Health Organization (WHO). *HIV/AIDS: HIV/AIDS and Adolescents*. Geneva, Switzerland: World Health Organization, 2005.

Wright, L. "Suicidal Thoughts and Their Relationship to Family Stress and Personal Problems Among High School Seniors and College Undergraduates." *Adolescence* 20 (1985): 575–580.

Wu, L. T., D. J. Pilowsky, and A. A. Patkar, "Non-Prescribed Use of Pain Relievers Among Adolescents in the United States." *Drug Alcohol Dependency* 94 (April 1, 2008): 1–11. Epub ahead of print December 3, 2007.

Yahoo! News. "1 in 3 Hit Songs Mentions Substance Abuse, Smoking." HealthDay. 4 February 2008.

Yesalis, C. E., and J. S. Cowart. *The Steroids Game*. Champaign, IL: Human Kinetics, 1998.

Zickuhr, K. "Who's Not Online and Why." Pew Internet & American Life Project., 25 September 2013. Available http://pewinternet.org/Reports/2013/Non-internet-users.aspx

Zuger, A. "Epidemic: An Overview." *The New York Times*. 8 August 2000. Available http://www.nytimes.com/library/national/science/aids/aids-overview.html

Photo by SSGT Jennifer J. Tovar, USAF. Courtesy of U.S. Department of Defense

Did You Know?

▶ Comprehensive prevention programs simultaneously involving the community, school, and family are more effective than single-unit programs.

▶ The harm reduction drug prevention model that is practiced in the Netherlands is a preventive model that meets drug users on their own turf in dealing with drug use and/or abuse.

▶ Drug prevention programs must distinguish among early experimenters, nonproblem drug users, undetected committed or secret users, problem users, and former users.

▶ Students in drug prevention programs who do not know how to say "no" need refusal skills training or peer resistance training.

▶ Drug education actually began in the 1830s with the temperance movement.

▶ Drug courts are a newer form of drug prevention in which drug defendants are more likely to undergo treatment (rehabilitation) than incarceration (punishment).

▶ Other strategies for dealing with drug use include the alternatives approach and meditation.

Learning Objectives

On completing this chapter, you will be able to:

〉 List the 10 most prominent factors influencing alcohol and other drug use surrounding the individual.

〉 List and briefly explain the three major types of drug prevention programs.

〉 List the five types of drug users that have to be considered before implementing a drug prevention program.

〉 List the five levels of comprehensive prevention programs for drug use and abuse.

〉 List the three family factors that can prevent initiation to drugs or extensive drug use.

〉 List five existing prevention programs largely found in higher education.

〉 Understand the main goals of the following large-scale drug prevention programs: the BACCHUS Network, D.A.R.E., and drug courts.

〉 Describe two alternatives to drug use.

Drugs and Society Online is a great source for additional drugs and society information for both students and instructors. Visit **go.jblearning.com /hanson12** to find a variety of useful tools for learning, thinking, and teaching.

Introduction

When someone tells another person "Just don't do drugs" and, if that person is addicted to, say, cocaine like I was, that comes across as an ignorant answer. You cannot just quit when you are addicted because even the idea of addiction continually blocks the possibility of casually deciding to stop using the drug. A lot has to go into the day you actually stop using the drug. First of all, the craving for the drug continually reminds you to do it maybe just a few more times. Then, your life appears to be less engaging because your body is missing the chemical properties of the drug that it became accustomed to and this affects your level of depression. So you have to sort of go through that slow abstinence period—you are without the drug and sometimes you can only deal with abstaining 1 hour at a time for the first week or so. Then slowly, ever so slowly, for me at least, the addict has to rebuild her or his daily living without the drug. It's just not easy. If it were, most people addicted to drugs would probably quit on their own. Especially when you realize that you are not controlling the drug, the drug is controlling you. Just remember, most addicts continually deceive [lie to] themselves and others that they are not "really" addicted. Do you know how hard it is to become aware that these lies are part of the addiction? Before the extended therapy I had, no one could convince me that the daily cocaine I was snorting and smoking was bad. *(From Venturelli's research files, female academic administrator in higher education who has been drug free for 3 years, age 37, June 21, 2000)*

A second interview revealed the following:

I started doing cocaine at age 52. One night, I was having a few beers with a friend of mine and another friend of his over at his apartment. I know I was older than both of them were since they were in their early thirties. After the first few beers, this friend of mine went into his bedroom and came out into the

living room with a bag of coke. Soon as he entered the room, he threw the bag into my lap and said, "Do you want to try some of this?" I told them I never did this drug and said, "Okay I will try it once." All I remember that night is that I kept doing lines and often said, "Boy, this stuff is so easy to do—nothing to it." When the night was over, I got back into my car and went home. After that night, I started buying the coke each week and for over 2 years had spent thousands of dollars. It became a nightly thing to do. One day, I decided to stop buying coke since I was very worried about all the money I had been charging to my credit card as cash advances. For the first few nights it was difficult to not go out and pick up coke from a dealer I had gotten to know quite well. This dealer kept calling asking who I was buying from since he hadn't seen me in over a week. I repeatedly tried telling him that I was quitting and had no other dealer but he would not believe me. This added to the difficulty in giving up the drug but I did it. It was "cold turkey" and I had succeeded since now it has been 5 years and I never bought my supply again since that one night when I decided to quit. It is so easy to do this drug and become attached to it. I don't think I was really addicted when I was doing it, but I sure did it often. My problem was more of a mental attachment to the drug. I think I was certainly close to a serious addiction but the cost of the drug, using money I did not have, forced me to quit. In my case, the best prevention is to never start doing this drug or any other drug that is easy to do and makes you feel so good when you are doing it. I have several friends who continue to use this drug mostly on weekends. I am glad I am not in their shoes anymore. *(From Venturelli's research files, male mechanical engineer, age 59, November 5, 2010)*

This chapter explores and provides information on doing *something* about drug use and abuse. With so many potential causes for the unnecessary and nonmedical use of psychoactive substances, it becomes increasingly important to discuss methods, programs, and strategies that prevent, delay, or at the very least moderate the habitual use of drugs. **Figure 17.1** shows many of the potential environmental factors involved in what influences alcohol and other drug (**AOD**) use. The core in this figure starts with the individual, and each concentric zone represents clusters of factors

KEY TERM

AOD
alcohol and other drugs

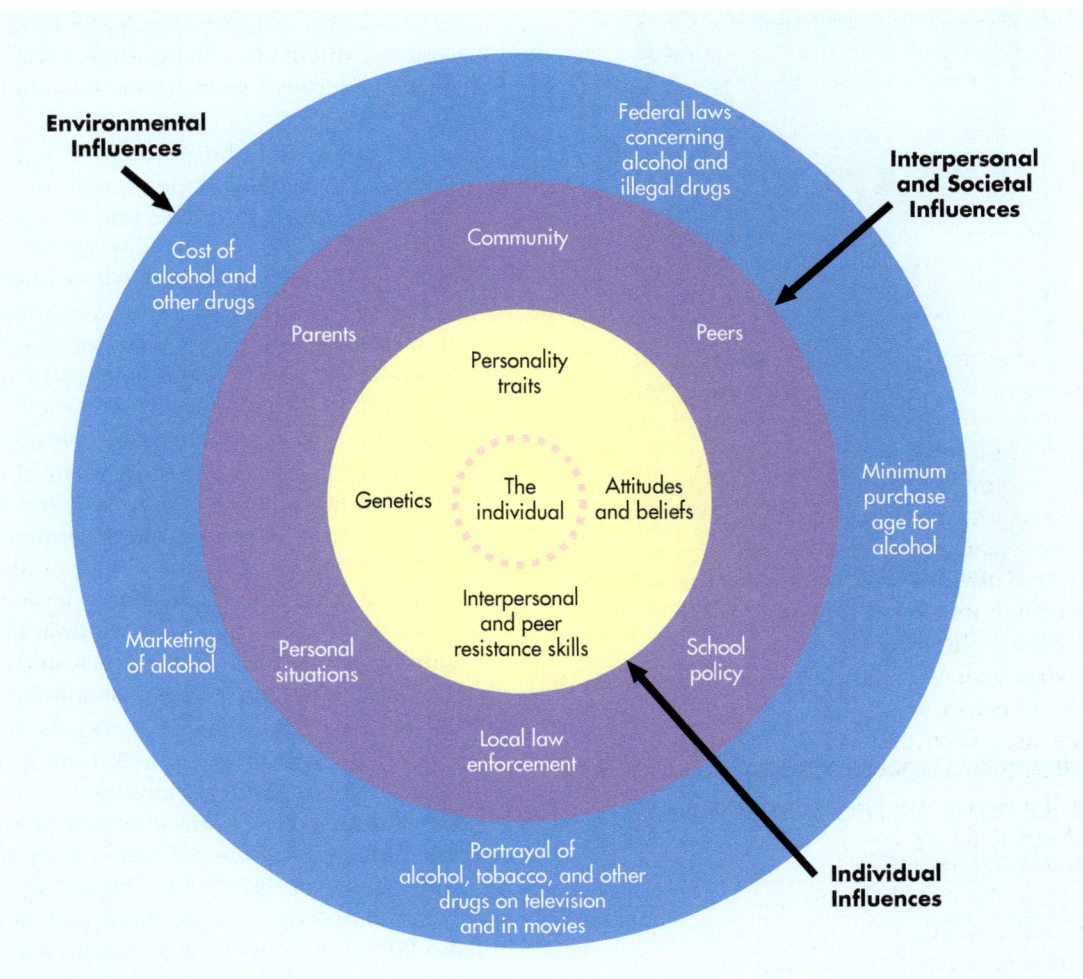

FIGURE 17.1 Potential factors that influence alcohol and other drug use.

Reproduced from U.S. Department of Health and Human Services, Office of Substance Abuse Prevention. "Factors that Influence Alcohol and Other Drug Use." In *Prevention Plus II: Tools for Creating and Sustaining Drug-Free Communities* (Figure 2.1, p. 19). DHHS Publication No. 89-1649. Rockville, MD: USDHHS, 1989. Distributed by the National Clearinghouse for Alcohol and Drug Information.

that influence an individual's views, attitudes, and behaviors toward drug use. With so many factors, each having an independent potential effect on the individual, you can see why comprehensive prevention programs involving the community, school, and family are more effective than single-unit programs, such as having a mandatory drug education program in elementary grades without other complementary and overlapping drug programs in the community and the family. Prevention research clearly shows that "we must attend to all factors; prevention that focuses on only one or two factors and ignores or discounts the rest is likely to fail to have a long-term, permanent impact" (Tinzmann and Hixson 1992, p. 3).

Through comprehensive prevention programs that are multifaceted and complementary, we are able to more effectively tease out which factors are most influential. The televised commercial in the early 1990s that showed two eggs frying in a pan: "This is your brain . . . this is your brain on drugs," sponsored by the Partnership for a Drug-Free America, was an early attempt at prevention through a disturbing analogy. Although its effect was poor on drug users, who had never felt their brains frying, it was an initial step toward innovative prevention efforts. Was it worth the airtime? Can the success of these programs be adequately measured?

In 1997, 15 states thought prevention of alcohol and other drug abuse was important enough to maintain certified prevention specialist credentialing. Today, a bewildering variety of programs exists from coast to coast in school districts, churches, and other communities, all with the goal of preventing initial drug use or halting use before it becomes a problem.

Example of an advertisement aimed at alerting parents about the dangers of early drug use.

How Serious Is the Problem of Drug Dependence?

In looking at drug dependence, the severity of this problem can be highlighted by the following current trends (Substance Abuse and Mental Health Services Administration [SAMHSA] 2012):

Substance dependence or abuse

- In 2011, an estimated 20.6 million persons age 12 or older were classified with substance dependence or abuse in the past year (8.0% of the population age 12 or older). Of these, 2.6 million were classified with dependence or abuse of both alcohol and illicit drugs, 3.9 million had dependence or abuse of illicit drugs but not alcohol, and 14.1 million had dependence or abuse of alcohol but not illicit drugs.
- The annual number of persons with substance dependence or abuse remained stable between 2002 and 2010, ranging from 21.6 million to 22.7 million. However, the number in 2011 (20.6 million) was lower than the number in 2010 (22.2 million).

- In 2011, 16.7 million persons age 12 or older were classified with alcohol dependence or abuse, which was lower than the number in 2010.
- In 2011, 6.5% of the population age 12 or older had alcohol dependence or abuse, which was lower than the rate in each year since 2002.
- The number of persons age 12 or older who had illicit drug dependence or abuse was similar between 2010 (7.1 million) and 2011 (6.5 million) and between 2002 (7.1 million) and 2011.
- Marijuana was the illicit drug with the highest rate of past-year dependence or abuse in 2011, followed by pain relievers and cocaine. Of the 6.5 million persons age 12 or older classified with illicit drug dependence or abuse in 2011, 4.2 million had marijuana dependence or abuse (representing 1.6% of the total population age 12 or older, and 63.8% of all those classified with illicit drug dependence or abuse), 1.8 million persons had pain reliever dependence or abuse, and 821,000 persons had cocaine dependence or abuse.
- The number of persons who had marijuana dependence or abuse did not change significantly between 2002 (4.3 million) and 2011 (4.2 million) or between 2010 (4.5 million) and 2011. The rate of persons who had marijuana dependence or abuse in 2011 (1.6%) was lower than the rates in 2002 (1.8%) and 2004 (1.9%), but was similar (very little difference) to the rate in 2010 (1.8%).
- The rate and the number of persons who had pain reliever dependence or abuse remained unchanged between 2010 (0.8% and 1.9 million) and 2011 (0.7% and 1.8 million) and between 2002 (0.6% and 1.5 million) and 2011.
- The rate and the number of persons who had cocaine dependence or abuse were similar between 2010 (0.4% and 1.0 million) and 2011 (0.3% and 821,000). However, they decreased between 2006 (0.7% and 1.7 million) and 2011.
- The rate and the number of persons who had heroin dependence or abuse were stable between 2010 (0.1% and 361,000) and 2011 (0.2% and 426,000). However, they increased between 2007 (0.1% and 214,000) and 2011.

Age at first use

- In 2011, among adults age 18 or older, age at first use of marijuana was associated with illicit drug dependence or abuse. Among those who first tried marijuana at age 14 or younger, 12.7% were classified with illicit drug dependence or abuse, which was higher than the 2.0% of adults who had first used marijuana at age 18 or older.

- Among adults, age at first use of alcohol also was associated with alcohol dependence or abuse. In 2011, among adults age 18 or older who first tried alcohol at age 14 or younger, 14.8% were classified with alcohol dependence or abuse, which was higher than the 3.5% of adults who had first used alcohol at age 18 or older. Adults age 21 or older who had first used alcohol before age 21 were more likely than adults who had their first drink at age 21 or older to be classified with alcohol dependence or abuse. In particular, adults age 21 or older who had first used alcohol at age 14 or younger were more than 7 times as likely to be classified with alcohol dependence or abuse than adults who had their first drink at age 21 or older (13.8% vs. 1.8%). The rate of adults age 21 or older who first used alcohol at age 21 or older and were classified with alcohol dependence or abuse in 2011 (1.8%) was lower than the rate in 2010 (2.7%).

- In 2011, during their most recent treatment in the past year, 2.4 million persons age 12 or older reported receiving treatment for alcohol use, and 872,000 persons reported receiving treatment for marijuana use. Estimates for receiving treatment for the use of other drugs were 726,000 persons for pain relievers, 511,000 for cocaine, 430,000 for heroin, 318,000 for tranquilizers, 309,000 for stimulants, and 293,000 for hallucinogens. None of these estimates changed significantly between 2010 and 2011.

- The number of persons age 12 or older who received treatment for the use of pain relievers and tranquilizers increased between 2002 and 2011. The number who received treatment for pain relievers in 2009 to 2011 ranged from 726,000 to 761,000 persons and was greater than the numbers in 2002 to 2005.

Age

- Rates of substance dependence or abuse were associated with age. In 2011, the rate of substance dependence or abuse among adults ages 18 to 25 (18.6%) was higher than that among youth ages 12 to 17 (6.9%) and among adults age 26 or older (6.3%). Both the rate among adults ages 18 to 25 and the rate among adults age 26 or older declined between 2010 (20.0% and 7.0%, respectively) and 2011. From 2002 to 2011, the rate decreased for youth ages 12 to 17 (from 8.9% to 6.9%), for young adults ages 18 to 25 (from 21.7% to 18.6%), and for adults age 26 or older (from 7.3% to 6.3%).

- The rate of alcohol dependence or abuse among youth ages 12 to 17 was 3.8% in 2011, which declined from 4.6% in 2010 and from 5.9% in 2002. Among young adults ages 18 to 25, the rate of alcohol dependence or abuse also decreased between 2010 (15.7%) and 2011 (14.4%) and between 2002 (17.7%) and 2011. Among adults age 26 or older, the rate was stable between 2010 (5.9%) and 2011 (5.4%), but it decreased between 2002 (6.2%) and 2011.

Gender

- As was the case from 2002 through 2010, the rate of substance dependence or abuse for males age 12 or older in 2011 was about twice as high as the rate for females. For males in 2011, the rate was 10.4%, which decreased from 11.7% in 2010. For females, it was 5.7% in 2011, which did not differ from the rate of 6.0% in 2010. Among youth ages 12 to 17, the rate of substance dependence or abuse among males was not different from the rate among females in 2011 (6.9% for each).

Race/Ethnicity

- In 2011, among persons age 12 or older, the rate of substance dependence or abuse was lower among Asians (3.3%) than among other racial/ethnic groups. The rates for the other racial/ethnic groups were 16.8% for American Indians or Alaska Natives, 10.6% for Native Hawaiians or Other Pacific Islanders, 9.0% for persons reporting two or more races, 8.7% for Hispanics, 8.2% for whites, and 7.2% for blacks.

Education

- Rates of substance dependence or abuse were associated with level of education in 2011. Among adults age 18 or older, those who graduated from a college or university had a lower rate of substance dependence or abuse (6.4%) than those who graduated from high school (8.0%), those who did not graduate from high school (9.3%), and those with some college (9.5%).

Employment

- Rates of substance dependence or abuse were associated with current employment status in 2011. A higher percentage of unemployed adults age 18 or older was classified with dependence or abuse (14.8%) than were full-time-employed adults (8.4%) or part-time-employed adults (9.8%).
- About half of the adults age 18 or older with substance dependence or abuse were employed full time in 2011. Of the 18.9 million adults classified with dependence or abuse, 9.8 million (51.8%) were employed full time.

Criminal justice populations

- In 2011, adults age 18 or older who were on parole or a supervised release from jail during the past year had higher rates of illicit drug or alcohol dependence or abuse (35.1%) than their counterparts who were not on parole or supervised release during the past year (7.9%).
- In 2011, probation status was associated with substance dependence or abuse. The rate of substance dependence or abuse was 33.7%

among adults who were on probation during the past year, which was higher than the rate among adults who were not on probation during the past year (7.6%).

Geographic area

- In 2011, rates of substance dependence or abuse for persons age 12 or older were 8.9% in the West, 8.6% in the Northeast, 8.3% in the Midwest, and 7.0% in the South.
- Rates for substance dependence or abuse among persons age 12 or older in 2011 were similar in large metropolitan counties (8.4%) and small metropolitan counties (8.2%), but were higher than in nonmetropolitan counties (6.3%).

After reviewing such significant findings in terms of numbers and percentages of substance-dependent or -abusing populations, we can now understand the need for discussing drug prevention in this chapter.

Drug Prevention

"In the broadest sense, prevention is organized activity designed to avoid or decrease health problems" (Wilson and Kolander 2011, p. 7). In addition to this definition of prevention, we add that in this chapter, **drug prevention** is aimed at preventing and/or decreasing not only health problems, but also social and personal problems. When both licit and illicit types of drugs are used and/or abused for nonmedical purposes, they compromise psychological, social, and biological behavior. In the remaining sections of this chapter, we will review what drug prevention entails.

Risk Factors and Protective Factors

From a broad perspective, when considering any drug prevention program, both **protective factors** and **risk factors** have to be considered. "Protective factors are those associated with reduced potential for drug use and risk factors are those that make drug use more likely" (National Institute on Drug Abuse [NIDA] 2002). The following are the main principles that have to be considered

KEY TERMS

drug prevention
aimed at preventing or decreasing health problems, including social and personal problems, caused by drug dependency

protective factors
factors associated with preventing the potential for drug abuse such as self-control, parental monitoring, academic competence, anti–drug use policies, and strong neighborhood attachment

risk factors
drug prevention is aimed at reducing risk factors, such as early aggressive behavior, lack of parental supervision, the lure of gang membership, drug availability, and poverty

when planning effective drug prevention programs:

- Drug prevention programs should enhance protective factors and reverse or reduce risk factors. Protective factors include:
  - Strong and positive family bonds
  - Parental monitoring of children's activities and peers
  - Clear rules of conduct consistently enforced within the family
  - Involvement of parents in the lives of their children
  - Success in school performance
  - Strong bonds in institutions, such as school and religious organizations
  - Adoption of conventional norms about drug use
- Risk factors include:
  - Chaotic home environment, particularly in homes where parents abuse substances or suffer from mental illnesses
  - Ineffective parenting, especially with children with difficult temperaments or conduct disorders
  - Lack of parent–child attachments and nurturing
  - Inappropriately shy or aggressive behavior in the classroom
  - Failure in school performance
  - Poor social coping skills
  - Affiliations with peers displaying deviant behaviors
  - Perceptions of approval of drug-using behaviors in family, work, school, peer, and community environments (NIDA 2002)
- The risk of becoming a drug abuser involves the relationship among the number and type of risk factors (e.g., deviant attitudes and behaviors) and protective factors (e.g., parental support).
- The potential impact of specific risk and protective factors changes with age. For example, risk factors within the family have greater impact on a younger child, whereas association with drug-abusing peers may be a more significant risk factor for an adolescent.
- Early intervention with risk factors (e.g., aggressive behavior and poor self-control) often has a greater impact than later intervention by changing a child's life path (trajectory) away from problems and toward positive behaviors.
- Although risk and protective factors can affect people of all groups, these factors can have a different effect depending on a person's age, gender, ethnicity, culture, and neighborhood environment.
- Prevention programs should address all forms of drug abuse, alone or in combination, including the underage use of legal drugs (e.g., tobacco, alcohol), the use of illegal drugs (e.g., marijuana, heroin), and the inappropriate use of legally obtained substances (e.g., inhalants), prescription medications, or over-the-counter drugs.
- Prevention programs should address the type of drug abuse problem in the local community, target modifiable risk factors, and strengthen identified protective factors.
- Prevention programs should be tailored to address risks specific to population or audience characteristics, such as age, gender, and ethnicity, to improve program effectiveness (quoted extensively from Robertson et al. and NIDA 2003, p. 7).

There are three levels of drug prevention programs, each suited to different types of drug users. **Primary drug prevention programs** are aimed at either nonusers who need to be "inoculated" against potential drug use or helping at-risk individuals avoid the development of addictive behaviors. For example, primary prevention often targets at-risk youth who may live in areas where licit and illicit types of drugs are rampant, youth who may come from problem families, or youth who are surrounded by drug-abusing peers.

The other two major types of drug prevention programs are (1) **secondary drug prevention programs**, which consist of uncovering potentially harmful substance use prior to the onset of overt symptoms or problems and/or targeting newer drug users with a limited or early history of

KEY TERMS

primary drug prevention programs
drug prevention programs with a very broad range of activities aimed at reducing the risk of drug use among nonusers and ensuring continued nonuse and helping at-risk individuals avoid the development of addictive behaviors

secondary drug prevention programs
programs that consist of uncovering potentially harmful substance use prior to the onset of overt symptoms or problems and/or targeting newer drug users with a limited history of use; the main goal is to target at-risk groups, experimenters, and early-abuse populations

TABLE 17.1 Levels of Drug Prevention and Suggested Activities

Primary Prevention (Risk Reduction Before Abuse)	
Intrapersonal factors	Affective education (emotional literacy)
	Resilience training
	Values clarification
	Personal and social skills development
	Assertiveness skills training
	Refusal skills
	Drug information and education
Small group factors	Peer mentoring, counseling, outreach, modeling
	Conflict resolution
	Curriculum infusion
	Activities demonstrating misperception of peer norms
	Alternatives to use: recreational, cultural, athletic
	Strengthening families
Systems level	Strengthening school–family links
	Strengthening school–community group links
	Strengthening community support systems
	Media advocacy efforts, reducing alcohol marketing
Secondary Prevention (Intervening in Early Abuse)	
	Assessment strategies: identification of abuse subgroups and individual diagnoses
	Early intervention coupled with sanctions
	Teacher–counselor–parent team approach
	Developing healthy alternative youth culture
	Recovering role models
Tertiary Prevention (Intervening in Advanced Abuse)	
	Assessment and diagnosis
	Referral into treatment
	Case management
	Reentry

drug use, and (2) **tertiary drug prevention programs**, which focus directly on intervention and target chemically dependent individuals who need treatment. Tertiary prevention involves treating the medical consequences of drug abuse and facilitating entry into treatment so further disability is minimized.

Usually primary, secondary, and tertiary programs are used in combination because, in most settings, all three types of drug users constitute the targeted population. **Table 17.1** further illustrates these levels of drug prevention and corresponding suggested activities; what can be accomplished is listed under each of the three types of prevention (primary, secondary, and tertiary).

KEY TERM

tertiary drug prevention programs
drug prevention programs focusing on intervention and targeting chemically dependent individuals who need treatment; tertiary prevention involves treating the medical consequences of drug abuse and facilitating entry into treatment so further disability is minimized (basically the same as drug abuse treatment)

Considering the Audience and Approach

It is important to be aware that drug users vary in their exposure and past histories of substance use and/or abuse. The audience for drug prevention comprises both users and nonusers. In analyzing the population of users, categories include the following:

- Nonusers
- Early experimenters
- Nonproblem drug users—those who abuse drugs on occasion, mostly for recreational purposes
- Undetected, committed, or secret users— those who abuse drugs and have no interest in stopping their drug use
- Problem users who are often drug dependent and/or addicted to drugs
- Former users

It is important that role models, counselors, teachers, and anyone else involved in drug prevention programs take into consideration that there are different types of substance users/abusers. Therefore, drug prevention programs must cater to the specific needs of these groups. For nonproblem users, drug education programs should examine the abuse of drugs and reinforce the message that uncontrolled use leads to abuse. For committed users, drug education should aim to prevent or delay drug abuse. Former users should be given information that will reinforce their decision to stop abusing drugs.

A number of questions should be considered by a professional planning a prevention program. To what type of audience should the drug information be targeted? Youth or adults? Peers or parents? Should information focus on knowledge, attitudes, or behavior?

Should the program emphasize and recommend abstinence or responsible use? In most cases, it is appropriate for drug prevention to focus on knowledge, attitudes, and behavior; the three are clearly related. For instance, if the goal is to increase knowledge, should we assume that attitudes and behavior would change accordingly, or should knowledge about the harmful effects of drugs be kept separate from attitudes and behavior? For example, if you learn that smoking marijuana is a health hazard, equal to or more destructive than smoking cigarettes, does this knowledge limit the satisfaction you derive from smoking marijuana with friends? Some would say yes. Unfortunately, many would say no. In fact, knowledge about the harmful effects of certain types of drugs has very little effect on the personal attitudes and habits of most people. Most cigarette smokers are aware of the health hazards before they start smoking, but this does not always stop them from starting or becoming addicted.

Drug education programs have to direct their attention to a small range of behavioral objectives. They will not be effective if they address too many issues. Drug prevention programs also must decide whether they will stress total abstinence or responsible use. Abstinence is radically different from responsible use. A program cannot advocate both. Information and scare tactics alone have no effect on drug use. Educational prevention models have been modified lately to achieve the following goals:

- Convey the message that society is inconsistent concerning drug use. For example, certain drugs that cause serious harm to a large percentage of the population are legal, whereas other drugs that have less impact are illegal.
- Convey that the reasons for drug use are complex and that drug users vary.
- Demonstrate to youth that young and old alike are affected by role models, in that attitudes regarding drug use are often patterned from family members who are role models.
- Acknowledge that other influential role models in music, sports, art, drama, business, and education who use and abuse drugs can affect attitudes toward drug use.

Prevention Research: Key Findings

"Each year, drug abuse and addiction cost taxpayers nearly $534 billion in preventable health care, law enforcement, crime, and other costs" (NIDA 2007). Another study reports that "[G]overnment spending related to smoking and the abuse of alcohol and illegal drugs reached $468 billion in 2005, accounting for more than one-tenth of combined federal, state and local expenditures for all purposes" (Eckholm 2009). Most spending for drug abuse went " . . . toward direct health care costs for lung disease, cirrhosis and overdoses, for example, or for law enforcement expenses including incarceration . . ." (Eckholm 2009).

Three major outcomes regarding drug abuse prevention are listed as key findings from the National Institute on Drug Abuse (NIDA 2007).

- *Addiction is a complex disease.* No single factor can predict who will become addicted to drugs. Addiction is influenced by a tangle of factors involving genes, environment, and age of first use. Recent advances in genetic research have enabled researchers to begin to uncover which genes make people more vulnerable, which protect a person against addiction, and how genes and environment interact.
- *Addiction is a developmental disease.* It usually begins in adolescence or even childhood when the brain continues to undergo changes. The prefrontal cortex—located just behind the forehead—governs judgment and decision-making functions and is the last part of the brain to develop. This may help explain why teens are prone to risk-taking, why they are particularly vulnerable to drug abuse, and why exposure to drugs at this critical time may affect the possibility of future addiction.
- *Prevention and early intervention work best.* The developmental years might also present opportunities for resiliency and for receptivity to intervention that can alter the course of addiction. We already know many of the risk factors that lead to drug abuse and addiction—mental illness, physical or sexual abuse, aggressive behavior, academic problems, poor social skills, and poor parent–child relations. This knowledge, combined with better understanding of the motivational processes at work in the young brain, can be applied to prevent drug abuse from starting or to intervene early to stop it when warning signs emerge.

▮ An Example of Drug Prevention at Central High in Elmtown

This section describes how a school-based prevention program is implemented and demonstrates that programs must be comprehensive and multifaceted to be successful.

Let us stand in the shoes of a parent and teacher committee trying to design a primary prevention program for students at Central High in Elmtown. The group has some prevention research materials that it received from the National Clearinghouse for Alcohol and Drug Information. After some

thought, most members of the committee decide not to address individual, personal risk factors that may generate anxieties, conflicts, or painful or threatening feelings. They have spoken with some students and ascertained that most of the 9th and 10th graders—even those who tend toward rebelliousness and avant-garde styles—are against taking drugs. Although many students feel this way, there are trends in the school that worry the committee members. Some popular 11th- and 12th-grade peer group leaders are drug users, and drug sales have been occurring on school grounds. The presence and availability of drugs and the beginning of a drug-using atmosphere make it more likely that some of the younger students will initiate use.

In brainstorming sessions, different committee members suggest ways to help these students avert initiation of drug use. Depending on their thinking, theoretical perspective, and exposure to prevention models, members come up with the following ideas:

- Students need to be grounded in good, solid knowledge about the negative effects and dangers of drugs (1) as provided in a drug education course or (2) more subtly, in a curriculum concerning drug effects and drug-using behaviors (also covered later in this chapter in the section on higher education).
- Students with low self-esteem will feel uncomfortable asserting individual choices or points of view that deviate from those held by peers or peer leaders. Bolstering a positive self-image would allow such students to refuse drugs.
- Students who have low expectations regarding their ability to refuse drugs will be least likely to actually refuse. The school might try to increase their *self-efficacy*—that is, their belief that their behaviors are powerful and will have results.
- Students just do not know how to say "no" and need refusal skills training or peer-resistance training.
- Although a clique leadership may set a pro-use tone, it is probable that the quiet antidrug students represent a silent majority. They may misperceive the amount of drug use that occurs in their school. If the antidrug students are shown that their own attitudes and beliefs are actually in the majority, they will see that the "emperor has no clothes."
- A more confrontational approach involves removing drugs from the school environment

by infiltrating the student body or using informants to gather information about who is distributing drugs. Dealers and users can then be identified or counseled and their parents notified. The school could make the decision to go as far as having the student arrested or expelling him or her.

With so many options put forth, some of the committee members become frustrated and fear that a sufficient program will never be created. Some of them have experienced alcoholism in their families and fear that many of these approaches are too ineffective for helping the students who are already experimenting.

Seeing a disaster brewing, the committee chair makes a call to the Division of Substance Abuse Services in the state Department of Health to inquire about drug prevention programs. The operator refers the call to the prevention specialists at the agency, who are linked to the National Prevention Network, which is part of the National Association of State Alcohol and Drug Abuse Directors. A specialist schedules a meeting with the committee, in which she makes the following points:

- A prevention needs assessment is helpful and necessitates using validated survey instruments to determine the patterns of behavior and attitudes regarding drug use among the student body.
- A combination of primary and secondary prevention would be good for the majority of the student body, and group treatment for substance abuse should be made available at an adolescent outpatient clinic. The outpatient clinic will assess some students who are well on their way to addiction and refer them into inpatient treatment. Because this intervention occurs when the student is at an advanced abuse state, this is considered tertiary prevention.

Notice how all three types of approaches (primary, secondary, and tertiary) are necessary to implement a comprehensive prevention strategy.

The specialist brought along a staff member of the Local Council on Alcoholism and Drug Dependence, an affiliate of the National Council on Alcoholism and Drug Dependence (NCADD) branch serving a three-county region of the state. Thousands of branches of NCADD exist in the United States, and their goal is to help local groups design and implement prevention programs. Many branches have developed specialized programs for teens, children, women, and the elderly. The staff member conducts preliminary sessions with the prevention committee and arranges to sign an affiliation agreement with the school administration, whereby NCADD will act as consultants to the school, aiding it in designing a prevention program to fit its particular needs. It will design a project, which will be based on a needs assessment that incorporates a survey of chemical attitudes and use and interviews with parents, teachers, and students. The project design will include the program objectives, a method and management plan, a timeline, and an evaluation component.

To help those members bewildered by the many possible factors identified by the committee in its brainstorming session (such as self-esteem, self-efficacy, and refusal skills), the staff member invites the committee to sample a number of available, attractive packages of user-friendly activities, such as the following:

- Broad-brush packages, which cover a variety of personal choice and primary prevention areas (Holstein, Cohen, and Steinbroner 1995)
- More targeted strategies, which might include a training package to be implemented by a consultant hired by the school district to address issues such as assertiveness training

Assertiveness training skills, which include a variety of personal and social skills, enable people to communicate their needs and feelings in an open, direct, and appropriate manner, while still recognizing the needs and feelings of others. They make people feel more powerful and better about themselves (less like doormats), and they offer strategies for saying "no" without hurting, provoking, or manipulating others (Alberti and Emmons 1988). Assertive behavior contrasts with hostile or belligerent behavior, passive and helpless behavior, and passive-aggressive or indirect manipulation. The exercises included in assertiveness training are nonthreatening, concrete, direct, and enjoyable.

Many intrapersonal prevention concepts, or personal and social skills development concepts, have come and gone, with a trendy buzzword accompanying each in the year it was introduced. Many of these concepts overlap, such as life skills training, self-esteem, self-efficacy, resilience training, and assertiveness training (McIntyre, White, and Yoast 1990; Norman 1994). The danger lies in employing them as gimmicks or slogans that accomplish little. Nevertheless, as Botvin and others have shown, personal and skills training that is carefully based on known cognitive and behavioral change factors, if carefully put into place, can indeed make a difference (Botvin and Griffin 2005; Botvin and Wills 1985; Shiffman and Wills 1987). It also is true that almost any positive lifestyle activity is likely to act as an alternative to participating in a drug-using subculture.

Comprehensive Prevention Programs for Drug Use and Abuse

Comprehensive drug prevention programs range from very broad approaches at the societal level to community-based, to school-based, to family and individual-based drug prevention. Comprehensive prevention programs can include ideological and institutional approaches, methods, and perspectives regarding drug prevention. In essence, comprehensive drug prevention programs are broad-based, affecting both single and multiple groups in a society, and can also include entire societies in how they approach and deal with the problem of drug use and abuse. Next we explore major types of comprehensive drug prevention programs and varying levels.

▮ Harm Reduction Model

The **harm reduction model** is a very broad and comprehensive model that involves society-wide prevention. As an approach to drug use and addiction, this model is practiced in some cities in the Netherlands and the United Kingdom. It is described by Westermeyer as an addiction model that connects "with the addicted community, by having an 'open door policy' that welcomes addicts to take part in services, regardless of level of motivation for change, goals or personal ideology" (Westermeyer n.d.). In a sense, it is a model that meets addicts on their own level.

Westermeyer (n.d.) identifies three central beliefs of the harm reduction model:

1. Excessive behaviors occur along a continuum of risk ranging from minimal to extreme.

harm reduction model
a society-wide approach to drug use and/or abuse that focuses on reducing the harm experienced by the drug user and/or abuser as well as the harm to society

Addictive behaviors are not all-or-nothing phenomena. Although a drug or alcohol abstainer has a lower risk of harm than a drug or alcohol user, a moderate drinker is causing less harm than a binge drinker is; a crystal methamphetamine smoker or sniffer is causing less harm than a crystal injector.

2. Changing addictive behavior is a stepwise process, with complete abstinence being the final step. Those who embrace the harm reduction model believe that any movement in the direction of reduced harm—no matter how small—is positive in and of itself.

3. Sobriety simply is not for everybody. This statement requires the acceptance that many people live in horrible circumstances. Some are able to cope without the use of drugs; others use drugs as a primary means of coping. Until we are in a position to offer an alternative means of survival to these individuals, we are in no position to cast moral judgment. The health and well-being of the individual are of primary concern; if individuals are unwilling or unable to change addictive behavior at this time, they should not be denied services. *Attempts should be made to reduce the harm of their habits as much as possible.*

According to Westermeyer, the Dutch (who created this approach to prevention of drug use and abuse) have "an 80% connection rate with the addicted population," whereas in the United States we are 80% disconnected from our addicted populations. In fact, through our punitive model in dealing with drug users, the strongest connection we have with the addicted population in the United States comes when they are arrested and jailed.

"Harm reduction strategies meet drug users 'where they're at,' addressing conditions of use along with the use itself. . . . HRC [the Harm Reduction Coalition] considers the following principles central to harm reduction practice" (Harm Reduction Coalition [HRC] 2011). The HRC:

- Accepts, for better and for worse, that licit and illicit drug use is part of our world and chooses to work to minimize its harmful effects rather than simply ignore or condemn them.

- Understands drug use as a complex, multifaceted phenomenon that encompasses a continuum of behaviors from severe abuse to total abstinence, and acknowledges that some ways of using drugs are clearly safer than others.

- Establishes quality of individual and community life and well-being—not necessarily cessation of all drug use—as the criteria for successful interventions and policies.

- Calls for the nonjudgmental, noncoercive provision of services and resources to people who use drugs and the communities in which they live in order to assist them in reducing attendant harm.

- Ensures that drug users and those with a history of drug use routinely have a real voice in the creation of programs and policies designed to serve them.

- Affirms drugs users themselves as the primary agents of reducing the harms of their drug use, and seeks to empower users to share information and support each other in strategies that meet their actual conditions of use.

- Recognizes that the realities of poverty, class, racism, social isolation, past trauma, sex-based discrimination, and other social inequalities affect both people's vulnerability to and capacity for effectively dealing with drug-related harm.

- Does not attempt to minimize or ignore the real and tragic harm and danger associated with licit and illicit drug use.

In essence,

Harm reduction seeks to reduce the harms of drug policies dependent on an over-emphasis on interdiction, such as arrest, incarceration, establishment of a felony record, lack of treatment, lack of adequate information about drugs, the expansion of military source control intervention efforts in other countries, and intrusion on personal freedoms. Harm reduction also seeks to reduce the harms caused by an over-emphasis on prohibition, such as increased purity, black market adulterants, black market sale to minors, and black market crime. A harm reduction strategy seeks to protect youth from the dangers of drugs by offering factual, science-based drug education and eliminating youth's black market exposure to drugs. A harm reduction approach advocates lessening the harms of drugs through education, prevention, and treatment. Finally, harm reduction seeks to restore basic human dignity to dealing with the disease of addiction. (AlcoholAnswers.org 2013)

■ Community-Based Drug Prevention

Community-based programs are very broad and take into account the community's youth, parents, businesses, media, schools, law enforcement, religious or fraternal groups, civic or volunteer groups, healthcare professionals, and government agencies with expertise in the field of substance abuse. The primary goal of community-based prevention is to provide coordinated programs among the numerous agencies and organizations involved in prevention.

Prevention requires communities to conduct a structured review of current prevention programs to determine (1) whether the programs in place were examined and tested according to rigorous scientific standards during their development and (2) whether these programs incorporate the basic principles of prevention that have been identified in research. Usually, prevention programs at the community level ask the following questions (Robertson et al. and NIDA 2003; Sloboda and David 1999):

- Does the program have components for the individual, the family, the school, the media, community organizations, and healthcare providers? Are the program components well integrated in theme and content so that they reinforce rather than duplicate one another?

- Does the prevention program use media and community education strategies to increase public awareness, attracting community support, reinforcing the school-based curriculum for students and parents, and keeping the public informed of the program's progress?

- Are interventions carefully designed to reach different at-risk populations, and are they of sufficient duration to make an impact?

- Does the program follow a structured organizational plan that progresses from needs assessment through planning, implementation, and review to refinement, with feedback to and from the community at all stages?

- Are the objectives and activities specific, time-limited, feasible (in terms of available resources), and integrated so that they work together across program components and can be used to evaluate program progress and outcomes?

Often, these programs set up prevention policy boards to oversee planning and implementation.

Boards should include representatives from law enforcement, juvenile justice, education, recreation, social services, private industry, health and mental health agencies, churches, civic organizations, and other community agencies that serve youth and families. They should also include one or several youth members. "The community can be a target group, especially when there is extensive community denial or lack of awareness, lack of clear policies, poor law enforcement, and so on. Public awareness campaigns, political action, and similar efforts are appropriate at this level of prevention" (Tinzmann and Hixson 1992, pp. 2, 3).

Community prevention programs can also direct their attention to changing the legal and social environment regarding alcohol, tobacco, and other drug (**ATOD**) supplies and toward youth (Center for Prevention Research and Development [CPRD] 2000). This effort also includes individual and environmental strategies. For example, an environmental approach to reducing underage drinking might involve training clerks to insist on proper age identification when selling alcoholic beverages. An individual approach might involve education efforts, such as a media campaign, aimed at discouraging young people from drinking (Silver Gate Group and Robert Wood Johnson Foundation 2001).

Other community-based strategies include the following:

- Strengthening the enforcement of existing legal regulations of ATOD sales and use
- Educating merchants and servers about alcohol and tobacco sales laws
- Regulating legislation regarding the sale of alcohol and tobacco to minors
- Implementing use and lose laws, which allow for the suspension of the driver's license of a person younger than 21 years of age following a conviction for any alcohol or drug violation (e.g., use, possession, or attempt to purchase with or without false identification)
- Imposing regulations on location and density of retail outlets—that is, monitoring the number of unsupervised vending machines dispensing cigarettes to minors in a given community and monitoring the number of retail establishments selling alcohol and tobacco near schools

Community-based prevention programs recently have been endorsed, supported as not only viable, but also cost-effective:

Drug use prevention programmes are effective when they respond to the needs of a community, involve all the relevant sectors, and are based on evidence; effective programmes should also incorporate strong monitoring and evaluation components. Such programmes are also cost effective. . . . If other costs to society were to be counted, such as the costs resulting from crime, unemployment, and ill health, the cost effectiveness of good drug use prevention programmes is likely to be even greater. (United Nations Office on Drugs and Crime [UNODC] 2011)

A community-based organization that has to be mentioned is Community Anti-Drug Coalitions of America (CADCA), which was organized in 1992. This organization

. . . has been training local grassroots groups, known as community anti-drug coalitions, in effective problem-solving strategies, teaching them how to assess their local substance abuse-related problems, identify root causes and local conditions and develop comprehensive plans to address them. Today, CADCA is the nation's leading national substance abuse prevention organization, representing the interests of thousands of community coalitions in the United States and around the world. (Community Anti-Drug Coalitions of America [CADCA] 2010)

CADCA's reach includes more than 5000 community coalitions and their affiliates across the United States, and a growing number of community groups around the world. It has 2000 dues-paying members and 17,000 subscribers to its e-newsletter; trains thousands of leaders, members, and volunteers; and even airs a televised program (CADCA TV) that reaches approximately 2.6 million households (CADCA 2010).

The core services that CADCA provides include:

- Training and technical assistance
- Dissemination and coalition relations
- Research and evaluation
- Public policy and advocacy
- Membership and communicating

KEY TERM

ATOD
alcohol, tobacco, and other drugs

- Special events and conferences
- International programs (CADCA 2010)

In conclusion, community prevention emphasizes comprehensive drug abuse prevention programs that include multiple components, such as the use of media, drug education in schools, parent education, community organizations, and formulation of drug-related health policy. In essence, community drug prevention seeks to reduce drug abuse by informing, coordinating, and decreasing the level of drug use at the community level.

■ School-Based Drug Prevention

Education has been used extensively in the past to control the use and abuse of drugs, especially alcohol and tobacco. Drug education actually began in the late 1800s, when most states required that the harmful effects of certain drugs be taught. An example of an early educational attempt to curb or stop drug abuse is the temperance movement in the late 19th century. The Women's Christian Temperance Union (WCTU) and the Anti-Saloon League taught that alcohol consumption was harmful and contrary to Christian morality.

Years ago, when drug prevention was first attempted, most substance abuse experts thought that schools should be responsible for educating the public about the dangerous use and eventual abuse of drugs because education is school's main objective. Schools began teaching about drug use, but in the beginning, drug prevention focused on individual factors, such as the dangers of particular types of drugs, the dangers of trusting individuals who sell drugs, and other scare tactics. One problem with this approach was that students varied enormously with regard to their drug experiences. Often, the students had already tried the dangerous drugs and had experienced only pleasurable effects with few negative consequences. Their experiences occurred before their exposure to drug prevention programs that relied on negative information, which is generally known as the **scare tactic or fear-based approach**. Many self-reported use surveys revealed that these programs were not successful. With such audiences of drug users, the warnings are short lived, not believed, or perceived as exaggerations. Today the use of evidence-based drug education is ". . . based on life skills that offer personal, social, resistance and communication skills, as well as information about the short-term effects of drugs through a series of sessions offered by trained teachers" (UNODC 2011). Another more recent study reported that "[e]valuation has shown fear-based approaches not to be effective. Programmes depending only on information provision or only on boosting self-esteem also appear to be ineffective. Interactive teaching also seems to be necessary for success, with more didactic approaches generally unsuccessful" (Claire 2013, p. 23).

In conclusion, the school-based programs that are the most successful

> . . . [p]rovide information about drugs and alcohol, in particular correcting misperceptions about how common and acceptable substance misuse is among the young people's peer group (normative education). They also teach interpersonal skills to help handle realistic situations where alcohol or drug are available. Examples with strong evidence base include the Life Skills training programme, developed in the United States, and Unplugged, tested in a large scale evaluation across several European countries. (Claire 2013, p. 23)

Table 17.2 summarizes the most popular, common, school-based drug prevention programs by including the premise, strategies, and effectiveness of the following approaches: (1) cognitive, (2) affective, (3) combined cognitive and affective, (4) social learning/cognitive-behavioral, and (5) normative education. Table 17.2 also details the strengths (if any) and weaknesses of each approach.

Finally, two more recent successful school drug prevention programs that "speak" to their audiences are the Athletes Training and Learning to Avoid Steroids (ATLAS) for males and Athletes Targeting Healthy Exercise and Nutrition Alternatives (ATHENA) for females. These two programs target teenage athletes and specifically focus on addressing steroid abuse and other unhealthy behaviors (e.g., drinking and driving). These two programs leverage the influence of coaches and peer groups to highlight proper sports nutrition, strength training, and other positive alternatives to using drugs to improve performance and build confidence. ATLAS and ATHENA have now been adopted by schools in 29 states and Puerto Rico and have been endorsed by Congress as exemplary prevention programs (NIDA 2007).

KEY TERM

scare tactic or fear-based approach
drug prevention information based on emphasizing the extreme negative effects of drug use—scaring the audience of potential and current drug users/abusers into not using drugs

TABLE 17.2 Summary of Common School-Based Drug Prevention Approaches

Approach	Premise	Strategies	Effectiveness
Cognitive	If youth understand the dangers of AOD, they will not use them.	Teach pharmacology of alcohol and other drugs, how they are used, long-range consequences of use—usually through scare tactics.	Seldom effective; sometimes detrimental—arouses curiosity and encourages experimentation. Dire facts are not credible; knowledge alone does not counteract peer pressure. Knowledge is necessary, but not sufficient; focus on more immediate physical/social consequences may work.
Affective	High self-esteem, values consistent with nonuse, and good problem-solving and decision-making skills help youth avoid AOD.	Raise self-esteem. Teach values and life skills. Typically, do not include AOD information.	Do not decrease rate of use. Some community members and parents protest teaching values and decision making. Need to include AOD information.
Combined cognitive and affective	Students need both information and life skills to avoid AOD use.	Teach problem-solving, decision-making, and peer pressure resistance skills and provide explicit information about AOD to connect life skills and AOD use and consequences.	Little consistent effect on reducing AOD use, although some successes have been reported.
Social learning/ cognitive-behavioral	AOD use usually begins in a social setting between grades 5 and 9, usually with peers, but sometimes adults. Youth need skills for resisting these pressures (based on Bandura's social learning theory).	Teach how to identify pressures from peers, media, advertising, and families. Teach resistance skills and model counterarguments. Students role play pressure situations and actively practice resisting.	Sometimes effective, especially if peers are involved in instruction and when students already have other fairly well-developed social skills. Little evidence that effects last.
Normative education	Youth overestimate the extent of AOD use among peers and thus may use AOD to feel part of the group.	Correct misconceptions, demonstrate actual norms through discussion, and develop nonuse norms.	Success with some drugs; not very effective with alcohol. Some youngsters may believe that fewer peers use AOD than actually do, and may come to feel AOD use is more acceptable than they did before entering the program.

AOD, alcohol and other drugs.

Data from Tinzmann, M.B., and J. Hixson. What Does Research Say About Prevention? Oak Brook, IL: North Central Regional Educational Laboratory, 2006.

SCHOOL-BASED PREVENTION POLICIES FOCUSED ON ENFORCEMENT

Grounded in **prohibitionist philosophy** and the law enforcement approach, and largely devoid of public health perspectives and strategies, the following measures have been used to prevent and reduce substance use among students:

- Antismoking policies
- Zero-tolerance policies
- Drug searches
- Drug testing

These law enforcement approaches aimed at middle school and high school students across the United States for the past 10 years and currently in force in many schools represent more hard-lined prohibitionist approaches for reducing and preventing drug use. In many communities

KEY TERM

prohibitionist philosophy (regarding drug use)
reducing and/or stopping unwanted drug use by legally banning and punishing drug use

across the United States as well as in many countries throughout the world there is an extensive variation of opinions regarding their success for curbing recreational drug use, which includes student use of tobacco, alcohol, and other drugs.

CURRICULUM-BASED DRUG EDUCATION OBJECTIVES

In an effort to educate students about the dangers of drug use, school-based drug education programs and objectives have been implemented in most U.S. school curricula. Specific educational topics have been established for elementary, middle school, high school, and college levels.

The elementary level includes the following topics:

- Drugs versus poisons
- Effects of alcohol, tobacco, and marijuana on the body
- Differences between candy and drugs
- Drug overdoses
- Dangers of experimentation
- How to say "no" to peers offering drugs
- Reasons for taking drugs: curing illness, pleasure, escape, parental use, and ceremony

At the middle school level the topics expand to include the following:

- How peer pressure works
- How to say "no" to peer pressure
- How drugs affect the body, physiologically and psychologically
- Where to seek help when needed
- Attitudes toward drug use
- How to have fun without drugs
- Harmful effects of tobacco, alcohol, and marijuana on the body
- Stress management and building positive self-esteem
- How advertisers push drugs
- Consequences of breaking drug laws
- Differences among wine, beer, and distilled spirits
- Family drug use
- Family drinking problems and family members who may have drug addiction problems
- Images of violence and drug use in rock and rap music
- Teenage drug abuse and associated problems

Topics at the high school and college level include the following:

- Responsible use of medications
- How drugs affect the body and the mind

- Legal versus illegal drugs
- Drinking and driving
- Drug effects on the fetus
- Recreational drug use
- Ways of coping with problems: anger and stress management
- How to detect problem drug users
- Drug education, prevention, and treatment
- Positive and negative role models
- How to build positive self-esteem
- Criminal sanctions for various types of drug use
- Binge drinking
- Drugs and driving
- Date rape
- Addiction to drugs and alcoholism

PRINCIPAL QUESTIONS FOR SCHOOL-BASED PROGRAMS

The following questions should be asked to improve the outcomes of drug education programs:

- Do the school-based programs reach children from kindergarten through high school? If not, do they at least reach children during the critical middle school or junior high years?
- Do the programs contain multiple years of intervention (all through the middle school or junior high years)?
- Do the programs use a well-tested, standardized intervention with detailed lesson plans and student materials?
- Do the programs use age-appropriate interactive teaching methods (modeling, role playing, discussion, group feedback, reinforcement, extended practice)?
- Do the programs foster social bonding to the school and community?
- Do the programs teach social competence (communication, self-efficacy, assertiveness) and drug resistance skills that are culturally and developmentally appropriate?
- Do the programs promote positive peer influence?
- Do the programs promote antidrug social norms?
- Do the programs emphasize skills-training teaching methods?
- Do the programs include an adequate "dosage" (10–15 sessions in year 1 and another 10–15 booster sessions)?
- Is there periodic evaluation to determine whether the programs are effective?

▪ Family-Based Prevention Programs

Primary family risk factors that predispose youth to find drugs attractive include the following:

- Chaotic home environments, particularly in which parents abuse substances or suffer from mental illnesses
- Ineffective parenting, especially with children with difficult temperaments and conduct disorders
- Lack of mutual attachments and nurturing

"Results from longitudinal studies of children, particularly those children most at risk for problems, indicate that families can protect children and youth against drug use and abuse through effective family management practices that impart skills young people can use in resisting social pressures to use drugs" (National Institutes of Health [NIH] and NIDA 1998, p. 49).

Although the just-listed risk factors are the primary risk factors, *protective factors*—the factors that can insulate against drug use—include the following:

- Strong parent–child bonds
- Parental monitoring with clear rules of conduct within the family unit and involvement of parents in the lives of their children
- Open communication of values within the family
- High levels of supervision and monitoring
- No inconsistent disciplining from lackadaisical to extreme enforcement of rules and no saying one thing and then doing another
- Consistent high levels of parental warmth, affection, and emotional support

In addition, research shows that protective family factors can moderate the effects of risk factors. The risk of associating with peers who use drugs can be offset by protective family factors, such as parent conventionality, maternal adjustment, and strong parent–child attachment.

Prevention at the family level needs to stress parent–child interaction strategies, communication skills, child management practices, and family management skills. Research has also shown that parents need to take a more active role in their children's

lives. This includes talking to their children about drugs, monitoring their activities, getting to know their friends, and understanding their problems and personal concerns (NIH and NIDA 1998).

PREVENTION PRINCIPLES FOR FAMILY-BASED PROGRAMS

In conclusion, family-based prevention programs need to do the following:

- Reach families of children at each stage of development.
- Train parents in behavioral skills to:
  - Reduce conduct problems in children.
  - Improve parent–child relations, including positive reinforcement, listening and communication skills, and problem solving.
  - Provide consistent discipline and rule making.
  - Monitor children's activities during adolescence.
- Include an educational component for parents with drug information for them and their children.
- Focus on families whose children are in kindergarten through 12th grade to enhance protective factors.
- Provide access to counseling services for families at risk.

▪ Individual-Based Drug Prevention and Treatment: Harm Reduction Psychotherapy

A more recent approach known as **harm reduction therapy (HRT)** uses several treatment models that ". . . can be used in outpatient settings, residential treatment, homeless programs, traditional drug treatment programs, medical services, community outreach programs among other service delivery settings" (Harm Reduction Psychotherapy and Training Associates n.d.).

HRT is based on the belief that alcohol and drug problems including substance abuse and dependence develop in individuals through a unique interaction of biological, psychological, and social factors. HRT is a non-judgmental approach to helping people experiencing alcohol and drug problems to reduce the negative impact of substance use, abuse, or dependence in their lives. Harm Reduction Therapy understands that people use alcohol and drugs for a variety of reasons. It addresses the complex relationship that people develop with these psychoactive substances over the course of their

KEY TERM

harm reduction therapy (HRT)
A nonjudgmental approach to helping people experiencing alcohol and drug problems to reduce the negative impact of substance use, abuse, or dependence in their lives

lives. In HRT, concerns related to drug and alcohol use are addressed simultaneously with their social and occupational impacts as well as their psychological and emotional implications in an integrated treatment approach to these "co-occurring disorders." (Harm Reduction Psychotherapy and Training Associates n.d.)

This type of therapy treatment emphasizes collaboration, respect, and self-determination, which differs from traditional addiction treatment. Traditional drug treatment generally follow a 12-step program (much like AA and NA) and often use varying amounts of confrontation and coercion in their treatment programs. (For another example of a semi- or *quasi*-type of harm reduction drug prevention and treatment method, see "Case in Point: A Departure from Conventional Drug Prevention and Treatment: A New Alternative—A Nontreatment Program for Alcohol and Drug Abuse.")

► CASE IN POINT

A Departure from Drug Prevention and Treatment: A New Alternative—A Nontreatment Program for Alcohol and Drug Abuse

Solving an addiction problem involving alcohol and other drugs without treatment? Addiction to drugs is *not* genetically inherited? A program for moderating or abstaining from drug use and/or abuse that flies in the face of Alcoholics Anonymous (AA) by claiming that drug addiction is *not* a disease? " . . . Treatment and 12 step based programs are less successful than no treatment at all?" (Baldwin Research Institute [BRI] 2010).

A program for moderating or abstaining from alcohol and other drugs with a better than 62% success rate verified by outside independent research organizations?

The Saint Jude Retreats, which offer the St. Jude Program, does not advocate belief in the disease of addiction myth. There is no disease of alcoholism; there is no disease of drug abuse; and, there is no disease of addiction! This is just one of many areas where the Saint Jude Program departs from treatment and why the Saint Jude Program is significantly more effective than the treatment model. Teaching our guests the need for personal responsibility for their actions rather than making excuses for poor behavior and choices, is the cornerstone to rebuilding their life. A disease by its very nature is out of the person's control. This is simply not the case with substance abuse. Substance abusers make the choice to abuse alcohol and drugs. Choice is a behavior, not a disease. (BRI 2013)

This program is based on the Freedom Model Law of Universal Motivation, which proves an individual's behavior is freely chosen. "The primary responsibility for one's life improvements is to be held by the individual rather than the program or staff" (BRI 2010). The program emphasizes learning through "doing" and "experiencing," and provides Certified Cognitive Behavioral Education Presenters to teach methods of self-change (BRI 2010). In contrast to Alcoholics Anonymous (AA), St. Jude replaces the disease model with cognitive behavioral change (through their proprietary Cognitive Behavioral Education, or CBE methods), in which participants set their own goals regarding either cessation from a drug or drugs or learning to personally moderate their drug use, as well as many other life-enhancing improvements. It is an educational/social-centered program, not medically staff centered. All detox services are completed prior to entry into the educational programs.

The Saint Jude Program is completely nontreatment based.

Treatment centers (many publicly funded) dispense a strange brew of indoctrination, religion, and medicine in a *faux*-hospital setting and admixture of medically supervised detox, three hots and a cot, misleading education, therapy and large doses of 12-step meetings. Discharge is marked by the admonition: "Don't drink and go to meetings." (BRI 2010)

None of this has been proven to be successful with heavy drinkers or drug users.

Finally, from a personal interview with one of the directors at Baldwin Research Institute, a significant proportion of clients enter the Saint Jude Program as a result of not succeeding in eliminating their drug use problems from previous treatment program stays. These individuals find relief in knowing that a nontreatment alternative exists.

Reproduced from Baldwin Research Institute (BRI). "The Saint Jude Retreats." Amsterdam, NY: Baldwin Research Institute (BRI), 2013. Available http://www.baldwinresearch.com/jude-thaddeus-program.cfm; Baldwin Research Institute (BRI). "Baldwin Research Project 1991." Amsterdam, NY: Baldwin Research Institute (BRI), 2010. Available http://www.baldwinresearch.com/baldwinproject1991-2.cfm

Drug Prevention Programs in Higher Education

The seriousness of alcohol and other drug use on college campuses is underscored by the following findings (Cal Poly 2013):

- According to the Core Institute, an organization that surveys college drinking practices, 300,000 of today's college students will eventually die of alcohol-related causes, such as drunken driving accidents, cirrhosis of the liver, various cancers, and heart disease.
- Of today's first-year college students, 159,000 will drop out of school next year because of alcohol or other drug-related reasons.
- Almost one-third of college students admit to having missed at least one class because of their alcohol or drug use.
- One night of heavy drinking can impair a person's ability to think abstractly for up to 30 days, limiting the ability to relate textbook reading to classroom discussions or to think through processes such as football plays.

As we can see, the use of alcohol and other drugs is a serious problem within the college or university environment. Major problems on college campuses resulting from such drug abuse include property damage, poor academic performance, damaged relationships, unprotected sexual activity, physical injuries, date rape, and suicide (Perkins 1997).

It is obvious that with all these negative findings regarding alcohol and other drug use on college campuses, prevention programs are vital. Next, we review the major prevention programs that currently exist in higher education.

▌ Overview and Critique of Existing Prevention Programs

This next section will review and critique four drug prevention program models in higher education. The four programs are information-only or awareness model, attitude change model or affective education model, social influences model, and the ecological or person-in-environment model. The first model, information-only or awareness model, is solely based on teaching about drug information, primarily the effects of using different types of drugs. This model heavily relies on making students knowledgeable about various drugs. The second model, attitude change or affective education model, works on attitude change and the role of self-esteem regarding drug use and abuse. The third model, social influences model, focuses on how to use resistance skills when drugs are readily available in a student's environment, taking into account such social psychological factors as prior socialization and peer pressure. The fourth model, ecological or person-in-environment model, looks at how changes in a student's social environment can affect attitudes about drugs and drug use.

INFORMATION-ONLY OR AWARENESS MODEL

One of the earliest preventive interventions, this model is based on the belief that if people are given extensive information about the harmful effects of drugs, it will change their attitudes about use and abuse. This model assumes that people are rational enough to seriously curtail or stop drug use based on information. Obviously, today we know that, at most, the majority of drug users exposed to the **information-only or awareness model** become more knowledgeable about the effects of drugs, but this approach has very little influence on the use of habitual or addictive-type drugs.

ATTITUDE CHANGE OR AFFECTIVE EDUCATION MODEL

The **attitude change or affective education model** assumes that people use drugs because they have poor self-esteem (Gonzalez and Clement 1994). As a result, prevention focuses on strengthening self-image, building up positive self-esteem, and boosting self-confidence. A problem with this model is that attitudes often are resistant to change and fluctuate depending on such environmental influences as peer and party settings. Attitudes that were formed in an educational setting (drug and alcohol classes) are abandoned in substance use settings.

KEY TERMS

information-only or awareness model
assumes that teaching about the harmful effects of drugs will change attitudes about use and abuse

attitude change or affective education model
assumes that people use drugs because of lack of self-esteem

SOCIAL INFLUENCES MODEL

The **social influences model** assumes that substance abuse results from multiple influences. Although outside influences are perceived as major influences, inner influences, such as prior socialization, a vulnerability to pleasing others, and a need to be accepted by friends and peers, are likewise taken into account. This prevention strategy emphasizes peer resistance and inoculation techniques. Techniques primarily include the following (Gonzalez and Clement 1994):

- Offering factual information about the consequences of drug use
- Guiding development of skills to recognize outer and inner pressures to use drugs and methods and techniques to resist usage
- Communicating correct information about the extent of drug use by students of similar ages
- Modeling, rehearsing, and reinforcing skills for resisting drugs when friends or peers expect compliance
- Persuading students to try these resistance approaches and techniques in classroom or group settings and in peer group settings away from the classroom

By far, this method has been more successful than the information-only and attitude change models. Although it works best when it begins at the junior high school level, refresher courses should be administered at least every 2 years. Some research findings indicate that although this method is least effective with alcohol consumption, it is effective with marijuana and cigarette smoking (Gonzalez and Clement 1994).

ECOLOGICAL OR PERSON-IN-ENVIRONMENT MODEL

This model is one of the newest types of prevention programs. "Interventions based on this model have multiple components and are designed to address individuals and the policies, practices, and social norms that affect students on campuses or in the community" (Gonzalez and Clement 1994, p. 3). Developed from human ecology, the **ecological or person-in-environment model** stresses that change(s) in the environment change people. Although the ecological or person-in-environment model does not ignore substance use from individual causes, such as personal beliefs and perception of risk, it does primarily focus on the causes from the social environment (Hansen 1997, p. 6).

"The central tenet [belief] of social ecology is that individual behavior is mainly the result of socialization; to change the behavior, we must change the social institutions that shape it" (Hansen 1997, p. 6). Hansen also stated "the strongest predictors of alcohol and drug abuse among young people are social" (p. 6).

This perspective emphasizes that it is important to take into account all of the environments that may have an impact on drug use. Friends, acquaintances, roommates, and classmates in dorms, sororities, and fraternities and at parties, cafes, and nightspots can influence students (U.S. Department of Education 1994).

As a result, this model advocates the following drug prevention strategies (Gonzalez and Clement 1994):

- Dissemination of drug information
- Cognitive and behavioral skills training for youth, parents, and professionals
- Mass media programming
- Development of grassroots citizen interest groups
- Leadership training for key organization and community officials
- Policy analysis and reformulation

In applying this model to the college campus, we find that college campuses have long served as an environment for initiating and perpetuating drug use and abuse. Fraternity drunkenness, for example, was decried as early as 1840 (Horowitz 1987). In 1988, an 18-year-old student attending Rutgers University died of alcohol poisoning at a fraternity party. In a television interview following the incident, then-Chancellor Edward Bloustein described fraternities as "organized conspiracies dedicated to the consumption of alcohol" (Hansen 1997, p. 5).

Using the ecological or person-in-environment model as a preventative measure can alleviate drug use and abuse on college campuses, lessening the vast majority of vandalism, fights, accidents, sexually

KEY TERMS

social influences model
assumes that drug users lack resistance skills

ecological or person-in-environment model
stresses that changes in the environment change people's attitudes about drugs

transmitted infections, unplanned pregnancies, racial bias incidents, date rape, and at least one-third of academic attrition often caused by drug use and abuse (Koss, Gidycz, and Wisniewski 1987). Although campus prevention programs and research date back several decades, such efforts remained isolated and sporadic until the late 1970s. All campuses now have medium to extensive alcohol and other drug prevention programs in effect. Tailoring this type of prevention to college environments is certainly worthy of consideration.

Finally, a variant of this model, which was originally formulated to focus on violence (Centers for Disease Control and Prevention 2009), takes into account other, larger factors regarding drug use and abuse. The **social-ecological model** considers the complex interplay among individuals, relationships, communities, and societal factors. This model (refocused by this author to more directly apply to drug use) emphasizes multiple interacting factors that put individuals at risk for experiencing and later becoming addicted to drug use. The main focus takes into consideration not just individual influencing factors, but also the particular drug users' types of social relationships (e.g., presence of many friends who use drugs), the community, and societal factors (e.g., chaotic drug-infested societies where drug dealing and drug use are common). The social-ecological model includes multiple influencing factors in a person's environment.

Examples of Large-Scale Drug Prevention Programs

▌ BACCHUS Peer Education Network

In 1975, an organization known as Boosting Alcohol Consciousness Concerning the Health of University Students (BACCHUS) was developed as a national student organization. Soon BACCHUS realized that many of its affiliates were members of sororities and fraternities; therefore, it renamed the organization, then known as BACCHUS and GAMMA (Greeks Advocating Mature Management of Alcohol), to the **BACCHUS Network** effective July 1, 2005. A more recent description includes the following:

> BACCHUS is a network of more than 8,000 student leaders and advisors who work with over four million peers on more than 330 campuses nationwide. Our Members are found on four-year public colleges and universities, private and two-year institutions, historically Black colleges and universities, predominantly Hispanic population campuses, and tribal colleges. (BACCHUS Network 2013)

The original goal of this program was to prevent alcohol abuse. Today, the program has broadened its goals to include other student health and safety issues, such as sexual responsibility, tobacco use, marijuana use, and sexual assault. The organization devotes a substantial portion of its resources and activities to the following goals on university-affiliated campuses:

- Create and foster a thriving network of institutions and young adult–led peer education groups supporting health and safety initiatives
- Empower students and administrators to voice their opinions and needs to create healthier and safer campus communities
- Develop and promote cutting edge resources and health promotion campaigns that support peer education, campus leadership, and activism on health and safety issues
- Provide exceptional conferencing and training opportunities for students, young adults, and professionals to support health and safety strategies
- Encourage national forums on young adult health and safety concerns
- Promote and disseminate research and effective strategies that better help campuses and communities address health and safety issues
- Advocate for effective and sensible policies and practices for campus and community health and safety issues (BACCHUS Network 2007, 2011)

The BACCHUS philosophy is that students can play a uniquely effective role—unmatched by professional educators—in encouraging their peers to consider, talk honestly about, and develop

KEY TERMS

social-ecological model
a variant of the ecological or person-in-environment model that takes into account multiple factors regarding drug use and abuse and focuses on the complex interplay among individuals, relationships, communities, and societal factors

BACCHUS Network
a national and international association of college and university peer education programs focused on alcohol abuse prevention and other related student health and safety issues

responsible habits and attitudes toward high-risk health and safety issues. The organization now hosts four web sites to assist students in their prevention efforts. Bacchusnetwork.org contains information about the organization's activities, services, conferences, campaigns, and resource materials. Smartersex.org addresses sexual health, features an "Ask the Sexpert" area, and offers complete information on sexually transmitted infections, human immunodeficiency virus (HIV), abstinence, and birth control. TobaccofreeU.org contains complete information on tobacco control, prevention, and cessation. Friendsdrivesober .org is the newest addition to the network and focuses primarily on highway safety and preventing impaired driving (BACCHUS Network 2007). The network:

> . . . is a university- and community-based network focusing on comprehensive health and safety initiatives. It is the mission of this . . . nonprofit organization to actively promote student- and young adult-based, campus- and community-wide leadership on healthy and safe lifestyle decisions concerning alcohol abuse, tobacco use, illegal drug use, unhealthy sexual practices, and other high-risk behaviors. (BACCHUS Network 2007, p. 1)

Currently there are 120 educational resources and training materials offered by our organization. In addition, each affiliate group receives health issue campaigns that, when used in combination, lay the foundation for a year-round prevention program:

- National Collegiate Alcohol Awareness Week (alcohol and high risk drinking)
- Tobacco Prevention and Cessation (control, policy, programs, advocacy)
- Impaired Driving Prevention (designated driver, safe ride, laws, awareness)
- Sexual Responsibility Awareness (sexual health, HIV/AIDS-STIs and relationship issues)
- Safe Spring Break (alcohol, impaired driving, predatory drugs, sun safety, personal safety)

Campaigns consist of health topic message promotion and resource manuals that contain the latest research and data, program delivery ideas, model programs, and marketing strategies. (BACCHUS Network 2013)

■ Fund for the Improvement of Postsecondary Education Drug Prevention Programs

In 1987, a huge explosion of campus drug prevention programs began. It was sparked by a $14 billion annual budget for college drug prevention placed in the Drug-Free Schools and Communities Act of 1986 (now titled the Safe and Free Schools and Communities Act). The funding was parceled out by the Department of Education, Fund for the Improvement of Postsecondary Education (FIPSE). FIPSE Drug Prevention Programs awarded about 100 grants per year from 1987 until 1996 via a grant competition that called for colleges to mount institution-wide programs. The guiding philosophy included the following points:

- A small, isolated program was seen as making little difference, but a comprehensive program reaching into several areas of the institution could send many consistent anti-use messages that would eventually reach critical mass and change the campus environment.
- There should be well-known, top-down administrative support for prevention programming.
- There should be well-written and carefully implemented policies about chemical use on campus.

The hundreds of new programs, whose administrators met and interacted in annual grantee conferences, generated the sense that there was a national prevention movement in higher education. The Network of Colleges and Universities Dedicated to Prevention of Alcohol and Other Drug Abuse was founded, incorporating 900 institutions. The network is supported by the Higher Education Center for Alcohol and Other Drug Prevention funded by the U.S. Department of Education, which provides a range of materials and newsletters (Ryan, Colthurst, and Segars 1995). Unfortunately, such large-scale efforts when evaluated years later (at the turn of the century) indicated that federally funded drug prevention on most college campuses had very mixed results often indicating weak success, and as a result most of the funding programs were discontinued.

More recently, ". . .many college and universities have implemented prevention programs, or, within counseling centers, intervention efforts to meet the needs of the institution and it students" (Larimer et al. 2005, p. 446). This finding by researchers also indicates that although implementing such individually based, specific college and university prevention programs is commendable, implementing new drug prevention programs without evaluating the impact of these programs is totally lacking on most college campuses. In other words, colleges or universities also need to rigorously assess and evaluate the effectiveness of their drug prevention programs—colleges and universities need to couple drug prevention programs with assessment.

From more than a decade of experience, several exemplary approaches emerged. These strategies might be the predominant focus of a program or one of a number of complementary components of a comprehensive effort. The strategies are addressed next.

PEER-BASED EFFORTS

Student peers can be involved in a number of ways: as educators, mentors, counselors, or facilitators of prevention and outreach work. Such an approach multiplies manpower tremendously, reaches the students who are apt to become lost in the flow, is not perceived as an outside or authoritarian intrusion, speaks the language of students, and works to change the predominant cultural tone on campus. Peers can conduct classroom presentations, work informational tables or drop-in centers, create prevention newsletters, and establish links to community groups. It is important to carefully train and supervise peer facilitators. Many peer programs are residence hall based, taking advantage of the training of residence hall assistants and peer facilitators (BACCHUS and GAMMA 1994).

CURRICULUM INFUSION

Infusion of a skill or topic across the curriculum has been used in conjunction with classes on writing skills, gender issues, and other areas. Curriculum infusion can be undertaken at individual institutions or as a consortium project. The advantage of curriculum infusion is that it involves faculty members, achieves open discussion of drug issues in the classroom as part of the normal educational process, and stimulates critical thinking about drug issues.

IMPROVISATIONAL THEATER GROUPS

Improvisational theater groups that tackle health and wellness issues can be lively, stimulating, and provocative, often breaking through peer and institutional denial and bringing issues home to students with a dramatic emotional impact.

Improvisational topics can include date rape, sexually transmitted disease, children of alcoholics on campus, and denial of chemical dependency.

STRATEGIES TO CHANGE MISPERCEPTIONS OF USE

Social psychologists Alan Berkowitz and Wesley Perkins, both of Hobart and William Smith Colleges, have conducted influential research illustrating that students often have incorrect estimates (exaggerated misperceptions) of drug use by their peers (Perkins 1991, 1997; Perkins and Berkowitz 1986). Thus, they misperceive the peer norms governing drug use, which may lead them to follow imaginary peers. This idea is a modification of the traditional understanding that peers influence peers. It follows logically that activities demonstrating the accurate use pattern to students and correcting misperceptions will indirectly affect overall use patterns. These efforts have included simply publicizing the results of alcohol and drug use surveys and awarding prizes for coming up with correct estimates.

ALTERNATIVE EVENTS

Alternative events, such as alcohol-free cocktail parties ("mocktail" parties), alcohol-free gatherings, and indoor rock climbing, especially as alternatives to presporting events and holiday parties, help avoid some events that are traditionally associated with chemical abuse.

PROGRAMS THAT CHANGE MARKETING OF ALCOHOL ON AND NEAR CAMPUSES

Until recently, institutions of higher education were a major focus of alcohol marketing. Alcoholic beverage producers sponsor many campus events, and these companies buy considerable newspaper advertising. One report indicates,

> Alcohol advertising is pervasive in college sporting events. According to a recent report in *USA Today,* "NCAA tournament games led all other sports events in alcohol-related TV advertising in 2002, with 939 ads costing $28 million. That compares with a combined 925 ads aired during the Super Bowl, World Series, college bowl games and the NFL's Monday Night Football." (StateUniversity.com 2011)

Beginning in 1991,

> The OIG [Office of Inspector General of the U.S.] . . . reviewed the voluntary codes then in effect under the auspices of the Beer Institute,

the Wine Institute, the Distilled Spirits Council of the United States (DISCUS) . . . , and an alcohol industry umbrella group, the Century Council. In particular, the review looked at the elements of the voluntary codes that were related to "youth appeal." . . . The OIG concluded: "While the industry advertising standards purport to guide alcohol advertisers towards responsible behavior, they fail to prevent advertising considered to have youth appeal" (Office of Inspector General, 1991:14). (Bonnie et al., 2004)

Further, "Like The Beer Institute, the DISCUS code calls for advertising not to be placed where most of audience is reasonably expected to be below the legal purchase age." In addition, distilled spirits companies are told not to advertise on "college or university campuses," including their newspapers; however, marketing activities are allowed if they are "in licensed retail establishments located on such campuses" (Bonnie et al., 2004).

From the findings above and the fact that most students on college campuses are underage with regard to purchasing and using alcohol, there is pressure on the alcohol industry to restrict influencing students about alcohol on college campuses with the likelihood that today it is "bad business to promote alcohol on college campuses."

Finally, it is better to embed prevention messages within an overall wellness perspective. Students are concerned about health and wellness issues, not programs that come off as dogmatic or preachy, moralizing, exaggerating, and nagging—perhaps reminding them of life at home.

■ Drug Abuse Resistance Education (D.A.R.E.)

One major drug prevention program that had high hopes for success was the school-based drug education programs incorporated into our nation's school districts—**Drug Abuse Resistance Education (D.A.R.E.)**.

Established in 1983, D.A.R.E. operates in about 75% of all school districts across the United States and in numerous foreign countries. In addition to the D.A.R.E. elementary school curriculum, the D.A.R.E. program includes middle school and high school curricula that reinforce lessons taught at the elementary school level. "In fiscal year 2000, the Department of Justice's Bureau of Justice Assistance, which supports various substance abuse

prevention programs for youth, provided about $2 million for D.A.R.E. regional training centers to support the training of new police officers that help deliver the D.A.R.E. program lessons" (quoted from U.S. Government Accountability Office [GAO] in Common Sense for Drug Policy 2009).

D.A.R.E. (Drug Abuse Resistance Education) administers a school-based substance abuse, gang, and violence prevention program in 75% of US school districts and in 48 countries (as of 2013). Since 1983, police officers have taught the D.A.R.E. program to over 200 million K–12 students worldwide—approximately 114 million in the United States alone. Proponents say that D.A.R.E. has helped prevent drug use in elementary, middle, and high school students. They contend that D.A.R.E. improves social interaction between police officers, students, and schools, is the most prevalent substance abuse prevention program in the United States, and is popular with kids and parents. Opponents say that dozens of peer-reviewed studies conclude the D.A.R.E. program is ineffective at preventing kids from using drugs. They contend that D.A.R.E. causes kids to ignore legitimate information about the relative harms of drugs, and that D.A.R.E. is even associated with increased drug use. (ProCon.org 2013)

Recent evaluations of this program show that, on a short-term basis, D.A.R.E. improved students' views of themselves and increased their sense of personal responsibility. However, the program has *not* yielded a measurable, significant change in drug use (Rosenbaum and Hanson 1998; Vogt 2003, p. 1). Moreover, this drug education program showed a strong inconsistency between students' self-reported attitudes about use and actual drug use (Clayton et al. 1991; Ennett et al. 1994; Vogt 2003). See "Holding the Line: D.A.R.E.: Frustrating and Poor Results from a National Drug Prevention Program" for more information on the D.A.R.E. program.

KEY TERM

Drug Abuse Resistance Education (D.A.R.E.)
drug education program presented in elementary and junior high/middle schools nationwide by police officers

HOLDING THE LINE

D.A.R.E.: Frustrating and Poor Results from a National Drug Prevention Program

In 1995, a disturbing study published by a group of researchers at the University of Michigan and backed by the U.S. Department of Health and Human Services (DHHS) and the National Institute on Drug Abuse (NIDA) showed that the use of illicit drugs by young people had been rising steadily since 1992. The results of this study were even more perplexing because overall drug use had been declining over the same period. The increase was happening despite several seemingly successful efforts to combat drug abuse with high-powered prevention programs.

Since the 1980s, most funds allocated for drug prevention have been spent in three areas: criminal justice, major advertising campaigns, and D.A.R.E. Law enforcement professionals who work with hard-core addicts, especially in poor urban neighborhoods, have favored compulsory preventive programs. According to William N. Brownsberger, former Assistant State Attorney General in the Massachusetts Narcotics and Special Investigations Division, addicts who are forced against their will to enter and remain in therapy can overcome their addiction. Roughly 90% of all addicts are arrested at least once every year, giving the criminal justice system plenty of opportunities to help them kick their habits.

One highly visible persuasive effort to end drug abuse has been the advertising campaign created by the Partnership for a Drug-Free America. The nation's advertising industry developed the partnership and funded it by collaborating with advertisers and a variety of health and educational agencies. The goal was to promote images designed to make drug use look "uncool," especially to younger people. In addition to the creative services donated by advertising agencies, media organizations donated more than $2 billion of public service and advertising space to the partnership between the late 1980s and 1990s.

In the early 1990s, the partnership commissioned surveys to measure the effect of its media campaign on students in the Los Angeles and New York City school systems. On both coasts, increased exposure to the partnership's messages appeared to dramatically change students' attitudes toward drugs. At the same time, however, the number of students who admitted using drugs actually increased.

Another high-visibility persuasive effort has been the nationwide D.A.R.E. program, which was launched in Los Angeles in 1983. "D.A.R.E.'s curriculum reflects mainstream theories about the best way to reduce drinking, smoking, and drug use by children. . . . The program began as collaboration between the Los Angeles Police Department and the city's school district" (Miller 2001, p. A14). Using role-playing techniques and resistance training, uniformed police officers become social workers, talking with students in their classrooms, educating them about the dangers of drugs, and giving them the tools to resist temptation or peer pressure. They generally teach 17 classroom sessions.

> Today most school-based prevention programs, including D.A.R.E., assume that adolescents need grown-ups' help in resisting social pressures to use [drugs]. Therefore, they try to correct children's exaggerated beliefs about the prevalence of drug use among their peers. They offer them information about the physical and social effects of using and they try to impart "resistance skills" for making and acting on thoughtful decisions. (Miller 2001, p. A14)

Although D.A.R.E. is the most popular drug education program ever developed for children, increasing numbers of critics claim that its benefits, if any, are short lasting. Most D.A.R.E. training begins in the fifth grade. At this age, students accept most of what they hear. By middle school, however, the effectiveness of D.A.R.E. begins to erode. By high school, many students resist participation in the program. According to a researcher from the Research Triangle Institute in Durham, North Carolina, which conducted a $300,000 study on the impact of D.A.R.E., "Unless there's some sort of booster session that reinforces the original curriculum, the effects of most drug use prevention programs decay rather than increase over time." The findings of numerous research studies conducted on D.A.R.E.'s effectiveness suggest that D.A.R.E. students were no less likely to use drugs than students who had not gone through the program (Ennett et al. 1994; Vogt 2003, p. 3). Some have even claimed that the D.A.R.E. program teaches kids to become curious about illicit drug use or actually motivates them to do drugs (Vogt

2003, p. 3). Further, "Among the notable quotations from researchers: 'is well established that D.A.R.E doesn't work' Glbert Botvin, Cornell Medical Center. 'Research shows that, no, D.A.R.E. hasn't been effective in reducing drug use' William Modzeleski, top drug education official at the Department of Education" (Plant et al. 2011, 147).

Another major negative finding came from the U.S. Government Accountability Office (GAO), which released a review of current research findings regarding alcohol and other drug abuse prevention programs, particularly D.A.R.E., in 2003. In brief, the six long-term evaluations of the D.A.R.E. elementary school curriculum that we reviewed found no significant differences in illicit drug use between students who received D.A.R.E. in the fifth or sixth grade (the intervention group) and students who did not (the control group). Three of the evaluations reported that the control groups of students were provided other drug use prevention education. All of the evaluations suggested that D.A.R.E. had no statistically significant long-term effect on preventing youth illicit drug use. Of the six evaluations we reviewed, five also reported on students' attitudes toward illicit drug use and resistance to peer pressure and found no significant differences between the intervention and control groups over the long term. Two of these evaluations found that the D.A.R.E. students showed stronger negative attitudes about illicit drug use and improved social skills about illicit drug use about 1 year after receiving the program. These positive effects diminished over time (U.S. Government Accountability Office [GAO] 2003, p. 2).

In this same report, seven school districts using the D.A.R.E. program were intensely analyzed. The findings indicated that "No statistically significant differences were observed between the intervention and control schools on students' past year marijuana use 2 years after the intervention" (GAO 2003, p. 5).

Further, "[a]s D.A.R.E. America celebrated its 20th anniversary, the nation's most widely used school-based drug prevention program was struggling with a credibility crisis that has devastated the organization financially and threatens its survival" (Vogt 2003). Reports indicate that a number of school districts throughout the country have abandoned the program, finding D.A.R.E. to be ineffective in curbing both licit and illicit drug use.

In light of the diminishing returns from various drug prevention programs, in late 1996 the Clinton administration proposed a compulsory drug test for teenagers who are applying for their driver's licenses. Like everything else, the proposal had both supporters and critics. Although this tactic may be part of the answer, prevention programs that have measurable, long-lasting effects remain difficult to find.

Data from Brownsberger, W. N. "Just Say 'Criminal Justice.' " *Boston Globe* (20 October 1996); Ennett, S. T., N. S. Tobler, C. L. Ringwalt, and R. L. Flewelling. "How Effective Is Drug Abuse Resistance Education? A Meta-Analysis of Project D.A.R.E. Outcome Evaluations." *American Journal of Public Health* 84 (1994): 1394–1401; Gordon, P. "The Truth About D.A.R.E." *Buzz Magazine* (July 1996); Gordon, P. "Can Madison Avenue Really Save America by Making Illegal Drugs Totally Uncool?" *Buzz Magazine* (August 1996); Miller, D. W. "D.A.R.E. Reinvents Itself—With Help from Its Social-Scientist Critics." *Chronicle of Higher Education* 48 (19 October 2001): A12–A14; U.S. Government Accountability Office (GAO). *Youth Illicit Drug Use Prevention: D.A.R.E. Long-Term Evaluation and Federal Efforts to Identify Effective Programs.* GAO-03-172R. Washington, DC: U.S. Government Accountability Office (GAO), 15 January 2003; Plant, M., R. Robertson, M. Plant, and P. Miller. *Drug Nation: Patterns, Problems, Panics, and Politics.* Oxford, UK: Oxford University Press, 2011: 147; and Vogt, A. "Now Many 'Just Say No' to D.A.R.E." *Chicago Tribune* (26 January 2003): 1, 3.

One major problem is that "over the past decade, a flurry of studies—by the U.S. surgeon general and the General Accounting Office, among others—found no significant difference in drug use between D.A.R.E. graduates and students never exposed to the curriculum" (Vogt 2003, p. 1; see also Plant et al. 2011). Further, regarding graduates of the D.A.R.E. program, one official said, "I can't tell you how many kids told me D.A.R.E. introduced them to drugs. The problem with D.A.R.E., other than that it's a multimillion dollar conglomerate in the business of selling T-shirts, is that it takes the burden off parents to raise their kids [drug free]" (Vogt 2003, p. 3).

Another major problem that has been identified is that the D.A.R.E. drug education program is presented in the classroom by fully uniformed police officers. Although the officers are well intentioned and their efforts are commendable, they are hardly a mechanism for transmitting new norms that would find converts among students, except perhaps those already successfully socialized (Gopelrud 1991). More importantly, uniformed police officers used as teachers "sends the wrong message that drugs are a law enforcement issue, rather than a public health issue" (Zeese and Lewin 1998, p. 1).

■ Drug Courts

Although these courts of law vary in organization, in scope, and at what point intervention occurs, the underlying premise is that drug possession and use is not only a law enforcement/criminal justice problem, but also a public health problem (Sherin and Mahoney 1996). "A drug court is a specialized or problem-solving court-based program that targets criminal offenders and parents with pending child welfare cases who have alcohol and other drug addiction and dependency problems" (National Institute of Justice [NIJ] 2011). Even though adult drug courts vary in target population, program model, and resources, they are generally based on a comprehensive model involving the following (NIJ 2011):

- Offender assessment
- Judicial interaction
- Monitoring (e.g., drug testing) and supervision
- Graduated sanctions and incentives
- Treatment services

In *drug court programs*, criminal justice agencies collaborate closely with the substance abuse treatment community and other societal institutions to design and operate the program. "Drug court programs are usually managed by a nonadversarial and multidisciplinary team. Recent research has shown that the stability of a drug court program and its judge play a key role in successful case management and reducing offender recidivism" (NIJ 2011).

The key goal is to divert substance abusers into supervised community treatment centers in an attempt to eliminate the destructive behavior. A committee usually composed of a judge, the district attorney, a public defender, the probation department, and treatment center officials determines whether treatment is needed and the type and length of treatment. A recent review of drug courts emphasizes that today such courts use a multidisciplinary team approach. "The most effective Drug Courts require regular attendance by the judge, defense counsel, prosecutor, treatment providers and law enforcement officers at staff meetings and status hearings" (Marlowe 2010, p. 4, quoting Carey et al. 2008).

Table 17.3 contains the results of a research evaluation of a multisite adult drug court program. The 20 sampled drug courts were evaluated based on the staffing characteristics and frequency of staffing, who attended the staffing, participation in the staffing, who ran the staffing, who made the

TABLE 17.3 Observed Drug Court Team Staffing Meetings at 20 Drug Court Sites

Staffing Characteristics	Results
Frequency of Staffing	
Every other week	10%
Weekly	75%
More than once a week	15%
Who Attends the Staffing[1]	
Judge(s)	100%
Project/resource coordinator(s)	85%
Defense attorney(s)	85%
Prosecutor(s)	80%
Treatment liaison(s)	70%
Case manager(s)	50%
Probation officer(s)	50%
Others	
Clerk(s)	20%
Law Enforcement (police/corrections)	15%
Drug court administration	15%
Mental health	10%
Health department	5%
Participation in the Staffing (scale of 1 to 5)	
Judge(s)	4.9
Project/resource coordinator(s)	3.7
Defense attorney(s)	2.7
Prosecutor(s)	2.7
Treatment liaison(s)	3.8
Case manager(s)	3.3
Probation officer(s)	2.9
Who Runs the Staffing	
Judge	55%
Project/resource coordinator	35%
Both	10%

TABLE 17.3 Observed Drug Court Team Staffing Meetings at 20 Drug Court Sites (*continued*)

Staffing Characteristics	Results
Who Made the Final Decisions on Participant Response	
Judge(s)	75%
Team consensus	25%
Length of Staffing Meeting (in minutes)[2]	
Mean across courts	64.85
Range across courts	13.00–170.00
Average Discussion per Case (in minutes)	
Mean across courts	2.64
Range across courts	0.60–6.00

[1]Multi-site Adult Drug Court Evaluation (MADCE) team observers rated the level of participation of each drug court team member on a scale of 1 to 5, with 1 being "did not participate" and 5 being "participated thoroughly."

[2]This reflects the length of the staffing meeting observed; the MADCE team made every effort to observe the whole meeting.

Reproduced from Zweig, J. M. "Chapter 2. Description of the Drug Court Sites in the Multi-Site Adult Drug Court Evaluation." In *The Multi-Site Adult Drug Court Evaluation: The Drug Court Experience*, by S. B. Rossman, J. M. Zweig, D. Kralstein, K. Henry, P. M. Downey, and C. Lindquist, 8–23. Washington, DC: Urban Institute Justice Policy Center, 2011.

final decisions on participant response, length of time in minutes of staffing meetings, and the average discussion time in minutes per case (Zweig 2011). Table 17.3 shows that 75% of the sampled drug courts held weekly staff meetings; that the judge(s), project/resource coordinator(s), defense attorney(s), and prosecutor(s) primarily attended the staffing; and that the judge(s) run the staffing meetings in 55% of the 20 courts sampled. (See Table 17.3 for more detailed findings.)

At the first National Drug Court Conference, one researcher reported, "These courts rely on strong collaboration among judges, prosecutors, defense lawyers, and related supporting agencies (such as case management, corrections, pretrial services, probation), on the one hand, and a partnership with treatment agencies (or providers) and other community organizations and representatives on the other" (Goldkamp 1993, p. 33). The treatment phase generally consists of: (1) detoxification (removal of physical dependence on drugs from the body), (2) stabilization (treating the psychological craving for the drug), and (3) aftercare (helping the defendant obtain education or job training, find a job, and remain drug free) (Office of Justice Programs [OJP] 2000).

As of 2011, there were over 2600 drug courts operating throughout the United States. More than half of these target adult offenders; others address juvenile, child welfare, and different court case types, serving well over 120,000 people (National Institute of Justice [NIJ] 2012). See **Figure 17.2** for drug court locations in the United States. "Drug courts exist at numerous entry points throughout the justice system" (National Association of Drug Court Professionals [NADCP] 2011b). The following drug court models are currently in existence (see also **Table 17.4** for the number of courts of each type in existence in 2011):

- Adult drug court
- Veterans treatment court
- Driving while under the influence court
- Family dependency treatment court (family drug court)
- Federal district drug court (federal reentry court)
- Juvenile drug court
- Reentry drug court
- Tribal healing to wellness court
- Back on TRAC: treatment, responsibility, accountability on campus

Eligible drug addicts can be sent to drug court instead of moving through the traditional justice system. Drug courts put individuals in treatment and closely supervise them throughout the process.

For a minimum term of 1 year, participants are:

- Provided with intensive treatment and other services they require to get and stay clean and sober;
- Held accountable by the Drug Court judge for meeting their obligations to the court, society, themselves and their families;
- Regularly and randomly tested for drug use;
- Required to appear in court frequently so that the judge may review their progress; and
- Rewarded for doing well or sanctioned when they do not live up to their obligations. (NADCP 2011c)

What is the target population of drug court participants?

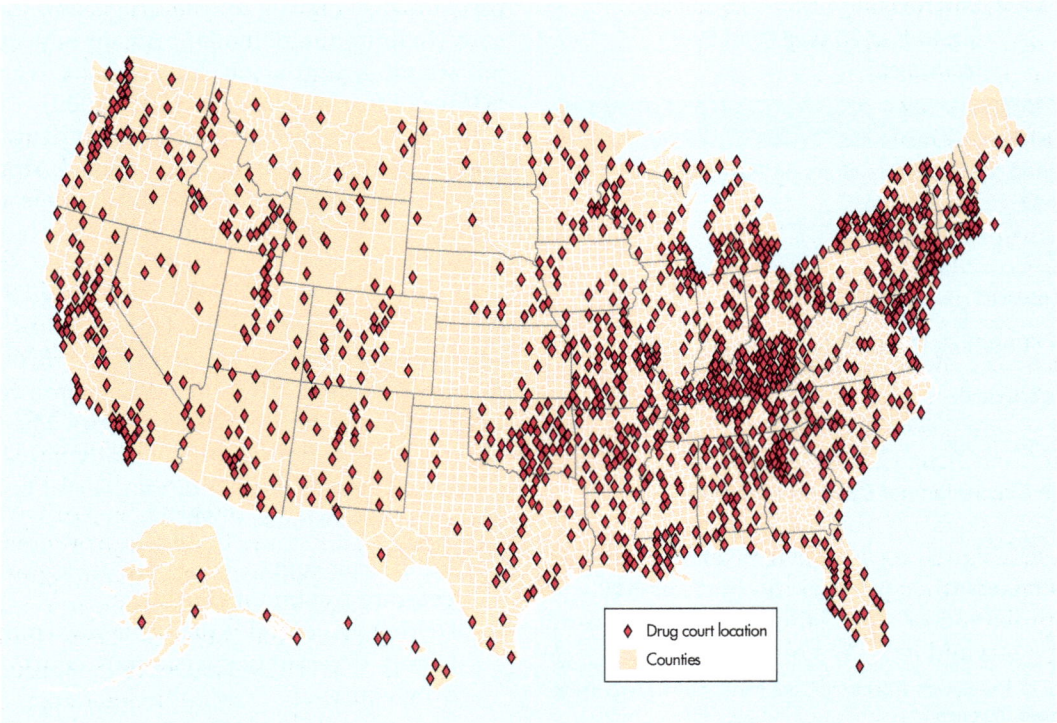

FIGURE 17.2 Drug court locations in the United States.

Reproduced from National Institute of Justice. "Drug Court Locations in the United States as of December 31, 2011." Washington, DC: U.S. Department of Justice (USDOJ), Office of Justice Programs, 2012. Available http://www.nij.gov/topics/courts/drug-courts/

TABLE 17.4   Number and Types of U.S. Drug Courts (as of December 31, 2011)

Type of Drug Court	Number
Adult drug courts	1435
Juvenile drug courts[3]	458
Family drug courts	329
Tribal drug courts	79
Designated DUI courts	192
Campus drug courts	5
Reentry drug courts	31
Federal reentry drug courts	46
Veterans drug courts	95
Co-occurring disorder courts	20

[3] Juvenile drug courts try to address the unique circumstances surrounding adolescent delinquency coupled with substance abuse.

Reproduced from National Institute of Justice. "Drug Court Locations in the United States as of December 31, 2011." Washington, DC: U.S. Department of Justice (USDOJ), Office of Justice Programs, 2012. Available http://www.nij.gov/topics/courts/drug-courts/

Drug courts are expected to have the greatest effects for high-risk offenders who have more severe antisocial backgrounds or poorer prognoses for success in standard treatments.

Such high-risk individuals ordinarily require a combined regimen of intensive supervision, behavioral accountability, and evidence-based treatment services, which drug courts are specifically structured to provide. Consistent with the predictions of the Risk Principle, drug courts have been shown to have the greatest effects for high-risk participants who were relatively younger, had more prior felony convictions, were diagnosed with antisocial personality disorder, or had previously failed in less intensive dispositions. (Marlowe 2010, p. 3)

A report stated that,

A recent survey of more than 120 evaluations of drug court programs showed that they outperformed virtually all other strategies that have been attempted for drug offenders within the 1 to 2 years that courts typically monitor offenders. Offenders who graduated from drug courts had significant reductions in rearrest rates and in charges for serious crimes. Data show that within the first year of release, 43.5% of drug offenders are rearrested, whereas only 16.4% of drug court graduates are rearrested. (Office of National Drug Control Policy [ONDCP] 2007, p. 25)

"Since the first drug court was established in 1989, drug court programs have been quickly adopted by communities and states across the country" (Franco 2010, p. i). Today, we are at the point where each state has multiple drug courts.

Overall, defendants participating in drug court sentencing have had lower rearrest rates, and there were statistically significant differences in disposition between those assigned to drug court and the comparison groups. Seventy-five percent of drug court graduates are arrest-free 2 years after leaving the court, and drug courts reduce crime 35% more than other court options (NADCP 2011a). "Rigorous studies examining long-term outcomes of individual Drug Courts have found that reductions in crime last at least 3 years and can endure for over 14 years" (NADCP 2011a).

Those assigned to drug court were more likely not to face further prosecution and less likely to serve probation or short jail terms. Finally, using a drug court and its system of administering treatment within a legal atmosphere is more cost-effective than criminal courts. In 2007, for every Federal dollar invested in Drug Court, $9 was leveraged in state funding. (NADCP 2011a).

One other finding stated that:

> Evaluations of the net costs and benefits of drug courts nationwide generally find that drug courts save taxpayer dollars compared to simple probation and/or incarceration, primarily due to reductions in arrests, case processing, jail occupancy and victimization costs. While not all persons diverted to drug court would have otherwise been sentenced to prison, for those individuals who are incarcerated, the average annual cost is estimated to be $23,000 per inmate, while the average annual cost of drug court participation is estimated to be $4,300 per person. (King and Pasquarella 2009, p. 7)

Past research showed that we should view the successes of drug courts with some caution because much of the effectiveness of these courts occurred very early—the courts were in operation fewer than 10 months, and these courts were very selective regarding the defendants allowed to participate—the criticism being that the courts tended to select violators who would have a better chance for rehabilitation. Today, however, evidence exists that past criticisms are no longer valid: "By 2006, the scientific community had concluded beyond a reasonable doubt from advanced statistical procedures called meta-analyses that Drug Courts reduce criminal recidivism, typically measured by fewer re-arrests for new offenses and technical violations" (Marlowe 2010, p. 1).

Further, at a 2009 Annual Conference of the American Society of Criminology, research showed that,

> In addition to significantly less involvement in criminal activity, the Drug Court participants also reported significantly less use of illegal drugs and heavy use of alcohol. These self-report findings were confirmed by saliva drug tests, which revealed significantly fewer positive results for the Drug Court participants at the 18-month assessment (29% vs. 46%, p < .01). The Drug Court participants also reported significantly better improvements in their family relationships, and non-significant trends favoring higher employment rates and higher annual incomes. These findings confirm that Drug Courts elicit substantial improvements in other outcomes apart from criminal recidivism. (Marlowe 2010, p. 2)

A very noteworthy and promising finding regarding drug courts is the emphasis on treating drug addiction and criminal behavior instead of simply punishing without treating drug-related juvenile delinquency and criminalistic behavior, as had been standard before drug courts were established.

Problems with Assessing the Success of Drug Prevention Programs

Both the National Institute on Drug Abuse (NIDA) and individual researchers have evaluated the multitude of drug abuse prevention programs in the United States. The general conclusions of these studies are as follows:

- Very few programs have demonstrated clear success or have adequately evaluated themselves.
- The relationships among information about drugs, attitudes toward use, and actual use are unclear in these programs.

Some key factors that are crucial to developing successful programs include the following:

- Prevention must be coordinated at different levels. Successful programs involve families, schools, and communities. In some cases, these efforts are not coordinated.

- The program must be integrated into the ongoing activities of schools, families, and community organizations. Superficial introduction of drug prevention strategies has limited effects. For instance, distributing literature door-to-door, making in-class presentations regarding the harmful effects of drugs, and posting banners and slogans warning of the consequences of drug abuse in communities are not successful methods. Instead, programs that are comprehensive and community-wide, integrated into neighborhood clubs, organizations, and church activities, are more likely to have a long-term impact on preventing drug use. A clear example is the yearly Great American Smokeout launched against tobacco use.

- Personal autobiographical and social experience accounts of former drug abusers should be included in drug information that is distributed. Recipients of drug prevention information should be given real-life accounts of use, abuse, despair, and successful drug rehabilitation. Just receiving drug information alone has little impact, either initially or over the long term.

Other Viable Alternatives to Drug Use

It has been suggested that people have an innate need to alter their conscious state. This belief is based on the observation that, as part of their normal play, preschoolers deliberately whirl themselves dizzy and even momentarily choke each other to lose consciousness (Wilson and Wilson 1975). Some young children progress to discovering and using chemicals (such as sniffing shoe polish or gasoline) to alter consciousness and learn to be very secretive about this behavior. They learn to be circumspect or come to feel guilty and repress the desire to alter consciousness when adults catch them in these activities.

KEY TERM

alternatives approach
an approach emphasizing the exploration of positive alternatives to drug abuse, based on replacing the pleasurable feelings gained from drug abuse with involvement in social and educational activities

If this desire to alter the state of consciousness is inherent in human beings, then the use of psychoactive drugs, legal or illegal, in adulthood is natural. Drug abuse is, therefore, a logical continuation of a developmental sequence that goes back to early childhood (Carroll 1977; Weil 1972).

One question in response to this is why, even if there is an innate desire to alter consciousness, only some people progress to abusing chemical substances. It appears that people who do not abuse psychoactive drugs have found positive alternatives to altering consciousness; they feel no need to take chemical substances for this purpose. Involvement in activities such as Boy Scouts and Girl Scouts, youth sports teams, music groups, the YMCA and YWCA, drug-free video game centers, drug-free dances, environmental and historical preservation projects, and social and service projects are viable alternatives to drug use. The rationale for these programs is that youth will find these activities engaging enough to forgo alcohol and drug use (Forman and Linney 1988).

This strategy is known as the **alternatives approach**. Workers in the drug abuse field tend to agree on its effectiveness. They note that young ex-abusers of common illicit drugs are more likely to stop when they gain satisfaction from exploring positive alternatives rather than from a fear of consequent harm. The alternatives approach assumes the following (Cohen 1971):

- People abuse drugs voluntarily to fill a need or basic drive.
- Most people abuse drugs for negative reasons. They may be dealing with negative feelings or situations, such as relieving boredom, anxiety, depression, tension, or other unpleasant emotional and psychological states. They may be rebelling against authority, trying to escape feelings of loneliness or inadequacy, or trying to be accepted by peers. Peer pressure is extremely important as an inducing force.
- Some people who abuse drugs believe the experience is positive. They may feel that their sensual experiences or music enjoyment is enhanced, or that they have achieved altered states of consciousness, or they may simply experience a sense of adventure. Some people may want to explore their own consciousness and reasons for the attraction to drug use.

Whether the reasons for drug use are positive or negative, the effects sought can be achieved through alternative, nondrug means. Such means are preferable to drug use and more constructive because the person is not relying on a psychoactive substance for satisfaction; rather, he or she is finding satisfaction based on personal achievements. Ideally, this approach should lead to a lifetime of self-satisfaction.

Table 17.5 lists various types of experiences, the motives for such experiences, the probable drugs of abuse with which they are associated, and alternatives to these drugs. As shown in the table, any constructive activity can be considered an alternative to drug abuse. For example, a young person who needs an outlet for increased physical energy might respond better to dance and movement training or a project in preventive medicine than working on ecological projects. In a large alternatives program established in Idaho, the following activities were planned during a month: arts and crafts, karate, reforestation, backpacking, Humane Society dog show, horseback riding, creating artwork for posters for various programs, astronomy, camping, and volunteering in a local hospital.

TABLE 17.5 Experiences, Motives, and Possible Alternatives for a Drug Abuser

Experience	Corresponding Motives	Drugs Abused	Possible Alternatives
Physical	Desire for physical well-being: physical relaxation, relief from sickness, desire for more energy	Alcohol, sedative-hypnotics, stimulants, marijuana	Athletics, dance, exercise, hiking, diet, carpentry, outdoor work, swimming, hatha yoga
Sensory	Desire to magnify sensorium: sound, touch, taste, need for sensual/sexual stimulation	Hallucinogens, marijuana, alcohol	Sensory awareness training, sky diving, experiencing sensory beauty of nature, scuba diving
Emotional	Relief from psychological pain: attempt to resolve personal problems, relief from bad mood, escape from anxiety, desire for emotional insight, liberation of feeling and emotional relaxation	Narcotics, alcohol, barbiturates, sedative-hypnotics	Competent individual counseling, well-run group therapy, instruction in psychology of personal development
Interpersonal	Desire to gain peer acceptance, break through interpersonal barriers, "communicate"; defiance of authority figures	Any, especially alcohol, marijuana	Expertly managed sensitivity and encounter groups, well-run group therapy, instruction in social customs, confidence training, emphasis on assisting others (e.g., YMCA or YWCA volunteers)
Social	Desire to promote social change, find identifiable subculture, tune out intolerable environmental conditions (e.g., poverty)	Marijuana, psychedelics	Social service community action in positive social change; helping the poor, aged, infirm, or young; tutoring handicapped individuals; ecology action; YMCA or YWCA Big Brother/Sister programs
Political	Desire to promote political change (out of desperation with the social-political order) and to identify with antiestablishment subgroup	Marijuana, psychedelics	Political service, lobbying for nonpartisan projects (e.g., Common Cause); field work with politicians and public officials
Intellectual	Desire to escape boredom, out of intellectual curiosity, to solve cognitive problems, gain new understanding in the world of ideas, research one's own awareness	Stimulants, sometimes psychedelics	Intellectual excitement through reading, debate, and discussion; creative games and puzzles; self-hypnosis; training in concentration

(continues)

TABLE 17.5 Experiences, Motives, and Possible Alternatives for a Drug Abuser (*continued*)

Experience	Corresponding Motives	Drugs Abused	Possible Alternatives
Creative-aesthetic	Desire to improve creative performance, enhance enjoyment of art already produced (e.g., music); enjoy imaginative mental productions	Marijuana, stimulants, psychedelics	Nongraded instruction in producing and/or appreciating art, music, drama, and creative hobbies
Philosophical	Desire to discover meaningful values, find meaning in life, help establish personal identity, organize a belief structure	Psychedelics, marijuana, stimulants	Discussions, seminars, courses on ethics, the nature of reality, relevant philosophical literature; explorations of value systems
Spiritual-mystical	Desire to transcend orthodox religion, develop spiritual insights, reach higher levels of consciousness, augment yogic practices, take a spiritual shortcut	Psychedelics, marijuana	Exposure to nonchemical methods of spiritual development; study of world religions, mysticism, meditation, yogic techniques

Data from U.S. Department of Health and Human Services, Office of Substance Abuse Prevention. "Factors that Influence Alcohol and Other Drug Use." In *Prevention Plus II: Tools for Creating and Sustaining Drug-Free Communities* (Figure 2.1, p. 19). DHHS Publication No. 89-1649. Rockville, MD: USDHHS, 1989. Distributed by the National Clearinghouse for Alcohol and Drug Information.

▪ Meditation

Some of the most intriguing research about the brain is being done on the state of the mind during **meditation**. In certain countries, such as India, people have long histories of being able to achieve certain goals through meditation. The word *yoga* is derived from the Sanskrit word for union, or yoking, meaning the process of discipline by which a person attains union with the absolute. In a sense, it refers to the use of the mind to control itself and the body.

Meditation involves brain wave activity centered on ponderous, contemplative, and reflective thought. An individual who meditates is able to decrease oxygen consumption within a matter of minutes by as much as 20%, a level usually reached only after 4 to 5 hours of sleep. However, meditation is physiologically different from sleep, based on the electroencephalograph (EEG) pattern and rate of decline of oxygen consumption. Along with the decreased metabolic rate and changes in EEG, there also is a marked decrease in blood lactate. Lactate is produced by metabolism of skeletal muscle, and the decrease is probably due to the reduced activity of

the sympathetic nervous system during meditation. Heart rate and respiration also are slowed.

▪ The Natural Mind Approach

Some people who take drugs eventually look for other methods of maintaining the valuable parts of the drug experience. These people may learn to value the meditation high and abandon drugs. In looking at Table 17.5, we can see how the use of different types of drugs can be replaced with possible alternatives by a drug abuser. Long-term drug users sometimes credit their drug experiences with having given them a taste of their potential, even though continued use has diminished the novelty of drug use. After these individuals become established in careers, they claim to have grown out of chemically induced altered states of consciousness. As Andrew Weil (1972, p. 67) put it, "One does not see any long-time meditators give up meditation to become acid heads."

Although chemical highs are effective means of altering the state of consciousness, they interfere with the most worthwhile states of altered consciousness because they reinforce the illusion that highs come from external, material agents rather than from within your own nervous system.

Some people have difficulty using meditation as an alternative to drugs because, to be effective, meditation takes practice and concentration; in contrast, the effects of drugs are immediate. Nevertheless, it is within everyone's potential to meditate.

KEY TERM

meditation
a state of consciousness in which there is a constant level of awareness focusing on one object; for example, yoga and Zen Buddhism

LEARNING PORTFOLIO

Discussion Questions

1. Figure 17.1 lists many factors that can influence drug use. Design and detail a drug prevention program by selecting any one of the concentric circles; include all factors within that circle and how you would deal with these factors.

2. Look at all of the findings in the section of this chapter entitled "How Serious Is the Problem of Drug Dependence?" Which two findings regarding dependence were the most interesting, and why were they the most interesting?

3. Comment on the harm reduction model as presented here and in other literature you may have. What are the major strengths and weaknesses of this model in comparison to the way the United States views drug users and/or abusers? Why do you think the U.S. government largely remains opposed to this approach? How do you think the United States would change if it were to adopt the harm reduction model?

4. What would you emphasize in a primary prevention program for junior high school or middle school students? High school students? College students?

5. How would you design a drug prevention program for undetected committed or secret users? What would you emphasize? Similarly, how would you design a drug prevention program for addicted drug users? What would you emphasize?

6. What do you think is more likely to work today in drug prevention programs for America's youth: teaching moderate use or total abstinence? Why?

7. Your boss says, "We received a much smaller amount of money than expected from the federal government to create a drug prevention program. Can you focus on either a community-based approach, a school-based approach, a family-based approach, or an individual-based approach/harm reduction psychotherapy prevention program?" Which would you select and why?

8. How effective has the BACCHUS Network been on your campus? Have you ever participated in any of its social gatherings? Do you think it is effective in curbing alcohol and/or drug use on your campus? Why or why not? Can you give specific experiences with the BACCHUS social activities?

9. List and explain three major strengths of drug courts in comparison with traditional criminal courts in the United States. Do you perceive any problems in preferring drug courts versus our criminal courts?

10. From everything you read in this chapter about the D.A.R.E. drug prevention program, what do you think are the major problems with this comprehensive drug prevention program? How would you improve it?

Key Terms

11. What is your assessment of using the alternatives approach and meditation for preventing drug use? Do you think it would be effective for alleviating drug use? Why or why not?

Summary

1. The 10 most prominent factors affecting an individual's use of drugs are as follows: (a) genetics, (b) personality traits, (c) attitudes and beliefs, (d) interpersonal and peer resistance skills, (e) community, (f) peers, (g) school policy, (h) local law enforcement, (i) personal situations, and (j) parents.

2. The seriousness of the problem with regard to drug dependence is highlighted by the fact that in 2011, an estimated 20.6 million persons age 12 or older were classified with substance dependence or abuse in the past year (8.0% of the population age 12 or older). Of these, 2.6 million were classified with dependence or abuse of both alcohol and illicit drugs, 3.9 million had dependence or abuse of illicit drugs but not alcohol, and 14.1 million had dependence or abuse of alcohol but not illicit drugs. Marijuana was the illicit drug with the highest rate of past-year dependence or abuse in 2011, followed by pain relievers and cocaine. Of the 6.5 million persons age 12 or older classified with illicit drug dependence or abuse in 2011, 4.2 million had marijuana dependence or abuse (representing 1.6% of the total population age 12 or older, and 63.8% of all those classified with illicit drug dependence or abuse), 1.8 million persons had pain reliever dependence or abuse, and 821,000 persons had cocaine dependence or abuse.

3. Three major types of prevention programs are primary, secondary, and tertiary prevention.

4. Five major types of drug users that drug prevention programs have to recognize before assembling a program are (a) early experimenters, (b) nonproblem drug users/recreational users, (c) undetected committed or secret users, (d) problem users, and (e) former users.

5. The five levels of comprehensive prevention programs for drug use and abuse are (a) the harm reduction model, (b) community-based prevention, (c) school-based prevention, (d) family-based prevention, and (e) individual-based drug prevention and treatment/harm reduction psychotherapy.

6. Proactive family factors can moderate the effects of drug risk factors. The risk of associating with peers who use drugs can be offset by protective family factors, such as parent conventionality, maternal adjustment, and strong parent–child attachment.

7. Five primary prevention programs that exist in higher education are the (a) information-only or awareness model, (b) attitude change model or affective education model, (c) social influences model, (d) ecological or person-in-environment model, and (e) social-ecological model.

8. Three of today's large-scale prevention programs are (a) the BACCHUS Network, a national and international association of college and university peer-education programs focused on alcohol abuse prevention and other related student health and safety issues; (b) D.A.R.E., a nationwide drug prevention program presented in middle and junior high schools by police officers that has shown severe shortcomings; and (c) drug courts, a promising and popular nationwide approach to prevention in which the primary purpose is to include treatment programs and options instead of only punishment for drug offenses.

9. Two additional possibilities for lessening or eliminating drug use are the alternatives approach and meditation. Alternatives to drug abuse are based on replacing the euphoria and pleasure gained by being high with involvement in social, recreational, and educational activities. Meditation is producing a state of consciousness in which there is a constant level of very satisfying awareness that is rewarding in itself without artificial inducements (drugs). Yoga and Zen Buddhism are examples.

References

Alberti, R. E., and M. L. Emmons. *Your Perfect Right*. San Luis Obispo, CA: Impact, 1988.

AlcoholAnswers.org. *Harm Reduction Philosophy*. Farmington, CT: The National Alliance of Advocates for Buprenorphine Treatment (NAABT), 2013.

BACCHUS and GAMMA. *Community College Guide to Peer Education*. Denver, CO: The BACCHUS and GAMMA Peer Education Network, 1994.

The BACCHUS Network. "Mission Statement." 2011. Available http://www.bacchusnetwork.org/mission.html

The BACCHUS Network. "About the BACCHUS Network." 2013. Available http://www.bacchusnetwork.org/about-the-network.html

Botvin, G. J., and K. W. Griffin. "School Based Programs." In *Substance Abuse: A Comprehensive Textbook*, 4th ed., edited by J. H. Lowinson, P. Ruiz, R. B. Millman, and J. G. Langrod, 1211–1228. Philadelphia, PA: Lippincott Williams and Wilkins, 2005.

Botvin, G. J., and T. A. Wills. "Personal and Social Skills Training: Cognitive-Behavioral Approaches to Substance Abuse Prevention." In *Prevention Research: Deterring Drug Abuse Among Children and Adolescents*. NIDA Research Monograph No. 64. Rockville, MD: National Institute on Drug Abuse, 1985.

Cal Poly (California Polytechnic State University). "Sobering Statistics." St. Luis Obispo, CA: Health and Counseling Services, 2013. Available http://www.hcs.calpoly.edu/content/pulse/sobering-stats

Carey, S. M., M. W. Finigan, and K. Pukstas. *Exploring the Key Components of Drug Courts: A Comparative Study of 18 Adult Drug Courts on Practices, Outcomes and Costs*. Portland, OR: NPC Research, 2008.

Carroll, E. "Notes on the Epidemiology of Inhalants." In *Review of Inhalants*, edited by C. W. Sharp and M. L. Brehm. NIDA Research Monograph No. 15. Washington, DC: National Institute on Drug Abuse, 1977.

Center for Prevention Research and Development (CPRD). *Research Based Approaches in the Community Domain*. Champaign, IL: University of Illinois Urbana Champaign, 2000.

Centers for Disease Control and Prevention (CDC). "Injury Prevention and Control: The Social-Ecological Model: A Framework for Prevention." 9 September 2009. Available http://www.cdc.gov/violenceprevention/overview/social-ecologicalmodel.html

Claire, J. "Drug Prevention Programmes in Schools: What Is the Evidence?" London, UK: Mentor, The Drug and Alcohol Protection Agency, 2013. Available http://www.mentoruk.org.uk/wp-content/uploads/2011/11/Prevention-Evidence-Paper-Nov-11-Final.pdf

Clayton, R. R., R. Cattarello, L. E. Cay, and K. P. Walden. "Persuasive Communication and Drug Prevention: An Evaluation of the D.A.R.E. Program." In *Persuasive Communication and Drug Abuse Prevention*, edited by L. Donohew, H. Sypepher, and W. Bukowski, 83–107. Hillsdale, NJ: Erlbaum, 1991.

Cohen, A. Y. "The Journey Beyond Trips: Alternatives to Drugs." *Journal of Psychedelic Drugs* 3 (Spring 1971): 7–14.

Common Sense for Drug Policy. "D.A.R.E. Admits Failure." 9 July 2009. Available http://www.csdp.org/news/news/darerevised.htm

Community Anti-Drug Coalition of America (CADCA). *Drug Free Communities Support Program Grantee Roadmap to Success: Training and Technical Assistance Support System*. Alexandria, VA: CADCA National Coalition Institute, 2010.

D.A.R.E. America (Drug Abuse Resistance Education). "About D.A.R.E." 1996. Available http://www.dare.com/home/about_dare.asp

Drug Policy Alliance (DPA). "Reducing Harm: Treatment and Beyond." 2013. Available http://www.drugpolicy.org/harm-reduction

Eckholm, E. "Governments' Drug-Abuse Costs Hit $468 Billion Study Says." *New York Times* (28 May 2009). Available http://www.nytimes.com/2009/05/28/us/28addiction.html?_r=0

Ennett, S. T., N. S. Tobler, C. L. Ringwalt, and R. L. Flewelling. "How Effective Is Drug Abuse Resistance Education? A Meta-analysis of Project D.A.R.E. Outcome Evaluations." *American Journal of Public Health* 84 (1994): 1394–1401.

Forman, S. G., and J. A. Linney. "School-Based Prevention of Adolescent Substance Abuse: Programs, Implementation and Future Direction." *School Psychology Review* 17 (1988): 550–558.

Franco, C. "Drug Courts: Background, Effectiveness, and Policy Issues for Congress." Congressional Research Service. Washington, DC: Government Printing Office. 12 October 2010. Available http://www.fas.org/sgp/crs/misc/R41448.pdf

Goldkamp, J. *Justice and Treatment Innovation: The Drug Court Movement*. Washington, DC: National Institute of Justice and the State Justice Institute, 1993.

Gonzalez, G. M., and V. V. Clement, eds. *Preventing Substance Abuse*. U.S. Department of Education. Washington, DC: U.S. Government Printing Office, 1994.

Gopelrud, E. N., ed. *Preventing Adolescent Drug Use: From Theory to Practice*. OSAP Monograph No. 8, DHHS Pub. No. (ADM) 91–1725. Rockville, MD: Office of Substance Abuse Prevention, 1991.

Hansen, W. B. "A Social Ecology Theory of Alcohol and Drug Use Prevention Among College and University Students." In *Designing Alcohol and Other Drug Prevention Programs in Higher Education.* Newton, MA: Higher Education Center for Alcohol and Other Drug Prevention, U.S. Department of Education, 1997.

Harm Reduction Coalition. "Principles of Harm Reduction." 2011. Available http://harmreduction.org/about-us/principles-of-harm-reduction/

Harm Reduction Psychotherapy and Training Associates (HRPTA). "What Is Harm Reduction Psychotherapy." n.d. Available http://www.harmreductioncounseling.com/therapy.html

Holstein, M. E., W. E. Cohen, and P. Steinbroner. *A Matter of Balance: Personal Strategies for Alcohol and Other Drugs.* Ashland, OR: CNS Productions, 1995.

Horowitz, H. L. *Campus Life.* New York: Knopf, 1987.

King, R. S., and J. Pasquarella. *Drug Courts: A Review of the Evidence.* Washington, DC: The Sentencing Project, 2009. Available http://www.sentencingproject.org/doc/dp_drugcourts.pdf

Koss, M. P., C. A. Gidycz, and R. Wisniewski. "The Scope of Rape: Incidence and Prevalence of Sexual Aggression and Victimization in a National Sample of Higher Education Students." *Journal of Consulting and Clinical Psychology* 34 (1987): 186–196.

Larimer, M. E., J. R. Kilmer, and C. M. Lee. "College Student Drug Prevention: A Review of Individually-Oriented Prevention Strategies." *Journal of Drug Issues* 35 (April 2005): 431–456.

Marlowe, D. B. *Research Update on Adult Drug Courts.* Alexandria, VA: National Association of Drug Court Professionals (NADCP). December 2010. Available http://www1.spa.american.edu/justice/documents/3067.pdf

McIntyre, K., D. White, and R. Yoast. *Resilience Among High-Risk Youth.* Madison, WI: University of Wisconsin, 1990.

Miller, D. W. "D.A.R.E. Reinvents Itself—With Help from Its Social-Scientist Critics." *Chronicle of Higher Education* 48 (19 October 2001): A12–A14.

National Association of Drug Court Professionals (NADCP). "Drug Courts Work." 2011a. Available http://www.nadcp.org/learn/drug-courts-work

National Association of Drug Court Professionals (NADCP). "Types of Drug Courts." 2011b. Available http://www.nadcp.org/learn/what-are-drug-courts/models

National Association of Drug Court Professionals (NADCP). "What Are Drug Courts?" 2011c. Available http://www.nadcp.org/learn/what-are-drug-courts

National Institute of Justice (NIJ). "Drug Court Locations in the United States as of December 31, 2011." Washington, DC: U.S. Department of Justice (USDOJ), Office of Justice Programs, 2012. Available http://www.nij.gov/topics/courts/drug-courts/

National Institute on Drug Abuse (NIDA). "Risk and Protective Factors in Drug Abuse Prevention." *NIDA Notes* 16 (February 2002).

National Institute on Drug Abuse (NIDA). *Drug Abuse Prevention: Drug Abuse Is a Preventable Behavior.* Bethesda, MD: National Institutes of Health (NIH), March 2007.

National Institutes of Health (NIH) and National Institute on Drug Abuse (NIDA). *Drug Abuse and Drug Abuse Research.* Washington, DC: U.S. Government Printing Office, 1998.

Norman, E. "Personal Factors Related to Substance Misuse: Risk Abatement and/or Resiliency Enhancement." In *Substance Abuse in Adolescence,* edited by T. P. Gulotta, G. R. Adams, and R. Montemayor, 47–56. Thousand Oaks, CA: Sage Publications, 1994.

Office of Justice Programs (OJP), Drug Court Clearinghouse and Technical Assistance Project (DCCTAP). *Looking at a Decade of Drug Courts.* Washington, DC: Drug Court Clearinghouse and Technical Assistance Project, 1999.

Office of Justice Programs (OJP), Drug Court Clearinghouse and Technical Assistance Project. *Summary of Drug Court Activity by State and County.* Washington, DC: U.S. Government Printing Office, 10 January 2000.

Office of National Drug Control Policy (ONDCP). *National Drug Control Strategy: The White House, February 2007.* Washington, DC: U.S. Government Printing Office, 2007.

Perkins, H. W. "Confronting Misperceptions of Peer Use Norms Among College Students: An Alternative Approach for Alcohol and Other Drug Education Programs." In *The Higher Education Leaders/Peers Network Peer Prevention Program Resource Manual,* 18–32. Washington, DC: Texas Christian University, U.S. Department of Education (FIPSE), 1991.

Perkins, H. W. "College Student Misperceptions of Alcohol and Other Drug Norms Among Peers: Exploring Causes, Consequences, and Implications for Prevention Programs." In *Designing Alcohol and Other Drug Prevention Programs in Higher Education.* Newton, MA: U.S. Department of Education, Higher Education Center for Alcohol and Other Drug Prevention, 1997.

Perkins, H. W., and A. D. Berkowitz. "Perceiving the Community Norms of Alcohol Use Among Students: Some Research Implications for Campus Alcohol Education Programming." *International Journal of the Addictions* 21 (1986): 861–976.

Plant, M., R. Robertson, M. Plant, and P. Miller. *Drug Nation: Patterns, Problems, Panics, and Politics.* Oxford, UK: Oxford University Press, 2011.

ProCon.org. "Is the D.A.R.E. Program Good for America's Kids (K–12)." Santa Monica, CA: ProCon.org, 6 November 2013. Available http://dare.procon.org/#Background

Robertson, E. B., S. L. David, S. A. Rao, and National Institute on Drug Abuse (NIDA). *Preventing Drug Use Among Children and Adolescents*, 2nd ed. Bethesda, MD: U.S. Department of Health and Human Services, 2003.

Rosenbaum, D. P., and S. Hanson. *Assessing the Effects of School-Based Drug Education; a Six-Year Multi-level Analysis of Project D.A.R.E.* Chicago, IL: University of Illinois at Chicago, Department of Criminal Justice and Center for Research in Law and Justice, 6 April 1998.

Ryan, B. E., T. Colthurst, and L. Segars. *College Alcohol Risk Assessment Guide.* San Diego: UCSD Extension, University of California at San Diego, 1995.

Sherin, K. M., and B. Mahoney. *Treatment Drug Courts: Integrating Substance Abuse Treatment with Legal Case Processing.* Rockville, MD: U.S. Department of Health and Human Services, 1996.

Shiffman, S., and T. A. Wills, eds. *Coping and Substance Abuse.* New York: Academic Press, 1987.

Silver Gate Group and Robert Wood Johnson Foundation. *Prevention 2000: Moving Effective Prevention Programs into Practice.* Princeton, NJ: Robert Wood Johnson Foundation, 2001.

Sloboda, Z., and S. L. David. *Preventing Drug Use Among Children and Adolescents: A Research-Based Guide.* Washington, DC: National Institute on Drug Abuse and National Institutes of Health, April 1999.

StateUniversity.com. "College and University Blog: Big Business—Alcohol Advertising and College Sports." 2011. Available http://www.stateuniversity.com/blog/permalink/Alcohol-Advertising-and-College-Sports.html

Substance Abuse and Mental Health Services Administration (SAMHSA). *Results from the 2011 National Survey on Drug Use and Health: Summary of National Findings.* NSDUH Series H-44, HHS Pub. No. (SMA) 12-4713. Rockville, MD: SAMHSA, 2012.

Tinzmann, M. B., and J. Hixson. *What Does Research Say About Prevention?* Oak Brook, IL: North Central Regional Educational Laboratory, 1992.

United Nations Office on Drugs and Crime. "Prevention of Drug Use." 2011. Available http://www.unodc.org/unodc/en/prevention/index.html

U.S. Department of Education. *Archived Information: Current Knowledge in Prevention of Alcohol and Other Drug Abuse*, edited by G.M. Gonzalez and V. V. Clement. Washington, DC: Government Printing Office, 1994.

U.S. Government Accountability Office (GAO). *Youth Illicit Drug Use Prevention: D.A.R.E. Long-Term Evaluation and Federal Efforts to Identify Effective Programs.* GAO-03-172R. Washington, DC: GAO, 15 January 2003.

Vogt, A. "Now Many 'Just Say No' to D.A.R.E." *Chicago Tribune* (26 January 2003), 1, 3.

Weil, A. *The Natural Mind.* Boston, MA: Houghton Mifflin, 1972.

Westermeyer, R. W. "Reducing Harm: A Very Good Idea." n.d. Available http://www.fullspectrumrecovery.com/fullspec/images/stories/pdfs/reducing%20harm.pdf

Wilson, M., and S. Wilson, eds. *Drugs in American Life*, Vol. 1. New York: Wilson, 1975.

Wilson, R. W., and C. A. Kolander. *Drug Abuse Prevention: A School and Community Partnership*, 3rd ed. Burlington, MA: Jones & Bartlett Learning, 2011.

Zeese, K. B., and P. M. Lewin. *The Effective Drug Control Strategy.* Washington, DC: Network of Reform Group and the National Coalition for Effective Drug Policies, 1998. Available http://www.csdp.org/edcs/edc.htm

Zweig, J. M. "Description of the Drug Court Sites in the Multi-Site Adult Drug Court Evaluation." In *The Multi-Site Adult Drug Court Evaluation: The Drug Court Experience*, by S. B. Rossman, J. M. Zweig, D. Kralstein, K. Henry, P. M. Downey, and C. Lindquist, 8–23. Washington, DC: Urban Institute Justice Policy Center, 2011.

CHAPTER 18

Treating Drug Dependence

© vm/iStockphoto.com

Did You Know?

▶ A variety of approaches to drug addiction treatment exist, including behavioral and pharmacological therapies.

▶ No single treatment approach is appropriate for all individuals.

▶ Relapse rates for addiction resemble those of other chronic diseases such as diabetes, hypertension, and asthma.

▶ Comorbidity between drug addiction and other mental illnesses is common.

Learning Objectives

On completing this chapter you will be able to:

❯ Discuss assessment of addiction severity and readiness to change.

❯ List several principles that characterize effective drug treatment.

❯ Discuss the role of comorbidity in substance abuse and its treatment.

❯ Discuss pharmacological and behavioral strategies to treat addiction.

❯ Describe the Mental Health Parity and Addiction Equity Act.

Drugs and Society Online is a great source for additional drugs and society information for both students and instructors. Visit **go.jblearning.com /hanson12** to find a variety of useful tools for learning, thinking, and teaching.

Treatment of Addiction

Individuals who are addicted to drugs come from all walks of life. Many suffer from occupational, social, psychiatric, or other medical problems that can make their addictions difficult to treat. Even in the absence of such complicating issues, the severity of addictions varies widely. It is essential to match treatment with the needs of the client. Further, it is valuable to intervene at the earliest possible stage of addiction with the least restrictive form of appropriate treatment. To accomplish this, it is important that treatment providers determine the severity of addiction as well as the readiness of an individual to change his or her behavior.

Assessing Addiction Severity and Readiness to Change

Addiction severity can be determined in many ways, including the administration of standardized questionnaires. Of these, the Addiction Severity Index (ASI) is among the most widely used assessment instruments in the field of addiction (McLellan et al. 1980, 1985, 1992). The ASI is one of the most reliable and valid measurements of the magnitude and characteristics of client problems. It focuses on possible problems in six areas: medical status, employment and support, alcohol and drug use, legal status, family and social relationships, and psychiatric status. The ASI provides information that can be used to identify and prioritize which problem areas are most significant and require prompt attention.

When assessing and prioritizing problems, one model of individual development that is often considered is Maslow's hierarchy of needs. This theory postulates that individuals are motivated by unsatisfied needs, and that lower fundamental needs must be satisfied before higher needs can be satisfied. These primary needs include food, drink, warmth, sleep, and shelter. These can be extended in the case of substance abusers to problems such as (1) unidentified or inappropriately managed health problems, (2) medication adherence issues (particularly in the presence of co-occurring mental or physical health disorders), and (3) physical alterations due to drug and/or alcohol dependence (Stilen et al. 2007). Once these fundamental needs are addressed, a second level of needs involving security and safety can be addressed.

Simplistically, these include such issues as stability, order, law, and limits. Examples of common problem areas reflecting this level include inability for self-care, management of mental health issues, personal/public safety issues, and legal issues. If these needs are not met, individuals receiving substance abuse treatment cannot move to higher levels wherein love and belonging, self-esteem, and self-actualization (i.e., fulfilling personal potential) can be attained (Stilen et al. 2007).

As important as assessing addiction severity and prioritizing problem areas on which to focus is consideration of a person's readiness to change his or her abuse behavior. Pioneering work by DiClemente and Prochaska (1998) revealed that behavioral change is a many-stage process, rather than a singular event. The stages described by DiClemente and Prochaska include:

- *Precontemplation:* An individual does not want to change or is not considering changing his or her behavior. The latter may be because he or she does not see a need for change.
- *Contemplation:* A person is considering changing his or her behavior.
- *Preparation:* A person is committed to a strategy for change.
- *Action:* A person is actively attempting to change.
- *Maintenance:* A person has changed his or her behavior. In order to complete the process of change, this behavior must become a part of his or her lifestyle.

Determining the stage of change at which an individual finds him- or herself can help providers select the best treatment plan to address a client's needs. This may help prevent the individual from refusing to accept all or parts of the treatment plan.

Principles of Treatment

A variety of approaches to drug addiction treatment exist. Some include behavioral therapy, such as counseling, psychotherapy, or cognitive therapy. Others include medications ranging from treatment medications (e.g., methadone, buprenorphine, nicotine patches, nicotine gum) to those intended to treat co-occurring mental disorders (e.g., antidepressants, mood stabilizers). The most successful drug abuse treatment programs typically provide a combination of therapies and other services to meet the needs of the individual

Treatment facilities provide a variety of services to people dealing with substance abuse.

abuser. They incorporate adequate assessment of treatment needs required not only as a direct consequence of the physiological and psychological effects of the drug, but also due to indirect problems, such as the need for housing, legal, and financial services; educational and vocational assistance; and family/child-care services. Such needs often are shaped by the gender, age, race, culture, and sexual orientation of the abuser.

Because drug addiction is generally a chronic disorder characterized by occasional relapses, a one-time, short-term treatment is often inadequate. Further, many individuals who enter treatment drop out before receiving all of its benefits; hence, and again, successful treatment often requires more than one treatment exposure. Of note, relapse rates for addiction resemble those of other chronic diseases such as asthma, diabetes, and hypertension (National Institute on Drug Abuse [NIDA] 2012). **Figure 18.1** illustrates these statistics.

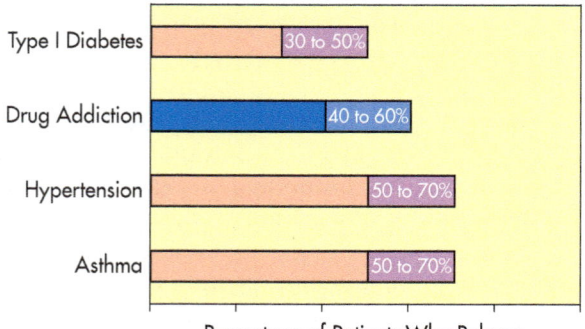

Percentage of Patients Who Relapse

FIGURE 18.1 Relapse rates for addiction resemble those of other chronic diseases such as asthma, diabetes, and hypertension.

Research has shown that good outcomes are contingent on adequate duration of treatment. Generally, for outpatient or residential treatment, participation for fewer than 90 days is of limited effectiveness; treatments lasting significantly longer are needed (NIDA 2012). For methadone maintenance, 12 months of treatment often is the minimum needed, and some individuals who are addicted to opiates require extended treatment lasting several years (NIDA 2012).

To best target treatment for an individual, the type and goals of treatment must be determined. Consideration must be given to the fact that both largely depend on the view one holds of addiction. For example, if the disease model is applied to addiction, total abstinence is generally required because this model views drug abuse as a biological condition that is largely uncontrollable. On the other hand, if responsible drug use is the goal, then occasional and moderate drug use can be the intended end result.

Effective treatment allows addicts to stop abusing drugs, returns them to a drug-free state of existence, and transforms them into employable and productive members of society. Measures of effectiveness typically include assessing levels of family functioning, employability, criminal behavior, and medical condition.

As summarized in the following list, the National Institute on Drug Abuse (NIDA) has delineated 13 overarching principles that characterize effective addiction treatment (NIDA 2012):

1. *Addiction is a complex but treatable disease that affects brain function and behavior.* Drugs of abuse can alter brain function and structure, resulting in changes that persist long after drug use has ended. This may explain why drug abusers are at risk for relapse even after extended periods of abstinence and regardless of potentially destructive consequences.

2. *No single treatment is appropriate for all individuals.* Treatment settings and services must be matched to each person's particular needs.

3. *Treatment needs to be readily available.* Individuals who are addicted to drugs are often uncertain about whether to seek treatment. Hence, it is important that services be available as soon as an individual makes the decision to seek help. Treatment opportunities can be lost if it is not immediately and readily accessible.

4. *Effective treatment attends to multiple needs of the individual, not just his or her drug use.* To be effective, treatment must address not only

the individual's drug use, but also any related medical, psychological, social, vocational, and legal problems. It is also important that an individual's age, ethnicity, gender, and culture be considered when implementing treatment.

5. *Remaining in treatment for an adequate period is critical for treatment effectiveness.* The appropriate duration of treatment depends on each person's individual problems and needs. As noted earlier, research indicates that for many, at least 3 months in treatment is needed.

6. *Behavioral therapies, including individual, family or group counseling, are the most commonly used forms of drug abuse treatment.* Such therapies often have different emphases. These may involve improving problem-solving skills, providing incentives for abstinence, addressing motivation to change, and building skills to resist drug use and facilitating improved interpersonal relationships.

7. *Medications are an important element of treatment for many patients, especially when combined with counseling and other behavioral therapies.* Specific pharmacological therapies for treating substance abusers are discussed later in this chapter.

8. *An individual's treatment and services plan must be assessed continually and modified as necessary to ensure it meets his or her changing needs.* In addition to counseling, an individual may require various combinations of medical services, family therapy, vocational rehabilitation, and/or social and legal services.

9. *Many drug-addicted individuals also have other mental disorders.* Because drug abuse and addiction often co-occur with other mental illnesses (see the discussion of comorbidity later in this chapter), patients presenting with one condition should be evaluated for the other(s). Treatment should address each identified issue, including the use of medications if warranted.

10. *Medically assisted detoxification is only the first stage of addiction treatment and, by itself, does little to change long-term drug use.* Medical detoxification is the process of safely managing the acute physical symptoms of withdrawal associated with stopping drug use. It can be an important first step toward abstinence, but alone is rarely sufficient to help individuals achieve long-term abstinence.

11. *Treatment does not need to be voluntary to be effective.* Sanctions or enticements in the family, criminal justice system, or employment settings can facilitate treatment entry and increase both retention rates and success of drug treatment interventions.

12. *Drug use during treatment must be monitored continuously, as lapses during treatment do occur.* The knowledge that an individual's drug use is being monitored can be a powerful incentive to withstand urges to abuse drugs. Monitoring also provides an early indication of a return to drug use, signaling a possible need to adjust treatment plans.

13. *Treatment programs should test patients for the presence of HIV/AIDS, hepatitis B and C, tuberculosis, and other infectious diseases, as well as provide targeted risk-reduction counseling, linking patients to treatment if necessary.*

Many treatment programs apply one or more of these listed principles as part of their therapeutic strategy.

Of note, the age of the substance abuser is an important consideration when designing treatment. This includes both the age of first exposure to drugs and the age at which treatment is initiated. Research indicates that from birth through early adulthood, the brain undergoes a prolonged process of development during which a behavioral shift occurs such that actions go from being more impulsive to more reflective and reasoned. Further, the brain areas most closely associated with judgment, decision making, and self-control undergo a period of rapid development during adolescence (NIDA 2012). Thus, adolescent drug abusers have unique needs that must be considered in developing a treatment approach to their addictions.

Gender-related considerations are also of importance in treating substance abuse. Treatment should attend not only to biological distinctions between genders, but also to the social and environmental factors that can differentially affect motivations for drug use, effectiveness of and reasons for seeking treatment, environments where treatment is obtained, and consequences of not receiving treatment. For example, many life circumstances predominate in women as a group, which may require specialized treatment approaches. These can, for example, include sexual and physical trauma followed by posttraumatic stress disorder. Research indicates that these are more common in women than in men seeking treatment (NIDA 2012). Other factors that can be (although are not necessarily) unique to women include issues involving financial independence, pregnancy, and child care. Each circumstance must be considered in developing a treatment plan.

Criminal justice–involved substance abusers are another population that often benefits from specialized treatment approaches. According to NIDA (2012), combining criminal justice sanctions with substance abuse treatment can diminish both subsequent abuse and associated crimes. Initiating treatment in prison and continuing that same treatment upon release also results in less drug use and less criminal behavior. Further, individuals under legal coercion tend to remain in treatment longer and do as well as or better than those who are not experiencing legal pressure (NIDA 2012).

Unfortunately, effective treatment for criminal justice–involved individuals is often unavailable. For example, as reported in a survey summarized by NIDA (2009), fewer than 10% of adults and approximately 20% of adolescents with substance abuse problems in the nation's prisons, jails, and probation programs can receive treatment on a given day. This survey also revealed that only 40% of adult facilities and 29% of juvenile facilities reported having full-time personnel to provide drug abuse therapy.

Therapeutic work environments that provide employment for abstinent drug-abusing individuals both improve life skills and promote a continued drug-free lifestyle. Further, some workplaces sponsor employee assistance programs that offer short-term assistance and/or counseling so as to link employees with substance abuse problems to local treatment resources.

Of note, several factors influence retention in treatment programs. These can include: (1) individual motivation to change drug-using behavior; (2) degree of support from family and friends; and (3) pressure from employers, the criminal justice system, and/or extensions of the court (e.g., child protective services). It also is important for treatment providers to ensure a transition to continuing care or aftercare following a patient's completion of formal treatment (NIDA 2012).

Comorbidity

Drug addiction is a complicated condition that often involves changes in the structure and function of specific parts of the brain. Changes in the structure and function of regions of the brain affected by drug addiction can also occur in other mental illnesses such as anxiety, psychosis, and depression. Noteworthy, overlapping factors including genetic vulnerabilities, trauma, stress, and/or underlying brain abnormalities can contribute to both substance abuse disorders and other mental illnesses.

Comorbidity is a condition in which two or more illnesses occur in the same person, simultaneously or sequentially. This term also suggests interactions between the illnesses that affect the course and prognosis of both (NIDA 2010). The *Diagnostic and Statistical Manual of Mental Disorders (DSM)* is a widely used authority for diagnosing such mental health problems (see "Here and Now: Tools for Diagnosis").

HERE AND NOW

Tools for Diagnosis

The *Diagnostic and Statistical Manual of Mental Disorders (DSM)* serves as a highly accepted and widely used authority for the diagnosis of psychiatric disorders. In May 2013, its fifth edition *(DSM-5)* was made available. Important changes include a revision of the chapter entitled "Substance-Related and Addictive Disorders." In particular, according to the American Psychiatric Association (APA 2013; the publisher of *DSM-5*), "substance use disorder in *DSM-5* combines the *DSM-IV* categories of substance abuse and substance dependence into a single disorder measured on a continuum from mild to severe." (APA 2013). Specific substances are addressed as separate use disorders (e.g., stimulant use disorder,

alcohol use disorder, etc.), but "nearly all substances are diagnosed based on the same overarching criteria." (APA 2013)

One important distinguishing feature of *DSM-5* is its clarification of the definition of "dependence." Many confuse the terms "addiction" and "dependence," and fail to recognize that dependence is a normal response to a variety of drugs—not simply substances of abuse.

Other important initiatives have been launched in order to further refine diagnoses of mental health disorders. In particular, the National Institute on Mental Health has launched the Research Domain Criteria project, which is designed "to transform diagnosis by incorporating genetics, imaging, cognitive science, and other levels of information to lay the foundation for a new classification system (Insel 2013)." This 10-year project holds promise for improving outcomes for the many individuals afflicted by mental health disorders.

Data from American Psychiatric Association, *DSM-5* Implementation and Support, 2013. Available http://www.dsm5.org/Pages/Default.aspx; American Psychiatric Association, Substance-Related and Addictive Disorders, 2013. Available http://www.dsm5.org/Documents/Substance%20Use%20Disorder%20Fact%20Sheet.pdf; and Insel, T. Director's Blog: Transforming, 2013. Diagnosis. Available http://www.nimh.nih.gov/about/director/2013/transforming-diagnosis.shtml

Comorbidity between drug addiction and mental illnesses is common. For example, individuals diagnosed with anxiety or mood disorders are approximately twice as likely to suffer also from drug abuse or dependence. This has also been demonstrated for individuals diagnosed with conduct disorder or antisocial personality. Similarly, individuals diagnosed with substance disorders are approximately twice as likely to also suffer from anxiety and mood disorders (NIDA 2010).

Mental illnesses can sometimes lead to substance abuse and addiction in that individuals sometimes abuse drugs in order to self-medicate an underlying medical condition (see "Here and Now: Schizophrenia and Cigarette Smoking: Self-Medication or Shared Brain Circuitry?"). However, the high incidence of comorbidity between substance abuse disorders and other mental illnesses does not mean that one necessarily caused the other. In fact, a causal relationship is difficult to establish for multiple reasons, including the fact that drugs of abuse can cause abusers to display one or more symptoms of, without actually having, another mental illness. Further, some symptoms of either a substance abuse disorder or another mental illness may not be recognized until the disease has progressed considerably, and by then, it often is difficult to retrospectively determine the precise onset of these disorders (for further discussion, see NIDA 2010).

Effective treatment of individuals with comorbid substance abuse and mental illnesses requires accurate diagnosis of both conditions. Individuals beginning treatment for substance abuse and/or addiction need to be screened for mental illnesses, and vice versa. Accurate diagnosis may require monitoring after a period of abstinence in order to distinguish the effects of substance intoxication or withdrawal from the symptoms of comorbid mental disorders. According to NIDA (2010), several fundamental barriers impede treatment of comorbid disorders. Among these, psychiatrists and physicians are the most common treatment

HERE AND NOW

Schizophrenia and Cigarette Smoking: Self-Medication or Shared Brain Circuitry?

Schizophrenic patients are more likely to abuse tobacco than the rest of the population. Various self-medication hypotheses have been proposed to explain this association. For example, it has been suggested that the nicotine found in tobacco may help compensate for some of the cognitive deficits experienced by schizophrenic individuals. Further, it may alleviate unpleasant side effects of antipsychotic medications and/or help people deal with the anxiety that can be associated with the illness. According to NIDA (2010), research suggests the possibility of the presence of abnormalities in particular circuits of the brain that may predispose individuals to schizophrenia, increase the rewarding effects of drugs like nicotine, or reduce an individual's ability to quit smoking. The existence of common mechanisms is consistent with the observation that both nicotine and the medication clozapine (which also acts as nicotine receptors) can improve working memory and attention in an animal model of schizophrenia. Further, clozapine is effective in treating individuals with schizophrenia, and it also reduces their smoking levels. Thus, understanding how and why patients with schizophrenia use nicotine may assist in developing new treatments for both schizophrenia and nicotine dependence.

Data from National Institute on Drug Abuse (NIDA). "Comorbidity: Addiction and Other Mental Illnesses." NIH Publication No. 10-5771. 2010. Available http://www.drugabuse.gov/publications/research-reports/comorbidity-addiction-other-mental-illnesses providers for mental illness, whereas a mix of professionals with varying backgrounds and credentials provides substance abuse treatment. Often, neither background is broad enough to address the full range of problems presented by patients. In addition, a bias exists in some substance abuse treatment facilities against using any pharmacological intervention, including those necessary to treat serious mental illnesses such as depression. Many substance abuse treatment programs do not employ professionals qualified to prescribe, dispense, and monitor medications. Finally, many individuals needing treatment are in the criminal justice system, and adequate treatment services for both mental illness and drug use disorders can be largely lacking in these settings.

Drug Addiction Treatment in the United States

According to the Substance Abuse and Mental Health Services Administration (SAMHSA 2012), in 2011, 21.6 million persons age 12 or older needed treatment for an illicit drug or alcohol use problem. This represents 8.4% of individuals age 12 or older. However, in 2011, only 2.3 million persons (0.9% of persons age 12 or older and 10.8% of those who needed treatment) received treatment at a specialty facility. (For this survey, specialty treatment was defined as treatment received at a hospital [inpatient only], drug or alcohol rehabilitation facility [inpatient or outpatient], or mental health center. It did not include treatment at an emergency room, private doctor's office, self-help group, prison or jail, or hospital as an outpatient.)

Based on SAMHSA data combined from 2008 to 2011 (SAMHSA 2012), among individuals age 12 or older who needed but did not receive illicit drug or alcohol use treatment, felt a need for treatment, and made an effort to receive treatment, the most common reported reason for not receiving treatment was a lack of health coverage and could not afford cost (37.3%). To address the issue of affordability, legislation such as the Mental Health Parity and Addiction Equity Act (MHPAEA) has been enacted (see "Here and Now: Insurance Coverage and Parity"). Other commonly reported reasons included the following (see also **Figure 18.2**): (1) a lack of readiness to stop using (25.5%), (2) a possible negative effect on job (10.1%), (3) had health coverage but did not cover treatment or did not cover cost (10.1%), (4) a lack of transportation or inconvenience (9.5%), (5) did not know where to go for treatment (7.3%), (6) perception that it might cause neighbors/community to have negative opinion (7.2%), and (7) a lack of time for treatment (7.1%).

Substance abuse costs the United States over $600 billion annually. Treatment can help reduce these costs. Research has demonstrated that treatment is far less expensive than simply incarcerating addicts. For example, the average cost per person for 1 full year of methadone maintenance treatment is approximately $4700, whereas 1 full year of imprisonment costs approximately $24,000.

HERE AND NOW

Insurance Coverage and Parity

In 2008, the Paul Wellstone and Pete Domenici Mental Health Parity and Addiction Equity Act (MHPAEA) was signed into law. This federal law supplemented the earlier 1996 Mental Health Parity Act (MPHA) by requiring group health insurance plans (involving greater than 50 insured employees) that offer coverage for mental illness and substance use disorders to provide those benefits in a no more restrictive manner than all other medical/surgical procedures covered by the plan. Of note, the MHPAEA does not require group health plans to cover mental health and substance abuse disorder benefits. However, when plans do cover these illnesses, coverage must be at levels that are no less and with treatment limitations that are no more restrictive than for the other medical/surgical benefits offered by the plan. Thus, by providing parity, the MHPAEA eliminates the practice of unequal health treatment by providing insurance coverage for substance use and mental health disorders equal to other chronic health conditions like hypertension and diabetes.

Reproduced from 2012 Report to Congress: Compliance With the Mental Health Parity and Addiction Equity Act of 2008. Available: http://www.dol.gov/ebsa /publications/mhpaeareporttocongress2012.html. Accessed May 11, 2013; Mental Health Parity and Addiction Equity Act, 2013. Substance Abuse Mental Health Services Administration. Available http://www.samhsa.gov/healthreform/parity/

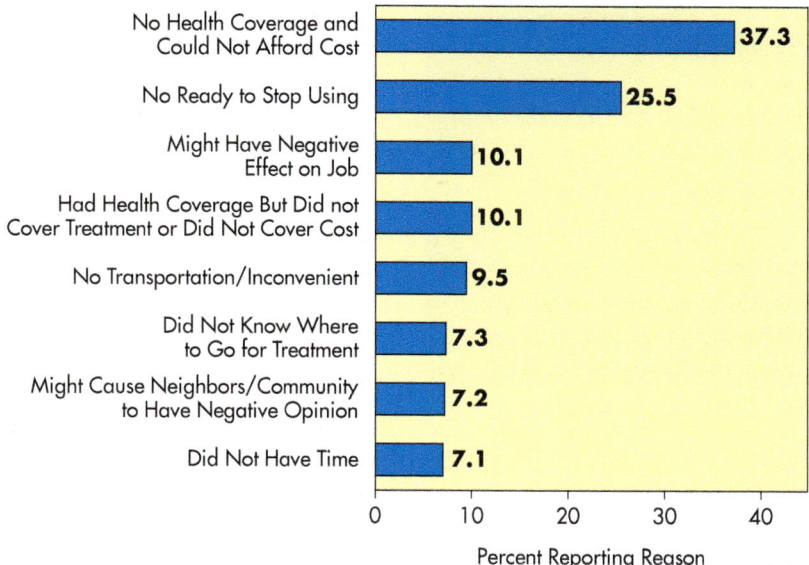

FIGURE 18.2 Reasons for not receiving substance use treatment among persons aged 12 or older who needed and made an effort to get treatment but did not receive treatment and felt they needed treatment: 2008–2011.

Reproduced from Substance Abuse and Mental Health Services Administration (SAMHSA). Results from the 2011 National Survey on Drug Use and Health: Volume I. Summary of National Findings. NSDUH Series H-44, HHS Publication No. SMA 12-4713. Rockville, MD: SAMHSA, 2012.

Treatment has other economic benefits to society. For example, it has been estimated that every $1 invested in addiction treatment programs yields a return of between $4 and $7 in reduced drug-related crime, theft, and criminal justice costs. With healthcare savings included, total savings can exceed costs by a ratio of 12:1. These savings do not include important benefits to the individual and society in the form of fewer interpersonal conflicts, improved workplace productivity, and reduced drug-related incidents among individuals who are treated successfully (NIDA 2012).

There is a wide array of general therapeutic strategies for treatment. Some involve pharmacological interventions, such as methadone maintenance or narcotic antagonist treatment. Other programs apply a drug-free approach. Programs can be short or long term and can be individualized or involve group participation. The following is an overview of various treatment approaches. It is important to realize that many treatment programs blend one or more of these approaches as part of their therapeutic strategy.

■ Historical Approaches

Considerable effort has been expended to find treatments for substance abuse. Several approaches, or at least components of them, continue to be utilized today. These include those discussed in the following sections.

ALCOHOLICS ANONYMOUS

Founded in the mid-1930s, Alcoholics Anonymous (AA) is now an international organization. The desire to stop drinking is the sole criterion required to join. The original founders of AA were strongly influenced by a religious movement known as the Oxford Group. AA outlines 12 successive measures, referred to as *steps*, that alcoholics should accomplish during the recovery process (Alcoholics Anonymous 2002). These steps include admitting that the person addicted to alcohol has no power over the drug. He or she must also believe in a greater power that can help him or her overcome shortcomings. Individuals must make initial and ongoing assessments of their life, and admit their wrongs. In addition, individuals must make amends to those whom they have adversely affected, except in situations where such actions could harm others.

AA has two types of meetings: open and closed. **Open meetings** are open to anyone who has an interest in attending and witnessing these meetings, and they last approximately 45 minutes to

KEY TERM

open meetings
meetings to which anyone having an interest in attending and witnessing is invited

Common alcohol abuse-related problems are shared at AA meetings.

1 hour. **Closed meetings** are for alcoholics who have a serious desire to completely stop drinking. These meetings are not open to viewers or "shoppers." At closed meetings, recovering alcoholics address, through testimonials, how alcohol has diminished their quality of life.

Some outgrowths of AA include Al-Anon, Adult Children of Alcoholics, and Alateen. These are parallel organizations supporting AA. Al-Anon is for spouses and other close relatives of alcoholics, and Alateen is exclusively for teenagers whose lives have been affected by someone else's alcoholism. Both relatives and teen members of alcoholic families learn means and methods for coping with destructive behaviors exhibited by alcoholic members.

REHABILITATION PROGRAMS

The first rehabilitation programs grew out of the work that AA members did with other active alcoholics. The "twelfth stepping" program involves reaching out to others in need and attempting to draw them in. The movement began in the early days of AA when the organization's founder, Bill W., had alcoholics trying to stop drinking or "dry out" living at his house in Brooklyn. At that time, "[his] home was stuffed, from cellar to attic, with alcoholics in all stages of recovery" (Al-Anon 1970). It was a natural transition to opening up "drying out houses" in the 1940s and 1950s.

Also during the 1950s, the **Minnesota model**, an inpatient rehabilitation model, was developed. It combined the AA philosophy with a multidisciplinary treatment team. A treatment plan was used, based on assessment of the individual and prioritization of goals. This model, which borrows from social work practice, is still used in treatment programs. Due to the vagaries of insurance reimbursement in Minnesota, the program lasted 28 days because that was the length covered by insurance; therefore, alcoholism programs traditionally were roughly 1 month long.

▮ General Therapeutic Strategies

In addition to the approaches mentioned previously, there are numerous strategies to drug addiction treatment. Some are individualized and some are group-based. Although not all treatment programs fit perfectly into any one of these categories, the following provides an overview of the general types of services available (NIDA 1999, 2012).

MEDICAL DETOXIFICATION

As noted previously, medical detoxification is the process of safely managing the acute physical symptoms of withdrawal associated with stopping drug use, typically under the care of a physician. Medications including benzodiazepines and other sedatives are often utilized. Detoxification can be medically necessary because untreated withdrawal from some agents (i.e., alcohol and barbiturates) can be fatal. Although detoxification is sometimes referred to as a distinct treatment modality, it is more appropriately considered a precursor to treatment because it is designed to treat the acute physiological effects of stopping drug use. It is not designed to address the psychological, social, and behavioral problems associated with addiction and, thus, does not typically produce lasting behavioral changes. Detoxification is often followed and is augmented by formal processes of assessment and referral to subsequent drug addiction treatment.

SHORT-TERM RESIDENTIAL TREATMENT

Short-term residential programs were originally designed to treat alcoholism, but have been used

KEY TERMS

closed meetings
meetings to which only alcoholics having a serious desire to completely stop drinking are invited

Minnesota model
a major model in the treatment of alcohol and drug abuse, involving a month-long stay in an inpatient rehabilitation facility, a multidisciplinary treatment team, systematic assessment, and a formal treatment plan with long- and short-term goals

to treat other forms of addiction. These provide relatively brief treatment based on a modified 12-step approach. The original model consisted of a 3- to 6-week hospital-based, inpatient treatment phase. This was followed by extended outpatient therapy and participation in a self-help group, such as AA, so as to reduce the risk of relapse once an individual leaves the residential setting.

LONG-TERM RESIDENTIAL TREATMENT

Long-term residential treatment provides care 24 hours a day, generally in nonhospital settings. The **therapeutic community (TC)** is the most recognized residential treatment model. TCs focus on the "resocialization" of the individual and use the program's entire community (e.g., staff, other residents) as important treatment components. Treatment is highly structured and can be confrontational. It focuses on developing personal accountability and responsibility. Activities are designed to assist individuals in examining damaging self-concepts and beliefs, and destructive patterns of behavior. An important goal is to implement new, more constructive ways to interact with others. Planned lengths of stay in TCs are often between 6 and 12 months. TCs often offer comprehensive services, which can include employment training on site. Research indicates that TCs can be modified to treat individuals with special needs, including women, adolescents, persons with severe mental disorders, and individuals in the criminal justice system.

OUTPATIENT TREATMENT PROGRAMS

The outpatient strategy varies in the intensity and forms of services offered. Such treatment often is more suitable for individuals who have extensive family and/or community support, or those who are employed. The intensity of programs varies from those offering simply drug education to those employing higher levels comparable to residential programs in services and effectiveness. Group counseling often is emphasized.

■ Behavioral Therapies

A number of behavioral therapies have been utilized successfully to help engage individuals in treatment and increase the likelihood for successful outcomes. These are described briefly in **Table 18.1** (for additional discussion, see NIDA 2012).

A patient recieves individual counseling in an alcoholism treatment center.

■ Pharmacological Strategies

Some treatment strategies employ pharmacological approaches to help patients with their addiction(s). These strategies are based on the properties of the drug to which they are addicted. Examples of these strategies are discussed in the following sections.

METHADONE

Treatment for opiate addicts is often conducted in specialized outpatient settings (e.g., methadone maintenance clinics) using methadone. Methadone is an opioid agonist (that is, a drug that activates opioid receptors). It is a long-acting synthetic opiate medication administered orally for a sustained period at a dosage sufficient to prevent opiate withdrawal and decrease craving. Patients stabilized on adequate, sustained dosages of methadone can function normally. They can hold jobs, avoid the crime and violence of the street culture, and reduce their exposure to HIV by stopping or decreasing injection drug use and drug-related, high-risk sexual behavior.

Patients stabilized on opiate agonists can engage more readily in counseling and other behavioral interventions essential to recovery and rehabilitation. According to NIDA (2012), the best, most effective opioid agonist maintenance programs include individual and/or group counseling as

KEY TERM

therapeutic community (TC)
inpatient treatment that focuses on the "resocialization" of the individual and uses the program's entire community as important treatment components

TABLE 18.1 Behavioral Therapies Shown to Be Effective in Addressing Substance Abuse

Therapy	Effective Targets	Description
Cognitive-behavioral therapy (CBT)	Alcohol, marijuana, cocaine, methamphetamine, nicotine	CBT is based on the theory that learning patterns play a critical role in the development of maladaptive behavioral patterns like substance abuse. A central element is anticipating likely problems and enhancing patients' self-control by helping them develop effective coping strategies. Techniques include exploring the positive and negative consequences of continued drug use, self-monitoring to recognize cravings early and identify situations that might put one at risk for use, and developing strategies for coping with cravings and avoiding those high-risk situations.
Contingency management (CM) interventions/ motivational incentives	Alcohol, stimulants, opioids, marijuana, nicotine	CM involves giving patients tangible rewards to reinforce positive behaviors such as abstinence. Rewards can include vouchers to be exchanged for goods or services that are consistent with a drug-free lifestyle, or incentives consisting of chances to win prizes. The rewards increase in value with evidence of sustained abstinence (i.e., consecutive negative drug tests), but reset to the lowest value with any evidence of a drug use recurrence.
Community reinforcement approach (CRA) plus vouchers	Alcohol, cocaine, opioids	CRA plus vouchers is an intensive 24-week outpatient therapy for treating people addicted to cocaine and alcohol. It uses a range of recreational, familial, social, and vocational reinforcers, along with material incentives, to make a nondrug-using lifestyle more rewarding than substance use.
Motivational enhancement therapy (MET)	Alcohol, marijuana, nicotine	MET is designed to help individuals resolve ambivalence about engaging in treatment and stopping drug use. The aim is to evoke rapid and internally motivated change, rather than guiding the patient stepwise through the recovery process. MET consists of an initial assessment session, followed by two to four individual treatment sessions. Motivational interviewing principles and coping strategies for high-risk situations are emphasized.
The matrix model	Stimulants	The model provides a framework wherein patients learn about issues critical to addiction and relapse, and receive direction and support from a trained therapist. The therapist fosters a positive, encouraging relationship with the patient and uses that relationship to reinforce positive behavior change. Treatment materials draw heavily on tested treatment approaches and include elements of relapse prevention, family and group therapies, drug education, and self-help participation.
12-step facilitation	Alcohol, stimulants, opioids	Twelve-step facilitation therapy is an active engagement strategy guided by three key ideas: (1) acceptance, which includes the realization that drug addiction is a chronic, progressive disease over which one has no control, that life has become unmanageable because of drugs, and that abstinence is the only alternative; (2) surrender, which involves giving oneself over to a higher power, accepting the fellowship and support structure of other recovering addicted individuals, and following the recovery activities laid out by the 12-step program; and (3) active involvement in 12-step meetings and related activities.
Family behavioral therapy (FBT)		FBT is aimed at addressing not only substance use problems, but also other co-occurring problems, such as conduct disorders, child mistreatment, depression, family conflict, and unemployment. FBT utilizes contingency management as well as other behavioral strategies, and involves the patient and at least one significant other.

Adapted from National Institute on Drug Abuse (NIDA). Principles of Drug Addiction Treatment. Publication No. 12-4180. Washington, DC: National Institutes of Health, April 2012.

HOLDING THE LINE

Expanded Options for Treatment of Heroin Addiction

Until 2000, opiate dependence treatments such as methadone could be dispensed only in a very limited number of clinics that specialize in addiction treatment. As a consequence of the Drug Addiction Treatment Act of 2000, the Food and Drug Administration (FDA) announced approval of Subutex and Suboxone tablets for the treatment of opiate dependence by specially trained physicians. Accordingly, the drugs can be prescribed in an office setting and, therefore, are more accessible to patients needing treatment.

Subutex and Suboxone treat opiate addiction by preventing symptoms of withdrawal from heroin and other opiates. Subutex contains only buprenorphine (a partial opioid agonist) and is intended for use at the beginning of treatment for opioid abuse once the individual has undergone detoxification. Suboxone contains both buprenorphine and the opiate antagonist naloxone and is intended to be used in maintenance treatment of opiate addiction. Naloxone has limited effects if administered sublingually, but is effective as an antagonist if administered intravenously. It has been added to Suboxone to guard against intravenous abuse of buprenorphine by individuals who are physically dependent on opiates.

well as provision of or referral to other needed medical, psychological, and social services.

NALOXONE AND NALTREXONE

An antagonist is a compound that suppresses the actions of a drug. Narcotic antagonists have properties that make them important tools in the clinical treatment of narcotic drug dependence (see "Holding the Line: Expanded Options for Treatment of Heroin Addiction"). For instance, the short-acting opioid antagonist naloxone (Narcan) is often used in the emergency treatment of opioid overdoses.

Naltrexone is a long-acting synthetic opioid antagonist used as a treatment for opioid addiction. It is usually prescribed in outpatient medical settings, although treatment initiation often begins after medical detoxification in a residential setting. Individuals must be opioid-free for several days before taking naltrexone in order to avoid withdrawal symptoms. Naltrexone is taken orally for a sustained period, and thus prevents all the effects of self-administered opioids. Naltrexone itself has neither subjective effects nor potential for abuse; however, patient noncompliance is a frequent problem, and thus, many treatment providers have found naltrexone to be most appropriate for highly motivated, recently detoxified patients such as professionals, parolees, and probationers, who desire total abstinence because of external circumstances. Of note, an extended release preparation of naltrexone (Vivitrol), administered monthly by intramuscular injection, has been FDA-approved to treat alcoholism.

BUPRENORPHINE

In 2000, Congress passed the Drug Addiction Treatment Act (DATA). This legislation allowed qualified physicians to prescribe specifically-approved Schedule III, IV, and V medications for the treatment of opioid addiction in general medical settings (e.g., primary care offices). Such office-based treatment of opioid addiction is a cost-effective approach that increases the span of treatment and the options available to patients.

Buprenorphine is a **partial agonist** (that is, a drug that has both agonist and antagonist properties) at opioid receptors. It reduces or eliminates withdrawal symptoms associated with opioid dependence but generally does not produce the euphoria and sedation caused by other opioids. It is available in two formulations—Subutex, which contains only buprenorphine, and Suboxone, which contains both buprenorphine and naloxone.

NICOTINE REPLACEMENT THERAPY

Nicotine was the first pharmacological agent approved by the FDA for use in smoking cessation

KEY TERM

partial agonist
a drug that has both agonist and antagonist properties

therapy. Nicotine replacement therapies, such as nicotine gum, transdermal patches, nasal sprays, and inhalers, are used to relieve withdrawal symptoms.

Other pharmacological therapies such as vareni-cline (Chantix) and bupropion (Zyban) are available by prescription to aid in smoking cessation.

DISULFIRAM

Disulfiram (Antabuse) is a drug used for treating alcoholics. This drug causes nausea, vomiting, flushing, and anxiety if an individual consumes alcohol while taking the drug. Thus, this drug is perceived as a deterrent drug.

ACAMPROSATE

Acamprosate (Campral) acts on the glutamate and gamma-aminobutyric acid (GABA) neurotransmitter systems. It is used to treat symptoms of alcohol withdrawal because it purportedly reduces associated symptoms such as anxiety, insomnia, restlessness, and dysphoria.

TOPIRAMATE

Topiramate is sometimes used off-label to treat alcohol addiction. Its mechanism of action likely involves the glutamate and GABA neurotransmitter systems, although its precise mechanism of action is not known.

LEARNING PORTFOLIO

Discussion Questions

1. Discuss the need to assess addiction severity and readiness to change.
2. List several principles that characterize effective addiction treatment.
3. Discuss the role of comorbidity in substance abuse and its treatment.
4. Describe Alcoholics Anonymous and its approach to assisting individuals addicted to alcohol.
5. Describe several therapeutic strategies to treat addiction.
6. Describe the therapeutic community approach to treating substance abuse.
7. Describe the Mental Health Parity and Addiction Equity Act.

Key Terms

Summary

1. Individuals who are addicted to drugs come from all walks of life. It is important that treatment providers determine the severity of a person's addiction as well as the readiness of that individual to change his or her behavior.
2. The process of determining addiction severity can be accomplished in many ways, including the administration of standardized questionnaires such as the Addiction Severity Index (ASI). The ASI provides information that can be used to identify and prioritize which problem domains are the most critical and require immediate attention.
3. It is important to assess a person's readiness to change his or her abuse behavior because this can help providers select the best treatment plan to address a client's needs. This may help prevent the individual who is receiving treatment from rejecting all or parts of the treatment plan.
4. Comorbidity is a condition in which two or more illnesses occur in the same person, simultaneously or sequentially. This term also suggests interactions between the illnesses that affect the course and prognosis of both.
5. Changes in the structure and function in regions of the brain affected by drug addiction can also occur in mental illnesses such as anxiety, psychosis, and depression. Overlapping factors including genetic vulnerabilities, trauma, stress, and/or underlying brain abnormalities can contribute to both substance abuse disorders and mental illnesses.
6. Effective treatment of individuals with comorbid substance abuse and mental illnesses requires accurate diagnosis of both conditions. However, several fundamental barriers can stand in the way of treating comorbid disorders.

7. One of the earliest real alcoholism recovery efforts was Alcoholics Anonymous (AA). Programs modeled on AA, known as 12-step fellowships, are major routes to recovery.

8. There are numerous approaches to drug addiction treatment, including outpatient and residential treatment. Medical detoxification is not a treatment per se, but rather a precursor to treatment.

9. Motivational enhancement therapy is a client-centered counseling approach for initiating behavior change by helping clients to resolve ambivalence about engaging in treatment and discontinuing drug use.

10. A major approach to heroin and other opiate addiction has involved the provision of methadone, a synthetic opiate.

References

Al-Anon. *Al-Anon's Favorite Forum Editorials*. New York: Al-Anon Family Group Headquarters, 1970.

Alcoholics Anonymous. "The Twelve Steps of Alcoholics Anonymous." 2002. Available http://www.aa.org/en_services_for_members.cfm?PageID=98&SubPage=117

DiClemente, C. C., and J. O. Prochaska. "Toward a Comprehensive, Transtheoretical Model of Change." In *Treating Addictive Behaviors: Processes of Change*, edited by W. R. Miller and N. Heather. New York: Plenum Press, 1998.

McLellan, A. T., H. Kushner, D. Metzger, R. Peters, I. Smith, G. Grissom, et al. "The Fifth Edition of the Addiction Severity Index." *Journal of Substance Abuse Treatment* 9 (1992): 199–213.

McLellan, A. T., L. Luborsky, J. Cacciola, J. Griffith, F. Evans, H. L. Barr, et al. "New Data from the Addiction Severity Index. Reliability and Validity in Three Centers." *Journal of Nervous and Mental Disease* 173 (1985): 412–423.

McLellan, A. T., L. Luborsky, G. E. Woody, and C. P. O'Brien. "An Improved Diagnostic Evaluation Instrument for Substance Abuse Patients. The Addiction Severity Index." *Journal of Nervous and Mental Disease* 168 (1980): 26–33.

National Institute on Drug Abuse (NIDA). *Principles of Drug Addiction Treatment*. Pub. No. 99-4180. Washington, DC: National Institutes of Health, October 1999.

National Institute on Drug Abuse (NIDA). "Research Addresses Needs of Criminal Justice Staff and Offenders." *NIDA Notes* 3 (1 April 2009). Available http://www.drugabuse.gov/NIDA_notes/NNvol22N3/nidaatwork.html#insert

National Institute on Drug Abuse (NIDA). "Comorbidity: Addiction and Other Mental Illnesses." NIH Pub. No. 10-5771. 2010. Available http://www.drugabuse.gov/publications/research-reports/comorbidity-addiction-other-mental-illnesses

National Institute on Drug Abuse (NIDA). *Principles of Drug Addiction Treatment*. Pub. No. 12-4180. Washington, DC: National Institutes of Health, April 2012.

Stilen, P., D. Carise, N. Roget, and A. Wendler. *Treatment Planning M.A.T.R.S. Utilizing the Addiction Severity Index (ASI) to Make Required Data Collection Useful*. Kansas City, MO: Mid-America Addiction Technology Transfer Center in Residence at the University of Missouri–Kansas City, 2007.

Substance Abuse and Mental Health Services Administration (SAMHSA). *Results from the 2011 National Survey on Drug Use and Health: Volume I. Summary of National Findings*. NSDUH Series H-44, HHS Pub. No. SMA 12-4713. Rockville, MD: SAMHSA, 2012.

INDEX

Page numbers followed by *f* and *t* indicate material in figures and tables respectively